Morality Tales

The publisher gratefully acknowledges the generous contribution to this book provided by the Institute of Turkish Studies, Washington, D.C., and by the General Endowment Fund of the University of California Press Associates.

Morality Tales

Law and Gender in the Ottoman Court of Aintab

Leslie Peirce

UNIVERSITY OF CALIFORNIA PRESS

Berkeley   Los Angeles   London

University of California Press
Berkeley and Los Angeles, California

University of California Press, Ltd.
London, England

© 2003 by
The Regents of the University of California

Library of Congress Cataloging-in-Publication Data

Peirce, Leslie
    Morality tales : law and gender in the Ottoman court of Aintab /
Leslie Peirce.
        p. cm.
    Includes bibliographical references and index.
    ISBN 0-520-22890-1 (Cloth) — ISBN 0-520-22892-8 (Paper)
    1. Women—Legal status, laws, etc. (Islamic law)—Turkey—
History. 2. Sex and law—History. I. Title.

    KKX 517.5.P45 2003
    346.56101'34—dc21   2002152228

Manufactured in the United States of America

11   10   09   08   07   06   05   04   03
10   9   8   7   6   5   4   3   2   1

The paper used in this publication is both acid-free and totally
chlorine-free (TCF). It meets the minimum requirements of
ANSI/NISO z39.48–1992 (R 1997) ∞

13064564

To my parents
and to my son, Kerim

CONTENTS

ILLUSTRATIONS

ACKNOWLEDGMENTS

There are many people to thank, since this book has been a long time in the making and has thus accumulated many debts. I am grateful to the staffs of the National Library in Ankara and the Ottoman Prime Ministry Archives in Istanbul, who facilitated my work in their collections. I am especially indebted to Dursun Kaya, director of the Rare Books and Manuscripts division of the National Library, who together with his staff assisted me in numerous ways as I read the court records of Gaziantep. Without the financial support of the Social Sciences Research Council, the Council for International Exchange of Scholars (Fulbright grant), and the Committee on Research at the University of California at Berkeley, this book would not exist.

My greatest thanks must go to the people of Gaziantep, to whom I am profoundly grateful for their hospitality, friendship, and help with my work. My first visit to Gaziantep, where I was a Peace Corps volunteer in the 1960s, gave me lifelong friends: the Arı family and Sabiha and Vehbi Dinçerler; these friends have generously allowed themselves to be enlisted in my research. Returning to Gaziantep in 1999, I made many new acquaintances who provided insights and information that caused me to recast parts of what I thought was a finished manuscript. I thank Ayşe Nur Arun for many things—for taking me to Rumkale, for giving me books, for providing me with introductions, and more. Akten Köylüoğlu has been my guide through the city itself and through several court records whose contents were obscure to me; her wide learning and her passion for Gaziantep's history make her a local treasure. I thank Rıfat Ergeç, former director of the Gaziantep Museum and now professor at Gaziantep University, for helping me imagine the spatial past of Aintab (the pre-twentieth-century name of the city). Ömer Karaman, the mayor of the municipality of Şahinbey, immediately grasped some of the critical questions in my work and helped me use the present as a window on the past. Nusret Çam, of Ankara University's Divinity Faculty, generously shared his knowledge of sixteenth-century Aintab and also helped me understand the social topography of the eastern parts of Gaziantep province. For acquainting me with his valuable work on Maraş, I am grateful to İsmail Altınöz. Ali Cenani of Istanbul kindly provided information about the early history of his family (the Demirci family, who figure prominently in the book). Dr. Barclay Shepard took me to wonderful monuments and also provided the hospitality of the Gaziantep American Hospital. Halit Ziya Biçer and Özalp Dündar generously shared their collections of old photographs. The Gaziantep Tourism Bureau was exceptionally helpful to me in providing information, suggesting people to meet, and guiding me around monuments; I especially thank Özgür Çinkay.

I am very grateful for my year in the Women's Studies in Religion Program at Harvard Divinity School, where my research material began to come together as a book. Constance Buchanan, then the program's director, helped give shape to the book by suggesting that the court of Aintab needed to be treated as a moral arena. Frank Vogel of Harvard Law School gave me much to think about in terms of the relationship of jurisprudence to practice. Talal Eid patiently answered questions as I tried to figure out that relationship for the sixteenth-century Ottoman world. During that year, I was fortunate to meet the poet Ellen Voigt, who suggested that the best way to untangle all the information in my head was to tell a story. And so the writing of the book began with Fatma's story, now its conclusion.

I am deeply indebted to Lynne Withey, director of the University of California Press, who at numerous junctures helped me think through how to shape the book so as to convey what I thought was important. It is a privilege to work with an editor who grasped the essence of the project before its author fully did. I am grateful to Suzanne Knott, senior editor at the Press, for her careful supervision of the book through the production process, and to Alice Falk for her meticulous copyediting of the manuscript.

To all the students on whom I tried out various court cases I give thanks for their ideas and for their occasional success in persuading me that my own readings were narrow. Likewise, I am grateful to the several audiences to whom various parts of this book were presented in lectures and talks for their insights and for saving me from error. I owe a large debt to the several friends and colleagues who read parts or all of the book or who answered my endless inquiries: I thank Iris Agmon, Peggy Anderson, Beth Baron, Edhem Eldem, Marian Feldman, Heather Ferguson, Fatma Müge Göçek, Daniel Goffman, Colin Imber, Nancy Özturk, Şevket Pamuk, Ruud Peters, David Powers, Najwa Al-Qattan, Amy Singer, Judith Tucker, and Sara Wolper. I also benefited from the suggestions of the Press's anonymous reviewers of my manuscript. If I failed to improve the book by neglecting some of their suggestions, the responsibility is mine alone. I am especially grateful to my son Kerim for his thoughtful reading of several chapters and for his much-valued support throughout this project.

Other kinds of help were critical. Amy Singer has been my longtime comrade in the quest to understand Ottoman culture and a friend of this book in countless ways. Lucette Valensi provided advice and support at a critical moment in the project. For deciphering passages in the court records, I thank Şinasi Tekin of Harvard University, and Margaret Larkin and Hamid Algar of my own university, the University of California at Berkeley. Hülya Canbakal lent me a hard-to-find text and, more important, shared her wisdom about Gaziantep with me. Charlotte Jirousek helped me choose illustrations, and Carel Bertram animated the city of Aintab in map 4. Fatma Müge Göçek inspired the title of the book. Natalie Balikciyan alerted me to the existence of an Armenian history of Gaziantep, while Stephan Astourian generously translated parts of it for me and helped me with the Armenian names in the court records. I am indebted to the exhaustive work of Hüseyin Özdeğer in the cadastral survey archives for Gaziantep, which aided my research enormously.

To Sara Wolper, Marian Feldman, Linda Robinson, and Amy Singer, companions in exploring regions traversed by the book, I am grateful for the pleasure of shared enthusiasms and for all I learned with and from them during travels in Turkey and Syria. I often failed to ask the names of the many people along the way who aided and informed us, but their words are alive in my notes and in my memory. Last, but in some ways first, I thank Joanne Omang and Lynda Özgür for the friendship and memories that began in Gaziantep.

Berkeley, California
August 2001

NOTE ON TRANSLATION AND TRANSLITERATION

All translations within the text are my own, although I have been helped by a number of individuals who have offered suggestions of what a particular Turkish word or phrase might have meant in sixteenth-century Aintab. In translating voices in the court records, I have tried to remain as close as possible to the language of the text, but I have taken liberties when it seemed important to find an English expression that renders the tone or idiomatic use of the original.

I have been somewhat eclectic in the transliteration of Turkish and Arabic words. I have generally used modern Turkish orthography for proper names used in a Turkish cultural context and for administrative terms used in an Ottoman context (e.g., Ayşe, *subaşı*). Names and terms with broader usage in the sixteenth-century Middle East I do not transliterate (e.g., Kizilbash, mufti). Occasionally, however, I have included Arabic ʿ, ʾ, and long vowels where modern Turkish orthography eliminates them; it is hoped that this will help those readers with a knowledge of other Middle Eastern languages who are not familiar with modern Turkish.

PRONUNCIATION OF MODERN TURKISH LETTERS
THAT ARE NOT TRANSLITERATED

ç	*ch,* as in *church*
ş	*sh,* as in *ship*
ı	*io,* as in motion, or *e,* as in *women*
ö	French *eu,* as in *deux*
ü	French *u,* as in *durée*
ğ	unvocalized, lengthens preceding vowel

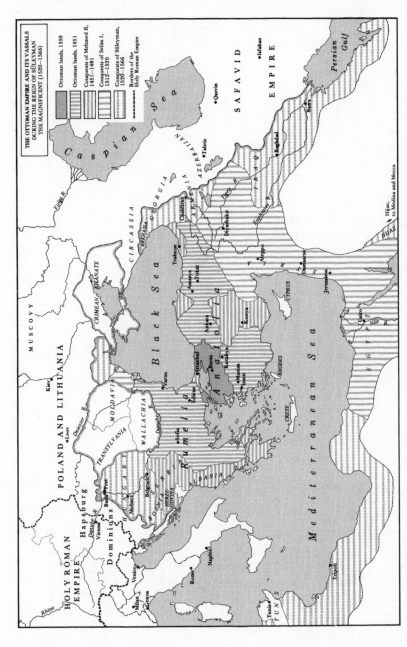

Map 1. The Ottoman empire in the reign of Süleyman I. From Leslie Peirce, *The Imperial Harem: Women and Sovereignty in the Ottoman Empire* (New York: Oxford University Press, 1993), xix.

THE OTTOMAN EMPIRE AND ITS VASSALS DURING THE REIGN OF SÜLEYMAN THE MAGNIFICENT (1520–1566)

- Ottoman lands, 1359
- Ottoman lands, 1451
- Conquests of Mehmed II, 1451–1481
- Conquests of Selim I, 1512–1520
- Conquests of Süleyman, 1520–1566
- Borders of the Holy Roman Empire

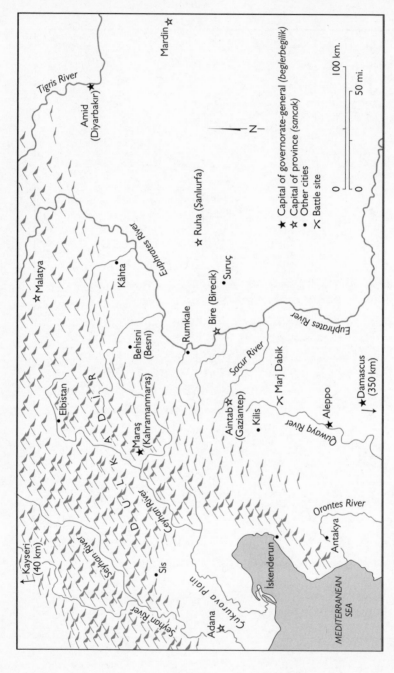

Map 2. The greater Aintab region.

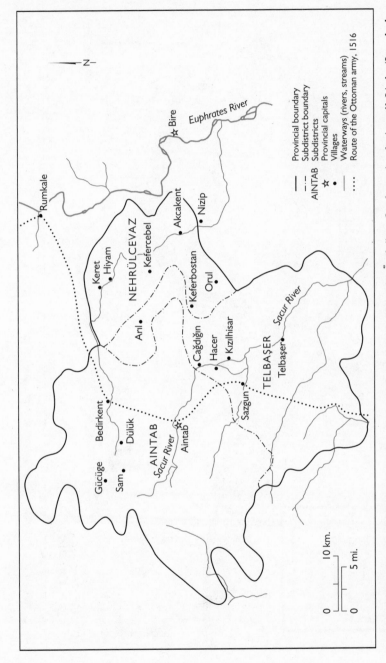

Map 3. Aintab province, mid–sixteenth century. Adapted from Hüseyin Özdeğer, *Onaltıncı Asırda Ayntâb Livâsı* (Istanbul: Bayrak Matbaacılık, 1988), endmap.

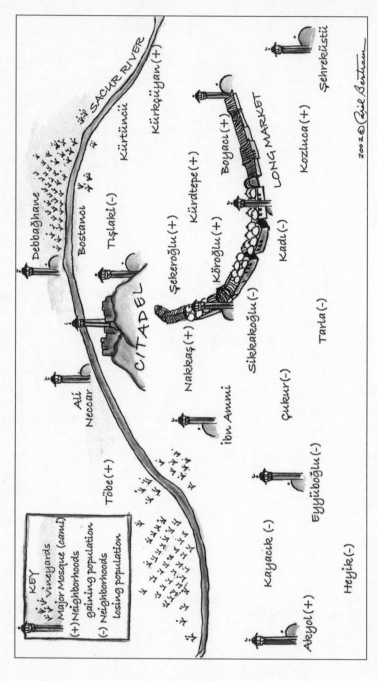

Map 4. Aintab city and its neighborhoods, 1536–1543.

Introduction

In late June of 1541, a new judge arrived to take up office in the city of Aintab, an Ottoman provincial capital located in southeastern Anatolia. Almost immediately, things began to change at the court. Within two days, the judge's residence—also the site of the court—was enlarged. Over the course of the summer, the caseload of the Aintab court doubled from what it had been before. And new kinds of cases began to be aired at court: women brought property suits against male relatives, murder cases began to be adjudicated under the judge's oversight, and sexual misconduct was increasingly prosecuted under the auspices of the court. What caused these changes, and how did the people of Aintab figure within them?

This book is about one year in the life of a provincial court. It follows the people of Aintab and its hinterland as they used their court to solve social problems and also as they were called to account by legal authorities for breaking the law. While the book takes an interest in the Ottoman legal system as a whole and in the laws that it enforced, it is primarily an attempt to understand the culture of a local court: that is, the nature of dispute resolution that occurred within it and its vision of social justice. Legal codes—Islamic sharia and Ottoman imperial law—were of course critical in shaping the legal life of communities like Aintab, but it was only in local interpretation that formal rules acquired vitality and meaning. The chapters that follow argue that it was the people of Aintab who, negotiating with and through the court, were responsible for much of that interpretation. Even during the year studied here, when the Aintab court was increasingly drawn into the Ottoman empire's expanding legal system, local individuals used the court to create a dialogue with the ruling regime over mutual rights and obligations.

Although the judge of Aintab was clearly a pivotal figure in local legal life, his judgments necessarily rested on the input that he obtained from members of the community. The latter were ever-present as witnesses, supplying the testimony that Islamic law regarded as the bedrock of the legal process. Members of the community often acted as mediators whose solutions to local disputes were then validated by the judge. And several local residents signed off on each and every case recorded by the court's scribe, thereby acting as witnesses to the court's proceedings in that particular matter. Ultimately, it was the judge who judged, but he did so with the aid of a court that was largely composed of members of the community.[1]

Women used the Aintab court in significant numbers, if not as frequently as men. The openness of Ottoman-period courts to women is a well-known fact, documented in numerous studies of women, the law, family, and property. However, most of these studies do not take into account the obstacles women faced as they presented their cases to the empire's judges. Women performed none of the procedural roles described above that were filled by their fathers, brothers, and sons. And while both Islamic law and imperial law protected the various rights to which women were entitled, at the same time they reinforced the overall subordination of female to male in this hierarchical society. Women had to fight harder to claim their rights. But challenges produced strategies. This book focuses on women not only for the intrinsic interest of their own encounters with the law but also for what their conduct at court reveals about the variety and flexibility of legal practice as a whole in this time and place. The three stories that open the different sections of the book—the domestic predicament of the child bride İne, the heresy trial of the teacher Haciye Sabah, and the pregnancy of the peasant girl Fatma—are in some ways the core of the book, since they suggest in specific ways how women negotiated the legal terrain in attempting to solve their personal problems. These stories are also a lens through which wider questions of justice, community, and empire become visible.

ENCOUNTERING COURT RECORDS

Morality Tales differs in a number of ways from other studies that are based on Ottoman court records. Most such works have tended to use court records as a source for studying local political economies or local social practices. Rather, I am interested in the work of the court itself—what problems people brought to it voluntarily, what crimes the court prosecuted, what strategies people devised to deal with the interventions of the law in their lives, and how shifts in the legal climate affected people's lives. The chapters and stories that follow place a good deal of emphasis on how people spoke at court and on what caused male and female voices to differ in some matters but not in others. There is a wide and sometimes curious range of talk in the court records, from crude cursing to remorseful pleas for absolution, from harsh condemnation of wayward wives to despair over a marriage unintentionally dissolved. A notable talent of the court was its ability to accommodate and mediate the often discordant voices that appear in its records.

Despite its critical role in local affairs, the court was not a place that everyone was eager to visit. People could take their problems to a variety of other local authorities—religious dignitaries, neighborhood and village headmen, tribal elders, urban magnates, or local officials such as the governor or the chief of police. The court, in other words, was only one of several legal resources in the city and province of Aintab. One reformist aim of the Ottoman government in this period was to encourage people to patronize the courts. Many cases in 1540–1541 were brought to the judge voluntarily, suggesting that some Aintabans used the court proactively as a resource in managing their lives. We will be interested in what advantages the court offered, and whether it was becoming more "user-friendly" as a result of incorporation into an imperial legal system. At the same time, courts could never be autonomous. Judges inevitably interacted with other authorities and other venues of dispute resolution, sometimes in concert, sometimes in conflict. An important project of this book is to look at the court as only one node, although a central one, in a local legal network, rather than regarding it as a legally autonomous, isolated institution.

Another novel aspect of the book is that it takes up a single year in the life of a court, in contrast to the typical approach of using court records to study long-term developments in a particular place. Here, we trace the work of the Aintab court from September 1540 to October 1541. The backdrop to our study of Aintab is the rapid Ottoman conquest of much of the Middle East. From 1514 to 1517, the empire's European and western Anatolian base was more than doubled through the acquisition of eastern and southeastern Anatolia, Syria and Palestine, Egypt, and the Hijaz, the western coastal area of the Arabian peninsula that included the Muslim holy cities of Mecca and Medina. The Ottoman empire was now the dominant power in the eastern Mediterranean and the Middle East, and the greatest Muslim power in the world. Located in a transition zone between southeastern Anatolia and northern Syria, Aintab was a small piece of the conquest. Our story takes place a generation later, when the city and the province that bore its name were in the process of becoming fully assimilated into the empire's networks of administration. The arrival in June 1541 of the new judge, appointed directly by the government and more powerful than his predecessors, was one sign of this process of assimilation. So while this book is a study of local dynamics, it is also about a moment when Aintab was in dialogue with an expanding imperial regime, a regime that, some have argued, was approaching its zenith in the years examined here.

Because of my interest in this meeting of local community with imperial regime and its impact on the people of Aintab, I chose to work on the earliest available registers in the long and rich series of court records that survive from Ottoman Aintab. The records from the year studied here are contained in two registers, the first covering the period from September 14, 1540, through May 18, 1541 (in the Islamic calendar, 12 Cemaziülevvel 947 to 22 Muharrem 948), and the second from May 25, 1541, to October 2, 1541 (29 Muharrem 948 to 11 Cemaziülaher 948).[2] These registers contain some 2,700 items, which range from three-line entries concerning a debt paid or a vineyard purchased to the lengthy entries detailing criminal cases or acrimonious disputes. The bulk of these records is made up of the testimony of Aintabans at court. Their voices create a record of the past that is sometimes humorous, sometimes heartrending, but always lively.

Finally, the book offers a sketch of a particular place at a moment in time. This in itself is nothing new, since we have full portraits of cities such as Aleppo, Izmir, Damascus, Salonica, and of course Istanbul. But there is little that looks closely at a sixteenth-century community—a community, moreover, that was not one of the powerful or glamorous urban centers of the empire. Rather, Aintab was a *regionally* cosmopolitan center. My sketch naturally extends to the broader domain in which Aintab played a role, since the concerns of its court stretched beyond the official boundaries of this rather small province. Under the "pax Ottomanica," Aintab functioned as a significant link in the various networks—economic, cultural, administrative, and even criminal—that constituted the region bridging southeastern Anatolia and northern Syria. Although the Aintab court was one of several in the area, I suggest that it may have been targeted to play a regional function because of the combination of features that characterized the city. Aintab was a commercial center, yet it had experience in accommodating a sizable tribal and nomadic population. It was both fortified with a citadel and centrally located among smaller fortified settlements. Moreover, the city enjoyed a reputation for religious and legal learning, or at least it had in recent centuries. Finally, it is probably not going too far to say Aintab was a stubbornly independent and self-sufficient place.

LAW, MORALITY, AND GENDER

The emphasis in this book is on the local delivery of the law and the uses that local populations made of legal resources available to them. The book concentrates on consumers of the law, individuals who of necessity developed strategies to aid them in their encounters with the court. The records of the Aintab court virtually demand such a focus, for they make clear that legal processes at the grassroots level were much more complex than either Islamic jurisprudence or Ottoman statute books might suggest. Court cases often represented tangled instances of conflicting interests to which no single legal rule, or even a combination of rules, could bring a clear-cut resolution. As a result, the court frequently found itself listening to contradictory but compelling testimony from parties to a case. This does not mean that the local court disregarded legal norms. On the contrary, many cases in the Aintab court involved clear winners and losers, casting the innocent against the guilty, and it was a legal rule that decided who was which. But equally striking are the many cases where there was no clear winner or loser or where both parties might be "a little bit" guilty. The many instances of brothers who fought over houses they had inherited jointly from their fathers are one example. Cases like these were frequently resolved through communal mediation, which called for a measure of local custom and common sense to leaven the weight of rules.

On the occasions when the court itself sorted out such complex cases, its goal appears to have been the preservation of social order, and its guiding principle the assumption that the harmony of the community superseded any narrow particular right. Even when the court punished, it might simultaneously acknowledge the humanity or social worth of the objects of its justice. The three female protagonists whose stories open sections of the book, for example, were guilty to varying degrees, yet each achieved a degree of reintegration into the social world of the community. As Lawrence Rosen remarks with regard to the present-day Moroccan court of Sefrou, the judge's aim is "to put people back into the position of being able to negotiate their own permissible relationships[.]"[3] A basic assumption in the work of the Aintab court was that justice had to be provided at the level of the individual if social order was to be achieved, even if that individual was an obscure peasant girl not even in her teens. We might characterize the court's goal in such cases as social equity, an outcome whereby no one enjoyed a clear monopoly on justice, since to lose might mean to suffer a diminished capacity to participate in social life.

In other words, the view in Aintab seems to have been that participation in social life was not possible if an individual was robbed of his or her personal integrity. We will see again and again that a reputation for good conduct was essential to a person's standing in the local community. How one gave testimony at court was therefore critical. It was up to the court's users to persuade the judge of their needs and to justify their actions. Even when individuals were clearly guilty, they sometimes tried to give moral justification for their acts or at least to plead extenuating circumstances. In trouble with the law for accusing two men of making her pregnant, the peasant girl Fatma blamed the mother of one for the plot to accuse the other, and pleaded that she could not tell a lie for fear of eternal punishment. It is one of the commonplaces of this book that the court was a public forum that gave voice to those of marginal status in the community, enabling them to speak in defense of their conduct and to assert their honor and moral integrity.

The law was not a level playing field. The normative codes that framed the operations of Ottoman courts assigned diminished social stature to the masses, and to certain groups in particular, among them women, non-Muslims, slaves, and members of tribal societies. Islamic jurisprudence— particularly the Hanafi school of law that prevailed in Aintab—was elitist, protecting an ideal vision of a society made up of propertied households. Ottoman sultanic law replicated this notion of differential justice based on class and civil status. But class was not a simple matter of wealth or family lineage. In the writings of Muslim thinkers, morality had long been intimately associated with social hierarchy: elites, it was believed, had greater sensitivity to right and wrong and therefore a larger share of honor. However, we will see that while the people of Aintab recognized social hierarchy, members of more modest social circles resisted the notion that they were morally deficient.

One of the manifestations of class structures in Aintab was the relative absence of elites from the courts. The records of 1540–1541 suggest that the wealthy, educated, and otherwise privileged members of Aintab society held aloof from the provincial court. Elite males might act as court observers and conduct state-related business at court, but they avoided airing personal matters; elite women simply did not appear in the court. This phenomenon may have been widespread, since there is evidence that the Ottoman regime was uneasy about the degree to which elites were able to avoid public regulatory mechanisms such as the courts. Whether elites were simply able to escape the reach of the law, or whether other sanctions were called into play to discipline them, is not clear. That the majority of the Aintab court's users may have been of modest circumstances does not mean that the court was therefore populist in orientation, but its culture was inevitably affected by the demography of its clients.

These observations about the Ottoman legal system in the mid–sixteenth century have important implications for women. Islamic jurisprudence upheld the ideal of the secluded woman, by definition a woman of virtue whose improper appearances in public jeopardized the honor of her household. Such a woman might own property and deploy her wealth publicly, but her dealings were hidden. Jurisprudence failed to acknowledge the situation of the exposed woman, whose economic and social circumstances might require her to traffic the public avenues of her community. Yet, categorizing her as essentially "female," it imposed sanctions on her that derived from a different social world. Sultanic statutory law was closer to a recognition of the social variety of the empire's subjects. But while it recognized that not all women practiced seclusion, its protective impulses, like those of Islamic jurisprudence, were directed toward the elite lifestyle. An example of the gap between formal law and grassroots realities is the treatment of rape: in normative legal discourse (pronouncements of Muslim jurists, laws issued by the sultans), rape was envisioned as occurring when men broke into houses. The Aintab court records, however, reveal equal numbers of females assaulted at home and on the streets.

How did the local court respond to the elitist bias in normative law? The judge was mandated to observe the regulations of both Islamic law and sultanic law. But because the court's users varied in social position, in their attitudes toward what constituted ethical behavior, and in the range of problems that brought them to the judge, the court had to maintain some flexibility. The fact that one of its functions was to give hearing to voices from the community meant that space was opened up for individuals to argue their circumstances from a personal moral outlook. Faced with laws and local practices that were disadvantageous to them, women did not hesitate to occupy that space. They often used it to assert that virtue was not a monopoly of the socially privileged.

A different light is cast on women, then, if we focus on law as process rather than on law as normative prescription or administrative structure. Although it can be argued that Islamic law provided greater protection for women's rights than did other premodern legal cultures, legal codes and procedural rules drew sharp distinctions between women and men. But the legal disabilities women endured did not turn them into mere passive objects of the law. For a number of reasons, grassroots practice was less sharply gendered than normative law. That women were legally active in significant numbers was due in part to the traditional mandate of courts to keep their doors open to the less powerful. In Aintab, the same dynamic was at work in the small community of Armenian Christians, who used the court in disproportion to their numbers. In addition, individuals relied on the open-door policy of the court to develop strategies to get around the structural obstacles that confronted them. I argue in chapter 5, for instance, that some women turned the court into a theater of morality, dramatizing the ambiguity in complex cases to their advantage. Finally, because the lives of all women and men were embedded in family relationships, the separate interests of the sexes were offset by the web of concerns and ideals that family generated. In other words, women's interests were protected in part by a view of society as an intricately woven fabric in which individual rights could not be unraveled from mutual responsibilities, especially those of the family.

Focusing on women at court has the benefit of highlighting the gap between normative prescription and actual practice—or perhaps, more accurately, highlighting the complicated relationship between the two. How the court listened to women's claims, how it framed their obligations as well as their rights, how it punished their crimes, whether it even admitted their voices in the legal representation of incidents in which they were involved—all can help us understand the ideals, the limitations, and the compromises of the local court. Conversely, women's strategies at court, both defensive and aggressive, display to us the ways in which the court made space for interpretation of the laws it was mandated to enforce.

A REGISTRY OF VOICES

It is the lively presence of voices in the Aintab records that gives this book its substance. The very structure of the textual record privileges individuals and their words, for the bulk of the judge's summary of a case consisted of the testimony of plaintiffs, defendants, witnesses, and local police. Testimony was recorded in direct, "quotable" speech, often in a vivid vernacular. That individuals spoke directly in the record was perhaps inevitable in a legal system that made little use of lawyers. Moreover, what was often at stake in this sixteenth-century court was the question of honor and personhood, even when the matter in dispute appeared to be money owed or property violated—thus the necessity to speak out for oneself was even greater.

However, as various students of Ottoman-period court records have noted, these records cannot be read transparently.[4] They cannot, that is, be read as simple statements of fact or as a neutral mine of social data. The problem of reconstructing the past from court records may be especially acute for the mid-sixteenth-century records from places such as Aintab. They are short executive summaries, shaped to conform to requirements of Islamic judicial procedure. Much detail of "what really happened" is left out, and much is reinterpreted in the judge's act of summation. Yet if we read the records carefully—in combination with and against one another—they can tell us a great deal about the texture of social relations, the nature of local conflicts, and the motivations of individual actors.

Concentrating on individual voices inevitably raises the question of translation. We cannot read these records without accounting for the processes of representation whereby the tangle of testimony at court, at times discordant and confused, was rendered smooth and concise by judge and scribe in the written record. In the premodern period, the voices of ordinary people were almost always archived through such institutional translation. As David Sabean has noted, however, this very constraint can prove productive since it directs our attention to the relationship of the archiving institution with its clientele.[5] This constraint has in fact led to the focus of the present study on Aintabans as clients of the court. If we use court records as our source, we cannot really study the people of Aintab apart from their relationship to their court.

The question still remains (or will be raised by students of Ottoman history, who sometimes obsess over the power of the Ottoman state) whether court records are merely "state" documents, artifacts of a legal system that was an arm of the state and therefore not accurate reflections of local cultural practices. It is certainly true that the local court did not belong wholly to the community. It oversaw the state's business of taxation and the financing of local defense, and its judge was appointed and salaried by the state. But enough has been said above to demonstrate that the work of the court was carried out not only by the judge but also by members of the community working alongside him. Another argument for looking at the Aintab court registers of 1540–1541 as a locally produced record is the fact that the state's executive arm in the province was also largely local: apart from state-appointed governors, the enforcers of the law were residents of Aintab city and the province's villages. Indeed, the blurred boundary between state and society is another commonplace of this book.

It is perhaps an irony that the registry of voices that the court records offer their readers today is in large part a product of Ottoman imperialization. It was the process of administrative consolidation that made this study possible, since it brought into being the public records that now serve as sources for local history. We can "hear" the individual in part because the emphasis on oral testimony in the court led to attentive listening. Where legally compelling, court authorities replicated the moral rhetoric as well as the materially relevant content of people's suits. This privileging of testimony was a particular emphasis in the work of the Ottoman sultan Süleyman, who was active in legal reform during the years studied in this book. As we will see, Süleyman and his legal advisers stressed the separate but complementary roles of the court and of legal enforcers such as local police and Ottoman provincial authorities. The insistence of the sultan and his legal team that no crime be punished without a trial in a judge's court was one factor in the expansion of the court system in this period. Another reform, it seems, was the practice of preserving the court's records as a publicly available register. It was this emphasis on a public record of local voices that enables us to retrieve some knowledge of Aintab's past.

A YEAR IN THE LIFE OF THE COURT; OR, WHAT IS IMPORTANT ABOUT 1540

Because this study explores the events of a single year, that span has considerable significance as the frame of our textual sources. The year 1540, or 947–948 in the Islamic calendar, is not necessarily a date to memorize, but it is arguably an important moment in the evolution of the Ottoman imperial enterprise and in the evolution of Aintab as a recent object of Ottoman conquest. Incorporated into the Ottoman domain in 1516 as one fruit of the defeat of the Mamluk empire, the region in which Aintab was located began to undergo accelerated assimilation into the empire's administrative networks around the mid-1530s (see maps 1 and 2). Perhaps every individual year has defining characteristics that make it important in some way. From the perspective of this book, three features define the year 1540–1541 for Aintab: growing prosperity, stepped-up integration of the court into an empire-wide legal system, and a program of legal reform that was being scripted in Istanbul, capital of the empire. Reform at the center of course affected the whole empire; here our purpose is to study its impact in one locality.

The process of imperialization meant that Aintab was not only integrated into the military, fiscal, and judicial systems of the Ottoman regime but also subjected to cultural currents and tensions originating beyond its borders. Perhaps the greatest of these was the Ottoman confrontation with the rising power of the Safavid regime in Iran. This ongoing rivalry, ideological as well as territorial, caused shifts in identity and cultural practice at both the imperial and local levels. Central to Ottoman polemic against the Safavid regime was its branding of the Safavids' embrace of shiite (shi'i) Islam as heresy. The very real military and territorial threat posed by the Safavids was cast as a spiritual menace to the Ottoman regime's embrace of sunni Islam. Generally speaking, the targeting of heresy requires two things: a threat to the boundaries of one's community and the power to enforce the "correct" ideological catechism. A central dimension of ideological challenge and response observable throughout mid-sixteenth-century Ottoman society was an increasing emphasis on doctrinal and legal orthodoxies. For the regime's subjects, orthodoxy was spelled out largely in terms of social conduct—the religiously informed rectitude of Ottoman society versus the morally misguided behavior of Safavid society. But while the years around 1540 were marked by intensified activity in the domains of religious and imperial law, these efforts were met at the grassroots level with varying degrees of acceptance.

Aintab in 1540–1541 is an excellent example of the predictable consequences as well as the unpredictable vagaries of incorporation into an imperial enterprise. Aintab was an old Islamic settlement, conquered by Muslim forces four years after the death in 632 c.e. of the Prophet Muhammad. It was also well endowed for its size with institutions of Islamic learning. The city had no doubt had a functioning court for a number of centuries before 1540. That it was the years around 1540 when its court became a node in the expanding network of Ottoman courts is suggested by the fact that its records began to be kept systematically in the mid-1530s; in addition, by 1541 at the latest it was receiving judges appointed from the center. Indeed, Aintab provides a rare opportunity to examine processes of legal incorporation, since very few Ottoman cities have court records extant for this early a date. Aintab is an even rarer opportunity to study an already-established local court at the moment it joined an empire-wide system of legal administration.

What did "Ottomanization" mean for a provincial city such as Aintab and its hinterland? At the most obvious level, it meant a loss of some degree of autonomy but a gain of well-being through the pax Ottomanica that brought safety to local communities and secured the trade routes that allowed them to prosper economically. But how much change was the imperializing power able to impose on its new subjects? In commenting on Charles Tilly's observation that European social history has concentrated on "how people lived the big changes," Judith Tucker notes that social history is also, or should be, about "how people *made* the big changes."[6] The Aintab court records suggest that Tucker's qualification is critical, since they reveal that much of the process of Ottomanization was enacted by local people, not by the centrally appointed agents of the Ottoman regime. Local actors included both elites who were empowered by the regime and ordinary individuals who cooperated with, resisted, and exploited the Ottoman presence on a daily basis.[7]

It is certainly plausible to speak of an "Ottoman legal system" in 1540, but the systematic aspects of the regime's legal administration went only so far. Central authorities established courts, appointed judges, formulated laws, regulated their enforcement by local police, and investigated when local legal processes were deemed to have broken down. In other words, the regime established a legal infrastructure. But as Ronald Jennings has shown, legal culture was heavily influenced by local participation and local customary law.[8] This was perhaps less true of cities in the orbit of the capital, but in the provinces—which were, in fact, the bulk of the empire—regional cultures inevitably infused the practice of the law. In Aintab, legal culture was colored by the variety of religious orientations and social practices of its inhabitants. Aintabans were not a culturally homogeneous lot, and they did not all readily embrace the new orthodoxies promoted by the Ottoman regime. Some no doubt would have agreed with the historian Ahmet Yaşar Ocak, who has characterized the atmosphere surrounding resistance to the regime's program as "a general discontent and a state of despair among the population, especially around the year 1540."[9]

DOING MICROHISTORY

Since one writes an introduction only after finishing a book, I take this opportunity to reflect on the pluses and minuses of the kind of microhistoriographical approach that is entailed in studying a single year in a single locale. Some might contend that the scope of this work is too broad to be called microhistory, but in the context of Ottoman social and legal history, the boundaries of the book's inquiry are drawn narrowly.

If one is interested in the culture of the court and its relationship to the community it served, intensive scrutiny of a particular moment seems a necessary methodology. When one lingers, the court records offer up a richness of small knowledge. One learns, for example, who the power brokers in Aintab were and how the less powerful managed to join forces with them or found ways to assert their own counterclaims. Certain characters reveal aspects of their personality through frequent appearances at court—the litigious woman Esma, the rowdy Armenian Karagöz, the compulsive textile merchant Ahmed Çelebi. Villages too take on different characters—Kızılhisar, a center of animal rustling, and nearby Cağdığın, with its idiosyncratic social values. The end product of such lingering turns out to be a kind of historical ethnography of the Aintab court at a particular moment in its long life.

Microhistory is not easier but rather more complex than a larger-scale study, at least in my view. What at first appears to be a narrowing of focus has a contrary effect, since the microscope catches myriad forces and contingencies that impinge on the phenomenon under study. These range from the very local to the large-scale. While universal contingencies such as class and gender affected the legal culture of Aintab, so did local factors such as the season of the year, the size and location of the village where an incident occurred, and the personality of the actors. Looking locally makes one keenly aware of difference. Indeed, microhistory inevitably leads to the detection of microcultures within the already circumscribed boundary of investigation. The implications for this book are that justice varied considerably, even within the boundaries of a territorially small province.

Large-scale forces shaped the legal life of Aintab in equal measure. In addition to the obvious factor of Ottoman imperializing, the most powerful of such forces was the contest over Muslim religious identity intensified by Ottoman-Safavid rivalries. The newly drawn boundaries separating Ottoman from Safavid territory did not yet define separate ideological communities (if indeed they ever fully did). Many in Anatolia sympathized with the early Safavid movement or were accused of such sympathies. Historians of early modern Europe such as Carlo Ginzburg, Natalie Zemon Davis, and Giovanni Levi have made us familiar with the ways in which religious controversies touched the lives of local communities.[10] In a similar manner, religious strife infected the neighborhoods of Aintab.

As for the limitations of microhistory, one is obvious: it is unfinished business. The court records of 1540–1541 reveal much about the years leading up to this study, but they say nothing about the future. Even if we wished to keep tracking the fortunes of Aintabans in their court, however, we would have to jump some eight years, since the extant Aintab court registers pick up again in earnest only in 1548.

From the reader's point of view, one aspect of the microhistoriographical approach adopted here may be frustrating. Several years of teaching and giving talks about these records have taught me that audiences want a resolution to stories such as those of İne, Fatma, or Haciye Sabah. Why *did* İne and her husband move to another village, did the pregnant and unmarried Fatma finally secure a husband, was Haciye Sabah guilty of heresy or not? It is this desire for closure about the past, I suppose, that causes most audiences to seek an interpretation of what was actually going on in a particular case or of what ultimately happened to its litigants. But the individuals who populate the chapters of this book, mostly women, can only be sketched lightly. Because of their procedurally determined nature, the court records tell fragmented stories. Nor do they always assign guilt or innocence, judgments that, if we had them, would make easier the attempt to reconstruct "what really happened." Moreover, the court is not always interested in the whole story, but rather concentrates on what is legally relevant. In sum, the records are resistant to narration, although each protagonist in a case may tell a story. And so the reader must live with indeterminacy and hypothesis. I offer a small excuse—that in the eyes of our sixteenth-century judges, indeterminacy was sometimes a good thing, since it helped achieve the goal of social equity. All history writing is a reconstruction of the past based on perceptions formed in the present, but I write this book acutely aware that mine are neither complete nor definitive readings of what happened in Aintab some four and a half centuries ago.

READING THE BOOK

As is undoubtedly clear by now, this book is composed of several interwoven themes—the court's relationship to its users, relations between women and men through the medium of the law, the Ottoman context of the Aintab court. To treat these themes separately, or to omit any one of them, would be to diminish the dynamic element in the life of the court. Different readers may wish to concentrate on specific aspects of the book, however.

The three case studies—the stories of the child bride İne, the controversial teacher Haciye Sabah, and the peasant girl Fatma—can be read independently, although they will of course mean more in the context of the book as a whole. The stories of İne and Haciye Sabah open parts 2 and 3, and reflect themes in the chapters that follow. Fatma's story frames the conclusion to the book.

Part 1 of the book provides the setting for our study of Aintabans and their court. Taken together, chapters 1 and 2 present a portrait of Aintab and its people. Chapter 1 locates Aintab both in place and in the passage of time, asking whether its conquest in 1516 was a rupture in the lives of the province's inhabitants and what the conquest meant for people's sense of identity and also for their well-being. Chapter 2 explores the variety of microcultures visible in Aintab by looking at communities defined by religion, urban or rural residence, and sedentary or nomadic lifestyle. The chapter also looks at crime, war, and pilgrimage as forces that drew Aintabans into worlds beyond their province's borders. The court is an element in the portrait drawn in chapters 1 and 2, but it is chapter 3 that introduces the court in detail—its work, the kinds of law it drew on, and its place in the varied legal landscape. The question of how the court translated the messy process of litigation into neat summary records is a particular focus of the chapter.

The chapters in part 2 are reflections on themes—social class, morality, and property. These chapters are particularly concerned with questions of gender and the similarities and differences in the experiences of females and males as they navigated the law locally. Chapters 4 and 5 move between normative law and grassroots practice in Aintab, asking to what degree local individuals tolerated the hierarchical and gendered structures of various legal discourses. Chapter 6 sets property within a set of concentric circles, asking how property and the human relations it fostered affected women as individuals, within their natal and marital families, and in the context of the Ottoman regime's policies of taxation and land ownership. A theme that runs throughout this section is the variability of justice. The story of İne's troubled marriage that introduces the section is also the story of the unusual justice offered by one village in the province.

Part 3 examines the Aintab court in its relation to the Ottoman imperial enterprise. It begins with a story of heresy, considering the ways in which local individuals ran afoul of the religious and political fault lines that were dividing the Middle East. Chapter 7 looks at the court's role in the dialogue between the local and the imperial that shaped Aintab's entry into a vast empire. It is primarily concerned with the question of legitimation—that is, with the political contract between governing regime and subjects and the role played by the court in mediating tensions between them. Chapter 8 addresses the matter of punishment and the sometimes vexed relationship between the judge and the local agents of sovereign authority who enforced the law. The related problems of violence and its uses, both by private individuals and agents of law enforcement, were a concern to local citizens. They were also a concern to the Ottoman regime, which was attempting to create a monopoly over violence in its recently conquered territories.

In part 4 the themes of the book are drawn together in the story of Fatma, which is followed by a brief conclusion. Fatma's attempts to deal with her pregnancy raise questions about the advantages that the local court might offer to such a woman. Her story is placed within the shifting terrain of economic recovery and its consequent effects on young people's ability to make marriages, of legal reform and its repercussions among the residents of a large village, and of the subtle but perceptible changes in the culture of the Aintab court that affected her dilemma. Ultimately Fatma's is a story about a local community making justice through its court.

PART ONE

The Setting

Aintab and Its Court

Locating Aintab in Space and Time

*I have chosen a banal place and an undistinguished story. . . . It is a tale of a
group of persons involved in local events (connected, however, to political and economic acts beyond their direct control) that is so very ordinary that it poses highly
suggestive problems of the motivations and strategies involved in political action.
Rather than open revolt, definitive crisis, profound heresy, or earth-shaking innovation, it was ordinary political life, social relations, the laws of economics, and
the psychological reactions of a normal village that led me to study the many relevant things that take place when nothing seems to be happening.*

GIOVANNI LEVI, *Inheriting Power: The Story of an Exorcist*

The city of Aintab was not so small a place as that studied by Giovanni Levi—
the Piedmont village of Santena in the seventeenth century. Yet as the center of one of hundreds of provinces in the sixteenth-century Ottoman empire, Aintab, like Santena, was not located at a hub of history. The city did
not inscribe itself into the empire's historical narrative until the latter's final
moments, when Aintab gained fame through its resistance in 1921 to occupying French forces. It then acquired the honorific title *gazi* (heroic warrior)—today's Gaziantep, the sixth-largest city in the Republic of Turkey.
But though the story of Aintab is not historically distinguished, it is, in the
richness of its daily drama, no less compelling than that of the more notable
cities of the Ottoman domain. It is simply written on a smaller scale. That
very scale is what I seek to explore, in the hopes that the "motivations and
strategies" of the people of Aintab and the "many relevant things" that took
place there will reveal themselves to us.

In 1540, when our study of Aintab's court begins, the city was the seat of
an Ottoman province of the same name. It had come under Ottoman control only twenty-three years earlier, when the sultan Selim I put an end to
the Mamluk sultanate in 1517. From Cairo, the Mamluk sultans had governed Egypt and greater Syria since the mid–thirteenth century, presiding
over the most stable and culturally prolific civilization of the late-medieval
Middle East. Aintab had been one of the Mamluk sultanate's northernmost
outposts; consequently it was one of the first cities to be taken by Ottoman
forces as they marched east and then south in the summer of 1516. It is said
that it was during his two-day stay in the city that Selim planned the battle

of Marj Dabik, which took place some 50 kilometers south of Aintab and sealed the demise of the Mamluk regime.[1]

In the first decades of Ottoman rule, probably few would have predicted the longevity of the dynasty and of its control of the region. Aintab's history had been one of a long succession of overlords and would-be overlords, some based to the north in Anatolia, some to the south in Aleppo, Damascus, or Cairo, and more rarely to the east (in Mosul, for example). The city was located in what we might call a buffer zone between southeastern Anatolia and northern Syria, a zone of strategic importance both militarily and economically (see map 2). The region, many of whose urban settlements were of ancient lineage, was crisscrossed by trade routes and dotted with fortifications (the citadel of Aintab had been in large part a Roman creation). While Aintab's fate depended significantly on that of Aleppo, the third-largest city of the Ottoman empire after Istanbul and Cairo, the city was not simply a secondary entity in this metropolis's hinterland. It in turn had its own hinterland, and was also an important node in the network that linked the several cities in this relatively urbanized region. Aintab, in other words, was a *locally distinguished* urban center.

If Aintab was ultimately "a banal place" in the now vast horizon of the Ottoman empire, there is one aspect of its history that *does* stand out in the written record of the Ottoman centuries: the fact, true for only a small handful of Anatolian and Syrian cities in the sixteenth century, that the province's court records are roughly continuous for a period of nearly 400 years (from the early 1530s to 1909).[2] This continuity may tell us something about Aintab right away: it suggests cultural and social stability and perhaps a certain civic-mindedness. Admittedly, the vagaries of fire, flood, war, and other hazards to the preservation of documents may account for the absence of court records in many cities where we might expect them for the sixteenth century.[3] Nonetheless, that the city of Aintab may well have taken deliberate care to preserve its court records is a cultural fact worthy of note.

This book obviously could not have been written without the court records, whose contents and interpretive challenges will be discussed in chapter 3. It also makes use of a second kind of historical record that illuminates the local history of Aintab: the cadastral survey register *(tapu tahrir defteri)*. Particularly numerous in the sixteenth century, these government-ordered surveys provided cadastral inventories of the taxpaying population of Ottoman provinces, together with their taxable lands, crops, animals, and services as well as other urban and rural revenues.[4] All this information allows us to sketch a picture of the demographic, economic, and even social complexion of the area surveyed. For Aintab, various cadastral registers exist, beginning as early as 1520, three years after the Ottoman conquest, when Aintab was surveyed together with the neighboring province of Bire (today's

Birecik).[5] In 1526, the province was surveyed in a cursory manner as part of a massive inventory of southeastern Anatolia, northern Iraq, and greater Syria, and then again, more systematically and thoroughly as a single province, in 1536, 1543, and 1574.[6] As Amy Singer has noted, the study of local history in the sixteenth century owes much to the felicitous existence of these two kinds of historical record, court record and cadastral survey.[7] Moreover, for Aintab, the density of such surveys in the first half of the century compensates somewhat for lack of other kinds of sources for local history, such as the registers of central government orders to provincial authorities, which came into being during the latter decades of the century, and the writings of travelers to the region, which exist for the seventeenth century.

A third and different kind of source is remembered history. Here we are most fortunate, for during the middle decades of the twentieth century, a serious effort was made in Gaziantep to collect local folktales, local legends about historical figures (including saints, conquerors, and scholars), and oral histories of local places (including monuments, city neighborhoods, bazaars, whole villages, and even the rivers and famed springs of the province).[8] Remembered history is obviously as much about the present as it is about the past, and it therefore might be thought to be less "reliable" than data gleaned from registers actually compiled in Aintab during the very years of this study. On the other hand, remembered history points us to those events of the past that affected people profoundly enough to inscribe themselves in living memory. The Ottoman conquest was one of these events.

Drawing on these varied sources, this chapter aims to locate the province of Aintab and its inhabitants in their historic environment. It recounts the vagaries of Aintab's fortunes in the decades before the Ottoman conquest, and the province's relative neglect in the first years of Ottoman overlordship. We then examine the beginnings of prosperity in the years leading up to 1540–1541, the focus of this study. Prosperity was not without its attendant constraints, and so we ask what price Aintabans may have paid for their improved circumstances and how Aintab's recent incorporation into the Ottoman domain affected people's sense of cultural and political location. The chapter concludes with a brief tour of the urban landscape to see what it can tell us about Aintab's response to its stormy history.

What we learn is that Aintab was a survivor. A city almost never graced by the presence of princes, it was long accustomed to looking after its own welfare. Its legends might recount the drama of conquest, but rather than surrender to invasion, the story they most often told was of local saints whose miraculous intervention made conquest possible. And as we will see in subsequent chapters, the records of the Aintab court in 1540–1541 suggest that the local population developed a flexible but tough-minded approach to dealing with the most recent of regimes to claim sovereignty over the city.

BUFFETED ON THE BORDER

Neither the recent past of Aintab nor its deep history was a simple story of movement from one relatively stable state to another. Control of Aintab was on the agenda of any power that wished to maintain its borders or create an independent state in the region straddling northern Syria and southeastern Anatolia. As a result the city's political history was one of a dizzying succession of overlords. In addition to Aintab's geopolitically strategic location (indeed, in part because of it), it was well-situated economically since it lay at the intersection of several trade routes. The city served as one of the gateways south to Syria and on through Palestine to Egypt. It also was a node in the network of eastern and southeastern Anatolian cities, which was in turn linked to trade routes east to Iran and southeast to Baghdad and the Persian Gulf. In addition, Aintab was linked to Anatolia through a number of different routes.

Aintab emerged on the stage of history under the aegis of the Byzantine empire. Its citadel was built up in the sixth century by the emperor Justinian as part of the consolidation of Byzantine control of the region. Aintab had already been part of the Roman system of defense in this eastern province guarding the Euphrates; it lay some 60 kilometers from the Roman city of Zeugma, which was situated at one of the few natural crossings of the river in the region.[9] As an urban settlement, Aintab was at first overshadowed by the ancient center of Dülük, 12 kilometers to its north, until the latter was ruined by an earthquake at the end of the fourteenth century.[10] Despite their combined strength, the Dülük and Aintab fortresses were unable to withstand the armies of Islam, who first took the area in 636 C.E., four years after the death of the Prophet Muhammad. Dülük/Aintab continued to operate as an important border post as it moved back and forth between the Byzantines and various Muslim states. The famed Abbasid caliph Harun Al-Rashid incorporated it into his border regime in 782, and in the early eleventh century, during a period of Byzantine revival of the empire's eastern Anatolian frontiers, Dülük became the center of a new "theme," or military administrative zone.[11] During the twelfth century, of the four Crusader states established in the Middle East, two—the principality of Antioch and the county of Edessa (Ruha)—occupied the transition zone between Anatolia and Syria; Aintab lay roughly on the border between them.

It would be a mistake to think that this region became more stable or peaceful with the decline of Christian political influence and the waning of interfaith conflict as Muslim rulers asserted control. After the demise of the Crusader states, Aintab found itself frequently traded back and forth among Muslim powers, small and large, who had ambitions in the region. The city was besieged in 1270 by the Mongols; in 1390 by Sevli Beg, leader of the local Dulkadir tribal federation; in 1400 by the Turko-Mongol conqueror Timur (Tamerlane); and in 1420 by Kara Yusuf, head of the Akkoyunlu tribal federation centered in eastern Anatolia. But despite the recorded violence and destructiveness of these attacks, Aintab was acquiring a reputation as a cultured urban center. Bedreddin Ainî, a native son who went on to a distinguished career under the Mamluks as diplomat, judge, and historian, testified to both aspects of the city's history. Writing at the end of the fourteenth century, Ainî praised the city of his birth as a center of learning. He commented that it was known as "little Bukhara," after the famed city in Transoxania, because of its ability to attract learned scholars.[12] Ainî also wrote an eyewitness account of the suffering of the city's population during the siege of the Dulkadir prince Sevli Beg, when he and his brother were trapped in the citadel.

Though Sevli Beg's siege of 1390 failed, in the century before 1540, the attempts of the Dulkadir tribal federation to gain and maintain recognition as a regional political power were an important theme in Aintab's history. In the narrative of Aintab's recent past, the Dulkadir principality appears as the main protagonist because it was the power most immediately able to affect Aintab's political destinies, despite being the weakest of players in the region. The brief account of regional politics that follows is critical not only in order to situate Aintab on the larger stage of sixteenth-century history but also because these events formed the backdrop to daily lives in 1540–1541, as individuals adjusted past habits and assumptions to new circumstances.

Like the Akkoyunlu federation and the Ottoman dynasty in its origins, the Dulkadir were Turkmen—that is, Turkish-speaking groups with strong tribal allegiance whose legends of migration into Anatolia traced their origin back to Khorasan in northeastern Iran or to Central Asia.[13] The Ottomans had largely shed any tribal characteristics by the time they emerged as a significant regional power in the fifteenth century, but the Dulkadir and the Akkoyunlu drew their strength and legitimacy from the continuous incorporation of tribal groups into their federations. The Dulkadir principality was a loose federation of tribes centered in Elbistan and Maraş. Aintab lay at the southern reach of the circumference of Dulkadir authority, and, like the city of Kayseri on the northern border of Dulkadir, it was a stronghold the principality could not always keep control of.[14]

For nearly two centuries, until the Ottoman conquest, the Dulkadir lords successfully maintained the state that their ancestors had carved out in the fourteenth century.[15] They were able to do so because their territory was a useful buffer among the major powers competing for control of the region: the Mamluks, who had laid claim to the area in the thirteenth century and who managed to keep the Dulkadir lords as vassals for much of the latter's existence; the Ottomans, who became a serious presence in the region in the later fifteenth century; and whoever held power to the east—first the Akkoyunlu and then the Safavids, who succeeded the Akkoyunlu dynasty in eastern Anatolia and Iran. However, the skillful diplomacy that had sustained the Dulkadir principality was no longer adequate to the task in the intensifying confrontation that took place among this triangle of powers in the second decade of the sixteenth century.

It was toward the end of the long reign of Alaeddevle, from 1481 to 1515, that Dulkadir diplomacy was severely tested and ultimately failed. The last Dulkadir prince to rule autonomously, Alaeddevle had cemented his relationship with the Ottoman regime by giving his daughter Ayşe in marriage to the sultan Bayezid II.[16] At the same time, he cultivated his ties with the Mamluks. In the foundation inscription for the great mosque he completed in Maraş in 1502, the Dulkadir ruler conspicuously presented himself as vassal to the Mamluk sultan: the inscription began, "This sacred mosque was built in the days of Sultan Al-Malik Al-Ashraf Qansuh Al-Ghawri[.]"[17] But while the Dulkadir had been able to balance their relationships with the Ottomans and the Mamluks, they could not handle the greater complexities precipitated by the emerging power of Safavid Iran. It was the increasingly heated confrontation between the latter and the Ottoman state of which Alaeddevle ultimately fell afoul.

In 1508, before his regime was even a decade old, the young Safavid shah, Ismail, issued a dramatic challenge in Anatolia by smashing the Dulkadir capital at Elbistan. The Ottoman prince Selim did not let this and other of Ismail's challenges go unanswered. Indeed, Selim's bloody path to the Ottoman throne—overthrowing his father Bayezid in 1512 and executing his three brothers together with their several sons—is typically explained as the result of his frustration with his father's inaction in the face of rapid Safavid expansion. In 1514, an Ottoman army under Selim scored an expensive but decisive victory over the Safavids at Chaldiran in eastern Anatolia, one of the major battles of Ottoman history. But Alaeddevle, who had made peace with the Safavids in the face of Selim's aggressive eastward moves, refused the Ottoman "invitation" to participate in the battle at Chaldiran. For this alliance with Selim's archenemy, Alaeddevle paid with his life.

Alaeddevle's "betrayal" at Chaldiran was used as pretext for his elimination: in June 1515 the ninety-year-old prince was confronted and defeated by the Ottoman eunuch general Sinan Pasha. His subsequent execution in the same year was a prelude to the Ottoman offensive against the Mamluks. Selim used a gruesome symbol of his victory to announce the death of the

Dulkadir prince to the Mamluk sultan Qansuh Al-Ghawri—the severed heads of Alaeddevle, one of his sons, and his vezir. When the heads were revealed by the Ottoman emissary to Al-Ghawri, those present at the royal audience were shocked at this insult to the Mamluk monarch, whose vassal Alaeddevle had been.[18] The sultan himself regained his composure sufficiently to imply that Selim's affront was unworthy of one Muslim's conduct toward another: "Why has he sent me these heads? are they Frankish heads that he sends as a trophy of victory over the infidels?"[19] Pressured by his generals to counter the Ottoman challenge, Al-Ghawri mobilized his forces and marched north to Aleppo. He himself died of a stroke during the fateful battle at Marj Dabik in August 1516. In January 1517, Cairo, and the whole empire with it, fell to the Ottomans.

Thus, within a period of four years, the Ottoman sultan and his soldiers had wiped out the Mamluk regime and removed the Safavids from Anatolia. By 1517, Selim had added a huge expanse of territory to the Ottoman state: eastern and southeastern Anatolia, Syria, Palestine, and Egypt, as well as vassal states in northern Iraq and the Red Sea coast of Arabia, which included the sacred cities of Mecca and Medina (see map 1).[20] The Ottoman sultan was now the preeminent Muslim sovereign in the world, and Muslims for the first time formed the majority of the empire's population.

And what of the Dulkadir principality? As was typical of tribal polities, the princely family often split into rival branches that pursued conflicting policies. A prime example occurred at Chaldiran, where Alaeddevle's nephew, Şehsuvaroğlu Ali, had assisted the Ottoman forces against the Safavids. Rewarded for his services with the governorship of the Dulkadir principality after his uncle's death, Şehsuvaroğlu Ali continued to support the Ottomans by joining their offensive against the Mamluks. He also played a prominent role in suppressing various anti-Ottoman rebellions that emerged in Anatolia and Syria once Ottoman hegemony was established. However, in 1522, when Şehsuvaroğlu Ali himself resisted discipline by the Ottoman administration, he and his four sons were brutally eliminated.[21] At that point, the Dulkadir domain was fully incorporated into the empire and turned into an Ottoman administrative unit, a governorate-general (beglerbegilik) that retained the name of the defeated dynasty.

As a city on the southern fringes of a buffer state, Aintab endured a good deal of buffeting during these years. This was nothing new, however. In fact, the city's suffering in the final years of Dulkadir rule was perhaps somewhat less than what it had endured a generation earlier, when the Dulkadir prince Şehsuvar (Alaeddevle's brother and the father of the last prince, Şehsuvaroğlu Ali) rebelled in the late 1460s against his status as vassal to the Mamluk sultan. Aintab figured all too frequently in the five-year confrontation that ended only with the prince's death. Let us look at this confrontation in some detail, since it provides an example of the assaults that punctuated Aintab's turbulent history. In May 1468, Mamluk forces drove the rebel Şehsuvar's supporters from Aintab. In a report issued by the governor of Damascus to the sultan in Cairo, it was noted that resistance had been fierce, and that an easy victory in the area was not in the offing. True to the governor's prediction, Şehsuvar reoccupied Aintab and drove out the Mamluks a month later, but it took four engagements between the opposing forces before the Dulkadir forces prevailed. Two years later, Şehsuvar offered to return Aintab to the Mamluk sultan, Qaytbay, if the latter would grant him a prestigious commandership in Aleppo province and overlordship of all Turkmen tribes in southeastern Anatolia. This proposition, admittedly audacious, gives us an idea of the importance of Aintab to Mamluk control of the region. It took the Mamluks three more years to subdue the Dulkadir prince, whose trial and execution in Cairo were the occasion for elaborate public spectacle.[22]

Aintab's fortunes had improved under Şehsuvar's brother Alaeddevle, locally known as Ali Devlet. A loyal vassal to the Mamluks, the prince controlled the city during his long reign through the grace of his patrons. Indeed, Aintab and its hinterland appear to have enjoyed a sustained period of relative peace until the events of 1515 and 1516. Considering Aintab an important addition to the Dulkadir domain, Alaeddevle built it a water reservoir as well as a large and centrally located mosque.[23] Repairs on the citadel were completed in 1481 at the outset of his reign. The inscription on the entrance portal hails the Mamluk sultan Qaytbay, who most probably ordered the renovation during a tour of inspection he made of his Syrian provinces in 1477. The tour took the Mamluk sultan as far north as Rumkale, a fortress on the Euphrates about 40 kilometers north of Bire and a day's march northeast of Aintab.[24] During this tour, Qaytbay no doubt visited Aintab, which had recently been restored to his control at considerable cost. To use Clifford Geertz's formulation, in journeying so far from Cairo, Qaytbay was "stamping [his] territory with ritual signs of dominance,"[25] one of which was the reinscription of fortresses in his own name. Nearly forty years later, the Ottoman sultan Selim would retrace Qaytbay's path, for he halted at Rumkale before entering Aintab on his 1516 campaign against the Mamluks. Memory of Selim's own "stamping" of the region can be seen in the present-day name of the area between Rumkale and Aintab—Yavuzeli, "land of the Stern"— after the sobriquet by which the conquering sultan came to be known.

Selim's choice of route in 1516 thrust Aintab once again into the throes of high politics (see map 3 for Selim's route). The seven days between the imperial army's arrival at Rumkale and the fateful confrontation with the Mamluks were no doubt momentous ones for the people of Aintab province. Perhaps to save the city from harm, perhaps to save himself, Yunus Beg, the province's Mamluk governor, defected to the Ottoman side. On August 20, 1516, he gave Selim the keys to the Aintab citadel, and on August 21 the sultan pitched camp "with great majesty and pomp" at the edge of the city. That day and the next, Selim held formal consultations with local military commanders to plan the battle that would take place on August 24 at Marj Dabik. Yunus Beg himself provided military intelligence during both the planning and the execution of the battle.[26] Aintab's alignment with the advancing Ottoman regime thus provided a critical opening to the rich and strategically located province of Aleppo, the first chunk of Mamluk territory to fall to Selim and his forces.

The demise of the Mamluk sultanate some five months later meant that princes would no longer use Aintab as a bargaining chip or a staging platform. Although inhabitants of the province could not have known it at the time of the Ottoman conquest, Aintab would enjoy nearly four centuries of relative freedom from assault, until the French invasion of 1921. For the first time in nearly a millennium, Aintab in 1540 was situated in the middle of an empire rather than in a borderland. This repositioning under the Ottomans of course lessened the strategic importance Aintab had enjoyed as a border province, rendering it a more "banal place." But banality may have been sweet to a city that had been so buffeted by recent history.

The Ottoman conquest did not mean complete stability for Aintab. A certain degree of flux was inevitable as the newly acquired territories underwent integration into Ottoman systems of military, fiscal, and judicial administration. As for Aintab, the ambiguity of its geographical identity and historical legacy was evident in its shifting administrative attachment during the first decades of Ottoman overlordship. Ottoman authorities first included the province (sancak, liva) in the beglerbegilik, or governorate-general, of Aleppo.[27] In so doing, they reaffirmed Aintab's late Mamluk identity as the northernmost post of a Syrian cultural and economic zone. However, at some point in the 1530s, perhaps as early as 1531, Aintab was transferred to the governorate-general of Dulkadir, whose capital was the city of Maraş.[28] The reasons for this transfer are not clear, although Dulkadir's relative lack of urban centers may have been one factor. Certainly the transfer of Aintab added a valuable economic and administrative node to a governorate-general largely populated by tribal groups. Aintab may also have been useful for its judicial potential, for, as we will see in chapter 3, its court was an important legal resource for the region.

Despite its administrative attachment to Dulkadir, Aintab continued to figure in the social and economic orbit of Aleppo, which was a major nexus of regional as well as international trade routes (in 1818, Aintab province would be returned to the governorate-general of Aleppo). As a culturally mixed province, where many inhabitants were bilingual in Turkish and Arabic (some spoke other languages as well), Aintab was characteristic of the whole ribbon of territory stretching from Iskenderun on the Mediterranean to Mosul in northern Iraq. The ambiguous geography of this region was still evident at the collapse of the Ottoman empire, as the states emerging after World War I quarreled over its destiny.[29]

THE PRICE OF STABILITY

The three-way battle among the Mamluks, the Ottomans, and the Dulkadir princes for control of Aintab in 1515 and 1516 adversely affected its material well-being, as might be expected. Moreover, the region was relatively neglected by Ottoman authorities until the mid-1530s, and it is only then that signs of prosperity begin to reemerge. By the cadastral survey year of 1536, the population of the province was growing, and by 1543 the economy was on an upswing.[30] Our study of the 1540–1541 court records is therefore situated in a time of recovering prosperity for the province as a whole (if not for every resident). In the following pages, we look briefly at the process of recovery as it is revealed in cadastral surveys. This process formed much of the background to what went on at court, since, for example, it fostered shifts in patterns of employment, in attitudes toward property and other material goods, and, perhaps most important, in social relations. All these were areas of human experience whose management might require recourse to the law. The relationship between changing material circumstances and local legal life was intensified because recovery was inseparable from the increasing intervention of the Ottoman regime in the affairs of its newly acquired province. Relations between Aintabans and their new overlord often sorted themselves out in court. The court's records suggest that in 1540 the people of Aintab were still occupied with adjusting their lives to the effects of conquest, which brought stability but at a certain price.

Before outlining the process of recovery in Aintab, I think it important to frame this discussion of change at the grassroots level with a generalization about the period. It would be a mistake to assume, as too often is done, that provincial and especially rural areas in the premodern period were static and unchanging—bound by "traditional" lifestyles and modes of problem solving.[31] Such a notion is clearly inappropriate with regard to the sixteenth-century province of Aintab. This notion unfortunately lingers in much current thinking about Ottoman history, where a fixity is ascribed to the "classical period" as if that constituted a stable and largely unchanging society. This tendency to locate meaningful change only in the later centuries of the Ottoman period results largely from the nearly universal view of the fifteenth and sixteenth centuries, in particular the reign of Süleyman (1520–1566), as a time relatively free of tensions and significant challenge to the modus operandi of the empire. In truth, however, Süleyman's reign was marked by challenge and contestation, and the lives of his subjects by change both subtle and overt. Moreover, vast territories were still in the process of being absorbed—not only the conquests of Selim but also Süleyman's own stretching of the European wing of the empire through the addition of Hungary and a number of vassal states. In other words, the Ottoman empire was still "becoming," as its foundations were expanded and reconfigured. Local courts were inevitably caught up in these shifting currents as institutions both shaped by and giving shape to new directions. As for the sultan's subjects in Aintab, users of the provincial court in 1540 were engaged in the process of adapting old strategies and devising new ones, seeking not only to cope with the encroaching state but also to take advantage of the province's increasing prosperity.

Despite the relative peace under Alaeddevle's long reign, Aintab was located in an area that suffered depredation during the conquest years in addition to the general depressive force of political uncertainty. The large cadastral register of 1526, which surveyed most of the territories conquered by Selim, suggests that Dulkadir was by far the poorest of the four governorates-general spanning southeastern Anatolia and Syria.[32] The register provides consistent enough data across the provinces surveyed to permit the use of estimated tax revenues as a rough comparative measure of wealth (revenue was given in *akçe,* the standard silver currency of the empire). For the governorate-general of Damascus, revenue per taxed household was 338 akçes; for wealthy Aleppo, 567 akçes; for Diyarbakır, 307 akçes; and for Dulkadir, a low 165 akçes per household.[33]

Had the Dulkadir princes left a legacy of poverty? Disruption and disorganization experienced as the Dulkadir principality unraveled no doubt played a role in its relative poverty. But other areas in southeastern Anatolia and Syria also suffered from the neglect of faltering states and the wages of conquest. Two other factors may help to account for the low tax revenue from Dulkadir. First, the territory of Dulkadir was intrinsically less productive than the other governorates-general since it was largely mountainous and lacked either a major commercial and cultural center such as Damascus or Aleppo or the abundance of middle-sized cities that Diyarbakır enjoyed (Ruha, Amid, Mardin, and Mosul, for example). Second, it was harder to collect taxes in Dulkadir because of its large tribal population. Tribal groups were not only dispersed and more mobile than peasants or city dwellers, but also notoriously resistant to taxation by state authorities. In other words, the data from Dulkadir suggest both a poorer population and one that was less taxable.

How should we place the province of Aintab in the context of the 1526 survey? Although it belonged to the Aleppo governorate-general in 1526, it was considerably poorer than Aleppo's other provinces: Aintab's revenue yield was an estimated 246 akçes per household.[34] On the other hand, the province was notably better off than other parts of the Dulkadir governorate-general, to which it would be transferred around 1531. It seems that relative peace in the decades before the Ottoman conquest may not have translated into prosperity for Aintab. This is not surprising, given the waning attention of the Mamluks to their northernmost territories and the struggle of Alaeddevle to save his principality in the face of Ottoman and Safavid designs on it.

The court records confirm that Aintab experienced dislocation and loss of population in the years preceding and following the conquest, perhaps in the rural areas of the province more than the city itself. A dispute over ownership of a vineyard in the village of Keferbostan, recorded in the court register for December 1540, gives us one chronology of flight from the land followed by resettlement. When the peasant Yakub came to court to lay claim to a vineyard he had planted and apparently left in the care of Haci İdris, the latter defended his ownership by demonstrating in his testimony that Yakub's claim to the vineyard exceeded a fifteen-year statute of limitations: "After Yakub planted the vineyard, the village went into decline. It's been about seven or eight years since the village started to prosper again after being abandoned, and the place was recultivated and then the vineyard reestablished. It's been twenty-five years since I took over the vineyard."[35] According to Haci İdris's timetable, Yakub abandoned his vineyard (and his village) around the time (1515) that Ottoman authorities executed Alaeddevle—a time when anxieties about the fate of Aintab and its hinterland must have been high. Haci İdris's testimony suggests that the contest over the region initiated a period of dislocation whose effects were felt through the early 1530s.

Another example of decline and recovery emerges from the 1543 cadastral survey. Among the list of estimated tax revenues for Hiyam, the most populous of the province's villages, were entries for a butchers' workshop and a dyers' workshop. However, no revenue figures were entered for either establishment: the dyers' workshop was described as abandoned and fallen into disrepair, while the blank entry for the butchers' workshop tax suggests that butchering activities had once, but no longer, existed at a taxable level. The dyers' workshop was to reappear in the 1574 cadastral survey with a healthy tax revenue, indicating that at some point textile dyeing revived as a productive occupation in Hiyam. Taken together, the vagaries of the Keferbostan vineyard and of Hiyam's workshops suggest an upswing beginning in the mid-1530s and continuing through the middle decades of the century. But the pace of recovery was uneven, and some outcomes of the region's post-conquest decline, no matter how temporary it might have been, permanently altered the complexion of local societies and economies. A small example is the demise of Hiyam as a meat-processing center.

Recovery in the Aintab region was in part a function of post-conquest consolidation, but consolidation did not follow immediately upon the Ottoman conquest. It is no coincidence that the mid-1530s emerge as a time of upswing, since it was only then that the Ottoman regime turned its close attention to the region. A critical event affecting the fortunes of southeastern Anatolia as well as of northern Syria and Iraq was the victorious and much-celebrated military campaign against Iran undertaken by the sultan Süleyman between 1534 and 1536. By the 1530s, it had become clear that the Safavid whirlwind was not a passing phenomenon: the Iranian state had established itself as a formidable and seemingly permanent rival. Süleyman's extended eastern offensive was a second major victory of the Ottomans over the Safavids, a contest now played out between the sons and successors of Selim and Ismail, the original combatants at Chaldiran. Since it was Süleyman's first eastern campaign, it also provided an opportunity for the sultan to stamp the vast areas through which he and his army marched with his own sovereign legitimacy.

One of the principal outcomes of the campaign of 1534–1536 was increased security of trade and communication routes that passed east through the southeastern Anatolian cities of Aintab, Bire, Ruha, and Amid (today's Gaziantep, Birecik, Urfa, and Diyarbakır). Part of the trade was destined for Iran, part would pass through Mesopotamia to Baghdad. The ancient seat of the prestigious Abbasid caliphate and a city of great political and economic as well as historical importance, Baghdad was the principal prize won by the sultan and his armies in 1535. Control of Baghdad gave the Ottomans access to the Persian Gulf and to trade routes that enhanced the value of those already incorporated into the empire by Selim.

To what extent was Aintab province integrated into this larger world? The court records provide us with evidence about Aintab's connection to trade routes linking eastern and southeastern Anatolia to Baghdad and Iran. In 1541, the Aintab court was the site of investigations into two crimes against traders plying these routes: the robbery and murder of two Christian merchants carrying linen cloth from Erzincan to Diyarbakır and the robbery of a member of the sultan's provincial cavalry, who was also carrying linen cloth, on his way from his base in Konya to Baghdad.[36] While neither of these crimes was *committed* in Aintab (the murder took place near Malatya and the timariot was robbed in Bire, the province directly east of Aintab), that they were *tried* there suggests the role played by the city in securing regional networks. Aintab also had links to the trade south. The return of Venetian traders to Aleppo in the early 1530s, after a fifteen-year absence, suggests a general revitalization of trade and manufacture in the formerly Mamluk world to which Aintab had been connected.[37] The court records of 1540–1541 show that textiles from as far away as Damascus and Egypt were being bought and sold among leading merchants and officials of the city, as well as between city merchants and village chiefs.[38]

While the specific geopolitics of Ottoman-Mamluk and then Ottoman-Safavid relations were critical in determining economic and social well-being (or lack thereof) in the Aintab area, they were not the only relevant factors. Patterns of decline and recovery were more than regional. Stagnation in the early sixteenth century resulted not only from the contest for control of the area but also from a general decline in Mediterranean trade. Likewise, recovery in the Aintab area was linked to the growth of the Mediterranean region as a whole between 1520 and 1580, a phenomenon observed by Fernand Braudel and confirmed for the Ottoman domain by a number of scholars.[39] In the case of Aintab, the cadastral registers give evidence of substantial population and revenue increase between the survey years of 1536 and 1543. For example, the number of rural households in the district surrounding Aintab city grew from 1,151 to 1,500, an increase of 30 percent, while in the same period tax revenues increased by 56 percent. In Aintab city, while the number of households increased by a small margin, from 1,836 to 1,896, city tax revenues increased by a dramatic 73 percent.[40]

We need to be cautious when studying economic and social change through cadastral surveys, since it is hard to be certain how much the figures reflect real growth and how much they are the artifact of more efficient counting by government bureaucrats. In evaluating these figures, we must also keep in mind the expansion of government regulation and taxation, which harnessed growth in order to divert a portion of it to state coffers. In other words, these figures suggesting recovery and growth may rest in part on more vigorous tax assessment and collection. An example of this phenomenon is the Aintab market inspectorship *(ihtisap)*, a vital and lucrative office that collected taxes on the scales and stamps used by shop owners as well as fines on substandard products; additionally, it was responsible for levies on merchandise coming into Aintab's markets to be sold and purchased goods going out.[41] The potential annual revenues of the market inspectorship had clearly been underestimated at 40,000 akçes in the 1536 survey of the province; the error was rectified in the survey of 1543, where the market inspectorship was listed as generating 136,000 akçes annually, or more than triple the previous estimate.[42] Moreover, in 1543 revenues from the market inspectorship were no longer listed as part of the provincial governor's income, but instead had been transferred to the state administration, where presumably they could be more directly and effectively supervised. The point here is that failure to read the huge jump in market inspectorship revenues in the context of increasing government scrutiny and control of the local economy may lead to an overestimation of economic expansion.

If tax assessment and collection were less efficient before 1543, it is in part because the Ottoman regime did not yet have sufficient control over Aintab (and provinces like it) to implement its fiscal systems. But it also

seems likely that the regime deliberately practiced a degree of benign neglect for the first twenty years or so of its rule. For example, it appears to
have lowered tax rates in Aintab after the conquest and then raised them
sometime between the survey years of 1536 and 1543 (the market inspectorship is only one example of this). The first survey of Aintab in 1520,
which probably reflects rates in effect at the time of the conquest, reveals
tax rates considerably higher than those applied in 1536: for example, the
annual head tax on farmers *(çift resmi)* was 80 akçes in 1520 but half that in
1536, the head tax on landless rural laborers *(bennak resmi)* was reduced
from 16 to 12 akçes, and the vineyard tax was reduced from 30 akçes per
thousand vines to 20 akçes in 1536.[43] This reduction of taxes following conquest was a standard policy of the Ottomans.[44] Not only did it placate local
antagonism toward the conqueror, but it also provided incentives to repopulation and helped people get their local economies rolling again. Then,
when the regime was more firmly entrenched in the conquered area and recovery was moving apace, taxes might be raised: in Aintab, the vineyard tax
was doubled from 20 to 40 akçes per thousand vines between 1536 and
1543, while the taxes on wheat and barley (the principal staple crops) were
increased by 20 percent and 33 percent respectively.[45] The head tax on
farmers and landless laborers remained at its lowered rate, however, a continuing incentive to the repopulation of rural areas. In short, the figures
cited above demonstrating population and revenue increase appear to illustrate the workings both of Ottoman fiscal manipulation and of the general prosperity of the eastern Mediterranean in these years. If Aintabans
were unhappy with the Ottoman regime's managerial approach, their re-
sentment was perhaps softened by good times.

A time of economic recovery and growth was also a time of social
change—change that might be accompanied by strains in social relations
as individual roles and expectations underwent transformation. The cadastral surveys, and to a lesser extent the court records, yield a wealth of information testifying to shifting economic and social structures and relations.
For one thing, settlement and occupational patterns within the province
were shifting. One rural trend observable in the various cadastral registers
belonging to Aintab was the movement of agricultural production, particularly of the staple crops of wheat and barley, from the farms of larger villages to those of smaller villages.[46] And in the larger villages, increasing
numbers of people were employed in cash-crop farming, sharecropping,
and nonfarming occupations such as textile production and food processing. As grain production shifted to smaller villages, unfarmed land was being brought into cultivation: the court records of 1540–1541 contain numerous grants to peasant cultivators and gentlemen farmers of title to virgin
land. Moreover, areas previously abandoned were coming back into culti-

vation. Known as *mezraa*s, these were tracts devoted to agricultural production, boundaried and often linked to specific villages, on which settlement
appears to have been forbidden (*mezraa* might best be translated as "cultivated field"). Mezraas have been described as a kind of agricultural reserve,
that is, land that went in and out of production according to demand.[47]
That Aintab was in the process of recovering mezraa lands is revealed in several grants of title to mezraas in 1540–1541, where the land is described as
"abandoned and in decline" and "suitable for cultivation."

These changes in land use had implications for the tribal population of
the province. The opening up of agricultural land facilitated the settlement
of tribal groups. Sedentarization was certainly a policy encouraged by the
Ottoman regime, for whom the pacification of rebellious tribes in Dulkadir and elsewhere was a challenge in the decades immediately following
the conquest.[48] As traditional agriculturalists diversified or moved entirely
into other occupations, space was opened up in the villages and mezraas
of the province for new labor, agricultural or otherwise. While tribal loyalties might still persist, settling down to a life of mixed pastoralism and agriculture transformed an individual from the status of nomad, identified
through the tribe, to that of householder, identified through the land. This
transformation was not a simple one, however, and we will see that a significant amount of criminal prosecution at court had to do with tribal practices
such as abduction and private vengeance that sat less well with more urbane
segments of the Aintab population.

These shifts appear to have been related in turn to changing household
structures and changing roles for both females and males. Where the employment pattern of male heads of household changed, so did that of
women and children. For example, females were likely to have a greater variety of work experiences in larger villages, with their more diversified
economies. Moreover, it is difficult not to relate shifting rural employment
patterns to the chronologically parallel rise in the number of bachelors
(*mücerred*). Why the numbers of bachelors increased is a complex question
beyond the scope of this study, but the phenomenon may have been one of
the outcomes of prosperity, as demand for land as well as for nonfarming
jobs outpaced availability.[49] The resulting financial inability of men to establish an independent marital household thus pushed up the age at which
they married. And where there were more bachelors, marriage strategies of
young women and their families compensated accordingly.[50] We can imagine a further effect of greater numbers of bachelors on household structures and gender roles: because of the general social discomfort with allowing unmarried males to live independently in neighborhoods of married
householders, these bachelors remained in the homes of their parents or
elder brothers. All of these issues—employment, land, marriage—were cri-

tical to individual well-being and frequently caused problems that required adjudication, as the court records so clearly demonstrate. The stories of İne and Fatma highlight the problems of young peasant girls in the often difficult process of negotiating marriage.

Social and economic life were not the only domains of change. Rivalry between the Ottoman and Safavid states carried with it profound religious tension that might reach down to local communities such as Aintab. This tension stemmed from the Safavid dynasty's declaration of shi'ism as the religion of state, a move that placed Iran in doctrinal opposition to the sunni allegiance of the Ottomans. The Islamic world had not seen a powerful shi'i state since 1171, with the fall of the Fatimid dynasty in Egypt. This fact in itself rendered the Safavid adoption of shi'ism an ideological challenge the Ottomans could not leave unanswered. Moreover, ideological rivalry was in part fueled by rivalry over the allegiance of the populations of eastern and southeastern Anatolia and northern Syria, in particular that of Turkmen tribal groups spread throughout these regions. It was these Turkmen tribes who had given their religious allegiance to the Safavid movement in the second half of the fifteenth century and had moreover formed the armies that turned it into a conquering dynasty. But others too were sympathetic, or perceived to be sympathetic, to the religious preaching of the Safavid shahs. The latter claimed allegiance not only as monarchs but also as charismatic sufi sheikhs, for the Safavid movement had its origins in a sufi order that began to proselytize actively in the later fifteenth century, especially in Anatolia. Throughout the sixteenth century, many remained loyal to the Safavid house, either covertly or overtly, even though the Ottoman regime did not cease its prosecution of Safavid loyalists.[51] The confrontation between these two superpowers of the sixteenth century had repercussions throughout the region, creating as it did an ideological "cold war" that affected relations even among ordinary residents of communities such as Aintab. The story of Haciye Sabah revolves around a case in which social and religious tensions in Aintab erupted in an accusation of "heresy" not unlike accusations of witchcraft in Europe at the time.[52]

The intensification of religious politics and polemic between the two rival powers meant that religion acquired a more central role in government than it had played in recent centuries. Greater attention was paid, for example, to Islamic jurisprudence and its practitioners, and to "correcting" the beliefs of ordinary subjects. From this perspective, Süleyman's military victory against Iran in 1535 was a watershed in his reign, since it initiated a period during which the sultan's concern with religio-legal orthodoxy became a central focus of his activities. The issuing of Süleyman's comprehensive law code and the interest he showed in religious law during the years with which this book is concerned were manifestations of his heightened attention to religious politics. These years were also a period of strengthening and expanding the system of provincial courts and of introducing the new law codes to them.

Indeed, it was impossible to separate religious orthodoxy, legal administration, and consolidation of the state's military and fiscal control over territories recently conquered. The very conditions that yielded greater economic security and stability in the Aintab region were in part the result of tighter control by the state of its provincial domains. It is probably no coincidence that the series of Aintab court registers kept as a public record dates from the early 1530s, that the first two cadastral surveys occurred in close succession in 1536 and 1543, and that a powerful judge was appointed in 1541. While a strong court was in many ways a good thing for its clients, it also facilitated greater control by the government. The court was the principal venue not only for the legal affairs of the population but also for the state's fiscal affairs, since the business of taxation—collection, disbursement, and any related disputes—was registered there. As we have seen, court records and surveys do not merely record growth in the province; they also reveal the state's stake in documenting and controlling growth. Indeed, documentation for the Ottomans was the handmaiden of control.

LOCALISM, HISTORICAL MEMORY, AND IDENTITY

How did individuals in the city of Aintab and in the villages and tribal settlements of its hinterland see their place in the world in 1540? Had they acquired a sense of "being Ottoman"? or were memories of the Mamluks or of the Dulkadir interlude still part of their cultural baggage? Perhaps, as citizens of a volatile border region, their loyalties were perforce more local. The court records do not address such questions of identity and allegiance directly, just as they do not purposefully elicit our subjects' views on matters at the heart of daily life, such as family and marital relations or religion and spirituality. They do, however, provide us with enough clues to point toward some answers. The most useful clues come from the ways people in court talked about the past. Their framing of past time suggests that Aintabans' loyalties were indeed local, and that they did not construct their identities in relation to the regimes that ruled them.

Historical time as people invoked it at court did not extend back much beyond a single generation. The chronology of Haci İdris cited above, reconstructed to enable him to lock in his claim to Yakub's abandoned vineyard, is not untypical in citing the span of an adult lifetime as evidence in support of a particular suit. For many, the Ottoman conquest of the region served as a prelude to their adult lives, figuring as it did as a signal event of their childhood or youth. While Haci İdris did not explicitly mention the conquest (although it clearly figured as the catalyst for the chain of events he recounted), other individuals at court invoked it as a convenient point from which to reckon time. When, for example, the death of an old man who was an expert on horses was reported in court, it was explained that he had "come and taken up residence in these parts around the time of the conquest[.]"[53]

Another way in which voices in the court record marked time was by reference to local governors and their terms in office. In a suit brought by one İncebay and her stepson Mehmed to evict the occupant of a house that they claimed was their inherited property, İncebay dated the period of occupancy from "the time when the late Mihaloğlu was governor of Aintab," while Mehmed stated that the occupant had lived there for forty years.[54] Mihaloğlu (whose name was actually Mihaloğlu Yahşi Beg, or Yahşi Beg son of Mihal) would have been a governor difficult to erase from the city's memory, if only because of the college he had founded in his family's name; the Mihaliye, as it was known (the equivalent of our calling something "the Carnegie" or "the Rockefeller"), commanded the largest budget of any urban institution in Aintab, according to a 1557 government survey of public institutions in the province.[55] In another case involving a dispute over the status of a piece of government land, a leading Aintab official insisted that the land was *timar*, that is, land whose revenue supported a member of the Ottoman provincial cavalry. The parcel in question, he emphasized, "had from the royal conquest through the term of Ali Beg been farmed as *timar*"—Ali Beg being the current governor-general of Dulkadir.[56] The official thus framed the period of Ottoman administration in terms of local avatars of Ottoman dominion: the conquering sultan and the current delegate of sultanic authority in the region. In other words, what mattered was not the sovereign power in a faraway capital but who represented it.

Distinguished individuals, it seems, and the events associated with them were useful markers in the measurement of time. The same tendency to count time by individuals and life spans, rather than by a specified number of years or by actual dates, can be observed in government survey registers as well as in court records. In the surveys, the length of time that a piece of private property had been in the hands of a particular family was indicated by giving the genealogy of the family rather than dates or an approximate number of years. (In Ottoman sources, genealogy is recorded by listing the line of ancestors back into time; there "b." is an abbreviation of "ibn," or "son of," and "bt." an abbreviation of "bint," or "daughter of.") An example of length of ownership established by genealogy is the village of Arıl, owned by the Boyacı family, one of the three leading households of Aintab. In the survey register of 1543, the village was entered as "the property of Seydi Ahmed b. Alaüddin b. Mehmed b. İbrahim b. Hüseyin Boyacı."[57] The prominence of these families was signaled by their adoption of a lineage name—accomplished by prefacing the name of the eponymous ancestor with "İbn" or adding the suffixes -*zade* or -*oğlu,* all meaning "descendant(s) of."[58] Hence we find "Boyacıoğlu," descendants of "the dyer," or "İbn Sikkak," descendants of "the coiner," one of the other notable families.

Events occurring before the Ottoman conquest are sometimes described in the court record as happening in Mamluk time. Aintabans referred to these years as "the time of the Circassians," a label alluding to the ethnic origins of Mamluk rulers of the fifteenth and early sixteenth centuries. In two cases of disputed ownership, one regarding a house and the other a vegetable garden, the occupant and the vegetable farmer, respectively, won because they could prove that they had possessed the property since the "Circassian" period.[59] In the latter dispute, the farmer claimed to have worked the property "for twenty or thirty years" (an adult lifetime), while the witnesses for his case testified that his mother had acquired the property as the result of a distribution of land at some unspecified point "in the time of the Circassians."

In these two property cases, the Aintab court was most likely satisfied with these loosely established dates because they comfortably exceeded the statute of limitations on property claims. However, when the court and its users wanted to, they could be quite precise about dates. Specific dates typically appear in entries in the registers that recorded the receipt of annual taxes, stipulated the term for which a tax farm was granted, or noted the period over which a private debt would be repaid. If, as it seems, the strengthening of the court system was an aspect of greater Ottoman administrative presence in the later 1530s, people were perhaps becoming more used to precision with regard to dates. This no doubt went hand in hand with the growing importance of documents relative to oral evidence, especially in financial matters (a subject that will be dealt with at greater length in chapter 7). For a fee, users of the court could obtain a copy of the court record of their case. This document, known as a *hüccet,* was dated by the court scribe, and its contents might refer to other dates if they were relevant to the matter at issue. Such documents apparently were carefully preserved: people often brought them to court to prove a claim, and on occasion, when unable to prove a claim, were forced to admit that the documents had gotten lost. But while more precise dating was an aspect of Ottoman administrative consolidation, marking time by generations and by reference to known events and persons continued as a functional practice at court. Not only was it a familiar mode of recovering the past, but it struck a different cultural register from numerical dating in that it validated one's own relation to the past or present in terms of significant others.

As the examples above suggest, it was the settling of claims over property that most often required petitioners at court to cast their memory back over time. Otherwise, history was not much present at court. When locating points in the past *was* necessary, as in the cases above, there is a notable lack of reference to the period of Dulkadir overlordship of Aintab. Although the Dulkadir name remained alive administratively as the regional governorate-general to which Aintab now belonged, the Dulkadir legacy seems not to have entered the collective historical memory as worthy of defining a period in Aintab's past. Perhaps Aintabans had absorbed the view of the Ottoman and Mamluk superpowers that the Dulkadir lords were ultimately vassals, not princes. Moreover, the ignominious deaths of Şehsuvar in 1472, Alaeddevle in 1515, and the last prince, Şehsuvaroğlu Ali, in 1522 reduced them to the status of common rebels. All were denied a ruler's prerogative of burial in a fitting tomb, which would have helped preserve their memory as future generations came to recite a prayer of blessing. Perhaps to residents of Aintab, an old urban center with cultural pretensions, the Dulkadir lords were merely tribal chiefs. The citizens of Aintab probably considered their own city, with its reputation for learning and its connections with the cosmopolitan metropolis of Aleppo, culturally superior to the Dulkadir capitals of Elbistan and Maraş.

Historical hindsight suggests that it was the Mamluk experience that figured as the *longue durée* of the province's past. The memory of the Mamluks surely lingered after their political death. There were the physical traces they left in the urban structures they had built or rebuilt: Qaytbay's enhancement of the citadel, the neighborhood mosques endowed by his predecessor Khushqadam and his successor Qansuh Al-Ghawri (both of which carried their patrons' name), and the large fountain *(kastel)* constructed by Al-Ghawri.[60] In the countryside, there were a number of villages and mezraas that had been the private property of Al-Ghawri and were now managed by his granddaughter, Fatima. Fatima's late father, Mehmed Beg, who spent time in Aintab, had been an unforgettable character, a man who loved entertainment, stayed up all night and slept during the day, and was surrounded by performers and sycophants.[61] (Fatima's own son would later become *beglerbegi*, or governor-general, of Aleppo.) [62] And finally, there were Aintabans who owed their wealth and position to favors under the Mamluks. In short, Aintab—the city at least, if not all the province's villages—had no doubt acquired a habit of orienting itself politically and culturally to the south.

But it is important not to overestimate the sense of linkage that the people of Aintab felt to the dominant political powers of the region. Indeed, what is striking in the court record is the absence of a sense of larger political allegiance. This may not be so surprising given that Aintab had typically been located on the northernmost or southernmost border of political entities in the region, and was never fully integrated as a vital component in any imperial network. In other words, Aintab was accustomed to being a city of the marchland. Moreover, its recent historical experience was of waning states. Even so important a Mamluk administrative center as Damascus experienced a certain degree of isolation in the last decades of Mamluk over-lordship, as the powers in Cairo became increasingly unable to exert their influence beyond the capital. As for the Ottoman regime, it was a rising state that had only recently arrived on the scene. Not only was Aintab in 1540 on the cusp of a shift in imperial culture, but the Ottoman entity itself was deeply engaged in the process of "becoming"— of integrating into its already-established identity as a Balkan and western Anatolian power its new legacy as the heir to the Mamluk sultanate and, consequently, the para-mount sovereign presence in the eastern Mediterranean. The mantle of hegemony, in other words, was not yet fully embroidered with Ottoman design.

But there is an issue here larger than the location of Aintab relative to sovereign authorities. We often tend, mistakenly, to backdate the idea of the state as a corporate and integrative enterprise, as a medium providing an overarching identity to its citizens by means of the integration of disparate localities into a political whole. Governing authority was not, however, con-ceived in such terms in the sixteenth-century Middle Eastern world. Had we to render the term "state" into the language of the sixteenth century, we would most probably settle on the word *devlet* (*dawla* in Arabic), but it would not have signified then the modern notion of the state that it does today. Rather, a resident of Aintab in the sixteenth century would have under-stood the term *devlet* to mean the ruling dynasty and the government classes immediately dependent upon it. In this scheme, the dynasty was a source of authority imposed on a set of preexistent, ongoing local entities and en-terprises. Aintab might recognize itself as one of those localities, but it could by no stretch of the imagination have included itself in the concept of *devlet*.

This notion is embedded in the Ottoman dynasty's own self-representation. While asserting the dynasty's sovereignty over conquered territories, imperial rhetoric simultaneously acknowledged the separate identities of the various regions constituting its domain. Operative terms in the sixteenth-century language of this empire were *Al-i Osman,* the House of Osman, and *memalik-i mahruse,* the well-protected domains. The first rep-resented the dynasty itself, as its own corporate enterprise. Still popular in the early sixteenth century was the genre of "Histories of the House of Os-man," which recounted the glorious exploits of the sultans and, both im-plicitly and explicitly, proclaimed their legitimacy. As with the Boyacı fam-ily of Aintab, lineage defined identity and established historical claim to ownership. The sultans never spoke their own names without a train of their forefathers' names behind it: Süleyman, for example, in closing a letter to Francis I of France, identified himself as "Sultan Süleyman Khan son of Se-lim Khan son of Bayezid Khan."

However, when the sultan referred to the empire as a whole, as he often did in decrees addressed to an internal audience, he called it *memalik-i mahrusem,* "my well-protected domains." The phrase *memalik-i mahruse* emphasized the plurality of domains, not their unity, not their "Ottomanness." When the sultan wished to proclaim his own legitimacy, most volubly expressed to other rulers, he drew attention both to the multiplicity of his possessions and to the historical individuality of each. In the letter to Francis, Süleyman saluted the French king in a manner intended to point up the disparate scope of their sovereignties: "I, sultan of sultans, leader of the lords, crown of the sovereigns of the earth, the shadow of God in the two worlds, sultan and padishah of the Mediterranean, Black Sea, Rumelia, Anatolia, Karaman, Dulkadir, Diyarbakir, Azerbaijan, Iran, Syria, Egypt, Mecca, Medina, all the Arab lands. . . . And you Francis, king of the province of France . . . "[63] What reads today as arrogant bombast is an articulation of the sixteenth-century notion of imperial sovereignty: Süleyman ruled over many former states and peoples; Francis, in the Ottoman view, over only one.

The phrase *memalik-i mahruse* was no doubt intended to summon up the dynasty's role as protector of its domains, certainly one of the principal justifications of its sovereign hold on them. But the term "well-protected" was also an attribute of Aintab itself: the court register dating from May 1541 through October 1541 opens with an inscription naming the seat of the court as "Aintab *el-mahruse.*" When applied to an individual locality, the term connoted a fortified and garrisoned city.[64] In other words, the attribution *mahruse* highlighted a salient element of the city's own historic identity as a strategic bastion. The term thus acquired an ambivalence in the new relationship of Aintab to the imperial center: the city with its citadel was an asset to the dynasty, yet the dynasty now commandeered the project of protection. The dynasty itself was the bastion, a notion that Süleyman made visible on his return march to Istanbul after his victory in 1535 against the Safavids. Passing through the fortified cities of Diyarbakır, Ruha, Bire, Aleppo, and Adana, the sultan and his army did not halt at Aintab but traveled through the province's southeastern corner (see figure 1). One wonders how many Aintabans may have lined the route of his procession to catch a glimpse of the victorious monarch.

But did the sultan's appearance persuade Aintabans to see themselves as participants in a new imperial venture? It seems unlikely. Recent history amply demonstrated the vagaries of dynastic competition: the Mamluk sultans and the Dulkadir princes had disappeared from the stage of politics. While the Safavids suffered defeat in 1535, it was no doubt evident that it was only a matter of time before the two powers that had recently become dominant players in the region would come into conflict again (as they did in 1548). Who could say who would win the next round? Moreover, many of the armed uprisings that challenged Süleyman's legitimacy originated in the former Dulkadir domain or in central Anatolia, and Aintab undoubtedly felt their unsettling effects. Rebellious governors in Damascus and Cairo at the beginning of Süleyman's reign had been duly punished, but any instability in the region would open the door to future moves to free Egypt, Syria, or both from Ottoman overlordship. In 1540, it was probably not a safe bet that the Ottomans would claim sovereignty over Aintab for nearly four centuries to come.

As we will see throughout this book, there were many ways in which the presence of Ottoman authority was felt locally, and sometimes exploited by the people of Aintab to their own benefit. Certainly, prominent members of Aintab society might secure influential and lucrative positions as Süleyman's government sought local allies in administration, thereby identifying themselves with the Ottoman regime. But for the great majority of ordinary individuals, such incentives for identification were lacking. And the prominent would no doubt find themselves able to accommodate to a new ruling authority should the Ottoman regime be pushed out of the region. It was in the interest of most Aintabans to cultivate their own gardens.

LOCALISM AND CIVIC INITIATIVE

Travelers to Aintab city invariably noted its citadel, its green spaces, and its bazaars and merchants.[65] The city's horizon was dominated by the citadel, which was constructed on a natural rocky outcropping enlarged by millennia of local inhabitants and their settlements.[66] Turned into a minor fortification by the Romans, the citadel was subsequently expanded and enhanced by various Byzantine and Muslim rulers. Not far from the citadel, Aintab's northern perimeter was marked by a stream known as today as the Alleben, an upper branch of the Sacur River. The Sacur flowed across the province from northwest to southeast, bisecting it and eventually emptying into the great Euphrates River.[67] It was the Sacur's waters that made possible the green belt of orchards, vineyards, and vegetable gardens that formed a cultivated boundary surrounding much of the city (a boundary that was erased by urban expansion only toward the end of the twentieth century). Indeed, Aintab may have derived its name from the local abundance of water in the form of streams, natural springs, and underground channels: popular etymologies for the city's name include "land of springs" and, more plausibly perhaps, "sparkling spring."[68] As for the southern perimeter of the city, along it could be found a number of stone quarries that supplied building material for the city's houses, bazaars, mosques, and schools.[69]

In the mid–sixteenth century, Aintab was amply endowed with bazaars, shops, and workshops (it still today hosts one of the liveliest of traditional markets in Anatolia). According to the 1536 cadastral survey, the city contained some 1,300 commercial units (a figure that includes only shops [dükkân] and workshops [imalathane] located on public property, and omits the many units located on private property or property belonging to religious foundations).[70] Evliya Çelebi, a famous seventeenth-century Ottoman courtier and traveler, wrote that there were 3,900 shops and workshops in the year 1671.[71] Many shops were clustered along streets known as souks or bazaars. Some of these souk streets named the wares sold in them—for example, the souks of the coppersmiths, the jewelers, and the shoemakers.[72] Another market area popular in the mid–sixteenth century was known as "the souk of the merchants" *(suk el-tüccarin, suk-ı bezzazıstan),* which was most likely a large covered bazaar. Other shops were not located in the grand conglomerate of souk streets that constituted "the Aintab bazaar" but were scattered in the various neighborhoods of the city: the court records tell us of a broadcloth store in the Packsaddlers (Kürtüncü) neighborhood, and of a "public souk" in the large neighborhood of Ali Neccar, near the citadel.[73]

The most important market street of all was known, appropriately, as the Long Market *(suk-ı tavil)* (see map 4).[74] This street, which proceeded southeast from the citadel, constituted the main artery of the city. Along it were located several of Aintab's notable mosques, a sign that the Long Market was a choice and busy thoroughfare.[75] In this aspect of urban topography— the proximity of market and mosque, the intimacy between the material and the spiritual—Aintab was following well-established practices of Islamic religious patronage. But no single one of the Long Market's mosques dominated the others. In other words, Aintab did not have a "great mosque" *(ulu cami),* in contrast to other cities of the region, including Aleppo, Diyarbakır, and Maraş. Great mosques were built by sultans and princes, and while Aintab was occasionally the recipient of largesse from various of its sovereign overlords, no one had endowed it with a dominant mosque that might have functioned as a focal point in its urban landscape.

Indeed, one of the distinguishing features of Aintab's history is that it was not a prince's city.[76] Aintab was rarely visited by royalty except to be sacked or conquered. The one exception was the tenure in the second quarter of the thirteenth century of the prince Al-Malik Al-Salih Ahmad, whose brother was ruler of the Aleppan branch of the distinguished late-medieval Ayyubid dynasty.[77] During his governorship of the city, Melik Salih Ahmed (as he is known in Turkish) is said to have established gardens and orchards around the city, and to have built houses for its inhabitants, turning the city into "a little Damascus."[78] His major efforts, however, were devoted to the citadel, which he repaired and expanded; he is said to have built a pavilion in one of its towers, and he may be responsible as well for a mosque and the bath whose remains can be seen today.[79] The enhancement of the Aleppo citadel by Ayyubid rulers no doubt formed a model for Melik Salih Ahmed's work, and the striking resemblance of the two fortresses certainly gave Aintab the aspect of "a little Aleppo"[80] (see figures 2 and 3).

In the history of the Middle East, Melik Salih Ahmed is surely an obscure prince. We note him here because popular memory in Aintab credits him with embellishing his fiefdom and thereby giving the city an identity to be proud of. Other sovereigns left their mark on Aintab, but the patronage of Melik Salih, a prince *of* the city, was an exception in Aintab's experience of sovereign overlords.

Rather, Aintab was very much a city whose amenities were the product of local initiative.[81] The major "Friday" mosques as well as the dozens of smaller neighborhood mosques frequently bore the names of their local founders, which were typically lent in turn to the neighborhoods served by the mosques. While the citadel was an urban site claimed and periodically maintained by distant ruling regimes, the lasting contribution of sovereigns to the living infrastructure of Aintab was small—a couple of neighborhood mosques and a fountain financed by Mamluk sultans, and the Friday mosque of Alaeddevle. Overwhelmingly, it was local patrons who built Aintab's shrines, schools, and places of worship.[82] Local patronage was an ongoing process, and a number of public works were undertaken in the decades following the region's economic recovery: in 1548, for example, a pious family from Sam (a large village near Aintab) would complete the construction of a second college *(medrese)* in the city, with a primary school alongside it. To support the college, the patrons from Sam built a *han*—a large commercial establishment that contained space for workshops, offices, and secure warehousing—whose annual revenue of 9,600 akçes underwrote the salaries of the college's professor and administrator, student stipends, and building upkeep.[83]

Acts of local patronage were often inscribed in legend. The founding of the Ali Neccar and Boyacı mosques, both of which date from the fourteenth century, are two examples of local initiative that figured in Aintab's historical memory. These legends have fortunately been made accessible through the work of Cemil Cahit Güzelbey, the most prolific and best informed of local historians.[84] Foundation stories are useful to our portrait of Aintab for a number of reasons. The persistence of these stories tells us how important mosques were to people of the city, not only as places of worship but also as the nuclei of urban neighborhoods. They also inform us of popular notions of piety, a dimension of local culture that is largely inaccessible through the court records. And they have the virtue of animating the urban geography described above.

The story of the mosque of Ali Neccar centers on the pious devotion of Ali, a carpenter *(neccar)*, who decides to test the money he has painstakingly saved for the mosque he wants to build in order to be sure that it is *helal*, that is, legitimately acquired. Concealing the gold in the hollowed-out trunk of a tree, which he tosses in the Sacur at a moment when its waters are particularly turbulent, Ali then enters into a period of pious resignation and waits to see if the log will be recovered (a sign of the money's purity). When, months later, a peasant from one of the villages on the shores of the Sacur brings the log into his shop with the request that the carpenter repair his plow with a fragment from it, Ali gives thanks to God and embarks on the construction of the mosque.[85] The story of the Boyacı mosque, also known as the mosque of Kadı ("the judge") Kemaleddin, recounts the relationship between a reformed bandit who becomes learned in the Islamic sciences (the judge) and a local man, Boyacı ("the textile dyer") Yusuf. Boyacı Yusuf figures in the story as the person who saved the judge in his bandit days by cutting him from down from a hanging tree. Even during his life of crime, Kemaleddin's good character had been signaled by the fact that the young girl he and his band abducted (the crime for which the authorities sentenced him to hanging) forgave him his transgression. Years later, the successful judge sent money to the dyer, instructing him to build a mosque on the site of the hanging tree.[86] In 1540, the Boyacıs were one of Aintab's three leading families, with a fast-growing neighborhood bearing their name.

Mosques were not the only public institutions endowed by local individuals whose good deeds were marked in legend. Others included the several establishments in and around Aintab that welcomed and fed sojourners and the poor. Such establishments, or *zaviye*s, were associated with sufis, that is, Muslim "mystics" who were devoted to a contemplative life (such individuals were commonly referred to in Turkish as dervishes). Some of Aintab's dervishes were followers of the great sufi spiritual leaders familiar across the Muslim world, while others were followers of local saints (*evliya*) or prominent local dervishes acclaimed for their spiritual perfection. (These saints and charismatic dervishes might be called by a variety of titles, including sheikh, *baba, dede,* or *pir.*) The zaviyes of Aintab were typically named either in memory of a local saint or after the lineage of the dervish family who founded them. For example, the two best-endowed zaviyes (according to a 1557 survey) were the Dülük Baba zaviye, named after a local saint, and the Demirci zaviye, established in the early sixteenth century by another of Aintab's leading families, the Demircioğlu.[87] Some zaviyes grew up around, or incorporated, the tomb of a saint, thereby enabling the visitor to receive both material and spiritual succor.

Saints and dervish sheikhs were particularly salient as carriers of historical memory. In his study of Ayyubid Aleppo, Yasser Tabbaa has noted the important role of local saints in establishing "emotional attachment" to one's native city:

> In medieval Aleppo, this attachment was quite often linked to the city's commemorative history, which equally resided in hagiographies and popular myths as in the physical artifacts themselves. This sacred geography drew on

the deep cultural and spiritual associations of specific locations in the city and on the numerous patriarchs, saints, sufis, and other holy men and women whose charitable or miraculous acts constituted the pious history of Aleppo. Indeed, it is not an exaggeration to suggest that every significant location in the walled city and many outside of it were "protected" through their association with a particular memory, event, or saint.[88]

This is certainly also true of Aintab and the villages around it. Indeed, the "sacred geography" of Aintab encompassed the whole province, dotted as it still is with the graves of holy persons *(yatır)* that act as magnets for local pilgrimage. Remembered history in Aintab, particularly of the centuries before the eighteenth or nineteenth, is in large part popular hagiography. We can take Dülük Baba as an example of how saints' lives can localize the great events of history. Two stories are told about this very prominent local saint, each exemplifying a common hagiographic theme, or topos: the saint martyred during the Muslim conquest in the seventh century, and the saint who wins the allegiance of Sultan Selim by facilitating the Ottoman conquest of the Mamluk empire.[89]

According to the first story, Dülük Baba was a companion of the Prophet Muhammad whose real name was Davud Ejder. He was serving as a standard-bearer in the Muslim army when he was wounded and died on a hill near Aintab. Over time, however, his grave became obscured. It was rediscovered through the good graces of a mule driver who got lost in a storm on his way from Maraş to Aintab. When he appealed to his own spiritual guide, the great sufi sheikh Abdulkadir Gilani (founder of the Qadiri order), the latter appeared before him and said, "Why do you call on me for help when Davud Ejder lies here right beside you?" A flashing light suddenly appeared that signaled the whereabouts of Dülük Baba's grave and also enabled the mule driver to regain his bearings and make his way to Aintab. Later he returned to build a domed tomb over Davud Ejder's grave and provide an endowment for a lantern to be kept lit every night to guide wayfarers.

Dülük Baba was not the only companion of the Prophet identified with Aintab. Tabbaa's point about the ability of saints to protect local whereabouts is exemplified in a legend told about 'Umar, the second caliph, under whose leadership the early conquests were accomplished and who, in this story, has personally supervised the Muslim conquest of Aintab from the Byzantines. When the commander he appoints to guard Aintab proposes building a wall around it, 'Umar responds that the city is already surrounded by walls—spiritual walls, that is—in the form of five companions buried in the city's vicinity. One of these, of course, was Davud Ejder; another was Pirsefa, a Muslim from Medina who is said to have participated in the conquest of Aintab under the command of Ali, cousin and son-in-law to the Prophet. Pirsefa's tomb, preserved today in the Boyacı neighborhood of the city, continues to function as a pilgrimage site.[90]

In the second story about Dülük Baba, related in Evliya Çelebi's narrative of his travels, the saint appears as a dervish living at the time of the Ottoman conquest. As Sultan Selim marched through the province, Dülük Baba approached him to give him the good tidings of the conquest to come. The dervish predicted the date on which the Ottoman army would take Cairo and informed the sultan that he would become overlord of the holy cities of Mecca and Medina. When things turned out just as Dülük Baba predicted, the victorious sultan returned to Aintab to honor the dervish, only to find that he had passed away.[91] Before departing for Istanbul, Selim built a lofty tomb over his grave.

This theme of the local saint facilitating the Ottoman conquest also appears in other stories, most notably about a dervish sheikh of Sam (the same individual who actually founded the college mentioned above). The several versions of the encounter between Selim and the sheikh, Muhiddin b. Abdurrahman Erzincanî, all center on miracles performed by the latter through the dry grapevine cuttings he tenders the sultan and his men. The marvels range from the feeding of many from a single cutting to the appearance, at a crucial moment in the battle between the Ottoman and Mamluk armies at Marj Dabik, of a whole field of vines and the billhooks used to prune them, a miracle that rouses panic among the Mamluk ranks and leads to the Ottoman victory.[92]

Neither the stories about Dülük Baba nor those about Davud Ejder and the sheikh of Sam are necessarily "true." They draw on a widely shared narrative repertoire of trials, miracles, and ordinary human faith that can be found in popular legends as well as in scholarly hagiographies of renowned sufis. But the specific combination of elements that figure in the vernacular mythology of a particular place can alert us to matters of local concern. As we see, conquest is frequently a critical event in these narratives of Aintab saints and dervishes. This is not surprising for a city so often the object of power rivalries. One reason hagiography was so ubiquitous a strategy for narrating the past was that legends of local saints helped domesticate the cataclysmic events surrounding conquest and redress the balance of power in favor of the local. These stories were a vehicle for the people of Aintab to place themselves in the larger world and to make themselves actors in events beyond their control—in other words, they helped bridge the tension between conquest and local autonomy. By invoking the protective role of martyred Muslims during the Islamic conquest and miracle-working dervishes during the Ottoman conquest, legends asserted the continuity and security of place.

But in these stories another theme stands out: the responsibility of the living to shelter the pious dead by building and maintaining tombs for them.[93]

The process is reciprocal: saints cannot protect if they are not themselves protected. No doubt these stories were intended to play a didactic role. They repeatedly set the example of good works. Some of them asserted the worthiness of Aintab and its inhabitants to be graced by royal patronage. Indeed, sultans—Mamluk and Ottoman alike—*did* contribute to local zaviyes, and it was their contributions that enabled such establishments to survive as permanent way stations in the provincial landscape. The stories of Selim, the sheikh of Sam, and the tomb of Dülük Baba in fact contain some grains of truth. During their campaign halts in cities along their marching routes, sultans typically met with leading local dignitaries, including prominent spiritual leaders, and typically assigned funds to the repair, upkeep, and creation of local public structures such as citadels, city walls, mosques, and the shrines of saints. It is therefore not improbable that Selim met with the sheikh of Sam and received his blessing for the impending confrontation with the Mamluks.[94] In any case, at some point during his reign, the sultan exempted the village of Sam from all taxes and transformed it into a religious foundation *(waqf)* entrusted to the sheikh and his descendants.[95] It is no doubt this award of revenues that enabled the sheikh and his family to undertake the construction of the new college, primary school, and commercial building completed in 1548. As for Dülük Baba's tomb, Selim may well have ordered the repair or enhancement of the existing sanctuary, although it was his son, Süleyman, who in fact put the Dülük Baba zaviye on a sound fiscal footing by endowing it with the revenues of several mezraas and villages.[96]

Monarchs of the period were conspicuously attentive to the shrines of sufis and saints, in part because these figures were traditionally important as vehicles of political legitimation. For this reason, royal acts of patronage typically occurred at the moment of conquest, and one might think of them as acts of propitiation toward local communities through the gifts made to local worthies, both the living and the dead. One of Selim's gestures toward his newly conquered domain was to restore the tomb of Ibn Al-Arabi, the great thirteenth-century sufi thinker buried in Damascus. And when Selim's son and successor Süleyman took Baghdad from the Safavids in 1535, he would miraculously "discover" and then restore the neglected tomb of Abu Hanifa, celebrated jurist of the eighth century and founder of the school of law followed by the Ottomans. The Ottoman conquest of Constantinople in 1453 had been similarly blessed through the miraculous recovery of the alleged burial place of Eyyüb, companion of the Prophet and his own standard-bearer (the district of Eyyüb continues to be the major pilgrimage site in Istanbul today).

While saints and miracle workers inspired royal patronage, the stories of tombs, like those of Aintab's mosques, were also important in spurring *local* initiative. In them, a lowly muleteer might be the agent of a saint's recuperation from obscurity, just as a carpenter could build a mosque that would become the focal point of one of the city's largest neighborhoods. Local initiative was critical in a locale where investment by sovereigns was sporadic and limited. As we have seen, Aintab had neither a resident royal patron nor a great mosque to proclaim its stature as a distinguished city. Nor could it boast a major (and perhaps lucrative) pilgrimage site comparable to that of the neighboring city of Ruha (Urfa), which claimed to be the birthplace of Abraham as well as a stopping place in Eyyüb's travels.

Local good works by local individuals were necessary to sustaining both the amenities and the image of a flourishing city. Though Aintab lacked grand monuments other than its citadel, it had abundant human resources, not only in its prominent merchants, scholars, and spiritual leaders but also in the countless ordinary individuals who did their part to maintain an infrastructure of urban civilization. There was, it seems, a strong habit in Aintab and its hinterland of making charitable donations to local institutions. Our court records inform us that in July 1541, a certain Ayşe donated her share of a house in the Packsaddlers neighborhood to the local mosque, while Köse Bayram, from the large village of Hacer, donated a house to his village mosque.[97] Similarly, Aintab court registers from later decades and later centuries are full of such donations. Among the many individuals who made donations to the Boyacı mosque, for example, were Bekir from the town of Nizip, who in 1596 endowed the income of two agricultural tracts to the mosque's upkeep; the city dweller Ayşe, who established an endowment in 1650 that used the income generated by a flock of eighty sheep to purchase sesame oil for the mosque; and the three Mısırzade brothers, who in 1909 endowed the income of a shop near the mosque to its general expenses.[98]

Still today, citizens of Gaziantep frequently assert that theirs is a city where people invest locally and are not eager to become dependent on government support. This appears to be a habit born, at least in part, of historical necessity.

2

The People of Aintab
and Their World

Now that we have located Aintab in historical space and time, we expand our portrait in this chapter by looking at the people who lived within the province and the variety of communities in which they lived. We watch the people of Aintab moving among city quarters as well as between village and city. Pursuing the question posed in chapter 1 about local residents' vision of their place in the world, this chapter asks if the province of Aintab created Aintabans—in other words, if the provincial boundary defined a real entity in the minds of those within it. The chapter then turns to the traffic in persons, animals, and goods across the larger region of which Aintab province was an integral part: here we are interested in the variety of needs and desires that stretched people's lives beyond hearth and neighborhood. We also examine the infrastructures of communication—legitimate as well as criminal—that made contact across social and economic space possible. Finally, we look at two forces—war and pilgrimage—that induced individuals to undertake longer journeys that transported them far beyond the region. Throughout the chapter, we seek to understand how the recent Ottoman presence in Aintab influenced the shape of communities and the nature of communication.

THE PROVINCIAL LANDSCAPE

Aintab in the mid–sixteenth century was a compact province. No village within the provincial boundary was much further away from Aintab city than a two-day journey on foot, and many were closer. The rural population of the province was spread among some 225 villages that ranged enormously in size, from small hamlets consisting of only a handful of households to the twin villages of Hiyam and Keret with their combined population of nearly 2,000 souls.[1] Predictably, the province's largest villages—and no doubt its oldest—were located on waterways, near springs, and along the major routes that carried soldiers, caravans, pilgrims, and others.[2] According to the 1543 cadastral survey (the first to systematically inscribe the whole province), the villages of Aintab accounted for a little less than three-quarters of the province's total population of some 36,000.[3]

The province's capital was a sizable city according to the 1543 survey, with a population that was probably between 9,000 and 10,000.[4] To get a sense of what these numbers actually mean, let us place the city in a comparative context. Within Anatolia, Aintab ranked after old established urban centers such as Bursa, Ankara, and Kayseri, the largest cities in sixteenth-century Anatolia, whose populations at midcentury probably numbered somewhere between 13,000 and 20,000.[5] In the region spanning southeastern Anatolia and northern Syria, Aintab was the largest city exclusive of Aleppo, with the possible exception of Ruha (Urfa) to the east, also a provincial capital.[6] Aintab's closest neighbor as a provincial capital was Bire, a much smaller city (about a third Aintab's size) but strategically important because of its location at a natural crossing of the Euphrates; Bire's wharf taxes supplied substantial revenues[7] (see figure 4). As for Maraş, nominally the regional capital to which Aintab was subordinated, the city was smaller than Aintab in 1540, but its role as capital of the Dulkadir governorate-general probably explains why it grew more quickly, catching up to Aintab in population by around 1560.[8] Aleppo, the largest city in the region by far, had a population of around 60,000 in the years covered by this study.[9] To the south of Aleppo, the major metropolis of Damascus was inhabited by some 45,000 to 50,000 people in the same period,[10] while Jerusalem was somewhat smaller than Aintab.[11] Although Aintab city was not growing fast in 1540, its pace of growth would pick up, giving the city a population of somewhere between 14,000 and 14,500 by 1574.[12]

A caveat is in order here: all these figures are very rough estimates. They are based on the Ottoman regime's definition of the taxpaying household (*hane*), which might exclude any number of exempt households, such as those headed by the disabled, individuals employed in tax-exempt forms of service to the state, and imams, priests, and rabbis. Moreover, cadastral surveys did not count non-householders such as slaves, retainers, and transients, making it particularly difficult to estimate the populations of cities, where such groups were more numerous. The estimates above, therefore, may be on the low side, and those for the metropolises of Aleppo and Damascus particularly imprecise. A further challenge in estimating populations is the difficulty in comparing taxable household figures, since cadastral surveys were carried out in different years and sometimes used different categories in their counts. Some surveys, for example, indicated numbers of bachelors, and others did not; this variation in counting adult males is one

of the major problems in estimating household size. Not surprisingly, scholars have differed in how they have approached the problems of translating
inconsistent tax data into population estimates.[13] As for Ottoman officials,
they were more interested in how to estimate taxes than in how to estimate
population. What leads to "inconsistencies" in our eyes was probably a virtue to them—the attempt to honor local practice in the assessment of taxes.
Indeed, the very inconsistencies in cadastral surveying are an unexplored
subject with the potential to tell us much about local social structure and
agricultural practice.

Despite the flux in its early administrative attachment, Aintab province
remained more or less fixed in its borders and its administrative divisions
(see map 3).[14] The province was divided into three subdistricts (nahiye).
In the northwest was the subdistrict of Aintab, so called because the city of
Aintab—the provincial capital—was located within its boundaries. The
other subdistricts were Telbaşer in the south and Nehrülcevaz in the east.[15]
In the number and size of their villages, Aintab and Telbaşer were remark-
ably parallel, while Nehrülcevaz, the subdistrict smallest in area, had the
fewest villages but also the largest (including the twin villages of Hiyam and
Keret). The province's geographical complexion ranged from the agriculturally productive Euphrates valley in the east and southeast to grassy mountain plateaus in the west and northwest, with increasingly undulating terrain
in between. Aintab city was centrally located in the midst of these plateaus,
at an elevation of 800 meters. Insofar as reasons of geography, both natural
and human, joined Aintab province to the Dulkadir governorate-general, it
was the mountain highlands of Aintab subdistrict that was the common trait
linking the province to other provinces in Dulkadir. Such terrain was amenable to a mixed economy of agriculture and small-animal pastoralism;[16] it
is thus not surprising that of the province's three subdistricts, only Aintab
contained villages populated by individuals identified as belonging to tribal
federations, most notably the Dulkadir.[17]

In addition to the 225 villages of Aintab province, the cadastral surveys
for our period list some 256 mezraas. As we have seen, mezraas were non-
residential areas devoted to agricultural production, land that went in and
out of production according to demand. A notable example is the site of the
famous confrontation in 1516 between the Ottomans and the Mamluks,
Marj Dabik, which was recuperated as a productive mezraa by 1520.[18] That
use of such reserve agricultural land had languished but was now picking up
is suggested by the fact that several mezraas and an occasional village were
named "Ruins of such-and-such"—for example, Lake Ruins, Eighty Ruins,
Mountain Pass Ruins); the village of Karacaviran ("Dark Ruins") was elevated from the status of mezraa to that of village in the 1543 cadaster.[19]
(This pattern of shifting land usage has also been documented for Aleppo
in the same period.)[20] The court records for 1540–1541 are full of grants

of title to mezraa land going into cultivation; one such grant noted that title to the mezraa of Barmeluca had been awarded to the peasant Mehmed
"so that he might go and improve the mezraa and farm it."[21] Mezraas could
be quite large, accommodating the vineyards and orchards of as many as
eight individuals, who shared the tax imposed on the title grant.[22] The ratio of village to mezraa was lowest in the subdistrict of Telbaşer and highest in Nehrülcevaz, where a pattern of fewer but larger village settlements
working more extensive landholdings appears to have prevailed.[23] The expansion of mezraas during the years addressed by this study is a symptom
of the recovery described in the previous chapter: rural populations were
growing as trade and security picked up under Ottoman consolidation of
the region and as the Mediterranean region as a whole experienced a period of prosperity.

The villages of Aintab should not be thought of as a faceless mass of rural
units. Many of the larger ones were settlements of ancient origin; given the
antiquity of human habitation in the region, optimal sites for settlement
had been determined centuries earlier. The most recent historical layers of
settlement—Roman, Byzantine, Armenian, Crusader, Ayyubid / Mamluk—
were revealed in some sixteenth-century village names: these included cor-
rupted Greek and Latin names and names of Christian monasteries, as well
as Arabic and Turkish names. The antiquity of habitation had given rise to
the numerous tells—hills enlarged through millennia of civilizations that
dwelled upon them—that dotted the region. Many tells were, or had been,
fortified at various times in their past; the Aleppo and Aintab citadels were
examples of large tells whose defensive potential had kept them occupied
over long stretches of time. Some villages that were neither sizable nor of
other particular significance in 1540 had been more important in the past,
and often more urban—for example, Telbaşer, once a Crusader stronghold
and site of battles between Crusaders and Muslims, but in 1540 only a
middle-sized village.[24] By the end of the seventeenth century, however, Telbaşer would become the center of a judgeship (kadılık). This upgrading
testified not only to Telbaşer's own recovered importance but also to the potential latent within many older settlements to resume roles of significance
as human events rewrote local geography.

In other words, these older villages had character and history. When a
venerable tree in the large village of Mervana was destroyed in an act of
wanton violence, the court recorded testimony citing its local touristic fame:
"The natural spring in the village is a panoramic lookout (manzargâh). At
the source of the spring there is a great tree. From days of old, travelers
coming and going have benefited from the shade of the aforementioned
tree. Until now, no one has cut a single branch or a single twig from the
tree."[25] In a largely unlettered environment, the story of the past of villages
such as Telbaşer and Mervana was preserved in popular legend. Saints and

warriors figured in these legends, just as they figured in the legendary past of Aintab city. Particularly prominent in stories associated with the fortresses and citadels in the region was Ali, cousin and son-in-law of the Prophet Muhammad, fourth caliph in sunni Islam and first imam in shi'i Islamic genealogy. Scholarly focus on Ali's complex position in Islamic religio-political history often obscures the widespread popular veneration for him as a brave warrior, the "lion of God."[26] Traces of the footprints left by Ali's horse Düldül as he and his rider scaled the walls of rural fortresses are still pointed out to the tourist in Gaziantep today.

There is a notable aspect of rural narratives that distinguishes them from "city" narratives: the greater salience of females in them. This feature may reflect the more public roles that women tend to play in rural environments, or their tendency to take a larger role in storytelling than that played by their urban sisters. One such story is that of Ayşe Fatma, the sister (or, in some variants, the daughter) of Said b. Ebi Vakkaş, one of the five companions of the Prophet who, legend tells us, died during the Muslim conquest of Aintab and whose graves formed spiritual walls protecting the city. During the fray in which Said was slain, Ayşe Fatma was thrown to her death onto a large rock that split to become her grave. Herbs that grow in the rock's vicinity, used by local women in place of henna, are thought to spring from the roots of Ayşe Fatma's hair, some of which was left exposed when the rock enclosed her. According to the version of the legend recorded by the Aintab historian Cemil Cahit Güzelbey, children suffering from croup will be cured if they are passed through a hole in the rock on three successive Fridays.[27] Ayşe Fatma's grave was not unique in its powers, for sites in Aintab's legendary history often provide cures not only for bodily ills but also for difficulties in getting married or becoming pregnant.[28] This capacity of sacred places to offer solutions to life's problems adds a further dimension to Yasser Tabbaa's observation, quoted in chapter 1, that sacred geography can promote local identity and attachment. The purpose of relating the story of Ayşe Fatma here is not to suggest that it was recounted in 1540 in precisely the form in which it was told to Güzelbey (although the legend is no doubt of ancient provenance). Rather, it is to emphasize that peasants too have participated in the historical animation of their landscape—and have animated it in ways reflective of, and responsive to, their own social world.

In contrast to the rural area around it, Aintab city was hardly growing in population in 1540.[29] That slow city growth and rapid village growth went hand in hand between the survey years of 1536 and 1543 suggests that peasants who had fled to the city during hard times were returning to their villages and that some city dwellers saw greater opportunity in rural areas.[30] Perhaps the rapidly increasing tax burden borne by city residents in the years around 1540 spurred some to leave, though peasants were seeing some agricultural taxes go up as well.[31] This return to the land may have been a phenomenon particularly salient in greater Syria, since Aleppo and Damascus were unusual among major Ottoman cities at the mid–sixteenth century in experiencing population decline. In other words, the political contest described in chapter 1 may have taken a particularly significant toll in Syria, temporarily depopulating the rural hinterland as refugees swelled the region's urban settlements.[32]

But although new residents were not pouring into Aintab in 1540, people were clearly moving within the city's twenty-nine neighborhoods (*mahalle*), some of which were losing population, some gaining, and some remaining stable (see map 4). The largest neighborhoods in Aintab, each centered on a major mosque, were among the oldest and tended to be grouped around the citadel and the Long Market thoroughfare, the city's main artery.[33] Other neighborhoods spread out to the south of the citadel. The city's population had traditionally settled protectively below the citadel and the natural boundary of the Sacur River, which lay just north of it. What is striking about movement among Aintab's neighborhoods between the survey years of 1536 and 1543 is the city's rapid outward expansion. The fastest-growing neighborhoods—Akyol, Töbe, and Boyacı—were located, respectively, on the western, northern, and eastern edges of town, while the neighborhoods losing population were those to the south. The area around the citadel, the commercial and cultural heart of the city, was still heavily populated, but old neighborhoods were splitting to form new ones in this area as the population spread out to fill the core urban space. As expanding neighborhoods consolidated, local residents like those in the Kürtüncü ("Packsaddler") district rallied by making donations to enhance their local mosque.[34]

Two important factors were at work here: increased security and an expanding economy. Both were in large part a benefit of Ottoman overlordship. It was now safer to move further from the refuge of the citadel, which had sheltered the city's population during the numerous sieges in its past. The role of larger mosques as protective refuges probably also figured in earlier reluctance to move out from the older neighborhoods. Now people clearly wanted more room and were not afraid to seek it. The vectors of population redistribution within the city also suggest that Aintabans were able to take greater advantage of the green spaces on the banks of the Sacur, which supported numerous vineyards, orchards, and vegetable gardens.

Movement within city neighborhoods also reflected the growing opportunity for exchange between Aintab city and its hinterland as well as for trade with other urban centers in the broader region in which Aintab was located. It is no coincidence that the fastest-growing neighborhoods were located on major routes into and out of the city—Akyol on the Aleppo road, Töbe on the Maraş road, and Boyacı on the main artery east to the

Euphrates and beyond. Like the growth of rural population, the internal migration of Aintab's urban population suggests an orientation increasingly outward as the province sought to garner its share of the prosperity described in chapter 1.

Reading court records together with cadastral surveys, we observe that the spatial dynamics of urban growth reflected the dynamics of power among Aintab's leading families, or, more precisely, their shifting status. In 1540, there were three notable families in Aintab: the Sikkak, the Boyacı, and the Demirci—or, to give the English equivalents of their names, which presumably derived from the occupations of the lineage founders, the Coiners, the Dyers, and the Smiths.[35] The Demircis were less influential as urban power brokers than the other two families, perhaps because theirs was a sheikhly family (one of the two largest zaviyes in Aintab province bore the family name).[36] The current heads of the Sikkak and Boyacı families, however, were involved as tax-farmers for the state and played prominent roles in business. We will meet them frequently in upcoming chapters. For now, suffice it to say that the court records and, to a lesser extent, the cadastral surveys give the overall impression that the Sikkak family had enjoyed its heyday under the Mamluk and Dulkadir regimes, while the Boyacı family, in the person of its present head, Seyyid Ahmed, was more adept at making use of new opportunities afforded by the Ottoman regime. Although associated by legend with the mosque of Kadı Kemaleddin, and thus with the shrinking neighborhood that bore its name, the Boyacıs had their own neighborhood in the eastern reaches of the city. This city quarter was growing fast, in contrast to the centrally located neighborhood named for the Sikkak family. Though still one of the two largest city neighborhoods in 1543, the latter was declining in population. It is perhaps no coincidence that the Sikkak neighborhood would disappear by the late seventeenth century, while the Boyacı neighborhood still exists today.[37] No doubt a variety of factors explain the growth of population at the eastern edge of the city— more space, proximity to the Sacur, and a favorable location for taking advantage of the opportunities opened up by the increasing traffic into and out of the city. But might not another factor be an opportunity to reside in a neighborhood whose patron was recognized as a comer?

Local elites were accustomed to a degree of autonomy, and their habit of influencing the uses of urban property was sometimes a problem for the Aintab community. A dispute at court in mid-June 1541 reveals the vested interest of this elite in holding on to valuable agricultural properties along the Sacur. During their testimony in this case, some dozen individuals, including prominent religious dignitaries, military officers, and local merchants, openly admitted that they had been diverting water illegally from a mill belonging to the Mihaliye college in order to irrigate their own properties. Moreover, it came out at court that there had been earlier, unsuccessful, attempts to discipline them for flouting laws regarding water rights. What secured the college's suit this time around was the Mihaliye manager's trip to Istanbul, where he obtained an imperial order supporting the college's claim.[38] The recently enhanced authority of the Aintab court was no small factor in the effort to protect this important urban institution.

The scofflaw attitude of the gentleman farmers no doubt stemmed in part from the proprietary stake that they felt they could claim in the physical development of the city. Aintab's urban infrastructure was largely the creation of this elite: to read through the inventory of public foundations that was compiled in 1557 is to be overwhelmed by the number of private individuals whose cumulative good works had brought into being the eleven Friday mosques (cami), the sixty-plus smaller neighborhood mosques (mescid), the eight zaviyes, and the two colleges (medrese) and four schools (buka) that were operating in Aintab, only a small handful of which were the product of royal patronage.[39] Ira Lapidus has noted the remarkable degree to which local merchants, sheikhs, jurists, and judges in Damascus and Aleppo undertook to "sustain communal and religious life in the face of growing neglect by the Mamluk regime" in its later decades by assuming an enlarged share of the burden of "investment in maintenance of the urban physical plant."[40] As we saw in chapter 1, Aintab was not accustomed to the kind of royal patronage that had sustained the urban plant of cities such as Damascus and Aleppo in good times. Rather, it was Aintab's leading citizens who had steadily borne this responsibility over the centuries. The budget of many Aintab institutions depended in part on the income of urban properties that had been endowed to them by just such individuals as those now in trouble for stealing water from the Mihaliye's own endowment. Their attitude, which combined civic-mindedness with a certain disregard for the law—as if to proclaim "the city belongs to us"—was one that the Ottoman regime was attempting to undermine, as we will see in subsequent chapters.

THE HUMAN GEOGRAPHY OF AINTAB PROVINCE

Who were the people who lived in Aintab city and the villages in its hinterland in 1540? The answer to this question is not so simple, since we first have to consider how people "read" their social landscape in the sixteenth century—in other words, what social categories they regarded as important in making distinctions among individuals. The problem is that different kinds of historical record yield different human geographies. The cadastral surveys, for example, give us the important categories of religion (Muslim, Christian, Jew), residential community (city dweller, villager, nomad), and marital status. But because the surveys count only those who were taxed— resident adult males—they omit the majority of the population, including females, children, slaves, and sojourners. Moreover, administrative divisions imposed a static structure on communities that were in reality more fluid and more ambiguous, and thus resistant to neat categorization. Chapter 4 will explore in some depth the various ways in which Ottoman society of the mid–sixteenth century stratified itself; luckily, the court records let us listen in as people talked about difference and sometimes challenged prevailing notions of social position and human worth. For now, let us look at some cadastral categories and ask how reflective they were of everyday life in Aintab province. We examine first religious identity and then the distinction between nomad and sedentary, and in the next section we explore the divide between urban and rural.

Religious allegiance was one of the most fundamental, obvious, and pervasive ways of identifying individuals in the sixteenth century. The distinction between Muslim and non-Muslim was clearly central, but neither of these broad divisions was homogeneous. In what follows we look at Aintab's non-Muslims, virtually all of whom were Armenian Christian, and also at the varieties of Muslim identity that were locally observable.

Aintab's demographic makeup in our period stood out from that of most provinces surrounding it in that it contained fewer non-Muslims. Its non-Muslim population was relatively small and uniformly Armenian Christian. In this respect, Aintab contrasted with religiously more heterogeneous populations in surrounding provinces, particularly to the east and south, which included small Jewish communities and larger Christian populations.[41] Aintab appears to have had no Jewish community, although a Jewish financier *(sarraf)*, who was most probably based in Aleppo, figured prominently in the city's economic and administrative life. To contrast Aintab's non-Muslim demography with that of other areas in the region, we draw on the cadaster of 1526, which gives the religious breakdown for the *beglerbegilik*s, or governorates-general, of Dulkadir and Diyarbakır. While the governorate-general of Dulkadir was approximately 4.5 percent non-Muslim, that of Diyarbakır was approximately 15 percent.[42] The non-Muslims of Diyarbakır were overwhelmingly Armenian, with a small Jewish population; the religious identity of Dulkadir non-Muslims was not specified.[43] In the city of Ruha, some 120 kilometers east of Aintab and its rival in size, approximately one-quarter of taxpaying males in 1526 were Armenian (there was no Jewish population listed).[44] As one moved further east, both Armenian and Jewish communities grew in size: particular concentrations of Armenians were evident in the cities of Hisnkeyf and Arabgir, where they formed 50 and 61 percent of the population, respectively, and in Mardin they were also the majority (59 percent), while Jews made up 6 percent of the city's numbers; further east, in Mosul, non-Muslims (Armenians and Jews) constituted 32 percent of the population.[45] Unfortunately, the massive 1526 survey from which these numbers are drawn does not break down the population by religion for Aintab, or for any cities or provinces in greater Syria.[46] But in 1543, the non-Muslim population of Damascus was 13 percent, roughly divided between Jewish and Christian households.[47]

Of the twenty-nine neighborhoods in Aintab city, one was Armenian. It was listed in the cadastral surveys as "the neighborhood of the Armenians" (mahalle-i Ermeniyan), but was called Heyik in the court records (the name it retained into the twentieth century).[48] The 1536 survey recorded 44 households and 11 bachelors in this neighborhood, but the survey of 1543 listed only 28 households and 6 bachelors.[49] Were some Armenian families moving to other city neighborhoods or to rural communities, as were their Muslim counterparts? or were they emigrating from Aintab province altogether? It is difficult to answer this question.[50] It is worth noting that the village of Orul contained more Armenians than the city did. Orul, located in the Nehrülcevaz subdistrict, was the third-largest village of the province; in 1543 it had a total household population of 156, of which 60 paid the poll tax imposed on non-Muslims.[51] Perhaps the Armenian city quarter was shrinking in part because families were moving to Orul.[52]

According to the 1543 survey, Armenians constituted approximately 1.4 percent of the population of Aintab province.[53] However, it may be that the non-Muslim population of the province was somewhat undercounted in the surveys, since Armenians seem to have been recorded as such only when they clustered in an Armenian neighborhood. For example, there appear to have been Christians (Armenians?) living in the village of Mervana—an entry in the court record lists the poll tax paid by non-Muslims among Mervana's revenues—but the cadastral survey does not indicate their presence in its enumeration of the village's male inhabitants.[54]

That Aintab province once contained a larger Christian population than it did in 1540 is suggested by several village and mezraa names associated with Christian settlement: Three Churches, Little Church, Church Valley, Monastery of Rejim, Monastery of the Cave, Infidel Hill, Little Infidel. It is difficult to say whether the decline of the Christian population resulted from the demise of the Crusader states in the twelfth and thirteenth centuries or was a more recent phenomenon. Certainly the Mamluk conquest of the area in the late thirteenth century contributed to the attrition of Christians in the Aintab region. A notable event here was the prolonged siege of the Euphrates fortress settlement of Rumkale (called Hromklay in Armenian), seat of the Armenian Catholicosate since 1147 and a pilgrimage site for both Armenian and Jacobite Christians. When Mamluk forces prevailed in 1292, the inhabitants of Rumkale either fled or were taken prisoner. The fortress itself was "converted" through its renaming as "Citadel of the Muslims."[55]

To what extent do the court records yield a portrait of Aintab's Armenians? Recent studies of non-Muslims in the Ottoman courts are challenging

the long-unquestioned assumption that non-Muslims used their own communal courts except when they were involved in legal matters with the state
or with those not of their faith. In virtually all accounts of Ottoman courts,
Christians and Jews can be observed using the court voluntarily for a variety
of personal matters.[56] Recently, Najwa Al-Qattan has questioned the very
concept of the "legal autonomy" of non-Muslims. She suggests that the use
of the courts by non-Muslims in eighteenth- and nineteenth-century Damascus was virtually a strategic necessity: "Their behavior was based on the
correct perception of the court as the registry and depository of all official
documentation. In addition, by availing themselves of the courts in pursuit
of personal interests, they demonstrated an impressive knowledge of Islamic legal practice, an acceptance of shared cultural-legal norms, and a
pragmatic outlook on marital and familial issues."[57] Much the same could
be said about the Armenians of mid-sixteenth-century Aintab, who were
quite visible in the court in proportion to their small numbers in the population. They used it to negotiate routine transactions such as purchases,
loans, and joint business ventures, the majority of which were transactions
with their Muslim colleagues. But they also used the court to mediate delicate family matters such as a wife's alleged sexual indiscretion or a quarrel
between brothers. In other words, like their Muslim cohabitants, the Armenians of Aintab approached the court as a resource in the management of
myriad aspects of daily life.[58] By doing so, they revealed themselves to be a
typically diverse social group, ranging from pillars of the small community
to troublemakers and an alleged murderer.

It is also worth noting about the Armenians of Aintab that they did not
hesitate to use the court to protect themselves when their minority status
put them at risk, as we will see in chapter 7. Indeed, this defensive Armenian recourse to the court is evidence in support of the argument that the
local court was attentive to its less powerful constituencies. Yet it is striking
that only *urban* Armenians appeared in the Aintab court in 1540–1541: not
a single Armenian inhabitant of Orul came to court over the thirteen
months covered by this study, although several Muslim inhabitants of that
large village appeared before the judge. Whether the Armenians of Orul
simply had no business with the court that year or their rural residence allowed them to cultivate a deliberate distance from the law is hard to say. It
is possible that in times of social and political uncertainty, as the previous
decades had been for Aintab, living outside the city was safer for culturally
distinct and numerically marginal populations such as the Armenians of
Aintab.

To raise the subject of religious diversity and not touch on the heterogeneity of the province's Muslim population, which was far from uniform in
its religious status and spiritual orientation, would be to ignore a vital aspect
of local identity and local culture. To a certain extent, the range of Muslim

identity paralleled a hierarchy of social class. There were two groups of individuals in Aintab whose claim to religious distinction was strongly bound up with a claim to a privileged role in society: the "people of religious learning" *(ehl-i ilm)*, as they were called in the records, and those claiming descent from the family of the Prophet Muhammad *(seyyids)*. The former carried the title *Molla* and were educated in the religious colleges *(medreses)* that could be found in all cities of the region. The famous Bedreddin Ainî, who praised Aintab for its reputation as a center of learning, had acquired his own education in the cities of Behisni, Malatya, Kâhta, and Aleppo, after initial study at two medreses in Aintab.[59] Members of the large molla class in Aintab were employed as imams and preachers at the large mosques, teachers at local schools, muftis, and heads of local zaviyes. As might be expected, this class as a whole stood for scripturally based learning and moral rectitude based on observation of Islamic law. As for the seyyids—those claiming descent from the Prophet—they too formed a sizable group that included mollas as well as prominent merchants and tradesmen (the Boyacı family, for example, were seyyids).[60]

A second dominant form of Muslim religious identity was what we might call the dervish-baba stream of spiritual conduct and expression, in which devoted disciples, the dervishes, followed the person or the model of a baba, or dervish leader. As we have seen, babas were celebrated in legend for their miracle working and their saintly charisma. This form of religious expression was especially popular among Turkmen, who are thought to be responsible for having brought the culture of "dervish Islam" to Anatolia.[61] But rather than remaining the monopoly of popular saints and their often anti-establishment followers, this culture was brought into the mainstream, in large part through the model set by the Ottoman dynasty's cultivation of dervish leaders. Dervish babas were powerful, indeed indispensable, vehicles of legitimation, and figured prominently as such in the foundation myths of the dynasty. In chapter 1, we saw how Aintab's saints and dervish babas performed this function of sanctioning and thereby legitimating the Ottoman regime locally, at the time of its military occupation of the region. Dervish Islam was channeled into the mainstream institutionally through the innumerable zaviyes that provided social and spiritual succor throughout the Ottoman lands. It is no coincidence that zaviyes were conspicuously endowed by sultans, whose own reputation for charitable concern and spiritual enlightenment was bolstered as a consequence.

At first reading, it might seem that the Islam of the dervishes was populist in orientation, while the Islam of the mollas was urban and elitist. Such a distinction does not do justice to the complexities of religious identity in this period, though it is not wholly inaccurate and can help predict social tensions in Aintab society. Again, we might cite the model set by the Ottoman dynasty, which supported both streams of Islamic religiosity and endowed as many religious colleges as it did zaviyes. At the local level, the court records reveal the complex social hierarchies within each of these streams. Where, for example, was the boundary that defined "the people of religious learning"? Did this rubric, which clearly included leading teachers, jurists, and high-ranking mosque personnel, also encompass village imams, who could not claim the title *Molla* and who served unlettered congregations? Probably not.[62] And on the dervish side, the process of institutionalizing spiritual devotion led to distinctions between "molla" sheikhs and common dervishes. An example is the case of one Dervish Hüseyin, who used his own modest resources to build a shrine at the grave of Kurban Baba and to keep candles lit. Dervish Hüseyin was a figure reminiscent of the legendary muleteer who miraculously recovered the grave of Dülük Baba. But his act of piety was challenged by a molla, the sheikh of the Kara Abdal zaviye, who claimed that the right to light candles at Kurban Baba's grave belonged to his own zaviye. The dispute was resolved through mediation, and Dervish Hüseyin was paid 3 gold pieces to "disappear."[63] Authorities acting in this case upheld the local dervish "establishment" by preventing easy access to public spiritual mediation, the foundation of dervish authority. Important zaviyes in Aintab had important individuals at their head: a father-and-son pair, Seyyid İsmail and Seyyid Şemseddin, were sheikhs of the Haci Baba and the Dülük Baba zaviyes respectively,[64] and the Demirci family, hereditary sheikhs of the zaviye they had established, were one of the three leading lineages of the city.

It is probably fair to say that in 1540 the two streams of Muslim identity were strongly present, and present in multiple and sometimes overlapping manifestations. But it is perhaps significant that during his sojourn in the region in 1516 and 1517, the sultan Selim celebrated the graves of sufis and dervishes, while in 1535 it was the grave of Abu Hanifa, the founder of a school of Islamic jurisprudence, that was celebrated by his son Süleyman. In other words, in its larger Ottoman context, our study is situated at the cusp of a cultural and political shift toward the Islam of the mollas. In this shift, no small role was played by the threat posed by the Safavid shahs, hard-headed sovereigns but at the same time charismatic heads of a sufi order with proven appeal to Anatolian Turkmen.

Who were these Turkmen and to what degree was their social organization a part of Aintab's cultural heritage? From the eleventh century on, Turkmen nomadic tribes invaded or migrated from Central Asia into Anatolia as well as into northern Syria and northern Iraq. They were largely responsible for both the Islamization and the Turkification of the region.[65] The tribal bonds of many, however, were gradually eroded by the process of sedentarization, which substituted a local civic identity for that of Turkmen. At the same time, ongoing immigration as well as migration of Turkmen tribes within Anatolia meant that tribal practices and allegiances remained part of the cultural mix in much of the region. These processes shaped a critical aspect of Aintab's demographic makeup in the sixteenth century: the cultural distinction between sedentary and nomadic and the lived reality that this distinction could not be absolute because of the process of sedentarization.

The broad region in which Aintab province was located had a relatively large population of tribes (cemaat). Administratively, members of tribes were treated not as individually taxed heads of household, as villagers were, but rather as a corporate group. In other words, their allegiance was recognized not as that of a settled subject owed to the Ottoman state but rather as that owed by a tribal member to the tribal chief. It was the tribal leader who was answerable to the state for tribute or taxes and, when required, military aid. According to the massive cadastral survey of 1526, the governorate-general of Aleppo included 79 tribes, Diyarbakır 179, and Dulkadir 665.[66] No tribes were listed in that survey for Aintab, although, as already noted, the Aintab portion of this survey is sketchy and superficial; in 1526 Bire, the province directly east of Aintab and roughly the same size territorially, contained ten tribes. In the more careful survey of 1543, Aintab was described as containing fifteen tribes, that is, tribes whose pasturelands were located principally within the province and who were therefore administratively linked to it.[67] These were all Turkmen tribes. While the court records suggest that there were numerous settled Kurds, there is no cadastral evidence of Kurdish nomadic groups with administrative ties to Aintab officialdom. Many Kurdish tribes of the broader region had negotiated tributary status with the Ottoman regime soon after the conquest, a phenomenon that may account for their absence from official surveys.

Aintab's contact with nomads was not limited to those living within its administrative boundaries. The fact that the Aintab court handled a number of cases involving members of tribes from outside the province demonstrates the limitations of the cadastral surveys, which give us a static portrait of populations that in reality moved back and forth across administrative boundaries. Indeed, the whole point about nomads is that they were not stationary. Though they might be "registered" elsewhere, some tribes spent the winter months in Aintab province, while others passed through on their way to and from their summer quarters. However, this seasonal presence of nomadic groups appears to have diminished during the middle decades of the sixteenth century: estimated revenues from the "smoke tax," an impost levied on nomads wintering in the province, dropped from 18,000 akçes in 1536 to 10,000 in 1543 and to 5,500 by 1574. On the other hand, revenues from the "grazing tax" imposed on nomads simply passing through the province on their migratory routes remained more or less constant over these years.[68]

Although the "uncivilized" conduct of nomads—raiding caravans and pilgrim trains, abducting women and boys, carrying out blood feuds—caused the distinction between nomad and settled to be tenaciously asserted by the latter, symbiosis between the two was a deeply rooted historical reality. No community in the region could afford to shun nomads, since local economies and local consumers depended to a considerable extent on the goods and services they supplied.[69] Aintab may in fact have been an inviting place for nomads to settle. Part of the drop in wintering Turkmen tribes is probably the result of their settling down. We may in fact be looking at sedentarization-in-progress in a handful of villages in Aintab subdistrict whose populations were identified by their tribal name in the cadastral registers of 1536 and 1543: the village of Kayapınarı, for example, inhabited by the Koca Hacilû tribe, or Belankendi by the Kara Hamzalû and Bortu by the Küçük Hacilû.[70] All these tribes were members of the Dulkadir federation. To put this another way, the cadastral registers appear to acknowledge the transitional state of these settlements from tribal to peasant. The process of settlement was no doubt facilitated by the composition of the Dulkadir federation, the dominant tribal grouping in Aintab province, which was made up of a large number of smaller tribes. The suitability of Aintab subdistrict to a mixed economy of pastoralism and agriculture was also a factor. The same phenomenon of agricultural communities identified through their tribal structure can be seen to a much greater extent in the plain of Suruç in Bire province, where village fields and mezraas were farmed by clans subordinated to their Kurdish or Arab Bedouin tribal chieftains.[71] By contrast, the comparative paucity of such powerful chieftains in Aintab province may have hastened the absorption of nomads into settled society.

Sedentarization was a critical process in the area, and the social waves it set in motion are an ever-present if sometimes muted theme in our story of Aintab, its court, and its people. The process was not new to Aintab, for the sedentarization of Turkmen tribes had been going on since they began to arrive in significant numbers in the region. (Perhaps the sedentarization of the Kurdish tribespeople of Aintab was a similarly ongoing process, but it is harder to trace in the extant historical record.) Much of the Aintab elite—merchants, tax-farmers, landed gentry, the learned class—was originally of Turkmen origin.[72] This is not to say, however, that tribal affiliation continued to define their identity. On the contrary, the powerful cultural ideal of assimilation to urban civilizational norms acted to erase the memory of immigration. Sedentarization was clearly still going on in 1540, perhaps even intensifying under Ottoman pressure. But the transition from nomadism to the life of a peasant or city dweller was neither immediate nor always smooth. Although the cadastral registers are silent with regard to this process, the Aintab court records are not, for the court was clearly a place where the tensions surrounding sedentarization were confronted and sometimes mediated. While tribal identity was diluted by urban assimilation, it was not shed immediately. The court records are full of villagers and city dwellers called "Kurd So-and-so," and the names of others suggest a Turkmen identity—for example, one Sıdkı b. Mahmud, a butcher in the city who was popularly known as "son of the little Turkmen."[73]

The urban prejudice against nomads meant that attitudes and behaviors were unthinkingly ascribed to recent settlers. That people automatically perceived Turkmen to be nomads is suggested by the revised law code for Aintab in 1574, which ordered a correction in taxation practices discriminating against poor Turkmen laborers in the city. The new statute pointed out that these settled Turkmen were being mistaken for wintering nomads because they did not own their own homes.[74] Stereotypes of Turkmen as nomads were probably fed by the recognition that sedentarization was not an irreversible process—renomadization might occur for a variety of reasons. In our period, negative stereotypes were exacerbated by the association of Turkmen with Safavid partisanship and its religiously "deviant" practices (the story of Haciye Sabah deals at length with this problem).

Social tensions manifested themselves in a number of ways that will be apparent throughout the book, but for now two examples from the city will serve as illustrations. One telltale sign of social conflict was cursing, a tactic that the court records suggest was used by the less powerful against the elite. An example is a case in which the Turkmen Şah Hüseyin b. Allahverdi uttered a slanderous curse against a distinguished merchant who claimed descent from the Prophet Muhammad: the Turkmen accused the seyyid of being an adult catamite.[75] In another manifestation of tension, the traditional Islamic (Hanafi) legal prohibition against giving females in marriage to males of "inferior" social class (küfv) worked in Aintab against "ethnic" groups: one Yunis protested the marriage his mother had made for his sister Fatma because her fiancé was Kurdish; he stated in court that "there is no social equivalence—the aforesaid [fiancé] is of Kurdish origin and my sister is the daughter of a scholarly family (ehl-i ilm kızı)."[76] Both these incidents register antagonism between urban elites and those deemed lacking in urban sophistication because of their tribal backgrounds.

It is harder to judge the tensions of sedentarization in villages, since their social anatomy was less revealed at court than that of the city. Moreover, each village population was a different demographic and historical mix. But it is probably safe to say that memory of past nomadic or tribal identity remained alive longer among peasants than among city dwellers. The residents of one large and old village in Gaziantep told me in the fall of 1999 that, as their history has come down to them, their ancestors "lived up in the mountains" at some time in the past, "when animal hides functioned as money"; when they "came down," it was the availability of water that determined the settlement's location. This would seem to be a remembered history of an earlier pastoral life in which animal products were bartered for the goods produced by peasants and artisans, a way of life given up for a future as farmers. The villagers also confirmed what the work of local historians and folklore specialists suggests—that over time, tribal identity was attenuated but not lost; rather, it was broken down into family lineages and became a way of naming a line of descent *(sülâle)* rather than a larger loyalty to a tribal group or tribal leader.[77]

However, this means of tracing descent can preserve the antagonism associated with nomadic tribal habits of feuding: tensions between competing village lineages still erupt into intractable blood feuds in Gaziantep.[78] In 1999, a seventy-five-year-old feud between two tribal lineages *(aşiret)* that had resulted in the killing of twenty-some individuals was finally settled, in large part through the mediation of local state authorities.[79] To what extent these modern traces of the breaking down of tribal identity are relevant to Aintab in 1540 is hard to say, but the court records make clear that the most public manifestation of tensions around sedentarization was the conflict between residual "nomadic" habits and the legal culture of a sedentary polity.

CITY AND COUNTRYSIDE; OR, THE QUESTION OF PROVINCIAL IDENTITY

Did the province of Aintab create Aintabans? In other words, did the provincial boundary define a real entity in the minds of those within it? Clearly there was civic pride among some city dwellers, but what about the loyalties of the province's many villagers? To put this question another way, how intimately was Aintab city linked to its hinterland?

The cadastral surveys drew a sharp distinction between the urban and the rural. They grouped adult males by their city neighborhood, their village, or their tribal affiliation if nomadic. The court records too identified individuals by their address, so to speak, inscribing a litigant's village or tribe along with his or her name (city dwellers were marked by the absence of a rural address). But the categories employed by state documents do not necessarily reflect social habits. In fact, what the records reveal is constant traffic between village and city.[80] Moreover, the occupations and preoccupations of city dwellers and villagers in larger rural settlements overlapped, suggesting that there was a cultural continuum rather than a divide between rural and urban. In effect, the cadastral surveys imposed an administrative dichotomy on a more complex and fluid reality, just as they dichotomized the dynamic relationship between nomadic and sedentary.

City dwellers engaged locally in "farming" activities, cultivating orchards, vineyards, and vegetable plots located throughout Aintab city and particularly along the banks of the Sacur River.[81] Indeed, the city was celebrated for these green spaces: Bedreddin Ainî in the fourteenth century, as well as the polymath Kâtip Çelebi and the traveler Evliya Çelebi writing in the mid–seventeenth century, praised them as one of Aintab's attractions.[82] According to Evliya, they were the site of much leisure-time merrymaking (by men). The importance of urban farming was recognized in the agricultural taxes that were levied in the city as part of the provincial governor's income. These revenues were assessed at 7,000 akçes in 1536 and 13,000 akçes in 1543, and included taxes on grain, vegetables, beehives, grapevines, and mills.[83]

In addition, city people owned rural property. If modern practice bears any relation to that of the past, then we must imagine many city families repairing in the summer months to their village houses or small vineyard cabins. Rural property owned by city dwellers might range from entire villages to mezraas, houses, mills, and individual vegetable, vineyard, and orchard plots. One's rural domain might even consist of a single tree: the woman İl Hatun had acquired a walnut tree in the village of Ahmanus as part of her dower, which she proceeded to trade for a walnut tree in the village of Leylencik (walnut trees were valuable not only for their fruit but also for the dye that was rendered from their shells).[84] A mill, on the other hand, was a substantial rural investment: in September 1540, the court recorded the fact that a mill located in the village of Yona, inherited jointly by the relations of the city dweller Hüseyin Ağa—his mother, wife, sister, and brother—had been consolidated under the sole ownership of the brother, who bought out the female heirs for a total sum of 300 gold pieces.[85]

Rural residents, in turn, were linked to the city in numerous ways.[86] Since many villages were located fairly close to the city, its markets were available for selling surplus agricultural and animal products. Aintab was famous for its textiles and its fine leather, much of which was supplied by local villagers and pastoralists. Many villagers availed themselves of the ubiquitous networks of loans, borrowing sometimes from other villagers but more often from city people; debts typically ranged from 500 to 2,000 akçes.[87] Moreover, city dweller and villager might enter into a variety of partnerships. Two villagers from Mervana, for example, teamed up with Seyyid İsmail, the prominent sheikh of the Haci Baba zaviye, in a joint purchase of the tax-farm for the village's revenues.[88] A villager from the neighboring province of Bire invested 8,500 akçes in the commercial ventures of one Hoca Yusuf, who at the time of his death had debts to a range of individuals including a prominent timariot and the woman Rahime.[89] Finally, rural residents were important as consumers of goods produced and traded in the city. For example, the headman of the village of Tilşar (Telbaşer?) purchased twenty pieces of ordinary cotton cloth and four pieces of Damascene linen from the city textile merchant Ali b. Yusuf for 2,210 akçes, perhaps for resale to residents of Tilşar. Several days later, Ali sold 65 pieces of ordinary cotton and 130 pieces of Egyptian cloth to the son of the trustee of crown lands for 10,000 akçes, the payment due seven months hence.[90] Like the Bire villager's investment in a joint commercial venture, the Tilşar headman's cloth purchase placed him in a trading network that extended beyond the province's borders.

Marriage and local migration also bridged the divide between urban and rural. Families with both city and country cousins were well positioned to exploit economic linkages between village and city. Such a situation may be reflected in an inheritance settlement worked out by İbrahim and his two sisters—Sati, who, like her brother, was resident in Aintab city, and Saide, resident in Hiyam, the largest village in the province. From their father, Sati and Saide each inherited a half share in a textile shop specializing in broadcloth; they were now selling their shares to İbrahim for 662 akçes each.[91] While the court record does not make explicit whether Sati and Saide were married, it is difficult to imagine that Saide, the village sister, would be living in Hiyam without a husband or a branch of the family with whom she might reside. One might reasonably speculate that Saide and others of her household were engaged in the production of the broadcloth sold in the city shop: weaving it, spinning and dyeing the yarn, and purchasing the wool from local pastoralists or acquiring the raw materials from the city. Perhaps Saide did not dirty her hands in such activities, but rather supervised the work of recruits from the local village.[92]

Indeed, village populations exhibited a range of socioeconomic statuses. For this reason, I avoid using the word *peasant* to refer to village residents, although many Aintab villagers certainly could be characterized as peasants. Some village residents were wealthy enough to have households that included slaves. Kubad from the village of Süleyman proved at court that the runaway black male slave named Bereket, whom he had recovered from the chief financial officer of Damascus, was in fact his property.[93] Yusuf from the village of Suboğaz sold to a city official a female slave valued at 30 gold pieces, presumably white and possibly a concubine, in exchange for 8 gold pieces in cash and a horse valued at 20 gold pieces.[94]

In the court records for 1540–1541, the complex relations among urban and rural economies and networks are most richly exemplified by a case involving a grandfather's sale of property to his grandsons. In November 1540, Haci Mehmed, a resident of the Boyacı neighborhood of the city, appeared in court to register the sale of "real estate and livestock" *(emlak ve davar)* to the two sons of his daughter Ayşe, for a sum of 4,000 akçes. He may have been attempting to bypass the laws of inheritance, which mandated that two-thirds of a person's estate be divided among relatives according to legally fixed shares. Whatever his motivation, Haci Mehmed appeared to be divesting himself of a not inconsiderable rural enterprise. The sale included property in the village of Arıl consisting of a house, a vegetable garden, and a pomegranate orchard, along with the right to rent a pond and a well there. Also sold were two large vineyards in two different mezraas consisting of 500 and 700 vines respectively, and fifty head of sheep in the care of two men from the Turkmen tribe of Begdili.[95]

What does this transaction tell us? For one thing, it suggests that individuals who were officially classified as city dwellers could have a rural identity as well, moving between their roles as urban entrepreneur and rural gentry. The transaction also suggests an interdependence between this gentleman farmer and the local villagers, who were in all probability hired to work his land, perhaps to process his grape harvest into grape syrup (a staple of local kitchens), and to watch over his properties in his absence. Furthermore, it reveals a link between nomadic pastoralists and urban or rural entrepreneurs. This was not the only instance in which animals were farmed out to nomads for summer pasturing or perhaps on a permanent basis: Hasan, from the village of Sam, sued the Bedouin Mehmed over his horse, which had been stolen during its summer pasturing under Mehmed's supervision.[96]

Finally, the location of Haci Mehmed's urban and rural residences suggests some kind of relationship between him and the prominent Boyacı family. Not only did he live in the city neighborhood bearing their name, but the village of Arıl, where his country house and some of his agricultural properties were located, was owned by Seydi Ahmed, current head of the Boyacı family. Arıl was a large village that was strategically located on the main road from Aintab to Bire and on to the east, a route that is referred to today as "the old silk route."[97] This case again prompts speculation about the extent to which residents of urban neighborhoods named after local magnates might enter into joint networks or perhaps benefit from the magnate's patronage. By ensuring that his rural holdings passed safely into the hands of his grandsons, perhaps Haci Mehmed was consolidating his family's relationship with the Boyacıs for the future. Since the court record tells us nothing about Haci Mehmed's other properties or investments, it is difficult to do more than simply pose this question.

We have been speaking of the residents of Aintab city and the province's villagers and nomads as "Aintabans," as if the provincial boundary defined or encompassed a shared identity. In the case of urban dwellers, many people probably did identify with Aintab as the place where they had set down roots. Perhaps some of them experienced a sense of civic pride in this local center of trade, education, and law. But what about the province's villagers and, even more, nomadic elements who were identified in the court record not in relation to place but rather as a tribal entity? I have been arguing for a dense set of connections between rural and urban residents, but these connections were not necessarily confined within the provincial boundary. To a considerable degree, the provincial boundary would have seemed arbitrary to many, particularly those in the subdistricts of Telbaşer, whose orientation was toward the south, and Nehrülcevaz, close to the Euphrates cities of Bire and Rumkale. Moreover, a number of villages within the provincial boundary were directly connected to Aleppo, either owned by well-to-do Aleppans or belonging to pious foundations there. And as the site of a periodic market, the large village of Nizip (today a city of some 80,000 and a subdistrict in the province of Gaziantep) was a magnet for inhabitants of the eastern parts of the province, despite being administratively tied to the neighboring province of Bire.[98]

Yet there was probably a growing identification with the province as such, or at least a recognition of its potential, in the form of its officialdom, to affect one's life, both positively and negatively. The province was as close as the tax collector or the police agent who might appear to investigate a disturbance or complaint. In addition, each village, each mezraa, and each nomadic tribe was linked in a specific manner, through a specific individual, to the larger fiscal and administrative systems—be that link a cavalryman assigned to a particular village, a landowning family such as the Boyacıs, the trustee who supervised villages in the crown's domain, or the official assigned to collect the lump-sum taxes imposed on tribal groups. We can presume that most villagers and nomads, or at the very least those with local responsibility, understood how their particular community fitted in at the provincial level of administration, even if they had little grasp of the political economy of the empire as a whole. Last but far from least, the court of Aintab itself was a centripetal force drawing people's attention to the provincial capital. The steady stream of villagers, urban residents, and the occasional tribesman or tribeswoman who used the court on a daily basis, many voluntarily, demonstrated popular awareness of the court as a provincial resource. Nevertheless, for some, thinking of themselves as Aintabans was no doubt a new habit in 1540.

DEFINING THE REGION: NETWORKS OF CONTACT AND COMMUNICATION

How geographically extensive was the world of Aintabans? The court records, our only local source for this period, suggest that the city of Aintab in the sixteenth century might be considered "regionally cosmopolitan." It was tied into a network of cities spanning southeastern Anatolia and northern Syria. With Aintab at the center, the network's inner core was defined by Aleppo, Kilis, Maraş, Ruha, and Bire, and its outer circle by Damascus, the Çukurova Plain, Elbistan, Malatya, and Amid (see map 2).[99] In this section, we examine the linkages that knit the region together and the role played by Aintab in regional networks. One of the most important of these networks was the system of courts, and another the web of law enforcement officials that paralleled the judicial network. In addition, ordinary people created their own ties crossing the provincial boundary.

A large variety of legal problems and issues brought outsiders to the Aintab court, revealing the diverse nature of contacts among people across social and economic space. (Aintabans with business outside the province are less visible, their stories no doubt recorded in the registers of neighboring courts, which have unfortunately not survived.) Some of the networks crossing the region were the obvious ones: trade, family ties that crossed provincial boundaries, military communication among the several fortresses in the region. Travelers, traders, soldiers, relatives—all were channels of communication. The relative density of the urban network, the infrastructure of hostels and soup kitchens that most cities provided, and the possibility of lodging in villages overnight helped lighten the burdens of travel for the remarkable number of people who came and went from Aintab city and its villages.

The court record also reflects illicit networks, and at the same time hints at the links among agencies that controlled crime. There was, in effect, a kind of regional dragnet operating across the geographic area mapped above. Let us look in some detail at the problem of missing animals, since it gives the sharpest evidence of lines of communication crisscrossing the region. With the possible exception of negotiations over debts, the statistically most common issue at the Aintab court was that of horses, donkeys, and mules who had in one way or another left the hands of their masters and mistresses. An astonishing number of animals went astray, were stolen, or moved rapidly across large distances by means of serial trading. Indeed, a lively market for stolen animals appears to have connected many parts of the region (the village of Kızılhisar in Telbaşer subdistrict—today's Oğuzeli—figured often in both licit and illicit animal trading). Individuals claiming their animals in the Aintab court came from as far away as Harran (south of Ruha), Dayr Al-Zor further to the south, Sis and Kos in the Çukurova Plain, and even Karaman in south-central Anatolia.[100] Some claims were long-standing: Bozdoğan from Sis was in pursuit of a horse that had been stolen nine months earlier and had belonged to his sister's husband, while Ahmed from Dayr claimed to have spotted a donkey that had been stolen from him three years earlier. Since a number of these claims were made in the months of October, November, and December, it is possible that animals tended to go missing during summer pasturing or summer migrations across parts of the region. Or perhaps it was only after the harvest season that people had the free time to make the journey to the Aintab court.

How did these individuals trace their animals? The court records suggest that it was customary for strays or animals suspected of being stolen property to be turned over to the authorities in each provincial capital and large village. These authorities—the provincial governor's staff, and police officers in the city and in larger villages—were also responsible for fugitive slaves and other matters of law enforcement that crossed provincial bound-aries.[101] Their involvement in the recovery of lost animals was not simply to protect the interests of subjects. The state had its own stake in preventing a black market in animals: beasts of burden were customarily sold in desig-nated markets where a sales tax was imposed, whose revenues in Aintab went directly to the imperial treasury.[102] In Aintab city, this market was known, fittingly, as "the sultan's bazaar."[103]

Any number of cases in the record for 1540–1541 make clear that com-munications among authorities were efficient and reasonably rapid; often their networks seemed to parallel or coincide with those used by the courts. Stolen animals came to the attention of the authorities in part because pen-alties were imposed on anyone who failed to turn over a stray animal and then have the find publicly "broadcast."[104] It is not clear exactly what was in-volved in the process of "broadcasting," but city officials and the headmen of large villages presumably disseminated information by dispatching one of their numerous subordinates. (The distances between points within the province were not excessive: for example, it took approximately six hours on foot to travel from Aintab city to the village of Orul.)[105] It is not difficult, therefore, to imagine the sixteenth-century equivalent of an information hotline among the towns, villages, and tribal leaders in the region. How else, one wonders, would Ahmed from Dayr have come across his donkey in Ain-tab, a city of some 10,000 human souls and no doubt hundreds of donkeys; or how would Bozdoğan from Sis have known to look for the missing horse in a village in Kilis, a town (and judicial district) southwest of Aintab? Other cases in the records show owners of lost or stolen animals regularly applying to the authorities in order to recover their property; the court was a party to the events because the owner had to prove before the judge that the animal was hers or his. In August 1541, records were transferred from the courts of both Aleppo and Bire in order to substantiate a Bire resident's suit to re-possess a mule that had disappeared.

Clearly, the value of animals to both individuals and the state was an im-portant factor in animating this regional dragnet. But our interest here is not simply in the animal economy of Aintab. Examining the network for re-covering lost animals is useful for two reasons: it exposes the connections among economic, judicial, and administrative structures and, more impor-tant, it demonstrates one channel through which local people became fa-miliar with legal networks and grew accustomed to using them. People of-ten went to a great deal of trouble to recover a horse or a donkey, even though they might pay a fine for having failed to adequately supervise their animals. Two men from Kos, for example, whose horse had been stolen from a village in Aintab province, went so far as to obtain an order from the local "pasha"—the Dulkadir governor-general—to aid them in their legal suit. Ahmet from Dayr petitioned the court for a fifty-day postponement of his suit so he might fetch his witnesses from home; precisely two months later, the witnesses appeared in the Aintab court to testify that the "gray male donkey with clipped ears" was indeed Ahmet's property. All this trouble was taken for a donkey whose value was not very great; the man in whose possession it was found claimed he had purchased it for 194 akçes in the village of Kızılhisar.[106]

One reason that lost animals appear to have been returned to their owners with some regularity was that the punishment for theft was severe. The law code of Süleyman, issued around 1540, prescribed two possible penalties for the theft of horses, mules, donkeys, and cattle: a hefty fine of 200 akçes or the cutting off of the thief's hand; repeated theft could be punished by hanging.[107] As we will see in chapter 8, while physical mutilations and the death sentence may have been rarely carried out, their presence on the books functioned (in theory) as a deterrent to the crime of theft. That the theft of animals was a chronic problem in the region and one that past regimes had taken seriously is suggested by the fact that theft of horses and donkeys was the second item in the law code issued by the last Dulkadir ruler, Alaeddevle: the penalty for animal theft was 18 gold pieces, greater than the penalty for adultery but less than that for destroying someone's house.[108] (The first item in the law code was brigandage, or highway robbery, punishable by hanging.)

The network of communications among local authorities may well have predated the Ottoman regime, and in fact was probably an old regional arrangement. It was reinforced by Ottoman consolidation of the area. Indeed, Süleyman's law book gives the impression of simply *assuming* the existence of a legal infrastructure—of law enforcement mechanisms as well as of judges and courts. This assumption is evident in its regulations regarding missing persons and the widespread practice of personal surety, that is, the appointment of guarantors for criminal suspects. The role of such guarantors *(kefil bi'l-nefs)* was to ensure that suspects not evade the law by simply disappearing; in the language of the court record, they were "delegated to guarantee the presence of the individual whenever it might be requested." Should his ward go missing, a guarantor was required by law to search across seven judicial districts *(kadılık)* before he could be absolved of responsibility.[109] Such a requirement presumed the availability of officials who could facilitate the guarantor's search in each district.

This emphasis on the regional management of crime manifested itself in another practice whereby individuals from different regions could be drafted to act as guarantor for one another. When suspects from beyond the province's borders required surety, the Aintab authorities preferred to appoint guarantors from their home province. For example, two men from the Çukurova were appointed guarantor for the brother of one of them, while a third person—perhaps a local Aintab resident—was appointed guarantor for the two Çukurovans.[110] This practice of double guarantorship appears to have been employed only for suspects from outside Aintab. In an interesting pair of cases, Zenil from Kilis volunteered to act as guarantor for his fellow villager Ahmed, while the following day, Ahmed volunteered to act as guarantor to Yusuf from Mardin.[111] Were the two villagers from Kilis already acquainted with the man from Mardin? or was there perhaps a community of suspects, guarantors, and suspect-guarantors that coalesced around the local court? These cases suggest that the regional approach to ensuring legal order could foster a kind of localized solidarity among non-Aintabans.

The network of governors, judges, police, and their staffs was not aimed merely at controlling criminal activity; rather it operated to promote security in general. Order should not be taken for granted or assumed as the default state of affairs in this region and period. Indeed, if there was a state of relative security in 1540, it had been hard-won, and only recently. Conquest did not mean pacification, and it was only the critically important two-year offensive against Iran in 1534–1536 that put an end to nearly twenty years of Ottoman struggle to gain control over the areas conquered by Selim I in 1516 and 1517. Resistance can be documented throughout these years, during which numerous military expeditions were sent to quell disturbances. In securing social and legal order, the Ottoman regime was faced with troubles from two directions: on the one hand, challenges to its sovereignty from Turkmen tribal groups and, on the other hand, the lawless, and sometimes rebellious, conduct of its own soldiers and officers. The execution in 1522 of the last Dulkadir prince, Şehsuvaroğlu Ali, deprived the Ottoman sultan of perhaps the only figure who could control the Turkmen tribal chiefs (boy begleri). It also gave rise to a saying popular among Turkmen of the Dulkadir area, "the Ottoman is the oppressor of the brave."[112]

By 1530, the chronic pattern of armed uprisings, frequently inspired by militant dervish babas and sometimes attracting tens of thousands of supporters, was largely broken; but even after that date, tribal chiefs could still make it difficult for Ottoman governors to actually govern.[113] As for the regime's own undisciplined forces, a vivid example of the havoc they could cause is revealed in a complaint drafted by the people of Aleppo sometime in 1533 or 1534 and sent to the grand vezir. They alleged that troops stationed in and around the city were devastating crops, seizing animals without recompense, humiliating men by snatching their turbans from their heads, breaking into houses and abusing women and boys, forcibly occupying houses, and resisting all attempts at discipline for these violations. If the situation was not rectified, asserted the complaint, the people of Aleppo would simply abandon the city.[114] The celebrated campaign of 1534–1536 is usually thought to have been directed against Safavid power, but it was also a reconquest of the region aimed at purging it of internal challenges.

It is only in the later 1530s that we can begin to speak of a "pax Otto-

manica"—that relative degree of order achieved by a relatively lawful imperial rule over a vast territory. The renaissance of trade from the mid-1530s
on suggests that greater safety on the roads was one of the results of regional
cooperation in the interests of social and legal order. The court records
of 1540–1541 indicate that Aintabans traveled frequently for business, and
they demonstrate a range of occupations that took people on the road.
Major business deals among merchants were not, as a rule, conducted under the aegis of the court, but minor transactions, particularly disputes over
payment for goods received or repayment of loans, were often sealed at
court. These transactions indicate that intercity trade was frequently
handled by agents who were contracted by local merchants and dealers to
transport and sell their goods in distant markets. Things did not always go
as planned. The Aintaban Haci Mehmed, for example, was not pleased with
the performance of his agent Haci Bekir, who sold a herd of twenty-six goats
in Aleppo for less than his employer had instructed.[115] Some businessmen,
such as the Armenian İskender, took care of their long-distance contacts in
person. İskender used his travel as an alibi when accused of a crime: "I am
someone who travels on business," he told the court; "one day I'm at home
and the next day I'm out in the field."[116] In another case, an Aintab craftsman was sought for his skills: the stonecutter, Master Hüseyin, was hired for
16 akçes a day to aid in the construction of a bridge in a neighboring province. He was accompanied by his son and another worker, who were paid 12
and 8 akçes respectively; in addition, the master also negotiated travel expenses for his team.[117] Perhaps the easy availability of stone from the quarries to the south of Aintab city and the many mosques, covered bazaars, and
other buildings built from it gave its stoneworkers a regional reputation.

Greater security of the roads combined with economic expansion meant
a rise in the number of individuals coming from outside Aintab to its court.
In general, outsiders used the court to bring claims against Aintabans or
other individuals who happened to be living there at the moment. The
woman Sultan from Ruha appealed in vain to the judge of Aintab over a
seven-year-old debt that she claimed one Kuli, presumably from Aintab,
owed her for his purchase of a half share in a grove of trees.[118] While Ruha
and Aintab were some 120 kilometers apart, it is not unusual that two individuals separated by such a distance would co-own land (mills and horses
were other items sometimes held jointly). The owners might have a time-
sharing arrangement, for example, or employ agents locally to work the
property. In another case, the Egyptian Sharif Ahmed successfully claimed
a debt of 3 gold pieces from Abdulkadir of Aleppo.[119] Why cases such as this
last one, in which the litigants were identified as permanent residents of
cities other than Aintab, should come before its judge is rarely made clear,
although an obvious explanation is that they were temporary residents of
Aintab when the dispute came about.

A case involving an embroidered wool caftan suggests that plaintiffs sometimes had to travel to pin down their suit if the defendant or the object of dispute was to be found in Aintab. A certain Ahmed had rented the caftan in his home city of Aleppo to wear at a wedding held in Aintab, but apparently failed to return it. In Ahmed's first appearance before the judge of Aintab, he was summoned by a local policeman to court, where he formally acknowledged that he had rented and worn the caftan. A couple of weeks later, the caftan's owner appeared in court to claim his property.[120] As in cases involving the recovery of errant animals, a communications link among cities may be operating here: the sequence of events suggests that Ahmed and the missing caftan were first located by Aintab authorities, whereupon the owner made the journey from Aleppo to claim his property.

The reasons that brought women from outside the province to the Aintab court were less likely to pertain to business than to matters concerning family and personal relationships. It is not that women did not engage in business, but rather that the economic circles in which they operated were closer to home and their legal affairs were therefore managed through their local court (as we will see in chapter 6). From Ruha came Baki, whose purpose at the Aintab court was to act as proxy for the divorce of her daughter, who had become estranged from her Aintaban husband; Baki was accompanied to court by three women who served as witnesses to the validity of her appointment as proxy.[121] The villager Mehmet from Elbistan came to formally grant a divorce to his wife Fatma, who had been abducted seven years earlier and was now apparently living in Aintab with her abductor.[122] Indeed, as a relatively large city, Aintab may have been a haven for runaway lovers. The woman Zehra acknowledged at court that she had absconded from her village in Kilis province with the nomad Bayezid ("we ran away and came here," said Zehra).[123]

Perhaps the most consequential case that brought outsiders to the Aintab court was a long-standing dispute over compensation for bodily injury (*diyet,* in the language of jurisprudence). This case clearly displays the strength of regional links. Ten years earlier, a man from Aleppo had struck the left hand of a cavalryman from Damascus with a dagger, paralyzing three of his fingers. The cavalryman had then successfully sued the Aleppan for damages in the court of Aleppo, receiving several items of value (including a silver dagger!). Apparently unsatisfied with the amount of compensation, the cavalryman was now reopening the case in the Aintab court. The judge handed the case over to arbiters, presumably because he was unable to sort out the mutual recriminations that took place in his court between plaintiff and defendant (the cavalryman was unsure of the total worth of the items he had previously received). A judgment was ultimately made in favor of the cavalryman for the substantial sum of 150 gold pieces, of which he waived 60 (presumably the value of the previous settlement). To cover the remainder of his debt, the Aleppan then gave the cavalryman several more items, including two horses and a number of textiles pieces. The court record closed with the statement that the dispute between the two had been definitively resolved.[124]

This case again raises the question of why litigation that apparently involved no one identified as being from the jurisdiction of the Aintab court would be heard before its judge. That various networks of communication existed across the region—from Mardin to the Çukurova, from Elbistan to Damascus and even Cairo—should be evident from the many examples above. The court itself was one node in a critically important network: that of provincial judgeships. Procedurally, the network of judges and courts is revealed in the Aintab records through numerous instances of "transfer of testimony" (nakl-ı şehadet), whereby the history of litigation begun in one court was forwarded so that it could continue under another judge when necessary. In the case above, the cavalryman had requested just such a transfer of testimony from Aleppo in preparation for the Aintab hearing. Preparing these transfers was a regular duty of a judge and his scribes (the law book associated with Selim set the hefty fee for the necessary documents at 25 akçes).[125] As Nelly Hanna has pointed out in her study of Ottoman judicial administration in sixteenth-century Cairo, a major goal of the Ottoman regime was to systematize and standardize the judiciary throughout the empire, so that the work of one court could be conveyed to another.[126]

It is important to note that the jurisdictions of judges (kaza, kadılık) were congruent with those of provincial governors (liva, sancak), who in most regions of the empire represented both the military and fiscal infrastructures of the state. This deliberate congruency created parallelism among the three principal administrative hierarchies of the empire—the legal, the military, and the fiscal. But it is hard to tease apart these hierarchies in operation. The local court was a key element not only in the legal system but in all aspects of administration, since it was there that officials with a variety of responsibilities interacted, recording transactions and solving disputes. To put it another way, the court was the facilitator of shared responsibility among provincial representatives of the branches of government as well as between officials and the local population. The cavalry officer may have been able to locate his assailant ten years after the first court settlement because of the overlapping networks of judges and local police, the latter under the control of the provincial governor.

We might at this point indulge in preliminary speculation about the place of the Aintab court in this network of provincial judgeships. While it was the seat of a legal-cum-military province—simultaneously a sancak and a kadılık—Aintab was not the seat of a governorate-general. The smaller town of Maraş, 50 kilometers to the north, was the capital of the Dulkadir governorate-general to which Aintab belonged. Maraş also had its own judge. But it may not be surprising that the Aintab court handled business from a broad region that transcended such administrative boundaries. For one thing, Aintab was the largest city in the region, with the exception of Aleppo and possibly Ruha to the east. As we have seen, it was a magnet for entrepreneurs, as well as for those with less honorable purposes, the horse thieves and runaway lovers who perhaps hoped that the bustle of the city would offer anonymity. Moreover, the regularity of legal procedure revealed in the Aintab court records suggests a well-established judicial culture and a smoothly functioning judicial system. This impression is strengthened by the very neatness of the court records, which contrast with the more haphazard records from other Anatolian cities in this period.[127]

The Aintab court also worked hard: it held sessions quite regularly through the year, taking an occasional day off, breaking for two weeks at the end of October 1540, but hearing cases on the Muslim holy day of Friday. Perhaps the Aintab court enjoyed a reputation for processing cases quickly, attracting petitioners who preferred to avoid the courts of metropolises such as Aleppo and Damascus. It is also possible that particular courts were known for expertise in certain kinds of matters (missing animals, for example). As a city with a fortress and garrison, Aintab may have been regarded as qualified to hear cases involving military personnel, such as that of the cavalryman with the injured hand.

With regard to the question of Aintab's place in a regional network of courts, it is certainly important to remember that for the first time in several centuries, Aintab was located in the *middle* of a state. As a city whose identity had been influenced by its historical positioning in a marchland, Aintab under the pax Ottomanica may have acquired the role of integrating that marchland into larger regional networks. Relevant here is the fact that it was linked culturally and economically to Aleppo in the south, but administratively northward to a governorate-general with a considerable tribal population. The absence of court records before the Ottoman period makes it hard to know the extent to which the court's business was altered by its incorporation into the Ottoman domain, but their very existence from the 1530s on—that is, their existence *as a public record*—may point to a deliberately enhanced role for the Aintab court.

Although the great majority of cases heard by the judge of Aintab involved individuals from within the province, the foregoing brief sample of "outsiders" with business in the Aintab court should suffice to suggest that people of the region, or some of them at least, did not find travel an obstacle to accomplishing their ends. While the need for a legal settlement may have caused some to journey to Aintab reluctantly, others ended up in court because of their voluntary relationships that extended across space. Litigants at court were not limited to the wealthy and the powerful, whose mobility we might take for granted. Ordinary city dwellers, villagers, and those classified in the record as tribal nomads frequented the court with regularity. Women came for a variety of reasons and in substantial numbers, if not as often as men. Nor was a large material stake in a matter always the inducement that led people to appeal to the judge of Aintab. The challenge to today's reader of these records is to understand what other meanings their suits at court might have carried beyond their material consequences.

BEYOND THE REGION: WAR AND PILGRIMAGE

The citizens of Aintab province inhabited a region that was defined in part by personal and economic ties, and in part by administrative systems that were increasing in rigor during this period of Ottoman consolidation. We turn now to other aspects of their lives that transported them to physical and cultural topographies beyond the region. Were there forces that transcended the localism that has been so strong a characteristic of Middle Eastern identities, both then and now? The court records suggest that there were two ever-present magnets that drew Aintabans long distances away from their homes: war and pilgrimage.

War took men beyond regional boundaries, and no doubt caused the thoughts of the families they left behind to dwell on faraway places. Warfare was a staple of this period. The sultan Süleyman led seventeen military campaigns during the forty-six years of his reign between 1520 and 1566, and other expeditions took place under the command of his generals. Provincial officials were regularly called on to dispatch soldiers and supplies to meet the empire's defensive and offensive needs. Additionally, soldiers might be dispatched for security reasons—to guard pilgrimage routes, for example, or to combat the banditry that was endemic in areas with sizable nomadic populations.

Who made up the local military? In Aintab, the sultan's soldiers were a visible presence in the city and in numerous villages in the province. Some soldiers belonged to the garrison stationed in the fortress of Aintab *(merdân-ı kale)*, while others, known as *sipahis*, belonged to the provincial cavalry. Sipahis and their armed retainers were supported by tax revenues from the various villages to which they themselves were assigned. These temporary grants to sipahis of rights to village revenues were known as *timar*s, and sipahis were sometimes referred to as "timariot soldiers." Timariots were important not only for their military function but also because they were responsible for social and legal order in their villages. According to the cadastral survey of 1543, the fortress garrison numbered 53 men exclusive of officers, while the provincial cavalry stationed in Aintab province numbered 86, with an additional population of 109 armed retainers who served the cavalry members.[128]

The distances to which members of the Aintab military might be sent on imperial service can be measured in the court registers. An undated record from the fall of 1540 noted that ten members of the fortress garrison were dispatched on the "Erzurum campaign"; the issue that involved the court was the local requisition of ammunition and grain for the soldiers.[129] Whether another instance of military requisitioning was accompanied by the draft of soldiers is not clear: in October 1540, the city's copper dealers organized to meet an imperial order for copper to be supplied to Baghdad. They were instructed to set a price fair for the local market, to obtain the funds to buy the copper from the royal intendant for Aintab, and then to purchase copper from local suppliers.[130] In November, supplies that included 450 firearms were assigned to twenty soldiers who were being sent to Baghdad.[131] There are no other such records of military support coming out of Aintab for the year 1540–1541, but it may well be that men and supplies were steadily requisitioned from the province (the two records of soldiers dispatched on campaign were pasted in the fall of 1540 into the back of the court register and were not a part of its regular, daily accounts).

The Ottoman military in this period has generally been viewed as a professional military, which strictly forbade civilian entry into the ranks of combatants. Both the standing infantry in Istanbul—the famous Janissaries—and the provincial cavalry stationed throughout much of the empire have been assumed to be slave recruits serving the sultan directly. As this practice has been understood, the rationale for prohibiting a popular military was twofold: to provide a soldiery loyal to the sultan by eliminating any local allegiances and to keep taxpayers at their jobs—whether trading goods, tilling fields, or cutting stone—in order to finance the military and administrative requirements of government. It turns out, however, that this picture of a soldiery set apart from the civilian population is not entirely accurate for Aintab in 1540. A sizable number of the garrison soldiers as well as of the provincial cavalry were in fact local individuals.[132] Some were members of the local elite, or so their titles of *Beg* and *Çelebi* would suggest. Among these, for example, were the sons of Gazi Beg, who possessed timar rights to all or parts of six villages; the two sons of Tarhan Beg, who jointly possessed rights to four villages and a quarter share of two others; and the sons of Üveys Beg, who possessed rights to all or parts of five villages.[133] It is likely that Gazi Beg, Tarhan Beg, and Üveys Beg numbered among the tribal chiefs of the leaderless Dulkadir federation who were rewarded with timars as part of the Ottoman program of pacification of rebellious Turkmen chiefs during the 1520s.[134]

But how might we account for the local origins of soldiers of lesser status, particularly the members of fortress garrisons who often shared a timar village with two or three or four others? We can only speculate. Perhaps these individuals were retainers of such tribal chiefs as Gazi Beg and Tarhan Beg and their ilk. Or perhaps they were volunteers who had made good. A provincial governor might on occasion recommend that an outstanding military hopeful be granted membership in the cavalry assigned to his province. War could thus function as a magnet for adventurers, opportunists, and the discontented.

War may account for the men who simply disappeared from Aintab and did not return. Intentionally or not, some of these men who vanished left their wives utterly without resources. This predicament forced the wives to appeal for public assistance, which was by law disbursed by the local judge. Such was the fate of three women—Tatar, Meryem, and Fatma—each of whom petitioned the court in the summer of 1541 for financial support. Tatar and Fatma had heard no word from their husbands for seven years, while Meryem's husband had been missing for three.[135] The scope of this problem of disappearing husbands may have been greater than three instances in one year might suggest. For every woman who sought the court's help in the face of a husband's desertion or possible death, there may have been others who were taken care of by relatives or had sufficient resources to avoid seeking public assistance. That women were concerned over the possibility of desertion is suggested by the action of Uğurluhan, who took protective measures by getting her husband Bayındır to prearrange a divorce before embarking on campaign.[136] In August 1541, Bayındır made the following statement at court, recorded at his wife's request: "I am going on campaign; if I am unable to return and resume married life with my wife within three months, let her be divorced from me." The woman Şehzade had a similar arrangement, though in her case not necessarily related to war: on July 22, 1541, she had her prearranged divorce registered at court by proxy—her husband had failed to return to her by the date he specified (June 25), and Şehzade now wanted her divorce recognized.[137]

While war threatened social disorder for women, it could provide an opportunity for men. In the early 1540s, in Aintab at least, the post of timariot or garrison soldier was one offering in the repertoire of state-generated offices providing local employment. By admitting some local inhabitants into the sultan's service, the Ottoman regime may have won a degree of loyalty or at least a sense of shared interest from a segment of the local population. Once in the service of the state, were these soldiers eligible for promotion through the ranks, or were their offices merely honorary sinecures designed to satisfy local power brokers? Until we know more about how the provincial military was constituted in other places during this period, we cannot do more than hypothesize about the meaning of a military organization that incorporated more men of local origin than we have hitherto envisioned.

In the final analysis, the greatest inducement to travel beyond the provincial and regional boundaries was neither economic opportunity nor military service. What appears to have drawn the largest number of Aintabans out of the province—and taken them furthest—was their religious allegiance. The substantial number of individuals appearing at court who carried the title *Haci* for males or *Haciye* for females, signifying that they had performed the hajj, or pilgrimage to Mecca, suggests that more people undertook travel for religious purposes than for any other reason. The pilgrimage was especially significant for women, since it was for them the only regularly sanctioned travel over great distances.

The holy sites of Islam lay to the south of Aintab: Jerusalem, Hebron, Medina, and finally Mecca. Not only did Aintabans traverse hundreds of kilometers on their way to these sites, but the pilgrimage brought them together with Muslims from many other regions of the Middle East and beyond. Even those who did not make the pilgrimage may have had their horizons expanded while staying home, for some pilgrims from Anatolia and the Balkans passed through Aintab on their way to Mecca and, more important, back.[138] The Ottoman traveler Evliya Çelebi visited Aintab on pilgrimage in 1671, the occasion for a laudatory account of the city in his travel memoirs. Evliya's route took him from one fortress city to the next, from Tarsus in the Çukurova to Adana and on to Maraş, then southward through Aintab and on to Aleppo.[139]

The pilgrimage was not the only form of religious devotion that brought individuals from Aintab to other cities and into contact with other cultures. The woman İl left her accustomed life in Aintab in order to devote herself to serving the poor of Jerusalem. We know about İl's decision because she came to court to officially give over custody of her small daughter to her uncle.[140] (İl's title *Hatun,* or "Lady," suggests that she was a well-to-do individual; we have met her earlier, exchanging one walnut tree for another with the uncle who would raise her daughter.) The desire for religious knowledge was another quest that took individuals on the road. As we have seen, many men in Aintab carried the title *Molla,* the sign of a religiously learned individual. We may imagine that just as Aintab attracted the religiously learned in the fourteenth century, so the learned of Aintab (or some of them, at least) traveled to other centers of Muslim scholarship to expand their education. If Bedreddin Ainî had managed to garner an education in various cities of the region during the troubled times when conquerors seemed to be invading once a decade, the regional security underwritten by the Ottoman regime must surely have bolstered sixteenth-century educational networks, as it did judicial, economic, and military networks. Whether the same thing can be said for the small Armenian Christian community of Aintab in 1540 is not clear from the court records; but by the seventeenth century, Aintab itself seems to have been a noted center of Armenian learning, and the city produced individuals who left to take on leadership roles in the Armenian church.[141]

The coordinates of Islam's spiritual map tended to reinforce the association between the religious experience of Muslims from Aintab and the Mamluk past. For two and a half centuries, Mamluk rulers had held the prestigious title of "guardians of the holy places"—Mecca and Medina—which gave them the prerogative of constructing religious institutions and monuments in the holy cities. This title, perhaps the keystone of the Mamluk legacy, was one to which the Ottoman dynasty laid claim, and by 1540 it had just begun to visibly fulfill the obligations the title entailed. In 1537, Süleyman embarked on the refurbishment of Jerusalem, beginning construction of the great wall surrounding the city and making improvements to the water supply system. Over the next two decades, numerous endowments for the benefit of the religious sites of Mecca, Medina, and Jerusalem would be established by the sultan and prominent female members of his family, in particular his wife Hurrem and his daughter Mihrimah.[142] Had İl Hatun undertaken her quest to serve the poor in Jerusalem some years later, she might have lodged at the well-endowed complex established by Hurrem and completed in the early 1550s. This complex contained a mosque, a fifty-five-room dwelling for religious pilgrims, an inn and stable for travelers, and an area devoted to numerous charitable services for the poor, including a soup kitchen and public toilets.[143] As it was, departing Aintab in July 1541, İl Hatun most probably associated herself with one of the Mamluk-built retreats for female religious sojourners.

But while the hacis and haciyes of Aintab in 1540 passed through a built world of Mamluk-sponsored monuments, the living procession in which they participated was an Ottoman-guarded and Ottoman-facilitated phenomenon. Management of the pilgrimage was one of the major responsibilities—and at times, no doubt, one of the major headaches—of the Ottoman government. The pilgrimage involved strategic planning in several domains, including logistics and supply, security measures against Bedouin raiders of pilgrimage caravans, political relations with the Muslim aristocracy that controlled Mecca and Medina, and management of trade routes both local and foreign (for an enormous amount of business was conducted around the pilgrimage).[144]

The question of religious travel again raises the question of the pax Ottomanica: was there a reservoir of people who had feared to undertake the pilgrimage during the unstable conditions of the late Mamluk regime and the immediate post-conquest period? In the complaint submitted by the people of Aleppo around 1533, they expressed serious concern over the safety of the pilgrimage: the petition drew attention to the disgrace that the Ottoman regime would cause itself should the pilgrim caravans be attacked by nomad bands, and it recommended that traditional protective measures be reinstituted, such as sending purses of money to buy off tribal chiefs.[145] As security and prosperity increased over the 1530s, the pilgrimage surely became more feasible for individuals from Aintab and elsewhere. The upswing in Aintab's economy revealed in the 1543 cadastral survey may have translated into disposable income that enabled individuals to fulfill their religious obligations. Moreover, it is no coincidence that the Ottoman dynasty's program to fortify and adorn the holy sites of Islam was initiated on the heels of the great military campaign of 1534–1536 that bolstered Ottoman control of the former Mamluk domains. Given that an individual could choose when in his or her lifetime to make the pilgrimage, security was undoubtedly an element in the decision. The association between the "well-protectedness" of the sultan's domains and the ability to fulfill one's religious obligations would have been impressed on those hacis and haciyes of Aintab who had recently acquired their titles.[146] For women, and for many men as well, the pilgrimage may have been their most immediate experience of the benefits of being subjects of the Ottoman dynasty.

As for the region's Christians and Jews, whose sacred terrains fell within the Ottoman domain—indeed intersected with each other and with the Muslim spiritual map—the court record tells us nothing of their religious travel. However, sixteenth-century central government records dealing with the holy sites in Jerusalem portray Ottoman authorities as involved in a constant effort to regulate access of the many religious communities to their places of worship.[147] The memoir of Rabbi Moses of Basola, who spent three years in Jerusalem at the beginning of Süleyman's reign, described the varied Jewish community there,[148] and Joseph ha-Kohen, a Jewish resident of the city, praised the sultan's work (his enthusiasm made up for his factual errors): "In the year 1540 God aroused the spirit of Suleiman, king of Rumelia and Persia, and he set out to build the walls of Jerusalem, the holy city in the land of Judah. And he sent officials who built its walls and set up its gates as in former times and its towers as in bygone days. And his fame spread throughout the land for he wrought a great deed."[149] The religious balance in Mamluk Jerusalem had shifted toward the Muslims in the aftermath of the Crusades and the Latin occupation of parts of the Middle East. By contrast, the Ottoman regime, at least in the sixteenth century, enhanced opportunities for pilgrimage and settlement not only for Muslims but also for its own Jewish and Christian subjects as well as for religious sojourners from beyond the Ottoman domain.[150] It should be noted that facilitating the pilgrimage was for the Ottoman government not only a matter of sovereign pride but also a source of revenue: for example, the toll tax imposed on Christians and Jews passing through the province of Nablus on their way to Jerusalem generated a steady income of approximately 21,000 akçes a year.[151]

·   ·   ·

The province of Aintab was made up of a variety of settlements, a variety of peoples, and a variety of links that connected one to the other. The city of

Aintab was a critical resource to the villages and tribal groups that made up its hinterland, but its own status and prosperity were nothing without that hinterland. Nor was Aintab autonomous as a provincial unit, though for administrative purposes it was defined as a distinct entity within the empire and, as such, generated its own connective tissue. Aintab's links to neighboring provinces were multiple. Commercial networks, family ties, military coordination, regional agricultural markets, criminal contacts, the courts of judges—these and other connections overlapped and interacted to create what appears to be a dense web of communication across the region spanning southeastern Anatolia and northern Syria.

Much of this infrastructure existed before the coming of the Ottomans. Despite the vagaries of the early sixteenth century, it is possible that some of these links became stronger in the decades preceding the conquest as a necessary response to the waning of Mamluk attention and the need to shield the region from the impending battle over its control. What the Ottoman regime brought to Aintab and its surrounding provinces, at least in the middle decades of the century, was the force and the sovereign authority to stimulate, streamline, and further coordinate channels of communication. Aintabans paid a price for their diminished autonomy, but they were compensated by a period of relative prosperity and peace.

One who searches for mention of Aintab in Ottoman chronicles of the times will be disappointed. Its moment was the conquest. The staging ground for the victory of Marj Dabik over the Mamluks, Aintab then, as in previous centuries, played the role of a gateway to the critical domain controlled by Aleppo. Once Ottoman domination of the eastern Mediterranean was secured, Aintab ceded its strategic importance. Even the relatively small cities of Maraş and Bire figure more frequently in Ottoman chronicles—Maraş because of its militarily strategic location and its role as capital of the Dulkadir governorate-general, Bire because of its function as a Euphrates River crossing and thus a stage on an imperial highway. If Aintab had value to the Ottoman project in the post-conquest decades, it was as a stable regional center and an important node in regional networks of communication. That kind of steady sober performance is not the material of chroniclers.

This chapter has provided glimpses of the Aintab court and the work it did in sustaining the regional fabric. Much of that work was of a routine nature. But because the court was a local chronicler of sorts, its records are punctuated with stories of human drama. In the following chapter, we will become acquainted with the court itself.

3

Introducing the Court of Aintab

On Tuesday, July 12, 1541, the judge of the Aintab court heard fifteen cases, six of which involved women. Of those six, women were plaintiffs or petitioners in three: Tatar requested a daily allowance from the court on the grounds that her husband had disappeared seven years earlier, Minnet won a suit for slander against a man who had publicly accused her of promiscuity in the most obscene of language, and Kuddam won a suit against her brother, who had sold a mule from her dower but failed to give her a chemise and a hair ornament that he had promised in return. Kuddam's suit had been resolved through a process of community mediation, which resulted in her brother's giving her a black goat. In two other of the six cases, women were summoned to the court to give testimony. Fatma, the sister of an old man who had fallen into the moat of the Aintab citadel and drowned, testified that her brother had been senile and prone to collapsing, and that she wished to lodge no claim for wrongful death. The villager Haciye Zeliha recounted her part in the case of a missing copper serving dish: Hızır had given the dish to Durmuş for safekeeping, and Durmuş had lent it to Haciye Zeliha to use for a wedding celebration, during which the dish had gone missing. In the sixth case, the Armenian Harim was a silent participant in a dispute over her engagement to Vanis, who was sued in court by Harim's father for failure to get on with the marriage; Vanis prevailed, claiming that the men had agreed on a three-month waiting period.[1]

Fifteen cases was a heavy load for a single day in the Aintab court, and on July 12 the judge heard a greater proportion of disputes involving females than he usually did. But the cases that concerned these six women were typical of the range of matters that brought females to the court. Typical also were the hearings that did not involve women. Among these were three sales of animals (a horse and two donkeys), a loan negotiation, the sale of a house and stable, and the resolution of a dispute between two brothers over a house they'd inherited. In the latter, the judge validated a report submitted by a group of local citizens; the case was led by the headman of the city quarter in which the house was located, who had been delegated to investigate the disagreement. In another case, the judge accepted the opinion of local experts in resolving a dispute over water rights between a mill owner and several local farmers. Finally, the court recorded the fact that a butcher had sold meat in excess of the set price.[2] Even if we had only this single day's record of the court's proceedings, we could hazard some comment about life in Aintab in the summer of 1541—about family and neighborly relationships, about personal property (especially the salience of animals), and about the ways in which Aintabans made use of their court. Court records are strikingly effective as a source that opens windows onto local societies. It is only during the Ottoman period, beginning in the late fifteenth century, that such records survive in substantial numbers.

It is no wonder that in recent decades court records have become a popular object of scholarly research. This is particularly true for the premodern period, which is relatively lacking in first-person narratives or other sources that permit the historian of the Middle East to approach ordinary individuals. In addition to providing an enormous volume of data about economy and society, court records are especially seductive because they are replete with individual voices and stories—or at least the records from sixteenth-century Aintab are. But it is only relatively recently that the challenges of interpreting these texts have preoccupied their readers.[3] The records of the sixteenth century, fewer in number and much less studied than those of later centuries, have their own particular challenges. They may, however, be richer in personal narrative than those of late centuries.

This chapter is an introduction to the Aintab court of 1540–1541 and its records. It begins by considering the large range of business conducted at court, and what is actually meant by "the court"—that is, its personnel and its locale. The chapter then considers the nature of the court's written records as well as the obstacles one encounters in interpreting them. I argue first that we can begin to understand their social content only when we root the records in the terrain of Aintab as described in the previous chapters. I also suggest that their legal content is likely to remain obscure unless we read them together with other legal texts of the period. The chapter concludes by examining normative legal discourses—Islamic law, sultanic law, local customary law—as they shaped the deliberations of the court. Here I argue that the coming together of these discourses at the local level— the very process of their merging—created a considerable space in which members of the community could actively participate. One important factor here was that the court had to work to attract people into its orbit, since it was not the only community resource for solving legal problems.

Before moving on, we need to make an initial acquaintance with the court records. Since one of my interests in this project was to trace the impact of the court's incorporation into an imperial legal system, I chose to work on the earliest of the 174 registers that make up the extant court records of Aintab. This book examines the second and third bound registers in the series, which cover twelve and a half months in the life of the Aintab court. The first register is composed of 357 folios and dates from 12 Cemaziülevvel 947/September 14, 1540, to 22 Muharrem 948/May 18, 1541, and the second is composed of 330 folios and dates from 29 Muharrem 948/May 25, 1541, to 11 Cemaziülaher 948/October 2, 1541. There is one register that predates those studied here, catalogued as containing records from 938 through 946, but because of its delicate condition this register was unavailable for study.[4] The two registers from 1540–1541 measure approximately 10 by 30 centimeters, and the average number of cases recorded on one side of a register folio is slightly more than three (see figure 5).

The court met steadily during these months, breaking only for sixteen days in October 1540 and for six days in May 1541. Its volume of business was therefore considerable. Turkish was the principal language of the court records, with about one-fifth of the cases recorded in Arabic. Disputes and voluntary statements of fact are always recorded in Turkish, while the use of Arabic is confined to routine notarial business—for example, purchases and sales, debt negotiations, and appointment of bail agents. The language of the record is therefore not a clue to the native language of the speaker. Turkish was the principal language of the court because it was the language of the large majority of Aintab province's residents, and the lingua franca of those whose first language was Kurdish, Armenian, Arabic, or Persian.

THE COURT'S BUSINESS

Like other court records that survive from the late fifteenth century onward, those of Aintab reveal the enormous variety of business that was carried out under the auspices of the court. The premodern Middle Eastern court, as many have commented, was a multipurpose institution, a public registry as much as a judicial office. People used the court of Aintab to register all kinds of private transactions. For example, judge and scribe might be called on to record the amount of a debt paid and the amount still due, the sale of a house, or the return of a stray goat to its owner. The court might also register the contents of marriage dowers or estates of the deceased, although fewer people in mid-sixteenth-century Aintab used it for such purposes than did their counterparts in other times and places.[5] Individuals also used the court to record personal matters: the woman Seyda, for example, had the judge record her objection to the marriage her father had contracted for her without her permission.[6] The purpose for many in having such "facts" inscribed in the court's register was to create evidence that might later be useful should matters come to litigation (a technical term for this practice was "anticipation of consequences").[7] The utility of this exercise was demonstrated in the case of one Haci Mehmed, who had purchased a substantial house for 2,600 akçes from the woman Ayşe; the legality of his ownership had apparently come into question, and one of the ways he substantiated his claim was by informing the judge that he had had his purchase registered at court at the time of the transaction.[8] In this capacity as community registry, the court served local individuals in the management of their personal affairs, recording a variety of private issues at their request.

The court was also a judicial body that heard and judged disputes and investigated infractions of the law. In theory, only those crimes for which punishment was prescribed in the Qur'an were required to be prosecuted by the authorities. These crimes—theft, highway robbery, wine drinking, illicit sexual intercourse, and slander—were viewed as crimes against religion, and therefore claims of God (hakk Allah). In the prosecution of these crimes, the sovereign and his executive agents stood in for God.[9] In the Aintab court, accordingly, it was a variety of state-appointed officials who brought such cases before the judge. The officials with whom the court dealt most commonly were the agents of the governor-general (beglerbegi), of the provincial governor of Aintab (sancakbegi), and of the trustee appointed to manage crown lands in the province (hassemini). These agents were known as subaşı, a term somewhat awkwardly but perhaps most faithfully translated as "police." Local police were therefore an arm of the Ottoman government, since they reported to the regime's own representatives in the provinces.

In contrast to these state-prosecuted crimes, private claims had to be introduced by the aggrieved party. Known as hakk adamî, the rights or claims of the individual, private claims could be handled in a variety of ways: disregarded at the individual's discretion, settled amicably outside of court, or submitted to the court's jurisdiction. Such modes of settlement contrasted with the "claims of God," where, in theory, no abandonment or amicable settlement was possible. Individual claims in the Aintab court typically had to do with offenses against one's property (houses, animals, agricultural land, or personal possessions) or to one's person, through either physical or verbal attack. In the Aintab court records of 1540–1541, most criminal suits were the result of action by private individuals.

In practice as well as in legal theory, there was a middle ground between these two kinds of claims. Some crimes did not fit neatly into either category. For example, prosecution for slander, technically defined as an unfounded accusation of illicit sexual intercourse—and a "claim of God"—took place only in response to the demand of the slandered.[10] And a prominent sixteenth-century jurist's discussion of rape suggests that he viewed it as a crime against the individual, disqualifying it as a form of the Qur'anic crime of illicit sex because the latter's assumption of mutual consent could not be satisfied.[11] In addition, there was another sort of middle ground between the two divisions of rightful claims: individuals often alerted local authorities to alleged violations either of one of the Qur'anic crimes or of another's private rights. It is clear from the Aintab court records that police often became aware of criminal acts because people lodged complaints or informed against others.

Community surveillance, in fact, was built into the legal process. People had a real stake in how others conducted themselves, since they could be held legally responsible for the criminal acts of others. Several clauses in the law book of Süleyman, for example, held individuals, urban neighborhoods, or whole villages liable for crimes committed on their property if they could not find the guilty party.[12] The flip side of this collective liability was the collective right of neighborhoods to protest against and even expel residents known to have criminal reputations (in particular, thieves and harlots).[13] An example of this right in action was the protest of a neighborhood in Aintab city against a habitual liar, who was ostracized in October 1540 by the judge's order.[14] The story of Haciye Sabah explores a more serious and problematic instance of ostracism by collective protest.

In addition to its roles as public registry and arena of litigation, the court also served as the provincial nexus of empire-wide administrative networks. As a key provincial-level institution, the court coordinated various levels of government by receiving and registering orders from the sultan as well as the regional governor-general. The court also transmitted central government directives concerning the mobilization of troops and the requisitioning of military supplies. When a new provincial governor was appointed, it was the court that worked out the various financial and administrative details of transferring power (during the thirteen months of this study, two appointments of new provincial governors took place). In fact, the jurisdiction of a judge—the *kaza,* or judicial administrative unit—was by design congruent with the jurisdiction of the provincial governor—the *sancak* or *liva,* the basic unit of military-fiscal administration. The court's principal role as a nexus of administration was to serve as a link between military and fiscal systems at the provincial level, specifically between tax collection and defense. Many cases in the Aintab court dealt with registering, and when necessary adjudicating, the turnover of local tax revenues to the various fortresses in the region as salary for their garrison troops.[15]

Local courts like that of Aintab are often referred as "sharia" courts—that is, courts of Islamic law. This term is appropriate in that procedurally the court followed rules prescribed by Islamic law for such matters as the manner of introducing testimony or the order of testimony by plaintiffs, defendants, and their witnesses. Moreover, legal issues such as inheritance, divorce, and the purchase and sale of property were handled according to rules laid out in Islamic jurisprudence. And, as we have seen, the definition of criminal activity followed Islamic legal categories. But the term "court of Islamic law" does not describe all that the court did, since much of the business of its users, both private individuals and administrative officials, was of a mundane nature that had little or nothing to do with religiously based law. The court was also used by the Armenian Christians of Aintab on a regular basis. They had no choice in some matters, since as subjects of the empire they could be called to court for public crimes or for lapses in their tax obligations, and they could be sued by Muslims. But non-Muslims also voluntarily brought private claims that, in theory, came under the jurisdiction of their own religious or local customary law, such as divorce suits or inheritance claims. Commenting on the degree to which non-Muslims in early-seventeenth-century Kayseri used the city's court, Ronald Jennings remarks that "in effect, one law was administered in Kayseri for all the people."[16] In Aintab, the same could perhaps be said, but the court record was careful to "de-Islamize" the law when Armenian Christians brought private claims to the judge: the scribe followed Islamic legal procedure in recording the case but avoided the specific terminology of Islamic law, substituting synonymous language of a nonlegal nature.[17]

The court's multiple roles were generally managed locally. However, a series of events occurred in May and June of 1541 that suggest a major intervention of imperial authority. In late May, a government-appointed prosecutor was assigned to Aintab for the purpose of disciplining negligent tax collectors, in particular a member of the notable Sikkakoğlu family. It may not be coincidental that the prosecutor began his investigations just as Aintab received the news of the appointment of a new judge who, when he took up office a month later, proceeded to institute more rigorous scrutiny of local administration. And on June 18, five days before the new judge actually arrived in Aintab, a new provincial governor was appointed to the province, one whose rank outclassed that of his predecessor.[18] Aintab, it would seem, was coming under more vigorous government scrutiny in the early summer of 1541.

Despite the many functions of the Aintab court outlined above, its records do not provide us with a comprehensive panorama of life in the city and its hinterland. We do not see the many transactions, disputes, and settlements that occurred outside the compass of the court. The fact that private claims could be settled independently of the court meant that the judge was required to hold aloof even in cases of serious abuse. Sultanic law books ordered judges and deputy judges not to investigate matters that they were not invited to adjudicate; rather, according to the law book of Selim I, "those who are judges should station themselves in the traditional location of the court and not go out on rounds."[19] Moreover, the financial burden of coming to court was not negligible, since Selim's law book authorized Ot-

toman judges to charge petitioners for hearing and recording their cases
and to exact fairly steep fees for documents they issued and for copies of
court proceedings.[20] The existence of other, perhaps cheaper, venues for
dispute resolution and other authorities to whom one might appeal for decisions or for legal guidance in problematic moments meant that a good
deal of the legal life of the province took place outside the court.

THE COURT'S PERSONNEL

What is meant by "the court," or *mahkeme,* as it was called in the registers?
What personnel was essential to its constitution? The most critical question
here is the identity of the judge—the *kadı*—since the mentality and even
the personal quirks of provincial judges were critical not only to the practice of law but also to the quality of civic culture in the cities and towns
in which they served. In the case of Aintab, this question is only partially
answerable. We are fortunate in knowing the name—Hüsameddin—of the
new judge who served for the last three months of the period studied in this
book (from late June through October 1541), for the court register records
the news both of his appointment and of his actual arrival in Aintab. But the
judge who served during the preceding nine months is not similarly identified in the record (perhaps he took up office before the inception of the
first register studied). Some former judges of Aintab can be named—
Küçük Ali, Seyyid Cafer, Pir Mehmed—because litigants occasionally dated
a previous court appearance by stating who had been in office at the time;
the terms of service of these individuals cannot be dated, however.[21]

Although clearly a pivotal element in the court's work, judges are only
dimly present in the written record. Unlike Ottoman courts in some other
places and times, judges in the Aintab records did not sign their rulings.[22]
Their personal decision-making role is only revealed indirectly in the
phrase "it was ruled" *(hükmolunub).* Despite the apparent significance of
Hüsameddin's tenure as Aintab judge, we know his name only because his
appointment was conspicuously hailed in the court register on May 25,
1541, with the following notice on its opening page: "The news came that
the judgeship of Aintab, the well-protected, has been granted to Hüsameddin Efendi, may his virtue increase; read at the sitting of the court and
inscribed on the 29th of the month of Muharrem in the year 948.[23] Nowhere else in the 330 pages of the register was this judge named again, although on June 23 a brief line was penned announcing "the arrival of His
Honor" in Aintab. In other words, if one knew nothing about the structure
of the Ottoman legal system, one could not tell from the court records that
there was in fact a judge presiding. Litigants, witnesses, arbitrators, delegates
of the state's authority bringing cases to court—all these individuals are
named and verbally present in the court record, but the judge, situated at

the nexus of religion, state, and community, is, as an individual, virtually nameless and textually silent.

But who was Hüsameddin? and what kinds of individuals were the other judges referred to in individual records? Biographies of religious officials of this period, contained in collective works composed in the sixteenth and seventeenth centuries, rarely included men who made their mark as provincial judges. The biographic encyclopedia was a historically common Islamic literary genre, but it focused on the life stories of scholars, teachers, jurists, and more prominent judges.[24] The Ottoman compendia reflected the typical bias against provincial judges. They also exhibited a bias toward the imperial core of the empire—that is, toward figures whose careers circulated around Istanbul and the two former capitals, Bursa (in northwest Anatolia) and Edirne (in European Thrace). Even though judges, jurists, and scholars studied the same curriculum in religious sciences, the stereotype held that judges were inevitably compromised in their pursuit of a religious career by going on the payroll of the state and by having to make worldly concessions in their official judgments. Judges who won a place in the major biographical encyclopedias were therefore likely to have made their principal mark as scholars and teachers. In short, the provincial judge had a harder time creating a reputation that was thought worthy of being memorialized. But the reality was that many sixteenth-century products of Ottoman educational institutions who began their professional lives as teachers soon opted for the career of provincial judge because the salary of a judge was higher in the short run, although the ladder of opportunity was considerably shorter in the long run.[25]

Ideally, in a study of this sort one should know the identity of the provincial judge, the quality of his education, and the trajectory of his career. In the case of Aintab, the biographical compendia offer us no clues about the identity of the judges preceding the appointment of Hüsameddin in the late spring of 1541. There is, however, a Molla Hüsameddin whose brief biography in the early-seventeenth-century compendium composed by Nevʿizade ʿAtaʾi, *The Gardens of Truth,* makes him a possible candidate for the judgeship of Aintab. (*Molla* was a title for individuals with a religious education and employment as judge, teacher, or jurisconsult; all the judges of Aintab carried the honorific title *Efendi* after their given names—e.g., Molla Hüsameddin Efendi.)

The Hüsameddin described in *The Gardens of Truth* was clearly a successful provincial judge who may have originally wished for the preferred career of scholar and teacher. Born and apparently educated in central Anatolia, Hüsameddin devoted himself to the career of judge shortly after entering professional life in 1523 with a brief stint as teacher. He had begun his career, not atypically, by acquiring a patron: he entered the personal service of a retired judge of Edirne. When the latter died, Hüsameddin received an entry-level teaching post, from which he resigned shortly thereafter to become a judge. According to his biographer, he served in a great many choice assignments until his death in 1554, making him "an envy-inspiring high-ranking molla." But 'Ata'i gives no specifics about where Hüsameddin actually served, perhaps because he recorded only what was remembered about this figure from a century earlier. Whatever the case, Molla Hüsameddin was recalled as a stern and dignified individual, "notorious for his firmness and integrity in the performance of his office, counted among judges as grave and well-mannered, a dread-inspiring, venerable magistrate." Given his reputation for toughness, he was well named, for *Hüsameddin* means "the sharp sword of religion." 'Ata'i's Hüsameddin appears to be a judge's judge—knowledgeable, experienced, and decisive. It seems that the molla's appearance was as impressive as his demeanor, for he was nicknamed Papas ("the Priest") Hüsam "because of the thickness of his beard, which had an extraordinarily noble and pleasing appearance."[26]

This is not to claim that the Hüsameddin of 'Ata'i's biography was the individual dispatched to Aintab in the summer of 1541. We have only plausible dates, Anatolian origins (Hüsameddin's patron was also from central Anatolia), and a personality that could explain the increased rigor observable in the court during the summer of 1541.[27] But even if 'Ata'i's judge is not the individual who came to Aintab in 1541, he serves as an example of what the historical record can tell us about provincial judges of the sixteenth century. If, on the other hand, the Hüsameddin of the biography should happen to be our man, his appointment to Aintab tells us that the Aintab judgeship ranked as a relatively important provincial post. According to *The Gardens of Truth*, Hüsameddin was a "300-akçe judge," or someone who held a middle to high rank for provincial service.[28] That Aintab was an important provincial post is confirmed for the mid–seventeenth century by the famous Ottoman courtier and traveler Evliya Çelebi, who noted that it was by then a 500-akçe judgeship.[29]

As we will see more than once in subsequent chapters, the appointment of Hüsameddin had a discernible impact on the Aintab court, whether he was the stern and authoritative figure of the biography or not. It is not coincidental that his appointment was accompanied by the appointment to Aintab of a higher-ranking provincial governor as well as the assignment of a special government prosecutor dispatched to discipline errant tax-farmers. Moreover, the new judge arrived just as the prosecutor finished his month's work. Shortly after Hüsameddin took up office, new kinds of cases began to be recorded in the court's register: for example, women began to bring property claims against male family members, something they had not done in the preceding nine months, and scrutiny of male-female contact in public spaces was intensified. And the increase in the caseload of the court was striking: during the four and a half months following the special prosecutor's arrival (from May 29 on), the court averaged twice as many cases per week as it did during the preceding eight months.[30]

I would like to suggest the possibility that Hüsameddin Efendi was among the first judges—perhaps the very first—to be appointed to Aintab by the Ottoman government. In the traditional practice of Islamically ruled states, followed by the Ottoman sultanate, judges were appointed by the ruling authority. But we need to be careful about assuming that this practice was applied immediately in the vast heartland of the Middle East following its conquest in 1516–1517. Naturally, the Ottoman regime moved quickly to control the metropolises of the newly conquered territories—the sultan Selim appointed a governor, a judge, and a treasurer for Aleppo right after the victory at Marj Dabik, before the Ottoman army moved on to take Damascus and Cairo.[31] But it took time for the regime to turn its attention to the full administrative incorporation into the empire of lesser provincial cities like Aintab.

This is not to say that the judges preceding Hüsameddin Efendi were weak or incompetent. The records of 1540–1541 give every sign that Aintab's was a well-functioning court. Court users in 1540–1541 sometimes brought copies of judicial decrees issued in earlier years to support their suits, demonstrating that the practice of "anticipating consequences"—a practice that assumed the continuing effectiveness of the court—was not new.[32] Rather, I am suggesting that previous judges may have been local in origin. In the period of relative political insecurity preceding the Ottoman conquest, the cosmopolitan networks of training and appointment of religious officials characteristic of more settled times were breaking down. Jon Mandaville has shown that judicial offices in the Syrian cultural and administrative center of Damascus were becoming the monopoly of a closed corporation of local families.[33] The same was likely to have been true of Aintab, which may have drawn on its own educational resources and those of nearby urban centers. While the Ottoman regime moved almost immediately to appoint its own officials, including judges, to the major cities, Aintab's administrative incorporation began in earnest only around 1536. One clue that Hüsameddin Efendi may have been an early imperial judicial appointment to Aintab, or even the first consequential judge posted to the city, is the fact that the judge's residence was enlarged immediately after his arrival.[34]

While the judge was the pivotal figure at court, he was not the only person on its staff. Like the judge, other functionaries of the court were nearly invisible in the written record. During the year studied here, Aintab had a deputy judge (naib), Molla Veled. Although the usual job of a deputy was to serve outlying areas of a jurisdiction, there is no evidence that the Aintab deputy traveled. On the contrary, the court records suggest that villagers routinely made the one- or at most two-day journey to the court. The deputy did serve occasionally as communal witness, and it is only because of this role, also performed by hundreds of other Aintab residents, that we know of his existence, since the title *naib* was occasionally recorded along with his name. As for lesser functionaries, the court employed a summons officer *(muhzirbaşı)*, whose job was to bring litigants to court; however, he was mentioned only once during the course of the year, as the middleman in the payment of a debt, a role that was probably a private arrangement unrelated to his official duties, except perhaps as a reflection of the reputation he may have enjoyed because of his office.[35] In other words, these two court functionaries—deputy judge and summons officer—are revealed to us only through indirect evidence, not through any representation of their roles in the legal process. Hence it is difficult to know what, if any, influence they had in shaping local legal practices.

More important to this study, the court employed a number of scribes who were responsible for recording case summaries in the court's register and for issuing copies of case records and of documents such as certificates of marriage and manumission papers for freed slaves. In the schedule of fees to be charged by local courts for their services, laid out in the law book of Selim I, a portion was stipulated for the scribe: the fee for recording a hearing was 8 akçes (5 of which went to the judge, 2 to his deputy, and 1 to the scribe) and for issuing a copy of the record 14 akçes (10 to the judge, 3 to the deputy, and 1 to the scribe); for issuing a certificate of manumission, the scribe received 4 akçes, for a marriage certificate 2, and for a transfer of testimony 2.[36] If these fees were in fact applied in Aintab, a court scribe was hardly an impoverished bureaucrat.[37]

The shifts in calligraphic and narrative style that occur periodically in the texts of the records suggest that more than one scribe served the Aintab court in 1540–1541. Some scribes employed wordy legal locutions, repetitive phrases, and elaborate titles for notable figures appearing at court, while others adopted a streamlined, almost shorthand, approach. At least one scribe used no Arabic, recording all cases in Turkish.[38] One used the term *firengi* (frankish) rather than the typical *filori* for coins of gold, or florins. Another seems to have been fascinated by the business of taxation: he copied numerous official documents *(tezkire)* into the register and employed his own vocabulary when recording matters to do with tax-farms and land grants.[39] A scribe's stylistic preference appears irrelevant to the type of case, although it may be related to the annual rhythm of the court, whose load increased significantly in the summer and early fall months, a shift reflected in shorter and sparer records. It should also be noted that some scribes took fewer pains over their penmanship than others; poor penmanship generally went together with shorter records, and was therefore likely produced by the pressure of work. Scribes might occasionally doodle: a back page of one register displays a scribe's experiments with calligraphic styles. They might also amuse themselves with wordplay as they composed case records: in the case of the woman Teslime, who came to court to prove ownership of her donkey, the scribe first entered then altered the standard formula for assigning ownership—"the donkey was ruled to Teslime" *(Teslime'ye* hükmol-*unub)*—by crossing out the word "ruled to" and substituting "handed over to" *(Teslime'ye* teslim *olunub),* resulting in a pun on the woman's name.

Once in a while a scribe names himself: for example, Şemseddin, "scribe of the records" *(kâtib ül-huruf),* who appeared as one of the case witnesses for the donation of land that enlarged the new judge's residence.[40] Other than random mentions of a name, however, scribes, like judges, were anonymous figures in the court's record. Were scribes graduates of one of the several schools in Aintab? Or were they members of the judge's personal suite? Their identity is hidden from us—an unfortunate circumstance, since they played a significant role in creating the texts on which this study is based.[41] Evidence from the eighteenth century suggests that the position of court scribe was a distinguished one, at least in that period: in 1732, Cenanî Mehmed Efendi, a scion of the sheikhly Demircioğlu family and remembered as a noted poet, historian, and philologist, took up his deceased father's post as scribe to the Aintab court, and went on to serve the court over the next forty years in this capacity and as deputy judge. During the years of Cenanî Mehmed's service, the court records were often adorned with his poetry.[42]

While the court record says little about the identity of its staff, it makes explicit the identity of community members who participated in court hearings. Every case recorded at court had "case witnesses" *(şuhud ul-hal),* usually three or four in number, whose names were inscribed in the court register following the record of the case. Their function was to act as a check on the correctness of legal procedures observed in the case as whole, and to serve as repository of communal memory of the incident at issue. Different cases had different case witnesses, although some individuals performed quite regularly in this role; these included, for example, a certain Mehmed, known as "the man from Bire," the neighboring province to the east. Case witnesses ranged across the social population of the province, from state-appointed officials and city magnates with no personal connection to the case to parents and other relatives, friends and compatriots, and neighbors—parties, that is, with a personal connection to one of the litigants. In addition, some individuals appear to have been drafted into acting as case witness because they happened to be present in court that day on some other matter. In sum, case witnesses may or may not have been neutral with regard to the records to which they appended their names: some represented the general interest of the state or the urban community, some the interests of a litigant, and some no identifiable interest at all.

Ronald Jennings has pointed to the importance of these witnesses in bringing the local community into the legal process and in checking the powers of the judge. In sixteenth-century Aintab, as in the seventeenth-century Kayseri court studied by Jennings, the function of case witness should be considered an element in the formal legal structure of the court.[43] The diversity of Aintabans (all male) who acted as case witnesses suggests that specific legal knowledge was not a requirement, though it would seem that a basic familiarity with legal procedure and a basic grasp of the legal reasoning behind the particular case's outcome were necessary. Nevertheless, the consistent inscription in the record of the names of case witnesses gives it a very local geography. This practice of explicitly naming local participants at court while maintaining the anonymity of court personnel may reflect an underlying assumption that the outcome of a case was determined by the operation of the legal process as a whole rather than by the directives of an individual judge. We should keep in mind, however, that the near invisibility of the Aintab court personnel was not a universal feature of Ottoman-period court records.

Aintab was an old Muslim city, unlike many seats of judgeships in western Anatolia or in the European lands of the empire. The latter had shorter genealogies as Islamic judicial centers, even though they might have been "Ottoman" cities for a century or two longer than Aintab. The empire's capital, Istanbul, for example, had been Christian Constantinople until 1453, less than a century before the year studied here. Aintab had most probably had a functioning court since the mid–thirteenth century at the latest, when the Ayyubid prince Melik Salih Ahmet took up residence there. But while Aintab was intimately acquainted with the culture of Islamic law, incorporation into the empire's judicial networks brought a degree of change.

Under the Ottoman regime, certain modifications were introduced in the administration of local courts that should be considered a set of legal reforms. The judge was now to hold court in a specific and permanent location. As we have seen, the law book of Selim I was adamant in requiring the judge to remain stationary in a location familiar to the community he served. While it is difficult to know what earlier practice had been in Aintab (in many places, judges traditionally held court in mosques),[44] by 1540 the court appears to have met at the residence of the judge, which functioned as a kind of courthouse. As Nelly Hanna points out in her study of Ottoman-period courts in Cairo, one of the Ottoman regime's first efforts in the area of legal administration was to establish several courthouses throughout the city, beginning in 1522.[45] With the appointment of the forceful judge Hüsameddin in June 1541, the "residence-courthouse" of the Aintab judge was enhanced through a grant that enlarged its property, perhaps in anticipation of an increase in the volume of the court's work. Locating the court in a nonreligious space no doubt had the advantage of making it more accessible to women, non-Muslims, and others for whom there were taboos against entering the protected space of the mosque.

Another apparent innovation was the practice of keeping the court's records as a *public* record. There was nothing new in the keeping of written records per se: Wael Hallaq has demonstrated the centrality of this practice from early Islamic times onward,[46] though few records actually survive from pre-Ottoman times. Donald Little notes that there is no equivalent of a public record from the Mamluk period, although copies of documents related to a late-fifteenth-century Jerusalem judge do survive. Rather, the first public compilation of court records in Egypt dates from the second decade following the Ottoman conquest.[47] The Ottoman innovation was to require that records "should be deposited in a public domain," to use Hallaq's phrase. In the past, records had most probably remained in the possession of judges; some degree of continuity was theoretically maintained by the requirement that a new judge obtain records kept by his predecessor. The records from Aintab suggest that individuals insured themselves against the possible loss or inaccessibility of the court's records by obtaining and guarding copies of judges' decrees, the technical term for which was *hüccet*. Likely reasons for the disappearance of court records, argues Hallaq, include the problem of storage, the fact that they tended to be kept as loose leaves rather than bound registers, and the fact that "they were of highly limited interest to literate individuals."[48]

If Hallaq's final point is indeed correct, one consequence of the Ottoman practice of maintaining a public record was to give individuals, literate and otherwise, a decided and vested interest in the record of the court. Their words and actions were, in theory, recorded for all posterity to consult. This transformation in the mode of keeping records must have had considerable impact on how individuals chose to make use of the court (when they had any choice in the matter) and on how they framed their testimony before the judge. Whether the behavior of Aintabans had as yet been affected in 1540, when the practice of public record-keeping was just beginning, is not easy to say, but it *is* clear that the arrival of the centrally appointed judge Hüsameddin marked a signal change in the kinds of cases heard in court.

Yet if the Ottoman regime intended that all of the courts under its control keep public records and protect them well, it was not everywhere successful. In some places where there were most certainly courts, there are no extant records—for example, Maraş and Ruha/Urfa, whose courts are frequently mentioned in the Aintab records studied here.[49] In other places the records are incomplete. In Aintab, the extant collection is made up of 174 registers, covering the period from 1531 to 1909, but there are many gaps: in the sixteenth century, for example, these include 1541 (the end of the second register studied here) to 1544, 1551 to 1557, and 1576 to 1584.[50] On the other hand, the Jerusalem court registers were continuous through-out the Ottoman period: the collection contains 416 registers beginning in 936/1530, with only a single twenty-eight-month gap (between 1574 and 1576).[51] Was it simply the inevitable problems of conservation and storage that led to the disappearance of records in some times and places?[52] Or did old habits persist in places where there are gaps in the records or no records at all—that is, did records continue to stay in the possession of judges in some times and places during the Ottoman period?[53] Aleppo's public rec-ord, for example, did not begin until 1548. Did it matter who the judge was? Might it be that if the judge was of local origin, he favored traditional prac-tices, while if centrally appointed by the regime, he was more likely to pro-mote public record-keeping, particularly during a transitional period like the sixteenth century? These questions are impossible to answer at present, but they are important to keep in mind, given the impact that modes of record keeping might have on local legal cultures.

The practice of keeping a public record was obviously linked to the push to define a fixed location for the court. It was also tied to another goal of Ottoman judicial administration: to standardize procedures across the em-pire so that legal transactions could be universally recognized. As Hanna notes, "a person could, in one of the courts of Cairo, buy a house in Dam-ascus."[54] Numerous examples can be found in the Aintab records of 1540–1541 of the transfer of records—called "transfer of testimony" *(nakl-ı şehadet)*—to the Aintab court from other courts in the region. And while not an Ottoman innovation, the assignment of judges through centrally con-trolled appointment procedures contributed to this process of standardiza-tion, as did the rotation of judges from post to post every two or three years.[55] Finally, reversing the Mamluk practice of officially honoring all four schools of sunni jurisprudence, the Ottoman regime elevated the authority of the Hanafi school of Islamic law over the other three. The regime did not force adherents of other schools to follow Hanafi law, but in larger cities where there was more than one judge, the Hanafi judge was made head of the local judiciary. With only one judge and as a predominantly Hanafi city, Aintab no doubt felt the impact of this change less than did other cities that had also fallen to the Ottomans in 1516–1517.[56] But the appointment of Hüsameddin may signal a critical legal moment when Aintab, an old court, was more firmly integrated into the systematic structures and practices that the Ottoman regime was refining during these years.

THE COURT'S TEXTUAL RECORD

What was the nature of the textual record crafted by the judge and the scribe? The Aintab court records from 1540–1541 are short summaries rather than detailed accounts of what happened at court. As a summary, the written record of a case was a representation constructed after the fact, re-composing events and acts of speech. The brevity of these records poses a number of challenges to our understanding of local legal culture and of what Aintabans were attempting to accomplish at court. This and the following section consider these challenges and some possible means of addressing them.

Almost certainly it was the judge who was responsible for the core content of the record. Since the principal task in authoring the written record was to shape a compact narrative from sometimes lengthy court proceedings, the judge's expertise was essential, for the critical act in summarizing a case was to extract the elements of the proceedings that satisfied the requirements of correct legal procedure. Most likely the judge dictated the essence of the record, leaving it to the scribe to format it and fill in the requisite legal phraseology. Scribes were assisted in this task by manuals demonstrating typical formats for different kinds of cases, and it was perhaps these models that inspired the Aintab scribes to greater verbiage when they were not unduly rushed.

In the Aintab registers of the mid–sixteenth century, the individual record of each case was typically spare. However, a particularly complex case was frequently recorded in the register as two or more entries, each focusing on a separate claim or issue stemming from the case. (A single entry, or record, was known as a *sicil,* and Aintabans commonly referred to the court records as a whole by its plural, *sicillât.*) [57] The few entries in the registers that fill one side of a folio or more tended to be verbatim copies of written decrees from the sultan himself or the regional governor-general of Dulkadir, whose jurisdiction spanned several provinces including Aintab.

Because many particulars of a case are collapsed in the court record, it cannot be read as a complete and faithful account of what went on at court. Nor can the speech recorded in the register be assumed to be a verbatim account of what people said. Each case is set down as if it had been resolved in a single session of the court. Yet closer examination suggests that this apparent unity of time is illusory.[58] Complex and multiphased cases were often recorded in a manner that collapsed their time frame. A record presenting such a case was usually a condensed narrative of proceedings that had in reality been drawn out over more than one session of the court, and that perhaps included interim measures such as the dispatching of agents to seek additional evidence, to examine physical evidence that could not be transported to the court, or to mediate an intractable dispute. Thus, it was not deemed vital to represent in the court record the unfolding of events over time. Rather, what was important was the final summary of critical points in a case. Considerable verbal interaction might be omitted from the written record, which contained only that testimony necessary for a satisfactory resolution of the case. The written record of a case, shaped by these requirements, cannot then be viewed as a mirror of human events and emotions but rather as a prism that transforms separate streams of experience into a narrative focused to satisfy a particular set of requirements.

The cursory nature of these sixteenth-century records may lead some to dismiss them with the objection that we can never know what really went on. But the very brevity of the case records can be instructive: the bare essentials included in the official summary of a case point to what was legally at stake in a dispute. In other words, the selective, therefore constructed, nature of the record alerts us to the central issues of the case as conceived by the local court. It is a mistake, in fact, to expect the judge's framing of a complex case to mirror "reality," since in a litigated matter there could be no uniform narrative of events or their meaning. What the court crafted as the permanent record of a case is a significant piece of historical evidence in and of itself.

The saving grace in the records, the feature that enables us to make observations at the level of individual action and agency, is the preference in Islamic legal procedure for oral proof. To be sure, it would be an exaggeration to say that written instruments did not figure in the proceedings of the Aintab court in 1540–1541; numerous cases required that litigants produce a document—title to a piece of land, for example, or a certificate of manumission.[59] And as we will see in chapter 7, a case can be made that under the Ottoman regime written documentation was proving superior to oral testimony, and therefore edging the latter out, at least in matters pertaining to property. Moreover, the court record itself gained authority as written proof simply because it publicly preserved records of legal proceedings that might later be consulted for their factual relevance to future cases.[60] Nevertheless, the verbal testimony of individuals was the principal stuff of the court's daily operation.

The absence of lawyers in premodern Islamic legal practice meant that plaintiffs and defendants were their own advocates. While litigants in the Aintab court could be represented by proxy (*vekil*), they most often pleaded their suits themselves (or so the court records suggest). To support his or her suit, a plaintiff most often called on individuals whose oral testimony was usually based on eyewitness knowledge, although occasionally written documents acted as plaintiff's proof. Defendants too often produced witnesses who testified similarly. Procedure at the Aintab court followed the rules of Islamic jurisprudence for presenting claims and evidence.[61] Action was initiated by the claimant or plaintiff, and the defendant's denial or counterclaim typically followed. The burden of proof lay with the plaintiff, who then produced witnesses or, less commonly, documentary evidence. Should the plaintiff be unable to provide evidence, he or she might direct the judge to offer an oath of innocence to the defendant; the defendant had the right to refuse the oath, although the Aintab records suggest that it was rarely exercised. In the case of criminal accusations such as adultery, in which state officials acted as prosecutors, the accused typically responded with a confession, an alibi, or a plea that there were exonerating circumstances surrounding the offense. In the Aintab records, the most colorful or dramatic testimony is generally rendered by defendants.

The testimony of plaintiffs, defendants, witnesses, and officials is more often than not represented in the written record as direct speech (i.e., speech that can be framed by quotation marks). Similarly, the many voluntary statements people made at court—those bits and pieces of information that they wanted registered—are most often represented as direct speech (the technical term for such single-party statements is *ikrar*).[62] This apparent preference of the court for not tampering with the integrity of a speech act by rephrasing it into reported or indirect speech suggests that the court valued the act of testifying as well as the factual content of the testimony. Certainly inscribing oral evidence in direct speech had the virtue of making it possible to recuperate the oral nature of proceedings through the written medium of the court record. In other words, judge and scribe were to a degree able to finesse any tension that might have been felt between oral authority and written authority in their record-keeping responsibilities.

To be sure, faced with the task of creating a seamless narrative from the statements of litigants who may have found themselves less than articulate in the presence of the court, judge and scribe no doubt often rephrased a person's testimony. But there appear to have been rules governing such rephrasing. An important consideration seems to have been whether to record a statement in direct or indirect speech. Let us return to the case of Teslime, who brought to court two witnesses and her donkey, identified in the record as a small gray animal with a hole in its right ear, to have it confirmed as her property. She took this action after an incident in which one Mahmud had unlawfully seized the donkey, giving it back to Teslime only when she threatened to go to court. Mahmud's response, recorded "verbatim," was "I will *not* go to the judge" *(ben kadıya varmazum).*[63] Contrast this direct-speech statement with the kind of indirect-speech rephrasing often encountered in the Aintab records—"whereupon Mahmud declined and returned the donkey to Teslime." The indirect-speech version (my recreation) would have highlighted Teslime as the featured actor in the case, and it would also have erased Mahmud as a person with attitude. By representing Mahmud's actions through direct speech and thereby translating his adamancy straight into the record, the judge and the scribe have provided a context for understanding why Teslime has come on her own to prevent future challenge to her ownership of the donkey. Deciding whose testimony to represent as direct speech and whose in indirect speech thus put a spotlight on one litigant as the critical protagonist in a case; conversely,

voicing their testimony in a parallel fashion helped place two or more protagonists on an equal footing.

A second level of discretion employed by judge and scribe in reconstructing the voices of individuals is what we might call rhetorical tone: that
is, the degree to which the emotional or rhetorical content of the speaker's
statement is written into the record. Compare the following representations
of three husbands' divorce of their wives, using the formula for an irrevocable ("triple") dissolution of marriage:

> —Mehmed: "Let this Şahzade be irrevocably divorced."
> —Kasım: "This Nane obeys neither the imam nor me. Let her be triply
> divorced."
> —Ali: "Ayşe is my wife; she is no good for me, she doesn't obey me, she follows
> immoral ways, she is trouble. . . . I divorce her."[64]

Mehmed's formulaic statement is typical of the records of such divorces,
while Kasım's additional comment about his wife's disobedience is less
usual. But when a voice like that of Ali breaks out of the normal register of
speech to inscribe itself in the court record, we must ask what that public ut-
terance accomplishes for its speaker and why judge and scribe show deference to the power of those particular words. To put the question another
way: if Ali did not actually utter those particular words, we must ask why
judge and scribe chose to rephrase what he did say in such vivid and insistent language.

In this case, the answer to why the rhetorical tone of Ali's statement was
amplified is not difficult to discern: his wife Ayşe was suspected of adultery.
The cultural norms of the sixteenth century required Ali's vehemence as a
move to repair his diminished honor. What seems repetitive to today's
reader—she doesn't obey, her habits are immoral, she is trouble—may not
have struck the sixteenth-century observer the same way. Each phrase in
Ali's castigation of his wife's conduct perhaps communicated a separate flaw
in Ayşe's alleged failure as a wife. In other words, this was not a straightforward case of a husband's decision to divorce his wife, a fact that was signaled
in the court record by the force of Ali's statement.

But what about Ayşe, who claimed she was raped? Because the law permitted men to divorce their wives unilaterally, the court was not required to
listen to Ayşe on the matter of divorce per se. But this was a more complex
situation, and, as we might expect, the gravity of the accusation of adultery
demanded an inflected response from her as well as from Ali. The record
inscribes Ayşe's claim of rape—"I didn't consent, he pushed me into the
storeroom and shut the door, and forced me to have sex with him," as well
as the testimony of her five witnesses (two women and three men), recorded
as a collective voice: "Ayşe came crying to us, and when we asked her, 'Why

are you crying?' she said, 'Hızır pushed me into the storeroom and forced me to have sex with him.'"[65]

The record of this case yields a rare glimpse of personal distress and a small narrative as well. Both are typical of the defense of honor, when the dishonored must, if possible, tell an exonerating story. Raised voices in the records convey moments of disequilibrium not only in individual lives but sometimes in the life of the community as well; in this case, another individual, Hızır, has been implicated in the scandal. But the records are often silent on the outcome of such incidents. The court record gives us some clues about Ali and Ayşe—that she was quite young (perhaps fourteen or so) and that the couple had recently moved to Aintab from the city of Ruha—but it tells us no more regarding the denouement of their story. We will return to the case of Ayşe and Ali shortly as an example of how one can read through such ellipses in the court record.

How should we meet the challenges of such records? I originally set out to explore the Aintab court registers with the goal of investigating the dynamics of households and families in a provincial setting; that interest was an outgrowth of my first book, which studied relationships among members of the Ottoman dynastic household, with a particular focus on its female members. Within a month or two of reading the Aintab records, however, I was struck by a number of their features that eventually altered the direction of my research: the paucity of whole categories of "information"—for example, relationships between wives and husbands or between parents and children; the unexpected frequency of certain kinds of cases—for example, sexual crimes (unexpected because formal rules of evidence make them virtually impossible to prove); the briefness of the records, unlike the verbatim depositions recorded by contemporary European courts and by Ottoman courts in later centuries; and the variation in the representation of individual voices—the formulaic versus the personally revelatory. Another of the confounding silences in the Aintab records is the absence of a resolution, for the records often do not state the outcome of a dispute or the punishment imposed for an illegal act.

Given these presences and absences, I began to realize that the more productive questions to ask of the records had to do with the role of the court itself, both in the life of the community and in the legal system as a whole: how it maintained accountability to its constituents and simultaneously to the laws of religion and the laws of the state; why individuals made use of the court in the ways that they did; and what it was about legal processes that made the court receptive to their voices. Focusing on Aintabans as consumers of the law prompted questions about popular legal knowledge. It was surely not coincidental, for instance, that Ayşe ran crying to precisely the number of witnesses legally required to establish her claim of rape.[66] Because people appeared in court both voluntarily and involuntarily, we can—indeed, must—ask questions about their strategies in deciding what issues to submit to the judge and in framing their defense when unwillingly summoned before him.

The question of institutional translation remains, however. It is ultimately impossible to know what people actually said in court. But when the body of records is taken as a whole, patterns emerge that demonstrate consistency of testimony—a shared rhetorical tone—among similar cases. In other words, verbal testimony is recorded not randomly but rather in a manner integral to the nature of the matter at hand.[67] Patterns of speech representation can thus signal issues that were chronic concerns for Aintabans. An example of an issue that draws our attention because of the hyper-rhetorical tone in which people's testimony is recorded concerns the boundaries of dwellings and the dangers in crossing them without proper notice—to fetch wood from a neighbor, to leave a bundle of goods, to return a borrowed tray, to ask for a drink of water. What signals this concern with domestic boundaries is not how the legal issue at stake is articulated in individual cases, but rather the heightened tone of people's talk in general about crossing thresholds.[68] Cursing is another example of how attention to rhetorical tone can yield insight, for while cursing occurs in a variety of situations—brawling, negotiations over marriage alliances, family quarrels—it reveals itself over the totality of cases as a tool of the relatively powerless, a way of getting heard in the public arena of the court.[69]

The point here is that judge and scribe employed a variety of representational practices as they translated words spoken at court into the written record. To put it another way, the court employed a "grammar of representation" as it mapped legal rules for presenting testimony and evidence onto the local vernacular for speaking about oneself and one's relation to others. That the less powerful spoke in emotionally or rhetorically inflected voices more often than did established members of the community suggests that this was a way of compensating for disparities of power within the provincial community—between women and men, peasants and city dwellers, commoners and elite.

AMPLIFYING THE TEXTUAL RECORD

How can we penetrate the opacity of these records? Although their brevity points to key elements as construed by the judge, the purely legal content of a case does not always cast light on what was at stake in the lives of the litigants involved or on the strategies that lay behind their claims at court. At times, the legal surface of a case may even obscure its underlying dynamic. A dispute, in other words, may not ultimately be "about" what its written record suggests. Take divorce cases as an example. Rarely are they simply about a failed marriage. Rather, they involve culturally universal issues such as custody, child support, and in particular the control of property, as well as culturally specific linkages—in sixteenth-century Aintab, to adultery and rape, severe illness, the absence of husbands, and the pervasive habit of swearing. Fortunately, there are other contemporary sources that, when combined with the court records, help clarify their substance. We have already encountered the numerous cadastral surveys for Aintab, which contributed much to the portrait of the province sketched in the previous two chapters. These surveys can also aid in analyzing the court records. Other sources are more specifically legal: for example, the imperial law books issued by the four sultans from Mehmed the Conqueror through Süleyman, and the collections of fatwas issued from the increasingly influential office of the empire's chief mufti.

Asking what the court records can tell us about people's strategies for dealing with the law inevitably leads to questions about the identity of speakers at court. The cadastral surveys carried out in 1536 and 1543 have the virtue of helping to situate some of the individuals who came to court, both spatially and socially. As we saw in chapter 2, the surveys yield useful information about the size of city neighborhoods and villages and the nature of individual village economies, which helps us place incidents litigated at court in their local milieus. Cadastral registers have the additional merit of naming virtually all men in the province, listing them village by village and city neighborhood by neighborhood. These lists also indicate whether a taxpaying male was the father, brother, or son of other males named in the same village or neighborhood, and also whether he was a farmer or landless worker (both assumed to be married heads of household) or an unmarried young man living with a male relative. Evaluated in the aggregate, this information can suggest patterns of family structure and marriage practices, while the existence of surveys in the two years of 1536 and 1543 enables us to see trends in progress around 1540. All these data provide social context for a variety of matters treated in the court record.

Another kind of contextualizing information supplied by the surveys is the identity of the fiscal and legal authority for each village—that is, the official to whom local taxes were paid and who was also responsible for local law and order. For example, the village of Hiyam, the largest in the province, belonged partly to the imperial holdings in Aintab *(hass-ı şahî)* and partly to the pious foundation *(waqf)* of an Aleppan family; it paid taxes to both, but was legally bound to the provincial administration through the agency of the trustee for crown lands. In contrast, fiscal and legal authority for the smaller village of Kefer-Cebel, not too far from Hiyam, was shared among three timariot soldiers.[70] This information is helpful in situating the local delivery of the law in the rural hinterland of the province, since knowing who was entitled to collect the tax revenues of a village—be he gentleman farmer, timariot soldier, or agent for the crown—informs us about one level of dispute resolution. These local authorities acted both as legal resource for their subjects and at the same time as enforcer of the law. They were, in fact, part of the greater police force in Aintab.

This happy confluence of court records and cadastral surveys around the year 1540 is no coincidence.[71] The timing suggests the beginnings of a significant shift in imperial emphasis from territorial expansion to administrative consolidation, that is, from conquest to colonization.[72] By the early 1540s, the Ottoman regime had achieved relative control over both its eastern and western frontiers. In the east, the major military campaign in 1534–1536 against the Safavid regime in Iran secured the large region encompassing eastern and southeastern Anatolia and Iraq. At the other end of empire, Hungary was firmly integrated into the Ottoman domain in 1541: with the death of King Louis, a tributary of the Ottoman sultan since 1526, Süleyman brought the kingdom under direct Ottoman rule. This securing of frontiers marked a shift of emphasis in Süleyman's sultanate, initiating an increasingly visible role for the sovereign as legislator and administrative regulator. While Süleyman never gave up his career as military chief (he died at the age of seventy-four while leading his last campaign), his responsibilities in the arenas of law and religion began to be more conspicuously cultivated in the years around 1540. It is hardly surprising that the sobriquet by which Süleyman became known was *kanunî*—the lawmaker, the legally minded regulator.

Specifically, these new emphases brought into being legal texts that help us contextualize our court records. Süleyman's own principal contribution to the legal corpus of his reign—his law book, or *kanunname*—is generally dated to around 1540.[73] It is in effect a summa expanding on the law books issued by his father, grandfather, and great-grandfather. In his legal work, Süleyman was helped by a team of advisers he had assembled in the late 1530s, mainly the jurist Ebu Suud and the chancellor Celalzade Mustafa. The chancellor was most probably the compiler of the sultan's law book,[74] while Ebu Suud was principal author of the regulations issued for the administration of Hungary in 1541—the kanunname of Buda. The latter was a major advance in its regulation of land tenure and taxation (it would remain the basic Ottoman formulation on these matters until 1858).[75] The Buda regulations are not directly relevant to this study, but they alert us to the intimate relationship of law and land management so commonly associated with Süleyman's reign.[76] The density of cadastral surveys in the years around 1540, not in Aintab alone, can be seen as creating a documentary foundation on which the newly refined thinking about law, sovereignty, and the control of land might build. Many of these surveys were accompanied by local kanunnames.[77]

Fatwas issued from the office of the empire's chief mufti are another

genre of legal text that became increasingly salient during the reign of Süleyman. The nexus of law, religious consciousness, and administrative needs
can be seen in the growing importance of this office in the interpretation of
the Islamic legal underpinnings of the state. Technically the mufti of Istanbul, the chief mufti was increasingly called on to rule on legislative matters
affecting the conduct of government as a whole.[78] The influence of his position was reflected in the exponential increase in the number of fatwas he
issued and in the parallel elaboration of a fatwa office. In the beginning of
sixteenth century, the chief mufti Ali Cemali, known as "the basket man," is
said to have received questions by hanging a basket from his window, haul-
ing up it up when a petitioner tugged on the string, and writing his answer
on the same piece of paper. Later in the century, the office had been sufficiently bureaucratized that Ebu Suud, famed jurist and the chief mufti from
1545 to 1574, could claim to have issued over 1,000 fatwas in a single day,
with the help of a staff of assistants.[79] That local communities such as Aintab
were up on recent fatwas of the chief mufti is evident from their citation in
court, particularly in the matter of water rights.[80]

Accompanying the production of these various texts—fatwas and imperial laws—was the expansion of an infrastructure to apply them. The
mushrooming construction of new schools to train judges, jurists, and other
religious professionals was led by the dynasty, whose numerous building
projects under Süleyman began in earnest in 1537. Although the formal
structuring of a religio-legal hierarchy with well-defined career lines, established salaries, and rules for appointment and promotion would come later
in Süleyman's reign, its foundation was being laid in the years around 1540
with the expansion of the court system and the proliferation of educational
institutions. In Aintab, the local fruits of this process were the issuing of a
local law book for the province in 1536, the inception of regularly kept
court records in the early or mid-1530s, the cadastral surveys of 1536 and
1543, and possibly the first centrally appointed judge (Hüsameddin Efendi)
in 1541.

What this intensity of legal activity both locally and at the center of the
state means for the study of an individual provincial court in 1540 is that
the latter's processes can be framed in a larger perspective. The interplay
between the operation of the court and broader legal and political developments is a theme permeating this book. For now, let us look at one way in
which these connections can provide insight: namely, by shedding light on
the issues at stake in particular cases. The judge of Aintab almost never
spells out the pertinent legal and cultural considerations in a case, but contemporary normative law—a fatwa, for example, or a statute in the law
books—often makes plain the considerations that influence how litigants
and judge approach a legal case.

The unresolved situation of Ali and Ayşe can provide a test case for this contextualized exploration of the court records. The cultural constraints brought to bear on Ali because of the alleged sexual misconduct of his wife are illuminated by a statute in Süleyman's law book that penalizes a man who does not divorce his adulterous wife. The statute noted that while the penalty, known as a "cuckold tax" *(köftehorluk)*, had previously been 100 akçes, "it has become the custom to take 300 akçes."[81] In other words, the law book implied that popular morality was making it increasingly difficult for a man to stay married to an adulterous wife, or, as in Ali's case, to a wife caught in circumstances sufficiently compromising to give rise to suspicion of adultery. That five such "cuckold divorces" came to the Aintab court over the course of a single year suggests that the cultural pressure mirrored in the sultan's statute was felt locally.[82]

However, other elements in the law books and in texts of jurisprudence point to a more complicated scenario that might underlie the story of Ali and Ayşe. They suggest, for example, that the couple's divorce might have been staged. Süleyman's law book penalizes authorities who allow adulterers to marry, a prohibition hinting that committing adultery was sometimes a strategy to get out of marriage (remember that it was difficult for women to initiate divorce): "If a woman is spoken ill of with a certain man and her husband divorces her, that ill-reputed woman shall not be married to that man. If a marriage *has* been contracted, the judge shall immediately separate [them] by force and compulsion and shall severely chastise and heavily punish the cleric who married [them]."[83] In three of the five instances of cuckold divorce in Aintab, the adultery was consensual, and we have therefore to wonder if the community tolerated the marriage of adulterers. The plausibility of women's (and their lovers') willingness to exchange the dishonor of adultery for freedom to marry becomes greater when we learn that women cultivated other strategies for escaping marriage. They might, for example, refuse to remarry their husbands when the latter uttered a profanity (thereby rendering themselves apostates in the eyes of the law, a state that was rectified through "renewal of faith" and "renewal of marriage"). Indeed, this strategy of women was widespread enough to cause İbn Kemal, chief mufti from 1525 to 1534, to offer the opinion that women could be coerced back into their marriages:

> Query: If Zeyd [i.e., John Doe] pronounces something by way of a curse and must later remarry his wife, and she will not agree to the marriage and will not accept it and says "I'm divorced, I won't ever return to my husband," what must be done according to the law?
> Response: Force can be used.[84]

Both this fatwa and the sultanic statutes regarding adultery point to the intimate relationship between normative legal pronouncements and trends in social behavior.

The complexities of Ali and Ayşe's case underline the important observation that the judge sometimes had to sort out conflicting testimonies in
order to achieve "justice." One challenge in this case was to evaluate Ayşe's
allegation of rape. Here again, contemporary developments in legal thinking cast light on her situation. The judge's task was to navigate the conflicting legal principles that the question of rape brought into play. The crime
of illicit sex *(zina)* was classically defined by Islamic jurisprudence as consensual and heterosexual, but jurists well before the sixteenth century had
recognized the need to address the problem of rape (as well as same-sex li-
aisons).[85] The stumbling block of requiring four eyewitnesses to the sexual
act in order to prosecute rape, or in fact *any* form of illicit sex, was gotten
around in both sharia and sultanic law by the legitimation of circumstantial
evidence. Accordingly, the Aintab judge would seem to have absolved Ayşe
of the accusation of adultery (the three males and two females who witnessed her distress after the alleged rape provide the circumstantial equivalent of four eyewitnesses to the actual act).[86] But what about Hızır, who
would now seem liable to conviction as a rapist? The court record is silent,
as it is regarding other alleged rapists during the year. This silence suggests
that Hızır, like the others, was not prosecuted. Once again, it is reference to
sharia and sultanic law that helps us find an answer: a person with a reputation for moral probity is freed from suspicion of illicit sex if he or she de-
nies the accusation.

The point here, methodologically speaking, is that working between
the court cases and normative law helps us bridge the gaps in our ability to
grasp what was really going on in situations that were litigated. Such a meth-
odological approach also enables us to flesh out the sociolegal culture in
which all were operating, a culture in which normative law responded to the
messy complexity of real life, the judge considered each case on its individual merits but in reference to normative law, and individuals strategized by
drawing on local knowledge of the meaning and mechanics of legal rules
and processes. In other words, neither legal practice in the local courts nor
contemporary formulations of normative law can be understood apart from
the symbiotic relation between them.

Such an intertextual approach to reading court cases gives rise, when we
consider Ali and Ayşe, to another important observation. It may strike many
readers that the outcome of the case does not add up: Ayşe has been raped,
Hızır is freed of suspicion of raping her, Ali divorces Ayşe to rid himself of
a dishonored wife. The attempt to understand how this might have made
sense in sixteenth-century Aintab leads us to a central feature of the legal
culture of its court. Guiding the judge in his disposition of the case is what
we might call the principle of separate justices, whose goal is social equity
rather than a neat solution in which all relevant legal rules are brought into
harmony and satisfied. The judge invokes different sets of principles and

statutes as he approaches the legal situation of Ali, Ayşe, and Hızır separately. No one is a winner in this case, but neither is anyone clearly a loser.
Although Ayşe has probably lost more than anyone else, she has restored
some modicum of her honor with the help of sympathetic bystanders. This
approach to the law—the pursuit of separate justices—is characteristic
of the court's representation of other obviously complex and contentious
issues admitting no unified solution; these conflicts tend to be teased apart
in the record, which takes up the situation of each of the protagonists
independently.[87]

However, the case of Ali and Ayşe still is not a complete story. Indeed, it
is one of the most incomplete and puzzling stories in the records studied in
this book. We still don't know why the couple moved from Ruha to Aintab.
Armed with the knowledge outlined above, however, we can construct plausible scenarios from the ultimately opaque record—or opaque to us, for
contemporaries would no doubt have been more astute readers of the story
excerpted in the court's record. Perhaps Ali and Ayşe moved from Ruha to
stage the incident, which occurred very soon after the records of their marriage and the contents of Ayşe's dower were transferred from the court of
Ruha. Or did the couple come to Aintab to get a fresh start? If so, Ayşe may
have proved herself, perhaps once again, just too young to be married, too
young to conform to the comportment expected of a married woman. It is
indeed tempting to spin out such scenarios from cases like Ayşe's. But the
effort to pin down a precise chain of events may be misplaced, since the
court itself was not concerned with constructing a narrative of "what really
happened." Indeed, it was as a problem of conflicting narrative strategies
that the court record approached Ali and Ayşe's case, one that elicited from
its protagonists different constructions of its meaning. The court took each
protagonist's version of the events and evaluated it on its own merits.

THE VARIETIES OF LAW—ISLAMIC, IMPERIAL, CUSTOMARY

What is it about legal structures and processes at the local level that allowed
space for the persuasive agency of individuals? This question is another
pervasive theme in this book, but some preliminary answers can be considered at this point. One factor was the obvious need to make the court user-
friendly, since it relied for a large volume of its business on voluntarily submitted petitions. The hearings that took place in court on July 12, listed at
the beginning of this chapter, were typical in that there were two matters
submitted voluntarily for every matter brought by a local official. Cornelia
Dayton's comment about seventeenth-century New Haven, that "the colonial court's effectiveness in keeping the peace depended on the public's
willingness to bring complaints and testimony to it,"[88] is equally true of the
Ottoman provincial court of the sixteenth century. Given the availability of

a variety of other communal modes of dispute resolution, some at the neighborhood level, the court had to demonstrate that its services were at least as good if not better.

The court's willingness to entertain individual narratives of injury, dishonor, abuse, or moral outrage is also the product of a universal characteristic of the early modern period, when the domestic and the personal were public; when ethical qualities such as honesty, piety, charity, and a reputation for moral rectitude were civic, not private, virtues; and when public humiliation was as serious a punishment as a hefty fine, a severe flogging, or jailing. In sixteenth-century Aintab, personal reputation was quantifiable, since the collective memory of the neighborhood or the court record could tell how many, if any, negative marks an individual had acquired and in what manner. Thus, after Ayşe's rape and divorce, the honor of each of the protagonists was protected or restored, albeit to unequal degrees. It would not be forgotten, however, that Ayşe and Hızır had drawn suspicion of sexual misconduct, and the ambiguity tolerated in the present case would not be repeated should either become involved in a future scandal. The consequences of acquiring such a negative mark—a *töhmet,* in the language of the court—went beyond loss of immunity from allegations of sexual misconduct. They also included disqualification from a variety of civic responsibilities, such as serving as witness at court, communal mediator, or guardian of the property of minors. Arguments about honor and reputation were therefore as concrete as arguments about the boundaries of property or the size of a debt. The notion of separate justices meant that individuals needed to make a good case about the integrity of their conduct or about the constraining circumstances that made misconduct unavoidable.

These two factors—the court's lack of a monopoly on the business of justice and the importance of speaking out about character—are not exclusive to premodern Muslim societies. But a third factor that accounts for persuasive testimony is particular to Aintab's place and time: the constellation of forces operating in the local court. Much literature has been devoted to explicating the legal discourses—sharia, sultanic law, local custom—that impinged on the court. Yet how they came together in the lives of ordinary individuals is a critical question that has been little explored.[89] In telling the stories of İne, Haciye Sabah, and Fatma, which introduce the parts of this book, I attempt to fill this gap through three case studies of females involved in situations of legal and cultural complexity. What I want to do now, in the remainder of this chapter, is to outline each of these legal discourses, with an emphasis on their local manifestations. While they are presented here as separate strands of legal tradition, I hope that the overlapping, indeed symbiotic, relationship among them will become clear. In the final section of this chapter, we will return to the question of how the intersection of these discourses made room for the persuasive agency of individuals.

The most obvious force influencing legal processes in Aintab was Islamic law—sharia—which functioned in the court of Aintab as the matrix for the decision-making process. The majority of cases that came to the Aintab judge appear to have followed sharia in their legal prescriptions, legal terminology, and court procedure. The Aintab judge followed the Hanafi school of sunni jurisprudence, though not all Aintabans were Hanafi adherents; some appear to have been Shafi'i and, when necessary, a Shafi'i deputy judge might be appointed to hear cases according to Shafi'i legal teachings.[90] As for legal texts that informed the court's work, the most commonly studied, if far from the only, text among students of jurisprudence of the period was *Hedaya (The Guide)*. One of the most popular Hanafi texts of all time, the *Hedaya* was authored by the twelfth-century Central Asian scholar Burhan Al-Din Al-Marghinani.[91] However, a relatively recent Hanafi legal manual, commissioned by Selim I and completed in 1517 by Ibrahim Al-Halabi, would go on to displace others as the standard authority in the Ottoman domain.[92] This work, *Multaka Al-Abhur,* may have reached Aintab by 1540, but since it generally took more than one generation for scholars to recognize, study, and then begin to teach a new text, Al-Halabi's manual may not yet have come to influence the work of a provincial judge.[93]

For the inhabitants of Aintab, sharia was more than a legal discourse confined to the court. For one thing, it was a scholarly tradition taught and studied by local citizens. Aintab had a remarkable number of residents who carried the title *Molla;* some of them taught in the city's several postprimary educational institutions, where the study of Islamic jurisprudence and other religious sciences formed the core of the curriculum.[94] It is not clear whether there were libraries of legal texts in Aintab, either in the private collections of mollas or in the city's colleges.[95] Nevertheless, a degree of knowledge of textual legal traditions was clearly part of the culture of the educated in Aintab. As noted in chapter 1, a well-known native son of Aintab, Bedreddin Ainî, writing at the end of the fourteenth century, observed that Aintab's ability to attract learned scholars earned it the nickname "little Bukhara," after the famed city in Transoxania.[96] Aintab's stature as a center of Islamic learning might have diminished since that point, but its population of mollas in 1540 was far from thin.

Sharia was also a living tradition, "the right path," an ethical code as well as a body of law.[97] Ordinary people did not have to apply to the court or the local colleges to obtain guidance along this path. Instruction was available at the neighborhood level from local muftis and imams, though no doubt delivered with less learned expertise than if dispensed by the judge or a resident teacher at one of the colleges in Aintab. A mufti is an individual sufficiently versed in jurisprudence to deliver an opinion—a fatwa—on a matter falling within the purview of sharia. People could apply to muftis for answers on matters of doctrine or for particular problems for which they were seeking a religiously or morally correct course of action. Muftis were unlike judges in two respects. First, while a judge's ruling *(hükm)* was binding, a mufti issued a "non-binding advisory opinion to an individual questioner."[98] In other words, muftis might differ in their answer to a query. Second, while judges were officially appointed to their office, muftis might or might not hold official appointments, and in fact the majority most probably did not. There was a range of muftis in the sixteenth-century Ottoman empire, from the chief mufti, a prominent legal scholar and practitioner whose reputation for expertise earned him appointment to this post by the sultan, to local individuals with no official capacity who were simply sought out by others in their communities because of their reputation for religious knowledge.[99] Because muftis often delivered opinions on disagreements or conflicts between individuals, they were a kind of legal resource that helped satisfy the community's need for mechanisms of dispute resolution.

Aintab had its own mufti, Molla Hasan Efendi, although it is not clear whether he held an appointed office or was instead a locally respected scholar whose opinions were considered weighty enough to influence the judge's decisions. Whatever his precise status, Molla Hasan's presence provided a sanction for interpretations of sharia that might run counter to those of the chief mufti in Istanbul. When the hapless Derviş Ali, apparently delirious from illness, uttered the irrevocable divorce formula and then went to court to try to rescue his marriage, Molla Hasan opined that divorce had not been precipitated.[100] This reading of sharia appeared to go against the fatwa of a recent chief mufti (İbn Kemal), which stated that the divorce formula was valid even if spoken in delirium.[101] Another case, this one involving a stolen kilim, suggests that Hasan Efendi was not the only mufti who served the inhabitants of Aintab. When the kilim disappeared from the mosque of Ali Neccar, it was the mosque's "fatwa giver" *(fetvacı)* who accompanied a large delegation from the congregation to testify at court that the kilim had been found in the hands of a certain Mehmed.[102] This is not to say that every mosque had its own fatwa giver—the mosque of Ali Neccar was fairly well endowed and served one of the city's largest neighborhoods—but it is clear that appealing to muftis for guidance was a familiar practice in Aintab. The muftis of mid-sixteenth-century Aintab did their work outside of the court, although the fact that people occasionally brought fatwas to court to bolster their case suggests that the court was open to their legal expertise.[103] Indeed, if one of the judge's tasks in this period was to make the local court user-friendly, accommodating people's habit of consulting muftis was a sensible practice.

Basic knowledge of sharia was also offered by the imam of the neighborhood mosque, who functioned as prayer leader and religious guide to his congregation. Imams might teach children, as we learn from the case of Molla Hüseyin, imam of the city's Tarla Mosque, who doubled as imam in the village of Sebilhan. He came to court in July 1541 to register his resignation from the Tarla imamship on the grounds that he was incapable of fulfilling his duties there because of his responsibilities in the village: not only did he serve as imam, but he also gave instruction in the Qur'an to the village boys.[104] The case of Haciye Sabah suggests that girls too might receive basic instruction in religion from female teachers. The teachings of such neighborhood figures no doubt conveyed the basic precepts of religiously prescribed behavior and belief, although as expositions of jurisprudence they were probably far from systematic.

While the court was the principal channel for enforcing sharia locally, it was also an instrument in the application of *kanun,* imperial or sultanic law. Kanun manifested itself in Aintab in various forms: individual decrees sent to the court from the sultan's chancery, a law book *(kanunname)* specifically for Aintab, and, of course, the comprehensive imperial law book that applied throughout the empire. The responsibility for seeing that kanun was observed locally lay both with judges and with provincial governors and governors-general. This system of parallel judicial enforcement is evident in the practice of directives addressed from the imperial capital in Istanbul to both the judge and the provincial governor, and sometimes to the judge alone.[105] In this connection, it is important to remember that judges were appointed by the state. In a summary account of the 1543 cadastral survey of Aintab province, the judgeship was listed in the inventory of government-appointed personnel along with the provincial governor and locally stationed cavalry officers.[106]

Lawmaking by the Ottoman dynasty was more than the routine task of dispatching individual decrees and periodically assembling various laws and administrative regulations into kanunnames. Issuing laws that imposed a regulating order throughout the imperial domain was a classic marker of sovereignty. The central role of lawmaking as both a symbolic and a practical quality of rulership, particularly critical at the foundation of the state, is often attributed to the Central Asian heritage of the Ottoman dynasty. But we should note that it was a pronounced element in the Ottomans' Byzantine heritage as well. In this respect, the model of Constantine and Justinian was not so far from the model of Genghis Khan, famed not only as conqueror but also as lawgiver and consolidator of empire. To put it another way, the Ottoman sultans were surrounded by historical models of legally minded rulership. Indeed, justice as a quintessential attribute of kingship was a broadly shared value among Mediterranean and Near Eastern civilizations, much vaunted, for example, in the histories of ancient Persian rulers.[107]

Lawmaking was a sovereign function conspicuously performed by the four sultans from Mehmed II, conqueror of Constantinople in 1453, to Süleyman, collectively the architects of the imperial foundations of empire.[108]

Their kanunnames were of two types: imperial compendia for universal application, and local codes for provincial administration tailored to the local economic and demographic base of an individual province as well as to local needs and customs. (As we have seen, the kanunname for Aintab was issued in 1536, at the time of the province's first systematic cadastral survey.) [109] The imperial law books included sections on criminal penalties, market organization and urban taxes, agricultural taxes and regulations for the peasantry, organization of artisanal and manufacturing activities, taxes on nomads and their regulation, and regulations for the military (infantry corps and provincial cavalry). They functioned as a kind of administrative constitution, laying out a blueprint for organizing and administering the vast agrarian and commercially based domain that was the Ottoman empire.

A fundamental aspect of these imperial law books is the organic, cumulative process by which they developed. A sultan honored his ancestors' legacy by retaining their laws, while at the same time he added laws of his own. Süleyman earned the nickname "Kanunî" in part because he was the last of the great compilers of his ancestors' laws. The law books of the sultans are, strictly speaking, not "codes" in the sense of providing a systematic and consistent statement of a body of law, for they contain internal inconsistencies as a result of their cumulative production. Rather, the guiding principle of their organization was the collecting and collating of existing laws issued for the various regions of empire, and the weeding out of those that had lost their applicability. This spirit of inclusion enabled the Ottoman sultans to absorb the laws of former rulers of the domains they conquered; indeed, they considered themselves heirs to certain of these rulers, particularly those sultans, such as the Mamluk Qaytbay and the Akkoyunlu Uzun Hasan, who combined success in conquest with success in bringing about stability through legal regulation.[110] In terms of their cultural import, then, the Ottoman law books reflect a concern less for theoretical consistency than for historical rootedness and sustained awareness of the variety of local practice within the empire.

One aspect of kanun is routinely visible when we look at grassroots legal administration through the lens of the court records: the granting of rights to farm the land. In the many cases in which title to farming rights is bestowed, a ritual linguistic feature is the phrase "in accordance with the imperial kanun" *(kanun-ı padişahî muktezasınca).*[111] Reflected in this verbal framing is the critical role of kanun in underpinning the regime's tight control of non-urban land. Less visible at the grassroots level is another important aspect of kanun—its criminal prescriptions. No records of sentencing and punishment exist to parallel the records of court hearings, if indeed such police records were ever routinely kept. Trial and punishment were distinct domains of legal administration, a division that was emphasized in

Süleyman's legal reforms. Sharia rules of procedure structured hearings at court, while it was mainly kanun that structured law enforcement and punishment. And so, for the most part, we have to look between the lines of the court's proceedings to discern how kanun worked as the blueprint for law enforcement. Chapter 8 takes up the domain of law enforcement in detail, but let us take a brief look at some of its key aspects here.

Although no record exists of the actual penalties assigned in Aintab in cases of criminal infraction, we are informed by the 1536 kanunname for Aintab that penalties were to be assigned according to the imperial law book: "For every crime that occurs, no matter how great or small, [the penalty] shall be decided with reference to the Ottoman Kanun (*Kanun-ı Osmanî*). Force shall not be used to exact anything more than that."[112] While there is no explicit proof that these procedures for enforcement were actually applied, we have no reason to doubt that they were. A case that came to court in the summer of 1541 gives us a clue that kanun was the authority for deciding punishment: when the nomad Ahmed b. Mehmed was charged with harboring a relative who had struck another with a rock, he pledged to bring him before the judge; "If I don't," he said, "I'll pay the penalty that kanun prescribes."[113] Punishment by kanun could take the form of fines, floggings, imprisonment, public humiliation, and temporary banishment, and these all can be observed in the Aintab record. Two other punishments that, in theory, could be prescribed in dire cases—amputation of limbs and execution—are not mentioned in the Aintab records. In short, Süleyman's law book endorsed a range of penalties, though the regime appears to have preferred fines for routine crimes, one reason being that they provided revenue for the state. The nomad Ahmed apparently expected to pay such a fine if he failed to fulfill his legal charge.

Enforcing criminal penalties locally was the job of the sultan's men. The most important chain of command flowed downward from the regional governor-general through the provincial governor to the provincial chief of police and finally to the lesser officials who reported to him. A second chain of authority, less broad than the first, was headed by the trustee for crown lands in Aintab province. Collectively these men were known as *ehl-i örf*, "people of executive authority," or more simply, "the authorities."[114] All these individuals appear at court as prosecutors of the law, but the absence of police records makes it difficult to say precisely where in the chain of command specific penalties were assigned and applied.

As designed by the sultans and their advisers, the Ottoman legal system of the mid–sixteenth century was to contain checks and balances: judgment by the judge according to sharia rules of procedure and sharia-defined categories of criminal action, enforcement and punishment by the executive officials according to kanun. But the relationship between the legal realms of sharia/judge/hearing and kanun/police/enforcement was not untroubled, as chapter 8 will explore further. The efforts during Süleyman's reign to standardize legal practice and to give a larger role to the courts exacerbated whatever natural tensions existed between these two arms of justice. Imperial law attempted to regulate these tensions, especially the extralegal actions of police in torturing suspects and extorting excessive fines. These attempts are evident in the statute quoted above and more explicitly in the following statute, also from Süleyman's law book, which insisted that no penalty could be imposed without a court hearing and judgment: "The executive officials shall not imprison and injure any person without the cognizance of the judge. And they shall collect a fine according to [the nature of] a person's offense and they shall take no more [than is due]. If they do, the judge shall rule on the amount of the excess and restore it [to the offender]."[115] While kanun could not directly regulate the workings of Islam's holy law, it could hope to discipline its own enforcers.

The phrase "by kanun and sharia" is common in texts of the fifteenth and sixteenth centuries. When news of a murder committed by two Aintabans began to leak, local conversation marked its gravity by noting that it needed to be "tried by sharia and kanun."[116] In other words, people recognized that they were living under two legal authorities but that the two marched together. In truth, the long history of Muslim sovereigns fulfilling (or failing in) their duty to enforce religious law had drawn these two sources of law into symbiosis, at least in the eastern Mediterranean region and by the late medieval period. In Aintab, the "people of executive authority" who punished were the same individuals who prosecuted the Qur'anic crimes in the name of protecting the "claims of God." And in striving to compile a comprehensive penal code, Süleyman's law book prescribed penalties both for crimes defined under sharia and for those ignored by sharia. This comprehensiveness inevitably created a significant overlap between kanun as criminal law and sharia.

While the court was charged with accountability to both sharia and kanun, there was a third contender in this local arena of justice. Local customary practices were admitted into court proceedings as yet another form of normative law. The idea that customary practice was a necessary if not theoretically authorized source of law was an old notion in Islamic legal thinking. As Abraham L. Udovitch has pointed out, "Local custom . . . comes in, as one might say, through a side door as a source of law, without being explicitly recognized as such."[117] Classical terms for customary practice were *urf* (Turkish *örf*) and *adet,* but in the sixteenth century the term *kanun,* most often associated with sultanic legislation, also appeared in Ottoman texts with the meaning "custom" or "practice"; in this usage, it was often paired with the word *kadim,* "old" or "ancient," to mean traditional or customary practice, *kanun-ı kadim.*

In Aintab, customary practice did not have to be written to serve as legal referent, so long as trustworthy spokesmen could be found to testify to its historic validity. Local residents who possessed expertise in a particular matter might be summoned to inform the judge of professional norms to facilitate his ruling in a dispute whose grounds were unfamiliar to him. Because Ottoman judges were rotated frequently, they were inevitably dependent on local information: the success of their custodianship of the court depended on their working together with leaders of the community. One arena where local leaders *(ayan)* set legally enforced standards was the pricing of goods sold in the markets of Aintab, which the court record informs us were established "according to traditional practice" *(adet-i kadim üzere)*. For example, in the setting of meat prices, the record relates that "the *ayan* of Aintab gathered, came to the court, and gave the following testimony: 'It has come about from old that in the current season [June], a *batman* of lamb is [sold] for nine Aleppo akçes and a *batman* of goat meat for seven Aleppo akçes.'"[118] The cultural importance of traditional practice is reflected in the existence in the Turkish language of a verbal formation indicating ancient origin or traditional practice, a form that is employed in the testimony quoted *(olagelmişdir*—"it has come about").

Another way in which community members brought local practice into play at court was through their role as arbitrators in cases resolved by communal mediation. This process was known as *sulh*, "peacemaking" or compromise; mediators were known as "peacemakers" *(musalihun)*. Disputes in Aintab were handled in this manner quite frequently, and issues that underwent communal arbitration ranged from personal insults to disputed inheritance claims. An unusual case that was arbitrated concerned a horse who was attacked by a swarm of bees and died; the settlement required the owners of the beehives to pay 10 gold pieces to the owners of the horse.[119] In cases amenable to a negotiated settlement, the disputing parties typically chose the arbitrators, whose recommendation the judge then validated in court, so long as it met with his approval. In the view of Hanafi law, arbitrators were likened to the judge in their function, which required "wisdom and judgment."[120] The court records do not preserve the identity of individual arbitrators; rather, they introduce a record of arbitration with the phrase "arbitrators entered the breach" and follow it with the terms of the compromise reached. The records also do not spell out the arbitrators' criteria for arriving at a settlement, but we can assume that they drew on local custom, knowledge of the disputants' relationship to one another and their place in the community, and ethical common sense. What is significant about arbitration is that sharia authorized dispute resolution by and among local individuals according to methods of their own devising, so long as the solution was acceptable in the judge's view. Indeed, if Muslim judges were to attract the legal business of communities under their jurisdiction to their courts, co-opting common practices like mediation was a strategic and perhaps inevitable move.[121]

LOCAL JUSTICE

As we have seen, legal processes at court relied to a considerable degree on input from the local community. In the court, therefore, we are often closer to *choices* about justice than to *rules* about justice. Hence we may come closer to an appreciation of the moral and ethical outlook of a Muslim society by looking at its courts than by examining its formal legal codes. Some might object that the notion of justice that prevailed in Aintab in the year 1540–1541 is a highly particular one, perhaps shared not even by other Anatolian communities of the times. The argument can be made, however, that the variability in the definition of what constituted justice not only was tolerated in the sixteenth century but was an intentional design of the legal system as a whole.

Islamic law, particularly the Hanafi school of jurisprudence, gives the judge guidance on rules and procedures but deliberately leaves him latitude to incorporate local circumstances and customs. This acknowledgment of the role of the local was articulated in a fatwa of the chief mufti İbn Kemal (d. 1534), a brilliant and versatile scholar and one of the critically important legal appointments of Süleyman's reign.[122] The question posed to İbn Kemal concerned the definition of *tazir,* the discretionary assignment of penalties outside of those definitively fixed by sacred scriptural sources.

> Query: What is tazir?
> Response: There is a tazir *appropriate for each person's situation.* The decision in that matter belongs to the judge[.] [123]

The point is that judgment was to be achieved through a localized reading of formal jurisprudence. İbn Kemal's response also underlines the point about separate justices made above: individual consideration should be given not only to each case, but to each person.

It would be a mistake, however, to see such local grounding of normative law as risking a breach between legal "theory" and "practice," that is, between jurisprudence and the actions of the court. One of the central concerns of Islamic jurisprudence was the question of how its formulations— viewed as an ongoing effort to discern God's will for humankind, a truth always beyond human reach—might be responsibly applied to particular problems.[124] The problem was addressed in part through the existence of a number of genres of legal interpretation that spanned the spectrum from academic to applied: theoretical works of jurisprudence hewed more closely to sacred sources and to the opinions of the founders of the school, while commentaries, especially shorter ones suitable for use as manuals, had a more practical orientation.[125] Of the four schools of sunni law, the Hanafis gave perhaps the most consideration to local particulars in the application of the law. It is no wonder that this was the school officially adopted by many rulers of late-medieval and early modern Muslim empires in the Middle East, Central Asia, and India, given its greater capacity to accommodate the variety of local cultures populating these empires.

Scholars customarily emphasize the differences between sharia and kanun, but even more striking, if one considers their application rather than their genesis in religious versus imperial sanctions, are their similarities. Hanafi legal tradition shared with sultanic kanun a number of features that gave them an epistemological kinship. Both had strong loyalties to the founders of their respective legal traditions, yet both acknowledged from the beginning the notion that there could be differences of opinion among the founders. Both were moored to original texts while recognizing the need for continual commentary and practical flexibility. Both emphasized local knowledge, sharia with its caution to judges to recognize legitimate local practice and kanun with its separate law books for different provinces. Both would appear to have similarly viewed normative law as a statement of the limits of the tolerable rather than a set of inflexible rules to be imposed regardless of circumstances. Both had mechanisms for updating and modifying existing textual prescriptions. Cornell Fleischer's comment about kanun—that "sultans built upon and adjusted, but never fully abrogated, the laws of their fathers by issuing their own supplemental codes, reaffirmations, and revisions of standing legislation"—is similar to the arguments scholars today are making about the role historically played by fatwas and other genres in the expansion of sharia; thus Baber Johansen observes that "While the early tradition is upheld in the textbooks for teaching purposes and is used as a yardstick by which to measure the unity of the legal system, new solutions are widely accepted in other literary genres like the commentaries, the *responsa* [fatwas], and the treatises on particular questions."[126]

It is not surprising that Hanafi sharia and Ottoman kanun shared cultural assumptions and attitudes, given the long history of accommodation between religious and ruling authorities that accelerated with the eleventh-century empire of the Seljuks. Indeed, the guiding formula of *din wa dawla,* "religion and imperium," translated in practice into a mutual reinforcement between the two sources of legislative authority. The division of labor between judgment and punishment in the court of Aintab is a concrete example of this symbiosis. The plausibility of the oft-quoted dictum of Joseph Schacht, historian of Islamic law, that the Ottoman sultans of the sixteenth-century "endowed Islamic law, in its Hanafi form . . . with the highest degree of actual efficiency which it had ever possessed in a society of high material civilization since early Abbasid times . . . ,"[127] depends largely on the compatibility between sharia and kanun at both the conceptual and the grass-roots level. This study is, in a sense, witness to that compatibility.

This chapter has underscored the importance of community participation in the effectiveness of the local court. Normative legal discourses were designed not to be rigidly applied but rather to be used as legal guidelines whose interpretation depended on local particulars. Members of the community played a variety of significant roles in that process of interpretation, acting as reliable sources of customary practice, as mediators employing familiar means of reconciliation, and as court observers. Local knowledge, in other words, was a critical link between Islamic jurisprudence and imperial lawmaking on the one hand and the achievement of communal "law and order" on the other.

Another crucial aspect of local participation in the legal process was the responsibility delegated to neighborhoods and individuals for monitoring morality and conduct. While this responsibility was in part a product of the fear of being held accessory to the criminal acts of others, it promoted local initiative in the resolution of disputes. In all of these functions, a capacity for legal knowledge and judgment was attributed to the local population. The state-appointed judge of course regulated community participation in the legal processes, providing a kind of quality control over the local administration of justice, but he could not function alone. In this sense, the court was much more than a judge and a set of laws: it was a local institution that was very much the product of its users' actions.

As the focal point where normative legal traditions came together, the court was most certainly a critical arena. But many studies of Ottoman legal practice err in failing to locate the court in its relation to other venues of dispute resolution. A final point to consider in this chapter, then, is the interaction of the Aintab court with other local legal venues. In Aintab, other communal mechanisms for problem solving existed to which the court had to more or less accommodate itself. The court records indicate that people often tried other venues first, or that other authorities might first intervene in local problems before they ended up in the court. And for every case that eventually came to court, there was probably another, or maybe several others, that were resolved locally. Village and neighborhood imams, for example, were commonly arbiters of disputes (Fatma's story involves a case that was first handled by a village imam). Elders of nomadic tribes arbitrated disputes among their people, and Ottoman authorities generally respected their legal autonomy except when intertribal tensions threatened to erupt into larger conflict or when tribal leaders themselves sought government intervention. Timariot cavalry assigned to villages had as one of their responsibilities the maintenance of local law and order, but when they encountered difficult cases, they, like local imams, either referred them to the court or personally brought them there. Moreover, individuals might create their own path to justice, as did the intrepid Şahpaşa, who established her claim to an oil press by first obtaining a fatwa, which she then took to the governor-general, who ordered the provincial governor of Aintab to see to its execution, whereupon the case finally came before the judge.[128] In sum, the court was only one, albeit the central, arena of justice in the province; and as the central arena, it necessarily cooperated with other local and regional arbiters of justice.

The question of judicial appeal often arises in connection with premodern Middle Eastern legal practice, where such recourse is perceived to be more or less lacking. Although Ottoman courts and judgeships were arranged in an order of precedence, there was only one level of courts and no higher judicial apparatus to reconsider the decisions of court judges. Strictly speaking, a judge's ruling could not be overturned, though a complaint could be lodged with regard to the judge's abuse of his office through corruption, bias, or failure to admit cases (see chapter 5 for further discussion of the problematic judge). Complaints could also be lodged against representatives of state authority in the province, the executive officials, for failure to enforce judicial decisions (see figure 6). Because both these types of complaint were about employees of the state, the process of appeal passed through the executive line of state authority rather than through the religious establishment. In other words, it was ultimately the responsibility of the sultan to ensure the integrity of the courts. In theory and sometimes in practice, even a poor peasant enjoyed the right to appeal through the chain of executive authority. The limited evidence in the Aintab court records suggests that people went above the provincial level of administration to appeal, petitioning either the regional governor-general or, more rarely, the sultan himself.

Islamic literature and art celebrate rulers who respected the mandate that sovereigns personally dispense justice, mainly corrective justice, to the lowliest of their subjects. However, the question remains of how available the option of petition was in practice for those who lived at a distance from the regional or imperial capital. The two or three Aintabans who actually petitioned the sultan, or more likely his council of ministers, in 1540–1541 were among the elite of the province. Ordinary individuals tended to go to the governor-general, Ali Pasha, who resided in the Dulkadir capital of Maraş. In pre-Ottoman times, the court of the governor-general had played a larger role in the administration of justice. As one of its reforms, the Ottoman government encouraged its subjects to take their legal problems to the local judge, thereby emphasizing the legal division of labor between judgment and enforcement. Indeed, the court records of 1540–1541 demonstrate that when Aintabans appealed directly to the governor-general, he almost always referred the trial phase of the matter to the Aintab judge. In sum, there appears to have been no real appeal of the legal merits of a decision itself, although, to repeat, a dissatisfied individual could protest the judge's personal competence or a lapse in the enforcement of a decision.

However, the case of Aintab, with its overlapping and interconnecting legal venues, suggests that raising questions about appeal might not necessarily be the only, or even the right, way to approach the structure of the legal system in the early modern Ottoman state. Rather, it was through the menu of local options, not through channels that took one outside local venues, that ordinary people enjoyed a degree of legal maneuverability. Where recourse to the law was voluntary (as it was in many private claims), Aintabans could choose among or combine legal resources, now preferring this one, now that. Making such choices required a degree of legal sophistication on the part of the court's constituency. People needed to recognize when it was appropriate or necessary to go to court, and what the advantages or disadvantages were to the various legal options available. Faced with a brewing dispute, for example, a person might have preferred to first obtain a fatwa ruling on the problematic issue, then go to court if the dispute proved intractable. The fact that the judge's ruling could not be appealed meant that going to court required careful calculation (so long as recourse to the judge was voluntary, of course). All this underlines the imperative that our study of the court records be firmly rooted in the local social, political, and moral terrain.

This is not to say that the court of Aintab was solely a community institution. It also "belonged" to the Ottoman regime as a part of its legal apparatus. We might think of the local court as the meeting place between subjects and sovereign where the two negotiated a balance of control over the management of local society. As we will see in chapter 7, the provincial court was an arena where the dialogue between ruler and ruled was conducted in a mutually intelligible language of duties and expectations. But the court was not only about sovereigns and subjects. It was also a place where Aintabans addressed each other. The presence of the court promoted interconnection among local legal resources, thereby adding a certain rigor and coherence to the grassroots delivery and consumption of the law. For Aintab, incorporation into the Ottoman regime's judicial system meant neither a justice imposed nor a justice bestowed, but rather a justice carefully and strategically facilitated.

PART TWO

Gender and the Terrain
of Local Justice

İne's Story
A Child Marriage in Trouble

In December 1540, the court of Aintab heard testimony from a village girl whose young life appeared to be troubled by a dangerous domestic situation. This chapter attempts to reconstruct the story of the child bride, İne, and her child husband, Tanrıvirdi. As her case opened, İne was living in the household of Tanrıvirdi's father, presumably until the time that the two were old enough to consummate their marriage and live together as a couple. What had apparently gone wrong in this arrangement was that Tanrıvirdi's father had raped İne, or so she accused him in court. İne's story is one of various interventions by the local court and the local community to save both the young marriage and the reputation of those involved. But the attempt to rescue the marriage ultimately failed, as İne and Tanrıvirdi appeared in court for a second time, nine months after the rape accusation, to register their divorce.

How did these events affect İne and others involved in this rupture of domestic relations? Unfortunately, their lives after the divorce recede into the unrecoverable past. The court record gives us only two scenes from the drama of İne and Tanrıvirdi—two stills, if you will—shutting down its camera when its involvement is done. But connecting the two stills is a narrative that can be plausibly reconstructed by situating clues from the two case records in the context of what other court cases and other sixteenth-century sources tell us about the local culture. The events that appear to have occurred in the lives of İne and Tanrıvirdi between their two court appearances—İne's accusation and the couple's subsequent divorce—suggest that much of the responsibility for resolving the family crisis was placed in the hands of the local community.

İne's story is a microexample of relations between an individual and her society. It suggests that the most insignificant of individuals—one who, on the surface, would not appear to be an influential member of her community or even of her family—can harness society's attention to resolve a situation that threatens her well-being. İne is able to do so, I argue, as much because her circumstances jeopardize the well-being of others as because her own social persona is at risk. It is the embeddedness of the individual in the fabric of local society—the danger that an individual rupture, a broken thread, might cause the whole fabric to unravel if left unmended—that provides İne with some leverage in her community.

The case of İne, Tanrıvirdi, their families, and their community underlines several of the themes developed in this book. The denouement of İne's accusation illustrates the notion of separate justices for individuals in conflict, for it would appear that İne's father-in-law is exonerated at the same time that the marriage is judged to be endangered in his household. Another theme echoed in İne's story is the interrelationship among the different resources in the community for dispelling social conflict: following the judge's hearing, mechanisms of dispute resolution beyond the court seem to be put into operation. The issue of the child marriage also points to the importance of place and its implications for the nature of justice: at the time of their divorce, Tanrıvirdi and İne have moved to the village of Cağdığın—a place with an unusual character in the provincial landscape. My reading of the role that Cağdığın plays in İne's story is derived in part from the fate of another young girl living in the village who is also thought to be at risk in marriage. Taken together, these two cases exemplify the variability of legal enforcement, and of legal thinking, across the provincial domain.

THE ACCUSATION

The scant facts of the domestic situation revealed in the first case record constituting İne's story suggest that the girl was present in her father-in-law's home as a result of a marriage arranged for the two children by their parents (in İne's case, one was a stepparent). Here is the text of the first court appearance involving İne and other members of the two households.

> İne daughter of Maksud, from the village of Hacer, came to court. Her father-in-law Mehmed son of Ümit was also present. The aforementioned [female] brought the following suit: "My father-in-law Mehmed raped me [lit., 'had illicit sex with me by force']; he destroyed my virginity." When Mehmed was questioned, he denied [this]. When the people of the village were questioned, they said: "Mehmed has been together with us from the time we were all children. We have never observed or heard of any wrongdoing on his part. We consider his people as friends." The girl's stepfather Hüdavirdi said: "Previously, several times I asked her, and İne denied [that anything was going

on], and never said anything. Now she is saying this." It was recorded as it happened.

Witnessed by: Mehmed b. Hüdavirdi, secretary; Ömer b. Haci; Haci Ahmed b. Halil, steward; Haci Ahmed b. Demircioğlu[1]

How common were such child marriages? Certainly the practice of parents "promising" a daughter to another family as future wife for their son was not uncommon in sixteenth-century Anatolia.[2] What is less clear from our sixteenth-century sources is how often the young couple was actually married, as İne and Tanrıvirdi appear to have been. In the case of promising, the child couple were *namzed,* pledged to one another, a status that appears to be distinguished from that of being engaged *(nişanlı),* the relationship between a couple of marriageable age before they wed. Our midcentury court records from Aintab as well as late-sixteenth-century records from Ankara give evidence of the practice of promising young children; this evidence comes mainly from arrangements that went awry and thus ended up in court. A pledged relationship might collapse, for example, when the future father-in-law decided to take another bride for his son,[3] or when the daughter, now of an age and degree of physical maturity to assume actual married life, rejected the husband chosen for her by her family.[4] Disputes over the money exchanged at the time of pledging (usually a payment in cash or kind by the future father-in-law to the girl's father) sometimes landed people in court, particularly when a pledging collapsed and one household attempted to recover its investment from the other.

While the practice of promising children was common enough, it is not clear how often it led to the girl taking up residence with the family to which she was pledged. That such an arrangement was not unknown in Aintab is suggested by a court case from July 1541 in which a father attempted to recover his daughter from the household of her husband-to-be, since the boy's father had chosen another bride for his son; the boy's father, however, refused to release the girl until her father paid the debt he had incurred for three and a half years' worth of his daughter's expenses. The sum that the girl's father had pledged for his daughter's support—3 akçes a day—was generous by Aintab standards, suggesting that these were relatively well-to-do households.[5] In Aintab, then, marriage practices that entailed a female child's move to her husband-to-be's home were not necessarily inspired by poverty, that is, by the desire to relieve the family of an extra mouth to feed.

An initial and important question arising from the above case, how İne managed to bring her problem to the court, may be unanswerable. The structure of Ottoman legal procedure—as we have seen, an amalgam of Islamic jurisprudence and sultanic law—required that an accusation of rape be made by the alleged victim and on her or his own initiative. Rape in sixteenth-century Ottoman legal thinking and practice stood somewhere between the category of private claims *(hakk adamî)*—that is, crimes of personal injury—and the category of crimes against God *(hakk Allah)* and, by extension, against society.[6] Private claims had to be brought before the judge by the aggrieved individual, while crimes against God—which included the crime of consensual illicit sex *(zina)*—were prosecuted by the sovereign authority and its delegates. Rape shared characteristics of both categories: the injured party had to initiate the suit, while local agents of imperial authority were generally also involved. In İne's case, the procedural requirement that the alleged victim bring the accusation herself was satisfied: the court's record opened directly with her accusation.

The record of İne's case, however, was typical of the Aintab registers from 1540–1541 in that it incorporated only the elements of the incident required by legal procedure. Thus it leaves us in the dark about many aspects of the case of great interest to us—for example, what provoked İne's journey from the allegedly abusive household to the provincial capital and its court. One plausible explanation is that members of İne's own family guided the case to court. Or perhaps a local authority in the village of Hacer, wishing to remove the dispute from his venue, prevailed on them to take İne's accusation to the Aintab judge. Another possibility is that the accused father-in-law Mehmed took the initiative in getting the case to court, in order to clear his name. This is a less likely scenario, however, because the court record frames the case as one of İne accusing Mehmed of rape, rather than Mehmed accusing İne of slander. One last possible explanation of İne's journey to the Aintab court is that the dispute simply erupted locally, threatened to get out of hand, and was inevitably dragged before the judge. The neatly ordered testimony of the written record, in other words, may mask a disordered conflict characterized by mutual recriminations.

The thrust of the protagonists' first appearance at court is, in fact, the clearing of the father-in-law's name. While no resolution of the question of whether Mehmed raped İne is explicitly stated, the structure of the record indicates that he was not found guilty. There were two legal principles at play in the disposition of the case. The first was that an accusation of illicit sex (whether the accuser was complicit in the act or coerced) was not valid without corroborating testimony.[7] The Qur'anic requirement of four witnesses to the illicit act, which had the effect of rendering prosecution of sexual crime virtually impossible, was relaxed in sixteenth-century Ottoman legal practice. Indeed, Hanafi jurisprudence itself acknowledged the need for admitting circumstantial evidence in order to prosecute illicit sex. The twelfth-century Hanafi jurist Al-Marghinani, whose legal manual was widely used in sixteenth-century Ottoman legal practice, noted that "whoredom being an act the nature of which most frequently excludes the possibility of positive proof, it is necessary that circumstantial evidence be admitted as sufficient to establish it, lest the door of correction might be shut."[8] However, Al-Marghinani's lengthy discussion of *zina* never considers how such evidence might work in practice. Prosecution of sexual crime in sixteenth-century courts was accomplished by allowing fewer than four witnesses and by admitting circumstantial and hearsay evidence, practices that were sanctioned by Süleyman's law book (dating from around 1540); the case of Ali and Ayşe in chapter 3 is an example. In the case at hand, the indirect evidence appears to be the "several times" that İne's stepfather Hüdavirdi asked her if all was well, and her several denials that anything was wrong in the household of her child husband. The weight given to this testimony of the stepfather suggests that had İne previously spoken of her father-in-law's illicit intentions, her statement would have been accepted by the court as corroborating evidence. Lacking any such evidence, İne's accusation stands uncorroborated.

The second legal principle informing the case was that a person with a reputation for sexual probity—that is, a person with no known suspicion or conviction of prior sexual misconduct—was protected against accusation of sexual crime. (Such a person was known by the legal term *muhsan/muhsana*.) That this principle was observed in the Aintab court is demonstrated by other cases, similar to this one, involving accusations of sexual misconduct (rape, attempted rape, or physical harassment). In those cases, the accused were safe unless they had a *töhmet*—a previous instance of publicly articulated suspicion of, or conviction of, wrongdoing. Here are summaries of two such cases:

> —The married peasant woman Canpaşa accuses one Hamza of entering her house at night, climbing into her bed, and assaulting her. Hamza denies this, whereupon investigation among the people of the village shows that he has been similarly accused with regard to another woman in the village and therefore has a *töhmet*. Hamza is sentenced to punishment by the judge.[9]

> —Mezid brings a case against Hüsniye, wife of Şeyhi, saying that when he was staying at their house, Hüsniye came to him in bed after Şeyhi had fallen asleep. Hüsniye's character is investigated, and three men of the neighborhood testify that "we have never known any ill conduct on her part, and we cannot say she is prone to bad behavior."[10] (Note that a woman could be accused of unwanted sexual aggression.)

In these two situations, the court sought the opinion of fellow villagers or residents in the same city district in order to establish the reputation of the accused. The same procedure was followed in İne's case: the residents of the village of Hacer gave testimony regarding the stepfather Mehmed's character, stating that as far as they knew, he was an individual of moral probity. These cases demonstrate the importance of reputation, which, as we see, was reified through the testimony of the community.

A note regarding terminology is perhaps in order here. The terms *töh-metsiz* (free of *töhmet*) and *töhmetlü* (having a *töhmet*) appear to be the legal vernacular for dealing with the concept of *muhsan/muhsana,* used in jurisprudence to mean a free person (i.e., someone not a slave) with no prior conviction of illicit sex.[11] In the court records, however, the term *töhmet* appears to encompass suspicion as well as conviction of illicit sexual activity (for further discussion of *töhmet,* see chapter 5).

THE COMMUNITY'S INTERVENTION

With an uncorroborated accusation and an accused with a communally certified good reputation, İne would seem to have lost her case. Moreover, she could be fined, at least in theory, for having made the accusation: wrongful accusation of illicit sex was a crime punishable, according to sultanic statute, by a flogging as well as a monetary fine.[12] Had the court record not contained a second case offering us clues to other modes of intervention into İne and Tanrıvirdi's situation, we might have concluded that İne was left defenseless in a domestic arrangement whose abusive threat had not been conclusively disproved. (Indeed, I worked with these court records for two years before I realized that the two cases were related; they are separated in the court registers by approximately 1,800 intervening records.)

While it is true that the formal intervention of the court ceased once it adjudicated the rape accusation, the process of dispute resolution appears to have continued beyond the appearance of the villagers from Hacer before the judge of Aintab. Even during the court hearing, the watchful eye of the community was already focused on them. The court proceedings were witnessed by two influential members of the Aintab community: the city steward *(şehir kethüda)* and the head of the Demirci family, one of the city's three most prominent families. A third witness, the secretary *(kâtib)* Mehmed b. Hüdavirdi, appears to have been a minor clerk in the provincial governor's service.[13] These individuals acted as case witnesses, or official signatories to the case record, whose responsibility was to ensure that the judge's handling of the case had been procedurally correct; as noted in the previous chapter, such individuals might or might not have a personal interest in the case. While the presence of four case witnesses was conventional for the Aintab court, such a high proportion of local dignitaries was not. In the view of both court and community, then, İne's case was recognized as being one of more than private concern.

This acknowledgment of the "public" aspect of İne's case stems in part from the historical role of the governing authority in prosecuting sexual crime or allegations thereof. In the Aintab court, instances of sexual crime regularly entailed the intervention of local officials whose authority derived ultimately from the Ottoman sultan, officials collectively designated as

"people of executive power" *(ehl-i örf)*. But more important to understanding İne's situation is the cultural thinking that undergirded this legal practice: the recognition that sexual crime was profoundly disruptive of social
harmony. Local order could be disturbed not only by criminal *acts* but by
words as well. The number of legal rules protecting people from accusation
of sexual crime reflected society's extreme concern with shielding the reputation of the individual against potentially slanderous talk. In İne's case,
harmonious relations within her larger family were doubtless disturbed by
her accusation of rape against her father-in-law. Even if the allegation was
not true, it suggested an unhappy child and an embryonic marriage at risk.
The potential failure of the marriage would in turn endanger relations between the two households and possibly precipitate a dispute over money.
And it was not only the male heads of household who might clash: while İne
and Tanrıvirdi's mothers were invisible in the court register, it is difficult
in the world of these records to imagine a mother unconcerned about her
child's well-being or, at the very least, unconcerned about how a child publicly in distress might affect the social well-being of her household.

The subsequent record of İne and Tanrıvirdi's divorce suggests that the
gravity of İne's accusation and its implications mobilized local attention
beyond the court's adjudication of the rape accusation. In the narrative
connecting İne's two court appearances, the community appears to have assumed responsibility for mending the social rupture. Here is the case record of the divorce, entered in the register on September 20, 1541:

> When Tanrıvirdi son of Mehmed and his wife İne daughter of Maksud, both
> from the village of Cağdığın, were present [at court], Tanrıvirdi said: "İne
> here is my wife. She has no pleasure in life living together with me. I gave her
> a cow worth 1,000 akçes, let her give it back to me and I'll give her a divorce;
> and let her also give up her waiting-period support and her dower and her
> other rights." When the said İne forfeited the cow and her waiting-period sup-
> port and her clothes right and her dower and her other rights, the aforemen-
> tioned Tanrıvirdi said, "I divorce İne with an irrevocable divorce." There re-
> maining no claim or suit by either against the other, they were separated from
> each other and it was recorded.
>   Witnessed by: Mehmed b. Ümit; Hüdavirdi b. Pir Ömer; Ömer b. Haci
> Mehmed; Mahmud b. Ahmed; Ustad Ali b. Hüseyin; Ali b. Abdullah[14]

Once again, what governs the construction of the written case record is the
requirement of correct legal procedure—that the divorce itself be enacted
according to law. And once again, details crucial to our understanding of
İne's story are not included. Absent, for instance, is an account of how İne
and Tanrıvirdi came to be living in the village of Cağdığın rather than in
Hacer. One clue we *do* have is the gap of nine months between İne's accusation and her divorce, the implication being that everyone was waiting just

to be sure that İne was not pregnant. And the fact that the judge pronounced a "separation" *(tefrik)* suggests recognition of the case's special circumstances. The permissible grounds for separation were limited, including the husband's impotence and the wife's right to repudiate the marriage on coming of age, but a judge might act on his own initiative if he perceived a serious impediment to the marriage.[15]

At first glance, it might seem that İne's life was not much improved in her new residence, even though the young couple were now removed from direct exposure to the tensions present in Tanrıvirdi's paternal household. Tanrıvirdi's brief statement in the divorce proceedings was unusual in these records in citing an emotional state of mind, and it revealed a girl who continued to be so unhappy in her marriage that the only solution was to dissolve it.[16] Fortunately, the court record carries clues to suggest how the community intervened in an effort, however vain it might have been, to repair İne and Tanrıvirdi's domestic lives. The most important clue is the village to which they moved, Cağdığın.[17]

THE VILLAGE OF CAĞDIĞIN

Cağdığın may have had a special character among the villages close to Hacer, where İne and Tanrıvirdi's own families lived. It was considerably smaller than Hacer, which was one of the most populous villages of the province. The distance between the two villages was about 4 kilometers, not so great as to prevent the children's families from regular contact with them, or even from daily supervision over them.[18] Indeed, that the families continued to have a stake in their children's lives is suggested by the appearance of Tanrıvirdi's father and İne's stepfather as the first case witnesses of the divorce.

What is important about Cağdığın for our purposes is that it may have had a reputation for more rigorous ethical standards than did the surrounding communities. This is suggested by another case, entered into the Aintab court register on August 16, 1541, in which the village elders of Cağdığın acted to protect a young girl about to be given in marriage.

> Ali son of Mahmud, from the village of Cağdığın, summoned Hüseyin Fakih son of Ali to court and said: "Previously this Hüseyin Fakih got permission from the judge of Aintab, His Honor Seyyid Cafer, to marry his stepdaughter Sultan daughter of Haci Mehmed to me. When we arrived at the above-named village, the elders of the village declared: 'The girl is too young, be patient, let her grow up. You are moral people [lit, "you are Muslims"].' I have been waiting since then. But our official betrothal did not take place at that time." Because he made this statement, it was recorded.
>
> Witnessed by: Haci Ahmed the steward b. Halil; Haci Ali b. Cüneyd; Mehmed b. Hızır[19]

Here we have another case of a child bride given in marriage by her stepfather. The latter may have anticipated the resistance of the village community, given that he went to the trouble of securing the judge's permission. Nonetheless, the leading members of the village *(köy devletlüleri)* intervened to postpone the formal marriage and its consummation until the girl matured. What finally brought Ali to the judge to register the statement above is that he got tired of waiting, as is demonstrated by subsequent cases involving his suit to recover the dower he had given Sultan.[20]

What is significant in this case is that the village, in the form of its leading citizens, stood up not only to the two households involved in the marriage arrangement but also to the office of the provincial judge. In preventing the giving in marriage of a girl it considered too immature, the village demonstrated the ability of a local community to set its own standards of social and moral conduct as well as to enforce them. In this regard, it is noteworthy that it is to Ali's moral standards—"you are a good Muslim"—that the village elders appeal in persuading him to postpone the marriage. This case stands out in the court records for 1540–1541 for the boldness of its protagonists in resisting established authorities—indeed, it is unique.

How does this incident connect to İne's case? My hypothesis is that the child couple was deliberately placed in Cağdığın as a measure intended to be both protective and rehabilitative. It was a common custom in Aintab, as elsewhere, to involve people of good repute in the resolution of disputes. The court records often label such persons "Muslims," indicating not their sectarian identity but rather their righteousness. Sometimes such persons are called *musalihun* (peacemakers), especially when they act as arbiters in a formal process of mediation recognized by the court. A fatwa from a late-sixteenth-century chief mufti, Sunullah Efendi, suggests that it was an accepted practice to entrust troubled domestic situations to the watchful eye of neighborhoods with a reputation for probity. The mufti was asked for a legally correct answer to the following question: A woman has married on the condition that she not have to leave her own home; now her husband is insisting that she move with him and is abusing her over the matter: can she refuse to accompany him? Sunullah's response: "No, she can't. To prevent [him] from depravity and dissolution, the judge should imprison him, and, after his release, order the couple to take up residence among righteous people *(kavm-ı salih)* so that [he] cannot torment [her]. If he persists, he should be punished according to the judge's decision and imprisoned again."[21]

What I want to suggest is that İne and Tanrıvirdi have been placed in Cağdığın under the supervision of the community in an attempt to rescue their marriage, or at least to protect them during the nine months' wait. Sheltering them in a safe space might help prevent a rupture in the relations between their families as well as in their own lives. Perhaps the young couple was living in the household of a Cağdığın relative or with a local family established as a kind of guardian. As mentioned above, Cağdığın was within fairly easy visiting distance of Hacer. One of Cağdığın's advantages was the relative smallness of the village (58 households vs. Hacer's 123),[22] making it easier to watch out for the welfare of individuals at risk. The arrangement may have been informal, but it may also have been worked out with the guidance of authorities. Perhaps the invisible architect of this structure of dispute resolution was the city steward, who appeared as case witness both at the beginning of the affair and at the dissolution of the child marriage.

Several aspects of the two Cağdığın court cases involving the protection of young girls given in marriage are worth noting. The city steward, Ahmed b. Halil, who apparently tracked İne's case, also appeared as a case witness in the case just cited. This does not argue for any explicit connection between the two incidents, since the steward often appeared as case witness, but it does suggest that problems stemming from child marriage were considered significant enough to warrant his involvement.

Another, more striking, commonality between these cases that links Cağdığın to the plight of young girls is that both İne and Sultan were given in marriage by stepfathers. Assuming that both females have lost their fathers (who otherwise would presumably be arranging marriages for their daughters), they were orphans in the eyes of the law. The welfare of orphans was the responsibility not only of their remaining relatives but also of the community at large and specifically of the judge, who had the authority to appoint a guardian from the community. In Sultan's case, the elders of Cağdığın may have stepped in to act as guardian. Whatever their role, official or not, the elders appear to have been resisting abuse of the practice of child marriage, either by mothers lacking the financial support typically provided by fathers or by stepfathers anxious to unload the burden of supporting their wives' children.[23] While it was suggested above that child marriage in Aintab was not a strategy resorted to only by those in need, some must have found tempting the monetary advantage usually gained by giving a girl in early marriage.

The village elders were not acting in an unduly conservative or anachronistic fashion in their attempt to forestall abuses in the contracting of marriage. The same concern can be observed in various fatwas on the relationship between guardians and their wards issued by the Ottoman jurist Ebu Suud Efendi. More than once Ebu Suud insisted that when a girl was given in marriage by a guardian other than her father or grandfather, the marriage had to be sanctioned by the local judge.[24] This regulation was part of a larger move at the center of empire to bring the contracting of marriage under the control of legal authorities. In 1544, some three years after the court records studied here, Süleyman, the reigning sultan and patron of Ebu Suud, issued a decree that no marriage contract was valid "without the cognizance of a judge."[25] In a fatwa rearticulating the sultanic decree, Ebu Suud gave as his rationale a concern for avoiding the disruptive aftermath when such marriages didn't work out: the approval of the judge was necessary, he commented, "lest dispute and litigation ensue." What the mufti wished to prevent, in other words, was the very scenario precipitated by İne's accusation against Tanrıvirdi's father.

In insisting on the maturity of the female as a prerequisite for marriage, the elders of Cağdığın shared with the sultan and the mufti an interest in imposing stricter rules on marital alliances. However, in resisting the judge-approved marriage, the village elders seem to have been saying that the judge's standards, particularly as they affected young brides, were not high enough. Perhaps the villagers were simply protesting an individual case, with no larger agenda behind their action. On the other hand, they may have been resisting the expanding scope of Ottoman legal administration, clearly visible in the changes that were taking place in the Aintab court. Although this case occurred three years before the sultan's decree on guardianship, there was already ample evidence in Aintab province of the increasing public regulation of what had traditionally been more private practices.[26]

A SEPARATE IDENTITY

There was another feature of the village of Cağdığın that may have contributed to its special character. Villages in Aintab, as elsewhere, varied in the status of their land: most were part of the state domain, while other villages were private property or *waqf* land—that is, the property of foundations established by local notables or by sultans. As the private property of an eminent family, the village of Cağdığın was hardly unusual. What *was* unusual was the identity of Cağdığın's owners: the heirs of the last powerful Mamluk sultan, Qansuh Al-Ghawri. It was Al-Ghawri who in 1516 died defending the Mamluk empire against the Ottoman military engine on a battlefield not far from Aintab. Like the descendants of other royal families conquered by the Ottomans, Al-Ghawri's heirs were absorbed into the Ottoman elite. Or at least that was the fate of a branch of the family based in Aleppo: we learn from a 1574 survey of Aintab that the current head of the family was the governor-general of Aleppo, Mehmed Pasha.[27] Even more interesting, at the time of İne's case the Ghawri family's several holdings in Aintab province had passed from the former Mamluk sultan's son into the hands of a woman: Al-Ghawri's granddaughter Fatima Hatun, the mother of the future governor of Aleppo.[28]

In all probability Fatima Hatun did not often, or perhaps ever, visit the village of Cağdığın. The Ghawri family employed a local agent, one Haci

Hüseyin b. Abdullah, to manage their estates and collect taxes, as we learn from a case pertaining to a loan transaction in which he was involved.[29] However, physical absence does not mean that a powerful person's presence as overlord was not felt. Halil İnalcık has suggested that peasants on waqf lands, and particularly on imperial waqf lands, were often accorded privileged treatment.[30] This may have also been true of villages that were the waqf or private property of *local* notables, such as Al-Ghawri's heirs (the Ghawri family's possessions in Aintab province were in 1541 in the process of transformation into a family waqf).[31] What I am suggesting in connection with Cağdığın is that ownership of a village—either directly or indirectly as waqf—by a person of high status may have influenced the village's character.

That that person was female may have special relevance to İne's case. The sixteenth-century historical record of the women of the Ottoman dynasty contains a number of stories testifying to their compassion and concern for other women, especially those who were at risk or had fallen on hard times, such as prostitutes, convicts, and orphans. In May 1541, for example, midway between İne's two court appearances, the grand vezir Lutfi Pasha was dismissed from office after he was divorced by his wife, the sister of the sultan Süleyman, over a dispute concerning his inhumane treatment of a prostitute.[32] The influence of female patronage and protection might also manifest itself in the management of land. For example, Machiel Kiel tells us that even today, the inhabitants of the Bulgarian village of Bobosevo, which had formed part of the holdings of Süleyman's granddaughter, still remember that their village was under the protection of a princess, or "under the veil of a sultana," as they put it.[33]

As for Mamluk royal women, Carl Petry has drawn our attention to the remarkable degree to which women of the Mamluk ruling elite were assigned custodianship over property. He underlines the authority accrued by such women through their roles in "the preservation of lineages over time as well as the integrity of estates."[34] Fatima Hatun was no longer royalty, but she was of a distinguished family, one whose reputation in the Aintab region, only recently conquered from the Mamluks, was still influential. It is not unreasonable to suggest that Cağdığın's protection of young girls at risk in early marriages may have owed something to her stewardship of the village.

Cağdığın was doubtless known in the area, by peasants and officials alike, as a Ghawri village. That identity might have enhanced the village elders' ability to defend different social standards and practices. At issue here is an important aspect of the variability of justice: namely, the fact that the administrative status of a village—to whom it paid its taxes, whether it was state land, freehold property, or waqf—could affect the cultural environment of the village, its moral outlook, and the nature of justice available to it. In other words, the Aintab court records suggest that enforcement of the law varied across the provincial jurisdiction, depending on the status of the local community. In the case of Cağdığın, it is worth remembering that while Aintab was a flourishing provincial center in its own right, it lay in the economic and political orbit of Aleppo. A village with direct ties to Aleppo may have enjoyed more leverage over Aintab officials than did other villages in the province. More important, the village's links to a notable family connected with the prestigious Mamluk sultanate, whose demise was a recent memory, may have helped it resist the enforcement of Ottoman regulations by local Ottoman-appointed authorities, such as the judge. The Mamluk sultans had supported all four schools of sunni Islamic law, an indirect acknowledgment of the autonomy of sharia. The Ottoman sultan, in contrast, not only supported a single school, the Hanafi, but would shortly himself undertake to interpret what was traditionally the domain of religious authorities.

I am arguing here not for a specific Mamluk loyalism in Cağdığın, but rather for a sense of identity that enabled the village elders to take a stand for moral and administrative autonomy. As depicted in court records and state surveys (the two principal sources for local history in the sixteenth century), Cağdığın was a distinctly unusual place. If indeed İne and Tanrıvirdi were deliberately removed from the household and village of Tanrıvirdi's father, it is perhaps no coincidence that it was in Cağdığın and not some other village in the area that we find them living in the months before their divorce.

·   ·   ·

The intervention of the court and other members of the greater Aintab community did not necessarily produce a victory for İne. She apparently endured much pain. Moreover, her association with rape and slander probably continued to plague her, perhaps making it harder for a satisfactory second marriage to be arranged for her as she matured. What İne gained, however, was what she may have wished for all along: a recognition that the child marriage in which she was placed was untenable and unbearable.

To what extent was İne herself responsible for this outcome? I have been arguing that her power consisted of her capacity to get a hearing from the community. But how much of a role did she herself actually play in having her plight acknowledged? As suggested above, while the court record honored legal protocol in framing the accusation of rape as a case initiated by İne, any one of a number of individuals might have been the party responsible for translating domestic tensions into a journey to the provincial court. On the other hand, a child could well have understood that an accusation of illicit sex was bound to attract the community's attention. In other words, it is not implausible that İne was in fact the central actor in publicizing her dilemma.

But İne's capacity to get a hearing is not solely a result of her own agency; it is also the result of her location in a network of relationships. İne has leverage insofar as she exists in more than one social dimension. The court record focuses on her as the pivot of the problem, but everyone else who is involved has a story as well. While the record portrays İne exclusively in her relation to men, the absence of the two households' females in the written representation of the case does not mean they were not central players in the drama. Moreover, İne's social location is not bounded by family relationships: her probable status as an orphan places her in a relationship with the community, who compensate for the absence of a father.

That the individual is empowered by virtue of his or her social location may seem a banal observation. The point I am underscoring is that the legal process focuses on the individual as only one element in the social whole. Its operations are based on the premise that a rupture in one relation puts numerous other relationships at risk. İne's case may begin as a potential instance of child abuse, but it is never exclusively defined as that. The overarching concern of this community—and the aim of its dispute-resolving mechanisms—is to preserve social order. It sees itself as safe when the individual is safe, and the well-being of the smallest is therefore the concern of the greatest. The corollary to this social vision is that the resolution of disputes must spread "justice" around. In other words, no one receives a monopoly on justice since others would by definition lose. At the same time, this zero-sum game tries to preserve some equity for all. The principle of separate justices is at work in İne's case: the stepfather is cleared of the charge of rape, but İne is removed from his household and ultimately freed from the marriage. What İne's story demonstrates is that in this sixteenth-century community, disparities of power, while inevitable, were not unchallenged. It is İne's ability to claim her share of social equity from the community that constitutes her power.

4

Gender, Class, and Social Hierarchy

It was not an ideal of the premodern Ottoman legal system that its justice be blind. Not until the mid–nineteenth century was the idea entertained that the law should encounter the individual as a notional entity rather than as a particular combination of social and civil attributes to be scrutinized and entered into the calculus of judgment. Gender was a fundamental one of these attributes. The boundary between male and female is immediately visible in the Aintab court in the labels employed by scribes to identify all litigants and witnesses who were not freeborn Muslim men—namely, Christians and Jews, freedmen, slaves, minors, and females. Of these categories of "others," that of female was the most populous at court and the focus of our interest here. What is not immediately visible, however, because it was not labeled, was one's place in the social hierarchy. Social class had a significant impact on the ways in which gender roles were defined in the world of the law.

This chapter looks at gender and social class as two aspects of identity that interacted to shape legal thinking and legal processes on the ground. The chapter moves back and forth between normative legal prescriptions and practices in the Aintab court. As social and legal categories, neither gender nor social class was monolithic or even stable. For example, the category of female was nuanced by one's place in the life cycle, with married female householders most active at court. And although social hierarchy was an inescapable element in legal culture, class boundaries fluctuated and people were uncertain as to how to place themselves and others. Knowing where one stood was important since social class affected certain aspects of legal process directly (for example, in the sliding scale of fines prescribed for the wealthy, the middle class, and the poor). Sociolegal thinking also attributed a greater capacity for moral awareness and moral conduct to the privileged classes, an assumption that led in turn to differential sanctions on certain kinds of crimes.

There was an integral relationship between gender and class, in part because female conduct was a prime marker of class identity. The most obvious distinction was that women of the privileged classes held themselves conspicuously aloof from public venues. A set of questions submitted to Ebu Suud, the Ottoman chief mufti from 1545 until his death in 1574, suggests that people were uncertain about what sort of female conduct identified one as privileged. The mufti confirmed the norm of female seclusion as a marker of elite status. But at the same time, Ebu Suud recognized a legal conundrum in the possibility that elite women might avoid the public arena of the court (as in fact they did in Aintab); their failure to participate in the legal system might lead to "the languishing of rights," as he put it. This was indeed a source of tension for the Ottoman regime, as it attempted to persuade people to patronize its expanding court system but at the same time was disinclined to disturb ingrained social practices of difference.

In other words, shifting norms of legal thinking at the center of empire were interacting with a varied landscape of gender and social class in the provincial setting. It should not be surprising, therefore, that this chapter argues for no certainties, no definite "conclusions." What it does claim is that fluctuation spelled a degree of flexibility. There was give in the court's practice that allowed different individuals to argue in justification for acts that on the surface implied contradictory norms. The final section of the chapter looks at a number of court cases for perspective on local debates about class, morality, and honor. Centering on the question of male-female contact, the cases suggest that there was a lack of uniform opinion among Aintabans on the key question of proper female conduct. Although it appears that Hüsameddin Efendi, the judge appointed in the early summer of 1541, introduced greater legal scrutiny of contact between the sexes, there was notable variation in the way instances of potentially illegal conduct were heard at court. But uniformity *can* be found in the concern of individuals at court to argue the moral propriety of their actions. In doing so, ordinary Aintabans challenged the notion that moral stature was a prerogative of the elites.

RECORDING DIFFERENCE: THE COURT'S VOCABULARY OF IDENTITY

The consistency with which scribes recorded more or fewer labels to identify various individuals at court suggests that there was a kind of standard or "default" identity. This was the freeborn Muslim male adult. It was against this standard that the identity of all others was defined. Adult males were labeled in the record only by name (including patronymic—for example, Osman b. Ali, or Osman son of Ali) and place of residence. Others, however, were additionally labeled by whatever attributes differed from this standard: sex, religion, status as slave, status as freedperson, nomadic tribal affiliation, and, if the litigant had not reached legal majority, status as a minor.

Women constituted the largest group marked by the court record as "not standard," as "other." There was a particular redundancy built into the court record's marking of women, since they were regularly labeled as female even though their gender was automatically indicated in their patronymic—*bint,* "daughter of" (e.g., Fatma bt. Ahmed, or Fatma daughter of Ahmed). An example of the court's labeling is its identification of "the female person named Tura bt. Musa" *(Tura bint Musa nam hatun kişi),* who came to court to claim her donkey, which had wandered off and been found in a cave.[1] This redundancy reinforces the point about the court's habit of ascribing difference. It was not enough, it seems, to leave the stipulation of a female's gendered identity to the patronymic embedded in her name; rather, as a fundamental category of difference from the male default, femaleness had to be explicitly acknowledged.

As it marked women in introducing them into the written record, so did court protocol mark non-Muslims, slaves, freedpersons, nomads, children, and sometimes villagers as "other." Tura bt. Musa was also identified as Kurdish, her comparatively long label—*Ekrâd taifesinden Tura bint Musa nam hatun kişi*—indicating a doubled otherness, tribal nomadic as well as female. When a young boy made a complaint at court about being harassed on the street, he was identified as "the youth Ali b. Uğur," while his assailant, an adult male, was simply Davud b. Mahmud. When "the black slave named Mubarek b. Abdullah" was summoned to court as accomplice to an abduction, his partner, the mastermind of the operation, was simply Hamza b. Mehmed Fakih. Another slave, "tall and black," was not even named in the record when he was arrested as a fugitive, most likely because, in the eyes of the court, his identity could not be confirmed (he claimed he had been freed by his former owner but had lost his certificate of manumission in the confusion of his arrest).[2]

As for non-Muslims, the Armenian Christians of Aintab were routinely referred to in the court record as "the *dhimmi* So-and-so." *Dhimmi*—"the protected"—is the general term for Christians and Jews in Muslim-governed states. When an Armenian woman and a Muslim male came to court to register his loan of 13 gold pieces to her, the record identified the man simply as "Ali b. Abdurrahman" and the woman with the double label of "the female *dhimmi* Hemdi bt. İskender."[3] Because Armenians were for all practical purposes the only non-Muslims in mid-sixteenth-century Aintab, their religion was rarely specified; only once in the 1540–1541 records was an individual identified as "the Christian So-and-so" *(nasranî).*[4] The term "Armenian" was not unfamiliar to Aintabans, however: on one of the occasions when members of the Armenian community of Aintab acted in court as a collective, they referred to themselves as Armenian *(Arameniya taifesi),*[5] and in the cadastral survey of 1543, the city neighborhood in which most of them lived, the district of Heyik, was referred to as "the district of the Armenians" *(mahalle-i Armeniya).*[6] The only Jew to figure in the court records of 1540–1541, the financier Matuk b. Sadullah, was routinely introduced as *yahudi,* "the Jew."

A word needs to be said about ethnicity, since it might be expected to figure prominently as a category of identity, given that the heterogeneous Muslim population of Aintab was made up of what today we would call Turks, Arabs, and Kurds, each with their own distinct language. Yet in the court's taxonomic hierarchy ethnicity was a label only for tribal nomadic groups unassimilated to urban culture, thereby reflecting what ethnicity connoted in the premodern Middle East. In Aintab, this meant Turkmens, Kurds, and the occasional Arabic-speaking Bedouin. In other words, no city or village resident was formally labeled "Turk" or "Arab," although the tribal past of settled Turkmens or Kurds was often remembered as a nickname, such as "the little Turkmen" or "Kurd So-and-so." Rather, ethnicity was a marker of nonsedentary cultures, a label of "nonresidency" and therefore, in the eyes of the "resident," of the absence of the civilizational attributes of the sedentary. This primacy of the sedentary and especially of urban cultural identity is revealed in the court's habit of sometimes omitting residence in its labels when the individual lived in Aintab city, making the urban Muslim male the ultimate standard of identity.[7]

The Aintab court's taxonomy of identity was not simply a locally generated aid in identifying and ranking social groups. Not surprisingly, it reflected legal categories laid out in sharia and kanun. The social hierarchy established by the court's labeling practice ran parallel, for example, to the hierarchy of who was eligible to act as witness in court. Bearing witness in court was fundamental both to the court's structure and to the legal processes it authorized. It was also an important marker of the individual's membership in local civil society. There were two levels at which witnesses functioned at court: personal witnessing and case witnessing. The first was the giving of testimony by witnesses who spoke in support of either a given plaintiff or defendant, confirming their statements or bringing forward supporting evidence. Case witnessing, in contrast, was testimony to the validity of the proceedings as a whole. Case witnesses for a particular case—the *şuhud ul-hal*—were members of the community, usually three or four in number, whose names were invariably inscribed in the court register following the record of the case. As we saw in chapter 3, case witnessing can be considered a structural element in local court procedure.

Only an adult Muslim male could perform the office of case witness. This restricted eligibility had the result of rendering the court taxonomy's "default" identity coterminous with the formal constitution of the legal system.

Persons labeled as "other" could not serve as case witnesses. They might act as personal witnesses, but only so long as they themselves enjoyed full legal personhood: thus slaves and minors were limited to speaking only on their own behalf at court.[8] Personal witnessing by adult women and non-Muslims was generally confined to instances when theirs was the only reliable testimony to be had. In fact, in the Aintab records for 1540–1541, women acted as witnesses on only four occasions. In other words, there was a preference for Muslim male testimony whenever possible, even when the plaintiff initiating a case was a woman. Except in connection with events occurring in an all-female environment, it took two female witnesses to equal the testimony of a single male, as in the case of Ayşe's alleged rape, described in chapter 3, where three men and two women constituted the requisite four witnesses for a case of sexual crime. One outcome of these restrictions on witnessing by females was that women sometimes had to take extraordinary measures if they wanted to have their voices written into the court record, as we will see later in this chapter.

Another area where the court's taxonomy of identity overlapped the prescriptions of normative law was the sharia penalty structure for various crimes. In the matter of compensation for bodily injury or homicide, for example, injuries to women and slaves were less heavily punished than injuries to males. When blood money *(diyet)* was due for homicide or intentional wounding, sharia prescribed that the amount paid for a woman should be half the amount for a man.[9] A female's status here was thus parallel to her status with regard to witnessing, as it also was with regard to inheritance, where, for example, daughters received half the amount of property that sons did and widows half that of widowers. In the case of abortion intentionally caused by another, the blood money owed for a female fetus was one-tenth that of a male, and for a slave one-twentieth.[10] Freeborn males, in other words, were more valuable in this cultural calculation of personal worth. The implicit rationale was the productive economic role men were assumed and expected to play and their legal responsibility for the support of their families. It is noteworthy that Hanafi law (but *only* Hanafi law among the four sunni schools of law) afforded dhimmi males protection equal to that of Muslim males in regard to personal injury and homicide.[11] This was a comment on the economic value of the labor and earning ability of free males in general and on the critical contribution of dhimmis to the economies of premodern states.

A similar attitude toward the differential valuation of "others" can be seen in kanun, where the clauses on punishment in the sultanic law books often fined them at lower rates. For example, in the areas of sexual crime (adultery and fornication) and crimes against the person, non-Muslims and slaves paid only half the fine imposed on Muslims.[12] (The question of women's accountability for criminal acts is less straightforward, since it is so closely linked to the question of social class; it thus will be taken up in the next section of this chapter.) The rationale for this attitude of kanun was most likely derived from social attitudes that had been inscribed in sharia.[13] The twelfth-century Hanafi jurist al-Marghinani, whose legal handbook was popular among sixteenth-century Ottomans, explained the disparities in sharia penalties for adultery on the grounds that the higher one's status in society, the graver one's transgression of its rules. Accounting for the lesser punishment of the slave, he stated, "[A]s bondage occasions the participation of only half the blessings of life, it also occasions the suffering of only half the punishments, because an offense increases in magnitude in proportion to the magnitude of blessing under the enjoyment of which it is committed."[14]

In sum, the Aintab court's taxonomy of identity reflected a hierarchy of valuing persons that was laid out in jurisprudence and in sultanic kanun. But this language of difference in the labeling of people at court does not tell the whole story of what actually went on there. While it parallels structural features of the court, such as witnessing, its relation to the status of users of the court is more complex. To a degree, the court's labeling practices predict frequency of use of the court—city dwellers appeared more often than did villagers and nomads, men more than women, slaves rarely, Armenian villagers never. But the court's taxonomy does not predict other phenomena: it does not explain why women were as vocal at court as men in certain matters (such as their property rights and their honor), why the Aintab elite did not use the court in many matters, why the court seemed to be more open to ordinary folk, or why a person from one village enjoyed easier access to the court than did someone from the next village. In other words, the Aintab court, like every other local court, operated within a particular set of historical, geographical, social, and political contingencies that affected the degree to which normative categories were predictive of actual patterns of use.

THE AGES OF WOMAN

Through its insistence on distinguishing female from male by labeling all women by their sex, the court record signals that gender is a category of analysis appropriate to mid-sixteenth-century Aintab.[15] Indeed, the records make it possible to trace differences in strategies employed by women and men, and also to trace the particular constraints operating on the two sexes within family and community that necessitated those strategies. Yet, as feminist studies in recent decades have taught us, we must interrogate the absolute category of gender by factoring into our analyses other categories that intersect it, such as race, class, sexual orientation, and slavery; for Aintab, religion and "residential lifestyle"—urban, peasant, or nomadic—are also relevant categories. Indeed, while the Aintab court records clearly de-marcate femaleness and maleness as fundamental determinants of social identity, they also suggest that to regard "female" or "male" as a monolithic category at court is to obscure other social divisions inscribed in legal dis-course. As we have seen, gender is only one element in the vocabulary of difference employed by the court.

Moreover, the court approached the representation of gender in a nu-anced way. In composing the records of legal proceedings, judge and scribe never used an abstract, all-encompassing term for "female"; rather, they la-beled females according to their life-cycle stage. Three such life-cycle labels appear in the records: *kız,* the female child or unmarried adolescent; *gelin,* the newly married young woman; and *avret* or *hatun,* the female adult, mar-ried or once-married and now divorced or widowed. Similarly, the court rarely had need for a general term for "male." Adulthood required no label for men, since it was a given in the default identity, but two other life-cycle labels were employed by the court for males: *oğlan,* the child or unmarried adolescent, and *pir-i fanî,* the senile.[16] This multiplicity of vocabulary sug-gests that gender identity continually transformed itself over the course of one's life span, as different normative behaviors were associated with each phase in the life cycle.[17] To be female or male was therefore to be charac-terized by a gender identity that was neither monolithic nor static.

The points where parallelism of vocabulary for male and female life cy-cles breaks down can alert us to some of the social contexts that determined gendered identity. Take, for instance, the new bride—the *gelin,* a category not found in formal jurisprudence but salient in popular usage. There is no parallel among males, no explicit language for the "new groom." The ex-planation for this discrepancy lies in the customary vector of physical move-ment at the time of marriage, when the new bride became a subordinate adjunct of her husband's family. It was generally she, not the young hus-band, who made the spatial transition into marriage by moving into the household of his parents (the term *gelin* derived from the verb *gelmek,* "to come," one of whose idiomatic meanings was "to marry"). The word em-phasized that the young bride had as yet no identity except as an affiliate to her husband's family.[18] It was she, not her husband, who was "new" to her environment.

The female adult, in contrast—the *avret* or *hatun*—acquired her identity from the establishment of her own household unit with the birth of chil-dren. This event was often accompanied by a physical move into a separate residence. The everyday adjective for the married person—*evli,* literally "having a house"—suggests that household-as-residence was seen as a fun-damental constituent of full adulthood.[19] This convergence of household and the production of children reflects the widespread view of parenthood as critical in establishing full personhood in the community. The conjugal tie possessed considerable social significance in that it legitimated sexual activity, but the newly married couple was an incipient household as yet lacking its own identity. More than marriage itself, childbearing and child-rearing transformed men and women into socially mature adults. There was, however, a gender disparity in this signaling of adulthood, as the existence of two labels for the married woman—new bride and female adult—suggests. It was the female member of the marital pair—the bearer of the child—whose changing status marked the inception of the new household. Correspondingly, it was she who experienced greater pressure to bear children, to move from the status of *gelin* to that of *avret*. Hence the life-cycle phase of the new bride ideally was brief; consequently, it is a category met infrequently in the court records and contemporary fatwas, where women are most often referred to as *avret*.

Inevitably, these definitions raise the question of childlessness. In theory, a wife's prolonged failure to produce children was justification for her husband to take another wife or a concubine (the children of slave concubines were considered freeborn under Islamic law, unlike Roman law). In other words, a (fertile) Muslim man need not remain childless, another disparity between the sexes. But the Aintab records yield no evidence of polygyny, though a few men possessed slave women who might have been concubines. In this respect, the records add to the evidence provided in other studies that polygyny was not widely practiced in early modern Ottoman Anatolia. (In fact, an influential treatise on ethics from 1564, Kınalızade Ali's *Ahlak-ı Ala'î*, opposed polygyny, arguing that "just as one soul cannot inhabit two bodies, one male cannot occupy two houses.")[20] Rather, there is evidence of small families and even of childlessness in several Aintab records detailing the settlement of estates; sometimes the deceased left only one or two, or even no, sons or daughters as heirs, as a result of either infertility or their children's untimely death.[21] For example, the heirs to the substantial estate of the former warden of the Aintab fortress, Hüseyin Ağa b. Yusuf, included his mother, wife, sister, and brother (Ali Çelebi, a prominent textile merchant), but no children.[22]

Childlessness did not mean that childless women were deprived of the status of female householder, however. A flexible notion of family that allowed children to be informally adopted by relatives other than their parents made it possible for women who lacked offspring of their own to add motherhood to their identity. While the law provided options for ensuring the possibility of fatherhood, social practice was what helped childless women. A powerful sanction for motherhood by adoption was provided by the Prophet Muhammad's favorite and childless wife 'A'isha: complaining that she alone among the Prophet's wives had no *kunya*, or honorary parental designation, Muhammad gave her the *kunya* of Umm 'Abd Allah, "the mother of 'Abd Allah," her nephew.[23] Perhaps İl Hatun, whom we met in chapter 2 as she gave up her infant daughter in order to assume a life of pious devotion in Jerusalem, enabled a childless couple to become parents. Similarly, the presence of slaves and other adjuncts to the domestic unit allowed a household to be constituted by dependents other than natural children. For example, a baby girl abandoned in the Alaeddevle mosque was taken in by one Mehmed b. Haci İbrahim, who had found her and who pledged at court to take on the responsibility of her support.[24] In another case, the woman Fatma bt. Cuma registered at court that Kamer bt. Ali was her *besleme*—a servant girl whom she was bringing up in her household.[25] Perhaps the foundling in the mosque was to play the same role as Kamer. Household heads, male and female alike, had a responsibility—indeed, an obligation—to ensure that their dependents made appropriate marriages; conversely, dependents continued either to serve the household directly or to remain linked with it in a kind of clientage relationship.

The distinction between the life-cycle stages of the newly married and the mature married woman observed by the Aintab court records is, interestingly, not found in sharia definitions of female maturity. Social usage, in other words, could modify or elaborate on legal categories. In Hanafi jurisprudence (the school of Islamic jurisprudence followed by the Ottoman state, though not all of its subjects), both males and females were traditionally considered to have come of age—to have arrived at legal majority *(buluğ)*—when signs of physical maturation were observable; in the absence of such signs, both females and males were considered legally mature at fifteen. In some sixteenth-century Ottoman interpretations of sharia, however, the age of maturity in such a case was deemed seventeen for females and eighteen for males. At least that was the opinion of the renowned jurist Ebu Suud, from 1537 onward a principal interpreter of religious law to the empire's ruler and subjects alike and chief mufti for nearly thirty years.[26] Whether Ebu Suud's preference for a longer period of minority reflected customary practice among his constituents or a deliberate attempt to raise the threshold of majority is difficult to say.

But simply reaching the age of majority was not sufficient to becoming a full legal actor, that is, to being able to enter into contracts or to incur punishment. One had also to display competence in making socially responsible judgments.[27] The term for this competence was *akıl* (in Arabic, *'aql*); in the discourse of jurisprudence, it had the basic meaning of "moral reason" or "social discretion." *Akıl* was what the senile person lacked, thus disqualifying him from full legal competence. A case from the 1618 Kayseri court records suggests that reaching the age of legal majority and displaying the competence to make rational decisions were intertwined in the definition of legal capacity: in refusing the marriage that was arranged during her minority (under Hanafi law, such right of refusal took effect when a female came of age), Ayşe bt. Mustafa Pasha claimed in court that she was now both legally and socially mature *(baliğa ve akila)*, and that she wished to terminate the marriage her uncle Mahmud had arranged.[28]

However, even if jurisprudence assigned legal capacity to the level-headed older adolescent, social practice in Aintab and elsewhere seems to have been unwilling to fully concede the label of maturity to any female but the married woman with a household. This insistence on equating maturity with householder status is reflected in the fact that the vast majority of female users of the Aintab court were identified as *avret* or *hatun,* that is, as mature adults. Parenthood—or its functional equivalent in obligation to dependents—was necessary to advance one along the scale of social responsibility, entailing as it did the creation of one's own domestic unit through the acquisition of persons for whom one was responsible. A household, in other words, provided a woman with the physical and moral center of gravity necessary to prudent conduct.

That married or once-married women were the majority of female actors at court may seem natural, given the restricted legal capacity of minors and the authority of the male guardian over an unmarried female of age. Yet the recognition of the legal personhood of adult women under Ottoman legal practice deserves comment, since willingness to allow the voices of married women in the public arena of a court was far from a cultural universal in the sixteenth century. In early modern Europe, for example, marriage was a reason for suspending women's legal rights and access to courts.[29] The necessity of a wife's obedience to her husband was invoked as a reason for disbarring her from public legal arenas and for subordinating her to his legal control. On the other hand, the widow and the single woman of legal majority (achieved around the age of eighteen) enjoyed legal standing before the courts. In most places, married women were unable to buy and sell property, enter into contracts, or sue anyone, and in some places, any property a woman brought into the marriage became her husband's. In English common law of the period, which would shape the legal culture of the American colonies, the rules of coverture, which dissolved her identity into that of her husband, denied the married woman the status of a legal person.[30] According to William Blackstone's explication of this feature of common law, "The very being or legal existence of the woman is suspended during the marriage, or at least is . . . consolidated into that of the husband: under whose wing, protection, and cover, she performs every thing; . . . in our law-french . . . her condition . . . is called her coverture[.]"[31]

Yet, as studies of different European societies have shown, there were ways around the ban on married women at court. Many European urban law codes permitted married women to declare themselves legally single for purposes of property and monetary transactions, while some courts simply ignored the law if the legal incapacitation of women were judged harmful to those involved.[32] Despite the tightening up of restrictions on women in the sixteenth century through the revival of Roman law, with its emphasis on the absolute rights of the paterfamilias, women were not entirely denied legal recourse. In England, for example, the Court of Requests, which based its decisions on principles of equity rather than strict interpretation of common law, allowed women to bring cases even against their husbands.[33] But the Ottoman regime, until the nineteenth century, provided a single, unitary, court system, where Islamic law and sultanic law met an infinite variety of local customary practices.[34] As a result, the reconciliation of the needs of the community with normative rules carrying the sanction of religion or imperial authority had to take place within the parameters of local courts such as that of Aintab. To what extent, then, can we speak of women's "right" of access to this court system in the sixteenth century?

That married women were under the control of their husbands was a view that early modern Middle Eastern societies shared with their European counterparts. This view is embedded in the legal culture of the period, where the marriage contract assumed the husband's control of his wife. The equation of rights and obligations within marriage posited the husband's right to obedience from and sexual access to his wife in exchange for her rights to material support and to children, with no obligation to spend her own resources on the household.[35] But there were limits to the husband's authority. Men could exercise control over their wives' bodies and over their movements outside the household residence, but, in theory at least, husbands could not usurp the rights and claims belonging to married women under the law. Central among these were property rights—the right to inheritance shares prescribed to women by Qur'anic mandate, the dower specified in the marriage contract, and the claims women had to material support within the marital household. In addition, a number of personal rights to which women were entitled were spelled out in the fatwas of Ebu Suud, among them a woman's right to see her parents on a regular basis, to not be moved without her consent to a place distant from her natal roots, to acquire religious knowledge, and to make the pilgrimage to Mecca.[36]

As for a woman's rights to "due process," an important fatwa of Ebu Suud declared that a husband could not prevent his wife from representing herself in court or appointing a proxy to represent her. This right to court access, declared the mufti, was necessary to the integrity of the legal process itself. The husband could not interfere with his wife's access to the court because, in Ebu Suud's words, "Rights must not be allowed to languish. If she does not come [to the court] in person, the sharia authorities must obtain a proxy for her by ordering that one be appointed."[37] The languishing of the law, in other words, risked denying women that legal capacity to which they were entitled. It should be noted that Ebu Suud was no feminist; rather it was the increasing emphasis on legal order in the mid–sixteenth century that caused him to insist on strict observance of legal procedure.

In practice, however, there were different attitudes toward this question of women's rights, including access to the courts. A critical factor in determining one's attitude was one's place in the social hierarchy. Normative legal discourses of the sixteenth century as well as actual practice in the Aintab court suggest that elite status placed married women closer to the norms of coverture prescribed in Europe. In contrast, non-elite women made freer use of the court and displayed greater flexibility in manipulating the law to their own ends. Indeed, in the fatwa just cited, it was the veiled and secluded status of his upper-class wife—her literal coveredness—that apparently caused the husband to prevent her from appearing in court or even appointing a proxy.

SOCIAL CLASS AND FEMALE CONDUCT

It was only natural that law and legal practice in the early modern Middle East reflected cultural assumptions about class—in part because legal discourse was itself a product of the broader culture, in part because its formulators and arbiters considered themselves members of an elite. One of the most profound divisions in Islamic social thinking was that of *hass* and *amm*—the elite and the common, the privileged and the masses. Islamic literature is replete with writing about social hierarchies and the qualities of different classes. Louise Marlow has shown how the egalitarian impulse in the formative years of Islam was soon overwhelmed by the aristocratic and hierarchical tendencies in the lands that were so rapidly conquered in its name from the Byzantine empire and from the Persian Sasanians.[38]As Marlow demonstrates, the role of religious scholars was critical in the elaboration of an Islamicized version of hierarchy.[39]

Two notions particularly strong in early Islamic hierarchical visions were eroded over the course of the centuries: the equation of nobility with piety and the superiority of Arabs. Piety was overtaken by definitions of eliteness that admitted to the roster of privileged classes the military, governors, merchants, the wealthy, and those of distinguished lineage. The honor accorded piety persisted, however, in the respect given to religious dignitaries, in the ubiquitous following that holy men and women attracted, and in the status acquired by pilgrims to Mecca. As for the notion of Arab superiority, it was resisted by converts in the first Muslim centuries, principally those in Iran and Central Asia, who made use of the egalitarian elements in the Islamic tradition to challenge ethnically based hierarchy. Piety and Arabness *did* combine in the ennobling of descendents of the Prophet Muhammad, who were typically known as *seyyid*s individually and collectively as the *eshraf*. This distinguished group enjoyed special privileges and formed a distinct class in most cities and towns. Over time, however, even the eshraf lost its

Arab identity, practically speaking, as its numbers grew and came to include Muslims across a variety of cultures.[40]

As the composition of privileged classes became more complex and cosmopolitan over time, literacy in the high urban culture of Islamic civilization came to be a sine qua non of elite membership. Noblesse oblige required members of the elite to engage in conspicuous patronage through the endowment of charitable institutions (*waqfs*) for the public welfare and in the commissioning of luxury textiles, ceramics, and metalwork. One reason that the cultivation of material goods did not challenge the important place accorded the religious classes was that spirituality was not thought to be opposed to economic savvy. In contrast to other religio-ethical cultures—for example, the Confucian—Muslim societies did not disdain the profession of merchant. Indeed, Baber Johansen has argued that "the proprietor became the prototype of the legal person in Hanafite law," in part because many early legal experts were themselves merchants and craftsmen in the cities and towns of Syria, Iraq (where the Hanafi school originated), and Transoxania.[41]

All this is reflected in sixteenth-century Aintab. With its notable families, its sizable religious elite, its population of well-to-do merchants and taxfarmers, and its old urban culture, Aintab was acutely aware of social rank. One way that Aintab's elite is made visible to us is through the variety of titles employed in the court record to signal important individuals: these titles consist of the term "pride of" (*fahr ul-*) and the occupational group to which the individual belonged. Interestingly, the titles fall rather easily into the classic categories elaborated by Islamic thinkers over the centuries. These groups were (in no particular order) military appointees (*ümera, zuema, fevaris*), local tax-farmers and others in state-supplied offices (*akran, muharririn*), wealthy merchants (*ayan*), and religious notables (*ulema, sadat* [pl. of *seyyid*], *suleha, müteberririn*).[42] While these titles pointed to occupational identity, there was occasional crossover between the categories: one of the three distinguished *ayan* families, the Boyacıs, were seyyids, and one of the leading dervish sheikhs was a tax-farmer.

For women, however, only one distinguishing title was used: *fahr ul-nisa'*, "pride of women." But when we look at the women who were graced with this title in the records, an interesting point emerges. The court record names the wives or the financial backers of males whom we might call the state-sanctioned elite (e.g., local military men, tax-farmers, other stateappointed officials). In contrast, it never speaks of the women in households headed by leading religious dignitaries or established merchants. Such women, it would seem, did not enter the communal arena of the court. While we can assume that both these groups of women were locally recognized as members of elite households, the court's silence with regard to

some women and not others signals a distinction between an old "aristocratic" elite and a "nouveau" elite, a distinction that reflected a pre-
Ottoman versus Ottoman-based achievement of elite status in Aintab.[43] In
this regard, the discursive invisibility of certain women provides us with a
clue to cultural divisions within the Aintab elite that are obscured by the
uniform public visibility of males.

The controlled mobility and visibility of the female were conspicuous
and defining elements in the etiquette of the elite. Historians and feminist
scholars today debate whether the practice of female seclusion was integral
to Islamic culture or an artifact of pre-Islamic patterns. But this question is
more or less irrelevant in the sixteenth century, since by then the practice
had come to be an intimate feature of Muslim societies. A household whose
female members did not observe protocols of veiling and seclusion could,
almost by definition, not claim elite status. At the same time, contrary to
popular stereotypes of the Middle Eastern harem, wealthy or noble women
were far from powerless. As we will see in chapter 6, well-to-do women in
Aintab invested in business ventures and acted as financial backers of the
city's male power brokers. The seclusion of elite women was predicated on
the ability of wealthy households to retain slaves, servants, and clients who
assisted them in carrying out their public business.

The etiquette of controlled visibility was not an exclusively female phenomenon. To a certain degree, elite males followed its dictates as well. We
must imagine the notables of Aintab dispatching agents to take care of routine business and surrounding themselves with underlings when they personally appeared in the public venues of the city. The greatest model of the
controlled visibility of the male person was, of course, the Ottoman sultan,
who left the imperial palace in Istanbul only to execute the most weighty
of imperial responsibilities: to wage war, to participate in the Friday communal prayer, and to preside over the rare public ritual. The late-fifteenth-
century historian Neşri described the walling of Mehmed the Conqueror's
palace in terms of its "haremization": "he had [a] castle built, he made it a
harem, and within it he built glorious palaces, and made it the seat of his
sovereignty."[44] The palace itself was the locus of government, with various
structures within its walls housing the imperial council, the imperial mint,
the imperial armory, and so on.

An interesting case in the Aintab records suggests that the practice of collapsing "public" business into the residence of a high official extended beyond the imperial palace in Istanbul. Aintabans apparently felt that the
judge's residence—the seat of the court—should be an imposing and accommodating one. Three days after the arrival of the judge Hüsameddin
Efendi in June 1541, a certain Mehmed made a donation of a piece of property that bordered the judicial residence: "I have donated . . . my property
for the soul of the Prophet, so that all judges who come [to Aintab] may oc-

cupy it."[45] Coming so soon after the assignment of an important judge to the city, the donation suggests that either the community or Hüsameddin Efendi himself thought that a larger residence was appropriate to the city's judgeship. Mehmed's response may have been inspired by pious devotion or perhaps it was the result of pressure by the community or the new judge. Whatever the donor's motivation, the expansion of the judicial compound was no doubt appreciated as the number of petitioners to the court increased over subsequent months. The enlarged judicial compound may have facilitated women's use of the court by providing a more appropriate waiting place where the sexes might legitimately come together.

But precisely where was the boundary between elites and non-elites located? Who in the sixteenth century was eligible to be counted among the distinguished classes? In view of the changing composition of elites over the centuries, it is not surprising that prescriptive and descriptive texts were regularly reformulated to explicate and validate contemporary social hierarchies. And, predictably, religious scholars and legal experts tended to be the ones who articulated the norms for present times. Since a critical index of membership in the elite was the comportment of its women, rules defining their public conduct inevitably shifted with changing social circumstances. It was perhaps predictable that there would be uncertainty among sixteenth-century Ottoman subjects about the definition of respectability for women.

Or so it would seem from a series of questions posed to the chief mufti Ebu Suud. While Ebu Suud might render his opinion on matters of jurisprudence crucial to the conduct of imperial affairs, he was also, like any local mufti, called on to judge matters of everyday social conduct.[46] The set of questions we are concerned with here asked the mufti to clarify who qualified for the status of *muhaddere*. This term, which might best be translated as "respectable," combines what in modern (but not premodern) Western usage are usually separate concepts: a reputation for chaste behavior and the practice of veiling and seclusion.[47] The term thereby links moral status with the controlled visibility of the female body.

The definition of *muhaddere* alerts us to the important point that the elite were defined not only by their material wealth and their distinctive conduct but also by their moral qualities. Underlying the distinction between *hass* and *amm*—the elite and the common—was a conception of society in which classes of people were distinguished from one another according to their capacity for moral learning and moral excellence. In this view, those who derived status from notable lineage, religious authority, wealth, political power, and the like were thought to have greater awareness of ethical norms than the common folk, and therefore might be expected to hew to higher standards of conduct. Accordingly, their claim to privilege carried with it an obligation to engage in morally distinguished behavior.

The questions posed to Ebu Suud concerned the degree of seclusion that was necessary for a woman to be recognized as "respectable."[48] The following three fatwas delivered by the mufti trace the status of muhaddere through a variety of social venues:

> 1. Query: Can [a woman] be muhaddere if she handles her own affairs with the people of the village and brings water from the spring?
> Response: No.
> 2. Query: Can [a woman] be muhaddere if she goes to the public bath or to the countryside [lit., "to villages"]?
> Response: Yes, if she goes in [such a way as to preserve her] honor and dignity and is accompanied by servants and attendants.
> 3. [perhaps a variant text of #2] Query: Can [a woman] be muhaddere if she goes to the public bath and to weddings and makes excursions to other neighborhoods?
> Response: Yes, if she is goes with a retinue.[49]

Ebu Suud insists here not on invisibility, but rather on the veiled visibility of the female person. In order to be respectable, a woman must transport her human household—her servants and retainers—with her as she moves outside the physical boundaries of its walls. The mufti's fatwas are thus a graphic equation of honor and wealth. Ebu Suud's responses also reveal an urban bias: their successful muhaddere subject is a city woman, while the woman who exemplifies failure to qualify is a villager.

The uncertainty that underlay the queries posed to Ebu Suud suggests that the issues of women's mobility in public, their physical appearance, and their contact with men were as contested in the mid–sixteenth century as they are in today's debates about Muslim identity. That there was confusion over social boundaries in this period is not surprising, given the shifting social formations attendant on imperial consolidation and the shifting definitions of orthodoxy and morality growing in part out of the sunni confrontation with Iranian shi'ism. Aintab was not free from contention over these issues. In the final section of this chapter, we will see one manifestation of this contention in the resistance that some women—and men too—put up against the authorities' monitoring of their appearance in the streets. We will also see, especially in Fatma's story, that formulations of moral etiquette reflected in Ebu Suud's fatwas had the effect of leaving "non-muhaddere" women exposed. Women whose labor was public—women who had no servants to handle their affairs or even to draw water—were less able than wealthier women to guard their reputation and honor. More visible, they were easier targets of social suspicion and censure, guilty or not. Accordingly, they were denied the honor that automatically accrued to women of greater wealth and status merely by virtue of their seclusion. It is a truism in studies of Middle Eastern societies, both premodern and contemporary, that women's bodies are critical markers of political, social, and moral boundaries. What is not always noted is the different costs this phenomenon exacted from different women.

But is it fair to blame Islamic jurisprudence for the social bias that automatically rendered honorable status to some women, while by definition denying it to the majority of women? In another fatwa, in which he provided a more comprehensive characterization of the term muhaddere, Ebu Suud suggested perhaps not. To the query "Can [a woman] be muhaddere if she lets herself be seen by her father's freedmen and by the sons of [these] freedmen and by her sisters' husbands?" Ebu Suud replied: "It is not conformity to the prescriptions of the noble sharia that is the essential element in being muhaddere. That is why non-Muslim women can also be muhaddere. A woman is muhaddere if she does not let herself be seen by persons other than members of her household and does not set about taking care of her affairs in person."[50] The mufti's rule of thumb here on who could be muhaddere was rather close to Qur'anic prohibitions on male-female contact outside of specified degrees of kinship (including quasi-kinship relations among family members and household servants).[51] Yet he was careful not to give the category muhaddere the sanction of sharia. By acknowledging that non-Muslim women could be muhaddere, Ebu Suud avoided assimilating the category to a catechism of Islamically prescribed conduct. (Indeed, the attribution *muhaddere* figured prominently in the honorific titles that opened imperial diplomatic missives to Queen Elizabeth I of England, who was hailed as "the pride of the muhaddere of the Christian faith.")[52] At the same time, however, Ebu Suud acknowledged the importance of clarifying the social and legal implications of this practice by answering the persistent questions about its boundaries. In other words, despite his insistence to the contrary, Ebu Suud inevitably gave it the imprimatur of sharia by virtue of his authoritative voice. That the mufti was asked repeatedly about the definition of muhaddere suggests that popular belief assumed it to be embedded in sharia.[53] Here we have an example of the process whereby customary practice might eventually insinuate itself into the canon of religiously sanctioned norms. This prospect clearly troubled Ebu Suud.

While the mufti gave the category muhaddere a definition, imperial law endowed it with material consequences. The law book of Sultan Süleyman contained a statute prescribing the penalties to be imposed on brawls among women that distinguished between non-muhaddere and muhaddere females: "If women fight with each other, pull each other's hair, or strike each other severely, the penalty for those who are not muhaddere is a severe flogging and a fine of one akçe for every two strokes; the penalty for those who are muhaddere is that their husbands will be upbraided and fined twenty akçes."[54] What is noteworthy in this statute is that the responsibility for a breach of conduct by a muhaddere woman was placed in the hands of her husband, while a non-muhaddere woman directly suffered the consequences of her behavior. Since the severity of a flogging was determined by the local authorities, who could in theory prescribe up to eighty lashes, the monetary penalty for a non-muhaddere woman could exceed the penalty of 20 akçes imposed on the muhaddere woman's husband. In other words, the non-muhaddere woman might suffer a severe flogging and a substantial fine, while the parallel punishment for the muhaddere woman was the public humiliation of her husband and the imposition of a comparatively lesser fine on him. In the eyes of the sultan's law, whether she had a husband or not, a female commoner was in charge of her own behavior and its consequences, while it was the husband of the elite woman who was publicly accountable for her actions and therefore he who was publicly dishonored by her transgressions. The locus of personal honor thus imposed a kind of moral autonomy on ordinary women, and it is no wonder that we hear their voices raised in the court records.

In endorsing the social variability of justice, the imperial statute books may have merely reflected widespread customary practice. However, by (re)inscribing such practice in a regulatory program for the whole empire, they gave it authoritative sanction. It is therefore not surprising that people were anxious for definition of the boundaries between social categories, since kanun declared that the law for women and their husbands varied according to their social status. For men, a reputation for moral probity was a requirement for participation in the life of the community, which was symbolized by the ability to perform as witness in court. That men might risk diminished standing in the community by failing to secure the norms of gender segregation was the opinion of İbn Kemal, the chief mufti from 1525 until his death in 1534, and, like Ebu Suud, one of the most acclaimed of Ottoman religious scholars. When presented with a long list of individuals exemplifying religiously or socially deficient, delinquent, or deviant behaviors and the query whether such behaviors could disqualify a person from giving testimony in court, the mufti answered in the affirmative. Included in the list, along with thieves, pimps, pederasts, habitual liars, cheats, astrologers, Gypsies, players of backgammon, heretics, and persons ignorant of the most basic elements of their professed faith, were "those who keep company with women who are not close relatives" and "those who do not prevent their wives from [associating with] men who are not close relatives."[55]

In İbn Kemal's view, disregard of what we might term muhaddere standards of behavior was a moral failing that disqualified a man from bearing one of the marks of full citizenship in the community and deprived him of an upstanding moral reputation. To be sure, the mufti's fatwa was not necessarily meant as an eligibility test for witnessing in local courts—otherwise many less well-to-do plaintiffs and defendants would have been unable to use the courts for lack of witnesses to the circumstances they needed to litigate. Rather, the fatwa should be situated in the climate of imperial consolidation, where structures of morality as well as structures of administration were undergoing articulation. The contrived nature of the fatwa, a precomposed list leaving the mufti an all-or-nothing option, suggests a rhetorical or didactic intent, with the result that the fatwa ends up outlining a set of undesirable, but not necessarily illegal, behaviors. Nevertheless, the point was being made by Süleyman's muftis and by his own law book that social class was an important determinant of one's status in relationship to the law.

ELITES AND THE LAW

It might be thought that the question of witnessing was irrelevant to women, since they rarely acted as witnesses themselves. However, the fact that elite women routinely employed agents to manage their business presented its own problem of witnessing. Ebu Suud's commentary on this issue points to a tension between the self-interest of the elite and the integrity of the legal process. The following discussion examines the critical question of the relationship between local elites and a legal system undergoing reform and expansion.

As Ebu Suud noted in his definition of the muhaddere woman, she might have "affairs to take care of," affairs that could become subject to litigation or other court procedures. Given females' control of their own property under Islamic law, women of wealth in particular frequently needed to participate in legal proceedings. The disinclination of the muhaddere woman to appear herself in the public venue of the court meant that she needed to rely on agents on such occasions. However, the act of appointing an agent as legal proxy *(vekil)* required witnesses, an apparently tricky procedure when it was a muhaddere woman making the appointment. In a fatwa concerning the proper means for appointing a proxy, Ebu Suud asserts the priority of correct legal procedure over the practice of seclusion:

> Query: If Amr and Bekr come to witness the muhaddere Hind's appointment of Zeyd to be her proxy in some matter, is Amr and Bekr's testimony that Zeyd is Hind's proxy legally acceptable if they only hear her make the appointment from the other side of a door and do not see Hind's face or do not know whether or not there is another woman in the house in which Hind speaks? Response: No, [their testimony] is not [valid], unless they see her person.[56] (Amr, Bekr, and Zeyd are the "John Does" of fatwas, while Hind is the "Jane Roe.")

Another situation addressed by the mufti, this one concerning a muhad-dere woman's apparent attempt to deny the validity of a marriage con-tracted on her behalf, demonstrates the role opened up for female wit-nesses in the problematic area of proxy appointment:

> Query: Hind denies that she made Zeyd her proxy for contracting marriage; the witnesses of the proxy appointment say "We didn't see Hind's face; a woman behind a curtain spoke [making the proxy appointment]. We testified to the proxy appointment trusting that it was Hind." If Amr, who has brought a suit claiming that Hind is legally his wife, brings two women who testify con-currently that the person who appointed Zeyd proxy was Hind, is Hind legally Amr's wife?
> Response: Yes, she is.[57]

The two female witnesses are probably servants or retainers in the house-hold where Hind is resident; as such, their status is apparently not elevated enough to exempt them from appearing in court. However, *as witnesses* their status is enhanced: though typically the testimony of two women was re-quired as substitute for that of a single male, strict observation of the rules of gender segregation rendered women the only reliable witnesses in a purely female environment.

These fatwas are noteworthy in revealing the extent to which the social structure of a community and of individual households within it condi-tioned the practice of law. Ebu Suud's concern here was that the elite's cultivation of seclusion might infringe on the operation of the law as a com-munal process. In refusing to permit a husband's interference with his mu-haddere wife's access to court through a proxy and in insisting that proxy appointment be carried out in a valid manner, Ebu Suud asserted the pri-ority of a general interest in the integrity of the law over the right of the hus-band to control his wife's movements or the right of a woman to refrain from showing her face. His opinions expressed various levels of concern, emphasizing not only that women perform their legal roles in one way or another but also that the practice of seclusion not be manipulated as a ploy to avoid responding to legal suits. (This may have been the point of the fatwa against a husband's preventing his wife's access to the court.) The mufti's statement that "rights must not be allowed to languish" reveals a general concern for defending the integrity of public law against the pre-tensions of privilege.

The chief mufti's fatwas take on greater importance for this study in light of the fact that the elites of Aintab practiced a similar aloofness from the court. The court records of 1540–1541 suggest, on the one hand, that the elite of the city generally refrained from using the court and, on the other, that government authorities were concerned about the evasion of public regulatory mechanisms at the provincial level. Men of status appeared in the Aintab court fairly regularly when their business overlapped the business of the state. This occurred particularly in the area of tax-farming, where wealthy and influential Aintabans bid competitively for the rights to collect urban taxes and taxes on the crown's landholdings in the province. Otherwise, wealthy landholders, merchants, and entrepreneurs made their business arrangements without the help of the court. Ali Çelebi, brother of the former warden of the fortress mentioned above, was unusual among the Aintab elite in habitually registering his business transactions at court. As might be expected, elite women were even rarer than their male counterparts in the venue of the court.

Concern for the consequences of unregulated dealings by the Aintab elite is revealed in the mission of a special agent *(havale)* appointed by the sultan in late May 1541. His mandate was to discipline two tax-farmers who were in debt to the state, one of them the scion of the distinguished Sikkak household. Over the course of the month, the agent presided over the liquidation of much of their property. During his tenure, other local dignitaries—among them some of the city's leading religious figures—were also summoned to court to account for their tax-farming debts. As chapter 7 demonstrates in greater detail, the agent's larger purpose, which dominated the court for the month of June, was to bring the activities of local officeholders into the domain of the court. This mission was carried on by the new judge, Hüsameddin Efendi, who took up office just as the special agent was concluding his business.

Ironically, it was this process of subjecting local entrepreneurs to government scrutiny that enables us to view the role of wealthy women in underwriting the enterprise of tax-farming. When the holder of the market inspectorship, the largest tax-farm in Aintab, fell into debt, it was two women, Tatar bt. İbrahim and Haleb bt. İlyas, who bailed him out.[58] And because of the special agent's scrutiny of large-scale private commercial dealings, we learn that women invested in joint commercial ventures. During the month of June, when the agent was carrying out his mandate, the estate of the wealthy merchant Hoca Yusuf was liquidated at court, during which process the woman Rahime bt. İbrahim collected the returns due her from her investment in the merchant's enterprise.[59] It was not typical for such estates to be settled at court, and thus the settlement provides another example of the expanding regulatory reach of this provincial court. Had the affairs of the wealthy not been exposed to the court's scrutiny during the agent's presence, the existence of women such as Tatar, Haleb, and Rahime would have remained veiled to us. Luckily, we as historical voyeurs benefit from the Ottoman regime's attempt to bring elites under the purview of its legal authority.

But how were elites to be disciplined if they avoided the arena of the court? When they erred in their relationship with the state, the answer was clear: send a state-appointed official (such as a special agent) to punish the local miscreant. But what about matters of social morality and comportment? If sanctions were brought to bear against members of Aintab's elite, they did not enter the court record, and so are invisible to us. Of necessity, then, we turn to normative legal discourse on this subject.

Criminal penalties set out in sixteenth-century fatwas and imperial statutes echo the view that moral accountability differed from person to person and was intimately connected to one's status in the community. Punishment, in other words, was one manifestation of the variability of justice according to class. Variable accountability before the law expressed itself in two ways: on the one hand, elites sometimes suffered higher penalties because their transgression of moral imperatives was seen to be graver than that of ordinary individuals; on the other hand, they sometimes enjoyed an immunity that exempted them from sanctions suffered by the masses.

In the area of sexual crime, for example, persons of privilege were more heavily penalized for adultery and fornication. The imperial law books used a complex calculus of punishment, factoring in an individual's wealth as well as basic aspects of civil status—whether he or she was married or single, Muslim or dhimmi, free or slave. In theory, the fine for adultery imposed on a rich Muslim was six times greater than that imposed on a poor Muslim, and twelve times greater than that imposed on a poor non-Muslim or a slave.[60] It should be noted that classical Islamic jurisprudence did not recognize material wealth as a factor in the calculus of punishment, suggesting that this was yet another popular notion of morality inscribed in the sultanic law books. A similar attitude was expressed in the penalties for bodily injury. For example, in the case of a fight in which two persons ripped out each other's hair or beard, a rich person was fined 20 akçes and a poor person 10 akçes; if the fight led to a head wound requiring surgery, the person inflicting the wound paid 100 akçes if rich, 50 akçes if moderately well-off, and 30 akçes if poor.[61] The different penalties for brawling women were also based on class, although the criterion for discriminating between female classes, as we saw earlier, was behavioral rather than monetary. The rationale for this sliding scale, once again, seems to be that it was a graver indiscretion for the privileged to brawl.[62]

In contrast to these examples of socially privileged persons suffering heavier penalties, distinctions between "the common people" and the elites sometimes resulted in the imposition of harsher punishments on the former. For example, the following fatwa of İbn Kemal pardoned a religiously distinguished person while punishing a commoner for what appears on the surface to be an equal, or even lesser, offense:

Query: If a seyyid [a person descended from the Prophet Muhammad] says to someone, "You idiot! you cur!" and that person in turn says "That's what *you* are!" legally what must be done to the two of them?
Response: The seyyid is pardoned, the other is sentenced to punishment by the judge.[63]

The ruling implies that the commoner had in fact committed the greater violation, by insulting a communally honored individual, whereas the seyyid's membership in a distinguished lineage appears to have afforded him immunity from a penal judgment. In another fatwa, İbn Kemal exempted those who were not "common" from the drastic consequences of a broken vow:

Query: If Zeyd says, "If I drink wine, may I no longer be the slave of God and a member of the Prophet's community," and subsequently he does drink, what must be done according to the law?
Response: If he is a common person, he must renew his faith.[64]

In this instance of the widespread practice of the "conditional vow"—calling down an undesired outcome on oneself if one were to do what one vowed not to do—the speaker risked his Muslim identity. He was now, if he was "common," an apostate, requiring that he formally reaffirm his allegiance to Islam.[65] Underlying these two rulings may be the assumption that privileged persons do not need to demonstrate religious conformity as stringently as do commoners because they "know" the rules by virtue of their status, whereas legal sanctions are necessary to instruct ordinary individuals in publicly desirable behavior. In other words, privileged persons are protected by their *class* identity from the consequences of any violation they may commit as individuals, whereas commoners enjoy no such immunity, lacking as they do any claim to shared moral distinction. Louise Marlow points out that the most striking feature of early Islamic descriptions of social hierarchy is "the extremely low opinion in which the common people are held," in part because, it was thought, their gullibility allowed them to be easily seduced into following rebels.[66] This hostility toward the *avamm*, the commoners, clearly persisted into the sixteenth century, and accounts for the emphasis on their constant need for religious instruction.

Immunity from the sorts of punishments imposed on commoners did not necessarily imply a license for loose behavior among the privileged. Rather, different kinds of sanctions were deemed effective for different classes of individuals. A statute in Süleyman's law book stipulated that religious functionaries who break the law should be exempted from the standard penalties and instead reprimanded verbally: "If those who by virtue of an imperial appointment hold the office and receive the salary of judge, seminary teacher, waqf administrator, waqf supervisor, dervish elder, mosque preacher, prayer leader, and the like become liable to criminal sanctions, such sanctions shall not be imposed. To prevent them from doing [the same thing] again, it is punishment enough for such people for the judge to speak harshly to them."[67] This statute negotiates the tricky status of members of the religious establishment who are in the employ of the sultan: they must be disciplined, yet, given the status deriving from their religiously oriented careers, it is not seemly to subject them to the same sanctions as ordinary folk. But is the verbal sanction delivered to these individuals a "light" sentence? For possessors and purveyors of the highest form of knowledge, to be publicly reprimanded with words may be more humiliating and therefore more punitive than the public imposition of a monetary fine. The notion of a hierarchy of punishment in which the highest-ranking members of society receive only a verbal reprimand may have been a feature of Islamic jurisprudence from its formative period, or at least it was remembered as such. Al-Marghinani cited the renowned ninth-century jurist al-Shafiʿi on the four degrees of chastisement; the first was restricted, in Al-Marghinani's words, to "the most noble of the noble" and consisted "merely in admonition, as if the judge were to say to one of them, 'I understand that you have done thus, or thus,' so as to make him ashamed[.]"[68] Shaming punishments were more potent against the elite because, in the hierarchical outlook of legal discourse, they had more honor to lose.

The moral force of words in sixteenth-century society cannot be overestimated. As we have seen, the integrity of one's word—symbolized by the eligibility to testify in court—was a principal measure of one's communal status. That the husband of a muhaddere woman guilty of brawling in public was exposed to the same punishment as a lapsed religious dignitary—a verbal dressing-down in a communal forum—is both an acknowledgment of his and his wife's status and an affirmation of the moral nature of the failure to conform to muhaddere norms. In contrast, legal discourse implied that the female commoner was herself accountable for her conduct and her moral reputation.

DEBATING HONOR AND CLASS IN AINTAB

We now return to the question raised at the beginning of this chapter: the extent to which people in Aintab accepted the divisions among social classes and the moral hierarchy delineated and debated in normative legal discourse, namely, the fatwas and law books of the sixteenth century.

As a cultural process, legal thinking—by theoreticians, practitioners, and consumers of the law alike—is naturally a combination of debate, contention, confusion, and accommodation. In sixteenth-century legal debates, the role of women was inconsistently delineated. Women's social and moral agency was largely missing from jurisprudential debates, which were articulated by the very men who attributed to themselves social and moral authority over the lives of the less esteemed. However, the further we move from theoretical legal formulations and the closer we come to actual legal conflicts, the more frequently we see females as actors. This is why, of the various genres of normative law, contemporary fatwas, based as they were on specific factual scenarios, most often allow us to see individual women portrayed in action—asserting rights, protesting violation of their rights, maneuvering for social or material advantage, or breaking the law. The court records take us even closer, in part because of the critical role of personal oral testimony, in part because of the element of volition in the many cases originated by individuals. In examining local legal practice, one way we can get at the question of whether Aintabans accepted the social prescriptions of normative law is by considering access: what women appeared in the local court and under what circumstances, if any, was their access limited?

As we have seen, elite women did not appear in the Aintab court, although their male relatives did, principally because the status of the latter tended to involve them in business with the state. If elite women had problems peculiar to their status, or if they really did tear each other's hair out, the court did not interfere. Nor did females below the age of legal majority appear in court, except when they were sexually assaulted or accused of sexual misconduct (there were half a dozen such cases in 1540–1541). Female users of the court, then, were adult married—or formerly married—women of a range of socioeconomic circumstances, excepting the elite. When and how they used the court, or were summoned by it, are issues of concern throughout this book. Here, I make one pass at answering the question of women's access to the court by focusing on some interrelated issues raised in this chapter: Did the "muhaddere impulse" interfere with women's ability to have their voices heard (and recorded) at court? If so, what silenced them—self-censorship, family pressure, communal pressure, or perhaps the court itself?

As Abraham Marcus has noted with respect to Aleppo, the number of households on whose elite status there was local consensus was actually rather small. He has pointed to a large "middle class," whose upper reaches bordered the recognized elite.[69] To be sure, Marcus's study focuses on the eighteenth century, but the hierarchy he describes is strikingly similar to that of Aleppo's smaller sister to the north. While the records give only indirect evidence of status and wealth, some women who used the Aintab court appear to have belonged to the upper reaches of the middle classes: for example, Rahime, the female investor mentioned above, and Sitt ("Lady") Laiş, who failed to win her dower at the time of her divorce. Another example is the interesting case of Esma bt. Hoca Hamza, who came to court to request structural alterations to her neighbor's house in order to make her own more private. A week or so after the court had settled the sizable estate of Hoca Hamza, a merchant, and Esma added to her share of the house she had inherited jointly with her two brothers by acquiring the share of one of them, she brought her neighbor, the woman Hadice, to court. There she complained that an open niche in Hadice's house permitted male members of Hadice's household to see into her own dwelling, which forced her to "be modest"—that is, presumably, to cover herself at home as she would before strangers. Hadice agreed to block up the niche, although she had apparently resisted doing so in earlier discussion of the problem.[70]

Neither Rahime nor Esma used a proxy in her suit. Proxy use is not, as one might at first think, a reliable index of class; the fact that men used proxies suggests there were other reasons than modest conduct to rely on representation by others. To communicate their status as they went to court, women of substance may well have employed a set of behavioral signals that were the functional translation of "going in honor and dignity," to use Ebu Suud's formulation in his muhaddere fatwas. Surely Esma, who was so concerned about the protocols of exposure to the gaze of men, would not have made a public appearance at court if it had put her honor in jeopardy. Indeed, court appearance seems to have been one of those activities, such as acquiring religious knowledge and making the pilgrimage to Mecca, that justified women's presence outside the home. In chapter 3, we noted that the Ottoman regime's insistence on a fixed and independent venue for the court may have made it more user-friendly for women. In this context, the expansion of the judicial residence for the new judge Hüsameddin Efendi acquires a particular relevance.

What about the allegedly inferior status of those who did not practice muhaddere norms, proclaimed in İbn Kemal's fatwa on witnesses? Did ordinary Aintabans—women and their husbands alike—accept failure to observe female seclusion as a mark of inferiority? The short answer, as one might expect, is that Aintabans displayed a range of behaviors that expressed different attitudes toward the question of contact between the sexes. At one end of the spectrum was a case of confrontation between two men, Bahşi and İskender, over İskender's wife Yenusa. When Yenusa was seen in public with Bahşi (she claimed that the wife of the town auctioneer called her into her house when Bahşi happened to be present), İskender not only attacked Bahşi with a knife but divorced Yenusa a month later; "I renounce the woman, she is no longer fit to be my wife," he stated in court.[71] İskender's behavior fits the model of the "cuckold divorce," like that of Ali and Ayşe described in chapter 3, where Ali volubly attacked Ayşe's character while divorcing her, although she claimed to have been raped. It is worth noting that Bahşi, İskender, and Yenusa were Armenian, confirming Ebu Suud's observation that keeping muhaddere standards was a cultural practice shared by non-Muslims and Muslims alike.

In contrast to this example of muhaddere standards of behavior upheld, the substantial amount of business conducted between men and women in Aintab suggests that many face-to-face encounters between married men and women were treated as acceptable by local standards. By one of Ebu Suud's definitions, women involved in such dealings were non-muhaddere women, "handling their own affairs with the people[.]" But the example of Esma and of others suggests that Aintab's evaluation of women's public behavior was more subtle than a simple distinction between women who did their own business and women who used agents or proxies. The crux of the matter was, it seems, signaling that one's public affairs were honest legitimate business, not purposeless lingering or indiscriminate socializing that could get one into trouble. It may have been a perceived lapse in "honor and dignity" on the part of Yenusa and Ayşe that caused them to be shed by their husbands in divorce, Yenusa in entering the town auctioneer's home when she knew Bahşi was present and Ayşe in being on the street, unaccompanied, and thus vulnerable to being swept into the storeroom where she claimed she was raped.

To a certain extent, then, honor and dignity were a matter of perception. This raises the question of who monitored the human traffic in the highways and byways of Aintab. Enough has been said about popular morality, and its power to insist on social distinctions that had no basis in legal theory, to suggest that appointed officials were not the only moral watchdogs. Evidence abounds in the Aintab court records of surveillance by ordinary individuals, who reported indiscretions to the authorities. To a degree, surveillance was built into the legal culture: it was neighbors who were consulted, when necessary, on a person's moral reputation, and the neighborhood enjoyed the legal right to protest against, and even to expel, individuals who were judged to behave improperly. Moreover, ordinary individuals assisted local police in their role as prosecutors of the Qur'anic crimes of adultery, drinking, slander, and even highway robbery, instances of which were more often than not drawn to the authorities' attention by local residents.

It was the role of the court to evaluate the evidence that came to it, not to act as prosecutor itself. It thus fell to the court to decide when communal surveillance exceeded comfortable levels and threatened to turn into overzealous moral policing. But what standards did the court itself invoke to make such judgments, particularly in matters like male-female contact, where there was no firm local consensus, and where even normative law attached different degrees of guilt depending on the social position of the individuals involved? The short answer is that the court seems to have taken a case-by-case approach, examining the extent to which each situation was disruptive of the larger communal order. Haciye Sabah's story involves a case in which the court perceived a serious threat to local order. Here we will look, in some detail, at a case in which no disruptive issues were perceived. This case, concerning a woman who was seen leaving her male neighbor's house in the early hours of the morning, brings together a number of questions broached in this chapter—the applicability of muhaddere standards to ordinary people, the attribution of moral responsibility for a woman's behavior, the custodianship of moral values. The case also demonstrates how the unexpected often merges with the expected in actual court cases.

In this double case, recorded on July 20, 1541, two neighbors—the man Sadeddin and the woman Ayşe—and the latter's husband Haci Mehmed were brought to court because of the suspected illicit association between Ayşe and Sadeddin. This first of the two related case records hinged on the prohibition of contact between males and females whose association was forbidden because they were outside the degrees of kinship permitting men and women to mix freely. Forbidden, that is, in the view of religious law, but not, clearly, in the view of the three neighbors. The hearing was then followed by a second case precipitated by Ayşe's cursing one of the two men who informed against the neighbors. The affair of Ayşe and her accusers is an obvious instance of social surveillance by members of the community. It is also an instance of resistance by the surveilled. Ayşe's attack on the informant Cuma (she calls him a pimp) can be read as her way of restoring her honor by slurring the character of the informants. Because of the "raised voices" in this case, I give the two records in full:

I. Arab, chief of the night watch, came to court and summoned the individuals named Sadeddin b. Haci Süleyman and Ayşe bt. Halil and her husband Haci Mehmed, and said: "This woman was seen coming out of Sadeddin's house at daybreak. They are not closely related. What business does she have in his house?" When the aforementioned Sadeddin was questioned, he answered: "I owed her 90 akçes; she came to ask for it. Also, my little son was sick. The previous evening I had sent my little son to ask for a [nugget of sandalwood];[72] I thought perhaps she had come to bring it." When Haci Mehmed was asked the question "What business did your wife have in his house?" he said: "It was I who sent my wife; I told her to go get the money." What occurred was recorded.

[note appended to the record] It was recorded that Haci Derviş and Cuma b. Derviş Mehmed said: "We saw the said woman coming out of Sadeddin's house during the day. . . . He owed us some money, we had come to collect the debt[.]"[73]

II. Cuma b. Derviş Mehmed came to court and summoned Ayşe bt. Halil, and said: "This woman slandered me by calling me a pimp *(gidi)*." When the woman was questioned, she denied [the allegation]. When Cuma was asked for proof, the individuals named Bozoğlan b. Abdullah and Ali b. Mehmed testified as follows: "The said woman slandered Cuma by calling him a pimp." Upon acceptance [of their testimony], the foregoing was recorded at the request of Arab, chief of the night watch.[74]

Let us first take up the question of how the case came to court—that is, the role of the night watch *(ases)*, a kind of security patrol through the neighborhoods of the city.[75] In the hierarchy of official authority in Aintab, the chief of the night watch, a frequent figure at court, reported to the police chief *(subaşı)*, who reported to the provincial governor *(sancakbegi)*. During the year studied in this book, a number of cases were recorded in which people were summoned to court by the chief of the night watch to question their presence on the streets at night or in the early hours of the morning. With the exception of Ayşe, all were men.[76] In one case, a baker who was apprehended in a dead-end street in front of the house of a woman (a widow?) claimed he was on his way to work.[77] In a case from Arablar, one of Aintab's villages, two men accused a third of being on the roof of a certain Ali's house in the early hours of the morning when Ali was absent; the man claimed he had gone to Ali's house to get a drink of water.[78]

We should note that all these cases brought to court through the auspices of the night watch occurred under the judgeship of Hüsameddin Efendi, which began on June 23, 1541. When we remember that Hüsameddin Efendi arrived just as the special agent appointed by the sultan was finishing his disciplinary business in Aintab and that the new judge carried on the effort to bring the work of local officials under the aegis of the court, we may better understand the resistance of some Aintabans to the policing of neighborhood traffic. In the context of stepped-up scrutiny of the work of local officialdom and the conduct of local residents, policing might now threaten to become more than the familiar authority of the night watchman. It might also open the door to an increase in "accusationism" among ordinary residents of Aintab. The narrow line between legitimate surveillance by civilians and potential harassment is demonstrated in a case from the village of Sam:

> Ümmet b. Kara, from the village of Sam, summoned Ramazan b. Karaca to court, and said: "This Ramazan slandered me by saying 'A man entered your house at night.'" When Ramazan was questioned, he answered: "I had gone for a walk at night. I saw that two people were coming along the street. I said to myself, 'Let's see what they're doing.' While I waited, one of these two people entered Ümmet's house and one kept on going." His statement was recorded at Ümmet's request.[79]

Here, Ümmet has apparently preempted an assault on his honor by accusing Ramazan of slander. One has to wonder if going for a walk was itself sufficient justification for being on the streets at night. Indeed, all cases of civilian surveillance raise the question of how the surveillers justified their own presence on the street!

In the case of the neighbors Ayşe and Sadeddin, do the informants Haci Derviş and Cuma deserve Ayşe's curses? The law book of Süleyman stated that an observer of an act of illicit sexual behavior was under no compulsion to report the incident, although an instance of theft, by contrast, had to be reported lest a fine of 10 akçes be imposed.[80] If opinion in Aintab matched the view articulated by kanun, Haci Derviş and Cuma were liable to be seen as busybodies and mischief makers, as Ümmet saw Ramazan. Other cases in the Aintab record suggest that accusations of illicit association were a way of calling down the authorities on someone one bore a grudge against or felt antagonism toward (in our case, Sadeddin's financial dealings with both parties may be an issue). On the other hand, we should not dismiss the possibility that Haci Derviş and Cuma were motivated by genuine moral scruples. In this regard, the fact that both informants have religious affiliations calls for consideration. The prominent role in local affairs played by the heads of well-endowed dervish lodges in Aintab suggests that the local dervish community, or some elements within it, enjoyed an "establishment" position within the community. The stereotype of dervishes as less concerned with the letter of the law than were religious scholars trained in the classical curriculum is, like any stereotype, sometimes but not always valid. In other words, an attitude of strict moral rectitude was not incompatible with dervish allegiance.

Our protagonists, however, resist the informants' implication that their behavior has been improper. Indeed, Ayşe's curse suggests extreme annoyance at the authorities' intervention in their affairs. The explanations offered the court for Ayşe's presence in Sadeddin's house demonstrate a comfortable freedom of movement in the neighborhood, or at least between the two households. Their contacts are characterized by neighborly assistance—lending a hand in illness. The two families also have financial dealings: Ayşe's loan to Sadeddin may be another instance of neighborly assistance, although given the frequency of loans among members of the Aintab community, it could just as plausibly be a business dealing. The court frames the challenge to the neighborhood residents in such a way as to give them the benefit of the doubt, implying that there is no problem if it can be shown that Ayşe had constructive business in Sadeddin's house: in the deputy's question "What business (*maslahat*) does she have in his house?" the word *maslahat* carries overtones of socially or communally beneficial activity. The structure of the case record, leaving the neighbors' defense of their conduct unchallenged, suggests that no one was fined or otherwise punished.

This case both confirms and reverses positions taken by normative law.

While the court summoned Ayşe as well as her husband and neighbor, it addressed its questions only to the two men. Ayşe was the one allegedly "out of place," but her own account of her movements was apparently not deemed necessary to include in the case record. Here, the court action conforms with the principle of holding men accountable for the family's honor. As husband, Haci Mehmed's statement that he was the instigator of the allegedly illicit contact is enough to clinch the case in favor of the neighborhood residents. Where the case does not conform with normative law is in its suggestion that if family honor is at all at stake here, what is being upheld in this neighborhood is the dignity of *men,* who send their wives and sick children into the streets to do their bidding. This case is only one of many in the Aintab court records that surprise by revealing patterns of behavior and perceptions of behavioral meaning that are not predictable from normative law. It exemplifies the point that local moralities may reinterpret legal principles to fit their needs and rearrange legal elements into a locally tailored code of conduct.

Is it the judge who has silenced Ayşe? Does Hüsameddin Efendi himself hold the view that husbands are responsible for their wives' public conduct? Or has he responded to his litigants by hearing and recording the case in a manner that reflects the customary habits of their neighborhood? That Ayşe is not entirely subdued or silenced in the affair is evident from the angry encounter between her and the informant Cuma. When and where she has called him a pimp is not clear—perhaps in the events leading up to the court appearance, perhaps in the course of the court hearings. The cursing is actionable because it constitutes slander, and Cuma indeed chooses to take legal action against Ayşe. (Cuma's action may account for the uncharacteristic note added to the first case summary; otherwise, it is possible that the identity of the two informers would never have been entered into the record.) The written summary of this second stage of the affair, with its endorsement of the two witnesses' support of the slander accusation, suggests that Ayşe will be fined for slander if the kanun penalty is applied.

But has Ayşe's cursing backfired? Not necessarily: she has been erased from the written summary but, even at the risk of punishment, she has publicly voiced her view of the affair. Indeed, Ayşe may feel compelled to speak out for her own honor, since the record pays her no heed while devoting its attention to restoring the moral integrity of her husband. Her cursing, in other words, may have been a calculated move to have herself written into the court record, to create a legal space for herself alongside that reserved for the males involved in the case. By labeling Cuma a moral reprobate, Ayşe suggests that dishonor lies with him, not with herself: calling Cuma a pimp implies that he has been complicit in his own wife's sexual immorality, casting Cuma's wife as in fact the adulteress, not Ayşe, and

Cuma as a cuckold, not Haci Mehmed. Thus, through her cursing, Ayşe has displaced the onus of sexual misconduct onto the informant.

·   ·   ·

This chapter has used sixteenth-century sources to reconstruct under-standings of personhood and identity in contemporary legal life. Our sources—court records, fatwas, sultanic kanun—make it immediately ap-parent that one's sex figured as a core component of legal identity. Labels at court, punishments that differed for men and women, the strong prefer-ence for male witnesses—such aspects of legal practice combined to create a gendered justice, thereby suggesting that bodies and lives were not equally valued. However, because females were only one class of individuals expe-riencing legal discrimination, it appears that this unevenness of the law had more to do with the privileging of the freeborn Muslim city-dwelling male than with qualities intrinsic to the female, or to the Christian, the tribes-man, or the slave. In this regard, legal discourse of the Ottoman sixteenth century reflected a universal premodern assumption of individual inequal-ity that privileged certain males, though it was long before the coming of the Ottomans that the Islamic ideal of the equality of believers had yielded to social pressures to write difference into the law.

Much of this chapter has been devoted to showing how gender was inflected by social class. Class was a powerful legal category in whose delin-eation the conduct of women was a defining element. Aintab was a class-conscious community with a complex set of markers for the privileged—re-ligion, occupation, lineage, place of residence. The absence of elite women from the Aintab court suggests that the ideal of the muhaddere woman shaped the conduct of at least some segments of Aintab's privileged classes. But the actions and words of the many women who *did* come to court make clear that there were discrepancies between the place designated for women in normative discourse and the actual place they occupied in the le-gal life of Aintab. The court was an arena where ordinary users made space for themselves, however ad hoc and constricted it might be in compari-son with the ampler and more comfortable space reserved by normative prescriptions for the more powerful. The people of Aintab were sensitive to matters of honor and dignity, but those sensitivities did not necessarily fol-low prescriptive blueprints. While the elite of Aintab cultivated their supe-riority by remaining aloof from the court, the large "non-elite" population appears to have ignored the view expressed in jurisprudential discourse that its social and moral stature was inferior. Rather, Aintabans were assertive about defending their honor, particularly in the matter of contact between the sexes.

Yet the variety of attitudes articulated before the judge tells us that there was no single standard of conduct accepted by this socially complex community. People might agree on the outer boundaries of acceptable behavior but they actively disagreed over the details. The code of conduct in Ayşe and Sadeddin's neighborhood, where it was acceptable for women to be on the street doing family business, would clearly not have met the approval of all Aintabans. I have suggested that the local population made their own distinctions between proper and improper contact between the sexes— that is, between contacts with legitimate purpose (business dealings, use of the court, neighborly assistance) and idle contact (lingering on the street, peering out a window into the next-door courtyard, dropping in spontaneously to another's home). In sum, social location and individual readings of legal and moral prescriptions combined to produce a textured justice in Aintab.

At least one unanswered question remains: Did Ayşe, the neighbor of Sadeddin, intended for her voice to enter the court record, or was she a hapless victim of her loose tongue? We cannot know. But the next chapter suggests that some women, especially those accused of dishonor, deliberately used the court as an arena to address their fellow citizens as they attempted to rehabilitate their reputations.

5

Morality and
Self-Representation at Court

Although women came to the Aintab court less often than men, they spoke just as much once they got there, and perhaps even more. When they spoke volubly, it was often because they experienced greater difficulty in addressing the law, which was less favorable to females than to males in a number of ways. Legal practice in Aintab, for example, rarely permitted females to give testimony in support of plaintiffs or defendants, with the result that women could not call on other women to support their cases in court. Moreover, the legal option of the oath of innocence was almost never offered to females. The challenge of getting around these obstacles meant that women's legal and rhetorical strategies at court were often different from men's. Yet the court was receptive to women's voices, inscribing in its records the various idioms they employed. Its receptivity was in part an outcome of the Ottoman regime's promotion of its courts as the principal venue for legal business and dispute resolution. Clearly, it was in the interest of the regime, and of the judges employed by it, to ensure that local courts did not create an environment hostile to females. Nor was it in the interest of the Ottoman legal system to privilege certain segments of local society over others. The court was open to a surprising range of strategies and legal rhetoric employed by constituents from a variety of social backgrounds.

Much of this chapter concentrates on the question of "voice"—the individual choice of language and rhetoric that was an intrinsic part of legal strategy. Of course scribal intervention played a role in the translation of actual statements made in court into written form, but the large range of self-representative remarks inscribed in the registers suggests that the court respected the individual voice. For now, let us note two general issues that affected the ways in which individuals approached the court. The first is the nature of the case at hand. When legal rules were not explicitly gendered, females and males spoke similarly at court, in language that appears almost formulaic—for instance, on matters of property. Similarly, when gendered rights were clearly spelled out in the law, speech was rhetorically uninflected. For example, young unmarried women and girls spoke plainly in questions concerning their betrothal, since sharia openly stipulated that a female's consent was necessary to a marriage arranged for her. But in other areas, especially when reputation and honor were at stake, the rhetoric and vocabulary of both sexes were heightened, and females often spoke differently from males. In short, one's biological sex was a critical but not a fixed determinant of how one spoke at court.

The second broad issue that influenced Aintabans' use of the court was resistance to the hierarchy of social and moral worth discussed in the previous chapter. The discourse of social class, articulated largely by the privileged, attributed moral superiority to elites, while the masses were considered to have neither the intelligence nor the refinement to achieve an exemplary life. But as we have seen, the Aintab court records demonstrate popular refusal to settle for the notion that ordinary folk belonged to a lesser moral community. Reputation was a critical social and legal asset for all, and people argued vociferously for their honor and rectitude.

The central theme of this chapter is morality and how it animated the work of the court and its users. Morality was a palpable element running throughout people's talk, and it drove a good deal of business in this mid-sixteenth-century court. Preserving reputation was a goal of much litigation at court and of many of the voluntary statements that Aintabans had the judge write into the court record. The theme of moral character also permeated the work of sharia experts, whose writings and pronouncements debated the moral qualifications of judges and witnesses. Earlier chapters have noted the importance of the ability to give testimony as a measure of civic membership. With so much at stake, it is no wonder that people were preoccupied with their public reputation as well as with the conduct of others.

DEFINING MORALITY AND HONOR

How did our sixteenth-century subjects understand the nature of morality? There are no specific words in the Aintab court records for "morality." Rather, moral awareness seems to be a phenomenon that permeated the court, so fundamental to its work that no label was needed. When the court record had occasion to note an individual's good reputation, it might use a phrase such as "trustworthy and pious." And when local citizens worked together with the court as mediators or bondsmen, scribes termed them "Muslims," less to indicate their religion than to signal their good moral repute. This usage suggests that morality was defined as hewing to a religiously prescribed code of behavior. But how did people understand the content of that code?

For all eras, models of Muslim conduct were perhaps most accessible through the lives of prophets and saints.[1] The content of scripture, the stories recounted by popular preachers, and modes of worship all kept these moral exemplars alive. Most influential was the model of the Prophet Muhammad and other Muslims of the first generation; the Prophet's *sunna*—his words, deeds, and habitual practices—were a universal and authoritative ideal for Muslim conduct.[2] For Aintabans, morality was localized through stories of local saints and also of those early Muslims who fought for Islam in the Aintab region, be they companions of the Prophet or local converts (see chapters 1 and 2 for stories of some of these saints and martyrs).

Contemporary views of morality are displayed in two mid-sixteenth-century texts whose influence would continue over the generations. These two works—*Tarikat-ı Muhammediyye (The Way of Muhammad)*, a popular guide by Birgivi Mehmed, and the more academic *Ahlak-ı Ala'i (The Aliean Ethics)* by Kınalızade Ali—furnished comprehensive expositions of proper moral conduct.[3] Portions of these texts were quite practical, detailing right and wrong ways to act in myriad daily situations. For example, each work enumerated undesirable behaviors in lists of "calamities" of the heart, the tongue, the body, and so on. Birgivi Mehmed named some sixty calamities of the tongue, including calumny, cursing, lying, backbiting, mocking another, revealing another's secret, talking while the Qur'an was being recited, and petitioning for the office of judge, governor, guardian, or executor of a public trust.[4] Kınalızade Ali, who named many of the same errors of speech, cast these "calamities" as illnesses and offered "cures" whose goal was the substitution of virtue *(fazilet)* for vice. Both authors assumed the possibility of discipline based on moral awareness and conscious intent. Drawing on Greek and Islamic classics in the field of ethics, Kınalızade Ali defined "justice" *(adalet)*—the most excellent of virtues—in personal terms as a self-aware moderation, the practice of an Aristotelian mean.[5] Morality thus consisted of the combination of specific behavioral guidelines with spiritual commitment.[6]

How was a community to judge the morality of its members? If spiritual commitment was ultimately knowable by the individual alone, observable conduct was the basis for the only concrete measure of morality: one's reputation. Aintabans were regularly consulted concerning their neighbors' reputations: when Hamza sexually assaulted a woman in his village (he climbed into her bed), his fellow peasants were questioned about his character; they told the judge that "once before he was involved with a woman in this village; he has a record of immoral behavior."[7] And when the woman

Şeyhi was similarly accused, consultation with her neighbors turned up a clean record: "We have never observed any bad behavior on her part, so we can't call her badly behaved."[8] This role of the collective—the neighborhood, the village, the tribe—as moral arbiter was also reflected in its legal accountability for the moral climate in its domain and its authority to request the expulsion of undesirable members.[9] In Aintab in 1540–1541, neighborhoods collectively petitioned for the expulsion of a man accused of chronic lying and deceitfulness and a female teacher accused of corrupting her female students.[10]

The natural outcome of the collective's moral accountability was surveillance. In turn, surveillance provoked the defense of moral reputation and honor. Again, no term for "honor" appears in the Aintab records, yet it was clearly at stake in many cases at court. We do find, however, a much-used term for a blot on one's reputation: *töhmet,* a known offense or suspicion of having committed an offense. To be *töhmetsiz*—"without töhmet"—was to be innocent, free of dishonor. To accuse someone was "to allege töhmet" *(töhmet etmek).* Aintabans fought to have töhmets erased from the public record of the court, defending their honor even at the cost of breaking the law in order to get themselves before the judge and tell their own version of events. In the context of the Aintab court, then, honor can be defined as a commitment to keeping one's reputation unsullied: honor was the compelling need as well as the defensive action taken to maintain an unblemished record of conduct. Even when one was clearly guilty of an immoral or criminal act, it was important to publicly recount the circumstances that impelled one to forsake the community's moral code, in the hopes of redeeming something of one's honor even in the face of punishment.

THE MORAL CONSTITUTION OF THE COURT: WITNESSES AND JUDGE

Morality and the assessment of individual moral character lay at the heart of the court's operations. The character of the judge, of course, was critical to the integrity of a community's legal life. But it is striking that Islamic legal tradition placed the greatest emphasis on the honesty and probity of ordinary witnesses. Legal texts conceded that the character of judges did not always meet ideal standards, but they were uncompromising on the necessity of the honest witness. Their reasoning was that the quality of a judge's ruling depended on the quality of the facts his hearing produced. In the words of Al-Marghinani, "the decree of the judge rests upon proof, and proof rests upon the integrity of the witnesses."[11] In other words, it was the morality of a court's users and the integrity of the act of testimony that constituted the bedrock of the court's viability. The work of local courts depended ultimately on the actions and words of the communities they served.

But how was the moral integrity of the witness to be defined, and what precautions should courts and their constituencies take to prevent immoral persons from threatening the legal life of the community? Legal practice in Muslim societies appears to have worked from an assumption of the essentially moral nature of humans rather than of their inherent sinfulness. This assumption underlay the critical legal procedures of witnessing and oath taking, as well as civic functions sanctioned through the court such as the guardianship of minors or providing surety for property and persons. Muslim societies and the law they produced were not naive about human nature, however, and they recognized the need to prevent those deemed dishonest from disrupting legal procedure. At the heart of the matter was establishing the truth of words spoken in testimony.

There was consensus in Islamic legal tradition on some basic qualifications for witnesses: they could not be blind, nor could they be slaves. In addition, a tradition attributed to the Prophet Muhammad (a *hadith*) asserted that a person guilty of having slandered another was disbarred from witnessing. As for non-Muslims, they could give testimony only for other non-Muslims. But beyond these strictures, the definition of who was lacking in the requisite degree of moral rectitude was a matter of opinion. Consequently, the qualifications for witnessing appear to have been regularly reformulated as moral standards underwent cultural shifts over time. Al-Marghinani himself noted the existence of historical tensions in the Hanafi school's attitude toward the question of investigating the character of potential witnesses. While the founder of the school, Abu Hanifa, believed that "the magistrate ought to rest contented with the apparent probity of a Muslim," his principal followers Abu Yusuf and Muhammad, less sanguine about human nature, believed that the judge should scrutinize all witnesses. Al-Marghinani noted that the difference among these three founding fathers was frequently attributed to "the difference of the times" between their generations, adding that "in the present age" (i.e., the twelfth century), "the doctrine of the two disciples" prevailed.[12]

It is difficult to know precisely what procedures for screening witnesses operated at the Aintab court—whether, for example, the judge personally scrutinized potential witnesses before conducting a hearing or had the assistance of other court personnel. Or perhaps the prevailing practice was more in line with Abu Hanifa's view that only the obviously unfit need be barred from testifying. Evidence from the records—specifically, a case recorded on October 6, 1540—suggests that ultimately it was the local community that was responsible for monitoring the civic performance of its members:

Yusuf b. Mehmed came to court and summoned the official, Mehmed b. Muhsin, and made the following accusation: "This Mehmed, the night watchman, attacked me at night and hit me with a mighty blow." When [Mehmed] denied the accusation and proof was requested of [Yusuf], Manend b. Hüseyin and Tarak b. Haydar gave testimony in a legally approved manner. [Whereupon] the imam and the neighborhood gathered, came to the court, and lodged the following protest: "We cannot trust either the actions or the words of the said Manend." It was decreed that he [Manend] should be banished from the neighborhood.[13]

As we see, the original question of the night watchman's alleged misconduct was displaced by the problem of a dishonest witness, Manend b. Hüseyin. It is his neighbors acting collectively, with their imam as their leader, who protest against him. Manend's public testimony may have been just the opportunity they were waiting for to exercise the legal prerogative of a city quarter or a village to petition that disreputable individuals be removed from its midst. The law books of both Süleyman and his father Selim prescribed banishment—either temporary or permanent—as an appropriate punishment for such persons.[14] (The court register never tells us what happened to Yusuf's suit against the watchman.)

Beginning with the Prophet Muhammad, powerful models emphasized that the act of witnessing demanded an uncompromising standard of moral integrity. This point is made forcefully in a popular anecdote about a judge of Bursa, the famed Molla Feneri, and the fourth Ottoman sultan Bayezid I (d. 1402). When the sultan claimed familiarity with a particular case, implying his suitability to act as witness, Molla Feneri refused to allow him to give testimony. The judge's refusal was based on the grounds that the sultan had "abandoned his community"; that is, he did not take part in Friday communal prayers. The legend tells us that the sultan, duly reprimanded, proceeded to construct a mosque beside his palace, where he appointed a special place for himself and never again missed communal prayer.[15] The importance of the story for our purposes is that moral lapses tolerated in the ruler of a Muslim community are intolerable in a witness. Giving testimony was a *civic* act, and the witness had to be an upstanding member of his or her own local community.

The affair of the sultan and the molla suggests that in the late fourteenth century, attendance at communal prayer was a behavior that moral authorities were anxious to inculcate. Al-Marghinani's own twelfth-century list of those disqualified from witnessing included slanderers, women who lamented or sang publicly, habitual drunks, usurers, those who engaged in base acts such as urinating or consuming food on a high road, and those who openly inveighed against the Prophet and his companions. "Where a man is not restrained by a sense of shame, from such actions as these," commented the jurist, "he exposes himself to a suspicion that he will not refrain from falsehood."[16] It is worth noting that this same linkage between inappropriate conduct and dishonest speech was made by the members of the Aintab community who distrusted both "the actions and the words" of their problematic neighbor Manend. Individuals engaging in disapproved acts were termed *fasik*, a word that, perhaps predictably, encompassed a range of meaning—indecorous, lacking in integrity, unjust. As we saw in chapter 3, İbn Kemal, chief mufti of the Ottoman domain from 1525 to 1534, issued a lengthy contemporary catalogue of the disqualified, ranging from astrologers to heretics to men who let their wives mix indiscriminately with male company. Like his fellow jurist Al-Marghinani, the Ottoman mufti combined doctrinal and behavioral lapses in his updated sixteenth-century catechism of unacceptable conduct.

So important was bearing witness to the integrity of a court's work that the qualifications of the judge were framed in terms of those of a witness. Al-Marghinani's section on the duties of the judge opens with the statement that "The authority of a judge is not valid unless he possesses the qualifications necessary to a witness; that is, unless he be free, sane, adult, a Muslim, and unconvicted of slander."[17] The rationale for deriving the judge's qualifications from the standard established for witnesses was that giving testimony and making judgments were both acts of speech that determined the fate of another. Moreover, in the hierarchy of those speech acts, testimony outranked judgment since the latter was dependent on the former.

Beyond these fundamental qualifications, deliberations about the worthiness of a judge were focused on his personal conduct in office rather than the quality of his legal knowledge or the nature of his decrees. A particular concern was the susceptibility of judges to bribery, either to obtain office or once in office—hence the prohibition on judges accepting gifts or invitations to private banquets and entertainments. Nor should judges show familiarity or favoritism toward one litigant over another. In sum, prescriptive etiquette for the office emphasized the judge's impartiality in relations with his constituency.

Much attention was also given to the question of whether an individual who actively desired the position of judge was worthy of being one. On the one hand, the professional culture of the religiously learned encouraged a posture of reluctance toward the office of judge both because of the worldly compromises and temptations it entailed and because of the daunting challenge of making just decisions. Indeed, according to Hanafi tradition, two of the school's founding fathers had to be beaten or imprisoned before they could be induced to accept the office of judge. On the other hand, an absence of confidence and a lack of devotion to the office meant that a judge might not possess the authority to create an environment of respect for the law in the community to which he was posted.[18] We saw above that the religious authority Birgivi Mehmed counted it a calamity of the tongue to request the office of judge. He went on to say that people have misunderstood this caution: it is not that the office of judge is forbidden, but rather that most individuals are unable to execute it with justice; it is best therefore to take the office only if no more qualified person can be found.[19]

The fatwas of Ebu Suud add some sixteenth-century flavor to this familiar if ambivalent discourse on the nature of the judge's office. In the following fatwa on the dilemma caused by a bad judge, the renowned Ottoman jurist implies a comparison between judges and muftis in which the former come off worse:

> Query: Zeyd, a judge, attends a wedding where there is music and, God forbid, [while there] he is socially intimate with base men (*fasik*). Subsequently, Amr requests a fatwa on the question of what should be done to the judge Zeyd, and the noble fatwa's response is that "Such a person is not worthy of being judge." If, when Amr makes the fatwa public, Zeyd seizes the fatwa and won't give it back to Amr and makes light of the fatwa by saying "I am not judge by virtue of a fatwa, I am judge by virtue of the sultan's letter of appointment," what should be done to Zeyd according to the law?
> Response: Zeyd is dismissed from office on account of the first action [his conduct in attending the wedding], and his decrees are not valid. The sultanic appointment to the judgeship is given on the assumption that [the judge] will behave in a righteous (*adil*) manner. Should his immorality (*fisk*) become apparent [after his appointment], he is dismissed; if it was already apparent and the judgeship awarded despite it, then he is not dismissed [although] he deserves to be. But if he makes light of a sharia ruling [the fatwa], he becomes an apostate, and is executed if he does not reaffirm [his allegiance to] Islam.[20]

The fatwa's protagonist "Zeyd" exemplifies the stereotypical flaws of a judge—lapsed sociomoral judgment and overconfidence. "Amr," who takes action against him, appears to be a local citizen outraged by the behavior of his community's magistrate. It might be thought that Ebu Suud, delivering this opinion as a mufti, was displaying a personal bias against judges, but he himself had served as judge—and in the top judgeships of the empire, Bursa and Istanbul. Although it castigates the immoral judge, Ebu Suud's fatwa also demonstrates the risk of intense scrutiny that was assumed by those who accepted judgeships. Implied in the fatwa was the perception that most muftis acquired their standing through popular consensus regarding their personal qualifications rather than through a system of imperial appointment, and that a mufti's opinion, unlike a judge's decree, was an opinion based on sacred scripture rather than mundane fact. All the more critical then, noted Ebu Suud, was the sultan's responsibility to appoint good judges in the first place.

We can now better understand the characterization of the provincial judge described in chapter 3. Hailed in his biographical notice as "notorious for his firmness and integrity in the performance of his office, counted among judges as dignified and well-mannered, a dread-inspiring, venerable magistrate," Molla Hüsameddin was projected through the text as a person bearing authority derived from moral conduct.[21] This was perhaps the greatest encomium that could be bestowed on an individual who had made his reputation as provincial judge rather than as mufti or teacher. The latter careers were traditionally more honored because those who followed them had a closer relationship to sacred texts and less susceptibility to worldly temptations and tribulations. What was critical in a judge was his ability to project an aura of authority, and its corollary—the ability to promote a climate of respect for the law. The judge was a public figure and his office, in the view of his constituents, an essentially communal one.

Other factors also help explain why etiquette was emphasized more than legal prowess as the hallmark of a good judge. For one thing, it was easier to evaluate a judge's professional behavior than the corpus of his work. Indeed, the very notion of contemplating a judge's legal approach or his interpretive acumen was, in a sense, inappropriate, since each judgment *(hükm)* was considered to be based on a unique set of facts, facts moreover that were established by the witnesses. In this regard, the judge was unlike the mufti, who might acquire a reputation on the basis of "the excellence of his answers" (an attribute that was cited as one foundation of the great reputation enjoyed by the seventeenth-century Syrian mufti Khayr al-Din al-Ramli).[22] Rather, it was the moral climate established by a judge that was critical.

An additional, and equally important, reason for the stress on personal conduct was that intellectual achievement was held to be meaningless if not conjoined with personal morality. Knowing the teachings of Islam without living by them undermined one's claim to authority over others.[23] That is why Al-Marghinani's and İbn Kemal's interleaving of bad doctrine and bad conduct in their catalogues of immoral behavior would not have struck their followers—as it may today's reader—as an oddly assembled mix.

The concern over judicial etiquette was intimately related to the question of authority. At the heart of the debate over judges was a profound yet troubled awareness of the impact of the judge on those upon whom he sat in judgment. Judges were key figures in the communities where they served, drawn daily into myriad mundane local concerns. No wonder then that the figure of the judge was a popular if ambivalent subject of literary representation in Muslim societies. On the one hand, people recognized that judges were necessary to a smoothly functioning society. This is demonstrated in another story about the early Ottoman sultans, in which it is the subjects of the nascent dynasty who urge the sultan to appoint a judge over them.[24] On the other hand, the judge was traditionally a frequent figure in Muslim literary culture, where he was portrayed as falling prey to lusts of the flesh, undone by overweening pride, or duped by the faked testimony of self-interested tricksters. Sixteenth-century Ottomans were treated to this theme in a biography of the Ottoman judge of Mihaliç, which graphically recounted the dignitary's disturbingly undignified obsession with a young man of the city.[25]

THE COURT AND THE MORAL CONSTITUTION OF THE COMMUNITY

It was the consequence for others of their authoritative pronouncements that linked the ordinary witness and the judge as persons whose conduct the community could legitimately scrutinize. But giving testimony in court was not the only morally charged civic act that citizens of places like Aintab performed. Other sociolegal responsibilities undertaken by ordinary individuals were similarly framed as serious moral undertakings—for example, assuming the guardianship of orphans or acting as bondsman for the property, finances, or whereabouts of another. These routine social duties were connected to the court because the appointments of guardians and bondsmen were frequently (perhaps routinely?) registered before the judge and the subsequent performance of their duties monitored by him. Such ties between the legal arena and the broader activities of local citizens in doing good and serving their families and neighborhoods are precisely what constitutes the organic relationship between law and local culture.

The guardianship of orphan children was surrounded with particularly strong moral injunctions. Orphans were defined as minors who had lost their father. A critical aspect of their guardianship was the protection of their inheritance. In Aintab, there was an apparent preference for mothers as guardians,[26] though by law the judge had the authority to appoint a guardian from outside the family if necessary. But because judges could not possibly know the life circumstances of all their constituents, they relied on community input in the monitoring of orphans' welfare, as they did in so many other aspects of their job. In September 1541, for example, two men reported to the judge that that the three orphan children of one Haci Abdullah were in "need of support—*extreme* need," and the judge authorized as "necessary and urgent" the sale of a house and part of a vineyard that they had inherited.[27] Records of appointment stressed the moral qualifications of a guardian: when another set of three orphan siblings required someone to manage their inheritance, one Emir Ahmed b. Haci Ahmed was appointed after "Muslims testified that he was a fit and recognized person because of [his] trustworthiness and piety *(emanet ve diyanet ile mahall ve ma'ruf kimesnedir)."* The gravity of Emir Ahmed's role as guardian was further underlined by the fact that the four case-witness signatories to the record of his appointment were persons of local repute themselves—three mollas and the sheikh (or headman) of the textile merchants.[28]

Mediation was another court-sanctioned service performed by community members whose discursive representation in the Aintab court's records signaled it as a morally charged act. During the year 1540–1541, a substantial number of disputes were resolved through arbitration *(sulh)* by court-recognized mediators. Such cases were recorded in a twin set of ritual phrases that marked first the presence of severe disagreement and disputation and then the stepping into the breach of "peacemakers." In several instances, the peacemakers were described as "from among the Muslims."[29] Additionally, about half the records of mediation in the year 1540–1541 included the hadith, or prophetic tradition, "Peacemaking is a good work *(el-sulh hayır)*."[30] A typical formulation is found in the suit of the villager Ramazan against İskender, a former slave, in which the plaintiff claimed that İskender had knocked out four of his teeth four years earlier. The case record twice noted the parties' "serious dispute and severe disagreement," and the case was turned over to arbitration when the testimony of witnesses could not put an end to the fighting: "Peacemakers intervened, and acting in accordance with the hadith *'el-sulh hayır,'* reconciliation was achieved for 15 gold pieces [paid by İskender to Ramazan], and both sides accepted the accord."[31]

The use of this hadith in the context of dispute resolution and the use of the term "Muslims" to mean upstanding persons whose judgment could be trusted are the only regular invocations of religious allegiance in the court records. But an assumption permeating the record, and presumably also the court itself, is that moral conduct is coterminous with piety and a religiously informed identity. Acts at court were imbued with religious meaning. Legal procedure required that witnesses use the formula "I testify" *(ashhadu* in Arabic, *şehadet ederim* in Turkish) to remind them that they were taking an oath, lest they be tempted to lie.[32] This act was the more symbolically powerful for the fact that the identical words open the Muslim profession of faith, bearing witness to the unity of God.

The oath was another element in legal procedure that was instilled with a religious character.[33] Oaths were a procedural option employed in the absence of material proof: when plaintiffs could not produce evidence to support their claim against the defendant, they could if they chose direct the judge to administer an "oath to God" *(yemin billah)* to the defendant. In the Aintab court records of 1540–1541, defendants taking an oath typically swore the truth of their own testimony, and judgment was then made in their favor on the strength of the oath alone.[34] Once it was put into legal play, then, the oath of innocence invariably settled the case in the oath taker's favor.[35] The integrity of such cases was staked on the honesty of a single individual, an individual moreover who was party to the dispute. The critical importance of verbal honesty was impressed on oath takers in the Aintab court by requiring them to place their hand on the Qur'an—"the ancient words" or "the divine words," as the court record put it. Christians at court were by no means exempted from the religio-moral aspects of the oath—they simply used a copy of the Bible to swear on.[36]

Words uttered at court resonated powerfully. By privileging oral evidence and, as a corollary, putting great stock in truth telling, the work of a local court inevitably assimilated the speaker's moral integrity, indeed his or her relationship to God, to words spoken in the presence of the judge. This centrality of speech acts to legal procedure was merely one manifestation of the broad cultural importance of the oral for demonstrating the integrity of the individual as well as of the community. Verbal statements played a crucial role in establishing and enacting ethical codes. The relationship between the oral and the moral character of the speaker is immediately evident to every student of Islamic culture. It begins with the Qur'an, whose literal meaning is "recitation": Muhammad, the perfect Muslim, was instructed by the angel Gabriel to recite God's revelations for the benefit of the community; only after the Prophet's death was God's message organized into a written text. The hadith, the orally transmitted reports of the Prophet's own actions and words as well as actions and words of which he approved, formed an essential basis for the development of law, ethical literature, and even history. This oral tradition at the heart of Islamic society linked acts of speech, the moral character of the individual, and the well-being of the community: the validity of a hadith, and hence the sociolegal regulations founded on it, depended on the moral reputation of each human link in its chain of transmitters, its *isnad* or "prop."

Embedded in the Turkish language is recognition of the cultural fact that to transmit experience of a social event through speech is to ally oneself to it as witness and thereby to assume a responsibility for the construction of the event's communal significance. There are two tenses in Turkish for reporting events that have occurred, one connoting eyewitness experience of the event and the other only hearsay or other indirect knowledge. Oral testimony in the Aintab court registers is always recorded in the first of these tenses. The second occurs only in the statements of police agents bringing offenders to court on the basis of the allegations of informants. An example is the statement of the police chief Sinan that opened a case of adultery: "He summoned the individuals named Kürdi Ahmed and Fatmena daughter of Ahmed . . . and brought a case against them, saying: 'The aforementioned Kürdi *allegedly* went to the house of the aforementioned Fatmena at night, lit a candle and entered the straw shed, and committed adultery with Fatmena at night *(Fatmenaya zina itmişdir)*.'"[37] The officer's use of the "reported" past tense—marked in the translation by the word *allegedly*—suggests that either circumstantial evidence or information supplied by others brought the incident to the authorities' attention. (Kürdi Ahmed and Fatmena went on to confess to their illicit rendezvous.)

The discourse on witnessing assumed the capacity of the ordinary individual to give testimony honestly and effectively. Indeed, the whole system of law in practice was predicated on this assumption and its corollaries, the possibility of social consensus on what was moral and what was immoral conduct and the possibility of identifying and eliminating the morally untrustworthy. The Aintab court records demonstrate that this emphasis on ordered testimony as the bedrock of the court's work was not merely an ideal of jurisprudential theory. Litigants in the year 1540–1541 brought with them as witnesses a host of individuals from their social circles—relatives, neighbors, business associates, and so on—and it is the speech of these community members that constitutes the great bulk of the court's record.

But how does this assumption of moral maturity square with the pervasive theme in jurisprudence and other formal discourses of the intellectual deficiencies of the *avamm*, "the masses," and their consequent moral inferiority? As we saw in chapter 4, the social hierarchies explicit in legal discourse frequently assumed that members of social, religious, and political elites had a greater capacity for moral behavior than did less privileged classes. Here we have two seemingly contradictory stances regarding the moral autonomy of the individual, one that saw "the masses" as inherently liable to misjudgment and one that saw most of them as capable of honest and discerning testimony. The fact that both stances were endorsed by Islamic religio-social tradition would seem to be an artifact of the tension between egalitarian and hierarchical impulses described in chapter 4. One might argue that the legal *process* restored the moral integrity of those whom normative jurisprudential representations of personal worth had the effect of marginalizing. In the Aintab court, both views are evident in practice, suggesting that perhaps they were not so contradictory as might at first seem. While "the masses" populated the court as plaintiffs, defendants, and witnesses, other more select legal duties (acting as mediator, guardian, or bondsman, for example) were reserved for "the Muslims"—the pious, the morally distinguished.

We have been focusing in this section on the connections between legal ethics and communal or religious notions of morality. Commenting on Islamic legal practices as evinced in the present-day Moroccan court of Sefrou, the legal anthropologist Lawrence Rosen remarks that "to scrutinize testimony is to apply social concepts of probity to legal constructions of fact."[38] In other words, whoever "screens" potential witnesses for their moral rigor must inevitably draw on broadly shared communal definitions of rectitude. Like other scholars, Rosen is here subscribing to the view that law is an integral part of a society's culture and not a body of rules, norms, and procedures apart from popular notions of right and wrong. According to this broadly shared approach to the study of law, legal debates and practices have their own internal logic but are in intimate dialogue with other discourses, be they religious, political, regional, cultural, and so on. This is certainly true of Aintab in 1540–1541. But this dialogue did not come about simply as a matter of course. No matter how intimately legal practice depended on the participation of local individuals, and hence on their understandings of right and wrong, the law was still something apart. In other words, the bridge between law and local culture required constant upkeep and repair if it was to bear steady traffic. An episode that took place in the Aintab court in August 1541 will help illustrate the point that maintaining legal cultures was an ongoing and self-conscious process.

The problem confronting the community was that the bakers of Aintab were purveying a shoddy product. Or at least some of them were, for six were investigated over the course of several days at the beginning of the month.[39] The flaws in each baker's bread were exposed one by one: İmamkulu's bread was stale, Baba Kalender's fell short of the standard weight, while Kara Ahmed's loaves were both stale and scorched. In disciplining the bakers, the investigating authorities invoked the language of morality by framing the poor workmanship as a lapse of responsibility to the community. The examination was carried out under the supervision of the market inspector *(muhtasip)*, Şarabdar Abdurrahman, and the bread was judged by the sheikh of the bakers, Haci Mehmed, and a master baker, Ustad Yusuf. When the sixth baker's bread was found to be insufficiently leavened and also stale, the sheikh appears to have lost patience. He exclaimed, "It is shameful to produce this kind of bread! Making bread like this and selling it to Muslims is not lawful in the sight of God *(Allah' dan helal değildir)*." Why the vehemence of the sheikh's speech? Certainly the critical role of bread as a dietary fixture rendered the bakers' task intrinsically susceptible to moralizing rhetoric.[40] In the sheikh's view, the failure of his fellow bakers was not simply negligent workmanship but a sin.

But there is something more at work here. An investigation of the bakers of Aintab was not unusual, since the monitoring of market products and practices was a principal duty of the market inspector. The office of the muhtasip was an old institution, one whose mandate under Islamic law also included the enforcement of moral conduct. Nor was the sheikh's admonitory language unusual, given the connection between ethics and market conduct. What was *not* a "natural" aspect of the affair of the bakers was the venue of the disciplining, which was carried out in the court. It is this point that highlights the deliberateness of efforts to mesh law and local culture, to link institutions of the law with the quotidian work of the community in maintaining an equitable society.

The key fact here is that the Aintab market inspector, the catalyst in the incident, figures only once in the court records during the eight months from October 1540 (the earliest records studied in this book) until the end of May 1541.[41] The muhtasip's next appearance, on May 29, coincided with a significant moment in Aintab's legal life: the simultaneous arrival of a special agent representing the Ottoman regime and news of the appointment of a new judge, who would take up office in person on June 23. The mission of the special agent was to recover tax debts to the Ottoman regime incurred by prominent Aintaban tax-farmers, and in general to bring matters of fiscal and economic management (such as the work of the market inspector) into the purview of the court. When the new judge, Hüsameddin Efendi, arrived, a figure more powerful than his predecessors, he continued the project of extending the scope of the Aintab court's jurisdiction and creating an invigorated climate of respect for the law. The investigation of the bakers' product is only one example in the records from May 29 on of the expanded and more fully articulated linkage between the court's work and the moral economy of the community. As I suggest more fully in other chapters, these two appointments at the end of May signal a new and more thorough stage in the integration of the Aintab court into an imperial legal system.

The very first case heard after the arrival of the special agent, on May 29, was a routine price-setting action by the market inspector (more precisely, by one of the two individuals who held the office jointly). Three days later, both holders of the office were summoned to court to settle their own debt to the state; although the market inspectorship was a lucrative tax-farm, the two inspectors owed sizable arrears of 26,000 akçes.[42] The message was that the court would now monitor two aspects of this important office: its fiscal relationship to the state and its routine work. Products regulated at court in subsequent weeks included soap, meat, bread, pastries, red grapes, peaches, and onions.

The integration of the market inspectorship into the jurisdiction of the court was only partly inspired by the Ottoman regime's interest in collecting revenue. By incorporating the work of the office into its ongoing business—and perhaps using force to do so—the court gained legitimation for itself and indirectly for the governing regime. In the episode involving the bakers, for example, the court acquired an aura of concern for the welfare of ordinary Aintabans, making sure they were supplied with good bread. Moreover, by ensuring that words such as those of the sheikh of the bakers were spoken before the judge, the court "naturalized" the moral standards and professional practices of the community as its own business. The point here is that links between the world of the court and the daily life of the community required constant and deliberate tightening in order for the court's legal culture to maintain continuity with popular mores. In this regard, we must not forget that the court was in competition with other legal authorities in Aintab, and its success therefore depended substantially on its attractiveness to potential clients.

MORAL COMMUNITY AND GENDER

In considering how gender figured in the debates about who was fit to participate in the legal life of the community, let us begin with the all-important question of witnessing. Authorities disagreed over whether and to what extent women could give testimony at court, in part because the subject of women's witnessing precipitated a larger cultural debate about the female intellect and women's place in society. These debates, of course, insofar as they were committed to writing, reflected the views of men. Women's inferior intellect was a major theme that was widely sounded in the literary heritage of early modern Muslim societies.[43]

With regard to jurisprudence, the Hanafi school (to which the Ottoman government if not all of its subjects adhered) took a more liberal view of women's capacity to bear witness than did the Shafi'i school, for instance. The latter held that women's intellectual deficiencies prevented them from giving testimony in all but the common matter of property, whereas the Hanafis accepted women's testimony concerning marriage and divorce, guardianship, and other matters. The Hanafis were not without reservations about women's observational acuity and memory, however. Women's testimony was accepted only as the last resort, in the absence of male witnesses. Moreover, it was barred from any case involving punishment—any criminal case, that is—because of lingering doubts about female powers of observation and memory outside an exclusively female domain. In non-criminal matters, the memory problem was addressed by requiring two females to serve the function of one male witness.

The Hanafi attitude reflects less a belief in the inherent mental incapacity of women than an implicit recognition that the sexes were socially constructed. Al-Marghinani, for example, insisted on a woman's innate capacity to witness because she had the requisite faculties of sight, memory, and the capacity to communicate. Nevertheless, he noted, the rhythms of women's daily lives made them less desirable witnesses than men. When challenged that four women should constitute a sufficient number of witnesses in an ordinary case (on the principle that two female witnesses equal one male), the jurist used social grounds to dismiss this "suggestion from analogy." Its undesirable consequence was that "there would be frequent occasions for [women's] appearance in public, in order to give evidence: whereas their privacy is the most laudable."[44]

Practice in the Aintab court in 1540–1541 paralleled the limits elaborated in jurisprudence. While women regularly came before the judge as plaintiffs, defendants, guardians, or bondswomen, only four times over the course of thirteen months did they serve as witnesses.[45] This near-ban on female testimony meant that a woman could not count on being able to call upon other women in support of her legal claims. This limitation was exacerbated by the ban in Hanafi law on family members testifying on each oth-er's behalf.[46] As a consequence, since women spent much of their daily lives in the company of other women or family, there was a whole range of female experience that was difficult to document and thereby render amenable to treatment by the court.

Women were sophisticated enough to anticipate when a problem might require legal intervention, and sometimes could arrange for male witnesses to be present at critical moments. Property issues, for example, were amen-able to such planning. But what of problems that erupted suddenly, when witnesses could not be arranged? Incidents of this nature often involved quarrels or insults that occurred between two individuals in isolation. When Kuddampaşa accused her stepson Tac Ahmed of attacking her with a dag-ger, she could bring no proof of her claim, and the young man cleared him-self with an oath of innocence.[47] Likewise, Esma's inability to substantiate her slander suit against her brother (she claimed he had called her a whore) led to his oath of innocence—"because she was unable to produce the req-uisite number of witnesses," noted the record.[48]

These two men were protected by the possibility of taking an oath. But only twice in some thirty cases of oath taking during the year 1540–1541 was a woman offered the option of the oath.[49] In other words, the oath ap-pears to have been a legal defense largely inaccessible to women. Female lit-igants therefore had significantly less opportunity than men did to clear themselves of accusation of wrongdoing. The striking gender discrepancy in the use of the oath in the Aintab court resulted in part because women were much more often victims of male aggression than vice versa, and thus statistically more often plaintiffs without witness than defendant. But it is hard not to draw the conclusion that there was a cultural bias against women taking the oath.

How does women's moral status figure in these questions of legal pro-cedure? The answer is ambiguous. In the Hanafi jurisprudential debate, women's *moral* capacity does not seem to be an issue: while their social roles may diminish their effectiveness as witnesses, their capacity *as women* for honesty and integrity is not questioned. It is the "laudability of their privacy," to use Al-Marghinani's formulation, that trumps the plausibility of their testimony. This social argument against women's witnessing is reflected in popular sixteenth-century readings of class difference, discussed in the pre-vious chapter, which endowed elite women with superior moral status be-cause their voices were publicly inaudible. A fatwa delivered by İbn Kemal underlined the problematic nature of women's voices: when asked if it was permissible for women to gather and pray in an audible manner, he an-swered that it was forbidden for women to cause men to hear their voices.[50]

Women and men faced the court on procedurally unequal ground. Vir-tually unable to enlist their own sex in their defense or to take the oath of innocence, women enjoyed fewer structural props for their suits and their voices at court. Moreover, unlike men, they had to resolve the tension between secluding one's voice to signify moral status and speaking one's own voice to defend one's reputation and general well-being. At the same time, women must have felt some pressure to confront these obstacles and ambiguities, since the local court was gaining prominence in these years as an arbiter of disputes and, more intangibly, of morality. In other words, anyone with something important to say had better say it before the judge and, in addition, have it inscribed in the community record maintained by the court. How did all this affect the status of women's voices as they gave testimony in their own behalf? One way to get at this question is to compare how women and men and girls and boys spoke at court and what strategies they used.

A striking aspect of speech as cast by the Aintab scribes is the similarity of male and female voices in some domains and their difference in others. Recorded testimony was largely formulaic and ungendered in questions of property (including money) and all relations surrounding it. This was true whether a case was situated within the locus of the family (inheritance, marital property), the local economy (animals, tools, orchards, and vineyards), commerce and finances (loans and debts, purchase and sale, tax liability and payment), and so on. Property disputes were familiar and, in Aintab at least, routine. Hence there was a certain comfort level when people litigated over money and property at court. Moreover, because court talk about property was shaped by familiar rules and customary practices, the persona of the property owner (and his or her sex) was less at stake than it was in other kinds of legal issues.

While far less frequent in the court records, adultery cases were also formulaic, recording men's and women's confession or admission of guilt in parallel language. Here are some examples. When Kürdi and Fatmena confessed before the judge, Kürdi said, "I went at night to her house, lit a candle in her barn, and had sex with the aforementioned Fatmena," and Fatmena said, "The aforementioned Kürdi had sex with me with my own free will."[51] When Ali and Huri confessed, Ali said, "I've been [attached] to the aforementioned Huri for a while, and I would come and see her, and I also had illicit sex with her," and Huri said, "The aforementioned Ali and I have had an attachment to each other for a while, and I had illicit sex with him."[52] As we see, the male had a slightly more active verbal role and he reported more facts, but the court recorded male and female voices in a similar register. In another case, the scribe recorded the voices of the two adulterers as one: "We have each had a passion for the other for a while, and we committed adultery with each other."[53] An obvious reason for this parallelism of voice is that admitting guilt is by definition ceasing to strategize, since there is nothing more to be said. Adulterers were typically brought to court by local police, and their accusation and confession appear to be a formality. Thus if strategizing to evade arrest took place in any of these cases, and if women and men protested differently, it was at an earlier and unrecorded stage of events.[54]

In contrast to the standard talk about property at court or the standard admission of adultery, in other legal matters the proliferation of rhetorical strategies and their gendering is striking. The "raised voices" and charged language described in chapter 3 are most often evident in areas of sexual misconduct that were less scripted than adultery. These matters included sexually loaded social contact between unmarried individuals, rape, and the widespread habit of cursing in sexually slanderous language. Not only were the rules less clear in such matters—most lay outside the traditional compass of sharia—but one's personal honor and reputation were explicitly at stake. We might speak of a gendered grammar of argument as males and females engaged in litigation in a legal terrain that was fraught with personal consequences.

MARGINALITY AND SELF-REPRESENTATION

Because there were no lawyers in the Islamic court system, the burden of self-representation was carried directly by ordinary women and men who sought to use the court or were summoned to account by it. Narratives of intent, motivation, and extenuating circumstances were unmediated by the formulations of experts. One might choose to be represented before the judge by a proxy *(vekil)* who was perhaps more conversant than oneself in the ways of the court, but even the latter spoke as a lay citizen. Particularly when honor was challenged, creating disequilibrium in one's sense of personhood, it was critical to speak words of self-exoneration in one's own voice. Men and women alike spoke out at such moments, but they did so from different rhetorical scripts. Men generally attacked those who were the vehicle of their dishonor. While females sometimes took a similarly aggressive tack, they more often used the language of pleading, repentance, or even self-censure.

Males often spoke with anger and indignation. When the little daughter of Muhsin b. Babacık threw stones at the house of Haci Mansur, the latter answered insult with insult. He attacked Muhsin both physically and verbally, grabbing his beard and saying, "Aren't you a man? Why do you bother wearing a turban? Discipline your daughter!" The Haci registered an affront that struck at two bodily zones of honor—beard and head covering.[55] Muhsin apparently regarded the insult as excessive, since he took quasi-legal action by having Mansur's statement recorded at court, a move that fell just short of bringing a suit against him.

Moral indignation also characterized the statements men made when they divorced wives admittedly guilty of adultery or caught in circumstances suggestive of sexual transgression. In these moments, it was critical that the injury to the husband's honor be erased by displacing the moral onus onto the sinful wife. The words of men repudiating their wives were varied, but they all made the point that the women had abandoned moral standards defined and upheld by the husbands: "I renounce the woman, she is no longer fit to be my wife" (the Armenian İskender); "A woman like this who can't behave morally is no good for me" (Şenok); "She doesn't obey me; she has injured my honor" (Mehmed); "She is no good for me, she doesn't obey me, she follows immoral ways, she is trouble" (Ali).[56] The requisite tone was harsh and condemning, since its purpose was to establish the male speaker as the measure of female worth.

Boys too spoke in tones of anger and censure when their honor was assaulted, even though they lacked the social and legal stature of the adult male. Boys were vulnerable because they were not infrequently the object of male sexual desire.[57] When the boy Ali was pursued and then attacked in the street by Davud b. Mahmud, he gave the following account of the incident in court: "As I was on my way home, this Davud said things to me like 'My soul, my life.' When he said 'I love you,' I said, 'Stop talking like you're out of your mind! Get away from me!' So he hit me and injured me.'"[58] Ali's narrative in court displayed the appropriate male response—expressing anger aroused by moral indignation and questioning the opponent's capacity for rational behavior.

It is noteworthy that the voices of boys were never heard at court except when their moral reputation was impugned. Because boys lacked beards, substantial headgear, households and family dependants, and business properties—all of which were zones of honor for the adult male (and therefore potential targets of insult)—their honor was vested in their bodies. Likewise, sexual assault brought a number of young girls before the judge in the year 1540–1541. Honor of the body, then, was a public legal concern in Aintab that required even children to speak up in court. The fact that its violation was the one sure avenue to court for the preadult suggests that dishonor followed one into adulthood if it was not dissipated through legal action. As we noted in chapter 3, reputation was a measurable entity, and communal memory (or court record) was charged with toting up an individual's moral violations. As a person's criminal record is carefully tracked today, so was one's "reputational record" tracked in sixteenth-century Aintab.

An insult allegedly delivered to the boy Abdulaziz accounts for a very interesting record in the court register since it permits us to observe the scribe at work transforming a messy story into a legally clean record. In the process the scribe literally erased the allegation that Abdulaziz was involved in a sexual encounter with an older man, thereby enacting a legal stratagem that protected the boy's honor. According to the confusing narrative of plaintiff, defendant, and witnesses in the case, Mehmed b. Hüseyin entered the shop of Mehmed b. Hasan at night and drew a knife on him; during the scuffle that ensued, the assailant's turban fell off before he managed to escape from the shop. When asked for his version of events, the assailant apparently justified his entry into the shop on the grounds that he had seen a boy within (implied was some form of sexual irregularity). However, the court scribe later crossed out this portion of the assailant's testimony ("there was a boy *[oğlan]* in the aforementioned Mehmed's shop"), and thereby rendered the first of the two entries recording the affair simply the story of one man making an unprovoked attack on another and fleeing. The second entry *(sicill)* consisted of a slander case brought by the boy Abdulaziz against the assailant Mehmed, apparently for the very allegation that the scribe struck from the assistant's testimony. Mehmed was unable to provide proof for his allegation, and Abdulaziz cleared his name by taking an oath of innocence.[59]

There is no way of knowing if the boy was actually present in the shop or not, since the assailant's inability to prove his statement made it legally irrelevant. But the original story of the assailant Mehmed had the ring of spontaneous truth, and the scribe's inadvertent recording of it suggests that he was caught up in Mehmed's recounting of the event. At some point, however, the scribe expunged the assailant's statement as legally untenable, thereby recasting the narrative as a legally treatable, although perhaps "untrue," incident. For our purposes, what is important in the court record's construction of the incident is its demonstration that questions involving honor had to be isolated and treated separately, not just as substories in complex events. This may remind us of the case of Ali and his young wife Ayşe, described in chapter 3, in which Ali divorced Ayşe for adultery while Ayşe appears to have convinced the court that she was raped. There I termed the court's seeming contradictory reconstruction of this case "the principle of separate justices" since both husband and wife were able to save face in a morally and legally vexed situation. Here too, the legal reconstruction of the incident in the shop acts to give the benefit of the doubt to an individual whose honor has been attacked.

Although the assailant Mehmed was perhaps acting sincerely to rescue the youth, his inability to substantiate his story rendered him guilty of two crimes, assault and slander. Likewise, men did not always win their suits to defend their *own* honor if there were loopholes—narrative or moral—in their representations at court. A pointed example is the suit brought by one Ali b. Mehmed against Ahmed b. Mehmed, whom Ali accused of sexual assault. Ali's story was that he had been with a group of friends when Ahmed linked up with them and suggested that they all go off to a stream in the Heyik district, at the southern edge of the city. It was there that Ahmed allegedly stripped off Ali's trousers and raped him. Despite Ali's two separate attempts to support his case at court, his witnesses failed to corroborate his narrative. With Ali lacking evidence, Ahmed took an oath of innocence, and Ali formally retracted what now constituted slander (technically, a false accusation of a criminal sexual act).[60]

We have to wonder why Ali persisted in his case against Ahmed in the face of deficient proof. Perhaps he was merely making mischief by engaging in "accusationism" against an innocent Ahmed (the retraction of his accusation would appear to clear him of the crime of slander). On the other hand, it is possible that Ahmed was actually guilty, and the case failed because Ali produced only three participants in the event rather than the four eyewitnesses necessary to prosecute a person charged with sexual misconduct. If so, Ali's three companions were wise to deny the truth of his allegation, since according to the law their insufficient number meant each would suffer the penalty for slander if they supported him.

The severity of this penal sanction against sexual slander—requiring four witnesses to an illicit sexual act—derived in part from its origins. This stringent legal requirement for proving fornication or adultery, laid out in the Qur'an, had its roots in malicious accusation: the verses containing them were revealed at a time when enemies of the Prophet Muhammad were engaging in polemic against him by accusing his young wife of sexually immoral conduct (these verses are found in Surah 24). In some ways, sexual slander was the worst of crimes since the Prophet had identified it as a deed that barred individuals from acting as witness; as we have seen, the capacity to give testimony was the emblem of membership in the civic community. Sexual slander was a socially destructive crime because it attacked the victim's moral reputation, the core of his or her personhood. The punishment in a sense fit the crime: the serious moral risk run by perpetrators of defective slander testimony was perhaps even more consequential than the actual penalty for the slanderous act.[61]

Ali's unsuccessful suit is of further interest to us for what the court's record of the case suggests about the intersection of physical space and honor. Ali's case was no doubt prejudiced by the fact that he was not in a protected zone, such as his home or his shop, when the alleged assault took place, or, like the boy Ali above, on his way home. Ali and his friends were hanging out on the streets, picking up companions (*yoldaş*) as they encountered them, following their fancy to the edges of the city. They were a "crowd" (*hemre*) of friends. I suggest that there was an ambivalent, even negative, sociolegal resonance to the image, conjured by the judge's summary, of a bunch of friends on the streets. They came dangerously close in the social imagination to a gang of rowdies, whose idea of a good time might include sexual predation. Süleyman's law book included a clause outlawing "disruptive young men" (*levend*) from public venues: "*Levend*s shall not come to places where women and boys come to fetch water or wash clothes, they must be prevented. If they resist, they should be punished by the judge: the penalty shall be one akçe for every two floggings. And they shall not gather in front of a public bathhouse or along the road to a bathhouse."[62] The clause reflects the widespread perception that men in unregulated spaces were social pariahs, sexual aggressors who destabilized moral boundaries.

This is not to imply that Ali and his companions were disreputable individuals. Indeed, the group of friends included the chief of the night watch and a prominent local Armenian. But the events recounted in the court record constituted a stock scenario for trouble, and Ali was perhaps thought to have been asking for it. Far from being a protected zone of honor, the waterside venue was a zone of danger and potential dishonor. A week before this incident was recorded, two theology students—the brothers Hasan and Hüseyin—were attacked and beaten as they studied and performed their prayers "by a waterside" (perhaps the banks of the Sacur). Reflected here may be a "town versus gown" tension, one that fed into a larger tension between the city's religious elite and less orthodox sectors of local society. Of the brothers' testimony, Hüseyin's had the greater narrative drama:

> "I am a poor theology student. I took my books and went off to study. While I was performing my ablutions at the waterside, this Ali and a companion came up and struck me a heavy blow with a tree branch and caused me injury." When the aforementioned Ali was questioned, he denied [the accusation]. When the plaintiff was asked for proof of his allegation, the upright Muslims named Sundek b. Ümit and Süleyman b. Durmuş gave testimony . . . saying, "We are witness, and we give witness in the manner prescribed by God, that, while the aforementioned Hüseyin was making his ablutions at the waterside, the said Ali and a companion came and hit the said Hüseyin and caused him injury."[63]

Hasan and Hüseyin, it would seem, were not alone in their outing; they were themselves part of a male coterie of friends. Outside the bounds of the regulated city, open to any and all males, waterside spaces in Aintab seem to have been fraught with the potential for conflict.[64]

For women, all space outside the protected domestic interior was a zone of potential moral ambiguity. As their presence at the waterside cast doubt on men's intentions, so too women, once outside the more restricted locale that defined female integrity, were vulnerable to suspicions about their character. (Recall, for example, the social disruption caused by the presence in neighborhood streets of the two Ayşes in chapters 3 and 4.) Here was yet another challenge to females wishing to preserve their reputations. How were they to compensate for their vulnerability in public spaces when legal defenses such as the oath of innocence or protective witnesses were less available to them? No wonder that women and girls at court often spoke in a different voice.

While men adopted typically adopted a stance of intransigent moral rectitude and a blaming of others, women's testimony in defense of their integrity was more varied than men's and less predictable. Women did not have a ready script. In her study of sixteenth-century pleas for pardon addressed to the French king, Natalie Zemon Davis notes that women were "impelled to be more inventive in crafting their story, to offer more detail to fit the constraints of mercy."[65] Likewise the women of Aintab, in accounting for their actions, frequently appealed to the sentiments of their listeners. This had much to do with the fact that normative law was not written to protect their honor, and so they lacked what men enjoyed: ready legal procedures within easy grasp.

The records of cases in which females attempted to extricate themselves from problematic situations are often confused in their facts. Indeed, women's strategies seem to rely on deliberate avoidance of a narrative representation of events. Fashioning a story of events required casting protagonists as innocent against guilty, or themselves as plaintiff against others as defendant. Women and girls alike were often unable or unwilling to make such distinctions. Instead, they tended to present the court with moral dilemmas and sometimes to enact repentance. Females seem to have found it useful to argue for themselves by creating ambiguity, both narrative and moral.

Such was the case of the peasant girl Fatma bt. Hasan, whose predicament will be explored at length in the story devoted to her at the beginning of part 3. Fatma was pregnant and, moreover, in trouble with the law for naming two men as responsible for her pregnancy and one of them as having raped her. The village girl was able to partially redeem her situation by working a tone of repentance into her testimony accounting for why she had falsely accused another villager of rape. Blaming the idea for the act of slander on the mother of the young man who had actually impregnated her, Fatma cast herself as the tool of the mother's legal strategy and ultimately incapable of harming another. To the assembled court, she declared, "The truth of the matter is that I am pregnant by Ahmed. I cannot slander another, it's this world today, tomorrow the hereafter. It is Ahmed who had illicit relations with me."[66]

Public repentance was a strategy employed by another Fatma, who also made a false accusation of rape in order to redress the powerlessness of guilt. When the woman Fatma bt. Cuma was brought to court by the man who was the object of her slander, her repentance took the form of a vow to correct her conduct. "If I ever complain again to the governor or to any of the authorities or to anyone else," she stated, "I'll pay penance of

1,000 akçes . . . and you can also publicly shame me by blackening my face."[67] By means of the vow, Fatma preempted the role of the authorities, imposing a double punishment on herself—a substantial fine as well as public humiliation. She was able to recover a degree of both punitive and moral control over her actions since it was she who created the legal bargain and set the terms of punishment.

Sometimes moral dishonor was unredeemable, however. When a prostitution operation was exposed in December 1540 through the sighting of a prostitute on the roof of a male client's house, the hapless woman pleaded only to be spared public exposure.[68] But she could not sustain her anonymity (although it took a while before the court record got her name straight), since her testimony was critical to uncovering the established nature of the operation; legally speaking, she was the only one who could identify her role in it. The case opened with the report of the chief of the night watch:

> "When the woman was seen on the roof of Abdi b. Mehmed's house, a crowd gathered, but no one could be found at home. Finally she cried out imploringly from the roof, 'Don't humiliate me!' We got her down and brought her [here]." One of the members of the large crowd, Yusuf [b.] Haci Resul, also said, "She cried out [to us]. We [brought] her to the authorities, together with the quilt and mattress [that were] on the roof."

The next entry making up the four-sicill case began the exposure of the woman, now identified as Paşa bt. Halil, and the client, Abdi b. Mehmed. They first insisted that there had been no sex between them. They blamed the pimp, Mir Mehmed, for the compromising incident: Abdi—"The person named Mir Mehmed came, took my 30 akçes, and brought her to my house, but I never touched her"; Paşa—"Mir Mehmed dragged me off the street and took me[.]" Then client and prostitute apparently capitulated, admitting that they'd had sex at another time. Finally, Mir Mehmed admitted that he was, in fact, a pimp: "I took her to his house and brought them together. And besides this, I take women to many other people." Even if she had been forced into service by the pimp, the prostitute's situation was one of unredeemable humiliation, leaving her no avenue to even a partial rehabilitation of her personhood. Her admitted guilt foreclosed any possibility of a plea of repentance.

Certainly women were not alone in finding themselves in situations that offered no route to moral recovery. But what stands out in the court record is the near absence of males who adopted a humbling stance in court. This suggests that people sought to address the court only when they could avail themselves of a "role," however marginal, that provided them legal or moral leverage in the court. Because it was out of character for males to adopt a posture of pleading or repentance, they could perhaps expect little sympathy from the audience at court. Further evidence of this point is the selectively voluntary use of the court by Armenian males, who rarely appeared in situations that, by connoting "difference," could exacerbate their religious marginality in a community overwhelmingly populated by Muslims.

If the male voice at court was one of self-righteousness and moral adamancy, then a man who lacked a full male identity could not employ this male idiom. Men's voices take on a pleading or repentant tone in only two instances in the court record for 1540–1541, and in neither case did the protagonist meet the criteria for full legal competence: one was a slave and the other in a state of delirium. When the black slave Abdullah b. Abdullah named his accomplice in the theft of three donkeys—one Mir Mubarek from the village of Kızılhisar—and a black freedman meeting the description was brought to court, Abdullah used extreme language to insist that the authorities had gotten the wrong Mubarek: "This is not the Mubarek I meant. I've never seen this person. You can slit my throat if I should falsely accuse another."[69] Abdullah's statement is reminiscent of the statements of the two Fatmas involved in false accusations, protesting his inability to slander another and invoking severe punishment should he do so. As an aspect of his marginal identity, the slave, like the female, employed a different language at court, one that surrounded the simple statement of fact ("this is the wrong man") with protestation and plea. It turned out, however, that Abdullah's act in calling down upon himself the most extreme of penalties was not enough to clear the freedman's name of association with the "real" Mubarek. When the judge required that Mubarek's character be investigated, "prominent citizens" of Kızılhisar testified on his behalf: "This Arab is a trustworthy Arab. We have never witnessed any unreasonable behavior on his part. He's an honest boy."[70]

The second instance in which the male voice was tuned to a different, more "female," register involved one Derviş Ali, who was in the unfortunate situation of having inadvertently divorced himself from his wife. Derviş Ali had unintentionally placed his marriage in jeopardy during an illness that had induced delirium. In giving his testimony, he spoke in a manner evocative of delirium, as if to give evidence of his unnatural state of mind when he took the regretted action:

> Some time ago, when I was ill and confined to bed, I apparently made Mehmed b. Hızır my proxy to divorce the woman Nigâr bt. Yusuf, who is my wife, with a triple divorce. Now I don't have any knowledge or any memory of this, I don't know what I said when I was ill, and I wasn't thinking about getting divorced, and [I didn't mean to turn us into divorced people].[71]

Derviş Ali's testimony, composed of repeated takes on the incapacity of delirium, echoes the multiple invective heaped on adulterous wives. Now speaking before the court as a man of sobriety, he needed to distance himself in every way possible from the aberrant behavior. But as in the case of Mubarek the freedman, Derviş Ali's testimony alone was not enough to erase the unintended outcome. It took the mufti of Aintab to assert that the words spoken in illness had not disturbed the validity of the marriage.

The only males to employ a rhetorical strategy of repentance were thus a slave and a man who was temporarily not himself. In other words, the more isolated the individual from protective social status, the less adamant the voice and the greater the need for a rhetoric of persuasion. We are not talking here about socioeconomic marginality, but rather about the marginality of "role"—the degree to which both social conventions and legal practices provide an already scripted language for petitions at court. If we situate the testimonies of the slave Abdullah and the delirious Derviş Ali in the context of cases discussed above, they suggest that the gendering of voice and rhetoric in the Aintab record may have less to do with the actual sex—or age—of the speaker than with his or her sociomoral location in the incident at stake.

When sexually abused, children made accusations in "adult" language, or so their speech was represented in the court record. And just as a man could speak imploringly, so a woman could choose to adopt a voice of righteous authority, even when accused of immorality: in the story of Haciye Sabah, we will meet a female teacher who defended herself adamantly against charges of corrupting her students and who furthermore accused the court of inconsistency in its rules of judgment. And although her indignation took the form of punishable cursing, Ayşe bt. Halil, accused of dubious contact with a male neighbor, found a way to turn the question of honor to her advantage (see chapter 4). What I am suggesting is that there existed a spectrum of voice positions ranged along a hierarchy of moral authority, from righteousness to repentance. In this light, the "female" idiom and the "male" idiom were available strategies rather than voices determined solely by biological sex.

It is certainly true that many more women than men employed the "female" idiom in matters of honor and reputation, in part because of the legal obstacles they encountered regarding supporting testimony and the oath. But when we look at rhetorical style in court as a choice of legal strategy rather than a dictate of biology, we are reminded that gender roles—and legal roles as well—are socially constructed and therefore subject to larger social, political, and cultural change. People in Aintab, as in other communities across the empire, were coping with changing legal mores. But Aintabans were not passive in the face of legal rules and legal trends they did not like. The following section explores one way in which they acted to rectify legal practices that did not match their social needs.

SOCIAL ABSOLUTION AND THE COURT

In her study of pardon pleas, Davis describes the ways in which pleas for mercy addressed to the French king made use of the tools of literary rhetoric and the conventions of narrative. Despite their brevity, the sixteenth-century records of the Aintab court also reveal deliberate rhetorical strategies, but their audience was not the sultan. As we saw in chapter 3, there was no process of appeal to the sovereign for a judgment of one's guilt. Rather, the audience was necessarily local. In their testimony, Aintabans addressed, first of all, the judge. The opportunity to plead for one's honor and integrity was provided largely through the division of labor in the Ottoman legal system of the sixteenth century, where the job of the judge was to establish the "facts" of the case by listening to various representations of the matter at hand. Users of the court and their witnesses necessarily chose their words carefully. But particularly in matters where honor was at stake, they were mindful that another audience was listening, one that would make its own judgment independent of the court, since the latter's rules sometimes led to punishment and pardon that went against intuitive local readings of justice. The community, in other words, might grant a kind of social absolution that the judge could or would not. Hence we find women frequently making theater in the venue of the court and playing to an audience made up of the larger community.

Because of a legal culture that presented them with greater obstacles than men faced, women sometimes had to go so far as to break the law in order to get the attention of the court. It was in these moments especially that kin, neighbors, and community were their audience. Why else pay the price of a criminal penalty if not to gain a venue to present one's own version of affairs and relate an exonerating narrative of events? Such appears to have been the intent of the woman Hadice bt. Bilal, who traveled from Aleppo to accuse Abdulkadir b. Hoca Hamza of entering her house at night and raping her.[72] Unable, of course, to provide witnesses, Hadice lost her suit when Abdulkadir took an oath of innocence. Unlike some of the individuals appearing above, Hadice took no action to withdraw or blunt her accusation. It is hard to imagine that she was not aware that she would lose the case and presumably pay the penalty for false accusation of fornication. But women who had been raped had no recourse except to suffer the punishment for slander if they wanted to make the rape public. Hadice's purpose in bringing the case in the Aintab rather than Aleppo court was no doubt to voice her accusation against the rapist in his own community. The gain of such an action was that it established a tentative base for a brief against Abdulkadir's character.

A similar strategy may have been behind the slander case brought by the woman Esma bt. Hoca Hamza against her brother Alaeddin, despite the fact that she was bound to lose it. She accused him of calling her a whore.[73] Such sexual cursing was actionable as an instance of false accusation of adultery. Like Hadice, Esma could not prove her allegation (the court noted that she "was unable to supply the requisite number of witnesses"), and Alaeddin cleared himself with the oath. This was the same Esma who two weeks later would trade the 1,200 akçes she inherited from her father for her brother Abdulkadir's share in the house that he and Alaeddin had inherited. Perhaps it was his sister's plan to acquire part of the family dwelling that caused Alaeddin to curse her.[74] As we will see in chapter 6, Esma was going against the norm of sisters yielding the inherited family dwelling to brothers. Immediately after acquiring her share of the house, the litigious Esma took her female neighbor to court to demand structural alterations in the latter's house so as to protect her own domestic privacy. Esma was, it seems, a woman intent on taking care of herself and a legally savvy and active user of the court. All the more likely, then, that her case against her brother was taken with full awareness of the price she might pay to make the slander public.

The strategies of language employed by individuals in the scenarios sketched above were often aimed at the community as much as at the judge. Yet the very fact that the verbally inflected representations of self crafted by women (and some men) were inscribed in the court record is evidence that the judge regarded them as integral aspects of testimony. Even when his summary of a case implied punishment of the protagonist, the judge might see beyond the strictly legal preoccupation of the case to the underlying social dilemma that brought the protagonist to court. Because the mandate of a judge in the Ottoman legal system of the mid–sixteenth century was to expand the jurisdiction of the court and thus to encourage its use as an arena for dispute resolution, he necessarily needed to work with communal efforts to keep social peace. İne's story explored such a case, where the court's role in a social problem—a child bride's accusation that her father-in-law had raped her—was only one aspect of what appeared to be a wider communal response to the resolution of the dispute. As for the situation of the girl Fatma who named two males as responsible for her pregnancy, her story suggests that she may have manipulated both her fellow villagers and the law to gain a solution to her problem. In neither of these cases was the community's role in the handling of sociolegal problems as clearly delineated as the court's, but its presence was obvious.

That the community weighed evidence and came to its own judgment is already evident in its role in the exposure of suspect or criminal behavior. An example is the would-be witness Manend, whose neighbors exposed him as a liar and had him expelled from their midst. The community appears to have been particularly vigilant in the matter of sexual morals, even though

Süleyman's law book did not penalize failure to report sexual misconduct.[75] Numerous instances in the records portray Aintabans exposing or threatening to expose individuals to public censure or humiliation. A term that figures in some of these cases is *rüsvay*, "disgrace." The prostitute stranded on the roof used the term: "Do not disgrace me!" ("*beni rüsvay eyleme*"). When rumors reached Aintab that a man from the city had murdered a caravan merchant, an influential local citizen threatened *rüsvay* if the suspect's brother did not turn over 200 akçes, presumably as a form of bail.[76] Public humiliation—*rüsvay-i amm*—was the penalty for pimping prescribed in the law code of the Dulkadir rulers who preceded the Ottomans in Aintab.[77] But public disgrace had another face: expiation and reintegration into the community. As it exposed, so too the community absolved its members.

The process of social absolution worked in part because of a consensus that some legal rules might have harmful consequences for society. The Aintab court records contain much evidence of people relieving others of the legal and moral responsibilities imposed by normative law. In chapter 6, we will see that people developed strategies for getting around inheritance laws that could create problems for families and sometimes precipitate disputes among heirs. In addition, several entries in the court records reveal the measures people took to absolve neighbors and kin of damages incurred under the law. These cases revolved around the legal responsibility of neighborhoods or individual property owners for the injury or death of an individual on their premises in the absence of an identified perpetrator. When a man dying of wounds appeared in the village of Mentur, he relieved the villagers of their legal responsibility to find his murderer or pay compensation to his family should they fail to do so. Before succumbing to death, he managed to explain how he had come by his wounds (during an attack by brigands on the caravan he was escorting to Mosul), and he specifically requested that the locals not be held responsible for his death.[78] Similarly, when Haci Mustafa fell from the roof of one of Aintab's covered markets, which he had been hired to repair, he made a formal statement at court that no one was responsible for his injury; he had merely fallen by accident. The insistent repetitiveness of his statement is an index to the importance of absolution: "I was cutting stone on the roof of Tahtalı Han. I fell *after* I was paid for the job. There was no foul play. I simply fell."[79]

Even in the anguish surrounding the death of a child, grieving parents attended to the problem of damages. The lengthy, detailed, and impassioned explanation that Davud and his wife Rabia offered at court for their baby's death freed their son-in-law, in whose home the death occurred, from responsibility. The couple had gone to the latter's house to bake bread, they told the court, and had rigged up a cradle for their toddler Mehmed; when the beam holding the cradle collapsed, the child was killed. "It was a divine decree," they insisted, "It was God's preordaining, and so be it. We make no legal claim on anyone."[80] It is of course possible that the potentially liable party in each of these cases—the villagers, the market overseer, the son-in-law—requested or even insisted on the exonerating statement. Even so, the point still remains that Aintabans made strategic use of the court to protect each other from liability for damages.

Like the normative rules defining inheritance and liability, the rules delineating the crime of sexual slander created new problems as they solved others. Strict monitoring of slander protected reputations, but it also made rape and sexual harassment difficult to prosecute: as we have seen, the unrealistic requirements of proof (four witnesses or confession) was compounded by the criminalization of "false" or legally defective accusations of illegal sexual conduct. Nevertheless, there seems to have been a broad consensus in mid-sixteenth-century legal discourse on the criminality of rape, despite its being much less clearly delineated in normative law than was personal injury or wrongful death. Rape was labeled with a standard terminology across communities in the empire, suggesting an established view of its criminal nature: the chief mufti Ebu Suud used the same words to refer to it—*cebran zina*, "illicit sex by force"—as did scribes in the Aintab court, and perhaps the litigants themselves. Once rape was identified as a crime, the inevitable next step was to expose it even if punishing it was legally tricky. The remarkable number of individuals who brought accusations of rape suggests that the community recognized the legal conundrum that rendered accusers guilty of slander and that it was receptive to the initiative of rape victims in exposing the crime. Moreover, the high incidence of rape accusations in 1540–1541 suggests that the judge allowed the court to be used as a venue where victims could make their case publicly. The question of rape and other sexual abuse, including victimization by slander, is perhaps the most salient example of the community and the court working together to solve a social and legal problem.[81]

.   .   .

This chapter has focused on the relationship between morality, the ways in which individuals understood the moral constitution of their community and their court, and the ways in which they addressed the court on matters of personal consequence. The litigants who have animated the pages above employed a broad range of strategies, language, and rhetoric to represent themselves before the judge of Aintab. Hardly any of them spoke in court through a proxy, a fact that suggests that when people had an unusual or compelling case to make, they relied on their own powers of persuasion.

It is clear that differences in male and female approaches to the court were determined by the ways in which men's and women's social roles were constructed. Yet each individual, male and female alike, was enmeshed in a complex set of family and community relationships and therefore in a complex set of roles and power relations. Consequently, a person might have occasion to speak from a variety of "positions" and in a variety of "voices," depending on the situation at hand. I have argued that the range of rhetorical positions displayed in the Aintab court, while they tend to cluster as idioms associated with male or female, were not entirely sex-based but were to a significant degree role-based. Hence men could speak "like women" and women could speak "like men."

Much work on Ottoman court records has rested on a facile assumption that courts were uniformly open to women. Yet as we have seen, there were some real structural and procedural barriers to women in the Aintab court. (While this book focuses on women, much the same statement could be made about non-Muslims, children, the propertyless, and so on.) Both jurisprudential debate and grassroots practice in Aintab communicated the message that female voices at court were problematic. At the same time, where females were not scripted into the court, they found alternate means to bring their voices to its stage. Sometimes those means were compromising: breaking the law in order to defend one's moral reputation. Yet females had the advantage at court of being able to deploy a strategy of remorse and repentance, one that was culturally available to only a small fraction of males. In other words, the court sanctioned compensatory mechanisms to rehabilitate the moral integrity of those whom its biased processes had the effect of marginalizing.

A secondary theme of this chapter has been the relationship between law and society in Aintab, or between legal culture and social culture. That relationship was neither simple nor static, as we have seen. In keeping with its efforts to expand the scope of its jurisdiction, the court had an interest in making morality a public matter and not one reserved for private mores and private justice. Given the amount of talk about honor and reputation in the Aintab court, one would have to judge the court successful in drawing the public debate about morality into its own forum. Much of the talk, of course, was exacted under duress—but not all of it. One might speak of a tacit bargain between the court and its constituency: while the court forced some of the community's business into its forum (the work of the market inspector, for example), local residents turned the court into a stage from which to read their own scripts.

There were a number of reasons for the court's success as a moral arbiter. One was the court's recognition that some of its formal rules required correction, hence its willingness to let the guilty exonerate themselves. Another factor is the central place of testimony in its proceedings. The judge's principal job was to hear individual narratives (a point that explains the silence, the textual invisibility, of the judge in the written records of the court). In the process of listening, the judge was exposed to and accepted a variety of self-representations. In this light, it is more accurate to speak of "moralities" rather than a prevailing morality in Aintab, a range of tolerable moral readings produced by the microcultures that populated the province. This tolerance for moral difference stemmed from another element in the court's success: its ability to balance competing views of social worth. While it endorsed markers of class identity, at the same time its mandate to resolve disputes and keep social peace required the court to take seriously the claims of the less privileged. The court allowed ordinary people to say that they too appreciated the fundamental moral dynamic of their community, yet might accomplish its purposes in their own way. The court, in other words, enabled people to claim a common moral citizenship across the lines of social difference.

6

Women, Property, and the Court

That the women of sixteenth-century Aintab dealt in property is hardly news. The Aintab court resembles other Ottoman-period courts in that property was the issue that most often brought women (and men) before the judge.[1] Hence the question of property is a critical one in understanding the overall place of women both at court and in the community. Procedurally, property issues in the Aintab court were handled in accordance with sharia regulations, principally those regarding inheritance, contracts of purchase and sale, and proof of ownership. But the larger question of the cultural underpinnings of property relations—*who* brought property cases to court, and *why* and *how* they did so—provokes some interesting observations about the strategies of women and men in their relations to each other through the medium of property.

Muslim women acquired property primarily through the fixed shares they inherited from the estates of deceased relatives and secondarily through the portion of their dower to which they were entitled at marriage. The Aintab court records show women involved in a range of relationships stemming from their ownership of urban and rural real estate—houses, shops, and mills as well as orchards, vineyards, and vegetable plots. Women also owned animals—donkeys more often than horses, goats more often than sheep. Additionally, women engaged in the apparently ubiquitous enterprise of making loans, participating at both the high and low ends of local lending networks.[2] In these capacities as property owners, women resembled men. Unlike men, however, women appear in the court records owning and trading a wealth of material objects—domestic items such as pillows, quilts, pots, and pitchers, and personal items such as jewelry, clothing, and hand-worked textiles.

Transactions involving a sale, purchase, loan, or investment often brought women to court. So did disputes relating to such transactions. When it came to court litigation over property and money, Aintab women initiated proceedings as often as they were summoned as defendants. Women's ownership of property had implications beyond the immediately transactional, however, since the implicit recognition of their competency to manage money and property was critical to other public roles they played—for example, as guardians of the estates of minors and orphans or as fiscal partners in the business ventures of others.

Was there any bias against women in the matter of property—in the ways in which they acquired it, in their freedom to dispose of it, or in their ability to litigate over it? Procedurally, the court of Aintab treated women and men equally in property cases, once their cases got to court. In contrast to social problems that provoked divergent female and male voices at court, property provided its own script: women and men at court talked about property in the same language. But the court records give us only a partial picture of property relations in Aintab, since we cannot fully know what went on among individuals before or after they appeared in court, and we cannot know at all what went on among those who handled property and disputes over it without ever coming to court.

A frequent assumption about women in Middle Eastern societies is that patriarchal structures and practices have prevented them from access to their legal property or from appealing to the law over abuses of their property rights. In other words, female property rights are recognized as laid out in sharia, but are often thought to be difficult to realize in practice. In the Aintab records of 1540–1541, numerous females came to court to appeal the infringement of their property rights, suggesting on the one hand that they had trouble controlling their property and on the other that the court was a resource accessible to them in their attempts to correct abuses. But the fact that males too encountered obstacles to getting and maintaining control of their property suggests that property relations were more complicated than a simple struggle between the sexes.

This chapter examines the ways in which women maximized their control of property within an environment of constraints and opportunities. Women's hold on property was weaker than that of men. Not only did Islamic inheritance law grant them smaller shares of the estates of relatives, but, as we will see, the Ottoman state barred them almost entirely from the land it controlled. Women compensated for these biases by manipulating what property they did control, exchanging some of it for social capital and using some of it to create a material world under their own control. One singular advantage that women in the premodern Middle East enjoyed over many of their counterparts in other areas of the world was that property relations were extensively inscribed in Islamic law, where they were embedded in a moral system imbued with notions of just exchange, charity, and responsibility for the propertyless.

Gender and property relations are viewed here in a set of enlarging contexts: property and the individual, the family, and the state. The chapter begins by looking at the difficulties women encountered in obtaining property to which they had legitimate claim, and then examines how women consolidated their property once it was under their control. Then it looks at women's property strategies within two sets of family relations, the extended natal family and the marital household. Finally, property relations are examined in the context of the shifting definitions that property itself underwent as Aintab was colonized by the Ottoman regime and the subsequent rush by local subjects to solidify their hold on their material world. The focus is primarily on women, but it is important to note at the outset that the embeddedness of property in a broader moral universe, one that valorized the rights of the weak, means that women's experience of property cannot be considered apart from a whole set of human reciprocities.

GETTING PROPERTY: RESISTANCE AND THE COURT

In mid-sixteenth-century Aintab, the preoccupation with property was not limited to privileged classes. It did not take much in Aintab to own a house (almost everyone did), and items as seemingly insignificant as bath bowls and hoes were deemed worthy of inclusion in estate registers. Nearly everyone's life was caught up in the ebb and flow of property, and hence nearly everyone needed strategies to cope with this most common of experiences. This section of the chapter examines conflict over property with the principal aim of showing where tensions occurred in the process of property devolution. To that end, it presents several cases grouped in three sets; these deal, respectively, with grievances voiced by or on behalf of women, men, and orphans. A secondary purpose in summarizing these cases is to give something of the flavor of daily life, since property cases draw us into the material environment of Aintabans. The women and men of Aintab city and its hinterland will perhaps be more readily envisioned in the courtyards of their houses, among their vines and trees, tending their donkeys and goats, guarding their gold, inventorying their implements, and sometimes making their way to the judge in order to be able to do these very things.

The separation of the cases summarized below into women's, men's, and orphans' claims is somewhat arbitrary, since it obscures the intricately interwoven fabric of rights and responsibilities surrounding property in Aintab. Nonetheless, it is useful first to explore the ways in which different social groups experienced property and the challenges in obtaining it, and then to proceed to the larger contexts in which property relations were shaped. We begin with several cases in which women or their proxies used the court to recover property illegally diverted from them. This list is not exhaustive, but it contains some of the clearest examples of interference with women's claims to property, given in the order in which they occurred during the year:

—The female Canin sues her former stepfather, Hüdavirdi b. Ali, for selling a donkey that she and her sister inherited from their father. The stepfather claims that he turned over the 3 gold pieces he received for the donkey to their mother (by now his ex-wife). He loses the case when he cannot prove that he paid their mother. The latter takes an oath that he did not.[3]

—The woman Kuddam bt. Cafer sues her brother Şeyhi for selling a mule from her dower but failing to give her a chemise and a head ornament promised in return. The case is turned over to mediators, and Şeyhi gives his sister a black goat "in exchange for peace."[4]

— Selçük, Ayşe, and Magal(?), three sisters from the village of Seylan, bring a suit against the current owner of a vineyard of 750 vines that they inherited from their father when they were children. The owner claims it was sold to him by their paternal uncle, Yusuf b. Hüseyin. Asserting that they have now reached legal majority, the sisters deny the owner's claim that they had given their uncle permission to sell (the uncle himself admits he sold it illegally). The current owner cannot provide proof that they had given their permission, the women take an oath supporting their claim, and the vineyard is restored to them. It is apparently left to the now former owner to reckon with the uncle.[5]

—Mehmed is his wife Hüsni's proxy to claim a share of the estate of her deceased father, Haci İsa. It seems that while Haci İsa was alive, he had given a great deal of property to his minor son Üvez and made his brother Haci Ali guardian over the boy. The property included a house, two vegetable gardens in the city, a one-third share of a shop in the tannery district, and a half share of a storeroom there. The case is turned over to mediators, and Hüsni is awarded 2 gold pieces "in exchange for peace." The grounds for Hüsni's suit would seem to be that by giving away so much of his patrimony, her father effectively deprived her of her inheritance rights.[6]

—Mehmet b. Yusuf is his wife Meryem's proxy to demand items she has inherited from her mother, Mahdumzade. These are in the possession of the woman Şahi bt. Beşaret (whose relationship to the mother and daughter is not specified). Among the items are gold earrings, a gold bracelet, a necklace chain, a mattress and mattress cover, pillow and quilt covers, a large tray, and a bowl for the bath. Şahi hands over the earrings, and states that Mahdumzade had given them to her daughter while she was still alive. The fate of the remaining items is not clear.[7]

—Saadet bt. Seydi Ahmed sues Ahmed b. Tanrıvirdi for her share of a vineyard she had inherited from her father. Ahmed claims he bought the 125-vine share from Saadet's brother for 125 akçes and a goat. Saadet wins her claim (the very short record gives no details as to the steps of the legal process involved). It is apparently left to Ahmed to settle with Saadet's brother.[8]

—Zeyneb and Gülbahar, two sisters from the village of Caberun, claim a vine-yard inherited from their father. It is now owned by one Ahmed b. Mehmed, who claims that the sisters had traded it to their brothers (for what it is not said), the implication being that Ahmed purchased the vineyard from the brothers. The sisters deny this, and request a five-day extension from the judge so that they can round up their witnesses, who are absent at the time of the hearing. The register comes to an end two days later, and thus the out-come of this case is unknown. (As in the previous case, the scribe is stingy with details.) [9]

What do we learn from these cases? First, consider the mode of women's (anticipated) acquisition of the property: in six of the seven cases, the prop-erty was (or should have been) acquired through inheritance, and in the remaining case, through the marriage dower. Second, the identity of the "usurpers" of property: within the family, women's rights were infringed by a variety of male relatives—stepfather, uncle, even father, and, most fre-quently, brothers; in one case, an unidentified woman interfered with the inheritance (of women's things, passed—or not passed, as it turned out—by a woman through a woman to a woman). Third, the nature of the illegal property disposition: in most of the cases, the property—animals and cul-tivated land—was sold. When the property in dispute was land, it was a spe-cific type—vineyards: women wanted them, male relatives sold them. Note also that female suits to recover vineyards were brought directly against the current owner and not against the male relative who had sold the land. The court's interest was to defend the women's claims; it did not concern itself with prosecuting the wrongful seller or compensating the loser. Exempli-fied here is the court's mandate to establish the facts in a case and not to pursue matters that were not explicitly brought before the judge.

There are a number of ways to go beyond the simple facts that emerge from these cases. If we place them in the context of the court's work over the course of the year 1540–1541, they suggest that shifts were occurring in the relationship of property to gender and family. It is the timing of these cases that forms a critical connection with what we might call the politics of the court. None is dated earlier than July 1541—that is, there were no significant claims by women against family members during the preceding ten months of court records. It is not that women weren't making property claims at court before July. In fact, they were regularly involved in property and money disputes with a variety of individuals outside their families, sometimes on their own, sometimes in league with a brother, a son, or other male relative. Rather, what stands out from July onward is that women and their proxies began to go to court against family members. The timing of this shift may be explained by the set of events taking place in the Aintab court in the late spring of 1541, already mentioned in earlier chapters. At the end of June, a new judge, Hüsameddin Efendi, arrived in Aintab to take up direction of the court. He had been preceded by the month-long tenure of a special agent appointed by the sultan, whose specific mission was to correct abuses in tax-farming. Over the course of the month, various prominent members of the Aintab community were arraigned before the court for abusing their tax-farms—that is, for not remitting to the state in a timely manner tax revenues whose right to collect they had bid for and purchased. By the end of the month, there was a remarkable increase in the degree to which management of state revenues was handled under the auspices of the court. The broader message of the agent's work was that property relations were henceforth legally accountable. In other words, illegal practices that may have been so common as to have acquired the sanction of customary usage would no longer be tolerated, whether they were abuses of the claims of the state or of the individual.

Hüsameddin Efendi continued this expansion of court oversight: his assumption of the judgeship at the end of June was followed by a significant increase in the volume of business recorded at court. However, the court itself could not aggressively pursue a policy of tightening up the regulation of private property. Sultanic statute mandated that the judge not go out seeking cases to try but rather adjudicate only what came to him.[10] Private property crimes came under the rubric of rights or claims of the individual (hakk adamî), claims that had to be brought by the injured party him- or herself. The incidence of property claims brought by women after June 1541 thus suggests a deliberate intent to use the court coupled with a recognition of the changes initiated by the special agent and the judge who followed him. These claims remind us that neither property nor property relations are inert. They also underline a larger theme of this book—that shifts in legal culture may stimulate shifts in social culture and vice versa.

These cases raise two further issues that deserve some comment. The first relates to the impact of changes in the court. The Aintab court, invigorated by its incorporation into an empire-wide legal system and reinforced in June as an arena of normative law, may have benefited women in certain matters. In other words, the intervention of the Ottoman regime may have opened up space for groups within the population who previously lacked a legal voice. As noted in chapter 4, this resulted less from any programmatic pro-female activism on the part of Ottoman legal authorities (for state intervention also proved disadvantageous to some women) than from the administrative and legal systematization so characteristic of the middle decades of the sixteenth century.

The second relates to the "abuse" of women's property rights. Were the brothers, uncles, and fathers who sold or refused to turn over women's property consciously conspiring to "break the law" for a narrow personal advantage? Before attempting to answer this question, we need to account for the striking incidence in the Aintab court of property disputes among family members in general. These disputes were in large part the outcome of Islamic inheritance law. The rules of inheritance prescribed by the Qur'an allowed a person discretionary control of only one-third of his or her estate, and distributed the remaining two-thirds among a large number of relatives. This process often resulted in small shares of a property going to a variety of extended family members. An example from the court of Aintab is the claim lodged by the villager Ömer b. Abdullah against Ayşe bt. Satılmış for a share of the estate of her deceased father; they were distant relations—Ömer was three generations removed from their common ancestor, and she four.[11] These rules of inheritance appear to have been both a blessing and a burden. On the one hand, they had the result of spreading wealth around, which was part of the Qur'anic intent. Women, for example, could not be disinherited, although their shares were smaller than men's. In contrast to European practices, eldest sons in the Islamic world were not privileged at the expense of their younger brothers. In addition, special attention was given to the rights of orphans (defined as children lacking a father), with the judge mandated to watch over their property and to ensure the appointment of responsible guardians. On the other hand, because these practices led to the fragmentation of property, they threatened the efforts of parents to provide for their children or the attempts of siblings to build the joint family enterprises so characteristic of premodern economic and domestic cultures. The several court cases in which heirs reconsolidated property after a death in the family suggest that the fragmentation of estates and the intricacies of multiple ownership were often an unwelcome hindrance that necessitated corrective action.

Muslims were thus served with a set of rules about property that were not always conducive to survival strategies and planning for the future. Sometimes the rules were ignored in the interest of keeping property together. In particular, traditions of patriarchal authority based on property, primarily land, were hard to dislodge, especially in an economy founded on male-directed joint family enterprises. The perceived need to protect male control of property furnished a practical argument for legitimate infringement of the "technicalities" of the law, in which the denial of one set of rights (e.g., women's) could be justified by pointing to a greater benefit for all, including those divested of their rights (the presumption being that women fared better in a strongly united family). This legitimized practice of "abuse" meant that a legal challenge over a donkey or a vineyard initiated by a female family member was at the same time an assault on family relationships. What the intervention of the Ottoman state accomplished was to assert the primacy of a higher law over what appears to have been customary practice at the local level. In other words, infringement of women's property rights was now explicitly criminalized through the court's reordering of the hierarchy of ethical practice. The fact that women, or at least some women, were quick to see the court as their ally in property matters suggests that their own strategies were *not* necessarily compatible with those of other family members. Or perhaps changing circumstances called for new strategies.

The relationships among women, their relatives, property, and the law did not come about in a vacuum. We can gain a better perspective on these relationships by looking at property relations among males, and also at cases involving the property rights of orphans. The latter are important both because orphans were obviously male or female and because these cases were so frequent that to omit them would be to neglect an important aspect of Aintabans' thinking about property in general. First, let us look a partial but representative selection of cases involving men and property that came to court during the year:

—Two brothers, Ahmed and Mahmud, are brought to court by the local police for fighting over a pomegranate orchard (which appears to belong to them both). Ahmed accuses Mahmud of destroying the fruit of his trees by throwing stones at them, while Mahmud accuses Ahmed of insulting him and his son with "unlawful words." (Presumably, the brothers are fined for brawling.) [12]

—The Armenian Yakub b. Hızır obtains a court order that his brother Bahşi turn over to him his half of a piece of real estate they own jointly. The brothers request that experts be appointed to divide the property, which consists of two dwellings, an underground cellar, and half of a shared courtyard and well. The exact dimensions of the divided shares are detailed in the record.[13]

—Two brothers, Hasan and Yunus, have quarreled over a jointly inherited house. The court sends a delegation headed by the headman of the city quarter where the house is located to investigate. The delegation reports that Hasan has spent the equivalent of 24 gold pieces on improvements to the house.[14]

—The four sons of Haci Hüseyin state that after their father's death, their paternal uncle usurped control of their inheritance. They managed to get control of their share, and have held it in common since then. They now request that the court make a legal division of the inherited property among them.[15]

—Hüseyin b. Yusuf states in the presence of his brother Hamza that he does not accept the division of their father's estate, which had been performed by "imams" at the time of the father's death. Hüseyin now requests a redivision by the court.[16]

—Hamza b. Sıdkı has obtained a sultanic order that appoints the regional governor-general Ali Pasha as agent to investigate Hamza's complaint that he has been unable to take possession of his share of his father's estate. At court, Hamza alleges that his paternal uncle, Seyyid Ahmed b. Boyacızade, has prevented him from acquiring his share of the village of Arıl and five shops that were the joint patrimony of his father and uncle. Seyyid Ahmed claims that his

brother is still alive and challenges Hamza to prove his father's death. The register ends a week after this case, and thus the outcome is unknown.[17]

One thing we learn from these cases is that Aintab families customarily
relied on local authorities to divide up their inheritance in accordance with
the dictates of the law. (Women too made use of the court to settle their in-
heritances: the two sisters Fatma and Ümmetülrahman, for example, requested official division of their share of their father's estate.)[18] In other
words, property was often passed down in an undifferentiated manner that
presented heirs with the challenge of dividing it peaceably and equitably. As
we see, this could be done either by local religious authorities (each Muslim neighborhood had an imam, the prayer leader who performed a number of pastoral duties that might include attending to inheritance matters)
or under the auspices of the court. The latter was apparently seen as more
definitive, perhaps more objective, perhaps simply more "official."

Second, what is striking in these cases and others like them is the prepon-
derance of disputes that occurred among male siblings *after* they had taken
possession of their inheritance. This is a corollary of the important if anticipated finding that males in Aintab had fewer problems in taking control of
their inheritance than did women. Rather, it was the *division* of property that
was the greatest source of friction among males. Houses in particular seem
to have posed difficulties: heirs were faced with the problem of dividing up
a domestic space that might lose its physical integrity on being split into
shares. For example, after the official division of a three-house compound
between the brothers Yusuf and Mehmed (Yusuf got one house, Mehmed
two, and the courtyard was split between them), Yusuf required the court's
intervention to ensure his access to the compound's common door.[19]

In the two cases above in which males were dispossessed of their inheritance, we find paternal uncles interfering with the property of their neph-
ews. In these cases, it was junior males who suffered from patriarchal control of the extended family's domain. Abuse of property rights within the
family, in other words, was not a simple matter of gender, although the Aintab court records suggest that females were more easily disadvantaged. The
final case—the dispute within the Boyacı family, one of the three most
prominent lineages in Aintab—is remarkable for a number of reasons. For
one thing, it demonstrates the resources at the command of the rich and
powerful, who could invoke the attention of the sultan himself and thus of
the pasha, the highest-ranking delegate of imperial power in the region.
Much was at stake for the nephew Hamza, for he was (allegedly) deprived
not only of his material inheritance but also of his stature as heir of a distinguished family. The honorific patronymic of "Boyacızade," the lineage
name, was currently monopolized by Seyyid Ahmed (sometimes referred to
as Seydi Ahmed), who was never in his many appearances in court identi-

fied as "the son of Alaeddin," his actual patronymic, whereas Hamza was merely "the son of Sıdkı." Indeed, Seyyid Ahmed's local stature may have stood in the way of his nephew's ability to obtain a local hearing for his grievance, forcing him to petition higher authorities. Yet there was legal justification, or at least legal pretext, for Seyyid Ahmed's treatment of his nephew: he could be expected to defend his brother's estate under the legal doctrine of missing persons, which in Hanafi law assumed a natural life span of ninety years, during which time the missing person was assumed to be alive unless proven dead.[20] In other words, Seyyid Ahmed could be viewed as protecting his brother's inheritance against his nephew's attempt to usurp it prematurely. Ultimately, this case is one of the intriguing mysteries in the court records, for it is hard to imagine how the death or even the whereabouts of a prominent individual could remain uncertain in a society that had equipped itself with the efficient regionwide network for turning up missing animals described in chapter 2. People died away from home, on the pilgrimage or on family or commercial business, but how could a man such as Sıdkı b. Boyacı, who no doubt traveled with a retinue, disappear without a trace?[21]

If we review the men's and women's cases together, the point made earlier about simultaneous shifts in the management of the court and the management of property becomes even more salient. Like the women's cases, all of the men's cases (except the first, which was really a police matter) occurred under the judgeship of Hüsameddin Efendi, during the last three months of the thirteen-month period studied here. Disputes among male relatives over the division of inheritance began to be resolved under the auspices of the court only when a new judge began to wield what appears to be a more powerful mandate. Was the court insisting that the work of "experts" in dividing property take place under its own supervision? Or did men and women alike recognize a new advantage in having the court supervise and record their property settlements?

Finally, we turn to a set of cases involving orphans and their property. These had a wider social context than cases involving adults of either sex, since the relationship between orphans and property frequently involved the community. Because the responsibility for protecting orphans rested with the local judge, the defense of orphan rights was less dependent on the individual initiative usually required in claims over private property. The judge could exercise discretionary choice as to the appropriate guardian (*vasi*) for a particular orphan and, if he saw fit, could appoint someone outside the family. In the cases below, there are as many non-family as family guardians. Occasionally it might be the community that took the initiative in looking after the welfare of orphans, alerting the judge to instances of need. The cases below resemble the women's cases more than they do the men's: clearly, orphans, like women, were more vulnerable to having prop-

erty expropriated than were men, a situation reflected in the greater number and precise detail of cases dealing with their problems. It is not surprising that some of the women whose cases were given above were orphans
when their property was misappropriated, suggesting that female orphans
may have been especially vulnerable.

The following set of cases are examples of the routine issues as well as the
problems that arose in settling the estates of orphans:

—The (male) guardian of the "orphans of the woman Halime" (i.e., both parents are now deceased) claims four pomegranate orchards for his wards. The
orchards, their mother's property, had been sold by their father Musa eight
years earlier to one Ali (presumably without the wife's permission). The case
is turned over to mediators, who split three of the orchards between the orphans and the current owner Ali, and award the remaining one to Ali on the
grounds that it was a legal sale. The number and sex of the orphans is not
mentioned.[22]

—The woman Paşa bt. Ahmed, guardian of the orphan girl Satu, authorizes a
debt of 240 akçes owed to Satu's father's estate by one Ali to remain unpaid
until Satu reaches legal majority, six years hence.[23]

—Zeliha, mother and guardian of the orphan boys Hamza and Sadi, is summoned to court by Haci Ali on account of a debt of 200 akçes owed him from
the boys' father's estate. The father has died "in the land of honor," perhaps
while on the pilgrimage. Zeliha acknowledges the debt.[24]

—Because the orphan girl Sare needs a guardian, the court appoints her
older brother Mehmed b. Receb to "take possession of and protect" her inheritance of two gold pieces and a vineyard of 270 vines. He is authorized to
lend out the money at 20 percent interest, supervise the vineyard's cultivation,
and keep an account of its earnings.[25]

—Şerife bt. Murad, the paternal grandmother and guardian of the Armenian
orphan girl Meryem, is summoned to court by the secretary of the provincial
governor. The secretary claims 2,000 akçes from the estate of the girl's father,
Babek, to cover Babek's debt for an earlier purchase of wheat. The grandmother acknowledges the validity of the claim. In another case, the secretary
sues Babek's guarantor, the Armenian İhtiyar b. İskender, for payment of the
debt. (The wheat was presumably the produce of the secretary's rural fief.)[26]

—The (male) guardian of the orphan boys Halil and Mehmed brings a suit
against their mother Zeliha, claiming that she has seized part of the property they inherited from their father, and moreover has taken the register of
the estate's contents. The imam of the village states that the goods taken by
Zeliha are in his house, and he produces a register that is proven to be an accurate list of the estate's contents. (Zeliha has remarried by the time these
cases come to court, and the children are presumably in the custody of their
father's family.)[27]

—Two men from the community state at court that the orphans of Haci Abdullah, two daughters and one son, are in dire need of support. The men re-

quest that permission be given for the children's inheritance, a house and a vineyard, to be sold, and they repeat that the situation is an emergency. The court gives permission for the sale. (It is not clear if the two men will act as guardians of the children.) [28]

—The woman Gülşah bt. Mustafa, guardian of the orphan girl Halime, is summoned to court by Ahmed, who claims that a vineyard in their possession is property he inherited from his father. Gülşah counterclaims that Halime inherited the vineyard from her father, and wins the case when Ahmed cannot provide proof of ownership. [29]

One notable aspect of these cases is the role played by women as guardians. [30] Females were guardians as often as males were, indeed more often if we include the case in which a mother acted as guardian to her two sons. Women's ability to assume the sociolegal role of guardian, whose principal duty was protecting the property of orphans, confirms the extent to which they were regarded as competent managers of property. It is perhaps no coincidence that it was either for their own children or for other females that women took on these responsibilities. The records of 1540–1541 reveal other instances when women took on the protection of younger females, presumably in the absence of male heads of household. Women represented their daughters in divorce appeals, for example: Ayşe pleaded at court for the release of her young daughter Fatma, unhappy in the marriage Ayşe had contracted for her, and the woman Baki came from the city of Ruha to seek the divorce of an unhappy daughter living in Aintab. [31] This apparent preference for having women represent young females at risk may be linked to custody practices, which favored leaving young girls with their mothers as long as possible; their protective role appears to have extended into marriage when daughters were betrothed at a young age. This small sample of cases from Aintab is not an isolated example of women protecting other females at risk, for the historical record of the women of the Ottoman dynasty contains several stories of their compassion and concern for females who had fallen on hard times. [32]

Let us now return to the question that inspired this review of property disputes at court: were females disadvantaged? On the one hand, the court record leads us to answer yes: females were more vulnerable than their male counterparts to having their property rights usurped, and while women could themselves usurp, it was generally male relatives who exploited females. That women used the court to assert their claims indicates that at least some of them cared about controlling their own property. On the other hand, no issue in the court records better or more amply demonstrates the embeddedness of women (and men) in the family, or the family in the larger community, than property. The frequency of disputes among siblings or between generations—regardless of sex—suggests that the problems inherent in the complex process of transferring property in this predominantly Muslim society preclude any easy conclusions about the relationships between gender and property.

Looking at men's, women's, and orphans' property cases separately helps establish the ways in which gender and generation shaped people's experience of property. Placing these cases under a different lens—the lens of kinship—reveals many ways in which harm done to one individual may jeopardize the welfare of others. At issue here is the general principle in Muslim societies that to divest an individual of property is to threaten his or her dependents and heirs. The disinheriting of a nephew, for example, diminishes not only the individual but a whole branch of the extended family. Likewise, the loss of a woman's property means that her heirs are ultimately deprived of benefit. Loss of property might also have implications during her lifetime: for example, resourceless widows or women whose husbands had gone missing were entitled to support from the public treasury, and were thus a burden on the community. Moreover, while a wife was not required to spend her own funds on the household, a woman was expected to support her children in the absence of her husband if other means were lacking. If we remember that a fatherless child was considered an orphan, it is not difficult to see that abuse of the orphan was also abuse of the mother, whose own smaller share of her husband's estate could well prove insufficient to supporting her children. Moreover, proven lack of resources could weaken a woman's claim on her children. A woman's right to custody of her children was already tenuous under Islamic law, which awarded custody of fatherless boys at the age of seven and girls at the time of puberty to their paternal relatives. Lack of resources may also have weakened a woman's candidacy to act as guardian of her children and their inheritance, while the appointment of an outsider as guardian no doubt further threatened her ability to sustain the integrity of her household.

Once women achieved control of their property, however, they seem to have fared no worse than men in managing it. Women's frequent participation in the routine activities of buying and selling and borrowing and lending demonstrates the extent to which they were involved in the local economy, as does their role as guardians of orphans. These nongendered dimensions of property relations help account for the court's even-handedness in dealing with men and women over property.

WHAT DID WOMEN REALLY WANT?

In the cases summarized above, a gender asymmetry emerges in the nature of the property that people quarreled over: men tended to dispute over houses, while women tried to gain possession of vineyards and personal or household items. Another difference that emerges between women and men is their use of property once acquired. It is striking that women sold a great deal of real estate, most often vineyards and houses, occasionally a shop or a share in a mill. Men sold immovable property as well, but they also purchased it, so that their transactions added up to a net exchange of real estate. Women, however, almost never appeared in the Aintab court records buying real estate. This does not mean, of course, that *all* women divested themselves of real estate, for the court records show female owners of houses, shops, vineyards, and orchards who kept their property, or at least kept it for the present. What it does mean is that some women who fought to gain control of their property did so intending not to use it but to sell it.

For the most part, women acted independently in these sale transactions. They sometimes sold real estate jointly with their siblings, children, or mothers, but most often they were the sole owners of what they sold. In other words, heirs sometimes jointly sold inherited property immediately upon the settlement of the estate, but more often women sold property after establishing control of their shares. Women occasionally sold property to a family member, but most often to non-kin.

Why did women tend to divest themselves of real estate? We can perhaps best answer this question by looking to see what they did with their gain. What women wanted to have, it seems, was money and material objects. The court records give us a portrait of women creating a world of property accessible and deployable within their spheres of mobility. In addition, certain forms of property enabled women to extend their social commerce beyond the confines of the home or neighborhood. Money in particular circulated where women themselves could not go or chose not to go.

Among the domestic goods valued by Aintab women were mattresses, quilts, pillows, and cushions, as well as covers for these items. The covers were a particular focus of women's labor and pleasure, for many were embroidered or edged with crocheting or tatting at home. Women might sell these items and other hand-worked textiles such as handkerchiefs and towels, or they might put them aside for their daughters' or granddaughters' trousseaus. While Islamic law required no material contribution by the bride to the marital household, customary practice assumed that brides came with trousseaus (*jihaz* or *çeyiz*), and jurists even regulated the practice.[33] Young girls were taught the skills of sewing and embroidering from an early age and contributed to their own trousseaus. While mattresses and quilts were typically bedding, rolled up and put away in cupboards during the day, pillows, cushions, and bolsters (all denoted by the single word *yasdık*) were often the only items of "public" furniture in the premodern Middle Eastern home. These domestic items thus had considerable importance both functionally and aesthetically. In Gaziantep today, hand-worked textiles are highly prized and fetch handsome prices in shops that cater to brides' needs.

The personal goods Aintab women valued were clothes and especially jewelry. Chemises and caftans were favored items of clothing (see figure 7). Two contiguous case records from December 7, 1540, demonstrate the range in quality of women's caftans: Sare's estate contained a simple black caftan worth 15 akçes, while the dower of Cansur Hatun, "pride of women," included a luxurious red satin caftan.[34] The woman Kuddam, whose case against her brother is cited above, was apparently investing in a wardrobe when she attempted to trade the mule she received as part of her dower for a chemise and a head ornament *(sorguç)*. Hand-worked handkerchiefs and hand towels (denoted by a single word *mendil*) should also be included in this category of clothing. That they were not merely modest items of daily use is evident from their place in gift giving.

Indeed, clothing and other textiles often figured in gift giving, even at the level of royalty. They were prominently featured in the lavish gifts made to other sovereigns that were a significant feature of premodern diplomacy. In our period, items worked or commissioned by Hurrem Sultan, the favorite concubine of the sovereign Süleyman, were important elements in Ottoman diplomatic contacts. To a renegade Safavid prince whose alliance Süleyman was cultivating, Hurrem Sultan gave silk shirts she herself had sewn, mattresses, pillows, sheets, and quilts embroidered in gold, as well as pieces of handwork designed for the women of the prince's harem. Ottoman chronicles not only itemized these intentionally conspicuous gifts but also informed the reader that their value exceeded 10,000 gold florins. In a letter to the king of her native Poland, Hurrem noted that she was sending a gift of two pairs of pajamas, six handkerchiefs, and a hand towel. Embroidery was the highest female skill cultivated among women in the royal palace, and it was a way for retired harem attendants to make a living.[35] Palace women were thus cultivating the same arts of the needle to which their contemporaries in Aintab's villages and urban neighborhoods were devoted.

In the few lists of Aintab women's dowers and estates that are copied into the court records, jewelry is named quite often. The most usual kinds of jewelry were bracelets and earrings, though necklaces and rings also appeared in the records. In Sare's modest estate, a pair of ankle bracelets was listed along with the black caftan. While women seem to have acquired jewelry most often as a part of their dower, they also received it as gifts or inheritance from their mothers (and perhaps from other female relatives). An amusing incident that occurred in the village of Süleymaniye reveals that women also bought jewelry. As Fatma bt. İbrahim was purchasing a pair of gold earrings from another woman, they were grabbed out of her hand by one Arabşah, who explained in court that he had seized the earrings because Fatma owed him 200 akçes; Fatma presumably got to keep her earrings, because she subsequently paid her debt to Arabşah in cash and wheat.[36] Aintab had its own jewelers' bazaar, so women may have purchased jewelry directly or from female agents selling jewelry to those whose social habits disinclined them to shop in public spaces.[37]

The court records yield a lively portrait of women amid their things. Nafise bt. Mehmed made a trade with her husband in which she gave up part of her dower and canceled a debt he owed her in exchange for several domestic objects: a pot, a basin and water ewer, a large round tray for serving food, and two cauldrons, one large and one small.[38] All these would have been substantial objects made of copper. When women usurped the property of others, as in the two cases cited earlier, it was domestic items that they usurped. Şahi delayed in turning over Mahdumzade's legacy to her daughter of jewelry, bedding, and copper vessels. What Zeliha seized from her orphan sons' inheritance were material things, though the record did not specify their nature.

Several case records portray women toting bundles of things. Possessions were contained at home and transported in a cloth wrapping known as a *bohça*, which was also the name for the bundle itself. Bundles were the domestic treasury of ordinary women, and so the bundle wrapper could itself be an item of value. Gülpaşa bt. Halil purchased a silk bundle wrapper from the man Tanrıvirdi for 12 akçes and a handkerchief.[39] Women watched out for each other's bundles: when the villager Güldane bt. Yusuf's bundle was stolen one night, it was Ayşe who spotted it three days later in front of the village headman's house; contained in the bundle were a blanket, a blue pillow and quilt cover, a pair of silver earrings, a ring, and a gold coin.[40] The village woman Sare, whose husband was in jail, placed two copper food bowls and two sacks of "things" (*esbab*) in the house of a certain Hamza, apparently for safekeeping in her husband's absence (but without Hamza's knowledge). When the sacks were opened at court, one was found to contain a box with 84 akçes in it.[41] Because these misplaced bundles and sacks put their finders and unwitting shelterers under suspicion of theft (*sarika*), defined in Hanafi law as taking something stored within the boundaries of a dwelling,[42] the bundles' migrations and contents had to be detailed in court. Hamza was so nervous about the goods suddenly appearing in his house that he temporarily buried them, while Güldane had to testify that Ayşe never carried the recovered bundle into her own house, but rather handed it over to Güldane at her threshold.

There were a number of advantages to women in possessing material goods. Such goods had liquidity within women's own economic networks. Gold jewelry in particular could easily be sold by one woman to another in time of need. Stockpiling goods also helped women in one of their most important family responsibilities, preparing for their children's marriages. Gold jewelry was a core element in the dower that the groom's household was responsible for providing, while textiles and household objects could be given to a daughter for her trousseau. Like Mahdumzade, perhaps, other women accumulated goods to leave their daughters when they died.

Money was also desirable, for, like all material goods, it lent flexibility to women's social and economic relations. Cash by itself or in combination with goods enabled women to purchase items for their own or their children's benefit. Women sometimes traded goods for money, perhaps when they were in need or wished to make a particular purchase: Halime gave her son Mehmed a house and four Qur'ans in exchange for 5 gold florins.[43] Money also made money. Interest-free loans were frequent in Aintab, but loaning money for as much as 20 percent interest was not uncommon.[44] Aintab women participated in local networks of borrowing and lending, doing both in roughly equal proportions. For example, the proxy of the woman Sultan bt. Haci Mehmed appeared in court to satisfy her debt of 11 gold florins to one Yusuf, while a few weeks later Haciye Hatun came to court to register that Mehmed b. Hamza owed her 10 gold florins, to be paid back within a year (Mehmed put up five grape vines as collateral).[45] Significant accumulations of cash enabled women to invest as partners in joint commercial ventures, as did the woman Rahime described below.

Money and property also helped women realize spiritual goals, as the actions of one Ayşe bt. İsa indicate. Ayşe came to court on August 17, 1541, to register the donation of her share of a jointly owned house to her local mosque. Two of the four joint owners, one of them female, had already endowed their shares to the mosque, and Ayşe's donation was immediately followed by that of the fourth shareholder. These charitable deeds took the form of *waqf*, the widespread practice of assigning income to the upkeep of a public institution (for more on waqf, see below). Earlier chapters have noted the long tradition in Aintab of ordinary people making endowments to create and sustain religious and charitable endeavors. The institution that Ayşe and her co-owners supported, the neighborhood mosque in the city's Packsaddlers district, was also the beneficiary of other donations from district residents.[46] Shortly after making her endowment, Ayşe turned to her own spiritual welfare: she sold a gold bracelet to her stepson for 200 akçes, and then used the money to finance the recitation of the Qur'an after her death ("for my soul," she told the judge).[47] The Qur'an was most likely recited in the mosque to which Ayşe contributed.

Women no doubt cultivated an economy of money and material objects at the expense of holding real estate in part because the latter was harder for them to gain control of and also to work. The question of liquidity was critical. The Aintab court records depict women involved in numerous small transactions, devoting a good deal of energy to planning the deployment of their resources. The fact that the records involving inheritance almost always deal with the estates of fathers and not mothers suggests that a greater portion of women's property was given away or sold during their lifetimes. Mobilizing material objects and cash gave women greater flexibility than did controlling real estate because it enabled them to take advantage of opportunities in their immediate social environment and to channel largesse where they wanted.[48] Often, it seems, they channeled it to other females. These forms of property increased power where it counted for women, in the household and its status in the community. To "bundle" wealth was to store up potential social capital for the family that could be expended in a variety of ways, perhaps most frequently in planning for the marriages of children. Real estate was not without its uses, but one of its primary functions was as a route to a female economy of things and money.

GIVING AND RENOUNCING: PROPERTY RELATIONS AS SOCIAL CAPITAL

Men and women in Aintab did a variety of things with their property once they had a hold on it—they kept it or sold it, but often gave it away. Women, moreover, sometimes renounced their property rights, while men appear never to have done so. In trying to understanding the meaning of Aintabans' gifting or renouncing of property, we can make use of Pierre Bourdieu's notion of symbolic capital, the nonmaterial resources that individuals can summon as they position themselves in relation to their environment.[49] This notion is particularly relevant for Aintab women, since they more often than men exchanged real capital for social capital.[50]

Giving or renouncing property was intimately related to the rules governing its disposition. Property occupied a place in the mental landscape of Aintabans that exceeded its physical boundaries or its monetary worth. In this regard, Islamic rules of inheritance had a profound cultural impact. At an abstract level, they posited a moral foundation for property by making it an essential element in the definition of human well-being. The Qur'anic affirmation of the rights of groups often marginalized throughout world history in their access to material resources—orphans, widows, younger sons, and females in general—had the effect of raising consciousness of entitlement to property. Linked to this was a heightened awareness of the dangers of propertylessness and of the moral responsibility of the community to help those at risk of falling into poverty. The ubiquity of waqf charity was an expression of this impulse. More pragmatically, Islamic inheritance law inspired strategies for maneuvering among the many linkages within the family as well as among the overlapping spheres of family, community, and polity.

Giving or giving up property might therefore have a range of objectives: tactical, reciprocal, charitable, spiritual. Men's giving as reflected in the court records was frequent enough to be predictable: apart from charitable giving, they routinely gave houses to their sons. Men's giving appears to be a strategy for channeling certain kinds of property toward specific heirs and thus evading the arbitrary splitting of property among numerous heirs prescribed by sharia. The city dweller Haci Muhsin, for example, gave a compound consisting of three adjoining houses to his three sons, specifying who was to receive which house and what parts were to be shared.[51] The villager Hasan gave his (only?) son a fig orchard of two hundred trees and the family's house.[52] In contrast to these two prudent individuals, some men did not register their gifts at court, necessitating proof at the time of their death that they had in fact made gifts of houses to their sons during their lifetime.[53] In an unfortunate variation on this theme, the brothers Hüseyin and Hamza told the court that their father had intended to give his house to a third son: "while he was alive and in full health, our father Kasım said to our brother Mehmed, 'Let it be yours,' but before he could vacate the house and turn it over, our father died[.]"[54] Although women sometimes inherited shares of houses, the frequency with which men gifted houses to their sons suggests that this was a strategy for preserving ownership of urban property in the male family line. It also suggests that the specific assignment of houses or parts of them to specific individuals was intended to preempt the kind of friction among male siblings over the division of inherited homes that we saw in cases summarized above.

The question arises why daughters did not protest when they were denied a potential portion of their fathers' estates. They would have had justification for doing so, since Islamic law disapproved of erosion of an individual's estate through excessive giving.[55] The one woman who did protest her father's gift of much of his estate to his son—Hüsni, whose appeal to the court to overturn her father's plan is cited above—draws our attention to all the women who did not.[56] What women were preserving for themselves in sanctioning their brothers' inheritance of family dwellings was most likely the expectation that their brothers would succeed their father as their protectors. The family home, now the brother's home, was shelter for a female sibling in time of trouble, if circumstances in her own household made remaining there intolerable or if divorce or widowhood left her without resources. In the light of women's dependence on males as heads of the extended family, securing bonds with male kin was an important protective strategy. By giving up real capital, sisters gained a valuable form of social capital.[57]

Women's giving was less frequent in the court records than men's, perhaps because the court is not the right window for viewing much of it. While gifts of real estate were generally recorded, the giving of the sorts of material objects women accumulated was not. But where women's giving *is* visible, it went to strengthen ties to male kin, to whom women sometimes gave whole legacies intact. Three sisters, Fatma, Hadice, and Esmame, each gifted her share of their father's estate—a house, a workshop, and vineyards—to a different brother (the three brothers then registered the details of the division among them of the large compound dwelling).[58] Ayşe bt. Ali gave her shares of the estates of her husband Ömer and her son Ramazan to her remaining son Ali.[59] And İnepaşa canceled the 700-akçe debt her son-in-law Ali owed her—in the language of the court record, she made a gift *(hibe)* of it.[60] Each of these women probably expected in return the support of the male relative. Ayşe and İnepaşa may in fact have been about to move in with, or perhaps already were living with, the male relative in question—Ayşe with her son and İnepaşa with her son-in-law.

Earlier in this chapter, property figured as an object of conflict among kin and the court as a vehicle for intervention and amelioration. But as we see, there is another, equally compelling, theme in the story of property and family—that of property as a medium for consolidating family ties. In addition to the evidence of women's giving to male kin, the court records contain many examples of family cooperation, as relatives acted jointly to sell property or initiate claims to it.[61]As in the two following examples, it was most often a male who took responsibility for court business over joint family property. In two cases stemming from the disposition of their father's estate, Kasım b. İbrahim and his sister Emine, together with their mother Muluk, sold a house in the Tarla district of the city for 620 akçes: two months earlier Kasım had successfully sued on behalf of himself and his sister to recover their inherited vineyard from another claimant.[62] Bedreddin from Aleppo was able to prove his mother's disputed ownership of a one-quarter share in a mill in the village of Hacer: he produced three separate documents to prove that she had inherited it from her father, while the rival claimant could furnish none.[63]

"Family," so far in this discussion, has most often meant a woman's blood kin—brother, uncle, mother, sister, son, or daughter, and on one occasion, a daughter's husband. In other words, property tended to emphasize women's bonds to natal family and children. As seen through the eyes of the court, women's most frequent ties through the medium of property were with their siblings, and then, as they grew older, with their children. Men's most frequent ties were with their siblings and other agnates. While marriage translated a woman's spatial orientation from natal to marital household, her ties to her natal family retained a material reality through links of property.

One reason why women's natal ties figure so centrally in property relations at court is that inheritance forms the great bulk of court records having to do with the acquisition of property. In turn, the frequency of inheritance cases at court results from the fact that the settlement of inheritance was so often a public effort, one whose results were validated by inscription into the record. The many legal issues implicated in the constant turnover of property meant that the community entered the lives of families because of it. Neighborhood imams and court-appointed experts in the division of estates were called on regularly. Court-appointed mediators were faced with the challenge of allocating disputed property judiciously and peaceably. Expert witnesses were sent to assess the merits of conflicting claims to trees, vines, and doors. Ordinary citizens were drafted as guardians to manage the estates of orphans. And other individuals were victims of property disputes—for example, the buyers of women's land sold illegally by their uncles, brothers, and stepfathers.

But what about women's property within marriage? Even though most individuals using the court were probably married adults, the domestic life of married couples is only dimly visible through the lens of the court records. Here, legal culture reflected social culture, which frowned upon asking about a man's wife; correspondingly, the court intervened in the domestic space only when petitioned to do so. Nevertheless, the marital household had a critical reality in sixteenth-century Aintab. Although the frequency of divorce lent it a certain fragility, marriage was the matrix within which the identity of women was constructed—and to a large extent, that of men as well. The nuclear family, in other words, was not a culturally anachronistic concept in sixteenth-century Ottoman society. The household units *(hane)* listed in Ottoman cadastral surveys are generally assumed to have contained an average of five persons.[64] As we saw in chapter 4, polygyny does not appear to have been widespread in Aintab. Furthermore, scholars have challenged the stereotype of the large extended family as the most typical Anatolian residential pattern, arguing that people may have lived in such a domestic environment for part of their lives, but that the conglomerate household tended to break up after the death of the male elder.[65] The Aintab court records support this picture, demonstrating that sibling heirs frequently reconstructed domestic space into discrete "nuclear" units.

While the court records are informative about women's property links to their natal kin, they are reticent about property conflict within marriage. Their silence with regard to the dower legally prescribed for females at marriage suggests that actually getting it was not a problem, in contrast to the challenges some females faced in claiming inherited property. Silence in the records might also indicate that wives and husbands had few property disputes over the course of their marriage and that wives' property was safe from husbands' designs on it. During the year studied there were only two incidents of husband-wife conflict over property: Fatma bt. Kara Hamza successfully sued her husband Kara Ali for a 1,000-akçe debt he owed her,[66] while another Fatma proved that she had sold a house inherited from her father to her husband Ali b. Alihan (what was at stake is not clear—the court was simply asked to validate the sale).[67] Rather, husbands appear as helpmates in securing their wives' claims as proxies in court. If they had an interest in the success of these claims other than enhancing the family's immediate security and well-being, it was the future welfare of their joint heirs. Likewise, the occasional gift of a vineyard from a husband to his wife may have been aimed at the same goal of providing "life insurance."[68]

There is a danger, however, in reading these silences in the records as an indication that marriage was a haven from the constant disputation over property that figured in the Aintab court of 1540–1541. One need not be a misanthrope to question this vision of domestic harmony in a society that was both canny about property rights and litigious. Marriage was not a secure institution, given that Muslim men could divorce their wives simply by uttering a verbal formula.[69] This fragility of marriage no doubt inspired female strategies to protect property in anticipation of divorce. Or so current practices would suggest.[70] Women in contemporary Gaziantep are said to exercise caution over what property they bring into their marriage and to make clear what is theirs at the outset of the marriage. Witnesses to the contents of the bride's trousseau are created through the rituals of displaying the trousseau in the couple's new home and transporting it there in a conspicuous processional. If this vulnerability of women's property to usurpation by Aintab husbands is a *longue durée* cultural assumption, protectiveness toward their property may explain sixteenth-century women's preference for gold jewelry, which could be carried on the body; it may also explain why women kept their valuable goods in mobile bundles. Likewise, if the cautionary modern custom that females should take no property from their natal family into marriage except their trousseau is a long-standing one, it helps explain the sixteenth-century practice of leaving houses to male offspring. And the enduring emphasis on the trousseau helps explain the importance of women's commerce in domestic goods and jewelry described above. These various strategies of women tended to be realized without recourse to the court and indeed in deliberate avoidance of it. They remind us of the extent to which customary practice in all its variety acted to flesh out the bare bones of sharia legislation on such matters as marital property.

Although the court records are silent with regard to property relations between wives and husbands, they are vocal in the aftermath of divorce. The divorce settlement frequently caused men to balk and women to strategize. Women were sometimes forced to resort to suing in court in order to receive the property settlement due them at divorce. Their principal goal was their dower *(mehr)*. This was given to them in two segments, half at the time of marriage (the "prompt dower") and half at the dissolution of the marriage (the "deferred dower"). The villager Habibe, for example, sued her ex-husband Hızır for 104 akçes and a bracelet in addition to her dower, and received 160 akçes in an arbitrated settlement.[71] Another important property right was support during the mandatory waiting period after the divorce *(iddet)* whose purpose was to determine if the woman was pregnant and to allow an opportunity for reconciliation. The wellborn city dweller Sitt Laiş bt. Seydi failed to recover her dower from Haci Nasir, her former husband, when two witnesses testified that she had previously made him a gift of it; however, Sitt Laiş was able to obtain the sum of 2 akçes a day as waiting-period support for herself and 1 akçe a day in support for her daughter Saliha.[72]

The ease with which Muslim men could obtain a divorce—and conversely the obstacles encountered by women wanting to end their marriage—caused some women to face hard choices regarding property when they wanted release from an unhappy marriage. For every woman who sued for her rights at divorce, the court records give us two or three who gave up their rights. Women renounced their marital property rights for one of two reasons—as the price of initiating divorce themselves or the price of gaining custody of their children. With the possible exception of adultery, renunciation of the dower is the issue at court that gives us the closest look into the problematic aspects of marriage in Aintab.

Escaping an unsatisfactory marriage was difficult for women, since the only type of divorce commonly available to them required the renunciation of their marital property rights. While Islamic law provided a complex set of means to accomplish divorce, most contained the core provision that the dissolution of a marriage was initiated or accomplished by the husband's unilateral pronouncement of a formula of divorce. In this presumably most common type of divorce, the husband was required to turn over the deferred dower and provide waiting-period support. For women who wished to take the initiative in ending their marriage, the form of divorce known as *hul* was the principal mechanism available. But hul divorce required the wife to surrender her material rights in the marriage—the dower, waiting-period support, and possibly household items she owned.[73] It was women seeking hul divorce who most often renounced their dower at the Aintab court. Hul divorce occurred with a frequency that suggests women were commonly willing to trade material security for freedom from an unsatisfactory marriage. In this light, we see more clearly how critical it was for women to cultivate ties with their brothers. The frequency of hul divorce at the Aintab court is no surprise, as studies of divorce in different times and places across the Middle East demonstrate a similar saliency.[74]

What is perhaps unusual in mid-sixteenth-century Aintab is the frequency with which women gave up claims on their husbands at the time of divorce in order to acquire custody of their children. In a divorce initiated by her husband, Cennet received her dower but gave up waiting-period support and child support in exchange for custody of their daughter.[75] When an Armenian husband and wife, Hüdavirdi and Mısır, chose to divorce according to Muslim practice, Mısır retained custody of their daughter in exchange for renunciation of her property rights.[76] Haci Abdulkadir gave up his son Halil to his ex-wife Halime on condition that she no longer request child support.[77] And Huri, who was accused of adultery and divorced by her husband Mehmed, acquired custody of their daughter on the condition that she not remarry (Mehmed thus prevented her from legitimating her adulterous relationship in marriage); here is the record of their testimony at court:

> When Mehmed said, "She is my wife. She doesn't obey me; she has injured my honor. Let her forfeit the remainder of her dower and her waiting-period support and her various household possessions, the quilt and mattress, and whatever else; let her keep my small daughter as long as she doesn't marry another, and take care of her without requesting support from me; and I will divorce her," Huri forfeited the remainder of her dower and her waiting-period support and all other rights belonging to her and consented to clothe and feed her small daughter, and declared, "Henceforth I make no claim and no demand on Mehmed with regard to my dower or any other matter, I renounce my claim to any suit whatsoever; and furthermore I will support with my own funds his small daughter who is with me."[78]

These cases suggest that customary practice in Aintab allowed husbands to exact a price for custody, demanding that their ex-wives forfeit child support and other rights. This violated sharia, which formally gave the mother custody rights *(hakk-ı hizane)* of boys until the age of seven or nine and of girls until puberty; at that point, the father's right to raise the child *(hakk-ı terbiye)* took over. Sharia law required the father to pay support for any child of his in the legal custody of its mother; in the event of nonpayment, he could be imprisoned, for, as a fatwa of the chief mufti Ebu Suud put it, "it is he who causes the ruination of a small child; [the situation] is not like [that of] an adult child."[79] The mother's importance to a young child was clearly recognized in the rule that the mother's mother (or nearest female kin) should assume custody in the event of the mother's death or remarriage to someone outside either family circle.[80] Although the Aintab court records did not specify the exact ages of the children in the cases above, they were described as "small."[81] All this suggests that customary practice in Aintab forced women to pay a price that was technically illegal.[82] Like the custom of giving of houses to sons, custody is another example of a local practice, apparently sanctioned by the court, that evaded the intent of formal Islamic jurisprudence. What social capital might women have gained in this tradeoff? The court record does not make it clear, but we can hypothesize that in addition to the emotional gain, acquiring custody enabled women to retain some degree of the status of female householder and to cement the ties that they hoped would sustain them in their later years.

STRATEGIZING PROPERTY IN AN
ENVIRONMENT OF IMPERIAL PENETRATION

Much of the reason both women and men came to court so frequently over property was its general insecurity in the period that is the focus of this book. Insecurity was manifested in the large number of conflicting claims to ownership of houses, agricultural land, and urban real estate. The usurpation of property described in earlier parts of this chapter occurred in the context of confusion and a certain amount of lawlessness in the world of property. One of the puzzling challenges for the reader of the Aintab court's records of 1540–1541 is understanding how there can so often have been conflicting claims to houses and agricultural property, that is, how so many people could have been wrong about the validity of their claims to ownership. An example of overlapping claims is provided by the final orphan case discussed above, in which both parties asserted that the vineyard was inherited from their father; in this case, victory went to the party able to bring secure proof of ownership. This final section of the chapter situates the relationships among women, men, and property in the larger relationship of land to the processes of imperial incorporation that Aintab was undergoing in the years around 1540. Everyone, from the sovereign regime down to the peasant farmer, was adapting strategies to deal with the shifting status of land and its management.

One critical aspect of the Ottoman regime's presence in Aintab was its assertion of control over—indeed, possession of—the vast majority of the province's terrain. Its theoretical claim to all but narrowly defined forms of privately owned land was backed up by the several mechanisms of administrative control that were being fine-tuned during these years. One of these was the judge's court and another the web of officials that carried fiscal and legal control into even the smallest of provincial settlements. These mechanisms facilitated the regime's ability to assert control over the land and its revenues. At the same time, however, they served as a resource for the local population in consolidating *its* protective control over the forms of property to which it could lay valid claim.

If we consider the role of chronological time in the confusion over property, some explanations for the large number of property disputes suggest themselves. Conflicts sometimes arose from claims that might date back thirty or forty years, pointing to the conquest as causal factor. The general disruption of the conquest years caused some to leave the area, putting their land in what they thought was the temporary guardianship of another, only to learn upon return that they had stayed away too long and that guardianship had now modulated into ownership (the peasant Yusuf, whom we met in chapter 2, stayed away twenty-five years and unwittingly lost his vineyard). Another factor was the lack of a strong governing power in both the final decades of the Mamluk regime and the first decades of Ottoman occupation of the greater Aintab region. In the absence of a uniform system for registering ownership of property and adjustments to it (e.g., placing it in temporary tenancy), people sought the approval of various quasi-legal authorities such as neighborhood imams and village heads. Now, when confronted with the invigorated court system of the Ottoman regime, many claims to ownership that had seemingly been validated no longer stood up to the judge's scrutiny. The frequency with which plaintiffs at the Aintab court won their suits through *written* proofs—certificates of ownership, copies of court decisions—suggests that oral promises and proofs, adequate in the past, were slowly giving way to material evidence of ownership. Finally, popular awareness that the Ottoman regime now supplied the local court with the authority not only to register but also to enforce property claims seems to have led to a rush to revive old claims that had been languishing for lack of agencies to enforce them. Unfortunately for some, their claims were too old or too weak to stand up to challengers who were savvier in the ways of the law.

Plaintiffs whose suits proved weak or invalid at court may have been sincere in their claims, if legally ignorant. But there is also evidence of deliberate encroachment on the property rights of individuals and institutions in Aintab during the relatively chaotic period leading up to Ottoman consolidation of the region in the 1530s. A startling degree of lawlessness is evident, for example, in the abuse of a major income source of the Mihaliye college *(medrese)*, the public institution with the largest budget in the city. Part of the college's income derived from a mill it owned, located within the city on the Sacur River. The problem was that nearly twenty individuals, among them some prominent local leaders, had been diverting the mill's water supply in order to irrigate their private vineyards and orchards. The Mihaliye's manager, unsuccessful in past attempts to correct this abuse, now tried new strategies. He had previously obtained a ruling by a former Aintab judge against the gentlemen farmers, but he was apparently unable to enforce it. Now he brought to court a firman from the sultan himself ordering that the problem be investigated and rectified. Two individuals from the religious elite of the city (one of them the sheikh of the prominent Haci Baba dervish complex) testified on behalf of all the guilty parties that they had in fact knowingly violated the law in this matter: "our garden plots *(bostan)* have no legal claim on the waters of the mill—our plots are recent plots, the mill is old, the water belongs to the mill."[83] Four days later, on June 16, the Mihaliye manager again appeared in court, this time to challenge the illegal diversion of the college's own water supply; the judgment in this case rested on a fatwa recently issued by the empire's chief mufti, Çivizade Efendi.[84] Twice then, the manager solved his problem by directly linking the local court to the ultimate legal authorities in the empire. New resources could now be brought to bear on chronic problems.

The court-sanctioned enforcement of the Mihaliye's water rights took place shortly after the arrival of the special agent in late May 1541. Perhaps the manager was aware of the regime's plans for "upgrading" the court of Aintab (he had been to the capital to acquire the firman and the fatwa) and deliberately waited to introduce them in court. If the manager of a prestigious institution in Aintab required the backing of officialdom to finally win his case, how were weakly positioned individuals to claim their rights? In this context, it is not difficult to understand how the rights of ordinary individuals—orphans, females, junior males—had been eroded in recent years, and why they and their proxies might now see the court as a vehicle for defending their ownership rights.

The rush to register existing claims and to resuscitate old claims so evident in the court records is only the most obvious strategy deployed by Aintabans in the shifting circumstances around the year 1540. In order to observe their other, less transparent, strategies, we must understand how land was classified and taxed under the Ottoman regime—or rather, how local individuals might have understood the status of land in the environment of uncertainty surrounding the processes of Ottoman penetration. Land was divided into three basic categories: private (freehold) property *(mülk);* endowment land—that is, land whose revenue was assigned in perpetuity to a public or family trust *(waqf; vakıf* in Turkish); and state land, controlled by the Ottoman sultan *(miri).*

Private property included movable goods (animals, domestic items, agricultural and artisanal tools), houses, mills, vineyards and orchards, and urban real estate (e.g., houses, shops, and undeveloped plots of land). Rural land, by contrast, was largely claimed by the sultan, with the exception of whole villages or shares of villages in the province owned by a small number of landed gentry in Aintab and Aleppo. Finally, a special word needs to be said about vineyards and orchards, so ubiquitous in Aintab province: there was agreement that the trees and vines were the property of their cultivators and could be passed down to heirs, but opinion differed on who owned the land supporting the trees and vines.[85]

Waqf land was endowment land, whose revenues were assigned to some charitable purpose designated by the founder. Waqf institutions, such as the Mihaliye college, derived their income from rural agricultural revenues and from urban rental property (shops and houses), mills, public baths, or any combination of such revenue-producing institutions and landholdings. Waqfs were of two types, public and family, depending on the object of the endowment.[86] The public waqf included any establishment that benefited the community: for example, mosques, primary schools and higher institutions of Islamic learning, dervish hospices, hospitals and insane asylums, inns for travelers and merchant caravans, soup kitchens, aqueducts and fountains, and charitable donations for the benefit of pilgrims, the poor, and prisoners of war. Founders of public waqfs ranged from sultans, who undertook the more elaborate and costly of such enterprises, to individuals of modest means, who might, for example, set up a waqf to provide oil for the lamps of the local mosque, or donate a piece of property to be rented out by the beneficiary institution. Alternatively, individuals might add to an existing waqf operation, as did Ayşe bt. İsa above when she donated her share of a house to the waqf of her neighborhood mosque. In short, the public waqf sustained vital social and cultural networks that formed the infrastructure of Islamic societies, and governments could hardly have functioned without them. Nor could cities have supported the urban amenities expected of them without the waqf system. Aintab's urban infrastructure, as we saw in chapters 1 and 2, was the product of generations of local waqf endowment. The city was richly endowed with waqf-based institutions supporting education, public charity, and communal spiritual life: a government survey in 1557 counted eighty-six public waqfs, albeit some of them quite small and not all of them fiscally sound.[87]

The second type of waqf was the family trust, whose income was assigned to the founder and then to his or her descendants in perpetuity. This seemingly self-serving form of waqf was legitimized through the requirement that the waqf's income be assigned to a charitable purpose if and when the founder's family died out. In mid-sixteenth-century Aintab, family waqfs typically named the holy sites in Mecca, Medina, and Jerusalem as ultimate beneficiary, while one waqf dating from 845 H./1441–1442 C.E. named "the mosque in the city of Aleppo next to the citadel."[88] Evidence of family waqfs comes both from the cadastral surveys of Aintab province and from the numerous court cases in which the current beneficiaries (some of them women) appeared in court to validate their claim to the waqf's revenue.

Both forms of waqf were useful in sheltering property from fragmentation at the death of the owner. Waqfs could be used creatively by women and men to allocate property and income in ways that inheritance laws would not accommodate. An important qualification of waqf, both public and family, was that it could only be created out of private property. The transformation of private property to waqf was an ongoing process, one that is amply visible in the cadastral surveys for Aintab. For example, the village disputed between Seyyid Ahmed b. Boyacı and his nephew, listed as private property in the 1543 survey, was converted to a family waqf sometime before the next comprehensive survey of 1574.[89]

State land might seem less relevant to the concerns of this book than waqf or private property, since it could not be owned by individual women or men. However, rural life took much of its shape from the status of the land, as peasants allocated their energies so as to maximize their private gain in the face of state management of the land they cultivated. During the medieval period, Islamic states, particularly Turkish-ruled states, absorbed increasing proportions of rural land into their domains, which they then assigned in the form of military fiefs to soldiers and various military-administrative officials. In return for service, these officials were entitled to the land's tax revenues but not the land itself. Much the same system was in operation in the late Byzantine empire, so the Ottoman administration was in effect dual heir to these practices.[90] As for the peasants who worked the land, they were entitled to the use of the land but not the land itself; in other words, they owned only the usufruct rights. These rights were inherited by the sons of the peasant owner and could also be temporarily assigned to others.

If tested against the strict letter of Islamic jurisprudence, these practices were of dubious legal status. Muslim jurists of the medieval period were faced with modes of land tenure and taxation that violated classical legal formulations, among them the principle that rural taxpayers were the actual owners of the land. In response, jurists developed interpretations that rationalized the practices of ruling regimes, typically by relabeling and reclassifying forms of land tenure and taxes to accommodate them to the legal canon—or, to put it another way, by interpreting the classical canon to fit new circumstances.[91] During the Mamluk and Ottoman periods, jurists systematized opinions that had been advanced in recent centuries,[92] creating a more coherent Islamic justification for practices that originally were non-canonical. One way to rationalize the claims of conquest regimes like that of the Ottomans was to label state (dynastic) lands the "Treasury of the Muslims" *(beyt ül-mal)* and the sultan the steward of this treasury.[93] During the reign of Süleyman, the process of systematization intensified, particularly in the various fatwas and legal writings of Ebu Suud, who served Süleyman from 1537 until the sultan's death in 1566.

How did these forms of landholding—private, waqf, state—relate to women? Obviously, women could own private property, acquired through inheritance, dower, and purchase or trade. They could also establish waqfs, act as their managers, and be the beneficiaries of family waqfs. Because Islamic law governed the management of private property and waqf, it was theoretically incumbent on judges to protect women's rights to these two forms of property. Muslim dynasties are studded with royal women who endowed magnificent waqf establishments in the capitals of empires and in the sacred cities that were the object of pilgrimage.[94] Women were also active in charitable waqfs, providing for the poor, for pilgrims, and sometimes specifically for women in need.[95] This held true across the empire, from royal women in Istanbul to ordinary women in Aintab and beyond. In a 1546 survey of Istanbul waqfs, large and small, women were the creators of more than one-third of the endowments listed, devoting proportionally more of their energies and funds to family waqfs than did men.[96] In the Aintab records for 1540–1541, a number of waqfs were established by ordinary folk: the woman Emine donated a workshop as a family waqf, Ayşe and her three co-owners donated the shares of their house to the neighborhood mosque, Mehmed donated a piece of land in order to enlarge the residence of the Aintab judge, and the village male Köse Bayram donated a house to the village mosque.[97] These cases hardly constitute a representative sample, but it is interesting that the woman Emine was the only one to establish a family waqf.

Women's relationship to state land was more vexed than their relationship to either private property or waqf. A peasant's title to the use of rural agricultural land could generally only be inherited by his sons. This practice, prescribed by sultanic statute, flouted the Qur'anic insistence on women's right to inherit shares of their parents' estate. The prohibition was not absolute, however, and in some times and places widows could retain possession of their husband's farming rights.[98] In his fatwas, Ebu Suud permitted a daughter to succeed to her father's title in the absence of sons, on two conditions: that she pay the "entry fee" *(tapu resmi)* that would be charged any new occupant of the land (but not a son), and that she be able to farm it, that is, that she have a husband or sons.[99] There is limited evidence that over the course of the sixteenth century Ottoman authorities became increasingly willing to allow women to acquire title to the use of rural land, one justification being that if title were to devolve outside the family, the money and labor spent by the father on the land would go for naught.[100] However, the prevailing arrangement in Aintab, at least in the years covered by this study, was male succession to peasant-farmed land. In the cadastral surveys from 1536 to 1574, there is no evidence of female control of rural land that was not freehold or waqf.

In its policies on rural succession, then, the state's predominant attitude was akin to that of the men who were cited at the Aintab court for attempting to evade the rights of their female relatives. In Aintab in 1540, the state, so to speak, was condoning the disinheritance of females from its own property while simultaneously underwriting the criminalization of the disinheritance of females from private property. This seeming paradox was a manifestation of the two systems of justice that will be described in chapter 8— one for the state and one for its subjects: private property and waqf were regulated by traditional sharia principles, while land tenure was ordered by state practices that had more or less acquired the sanction of sharia. Nevertheless, the question must be asked (although it cannot be answered): To what extent did the state's reinforcement of patriarchal attitudes toward women's inheritance of land permeate thinking in general about women and property in Aintab? Did the state, in other words, send a message that taking measures to reinforce male control of property was acceptable?[101]

The strategies of local residents were in a number of ways attuned to these structures of landholding and the ongoing efforts of government authorities to systematize and codify practice.[102] In October 1540, or more precisely between the 19th and 23rd of the month, numerous individuals appeared at court to register rural land as private property, family waqf, or public waqf. For example, Yahya b. Araboğlu's claim to ownership (*mülkiyet*) of three-quarters of the village of İkizce and two mezraas was confirmed by two witnesses; the entry on İkizce in the cadastral survey of 1543 indicates that the Araboğlu family claim was an old one.[103] The remaining one-quarter of the village belonged to Fethullah b. Abdülkerim, noted in the court record as "one of the notables of Aleppo," and formed part of a family waqf whose current beneficiary Fethullah was; the waqf also controlled a mezraa and shares in four other Aintab villages in addition to İkizce.[104] Numerous other individuals registered similar landholdings, as did waqf institutions such as the Dülük Baba dervish hospice, which recorded its ownership of a village and all or parts of eight mezraas. What does this clustering of cases between October 19 and 23 represent? Does it suggest a collective action on the part of the local landed gentry and waqf administrators to affirm their ownership rights in anticipation of some government intervention in land administration?[105] Or did it perhaps occur in response to a call put out by the judge for a reregistration of all nonstate rural property? Many of the claims inscribed during the four intensive days refer to previous confirmations of private rural property recorded by the provincial governor's staff or official inspectors of waqf lands. This repeated inventorying of private holdings was perhaps a state-initiated process, complementary to the cadastral inventories of state lands.[106] One reason for our difficulty in discerning the relationship of stimulus and response in these court cases from October 1540 is that both the Ottoman regime and local individuals had an interest in officially registering property.

The court's attention to family waqfs, an aspect of its overall attention to clarifying and registering property claims, could be to women's benefit in that it furnished a climate hospitable to bringing forth claims. Women's ability to control waqfs in Aintab was like their ability to control private property: limited, challenged by men, but defended in the 1540–1541 court. Only one of the waqfs registered in October, a comparatively small one, was in the hands of women: three sisters, the Haciyes (female pilgrims) Emine, Saliha, and Salime, controlled the one-third share of a mezraa endowed by their father, Ahmed b. Beyar.[107] Other female waqf beneficiaries appear in the court record mainly because of problems asserting their right of succession—that is, their place as the eldest of extended family members qualifying as named descendants of the waqf's founder. In order to establish her claim to the oil press established as family waqf by an ancestor from Ruha, Şahpaşa bt. Halil went to the trouble of obtaining a fatwa that she then took to the governor-general Ali Pasha, who ordered the provincial governor and judge of Aintab to see to its execution.[108] Clearly Şahpaşa would not have resorted to such a roundabout means of realizing her claim, obtaining both religious and executive sanction in her favor, had she not encountered resistance along the way. When Cennet bt. Hızır came to court to assert her claim to the orchard that had been a family waqf for several generations, it was clear that there was dissension among the many descendants of the waqf founder. At least they could agree that Cennet was "the eldest of us all" and hence entitled to the orchard for the present.[109]

Having surveyed the various forms of land classifications, we can turn now to more specific practices and claims of the Ottoman administration in Aintab and the effects they had on the strategies of local residents in consolidating their property. Here we must consider the local community at two levels: the elite, some of whom benefited from government-supplied tax-farms at the same time that they suffered from certain government policies, and ordinary individuals, who maneuvered within more limited parameters.

At the level of the elite, owners of the whole or parts of villages had to cope with the Ottoman regime's application of a special system of fiscal administration of privately owned rural land. Known as *malikâne-divanî* (loosely, "private-imperial"), this system had long been practiced in older Islamic areas of the empire, including central and southeastern Anatolia and greater Syria.[110] According to the malikâne-divanî system, the governing regime claimed certain tax revenues of freehold or waqf villages while the remainder went to the owner or waqf beneficiary.[111] The Ottoman practice of this system has been called a pretext for the state to intrude its agents into privately owned or managed rural settlements.[112] It was also a means by which the state could generate more revenue for itself (at the expense of local landed gentry) without hurting the peasant producer.[113] Margaret Venzke's study of Aleppo suggests that the malikâne-divanî system eroded agricultural productivity over the course of the sixteenth century: for example, a dervish institution in Aleppo saw its agriculturally derived income drop 38 percent between 1537 and 1570.[114] The same decline in revenue of private or waqf villages under the malikâne-divanî system can be observed in Aintab between the cadastral survey years of 1543 and 1574. For example, the Boyacı family's share of the revenues of its village of Arıl declined by 29 percent between 1543 and 1574, while the state's take increased by 39 percent. The waqf share of the largest village in Aintab, Hiyam, which was owned by two Aleppan family waqfs, declined by 64 percent during the same period, while the state's share decreased by 20 percent. Such decline in malikâne-divanî village production, though a general phenomenon in Aintab, was not universal: the village of İkizce mentioned above, held jointly by Yahya and Fethullah, increased its private and waqf share by more than 112 percent, while the state's share increased by 35 percent.[115]

While it is not a project of this book to delve deeply into the political economy of Aintab in 1540–1541, the workings of the malikâne-divanî sys-

tem raise some questions about the larger relationship of the Ottoman state
to the local community. Assuming it is true for Aintab that the system was a
hook by which the Ottoman regime inserted itself into rural administration
and shifted revenue to its own advantage, we might ask if this was the assault
of an imperializing power on local autonomy, resuscitating a traditional
regional practice favorable to ruling regimes. Was the Ottoman state seeking to erode an important base of the privileged status of a local elite, with
little regard along the way for the venerable Islamic institution of waqf, as
Venzke sees its operations in Aleppo?[116] Declining revenues from privately
owned land suggests that her conclusion holds true for Aintab as well. On
the other hand, it needs to be recognized that the expansion of locally imposed state revenues provided benefits to the provincial population, at least
in Aintab. A good deal of the revenue arrogated by the state was recycled locally, particularly in the defense of the region; much of the state's take from
rural Aintab was turned over to various fortress garrisons in the region. Affecting daily life more directly, a portion of local state revenue was devoted
to the support of important local waqfs: for example, the dervish hospice
(zaviye) originally endowed by the notable Demircioğlu family, which provided food and lodging for travelers and twice-weekly free meals for the local poor, or the Cedide medrese—"New College"—that would be founded
in 1548.[117] The impact of such local institutions was recognized by the level
of state support they garnered: the Ottoman regime supplemented the
original private endowments of both the Demirci zaviye and the Cedide
medreses with imperial endowments from its local rural revenues. The support of such prominent public waqfs was an old habit of Muslim sovereigns
that sometimes transcended particular royal regimes: the Demirci zaviye,
for example, had been endowed with land grants from the Mamluk sultan
Qansuh Al-Ghawri.[118]

The intervention of the Ottoman regime in the administration of local
waqfs had other benefits for the local community. In the unsettled early
decades of the sixteenth century, there appears to have been widespread
abuse of waqf endowments throughout the region. The problems faced by
the Mihaliye college in protecting its revenue sources from the encroachment of local gentry were not unique. A typical abuse suffered by waqf foundations, particularly larger ones, was usurpation of their income by the
elites who managed them and held prestigious offices within them. A law
code issued by the dynasty in 1540 for the governorate-general of Diyarbakır noted critically that when foundation income was down, staff
tended to pay itself at the expense of the upkeep of buildings and thus of
the long-term viability of the institution.[119] At the time of the Ottoman conquest, corruption was evident among some leading figures in the religious
elite of Damascus: the historian Ibn Tulun reported that the chief Hanafi
judge from 1505 until the conquest actually sold many endowments while

he was in office; another judge allowed mosques and cemeteries to be dis-
mantled so that he could sell the materiel as scrap.[120] Were waqf administrators in Aintab similarly corrupt? Perhaps the problems that the Mihaliye's
current manager was addressing were in part the result of the negligence—
or worse—of previous managers.

It can thus be argued that the malikâne-divanî system was a good thing
for the general welfare insofar as it contributed to state spending for defense and public charity. But what about its impact on local magnates? Were
state-sponsored benefits to the local population entirely at their expense?
Taking as examples the three most distinguished *ayan* families of Aintab—
the Boyacı, the Demirci, and the Sikkak—we find that each experienced a
net loss of income from its rural holdings between 1543 and 1574.[121] On
the other hand, these families cannot be said to have been impoverished
at the hands of the Ottoman regime. The court records demonstrate that
one way of compensating for erosion of agricultural income was diversification into other sources of income, particularly tax-farming. All three
families were active in contracting tax-farms from the Ottoman regime during 1540–1541. Perhaps this form of entrepreneurship had always been
an element in the diversified economic base of such notables (the lack of
earlier court records for Aintab makes it difficult to say). Nevertheless, it is
plausible to suggest that the shrinkage in income of some malikâne-divanî
villages and mezraas in the possession of these magnates that occurred over
the middle decades of the sixteenth century was in part the result of rein-
vestment in expanding sectors of the local economy. Between 1536 and
1543, state tax revenues in Aintab city increased by 73 percent, making the
farming of urban taxes a potentially lucrative business.[122] In the subdistrict
of Aintab, the 78 percent increase in rural revenues from state land made
rural tax-farming another investment opportunity, perhaps especially attractive to magnates already practiced in rural financial management.[123]
Thus it could be said that the Ottoman regime, like its predecessors, gave
with one hand while it took away with the other.

The expanding scope for investment in tax-farms provided an opening
for women. Although there were no female tax-farmers in Aintab, a number of women figured as high-stakes participants in the lively competition
for these investment opportunities. Two obviously wealthy females, Tatar bt.
İbrahim and Haleb bt. İlyas, appear in the court records as financial backers for the joint holders of the market inspectorship *(ihtisap)*, the largest
tax-farm in the province. On July 14, 1541, they were acknowledged by the
court as guarantors *(kefil)* for the large debt owed by the market inspectors.[124] It is not clear what the women's relationship to the market inspectors was, nor what they stood to gain. At the very least, it was expected that
a guarantor would be paid back for any debt he or she assumed, and there
may have been some additional compensation as well.

Women were clearly valuable partners in the local competition for tax-farms. An explicit example of their critical financial role is provided by Mustafa Çelebi b. Hamza, the trustee of state lands in Aintab *(hassemini)* and thus holder of the most influential and prestigious local office furnished by the state. Like many others involved in tax collection, Mustafa Çelebi had his own quite sizable debt to the state. Had he not been backed at a critical moment by his wife, Aynişah bt. Karagöz Ağa, he might well have lost his important office. Aynişah's large inheritance bailed her husband out of his predicament: in October 1540, Mustafa Çelebi recorded the sale of a mill, an orchard, and six of a group of twelve stores belonging to her, for a sum of 20,000 akçes.[125] The court record specifies that Aynişah, acting through her proxy, approved the liquidation of this portion of her estate. What was Aynişah's gain? The continued standing of her household in the provincial community was undoubtedly of importance to her as well as to her husband.

The examples of Tatar, Hüsni, and Aynişah suggest that the changes occurring in Aintab opened up places for women to put their money. Indeed, the smooth flow of business may have depended on their financial support. It is difficult to know if there were other women like these three, since the court records are generally silent with regard to elite women. We might ask, for example, about the female relatives of the enterprising brothers Hüseyin and Ahmet Çelebi, the one a former warden of the fortress and the other a prominent textile merchant. When Hüseyin died, he left his mother, wife, sister, and brother as heirs. The women's shares in one item in the warden's estate, a mill in the village of Yuneh, were purchased by Ahmed Çelebi for a total of 300 gold florins (or 24,000 akçes). This sum, together with other gains from the estate and property perhaps already owned, made them women of considerable wealth. The court record does not tell us what they did with that wealth, but we might imagine that they, like the woman Rahime bt. İbrahim, invested in the trade in textiles, one of Aintab's strongest commercial enterprises. Rahime appeared in court in June 1541 to make a claim of 5,320 akçes against the estate of the cloth merchant Hoca Yusuf, whose debts to various individuals (at least those claims made at court) totaled 654 gold florins.[126] These "debts" were probably investments in a joint venture—the contractual partnership known as *mudaraba,* similar to the European *commenda,* which was elaborated by Islamic law and widespread in the Middle East.[127] In such a partnership, profits were shared by the trader (here, Hoca Yusuf) and the providers of capital. Hoca Yusuf's several partners placed the woman Rahime in a network of investment that included, among others, a villager from the neighboring province of Bire and a prominent timariot, Kasım Beg, "pride of the cavalrymen," as the court record identified him.

Despite the declining profitability of rural landownership and the regime's tighter control over tax-farmers, all of the individuals named above benefited in one way or another from the expanding economy, the growth of trade in the Aintab region, and the increases in tax revenues that made tax-farming profitable. But what about ordinary individuals—the farmers, artisans, shopkeepers, day laborers, and pastoralists whose taxes furnished a substantial portion of the rising revenues? Individuals of more modest means had more modest choices regarding how best to safeguard their property and invest their resources.

In earlier parts of this chapter, we saw how important houses and domestic items were to the men and women of Aintab. Also vital to ordinary Aintabans were the vineyards and orchards so ubiquitous in the province. The frequency with which they figured in the registration of inheritance or sales and in litigation testifies to the importance of these forms of property in the strategies of many. In the years around 1540, much new rural land was going into cultivation, particularly in small parcels. Formal grants of usufruct rights to land typically did not specify the intended use of the land, but where they did, vineyards were the most common, with sites for mills in second place. Urban folk were not deprived of the opportunity to "grow wealth," since orchards, vineyards, and vegetable plots ringed much of the city, giving Aintab its reputation for abundant green space. The choicest urban locations were probably along the Sacur River, which curved around the northern half of the city (this was where the local gentry had been illegally diverting water from the Mihaliye mill). In fact, this area was kept free for cultivation until the city's expansion northward during the last thirty years or so of the twentieth century.[128]

Men and women acquired vineyards and orchards through inheritance, purchase, dower, and gift. Perhaps we should say "grape vines and fruit trees" rather than "vineyards and orchards," since an advantage of this form of private property was that one could possess it in small packages—the single walnut tree that formed part of the dower of İl Hatun, for example, or the five vines owned by a villager in a shared mezraa. Vineyards and orchards were desirable because they were an object of agricultural labor that actually belonged to the laborer. They were not exempt from taxes, but they were considered private property. A tenacious popular belief of the period was that if trees or grape vines were planted so densely that no other crop could be grown beneath them, the land on which they grew also became one's private property—in other words, cultivating vines or trees could convert state land into freehold. The official view of the Ottoman regime, however, was that vines and trees were indeed private property, but that the land beneath them belonged to the domain of the state.[129] Not surprisingly, the popular belief persisted, since Ottoman land-use laws were in flux as they underwent a particularly intense process of codification in these years, only reaching their mature formulation in the law code issued in 1541 when

Hungary was annexed to the empire. Moreover, Hanafi jurists of the six-teenth century disagreed among themselves on the status of land on which trees grew. Some, including Ebu Suud, conceded that the planting of an or-chard or vineyard established the cultivator's inheritable claim to its usu-fruct, although the land was not converted to private property.[130]

All this makes it difficult to know what the prevailing practice in Aintab was. The language of court scribes when recording sales of vineyards and or-chards suggests that for all practical purposes, land and crop formed a unit: "a vineyard of 750 vines," "an orchard bounded on its four sides by . . . " Moreover, the case of one Hoca b. Tahir suggests that land was considered part of a deceased person's property: registered at court, Hoca's estate in-cluded a horse, a donkey, six goats, two farms (çift) worth 400 akçes, half a farm worth 300 akçes, and two vineyards worth 300 akçes.[131] Throughout the records of 1540–1541, there is evidence of a strong sense among many Aintabans that putting labor into a piece of land created a claim to rights in the land, though such claims did not stand up in court against legal chal-lenges by actual owners. Such was the situation of one Bayram Kadı, who had apparently been cultivating a vineyard on land owned by Seyyid Ali; when Seyyid Ali sold the land and the new owner went to court to get rid of Bayram Kadı, the latter lost despite his claim that the vineyard "is de facto in my control."[132] Whatever the precise thinking of legal experts in Aintab, vineyards and orchards were a staple in "estate planning" in Aintab.

It is possible that the widespread cultivation of vineyards and orchards had an impact on the overall agricultural performance of the province. The cadastral surveys of 1543 and 1574 yield a province-wide picture of sharply declining agricultural production accompanied by increasing artisanal manufacturing and food processing as alternate forms of rural employ-ment.[133] This shift was in part the result of the "pax Ottomanica" and the integration of Aintab into larger regional trade networks. What is of partic-ular interest here is that within the picture of declining agricultural pro-duction, cultivation of the grain staples of wheat and barley was giving way to the cultivation of fruits and vegetables. The same decline in the size of wheat and barley crops in larger villages has been documented during this period for the rich agricultural area northwest of Aleppo.[134] Despite the population increase observable in Aintab and Aleppo in the middle dec-ades of the sixteenth century, people do not seem to have gone hungry, be-cause of the simultaneous expansion of land going into cultivation. As we saw in chapter 2, the production of wheat and barley in Aintab was shifting from the farms of larger villages to those of smaller villages and to mez-raas.[135] The fact that new mills were being constructed in these years is fur-ther testimony to the increase in grain staples.

To what extent were these developments related to popular pressure to create more vineyards and orchards? Peasants in other parts of the Mediterranean world were attempting to shift to more profitable crops, especially since wheat, the principal grain, required more acreage and was therefore less profitable.[136] In 1550, for example, wheat and barley were being exported from Syria to Cyprus, where peasants were turning from grain cultivation to the cultivation of grape vines, sugar, and cotton, despite the remonstrances of the authorities.[137] Officials in Aintab who issued titles to virgin or vacated land—timariots, rural gentry, the trustee of state lands—may in principle have had the authority to specify what crops were to be grown, but cultivators clearly had minds of their own. The chronic abuse of the Mihaliye mill waters is an example of powerful individuals collectively conspiring to protect their private green spaces, but lesser folk in large numbers, as the example of Cyprus suggests, also had the force to bend official practice to local usage. The authorities may have tolerated the shift to horticultural crops in large villages since there was sufficient reserve land in these years both to feed people and to furnish adequate levels of tax revenue.

If these shifts in quantity and location of different kinds of agricultural production are seen as related to local strategies of allocating labor devised in the light of imperial consolidation, we must recognize women's motives as an important part of the story. It was not simply the invigorated Aintab court that accounts for women's several suits to claim vineyards they had inherited, but also the general importance people attached in these years to freehold agricultural property. Women insisted on their rights to vineyard ownership in part because vineyards were easily sold. They probably also had a particular interest in vineyards because they were able to handle much of the care of vines, as well as the processing of grapes. Women's labor was critical in turning grapes into cash crops, in a series of stages that can still be observed today: first, the extraction of the juice of the grapes (*şıra*), then its reduction and treatment to yield a variety of products. The most common of these in the Aintab records of 1540–1541 was *pekmez*, which can take the form either of a molasses-like syrup or a paste-like solid.[138]

Another aspect of shifting labor allocation in mid-sixteenth-century Aintab that affected women was an increase in artisanal manufacturing, documented in the cadastral registers for larger villages in Aintab and no doubt taking place in some urban households as well (see chapter 2). Diversification in forms of rural employment offered women a wider range of potential occupations. That women had some degree of say in how they spent their time is suggested by a fatwa of İbn Kemal, chief mufti of the empire from 1524 to 1535. When asked the question "If [a man] buys cotton and his wife spins it and weaves cloth from it, who does [the cloth] belong to?"

the mufti responded that if the wife's labor was voluntary, the cloth belonged to the husband; otherwise, the wife received "fair recompense" for her labor, that is, the equivalent of the going wage rate.[139] Whether local practice in Aintab accorded with the mufti's pronouncement is impossible to say. But if it did, the shift in larger villages to artisanal work may have afforded women a direct income that the grain-growing peasant household did not.

.   .   .

None of the approaches to protecting property practices described above— converting property to waqf, investing in tax-farms, cultivating orchards and vineyards—was new in 1540. However, these practices were salient in the court record at a time when the Ottoman regime was engaged in tightening up both its legal system and its control of land tenure. The conclusion that individuals in Aintab were consciously advancing self-protective strategies, at least partly under the auspices of the court, is inescapable. But the interests of individuals clashed, and here the court assisted in sorting out disputes and establishing legal and moral priorities. Where the court system upheld women's interests, it was largely because of Islamic law, which regulated private property transactions, the creation and management of waqf, and inheritance. While the moral impulse in upholding the rights of women was a critical aspect of the workings of the legal system, an equally significant impulse was securing the integrity of the legal process itself. That both men and women began to use the court to solve property disputes after June 1541—that is, after the demonstration of state intent to add rigor to the Aintab court—points to the critical role of the invigorated legal system in the matter of property rights. Women's rights did not languish, because, in the words of Ebu Suud, the law itself could not languish.

This chapter has argued that women's experience of property cannot be considered apart from a whole set of human reciprocities that shaped the broader social and moral environment. In this light, we might hypothesize a kind of tacit bargain among men, women, and the state, a bargain over land and other forms of property that assumed a division of labor in managing property and also a willingness on the part of each to forgo some degree of control over it. The Ottoman regime barred women from state land (at least in Aintab) but upheld their rights to other forms of property. It demonstrated its own stake in the nexus of reciprocities directly by supporting waqf institutions and indirectly by allowing some local residents to enrich themselves from the management of the state's own property. Patriarchal privilege, against which women could muster little real resistance, yielded to women's control of their own world of property independent from that of their husbands. No doubt there was tacit recognition that women's creation of their own economy out of their inheritance shares and dower ultimately worked to the benefit of the family and its social reproduction. Clearly, women's strategies were constructed within a context that privileged men and in which the Ottoman regime privileged itself at the expense of both women and men. Nevertheless, because property circulated within channels of reciprocal obligation, women's responses and strategies were able to influence the shape of the whole.

Figure 1. The battlefield of Marj Dabik. In this view from the mid-1530s, the site of the Ottoman victory in August 1516 is depicted as a flowering meadow. At the top is the village of Cebel Halit, and at the bottom is the shrine at what was believed to be the grave of the Prophet Davud. The Ottoman army camped here for two days after the battle. From Matrakçı Nasuh, *Beyan-ı Menazil-i Sefer-i Irakeyn*, fol. 105a. Courtesy of Istanbul University Library.

Figure 2. The citadel of Aintab. Aintab and its citadel are seen from the west in this mid-nineteenth-century sketch. The Sacur River is visible in the foreground, as are the vineyards and vegetable gardens watered by it. From Lieut. Colonel Chesney, *The Expedition for the Survey of the Rivers Euphrates and Tigris* (London: Longman, Brown, Green, and Longmans, 1850), atlas. Courtesy of the Bancroft Library, University of California, Berkeley.

Figure 3. The citadel of Aleppo. A late-seventeenth-century view of Aleppo, with its prominent citadel. From Henry Maundrell, *A Journey from Aleppo to Jerusalem at Easter, A.D. 1697* (Oxford: "Printed at the Theater," & sold by J. Bowyer, [London], 1707). Courtesy of the Bancroft Library, University of California, Berkeley.

Figure 4. Crossing the Euphrates at Birecik, 1955. The ruins of the fortress of old Bire are to the left. Perhaps transport in the sixteenth century was made in similar poled boats. Photographed by Josephine Powell. Courtesy of Josephine Powell.

Figure 5. First page of the Aintab court register, dated 29 Muharrem 948/May 25, 1541. The new court register was headed by an inscription hailing the appointment of the new judge, Hüsameddin Efendi. The three cases recorded below it (of which two appear in the image above) involve a price setting and two confessions to adultery. From Gaziantep Sicili no. 2, fol. 1. Courtesy of Milli Kütüphane Başkanlığı, Ankara.

Figure 6. A woman seeks an appeal. The woman on the left with her hands raised complains about the onerous outcome of a case she alleges was not handled judiciously. She appeals to a janissary, a member of the royal infantry. Janissaries were called upon to perform urban services such as fire fighting and policing (see also figure 10); in the latter capacity, they figured in the line of executive authority. From *Hünername* (1588). Courtesy of Topkapı Palace Museum Library, Istanbul.

Figure 7. How Turkish women go about at home. The women in this sixteenth-century portrait, probably ladies of Istanbul, are wearing items of dress—caftans and head ornaments—valued also by the women of Aintab. From Codex Vindobonensis 8626. Courtesy of Öesterreischische Nationalbibliothek, Vienna.

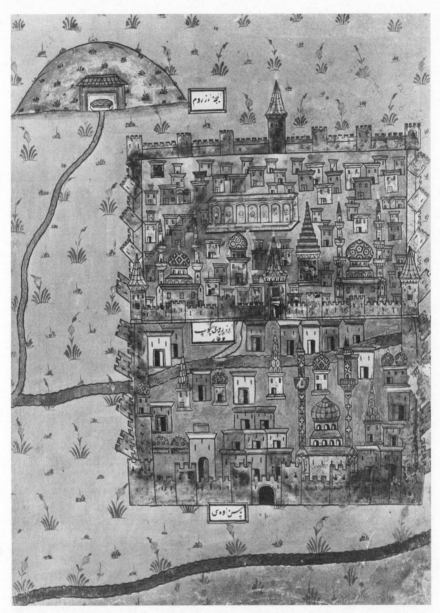

Figure 8. The city of Erzurum. This view from the mid-1530s depicts the walled city, relatively unpopulated in these years. The impressive domed buildings were constructed by various sovereigns and emirs from the twelfth through fourteenth centuries. From Matrakçı Nasuh, *Beyan-ı Menazil-i Sefer-i Irakeyn*, fol. 23b. Courtesy of Istanbul University Library.

Figure 9. Closing a wine bar. A bevy of authorities raid a winebar and administer a flogging to one of the guilty parties. From Franz Taeschner, ed., *Alt-Stambuler Hof-und Volksleben. Ein Türkisches Miniaturenalbum aus dem 17. Jahrhundert* (Hannover: Orient-Buchhandlung H. Lafaire, 1925), plate 23. Courtesy of Biblio Verlag, Bissendorf.

Figure 10. Caught in a rendezvous. A man and a woman are apprehended at a waterside rendezvous complete with refreshments cooling in the stream. Four janissaries, serving under police authorities, make the arrest. The woman appears to plead with her captors, while her partner is threatened by his. From *Album of Sultan Ahmet I* (1603–1618), fol. 20b. Courtesy of Topkapı Palace Museum Library, Istanbul.

PART THREE

Law, Community, and the State

Haciye Sabah's Story

A Teacher on Trial

On July 6, 1541, the judge of Aintab sentenced one of the city's residents, a woman identified in the court record as Haciye Sabah, to public humiliation and banishment from the city. This severe punishment ostensibly resulted from the court's finding that Sabah was guilty of violating the practice of gender segregation: she had allowed males to be present at the religious-instructional classes for females that she ran in her own home. Indeed, she had *hired* them to teach her female pupils. Her conduct in allowing the mixing of the sexes was characterized by the court record as "against the law and beyond reason" *(nâ meşru' ve nâ ma'kul)*. As if that unambiguous condemnation were not enough, a later insert to the text of the record added, "and it was forbidden" *(menhi)*. The teacher hired by Sabah, one İbrahim, was also punished with exile from the city.

With the sentencing, the court's work might have appeared to be complete. However, later that day (or at least in a later entry in the court record for that day) two male neighbors of the woman Sabah gave testimony that threw the case into a different light. They alleged that the instruction taking place in her home was actually initiation in heretical doctrines, which Sabah was instilling in her disciples with İbrahim's assistance. The neighbors went on to accuse the classes of devotional irregularities and excesses: the assembled females were so carried away by their swaying and dancing, charged the two men, that a little girl, unattended, had fallen off the roof and injured herself. Finally, the neighbors complained that suspicions of sexual misconduct had been voiced, bringing unwanted intrusion of the authorities into their midst.[1]

This was perhaps the most scandalous accusation and certainly the most unusual punishment recorded for the court of Aintab for the entire year. To be sure, the city and its rural hinterland were far from crime-free: during the course of the year, the court recorded five murders, two gang rapes, and numerous instances of adultery, slander, and assault. But the affair of the woman Sabah led to the most public punishment of a female and the sole case of exile from the city. To be exiled, as the court's judgment suggests, was to suffer the logical consequences of having placed oneself outside the boundaries of law and social reason.

For these reasons alone, the trial of the woman Sabah draws our attention. But it is of further interest for the rare evidence it provides of two other matters on which the historical record of the Ottoman sixteenth century is relatively silent: women's access to knowledge and education, and their involvement in the ideological controversies of the times. Moreover, it reveals the reactions that are provoked when a woman has influence beyond the conventional roles ascribed to her sex.

Basic education in this period, for males and females alike, meant instruction in scripture and in the catechisms of social conduct. Men were freer to get this kind of instruction from the neighborhood imam or from popular preachers. The court record depicts boys taught by the village imam and the more privileged tutored at home (for example, the material taught by one Molla Mezid to the boy Mehmed was registered at court by Mehmed's father).[2] Boys who wished to pursue a more advanced education might study in one of the several schools in Aintab. Perhaps sisters learned at home alongside their brothers, but it is only the education of boys that is visible in the court record. Because we have virtually no documentation of the education of females in the early modern Ottoman period, the trial of Sabah merits attention simply because it provides evidence of their instruction through the household learning circles that we know from other premodern societies of the Middle East. Whether or not Sabah was guilty of spreading heretical doctrine, it is clear that her religious-instructional classes were locally popular. Repeatedly in her testimony, she insisted that she made her living by organizing such classes, suggesting that she had a steady clientele.

Perhaps more intriguing, the case provides rare evidence of a female accused of heretical sympathies. Ottoman chronicles recount many examples of prominent figures executed for heresy, and central government documents throughout the sixteenth century give evidence of prosecution of individuals believed to have deviated from the orthodoxy of the state. All these individuals were men, however. This case offers an example of how ideological controversies might penetrate local neighborhoods and become the stuff of quotidian conflict through the society of women. Followers of the movement to which Haciye Sabah was accused of belonging were popularly called "the red heads," and her trial is reminiscent of the "red threat" that generated fear and anxiety during the McCarthy era in the United States. Her case exemplifies the familiar process of social and cultural fault lines exposed under ideological pressure, when accusations come to be based on matters other than questions of pure belief. The fault line made visible in the trial of Haciye Sabah divided the religious establishment, in the form of the city's mollas, from the popular faith so characteristic of Turkmen culture and its veneration of saints and spiritual leaders.

In the context of the court records, the case of Haciye Sabah is extraordinary by a number of measures. It takes us into a world beyond the material environment of property, the litigation of disputes, and the contractual networks of sale, loan, and bond that are the stuff of most court records. It does so by giving us a glimpse of how people came together around matters of faith and learning. The affair of Haciye Sabah also takes us briefly into a woman's world, although it was one that the authorities were eager to shut down. The record of this case comes closest in the work of the court to providing a formal deposition, since its protagonists give relatively complete accounts of their side of the story. Yet as with other complex events only dimly visible through the records, there is much more we would wish to know about this affair. The biggest mystery is whether Haciye Sabah was indeed guilty of heresy. Each reader will undoubtedly form an opinion, but this chapter will follow the lead of the judge of Aintab, who did not directly address the question of heresy but rather punished Haciye Sabah and İbrahim for violating codes of male-female contact. In fact, I argue, Hüsameddin Efendi's artful disposition of the case may have been deliberately designed to foster ambiguity over the matter of heresy.

THE KIZILBASH "HERESY"

The behavior of which Sabah was accused was "heresy" principally from the perspective of the Ottoman authorities. The specific accusation against Sabah was that she was instilling Kizilbash doctrines in her pupils. *Kizilbash* was the name given to the followers of the Safavid leader Ismail, who emerged on the stage of Middle Eastern politics in the last years of the fifteenth century. The label, meaning "redheaded" or "red-hatted," came from the headgear—a twelve-gored red "crown"—worn by Safavid partisans. Ismail's religious message was a melange of messianism, holy war, and celebration of martyrs and mystics of the Islamic past. These elements were fused through fervent attachment to his own person and his movement.[3]

From the Ottoman point of view, the Safavid threat was not just one more doctrinal skirmish that could be settled by eliminating the "heretic" leader. Ismail's Safavid patrimony was a sufi (or dervish) order that in the late fifteenth century adopted what today we would call a political agenda. By the turn of the century, the Safavid movement commanded an army of conquest. Under the leadership of the youthful Ismail, it created a new state on the territory leveled by the collapse of the Akkoyunlu dynasty. But while the

Safavids had begun in the fourteenth century as a sunni sufi order, Ismail made the surprising move of declaring shi'ism to be the religion of his nascent state. This declaration would bear fruit in the gradual consolidation of an orthodox shi'i religious establishment over the coming decades, but the latter would be quite different from the heterodox creed propagated by the Safavid movement as it first began to carve out a political domain.

The rise of the Safavid state was swift, perhaps unexpectedly so. The conventional date for the inception of Safavid rule is 1501, with Ismail's victory over the disintegrating Akkoyunlu regime. By 1507, the new sovereign was sufficiently master of the former Akkoyunlu domain in western Iran that he invaded southeastern Anatolia in a bid to claim the former dynasty's territories there, even attacking the Dulkadir prince Alaeddevle.[4] In 1508, Ismail took Baghdad. It looked as if the Ottomans were facing a renaissance of the classic political unit of western Iran, Iraq, and eastern Anatolia, whose latest incarnation had been the Akkoyunlu empire. In 1510, the Safavid forces shifted their attention to the east. There, Ismail and his army stopped the advance of the Uzbek dynasty, which had recently taken control of northeastern Iran. Defeating the Uzbek forces and killing their ruler, Ismail had the latter's skull fashioned into a drinking cup set in gold, which he dispatched to the Ottoman sultan, Bayezid II, as a trophy of his victory.[5]

It was Selim, the Ottoman prince stationed furthest east, in the Black Sea city of Trabzon, who understood the seriousness of the Safavid threat. A huge pro-Safavid uprising that swept across Anatolia in 1511 demonstrated the support that the victorious Ismail, now Safavid shah, commanded among populations claimed by the Ottomans as subjects.[6] Removing his father from the throne in 1512 and a year later eliminating his brother Ahmed, rival claimant to the throne, Selim led one of the most powerful and well-equipped armies of the time against the Safavids in 1514, delivering them a resounding defeat. It is often said that it was the sultan's fear of an alliance between the emerging Safavid state and the Mamluk sultan in Cairo that led him against the latter in 1516. The elimination of the Mamluks was, in this view, not a goal in itself but rather a move to consolidate the Ottoman hold on its newly acquired possessions in eastern and southeastern Anatolia, including the Dulkadir principality.[7] In 1518, Selim mobilized his forces again in an effort to eliminate the Safavid threat altogether, but his troops refused to move beyond the Euphrates. When Süleyman, unproven in battle, assumed the throne in 1520 upon his father's death, he chose to make his own reputation as conqueror on the empire's western frontier, and did not personally address the Safavid challenge until 1534.

In hindsight, it is possible to see the critical importance of these events for the future of the region. The problem of the Kizilbash lies at the heart of what was arguably the most profound development in the sixteenth-century history of the Islamic Middle East—the split of the region into distinct sunni and shi'i domains. Despite repeated military confrontations over the course of the sixteenth century between Ottoman and Safavid forces (and between the Safavids and the Uzbeks), by midcentury or so the wars of conquest so characteristic of late-medieval times had given way to the establishment of states that would prove more stable. With shi'i Iran positioned between the sunni Ottomans on the west and the sunni khanate of the Uzbeks on the east, parameters of identity were laid down whose ramifications are still observable in today's rivalries within the region. These developments brought to an end the centuries-long era of cultural and political fluidity across the Perso-Turkish world, stretching from Central Asia to the Balkans. The permanence of these shifts was not evident in 1540, but the impact of ideological change was soon felt. On both the Ottoman and the Safavid sides, the "confessional ambiguity" that had characterized religious identity before the sixteenth century gave way to increasing emphasis on the elaboration of orthodox positions.[8] Our protagonist—the woman Sabah—was only one of many individuals who were caught in the tensions and uncertainties surrounding the construction of these new identities.

What was the nature of the Kizilbash heresy? The shi'ism that would become the established religion of the Safavid domain and the antinomian preaching of Ismail's early years were initially indistinguishable. Scholars still debate the possible sources of Safavid shi'ism, particularly its declaration as the *juridical* base of the state.[9] Indeed, historical legend has it that the Safavid shah and his advisers had great difficulty locating shi'i texts, and that religious scholars had to be imported to Iran from centers of shi'i learning in Iraq. The Safavid dynasty was not the first to declare shi'ism the religion of state: the Fatimids in Cairo governed as a shi'i dynasty from the late tenth until the late twelfth century, inspiring a similar counterarticulation of a strong sunni identity on the part of rival powers. But the Fatimids had not attempted to convert the population over which they ruled to shi'ism. By contrast, the Safavids staked their survival in part on differentiating their subject population from that to the west and to the east. It was, in the main, a process of forced conversion that rendered the population of Iran shi'i.

To the Ottoman regime, the danger of ideological subversion from the east paralleled the threat of military encroachment. Particularly vulnerable were the regions of central, eastern, and southeastern Anatolia and northern Syria, because they contained a sizable Turkmen population. It was this population that had been targeted by the heterodox teachings of Safavid missionaries in late-fifteenth-century Anatolia. Their work was successful in creating a mass movement that ultimately propelled the Safavid house to political power. In other words, the state that would become the foundation of modern Iran was in its inception based on a successful appeal for the spiritual and political allegiance of tribal groups in Anatolia and northern Syria.

Safavid proselytizing in these areas was helped by the fact that they had only recently been incorporated into the Ottoman domain. The allegiance of Turkmen tribes to their new overlord was tenuous at best, hostile at worst, since they naturally resented the new regime's confiscation of their land and levying of taxes that tribal leaders had been accustomed to collecting for themselves.

The vehicle of Safavid proselytizing that won adherents in Anatolia took the form of poetry composed in the pen name of Ismail, Hata'i. These hymn-like declamations delivered in his voice preached holy war led by Ismail and devotion to his person, both as warrior and as divine embodiment of past heroes of the faith and martyrs to the excessive orthodoxy of Muslim authorities.[10] Devotional literature of this sort could spread rapidly in a largely nonliterate cultural milieu such as that of the Anatolian Turkmen. Ismail's hymns, if taken literally, were antithetical to the basic tenets of Islam, particularly its insistence on the oneness of God. They were also a political challenge to the sovereignty of the Ottoman sultan. Even after the Safavid regime eventually closed its borders to these fervently partisan but unruly Anatolians, it did not encourage their loyalty to the Ottoman sultanate.

Whether the author of antinomian hymns or the architect of a shi'i state, the Safavid shah was a heretic in the view of Ottoman authorities. So were his followers and any who might sympathize with them. The Ottomans regarded Kizilbash allegiance as a double heresy: religious, in that it challenged the sunni Muslim identity of the Ottoman sultan, and political, in that it recognized the Safavid shah as legitimate political overlord. In the first half of the sixteenth century, the discourse of political authority in the Middle East, as well as that of challenge and rebellion, was still one of legitimacy based on religious rectitude. In other words, political challenge was still articulated as religious rebellion. Conversely, any attempt to subvert political allegiance could be constructed as religiously deviant or heretical. The whole series of religiously articulated rebellions in central and southeastern Anatolia that challenged Süleyman's legitimacy in the 1520s and 1530s drew on this religio-political messianism so characteristic of the late-medieval Middle East.

What was Aintab's place in all this? As we have seen, it was a city that boasted a tradition of religious learning and a sizable population of mollas. This yielded an Islamic identity that was in tension with the antinomian and ecstatic tendencies among Turkmen, who followed the teachings not of mollas but of spiritual leaders known as babas or pirs. Aintab's rural hinterland included settled Turkmen in villages, and the city lay in the path of the annual migration of tribal Turkmen to the south. As an area on the southern edge of the former principality of the Dulkadir Turkmen, it had no doubt been drawn into the battles surrounding the rebellions that protested the legitimacy of Ottoman rule (a frequent target of these uprisings was the cadastral survey teams in whose wake came the hated taxation and regulation of tribal migration routes). One of the most violent of these was the rebellion led in 1527 by Kalenderoğlu, which originated in Karaman and gathered forces of 30,000 (or so the chronicles count them), including tribal chiefs from the Dulkadir federation.[11] The victory of the grand vezir İbrahim Pasha was due in no small part to his ability to win the Dulkadir contingent to the sultan's side by promising them the restoration of their fiefs (*timar*s), which had been confiscated by the Ottoman regime and converted to state land.[12] It is likely that the extensive rural holdings of individuals in Aintab who were titled *beg*—the sons of Gazi Beg, Tarhan Beg, and Üveys Beg mentioned in earlier chapters—were acquired as a result of this or a similar bargain with the Ottoman regime.

By the time of Haciye Sabah's trial, the danger to Aintab of invasion by Safavid forces was considerably diminished, but the Anatolian Kizilbash were still an internal presence in Anatolia. In 1536, Süleyman had emerged victorious after a two-year military campaign against the Safavids, with triumphs in both western Iran and Iraq. The Ottomans' principal prize was Baghdad, the ancient capital of the sunni Abbasid caliphate and an economically as well as politically strategic city. As for the Safavids, the dynasty had now come to share the Ottoman view that unruly Turkmen tribes were less useful in the process of state building than they were in conquest. The stabilizing of conflict between the two superpowers was reflected in the signing of a peace treaty in 1555. For the rest of the sixteenth century, their relations can be characterized as a kind of "cold war" vigilance, as zones of influence were demarcated and periodically contested in battle.

But though the Anatolian Kizilbash were now less threatening as a fifth column, they still had the potential to arouse anti-Ottoman loyalties. That Kizilbash proselytizing persisted throughout the sixteenth century is clear from the evidence of its prosecution. Most of our evidence of persecutions of suspected Kizilbash activists comes from central government records— the *mühimme* registers, or ledgers of directives from the imperial council to provincial officials—which are extant only from the late 1550s on. Many of these records from the 1560s and 1570s concern "disturbances" in southeastern Anatolia, northern Syria, and Iraq (areas with substantial Turkmen population). Several records concerned Aintab specifically.[13] It is therefore possible, even likely, that there were Kizilbash partisans in Aintab in 1540.

There is virtually no evidence in these central government records of accusations against women. Hence the value of the Sabah affair, to my knowledge unique in two ways: it reveals Kizilbash tensions from an earlier period and it points to women's role in the spread of sectarianism. As suggested above, this case also allows us to raise questions about representations of women's relation to heretical movements—to ask, for instance, whether an allegation of forbidden practices might indicate not so much a genuine fear of heresy as a plausible slander against women perceived to be too powerful, and therefore castigated as out of control and dangerously deviant. The case of Haciye Sabah casts a new light on the principal concern of this book, the work of the court, because the affair thrust the judge into a controversy that was at once religious, social, cultural, and political.

THE TEACHERS' TESTIMONY

If the length of individual testimony in the court record is an index of a case's gravity, then the affair of Haciye Sabah was most serious. The statements of the protagonists in this case are as close as the Aintab court records come to verbatim testimony, to voices not depersonalized through the scribe's use of formulaic phrases. The teaching colleagues defended their professional activities in precise detail, while the angry neighbors presented dramatic evidence in support of their case that Haciye Sabah was an undesirable presence in the neighborhood. Let us follow the lead of the court's record, and examine the case at two levels: first, the exposure of Sabah and İbrahim and their punishment for mixing the sexes, and second, the accusation of heresy by Sabah's neighbors.

The record of Haciye Sabah's trial consists of four entries (*sicill*s). First came a set of three statements (*ikrar*) by the leaders of the teaching circle, Haciye Sabah and İbrahim, and Şemseddin, another male who was present. Following the records of several unrelated cases but recorded on the same day, the fourth entry consisted of the neighbors' complaint, labeled in the record as *izhar-ı tekdîr*, "manifesting a reprimand." The same entry included the reappearance of Sabah and İbrahim before the court, during which they repeated their previous defense of their conduct. Although the testimony of Şemseddin made up the initial entry, I give the statements of Haciye Sabah and İbrahim first, as they establish the scenario:

> *Sabah:* The woman named Haciye Sabah, resident of the city of Aintab, came to the court and made the following statement: "I gather girls and brides and women in my home. I negotiated with İbrahim b. Nazih[14] and the two youths who are his apprentices, and in exchange for paying them a month's fee, I had them come every day to the girls and brides in my house and I had them preach and give instruction. There are no males at those sessions besides the said İbrahim and his apprentices; there are only women and girls and young brides. This kind of thing is what I have always done for a living." In accordance with the statement of the said woman, because the behavior that she had engaged in was against the law and beyond reason [and forbidden], she was publicly exposed and punished, and banished from the city and exiled. The particulars of the situation were recorded.

Witnessed by: Molla Veli b. Ali; Molla Abdulkadir b. Haci İbrahim, preacher; Molla Mahmud b. Halil, preacher; Molla Hüsam b. Mehmed; Haci Emir Ali b. Haci Ahmed; Muhsin b. Hızır, steward; Uzun Ahmed, market head

İbrahim: İbrahim b. Nazih, resident of the city of Aintab, came to the court and stated: "I preach and give instruction. No male is ever present at my sessions besides myself and my apprentices; only I and two of my apprentices are present. I do this preaching regularly. And so, as usual, I agreed to preach for a month in the home of the woman named Haciye Sabah; day after day women and girls and brides gather, and I preach and instruct them in this woman Sabah's home." Then some individuals of good repute [lit., "some Muslims"] testified as follows: "The said İbrahim used to preach in this manner regularly. Previously, the former judge of Aintab, Molla Habil Efendi, pride of the learned, banished the said İbrahim from the city." The said İbrahim acknowledged the correctness of their testimony. He was expelled and banished from the city on the grounds that gathering women, girls, and brides in such unattended homes and preaching is forbidden. The foregoing was inscribed and recorded in the way that it happened.

Witnessed by: Molla Veli b. Ali; Molla Mahmud b. Halil, preacher; Molla Hüsam b. Haci Mehmed; Haci Emir Ali b. Haci Ahmed; Muhsin b. Mehmed [*sic*], preacher; Uzun Ahmed, market head; and others who were present

The language of negotiation, hiring, fixed terms, fees paid for instruction (and presumably fees charged), regular attendance—all this suggests a routinized activity. Sabah's instructional classes appear to be an ongoing, well-organized enterprise. In other words, Sabah is in the business of women's education. Such education appears to be the basis of İbrahim's livelihood as well. His two apprentices—*şagird,* a word that may also be translated as "pupil" or "disciple"—may be present as training for their own such employment in the future.

The existence of a female educational circle in Aintab should not surprise us. By even the most conservative social standards of the times, reflected in the manuals of correct conduct written by traditionalist religious scholars, women might be allowed to leave the home for the purposes of gaining religious instruction. Or at least this is what we know from Mamluk-period sources.[15] As we have seen, Aintab was located within the northernmost reaches of Mamluk influence and was thus linked to the Mamluk cultural domain. Extant Mamluk sources are more literary than documentary, however: they reflect the elite world of scholarly circles, and the female educational activities of which they inform us involve women of scholarly families. The virtue of our court record from Aintab is its suggestion that women of more modest circumstances engaged in the same process. While the woman Sabah was a person of some religious distinction—her title *Haciye* suggests either that she had performed the pilgrimage to Mecca or that she enjoyed a reputation for religious learning and piety—she was a person of relatively modest means. This we know because she could not afford a house with its own private courtyard, but instead shared a courtyard with other households.

The testimony of Şemseddin gives us an idea of what went on at the instructional sessions organized by Haciye Sabah. Şemseddin was a *meddah*, a "eulogist," who probably recited stories recounting the life of the Prophet Muhammad and of the early Muslims, stories that dramatized the piety and good deeds of the new religion's first adherents as well as their trials and suffering. If the teaching sessions were in fact devoted to Kizilbash doctrine, then perhaps it was Ismail and the heroes celebrated in his poetry that Şemseddin eulogized. Here is the record of his testimony:

> Şemseddin b. Mehmed, resident of the city of Aintab, came to the court and stated: "When the woman named Haciye Sabah gathered women and girls in her home and brought the person named İbrahim b. Nazih among the women and had him preach, I too would be present at those sessions. I performed as *meddah.*" Because he made this statement, it was recorded.
> Witnessed by: Molla Veli b. Ali; Molla Mahmud b. Halil; Ahmed b. Halil, steward [of the city]; Molla Hüsam b. Mehmed

Şemseddin's testimony raises two questions: What was he doing at the sessions in Haciye Sabah's home and why wasn't he punished? Since both Sabah and İbrahim insisted no males were present except the two apprentices, Şemseddin was presumably one of them. Unlike İbrahim, who performed a more directly didactic function, the eulogist instructed through his narrative skill. İbrahim's duty was to "preach and advise," to give instruction on the proper conduct of a Muslim (female) and probably to answer the questions of Haciye Sabah's pupils. Sabah herself, it seems, was the organizer of the sessions, facilitating the interaction between the male specialists in religious instruction and the local female audience. As to why Şemseddin received no sentence, perhaps he was thought to have been misled by İbrahim, or perhaps he effected a sixteenth-century version of a plea bargain.

It is noteworthy that the court does not appear to challenge the claim of Sabah and İbrahim that the instruction of women constituted their regular employment. Moreover, the case record suggests that there was local tolerance of Sabah's educational enterprise, even a demand for it. After all, the families of Sabah's students—their husbands, mothers, fathers—appear not to have stood in the way of their attendance: the females came to class "day after day," and others had apparently been doing the same before the current month-long session. Someone in each family must have been paying for the classes, whether in cash or in kind. Moreover, we can assume that the women themselves would not have patronized the classes if attendance were perceived to put their respectability at risk. As we have seen in earlier chapters, women had a vested interest in protecting their honor, their most important social capital. In short, among the social groups represented by Sabah's pupils and their families, there was obviously some tolerance of male-female contact. The fact of male presence at her classes could hardly have been a secret.

The striking repetition in the court record of the phrase "girls, young brides, women" *(kız, avret, gelin)* deserves attention in this regard. Emphasizing the variety of females present, as Sabah and İbrahim repeatedly did in their testimony, must have been intended to aid their defense. Perhaps they hoped to establish the point that attending such classes was not considered dangerous or compromising by females at any stage of their life— unmarried girls, young brides, and mature married (or once-married) women. In the mouths of their detractors, this inventory of the female life cycle could have been a critical weapon, but because the record repeatedly ascribes it to the teachers, it appears to be an argument for the suitability of their instruction for all females. But the judge explicitly punished Sabah for violating norms of male-female conduct: her mixing of the sexes was publicly labeled "illegal, unreasonable, and forbidden." Whose norms were these, then, since they were apparently not shared by her pupils? This case clearly constitutes a site of conflict over the boundaries of male-female contact in mid-sixteenth-century Aintab.

In the court records of 1540–1541, a number of cases demonstrate that the local authorities as well as individual citizens of the city were attempting to regulate male-female contact by enforcing norms of propriety governing members of both sexes. The case of Ayşe and Sadeddin, described in chapter 4, and others like it suggest that some individuals resisted such attempts to regulate contact, especially when they interfered with the ordinary business of daily life in the neighborhood. This kind of resistance was found in more modest neighborhoods, where greater toleration of male-female contact was tied to its inevitability, given that families lacked servants to carry out their public business. Such seems to be the environment in which the woman Sabah operated. She was poor—*acize*—living on her own resources, possibly kinless; she and the two neighbors who complained about her were not wealthy enough to afford the privacy of a separate walled compound.

THE NEIGHBORS' TESTIMONY

Clearly the acceptable level of contact between females and males was a matter of contention in this city, just as the question of who was entitled to establish the rules of gender morality was contested. But even if there was greater toleration of male-female interaction in the milieu served by Sabah's classes—even if her clientele and their families were satisfied with her arrangements—something clearly got out of hand, provoking the neighbors to a public condemnation. Here is the record of the neighbors' testimony, with its accusation of Kizilbash heresy and indoctrination, and of Haciye Sabah and İbrahim's subsequent reappearance at the request of the court:

The individuals named Alaeddin b. Hoca Hamza and Ustad Mehmed Hayat, residents of the city of Aintab, were present at court and brought forth the following censure:

The poor woman who is known as Kara Sabah is our neighbor since we share the same courtyard. She holds gatherings of girls and brides and women in her home. She has hired the individual named İbrahim b. Nazih and the two youths who are his apprentices, and introduces him into the company of these girls and brides in her unattended house. While she says that she has him preach, she actually has him speak evil things. She has him conduct spiritual conversations with these girls and brides. She takes her own disciples (halife) and causes them to act contrary to the law: in the ceremonies, the girls and brides and women spin around waving their hands, and they bring themselves into a trancelike state by swaying and dancing. They perform the ceremonies according to Kizilbash teachings. We too have wives and families, and we are opposed to illegal activities like this. In particular, a little girl fell off the roof while participating in their ceremonies and was injured. And the authorities have gotten involved because some people have been accused of having sex with women.

When they said [the foregoing], the aforementioned Kara Sabah and İbrahim were invited [to come] to the court for examination. When they were questioned, the said woman Sabah stated: "I had my house vacated. I brought girls and young brides and women together with the said İbrahim and the two youths who are his apprentices. There were no males present at the aforementioned conversations besides the said İbrahim and the two apprentices. I brought them, and for the price of preaching, I had them conduct conversations with the girls and young brides. This is what I have always done for a living." When she had spoken, the said İbrahim confirmed [her testimony] in a legal manner. The foregoing was inscribed and recorded in the way that it happened.

Witnessed by: Molla Veli b. Ali, imam; Molla Mahmud b. Halil, preacher; Molla Hüsam b. Mehmed, imam; Muhsin b. Mehmed, steward; Uzun Ahmed, market head; Haci Emir Ali b. Haci Ahmed

In their litany of protest, the neighbors accuse the classes of following "Kizilbash teachings," but the list of problematic behaviors does not cite specifically Kizilbash expressions of deviance from the Ottoman sunni norm—whether a political heresy such as paying fiscal tribute to the Shah, or a doctrinal one such as ritually cursing the first sunni caliphs. Rather, the catalogue of transgressions is a conflation of the standard indictment of ritual excesses often alleged against sufis—swaying, dancing, becoming spiritually intoxicated[16]—with common characterizations of women out of control. The clichéd representation of the "deviant" tendencies of sufis may not be surprising when we remember that the Safavid movement's original presence in Anatolia was as an increasingly unorthodox sufi order. As for the linkage between deviant practice and the social disruption of family and neighborhood, it draws on a common trope about women—that they were prone to losing their grip on social reason *(akıl).* In the neighbors' depiction, both the bodies and the minds of the women are out of control: they spin, sway, wave their hands, and eventually abandon rational consciousness. This has mundane consequences: they are bad mothers, for their attention to their spiritual exercises causes the neglect and subsequent injury of their children. The final accusation—of illicit sexual activity issuing from a mixing of the sexes at the alleged rituals—is particularly characteristic of accusations against the Kizilbash, and appears in several of the cases recorded in the central government records.[17]

The two men's testimony was a serious accusation of unacceptable behavior. It was, in effect, a demand to have Haciye Sabah expelled from the neighborhood. The right of neighborhoods to make this demand was confirmed in Süleyman's law book: "If the people of a person's [city] quarter or village complain that he or she is a thief or a harlot and, saying 'He or she is not fit [to live with] us,' reject the person, and if that person has in fact a notoriously bad reputation among the people, he or she shall be banished, that is, expelled from his or her quarter or village."[18]

RELIGION, STATUS, AND POWER IN AINTAB

The case of Haciye Sabah exposed a number of social and religious fault lines within the population of Aintab. One is clearly suggested by the composition of the case witnesses—the *şuhud ul-hal*—that is, those individuals who signed off on each entry in the court register as witnesses to the proceedings as a whole. As we saw in chapter 3, case witnesses might be parties with a personal interest or stake in the issue at hand or leading members of Aintab society who lent a certain gravity to the court's activities. The large group of case witnesses in the record of Haciye Sabah's trial was dominated by mollas. More precisely, two imams and two mosque preachers witnessed the various stages of the case at court, an extraordinary representation of the city's religious establishment. The mollas of Aintab presided over the city's religious, educational, and charitable establishments. Trained in the formal disciplines of Islamic learning and in Islamic law, they included imams, muftis, teachers, and other staff of the city's colleges and secondary schools. The spiritual and educational influence of Haciye Sabah cannot have been to their liking.

The city's religious elite was not confined to the mollas, however. Aintab's established families included the heads of several *zaviye*s, or dervish institutions. Some were originally of Turkmen origin, since Turkmen had first come to the region as early as the eleventh century. As we saw in chapter 3, this elite represented a cultural hybrid of the *baba* spiritualist strain of Turkmen religiosity and the sophisticated mores of urban society. While the zaviye names reveal a Turkmen cultural origin—Haci Baba, Arduç Baba, Dülük Baba, Balluca Baba, Emin Dede, Ahi Ahmed—their current managers were among the leading citizens of the city.[19] Some were even *seyyid*s, claiming descent from the Prophet Muhammad. Members of the Demircioğlu family, one of the three notable families of Aintab, were perhaps the prime product of this hybrid assimilationist culture, and their zaviye, the best endowed, a notable urban amenity. In chapter 1, we saw that the sultan Selim patronized leading dervish figures after his conquest of Aintab, a testimonial to their local influence. Indeed, selective patronage had the effect of endorsing those local figures most acceptable to the regime's goals of religious orthodoxy, social order, and loyalty.

In other words, a distinction should be made between an Aintab elite of older families of Turkmen origin, assimilated to the traditions of urban Islam, and the less settled who found the message of the Safavid Ismail compelling (he was, in their view, a supreme spiritual guide, as well as a warrior). No doubt there were those in Aintab who shared memories of their own, their parents', or their grandparents' attraction to or perhaps participation in the Safavid movement. Were there widows whose husbands lost their lives in the Safavid cause? Haciye Sabah—"poor and resourceless," without the support of family, it would seem—was conceivably such a one. The names of many individuals appearing in the court records from 1540–1541 suggest a Kizilbash identity—for example, Şah Kulu, Hüseyin Kulu b. Cüneyd, Kutluşah, Pir Ali, and so forth). Such names, however, are not conclusive evidence of Kizilbash loyalty, as they may reflect latent or simply nostalgic identity, not necessarily active partisanship.

Tensions clearly existed in Aintab around some elements in the Turkmen population. That local stereotypes associated Turkmen identity with nomadism and poverty is suggested by a clause in the 1574 law code for Aintab issued by the sultan's bureaucracy. The clause suggested that poor Turkmen had been settling in the city, where they were being unfairly taxed as pastoralists because they did not own their own homes. The regulation pointed out that their lack of city real estate indicated *not* that they were winter pastoralists (that is, temporary city residents), but rather that they were simply poor. The impoverishment of nomadic Turkmen who chose to settle and the probable struggle they faced in adapting to city life was no doubt true in 1540 as well. Indeed, it was in all probability a continual feature of the process of Turkmen sedentarization that had been going on for centuries.

That such an identity could come into conflict with that of the religiously distinguished is suggested by a case recorded on September 14, 1541, in which the head of the night watch brought the Turkmen Şah Hüseyin to court for cursing a merchant seyyid in the most damaging of slanderous language—accusing him of being an adult catamite:

> Seyyid Fahruddin b. Seyyid Haci Hamza came to court, summoned the individual named Şah Hüseyin b. Allahveli, and brought the following suit against him: "This Şah Hüseyin said to me, in front of my store, 'You man boy who lets yourself be fucked,' and he said, 'You give it away to strangers, don't you have any for us?'"[20]

Şah Hüseyin's was a calculatedly public act. The curse was delivered in a space as imbued with a man's honor as his home—the area in front of his shop. It was overheard by at least three others, the eyewitnesses who supported Seyyid Fahruddin's case. Men frequently cursed each other, and women cursed men, in milder forms of the idiom used by Şah Hüseyin, but here the verbal attack would seem to be a manifestation of the cultural antagonism between these two groups. The curse was an invitation to reverse the social hierarchy that put seyyids at the top and Şah Hüseyins at the margins.

Where did Haciye Sabah and İbrahim fit into the complex socioreligious landscape of Aintab? By his own self-definition, İbrahim was a preacher and a religious teacher. As a preacher, however, İbrahim occupied a different place in the community from the two mollas who figured among the case witnesses and were also identified as preachers. They were *hatib*s, bearers of a recognized office among the ranks of religious professionals, officially employed to give the sermon that was a central feature of the Friday communal prayer. They too might preach more informally, like İbrahim, but there could be tension between those distinguished as mollas and popular preachers whose status was derived more from the size of their following than from their educational credentials. Jonathan Berkey has given a vivid account of this tension in Mamluk Cairo, where popular preachers were frequently accused of misconstruing the teachings of scripture through their imperfect command of religious texts.[21]

As for Haciye Sabah, there was historical precedent for both female learning circles and female leaders in the cultural heritage of Anatolia. In his biography of Jalaleddin Rumi, the saint and founder of the Mevlevi sufi order, Eflaki (d. 1360) described special sessions for the women of Konya in which Rumi would "reveal the hidden meaning of things and admonish them morally," and then perform the circular dance of the Mevlevis, bringing the whole gathering to a state of ecstasy. Recognizing the socially controversial aspect of this practice, Eflaki justified it on the grounds that the Prophet Muhammad had met with the women of his community to answer their questions about sharia.[22] According to Eflaki, during the generation of

Rumi's grandson's leadership of the order, the Mevlevi *halife,* or deputy, in the city of Tokat was a woman named Hoşlika, who served as spiritual leader for the area's prominent devotees of the order.[23] In his late-fifteenth-century history of the Ottoman dynasty, which idealized a time when the sultans had intimate relations with spiritual leaders, Aşıkpaşazade drew on the hagiographic tradition of the Bektashi order to note that the founder of the order, Haci Bektaş, honored a female disciple, Hatun Ana ("Lady Mother"), by making her his spiritual heir and "surrendering to her the revelations [that had come to him] and his miraculous powers."[24] Before her adoption as Haci Bektaş's disciple, Hatun Ana had belonged to a group known as the *baciyan,* or "spiritual sisters," of Anatolia. The historian Fuad Köprülü has tentatively linked this group to the armed female warriors serving the Dulkadir principality who were mentioned by the early-fifteenth-century traveler Bertrandon de la Broquière.[25]

How much factual basis there is for these legendary histories is hard to know, but there is no doubt that they reflected the cultural outlook of Turkmen society in Anatolia. Such honoring of female spiritual leadership was bound to come into conflict with the hierarchical ordering of society propounded by the religious establishment and reflected in legal categories that placed women in a subordinate and constricted role. The striking similarity of the story of Rumi and the women of Konya to the neighbors' description of the goings-on in Haciye Sabah's home suggests that they may have drawn on what had become a trope of sufi hagiography—a trope that in the hands of critics of women's independent spirituality magnified the problematic elements in Eflaki's account.

The point here is not that Sabah or her pupils were necessarily Kizilbash or even Turkmen. What I am suggesting is that there was almost surely an environment in some parts of Aintab conducive to keeping a Kizilbash identity alive, even if for some it was now a vague cultural allegiance rather than active partisanship or continuing loyalty to the Safavid shah. It is therefore plausible (but not certain) that the Sabah case *was* an instance of Kizilbash proselytizing or at least of communal celebration. If so, the case suggests an interesting phenomenon: the spread of "heresy" by women. It demonstrates how anti-establishment ideology might be propagated in a gender-segregated society through the agency of women. Women's learning circles, more shielded from public scrutiny than those of men, may have functioned as fertile ground for the spread of new or radical doctrines. The neighbors' use of the term "disciple" *(halife)* to describe Sabah's pupils' relationship to her underscores the possibility of a female identity outside women's domestic roles and kinship networks. The term connotes an allegiance to an authority external to the family as well as a solidarity among women through a shared set of beliefs and practices. In turn, the female pupils may have acted as a channel of knowledge back to their families—to both females and males in their visiting and kinship groups.

A CASE OF KIZILBASH SLANDER?

The neighbors' complaint of wrongdoing did not refer specifically to actual Kizilbash doctrine. Indeed, it was a kind of generic indictment of the religious excesses to which women were stereotypically thought to be prone. We are thus left to consider another set of questions: What sort of antagonism might have given rise to the neighbors' outburst? Might they have exaggerated or even fabricated the accusation of Kizilbash heresy? If so, what might their motive have been? And why was portraying Haciye Sabah as a Kizilbash proselytizer perceived as both plausible and effective?

In 1540, the Ottoman regime was engaged in the second phase of absorbing the territories and populations conquered a generation earlier. Administratively, this meant increasing standardization and controls exercised over officials and tax collectors. In terms of law and order, it meant the writing of new legal codes as well as an expanding system of courts and a police network to put laws into force. In the realm of religious belief and practice, it meant an increasingly detailed and rigorous formulation of the orthodox sunni position. Conversely, tolerance for the diversity that had been characteristic of Ottoman society in earlier times diminished. A number of heterodox sufi orders were suppressed in the sixteenth century, forced under the umbrella of the Bektashi order;[26] while it carried the flag for heterodoxy, so to speak, the Bektashi order itself was now more carefully scrutinized by the ruling regime. These changes were in part a response to the essentially administrative challenge of integrating vast territories recently conquered. But they were also, I would argue, an integral aspect of the fashioning of an Ottoman identity to counter the radical identity fashioned by the Safavids. The Ottoman turn at the mid-sixteenth-century to a more religiously oriented, legalistic posture has generally been attributed to the Ottoman incorporation of the Mamluk state and its new overlordship of ancient Islamic centers. But it was arguably as much a function of the Iranian challenge, of the cold war cultural politics between the Ottomans and the Safavids.

This attempt to impose what we might call "a new orthodoxy" inevitably led to alienation and protest. Ahmet Yaşar Ocak, who studies dissident movements in this period, argues that the years around 1540 were a time of widespread discontent in Ottoman Anatolia and Rumelia.[27] Kizilbash sympathizers were not the only dissident voices that the regime felt it necessary to silence. The reign of Süleyman was punctuated with trials and executions of schismatic or messianic figures who protested the sultan's legitimacy. On the other hand, the attempt by Süleyman and his advisers to elaborate an image of the sultan as sunni messiah, demonstrated by Cornell Fleischer, suggests that the Safavid challenge was being countered in more than one popular discourse.[28]

What I am underscoring here is the likelihood of widespread anxiety about public identities, of uncertainty over what beliefs and practices were legitimate and what were not. It would have been difficult for local communities such as Aintab to remain immune to these confusions over the definition of correct belief and conduct and the limits of tolerance. The temper of the times may therefore have made it easier for the people of Anatolia both to slip into the language of sedition and to perceive sedition among groups on the margins of urban culture.

The affair of Haciye Sabah erupted in a climate of uncertainty and even fear that permeated much of Anatolia in these years. It may have been unclear to many just what the label *Kizilbash* meant. By 1540, an allegation of Kizilbash allegiance could imply active pro-Safavid partisanship, but it was equally likely to indicate an internal opposition to Ottoman state policies and ideologies. Or it might intend a more specifically religious heterodoxy. Religious ideologies were the source of a good deal of confusion that had to be sorted out: the heterodox preachings of Safavid missionaries had to be separated from the jurisprudential aspects of established shiʻi doctrine, and matters of doctrine and conduct that could make a heretic out of an unwitting Ottoman subject needed to be identified. The unsettling effect of this ideological rent in the fabric of Muslim spirituality can be felt in the many questions addressed to the chief mufti İbn Kemal (d. 1534) that revealed uncertainty over what was now permissible and what was not. Certainly the accretion over time of various historical and rhetorical meanings around the term *Kizilbash* made its meaning potentially ambiguous or confusing, and consequently the label might easily slip into a popular repertoire of indiscriminate slander.

How might this climate of fear and uncertainly have affected the neighbors Alaeddin and Ustad Mehmed? They were clearly disturbed about Haciye Sabah's classes, and the legal thrust of their complaint to the court was a call for her removal from the neighborhood. In addition to the allegation of heresy, the two men pointed specifically to the threat to their families. Sabah's teaching circle may have tempted their own wives, or perhaps they feared the danger to their children. The neighbors may have objected less to the actual teaching imparted in Sabah's classes than to the constant disruption in the shared courtyard caused by the popularity of the classes. Perhaps the coming and going of the male instructors compromised their wives' and daughters' honor. Perhaps there were too many women trafficking in and out and too much potential gossip about the habits of the communal courtyard. The honor and reputation of poorer people were particularly vulnerable to communal scrutiny since their homes and domestic lives were more exposed. It was in part this vulnerability that lay behind the broad legal principle that neighborhoods had the right to police their residents and rid themselves of immoral or illicit influences. Involved here may also be a class issue: Alaeddin and Ustad Mehmed's defense of their families' reputation may reflect their view that they were socially superior to the woman they described as poor, as their patronymics and titles suggest: Alaeddin was the son of a tradesman, and Mehmed—*Ustad,* or "Master"— was a skilled craftsman.

The two neighbors also pointed specifically to the prior involvement of the authorities—the *ehl-i örf*—because of rumors of sexual impropriety. Here was a clear threat to the honor of their families, one that they could hardly leave unanswered. Taking action may in fact have been urgently required, particularly in view of the new emphasis on surveillance of male-female contact that is visible in the court record with the arrival of the new judge two weeks earlier. Instances of illicit sex certainly came in front of the court before the appearance of the new judge, but the evidence of stricter police monitoring was new.

But why bring an accusation of heresy? Of course, it is possible that the neighbors accurately assessed, or sincerely believed in, the Kizilbash character of the women's classes. Moreover, if rumors that Sabah and her colleagues were preaching Kizilbash doctrine were circulating locally, silence on the neighbors' part would suggest complicity in heresy. On the other hand, if the accusation of Kizilbash loyalty was a fabrication, then Alaeddin and Ustad Mehmed chose an effective slander. If their goal was to remove Haciye Sabah from their midst, a simple charge of sexual misconduct might have seemed insufficient, especially as the previous involvement of the authorities had apparently not led to punitive measures. The accusation of Kizilbash activism escalated the case to a higher level of wrongdoing, one that could not fail to catch the attention of court and community. This slander subsumed more than one kind of criminal behavior—illicit sex, disapproved modes of worship, and ideological subversion.

The vulnerability of the woman Sabah to communal suspicions and even hostility was linked to her relative poverty. The 1574 administrative reform that addressed the illegal taxing of poor Turkmen revealed a popular association of social marginality with Turkmen identity. Evidence from the mid–sixteenth century suggests that population shifts were occurring in the province's largest villages as well as in the city, and that migration and settlement were causing a variety of economic and cultural tensions. In chapter 2, we saw that there was considerable movement within city neighborhoods between the cadastral survey years of 1536 and 1543. Interestingly, the 1543 survey named neighborhoods by their main mosques rather than using their traditional names (many of which survive today), suggesting that urban flux was accompanied by administrative inducement to religious orthodoxy. In vocalizing hostility against poor (ex-)nomadic elements one might easily slip into attacking the heterodox proclivities associated with those of tribal background. In other words, representations of the culture of poverty in mid-sixteenth-century Aintab may have included anti-Turkmen and, more important, anti-Kizilbash rhetoric. In the neighbors' usage, then, "Kizilbash" may stand loosely for all that deviated from what was imagined to be normative communal behavior, for everything that the concerned neighbors did not want to be thought to be. The affair of the woman Sabah may have been generated within her own milieu, a product of uncertainty and anxiety engendered by and among marginal elements in a city that was located at a frontier of imperial self-definition and ideological boundary making.

The neighbors may have calculated that they would find a receptive audience for their complaint among the molla population of the city, for they represented Sabah as a woman of considerable religious influence over her pupils. Wittingly or unwittingly, they were drawing on the old trope that wrong knowledge in the hands of the ignorant led to rebellion. In their portrayal, Sabah gathered females in order to make them her disciples, whom she then proceeded to corrupt by teaching them heretical doctrines and modes of worship. The religious establishment of Aintab could hardly fail to respond to the challenge of this obviously charismatic female who threatened their authority in a number of ways.

The teaching circles violated many of the norms on which the status of the religious elite was staked. All of these violations were made worse because of the fundamental subversion of the male-female hierarchy that Haciye Sabah's enterprise represented. The allegation of Kizilbash worship implied that she challenged the doctrinal stance around which the Ottoman regime was currently fashioning its very identity. As a business, her classes challenged the monopoly of mollas over education in Aintab, since Sabah provided a forum where women could have the same access to instruction that men enjoyed at mosques. Moreover, the venue she provided enabled women to engage in forms of religious observance disallowed in mosques. The substantial numbers of women attending her classes challenged male authority over the spaces women occupied. From the mollas' point of view—a point of view presumably shared by a number of Aintabans—Sabah violated the moral boundaries of knowledge, space, conduct, and hierarchy. Her multiple transgressions no doubt explained why her sentence included a triple castigation of her behavior as illegal, beyond reason, and forbidden, while İbrahim's sentence merely stated his error in preaching among women, which was forbidden. Transgressing the boundary of knowledge, and therefore propagating false knowledge, was perhaps the worst of Sabah's sins in the eyes of her opponents, since it caused her and the women under her tutelage to loose themselves from the moorings of religious law and human reason.

THE CASE RECORD; OR, THE ARTFULNESS OF HÜSAMEDDIN EFENDI

The affair of Haciye Sabah produced a fascinating case record, several features of which call for reflection and comment. For one thing, it was rare for the judge to prescribe punishment himself (for more on this point, see chapter 8). In this case, not only did the judge himself sentence Haciye Sabah and İbrahim, but he pronounced a form of punishment rare in the court of Aintab in these years. Another unusual feature is that although the protagonists were punished for a publicly disruptive sexual offense, there was no prosecuting official present, in contrast to other such cases in the 1540–1541 records. Finally, the heavy presence of mollas among the case witnesses draws attention to the religious content of the controversy, yet the judge avoided formal comment on the accusation of heresy.

A key feature of the textual representation of events is the separation of the "trial" over the issue of illicit mixing of the sexes in Haciye Sabah's classes from the neighbors' accusation of Kizilbash proselytizing. The records of several unrelated cases heard on the same day intervene. But surely this representation of the case, with the neighbors coming to court *after* the sentencing, did not reflect the actual course of events. The judge's summary most likely imposed this order on what was no doubt a less episodic, more confused, and perhaps more drawn-out confrontation. In several other instances recorded in the court's register, the written record obviously collapses the time frame and separates into distinct testimonial narratives what was actually an acrimonious dispute full of mutual accusations. (An example is the dispute over the nighttime brawl in a bazaar shop—discussed in chapter 5—in which the assailant implied a sexual relationship between the storeowner and the youth Abdulaziz.) *Why* the record of this case isolated the accusation of Kizilbash sympathies, however, remains to be seen.

Unlike most case records, in which the initiative of either the local authorities or an individual petitioner in bringing the case to court is clearly spelled out, the record of this affair does not make it clear how the case came to the attention of the court.[29] Whatever its path to the court, it is certainly worth noting that Haciye Sabah's trial occurred two weeks after the arrival of the judge Hüsameddin on June 23, 1541. It may well be that the uproar over of the teaching circle had erupted earlier, and its settlement was put off pending Hüsameddin's arrival, as were other problematic cases (including a number of complex murders). On the other hand, it may have been the presence of the authoritative new judge that inspired the neighbors to make a legal suit out of a long-standing disgruntlement.

The affair of Haciye Sabah was not the first case of suspected sexual irregularity to come before the new judge: two instances of homosexual rape and a sexual slander case preceded the trial of Sabah and İbrahim.[30] In fact, Hüsameddin Efendi's court seemed to be targeting the problem of males and females thought to be dangerously present in each other's spaces. Two weeks after Haciye Sabah's trial, the judge would hear another case of suspected illicit contact, that of Ayşe and her neighbor Sadeddin (see chapter 4), although in that instance he apparently dismissed the charges as inconsequential. The Sabah affair, in contrast, was no routine matter, and people were no doubt curious, and perhaps apprehensive, to see how Hüsameddin Efendi would handle it.

For the purposes of argument, let us assume that the new judge was persuaded of the plausibility of the heresy accusation. One possible explanation for why he did not explicitly punish the teachers for heresy is that he was instructed not to. Certainly any judge on the payroll of the Ottoman sultan knew that one of his jobs in 1540 was to monitor public expression of dissenting or deviant opinion. But how was he to handle evidence of such sentiments? In the later central government records of Kizilbash prosecution, judges or other local authorities typically communicated their suspicion of subversive activity, and were then ordered by the sultan to initiate prosecution. Often judges were instructed to punish the guilty on grounds other than heresy.[31] Whether such a policy was followed before central records began to be kept is not clear, but the present case may exemplify the same procedure. Perhaps it is not going too far to speculate that news of suspected Kizilbash loyalism in the Aintab region was one of the factors underlying the appointment of a strong judge to the province's court.

A second possible explanation for Hüsameddin Efendi's decision not to prosecute Sabah and İbrahim for heresy is that he wished to avoid a Kizilbash witch-hunt. A distinguishing feature of the later central government records is that many date from around the year 1577, when the Ottomans were planning a major campaign against the Safavids in the Caucasus. The danger of the Kizilbash as a fifth column was a significantly greater strategic concern then than it had been after Süleyman's important victory in 1536. The years around 1540 were a time when the Ottoman regime was promoting consolidation and emphasizing the rule of law. The response of Süleyman's father, Selim I, to Kizilbash loyalism in Anatolia was to eliminate the problem through purges and the erection of an iron curtain between the Ottoman and Safavid domains. Süleyman's approach was less violent, since he could afford a guarded accommodation with the Safavids once Anatolia had been secured for the Ottoman regime. Süleyman did not hesitate to impose conspicuous punishment on the leaders of the several heretical movements that erupted in Anatolia in the first decades of his reign. But his policies toward ordinary subjects aimed at long-term correction, involving as they did a program of educating the population in the new sunni orthodoxy and using the courts as one vehicle of promoting it. From this perspective, the judge's summary of the case can be read as an attempt to acknowledge public concern over Kizilbash ideology and at the same time to prevent either a flaring up of sectarian strife or an outbreak of wrongful accusation. It was as much the judge's mandate to preserve local order and secure the well-being of his constituency as it was to root out heresy.

We will never know what Hüsameddin Efendi actually thought about Haciye Sabah's classes. What mattered was his disposition of the case, in particular the punishments he imposed on Haciye Sabah and İbrahim. Most Aintabans were not privy to the court's proceedings or its records. Rather, what they knew about the affair was probably confined to the judge's sentencing. The careful construction of the case record suggests that the punishments he decreed may have allowed him to satisfy all parties: the neighbors, who wanted Sabah gone; the mollas and the interests they represented; the female pupils, who perhaps feared they too would be punished; the defendants, particularly Haciye Sabah, who insisted until the end that she had done nothing that she had not done before; and, finally, the Ottoman regime, interested in promoting social as well as ideological order. There was, I suggest, a certain judicial artistry in Hüsameddin Efendi's settlement of the case that enabled him to calm local tensions and simultaneously achieve the state's goal of suppressing dissent. The key question here is how the punishments were read by the community—that is, how they were received outside the written record.

Neither of the forms of punishment imposed on Haciye Sabah and İbrahim—public humiliation and banishment from the city—was ordered by the judges in Aintab in any other case over the course of the year. This uniqueness and the double punishment imposed on Haciye Sabah, who was marked with ignominy before her expulsion from Aintab, demonstrated unequivocally to the community the seriousness of her crime. Hers was indeed an exemplary punishment. It may have been necessary in view of the lack of penalties imposed, at least publicly, on the females attending her classes, although they could be construed as guilty themselves of improper conduct. Haciye Sabah was isolated in her responsibility for the collective error, it was she who was the object of the neighbors' censure, and thus it was she who bore the burden of punishment.

What exactly was entailed in the penalty of *teşhir*—literally, "rendering notorious"—is not clear. A variety of specific humiliations were listed in different versions of sultanic law books and attested by European observers. They included being led through the streets while riding a donkey backward and holding its tail instead of a rein (the penalty for false witnesses and prostitutes), having one's beard cut off (for religious officials who married women to their abductors), being publicly exposed with a bird hung round one's neck (for the thief of a hen, duck, etc.), being paraded in the streets with a knife or arrow thrust through one's flesh (for cutpurses and people who knifed or shot another with an arrow), and so on. Sometimes public criers went ahead of the punished, announcing their crime.[32] But the only other mention of public shaming in the Aintab records came from the woman Fatma, who imposed the penalty of humiliation on herself should she break her oath to never again lodge a complaint against a man whom she had falsely accused of rape: "If I should complain . . . you can publicly shame me by blackening my face."[33] In the Dulkadir law book, public exposure with one's face blackened was the punishment prescribed for procurers. If this was the humiliation imposed on Haciye Sabah, then her punishment itself announced her crime to the community. She was explicitly a procurer in the eyes of her neighbors and implicitly so in the judge's condemnation of her actions.

The second punishment, banishment from the city, was imposed on both Haciye Sabah and İbrahim, and had been imposed on the latter once before. Banishment was a penalty frequently prescribed for Kizilbash sympathizers and activists, as central government records demonstrate.[34] However, it was also a possible punishment for sexual offenders, at least according to Hanafi law. The penalty of banishment did not typically entail permanent exile (as we see in this case, İbrahim was back at work in Aintab). For women in particular, who were thought to be at risk if removed from the home environment, banishment may have been temporary. The popular sharia manual by Al-Marghinani had the following to say about the exiled female:

> . . . her banishment is opening the way to the further commission of her crime, because people are under less restraint when removed from the eye of their friends and relations, as those are the persons whose censure they are most in dread of; moreover, in an unsettled situation, and among strangers, the necessaries of life are with difficulty procured, whence she might be induced voluntarily to prostitute herself for a supply, which of all kinds of whoredom is the most abominable[.] [35]

The law book of Süleyman suggests that not all sentences of banishment were actually imposed. Following the clause quoted earlier in this chapter, which envisioned banishment only from one's neighborhood, not from the city itself, the regulation continued:

> And if [the person] is not accepted in the place to which he or she moves, he or she shall be expelled from the city altogether. But [action] shall be suspended a few days to [see how things turn out:] If that person repents the former misdeeds and [henceforth] leads a righteous life, very well. If not, he or she shall be ejected from there too and be definitively expelled; he or she shall leave the town and go away.[36]

So it was possible that Haciye Sabah was not expelled from Aintab, although her insistence on her innocence did not bode well for a posture of repentance. If expelled, she most likely eventually returned to Aintab. Where she might have spent the intervening months is unclear. One probable effect of her banishment, however, was to close down her educational enterprise. If she resumed her former occupation on her return, it is unlikely that she hired male colleagues again.

Banishment, then, may have been read differently by different members of the Aintab community: as a plausible penalty for the illicit mixing of men and women, or as an appropriate penalty for Kizilbash heresy. Haciye Sabah's neighbors may well have been satisfied with the judge's handling of their accusation, while others of the community may have regarded the affair as a sexual scandal and nothing more. If my hypothesis about popular opinion in Aintab is correct, then we might speak of a deliberate and creative ambiguity on the part of the judge. He satisfied the aggrieved—the disturbed neighbors. He disciplined the allegedly guilty. He spared the female pupils by imposing an extraordinary penalty on their tutor. He thwarted a challenge to the hegemony of the city's mollas over the production of knowledge. And he reminded the community of the dangers in pushing the bounds of acceptable social behavior. Was the judge hunting heretics? We cannot be sure, since he artfully recorded this case for posterity in such a way as to allow future users of the court records to decide for themselves.

It was Haciye Sabah who had the last word in this case. Or perhaps we should say that judge and scribe allowed her to have the last word. Hers was the final testimony inscribed in the court register, and it ended, "This is what I have always done for a living." Sabah signaled that in her view, she had done nothing wrong, since no one had stopped her before for the same conduct. Rather, she implied that it was the arbiters of morality and the criteria by which they judged that had changed. Her insistence on this point in spite of the obvious inevitability of punishment was a means of defending her honor to the community at large. Sabah's message was that her guilt was in the eye of the beholder.

7

Negotiating Legitimacy
through the Law

Sometime after its conquest in 1514, the eastern Anatolian province of Erzurum underwent a cadastral survey carried out by Ottoman officials (for Erzuzum, see figure 8). This was a typical procedure in a newly conquered area and an early move in its incorporation into the Ottoman enterprise.[1] It was also customary Ottoman practice to temporarily retain the administrative infrastructure of the pre-conquest regime.[2] Since Erzurum had been part of the Akkoyunlu empire's Anatolian domain, Akkoyunlu tax codes were reaffirmed in this initial survey, as they also were for other formerly Akkoyunlu provinces in eastern and southeastern Anatolia.[3] In the prologues to the survey registers, these codes were referred to as "the laws of Hasan Padishah," after the greatest of the Akkoyunlu sultans, Uzun ("Long") Hasan, who died in 1478.[4]

But the people of Erzurum appeared less willing than Ottoman officials to honor the laws of the former monarch. In 1520, when another survey took place, they protested that the tax load under Uzun Hasan's code was excessive and unbearable. In the words of the survey register's prologue, their petition was granted because "under the wing of sovereignty, the protective shadow of justice, the shade of mercy, the peoples of the province . . . should enjoy protection and the circumstances of prosperity." Some taxes were duly abolished and some reduced, because, as the prologue went on to note, local prosperity was "a necessity for the survival of the regime and a cause of the right order of the realm."[5] This translation is a mere gloss of the Ottoman text—*mucib-i devam-ı devlet ü ba'is-i nizam-ı memleket*—with its rhetorically freighted locutions and its rhymed phrases (*devlet,* "regime," and *memleket,* "realm").

Reflected in this passage, buried in one of hundreds of local cadastral surveys, is a core element of Ottoman political discourse: namely, that local order is the prerequisite for the stability of the regime, and that local order is in turn dependent on the well-being of the population. The passage also portrays the dynasty in the age-old formulation equating rulership with justice and benevolence. The purposes of this formulation were of course rhetorical, but it encapsulates the paternalistic nature of the political contract as envisioned by Ottoman officialdom.

In reality, the protected were not always willing to settle in quietly under the wing of sovereignty. For one thing, they had the option of fleeing, which broke their part of the contract—to pay taxes and behave in an orderly manner. That is indeed what seems to have been happening in the environs of Erzurum in the years after the Ottoman conquest. While a new cadastral survey in 1540 repeated the story of the people's petition in 1520, it now called for the rigorous enforcement of local laws.[6] The reason for this new emphasis on authority in addition to benevolence was that most of the population near the Iranian border had fled their villages and towns.[7] (The clear context here is the rivalry in this vital frontier region between the two superpowers of the sixteenth century, the Ottomans and the Safavids.) Reinforcement of the law was necessary, the register asserted, in order to reassemble the inhabitants and restore prosperity to the region. By 1540, then, local law was more than a favorable tax code; it was also enforced residence and the production of revenue for the state.

In 1540, Aintab, like Erzurum, was undergoing the second phase of incorporation into the Ottoman empire, a broad shift in rhetoric and practice that we might term an imperializing phase in the domains conquered a generation earlier by Selim I. New cadastral surveys and new provincial law books of the years around 1540 dropped references to the laws of former rulers and spoke instead of Ottoman law and Ottoman administrative control. The transition was over. To local populations, incorporation into the domains ruled over by the Ottoman dynasty—that is, integration into its military, fiscal, and legal systems—was a trade-off. It meant both constraint and protection, both loss of autonomy and gains from the prosperity generated by the "pax Ottomanica." This was a time of conflict and resistance as well as opportunity and jockeying for a share of the benefits. In Aintab, some resisted the various manifestations of imperial authority, suggesting that the new regime undermined their own authority and status. Others were able to exploit to their advantage the province's new coordinates as one of the Ottoman sultan's domains. Whatever their reactions, few seem to have remained passive in the face of the changing political landscape.

For the political contract proposed by the Ottoman regime to work, channels of negotiation were essential. Negotiation was a reciprocal process, in which both province and dynasty aimed to establish legitimacy in each other's eyes—that is, each aimed to establish rightful claims over the control of local society and local resources. This chapter treats mid-sixteenth-century Aintab as a laboratory for examining the extent to which legal discourse furthered this process of mutual legitimation. It argues that the local court enabled a "lawful" construction to be put on the compromises that were necessarily fashioned between the local community and the central authority, however tense the relations between them might become.

Despite the dynasty's rhetoric of protective sponsorship, the years before 1540 had seen rawer forms of control. Ottoman chronicles tell us that Selim I executed thousands of Safavid partisans following his conquests. The first decades of Süleyman's reign, which began in 1520, were marked by a spate of revolts, many of them originating in central and southeastern Anatolia.[8] Woven together in these revolts, which were largely fueled by the Turkmen of Anatolia and northern Syria, were lingering religious allegiance to the Safavid dynasty and resistance to the Ottoman dynasty's program of surveying, taxing, and claiming much provincial territory for the crown. The Ottoman regime soon learned that it needed to reward as well as punish. Dispatched against a huge revolt led by one Kalenderoğlu in 1527, the grand vezir İbrahim Pasha was victorious in large part because he won over the Dulkadir Turkmen: he returned some of the land that had been seized from them in the form of timars granted to tribal leaders. The great military campaign against Iran between the years of 1534 and 1536, during which the sultan and the grand vezir traced much of central and eastern Anatolia, northern Syria, and Iraq, was in a sense the final Ottoman effort to quell unrest in these areas.

The campaign was also a watershed in Süleyman's reign. Government of these areas would henceforth rest as much on the rule of law as on the rule of force. As the principal site of this process at the grassroots level, local courts provided a venue where the contest for control of local resources was articulated in what might be called a civil discourse of legitimation. In Aintab, the presence of the court allowed people to pursue lawful strategies of resistance and thereby to engage local representatives of state authority in a dialogue about provincial governance.

In what follows, we take a microscope to the process of imperialization by looking at a number of events recorded at court in which different interests came into conflict. Taken all together, these events might be described as the politics of groups in confrontation with the state. No women figure overtly in this chapter, nor do any villagers. Its protagonists are principally individuals of some status and power in the city of Aintab, individuals who were able to take advantage of Aintab's incorporation into the empire. But, as with the dynamics of property described in chapter 6, there were also people who could do little more than simply strive to maximize their advantage within an environment of constraint. Their strategies, more difficult to discern, are no less interesting: rather than relying on personal resources, they protected themselves by creating group solidarities.

RECORDING THE EMPIRE: INSCRIPTION AS POSSESSION

A striking aspect of the imperializing process in the Ottoman sixteenth century is the centrality of writing and documentation. By midcentury, an explosion of writing of all kinds was taking place. From the capital, the sultan's bureaucrats ordered dozens of cadastral surveys, his chief muftis issued fatwas in increasing numbers, and his chancery compiled law books for individual provinces as well as a comprehensive administrative and penal code, the *Kanun-ı Osmanî*, for the entire empire. As for Aintab, its experience of official writing intensified in the 1530s and 1540s. The province was mapped in full detail in the cadastral surveys of 1536 and 1543. The first law book for Aintab *(kanunname-i liva-ı Aintab)* was issued in 1536, and inscribed in the survey register of that year.[9] Court records begin to be kept around 1531 (at least, the first extant records date from that year), and by 1540 the court's registers were kept with remarkable precision and regularity. These were, of course, all forms of writing issuing from state-appointed officials. But subjects too made use of the increasing salience of writing, as we will see below, rendering it a process through which the allocation of rights and duties was negotiated between sovereign and subject.

Writing was a powerful tool in the hands of the state. Take the cadastral surveys, for example, which provided the government with the data it required for implementing its systems of provincial administration. Where we today might stress the process of *counting*—the importance of figuring out how many people lived in a village, say, or how many dyehouses a province contained—the Ottomans stressed the act of writing. Obviously, counting was a critical part of the survey process, but the vocabulary of the survey highlighted the act of recording information in a register. Two terms for "recording" or "inscribing"—*tahrir* and *kitabet*—recur regularly. The local tax code for Aintab, entered into the 1536 survey register, began, "Formerly, when the aforementioned province was inscribed" *(mukaddema liva-ı mezbure kitabet olundukda),* and the 1540 survey of Erzurum, referring back to the events of 1520, used precisely the same formulation ("Formerly, when by imperial order the province . . . of Erzurum was inscribed").[10]

Inscription was an act of possession. Householder by householder, mill by mill, vineyard by vineyard, the sultan's officials provided him with a discursive panorama of his subjects and their productive output. Enumerating and registering the empire's human and material resources had an obvious utility to the fisc, but it was also a mechanism of control: the taxpaying population, once inscribed as resident in a particular place, was forbidden to move, and peasants lost their right to farm if they let the land go fallow. To be sure, counting resources was an act familiar to local people, who were very precise in court about how many vines their vineyards contained and how many head of sheep they had sold in the market. But to be registered oneself was to be defined and fixed in the cognitive scope of the sovereign authority. Inscription archived, and thus immobilized, the subject population.

It was not only the practical utility of registering resources that, from the government's point of view, drove the survey process. "Inscribing" a province was a symbolic act that was a necessary corollary of conquest, a ritual that was essential to the assertion of sovereign authority. In the early sixteenth century, to conquer was still to acquire vast territories through victory in one or two key battles (at the end of the century, in contrast, frontiers advanced slowly over disputed terrain, town by town). The process of inscription penetrated areas where the sultan had never appeared, marking every village of his domain with his sovereignty. It is this symbolic aspect of the survey process that helps explain why tax rates remained constant in successive registers, despite the effects of inflation later in the century: at one level, they were simply notional figures, artifacts of the act of "inscribing." It also helps explain why the frequency of surveys dropped off sharply after the 1580s, a phenomenon that some have seen as a measure of Ottoman disorganization and decline. In truth, they became less necessary, either symbolically or practically.

The timing of the surveys also points to their symbolic or ritual function. In Aintab, the dates of two of the three major sixteenth-century surveys—1536 and 1574—can be accounted for in part by their role in what we might call the semiotics of sovereignty. The surveys often took place at key moments in the assertion of sovereign control and can be construed as acts of "reconquest" or repossession. Thus the 1536 survey took place on the heels of the celebrated campaign against the Safavids, during which the Ottomans conquered Iraq and Kurdistan, and thereby secured a firmer hold on their possessions in southeastern Anatolia and northern Syria. The year 1574 marked the accession of a new sultan, Süleyman's grandson Murad III. In this matter of timing, the surveys are similar to the reissuing of patents to hold government office and of treaties with other nations that took place at the beginning of a new reign, symbolic of the new sultan's reassertion of his dynasty's sovereign control.[11] It is noteworthy that an updated law book accompanied the 1574 survey, marking both of these moments as legislative interventions by the dynasty. In other words, accessions were accompanied by the reinscription of the sultan's relations with his subordinates as well as with his royal peers. Though there was no accession in 1536, it was a watershed moment in Süleyman's reign, initiating new directions in policy and ideological emphasis.

In truth, until 1536 the Ottoman regime probably lacked the level of control in Aintab (and other parts of the region) necessary for a thorough survey. Practical obstacles included the economic dislocations of conquest, the persistence of old loyalties and orientations, revolts in Syria and Anatolia, and the complex process of sorting out administrative structures on the ground (remember that it was not until the 1530s that Aintab was stabilized as a province composed of three subdistricts under the governorate-general of Dulkadir). Moreover, postponing the survey process gained the Ottoman regime time to put new local alliances in place. It needed to identify and place in office local individuals who could facilitate the task of the Ottoman survey teams and the tax collectors who would follow them. (This process can be seen in the court records, and will be described shortly.) The significance of the year 1536 is that it was now both practicable to perform a survey *and* ritually necessary, as a corollary to Süleyman's "reconquest" of the area.

Long military campaigns were an opportunity for the sultan and his leading officials (who traveled with him) to attend to provincial administration as well as to display the sultanate as the supreme patron of the religion of Islam. During the winter of 1535, while the Ottoman army camped in Baghdad before resuming military operations against the Safavids, the sultan spent much of his time planning the legal and administrative reorganization of the region, including the surveys that would take place. Süleyman's four-month return march from Tabriz to Istanbul was a veritable royal progress that passed through much of Aintab's regional world—from Diyarbakır through Ruha and Bire to Aleppo, and then on to Adana and Konya. While the route from Bire to Aleppo did not encompass the city of Aintab, it took the sultan and his army through the large villages of Orul and Telbaşer in the southeastern reaches of the province. Clifford Geertz has drawn attention to the importance of the royal progress as a "ceremonial form by which kings take symbolic possession of their realm."[12] Wherever the army halted for more than a day, the sultan visited the major mosques, the local shrines, and the citadels of the area, ordering repairs and restoration as necessary.[13]

This pattern had been initiated in Baghdad, where even before settling into his camp, Süleyman paid homage at the tomb of Abu Hanifa, founder of the Hanafi school of sunni sharia. Indeed, taking Baghdad from the shi'i Safavids was a major goal of the campaign. Contemporary accounts of the campaign emphasize the ruined state of the grave's site, neglected by the "heretic" Safavids; it could be located only by the sweet fragrance that emanated from it.[14] Süleyman's first act of patronage was to order the construction of a tomb, a mosque, and a medrese honoring the jurist to whose tradition the sultan would soon turn his attention in earnest. Given the preoccupation with inscription that characterized the mentality of imperialization, it is no surprise that this campaign was documented in exquisite detail by Matrakçi Nasuh, a soldier, historian, and artist during Süleyman's reign. His lavishly illustrated history—*Beyan-ı Menazil-i Sefer-i Irakeyn (Proclaiming the Stations of the Campaign for the Two Iraqs)*—maps the campaign station by station, representing in miniature paintings the natural and architectural delights of the various cities now securely anchored in the sultan's domain (see figures 1 and 8). Matrakçı Nasuh's work was another genre of enumeration and celebration, another discursive panorama, and an echo of the sultan's self-proclamation as sovereign of many "well-protected domains."

While committing the art of government to writing was a project of Süleyman's reign, writing was a strategy that subjects could also master, whether they were literate or not. The court records for 1540–1541 demonstrate again and again the critical importance of written documents. As we have seen, property disputes were frequently won by the party who could produce documents—apparently, the more the better. When Bedreddin from Aleppo proved his mother's disputed ownership of a mill share in Hacer village, he produced three separate documents to prove that she had inherited it from her father: a copy of a court record, a waqf deed, and a copy of "the register" (perhaps the village's tax register or the register of the father's estate contents); the rival claimant, however, "had nothing in his hand by way of court copy, register copy, or land title."[15] When Emine and her brother Kasım sued to recover an inherited vineyard, the claimant could not produce a title deed and the siblings won their suit (the court did not record the nature of the siblings' documents).[16] As we saw in chapter 6, the large number of failed property claims were surely not all fraudulent. Rather, the process of imperialization, with its key technique of land inscription, rewarded those who kept abreast of the legal demands of the new administrative order and armed themselves with an arsenal of written documents.

The value of committing transactions to the court's own written record is made clear in the following case, in which the plaintiff Hamza "forgot" that the defendant Hızır no longer had obligations to him:

> Hamza b. Mehmed summoned Hızır b. Mahmud to court and said: "You are holding my half share of a horse, and now I want it." When Hızır was questioned, he said: "I *used* to hold your half share, but you appointed Haci İbrahim proxy, and he sold your share for 1,000 akçes to the Aleppo timariot Ahmed Beg. It's recorded in the court register (*musecceldir*)." When [the record] was discovered in the court register (*sicilden keşf olundukda*), it was found to be registered in writing (*mestur mukayyed bulunduğu*) that Haci İbrahim had sold the half share in the aforementioned horse to the said timariot for 1,000 akçes. [The foregoing] was inscribed in the court register (*sebt-i sicill olundu*).[17]

It is possible, of course, that Hamza was unaware of what his proxy had done. But whatever the circumstances, Hızır clearly understood the value of the court record. The several terms in this court record for registering, recording, and inscribing, like the varied terms for the documents Bedreddin assembled for the defense of his mother's mill share, demonstrate the multiplicity and complexity of legal writing.

The hazards of guarding documents are evident in several cases. The loss of documents could put a whole village at risk. When the trustee of crown lands demanded 15,000 akçes in taxes from the villagers of Nifak,[18] the latter claimed that Hamza and Mehmed, two men of·the community, had collected the moneys and turned them over to the trustee. When questioned, the two claimed to have delivered the money but were unable to produce the receipt that the trustee regularly stamped, signed, and remitted to village authorities on receiving their revenues. They were given a second chance when the judge ordered them to "see to the matter."[19] For a freed slave, losing one's manumission certificate was disastrous, particularly during travel, since it was impossible to prove one was not a runaway slave. Such was the fate of "the tall black slave" who claimed that he had lost his papers "while coming and going." The string of local authorities into whose hands he fell clearly believed he was a runaway, the presumption being that the first act of any freed slave who lost manumission documents would be to get them reissued.[20] If losing a document was bad, forging one could be worse: the penalty according to Süleyman's law book was "severe punishment," and the habitual forger's hand was to be cut off.[21] When the provincial governor's chief of police accused Haci Korkmaz of altering a judge's decree ("taking a pen to the noble decree of the court"), the accused, obviously unable to provide evidence that he had not forged the document, cleared himself by taking an oath of innocence.[22]

People understood the hierarchy of documents, seeking "power documents" such as an order from the governor-general in Maraş or even from Istanbul, when local authorities could not or would not enforce more parochial orders. As we saw in chapter 6, the manager of the Mihaliye college, unable to stop the abuse of his foundation's revenues, obtained a decree from the sultan and a fatwa from the chief mufti. In his efforts to recover a debt owed him of 15 gold florins (1,200 akçes), the merchant Hoca Maksud sought a decree from the judge of Istanbul as well as two imperial *adaletname*s, or orders for the correction of abuses. The heft of the three documents appears to have elicited an unusually prominent group of case witnesses as well as a special legal procedure—the city steward acted as intermediary in the repayment of the debt and also took possession of Hoca Maksud's documents at the end of the affair.[23] As with many cases in the Aintab court records, a hidden history to this case may be responsible for its unusual legal cast. Perhaps it was the principle of the thing that mattered to Hoca Maksud, since the debt hardly seems significant enough to warrant the journey to the capital.

For individuals of lesser means and lesser mobility, Maraş—the seat of the Dulkadir governorate-general—was the next best source of authoritative documents. In her efforts to get control of the oil press to which she claimed rights through a family waqf, the woman Şahpaşa bt. Halil exploited the complex relationship among various legal authorities by first obtaining a fatwa and then appealing to the governor-general, who ordered both the judge of Aintab and its provincial governor to see to her claim.[24] It worth noting that both Hoca Maksud and Şahpaşa appealed to sharia authority as well as to the executive authority of the state. In Şahpaşa's case, where the property came under the jurisdiction of Islamic law as waqf, the logic of dual legal protection is more obvious than in Hoca Maksud's. Nevertheless, the two cases suggest that local individuals may have sought redundancy in documentation as legal insurance.

The growing interest in documents no doubt helped privilege the judge's court over other local avenues of dispute resolution. The very rise in the number of cases over the course of the year 1540–1541 no doubt has something to do with a growing awareness among Aintabans of the utility of legal documentation and indeed of its necessity in the evolving administrative order of the Ottoman regime. People sought documentation primarily to secure ownership of real estate but also for loans and other forms of property. That the record itself served as proof of ownership accounts for such curiosities as the long and detailed descriptions of horses, mules, and donkeys—including owner-inflicted identifying marks such as clipped or pierced ears—that pepper the court records.

All this raises the question of literacy, since presumably many seekers of documentation were themselves unable to read. Literacy was clearly not a prerequisite for grasping the importance of committing legal relationships to paper. Just as individuals understood the importance of oral evidence at court, seeking witnesses to any incident that might spark future litigation, so they understood the need for documents, even if they themselves could not read them. The question of literacy may in fact be irrelevant in dealing with documents: given the oral acuity of largely nonliterate cultures, people probably could easily commit to memory the contents of their pieces of paper. At the same time, however, the increasing use of documents by the illiterate or semiliterate meant that local figures who *were* literate, such as the neighborhood imam, gained increased stature and influence in people's relationship to the legal process as a whole. Literacy was no doubt a requirement for those managing neighborhood or village affairs, given the critical role that documentation played in matters of tax collection. It is difficult to imagine that the headman of a large village, for example, could have been illiterate.

The expansion of the court system and the rising use of documents as evidence inevitably raises the question of fees. The law book of Selim I prescribed hefty fees not only for personal copies of court transactions (*hüccet*) but also for the recording of transactions in the court register.[25] On the other hand, the voluntary use made of the Aintab court by many local residents suggests that whatever fees were charged were not viewed as excessive. Indeed, it is possible that fees were not being charged for routine use of local courts in 1540–1541. Süleyman's law book, unlike earlier versions of Ottoman kanun, makes no mention of fees for the issuing of legal documents. The apparent shift under the Ottoman regime to the maintenance of the court's record *as a public record* may in fact have lessened the pressure on individuals to obtain and guard their own copies of cases legislated at court. Now, written evidence could be located by searching the court's records, as demonstrated by the case of Hamza and Hızır above.[26] Were one to travel, of course, it was critical to carry documentation of one's civil status—the plight of the hapless ex-slave who claimed to have lost his manumission certificate is a case in point. But it seems possible that the effort under Süleyman to build a network of courts and to encourage people to use them had as corollary a policy of reducing the cost of using the court, either by abolishing fees altogether for routine cases or by shifting their focus from charging for copies of documents to charging for recording the case in the court register (traditionally a lesser fee). Certainly making the court affordable was necessary if the Ottoman government was going to succeed in persuading people that the state's justice was user-friendly. The regime's policy of reducing taxes and penal fines levied by former regimes lends plausibility to the suggestion that it reduced court fees during the period of Süleyman's legal reforms.

AN OTTOMAN JUSTICE

The years around 1540 were critical for lawmaking in the Ottoman domain. Süleyman's law book, his much-expanded version of the *Kanun-ı Osmanî*, is attributed to these years.[27] The law book of Buda, issued after Süleyman's conquest of Hungary in 1541, gave mature formulation to Ottoman principles of land tenure and taxation. Behind this work stood a team of experts brought together after 1536—the jurist Ebu Suud, the chancellor Celalzade Mustafa, and the grand vezir Lutfi Pasha. We are already acquainted with the work of Ebu Suud in expanding the discourse of Hanafi jurisprudence to accommodate the inevitable demands of *siyaset*, the executive power that religious scholars before him had justified as necessary to the realization of sharia. Here we should remember that it was in 1537 that Süleyman appointed Ebu Suud to the post of military judge of Rumelia, then an office perhaps more influential than the chief muftiship (which would become the keystone of the religious establishment only during Ebu Suud's own tenure from 1545 to 1574). Celalzade Mustafa was appointed to the post of imperial chancellor *(nişancı)* in 1535, in the midst of the two-year campaign against the Safavids, of which he gave a lengthy eyewitness account in his history of Süleyman's reign.[28] Medrese-trained, Celalzade first served Süleyman as secretary to his grand vezirs. Because of his contribution to the administrative reforms in Egypt, reflected in the Egyptian law book of 1525, he was made chief secretary of the imperial council *(reis ül-küttab)*. In this office and then as chancellor, he established guidelines and models for imperial correspondence and played a central role in the expansion and codification of kanun. It was most probably he who compiled Süleyman's comprehensive law book; indeed, it was sometimes explicitly attributed to him as "the kanun of Celalzade."[29] A third influence on the intensive legal work of these years, although less directly so, was the grand vezir Lutfi Pasha, who served for two years from 1539 until 1541. Well educated in the palace school but lacking professional legal training, Lufti Pasha nevertheless was especially concerned with legal matters and considered himself something of an expert. He may well have been a motive force in the compiling of Süleyman's law book, which, as we have seen, is generally thought to have been issued in the period of his grand vezirate.[30] The collaboration of these men was critical in what appears to have been a self-conscious project to give definitive statement to Ottoman principles of law. Ottoman law could now aspire to superseding historical precedent, displacing the work of its imperial predecessors.

This new Ottoman justice was disseminated through new provincial law books issued in the years around 1540. The local code accompanying the second wave of surveys in the regions conquered by Selim I were a venue for representing the sultan, already registered in the public mind as a military victor, as the fount of justice. Notably, the reformed codes definitively displaced the laws of former rulers such as Qaytbay, the revered Mamluk sultan who ruled from 1468 to 1496, and the celebrated Uzun Hasan of the Akkoyunlus.[31] In Aintab, the shift in legal legitimation was made explicit in the 1536 law book, which opened by stating that "the corruptions *(bid'atlar)* introduced in the time of the Circassians"—the Mamluk sultans of the fifteenth and early sixteenth centuries—were now abolished.[32] As in the Erzurum law book of 1540, conspicuous reference was made in these second-wave codes to the suffering of populations under the laws of former regimes. In the 1540 code for Diyarbakır, the first statute reformed the practice of requiring agricultural taxes to be paid in cash (and at rates exceeding official commodity pricing). Drawing on the standard rhetoric of oppression and injustice now alleviated, in this case by permitting taxes to be paid in kind, the statute concluded, "Let the peasants in the realm of the padishah, refuge of the world, be free from care and farm to the extent of their capacity."[33] By displacing laws associated with Qaytbay and Uzun Hasan, both honored for their legal-mindedness as well as their soldierly talents, Süleyman's kanun proclaimed the maturity of Ottoman imperial culture and the sultan's superior justice.

Local communities may have paid a price for the advent of Ottoman legalism, however. Ömer Lütfi Barkan, the scholar who has studied provincial law codes of the sixteenth century most closely, has drawn attention to "the character of newness and uniformity that emerged over time, to the detriment of localism and regionalism."[34] It is beyond the capacity of a microstudy such as mine to evaluate the impact on regional economies of the new provincial law codes, which were primarily tax codes. But one thing this book can and does do is trace changes in Aintab's legal climate following the arrival of Hüsameddin Efendi, the state-appointed judge who, I have speculated, may have introduced Süleyman's new law book—the updated *Kanun-ı Osmanî*—to the city's court. The impact of his appointment is palpable in the court's register, from the enlargement of the judicial compound to a doubling of the court's caseload to shifts in the nature of cases coming to court. Yet Aintabans were far from passive in their reception of the new judge. Some were quick to see how they might make proactive use of "the Hüsameddin court," for example, the women who now initiated property claims against male relatives. And while others now found habitual modes of conduct questioned, particularly in the matter of male-female contact, individuals were able to persuade the court of the moral and legal defensibility of their actions. Although Hüsameddin Efendi was a state-appointed legal agent, the very nature of the Ottoman-Islamic court system required a judge to work in tandem with locals, as we have seen repeatedly in earlier chapters.

The same give-and-take shaped the larger process of negotiating legitimacy, our concern in this chapter. Aintab's history, as we have seen, was one of adapting its own interests to those of the regimes that ruled it. The city's accustomed autonomy and its regional self-sufficiency gave it the wherewithal to parlay its natural advantages—strategic location, a fortified citadel, a diversified economy, an enterprising and relatively stable population—into features attractive to rulers. And just as the legal apparatus of the regime—its laws, its judge—were absorbed into the local context, so the economic and social advantages offered by a vigorous new government were eagerly exploited by the local population. Moreover, the reciprocity critical to negotiating relations between a new sovereign power and its subjects was facilitated by the fact that it was largely local individuals who represented the Ottoman regime in Aintab, particularly in the day-to-day government of the city and province. Thus much of the dialogue about the rights of the imperial power versus the rights of the local population took place among Aintabans themselves.

Traditionally, it has been assumed that it was the direct delegates of the sovereign regime who carried the dynasty's authority and its message of legitimacy into the provinces. According to the model that many historians still employ to describe the pre-seventeenth-century period of Ottoman rule, the most locally powerful representatives of the sultan were the provincial governors (*sancakbegi; mir liva* in Arabic) and their superiors, the governors-general (*beglerbegi*), men of the rank of pasha who administered large regions of the empire. In turn, these governors were in charge of the provincial cavalry—that is, the *sipahi* soldiers of the sultan whose livelihood was provided by grants of the tax revenues (*timars*) from the villages and mezraas to which they were assigned. In other words, rural taxation, as well as rural administration, is assumed to have been in the hands of these timariot soldiers. But this picture is only partially true for Aintab in 1540–1541, and the realities of Aintab province challenge the neatness of the classical paradigm.

For most of the year, the provincial governor of Aintab was a weak individual, Cafer Beg b. Bali, who virtually never appeared in the court record as a figure of authority. Rather, he most often needed the court's assistance in straightening out his own affairs. In September 1540, for example, Cafer Beg appeared in court in a dispute with the heirs of a local timariot to whom he owed a debt; the case was settled by mediation. A telling prelude to the case was that the governor-general had had to send an emissary with an order that Cafer Beg pay off his debt.[35] A more commanding provincial governor was appointed in June 1541, but he remained in office for only two months. Indeed, the rapid turnover in the provincial governorship—three in one year—was hardly a formula for anchoring a legitimating voice for the sultan in this office. In contrast, the governor-general of Dulkadir, Ali Pasha, was a figure of consequence whose voice resounds in the court records through the authoritative language of his orders. However, from the perspective of the Aintab court, the pasha functioned mainly as a higher authority who heard cases deemed beyond the local capacity to settle. Ali Pasha could, and did, intervene in the affairs of Aintab on behalf of the sultan, but his interventions were acts of force rather than persuasion, acts of a colonizer rather than a legitimater.

The local delegates of sultanic authority who seem to have been most involved in the day-to-day life of the province—those who showed up frequently at court—were the trustee of crown lands in the province (*hassemini*) and the city *subaşı*, the "police chief" who was the executive agent of the provincial governor. Both of these individuals held state-generated jobs—that is, they worked for the imperial sector—but they did much of their business through their own delegates, all local individuals. Authority was thus diffused throughout the community, making it hard to point to an official other than the provincial governor who specifically represented state as opposed to local interests.

The point is that there was no clear line separating state and society in Aintab. The classical model of Ottoman organization presents a dichotomy between the *askerî*, the "military" or ruling classes, paid by the sultan and not subject to taxation, and the *reaya*, the ruled, the taxpaying subjects of the sultan. The local reality was that many *"askerî"* figures in Aintab were simultaneously committed to the interests of the local community and indeed rooted their own interests in the community. Moreover, many jobs that could be called "state offices"—the warden of the fortress, the trustee of crown lands, members of provincial cavalry assigned to Aintab—were allocated to local individuals and, more important, allocated according to the mechanics of local balances of power rather than by arbitrary design of the state. For example, several timariots—especially those with the largest timar grants—were local *beg*s, most likely former Dulkadir tribal leaders rewarded for their loyalty in the revolts that had marked the earlier years of Süleyman's reign.

In provinces distant from the imperial capital, therefore, it was not always easy to isolate a domain that could be labeled "state." Here, we define the state in the sixteenth century as the sum of the dynasty, palace, and bureaucratic cadres in the capital; the army standing in the capital; and the pashas, the highest-ranking members of the sultan's military slave corps. (In this book, the terms *state* and *regime* should be regarded as interchangeable.) The notion of the state's discrete presence in many provincial locales may make greater sense for later periods of Ottoman history (although recent scholarship has cast even this notion into doubt),[36] but for the mid–sixteenth century at least, the facile distinction between "state" and "local" obscures the complexities of power relations on the ground. Hence, when we talk about legitimation at the grassroots level, the emphasis should be on process and its relentlessly quotidian character, rather than on the local markers or bearers of sovereignty per se. It is instead in the microprocesses of shifting alignments and attitudes among local populations that questions of legitimation can most fruitfully be examined.

Tensions over control of local society and local resources in Aintab were most evident in matters of fiscal administration. They were a natural outcome of incorporation into the expanding Ottoman domain, a process whose principal local manifestations were the inscription of local communities in a state system of taxation and the redefinition of land ownership in favor of the sultanate (as we have seen earlier, the cadastral surveys of 1536 and 1543 reveal an increase in the crown's share of the province's rural areas as well as of its urban taxes). While these aspects of Ottoman imperialism were imposed by the central government, their implementation lay largely in the hands of local officials. Apart from timariots who collected a share of rural revenues, it was an army of local tax-farmers who negotiated the shifting fiscal terrain with the province's taxpayers. These individuals were local men who in turn distributed the fruits of their offices outward and downward in the form of smaller tax-farms and commissions.

A note on the terminology employed for tax-farms and on their structure is in order at this point. In referring to tax-farms, the Aintab records of 1540–1541 use interchangeably the standard administrative terms *iltizam* and *mukata'a;* they also employ the more common terminology of "leasing" the right to collect taxes *(icare almak, icareye vermek).*[37] In Aintab, the practice of tax-farming—subcontracting the actual collection of taxes from the legitimate recipient of specified tax revenues, presumably with some profit to the tax-farmer—does not appear to have required the farmer's advance payment of the entire purchase price of the tax-farm. While tax-farms were leased for specific sums stipulated in the farming contract, customary practice appears to have tolerated some flexibility in payment schedule. As we will see, abuse of this flexibility had led, in the view of the Ottoman authorities, to a widespread problem of debt owed to the state by Aintab tax-farmers.

The court records of 1540–1541 amply demonstrate the trickle-down effect of the benefits of state-generated offices through the granting of ever-smaller units of tax-farming.[38] Appointments to a number of city tax-farms dependent on the office of the provincial governor are recorded in the court records, among them the inspectorship of market practices *(ihtisap),* the tax on butchers, the tavern run by and for Armenian Christians, and, at a lesser level of revenue, headship of the night watch, the tannery, and the gut factory.[39] Tax-farmers whose position derived from the crown *(hass)* through the intermediacy of the local trustee of crown lands included a variety of local urban notables and village headmen who collected rural taxes on crown lands. Also farmed out by the trustee of crown lands were the tax on nomads wintering in the province and the taxes collected on fresh fruits and dry goods weighed at the municipal scales (including oils, cheeses, honey, grape molasses, rice, salt, henna, and alum).

In addition to generating numerous tax-farms, the offices of provincial governor and trustee of crown lands each employed a number of executive or police agents, who were known as *subaşıs*. In turn, the various tax-farmers and subaşıs were likely to have their own "men" *(ademi)* who, while lacking official titles, were acknowledged bearers of authority. Holders of larger tax-farms might subcontract segments of their revenues. The market inspector, for example, subcontracted the taxes on the medicine factory to one Ustad Ali for the sum of 40 akçes a month.[40] An example of a small rural tax-farm is the quarter share of a mezraa belonging to the crown whose revenues were subcontracted by one of the trustee's men to the saddler Mustafa b. Ahmed. Mustafa acquired the tax-farm by outbidding its previous owner for the year's taxes, 940 akçes to 860 akçes.[41] (This case illustrates the degree to which tax revenues estimated in cadastral surveys could be out of line with actual amounts: in the 1543 cadaster, the estimated revenue of the quarter share was 300 akçes.) [42] The right to the substantial taxes collected from the tribe (*cemaat*) of Kazak was subcontracted for the year 947 (1539–1540) by the secretary of Haci Cuma, the tax-farmer, to two members of the tribe, the brothers Pir Nasir and Pir Kuli. The brothers had outbid the previous subcontractees by offering 20,470 akçes for the year's taxes, 400 akçes more than the earlier contract, for the tax on sheep and the poll tax on bachelors and propertyless married men. In addition, they bid 7,000 akçes for a two-year lease on other taxes imposed on the tribe, including criminal fines and the marriage tax.[43] Clearly many individuals in Aintab wanted a share of the province's growing prosperity, and some were willing to speculate. That wealthy women used their money to finance tax-farms leased in the names of their husbands or other men indicates that gender was not a barrier to profiting from an investment in revenue raising.

In short, a considerable number of individuals were drawn into employment networks through the hierarchy of offices furnished locally by the central government. Indeed, the constant bidding for tax-farms in Aintab and the frequent turnover in some suggests that the demand for them exceeded their supply. If Aintab in 1540 was at all typical, our picture of the mid–sixteenth century must be altered to give significant space to local notables competing for local state-generated offices and to the trickle-down effects of tax-farming. This reality belies the classical model of sixteenth-century Ottoman political culture, which depicts provincial administration and tax collection as resting in hands of the askerî ruling class.

The evidence from Aintab suggests that tax-farms were nothing new; nor were they a sign of corruption, as has typically been the judgment of Ottoman historiography. The latter view has been amply and convincingly challenged by recent scholarship.[44] Indeed, the assumption that tax-farms were a natural linkage between subjects and state is encoded in the legendary histories of Ottoman origins composed at the end of the fifteenth century. One of the first issues that Osman Gazi, the first sultan, allegedly had to deal with was a request for a tax-farm. In the historian Neşri's version of the incident, "When the [signs of sovereignty] had been established in Osman Gazi's name, and judges and subaşıs had been appointed, someone came to Osman from the province of Germiyan and said, 'Sell me this market's taxes.'" What follows is a lengthy discussion between Osman and the man from Germiyan on the legitimacy of taxation in principle, with Osman cast as the innocent, protesting that he is not entitled to a portion of someone else's hard-earned profits and even threatening to punish the would-be tax-farmer for his outlandish proposition:

Osman Gazi replied, "What's a tax?" [The other] said, "You take money from whoever brings a load [of goods to sell] to the market." Osman Gazi said, "Hey fellow! what claim do *I* have on these people coming to the market that *you* should take money from them?" That person said, "It's the custom. It's true in every country that they take money for the ruler on every load [sold in the market]." Osman said, "Is this the command of God and the word of the Prophet, or does the ruler of every country make this up himself?" That person said, "It's always been a practice of sovereigns *(türe-i sultanî)*." Osman Gazi got angry and said, "Leave! Don't stand there any longer, or you may suffer at my hands! Why should someone who earns his living with his own hands owe me anything? Why should I take his money like a parasite?"

Only when "the people" convinced Osman of the social and economic necessity of taxation was the impasse was resolved:

When all the people heard what Osman Gazi had said, they said, "O Lord, even if *you* don't need [the taxes], it's the custom to give a little something to the people who monitor the market, so that their labor won't go for naught." [Osman Gazi] said, "Since you say so, let every person who sells a load [of goods in the market] pay 2 akçes. If he doesn't sell anything, he doesn't have to pay."[45]

One of the (several) implications of this story, a critical moment in Ottoman foundation myths, is that the collection of taxes is a *locally based function* that is latent until sanctioned and activated by a ruling authority with legitimate rights to the revenue in question. But with tax-farms thus positioned somewhere between the state and local society, there was bound to be some conflict over their regulation. As a domain of overlapping interests, tax-farms (like other state-generated offices) were vulnerable to competing claims to legitimate control.

The issues of balance of power studied here were relatively new in 1540, since it was only around 1536 that regime and province came into sustained dialogue. The inception of a public court record around this time was no doubt a feature of this dialogue. The court was a central venue where the business that the regime shared with the province was conducted. The court recorded the leasing of tax-farms (naming bidders and terms), the awarding of subcontracts to collect revenues leased, and the payback of delinquent revenues. It also oversaw the regulation of land and its revenues, recording such matters as title to usufruct of land going into cultivation, boundary disputes between timariots and civilian landowners, payout of revenues to fortress garrisons in the vicinity, and the registration of private and waqf properties in the rural areas of the province. If there is any validity to the speculation advanced in chapter 3—that the gaps in the series of court registers from Aintab during the sixteenth century may indicate that a public record was kept on specific request (either by the state or the local authorities)—then the call for a public record in 1540 and 1541 may signal recognition of a moment when contacts between the regime and its subjects in Aintab were particularly critical.

The authority of the state impinged directly on the court only at certain moments during the year studied here, but a review of those moments makes it clear that the state claimed the provincial court as a domain of action. The following discussion focuses on two points in time—October 1540 and June 1541—when the local population and the central government most closely confronted one another. The events of these months reveal some of the tensions and counterclaims inherent in the process of assimilation into an imperial system. They also reveal the mechanisms that each side invoked in court to articulate its own position and to strive toward some kind of accommodation among the various interests laying claim to this provincial community. Much of the argument below is based on chronology, that is, on attitudes and motivations suggested by events that occurred in close succession. The first set of cases, recorded in late September and October 1540, reveals an attitude of resistance on Aintab's part to the incursions of state authority. Nine months later, the sultan's appointment of a special prosecutor and a new judge appeared to inject the Aintab court with palpably enhanced authority. But in whose interest would that authority be exercised?

THE EVENTS OF OCTOBER 1540: RESISTING IMPERIALIZATION

That the local community was the matrix for exploiting the set of offices the state had to offer—indeed, that it may have felt it *contained* these offices—becomes even clearer when the contender for local office was an outsider to Aintab. The question of local entitlement came to a head in October 1540 when the Ottoman regime appointed its own candidate to an important office—that of *sarraf,* or city treasurer—and the community blocked the appointment. The tax-farm to the office of Aintab sarraf had been purchased by one Matuk b. Sadullah the Jew, as he is named in the court record. However, the Aintab community refused to let him take up his duties, as we learn from an order issued by the governor-general, Ali Pasha, and recorded in the court register at the beginning of October 1540. The governor-general, addressing himself to both the judge of Aintab and the trustee of crown lands, commanded them to facilitate Matuk's assumption of the office. His order was dated September 13 and recorded in the court register on October 1, two weeks after the register began to be kept:

> When this order arrives, let it be known that: The Jew named Matuk, who is the current sarraf of Aintab, has sent his agent to us, through whom he has informed us as follows: "I am the sarraf of Aintab, which position I hold as tax-

farmer from the head of the Aleppo Mint. But they do not permit me to act as sarraf over the revenues from royal lands and other occasional taxes; nor do they permit me to act as sarraf within the city proper. For this reason, I am unable to perform the functions delegated to me through the tax-farm or to furnish the requisite remittances. I will be held accountable for this." NOW, the aforementioned Jew is the sarraf in your area by virtue of the tax-farm from the Aleppo Mint. It is not permissible for any other individual to act as sarraf there. It is imperative that you see to it that whatever revenues are collected from the royal lands and as occasional taxes are handed over to the aforementioned Jew, and that you do not allow anyone else to act as sarraf within the city of Aintab proper.[46]

As we see, Matuk had purchased his tax-farm from the Aleppo Mint; accordingly, the office of fiscal manager of Aintab was not construed in the eyes of Ottoman authorities as a local one. The resistance Matuk faced in Aintab may have been less to him personally than to the prospect of relinquishing the functions of sarraf to an outside appointment. Although Matuk was probably from Aleppo himself and thus not a native Aintaban (there was at this time no Jewish community in Aintab), he was already known locally as a major player. He held one of the three largest city tax-farms, that of the tax on butchers, as well as the tax-farm of the municipal weighing scales, whose revenues belonged to the crown. It was most likely the aggrandizement of his local power base that was causing the community to protest Matuk's new appointment.

Just who the "they" is that resisted Matuk's assumption of the sarraf tax-farm is unclear. The judge and the trustee of crown lands were held responsible for correcting the situation, and, by implication, could be suspected of conspiring to resist Matuk's appointment in the first place. It is also possible that one of the leading families of Aintab, the Sikkaks, had a personal stake in this affair, assuming that their name in fact asserts their ancestral profession as "Coiners." The Sikkakoğlu family was one of three prominent notable families, or *ayan* lineages, in the city of Aintab (the others were the Demirci and Boyacı families—the Smiths and the Dyers, if you will). Combined with their local prominence, the Sikkaks' professional identity suggests that they in particular might have resisted the devolution of the city's financial affairs to an appointment made and held by outsiders. There is a hint of tension between Matuk and Ali Çelebi, scion of the Sikkak family: in early 1539, while Ali Çelebi held the office of secretary of crown lands *(hass kâtip)*, he received in that capacity the revenues of the weighing scales, whose tax-farm was held by Matuk. In documenting this transaction at court, Matuk stated that "henceforth there remains no legal dispute and no claim between us."[47] Whether this tension was simply over Matuk's payment to Ali as agent of the state or it was more personal is hard to say, but it is certainly deserves our attention, especially as Ali Çelebi was to be made a conspicuous object of the state's disciplinary efforts in a matter of months.

It is also worth considering briefly the fact that the sarraf is routinely referred to in the records as "Matuk the Jew" or simply "the Jew." At one level, this label is simply descriptive of difference from the standard of the adult male Muslim, who functions as a kind of default identity in the world of these records. As we saw in chapter 4, women at court are always identified as "the female So-and-So," the Armenians of Aintab as "the *dhimmi* So-and-so," peasants as "the villager So-and-so," persons not native to Aintab as "the Egyptian So-and-So," and so forth—nomads as nomads, Kurds as Kurds, and thus Jews as Jews.[48] Moreover, just as "dhimmi" in Aintab meant "Armenian Christian," because there *were* no other resident non-Muslims, Matuk was "the" Jew because there were no others in Aintab with whom he might be confused. But is something more going on here? Expressed in the identification of Matuk as "the Jew" may be a resistance to the growing role of Jewish municipal financiers, in part a product of the influx of Iberian Jews into the empire in the aftermath of the Spanish Inquisition. To be sure, Jews had been involved in tax-farming before the immigration of Iberian Jews at the end of the fifteenth century; and in late Mamluk and early Ottoman Cairo, Jews were associated with the tax-farm of the mint.[49] But the appearance of Jewish sarrafs in smaller cities may have been a new phenomenon. It was perhaps the *imperialization* of the office of city treasurer—its appropriation by the regime into a state-managed system—to which the powers in Aintab objected.

There are features of Matuk's dispute with the Aintab community that encourage us to ask further questions about the province's reaction to the display of authority by the state's enforcers. First, it was rare for the governor-general to intervene in the running of local administration, as he did in this case. Second, it was very rare for the city, with the apparent collusion of its court, to close ranks to resist someone. Third, and perhaps most interesting, the use in the court records of the ambiguous "they"—"they do not permit me to act as sarraf" *(bana sarraf itdürmezler)*—is most unusual.

The only other case in which the ambiguous "they" occurs is a complaint about the unjustified imprisonment of a Kurdish man recorded on September 26. In this case, too, the community was resisting a fait accompli initiated by an outside authority, for it was Ali Pasha's subaşı—his chief of police—who had imprisoned the man. Here is the record of this incident:

When they complained that the subaşı Davud, one of the Pasha's subaşıs, had seized and imprisoned Seyfeddin b. Musa, the Kurd, and was committing unlawful aggression against him on the grounds that he was a thief, the aforementioned subaşı was summoned to the court. After repeated questioning of him and the aforementioned Seyfeddin, nothing could be discovered that could be held [against Seyfeddin] and he was released. Mehmed b. Mustafa, a trustworthy person, was appointed guarantor for him.[50]

Who is responsible for Seyfeddin's release? Anonymous members of the community initiated the complaint, but the judge played a critical role by opening the case to scrutiny and thus revealing the Kurd's innocence. His actions were justified by sharia, for one of a judge's duties was to make sure that people in prison were there for just cause (strictly speaking, this review was supposed to take place when the judge first took up his appointment).

It may not be a coincidence that it was five days after the release of the Kurd that the governor-general's order concerning Matuk was recorded in the court register. Both situations were undoubtedly brewing for some time before their denouement was inscribed in the record. Each reveals popular discontent, though possibly among different groups in the population. It is not difficult to imagine that there was an ongoing conversation in the city— and possibly in rural circles as well—about the shifting alignments among the province's elites and about the future of Aintab in relation to the authorities in Maraş, Aleppo, and ultimately Istanbul.

That an atmosphere of uncertainty prevailed becomes clearer when we look at other events of October 1540. It was during this month, between the 19th and 23rd, that the court oversaw the registration and validation of waqf and freehold claims to villages and mezraas in the province, as described in chapter 6. This process of reviewing waqf and private landholdings was periodic (a comprehensive review of Aintab holdings would take place in 1557) and typically overseen by judges or other members of the religious establishment.[51] Shortly before the process began, between the 11th and the 14th, Armenians subject to the poll tax on non-Muslims in both the village of Orul and Aintab city were similarly registered. Evidence was brought to court that two individuals from Orul and four from the city were deceased, and that another had converted to Islam.[52] Moreover, four Armenians who appeared in both the Aintab and the Maraş poll tax registers brought documents from the governor-general and the Maraş judge attesting to their legal residence in Maraş; accordingly, they were removed from the Aintab register.[53] This latter confusion and the deaths of four men in an Armenian city population consisting, according to the 1543 cadastral survey, of thirty-four households suggest that the count of dhimmis in the province had not been updated recently, perhaps since the 1536 cadastral survey. In light of this attention to the poll tax, the registration of waqf and freehold villages in the days immediately following suggests that the intent was, at least in part, to gain a firmer fix on the revenues due the state from these villages and mezraas. The fiscal muscle of the Ottoman regime was clearly demonstrated in mid-October.

Other cases during these weeks suggest an attitude of resistance to the pressure of state authority. On October 18, three press owners were summoned to court by the provincial governor's subaşı and the market inspector to pay the annual tax on presses. Apparently assessed at a rate higher than they believed appropriate, the owners were adamant in their resistance: "In the past we have always paid 200 akçes for the presses; we will not pay a single akçe or a single grain more by way of other taxes or anything else."[54] Their determination and the presence of the subaşı, who had accompanied the market inspector to court, suggest that there had been some contention over the matter. However, the two authorities backed down, stating that "nothing is going to be requested besides the 200 akçes." But the record suggests that the compromise might only have been temporary, for it went on to conclude that "it was decided that nothing would be requested for now." This case points to popular awareness that the regime was exerting pressure to raise taxes, a reality that would manifest itself in increased levies attendant on the 1543 cadastral survey.

Even the most powerful local individual holding a state-generated office was under pressure from higher authorities. It was on October 23 that Mustafa Çelebi, the trustee of crown lands, appeared in court to pay off his arrears to the state, drawing on his wife Aynişah's considerable wealth to cover his debt of 20,000 akçes.[55] On the same day, he had to answer in court to an order from the sultan, issued in response an appeal by a local timariot who complained that his fief was wrongly claimed by the trustee. Accompanied by his son Bali Çelebi, secretary of crown lands, Mustafa Çelebi testified that in fact the fief had never been claimed for the crown, from the Ottoman conquest on.[56] One message conveyed by this incident was that the regime guarded its provincial revenues with care.

The court records for October suggest that marginal populations in Aintab might suffer from the disciplinary atmosphere that prevailed. Another record from October 23 echoes the popular sympathy displayed for the imprisoned Kurd Şemseddin. On that day, the governor-general's subaşı Davud, the official who had wrongly imprisoned Şemseddin, appeared in court to accuse a villager from Dülük of having aided in the escape of another Kurd imprisoned for theft by giving him a tool with which to cut his chain. The villager, one Ali, would seem himself to be indirectly associated with law enforcement, albeit of a more local nature: he was identified as son of the chief of the night watch (in Dülük).[57] And as so often in times of social stress, marginal populations become scapegoats: a murderer convicted in court on the 16th of the month unsuccessfully tried to pin the crime on his alleged Kurdish accomplice.[58]

Beginning on October 25, the court took a sixteen-day recess, the only such recess during the year. It is tempting to speculate that it did so to allow a respite during which tempers might cool down and people might get their affairs in order in anticipation of further scrutiny exercised through the court. With the possible exception of the prison break, all of these cases involved issues that had been developing before they were heard by the judge. News of the registration of land and poll tax payers would have gone out ahead of time, so that the individuals concerned might assemble their evidence and their witnesses in anticipation of going to court. Moreover, some of the landowners traveled from Aleppo along with their witnesses, journies that would have been arranged in advance. While these cases occurred after the controversy over the financier Matuk's appointment and the release of the Kurd Şemseddin from prison, they were part of the larger trend of events that appears to have aroused resistance to the work of the governor-general and of the provincial governor's officials in Aintab. Lack of evidence makes it difficult to discern the loyalties of the judge, if any, since the court register reveals neither his name nor whether he was a local man. At the very least, the case of Matuk suggests that no authority in Aintab was either able or willing to enforce the financier's appointment, the judge included. But the judge *did* command one instrument, the authorship of the permanent record of the events. The court record's singular representation of popular spokespersons as the ambiguous "they" dispelled the possibility of reprisals.

Before turning to the events of June 1541, let us pause to look at two cases recorded during the winter that cast light on the twin issues of executive intervention and legal mechanisms for self-protection. In both, representatives were identified to act as spokespersons or mediators for individuals in the community. The cases suggest a kind of protective reaction among the local populace, born perhaps of a sense of uncertainty over the future. The first case records the communally requested appointment of a "market chief" *(bazarbaşı)* on December 23. The record of this appointment is tantalizingly brief: "Because Muslims agreed, with regard to Ahmed b. [Halil], that he should be made head of the market, this was done. With the cognizance of the subaşı, he was ceremonially invested with a robe of office and officially appointed chief of the market.[59] In this case, it is not the ambiguous "they" but an equally ambiguous group of "Muslims" who give voice to the communal opinion. As noted in chapter 4, the term *Muslims* in these records generally means upright citizens of the community, those entrusted with representing public morality and relaying the tenor of public opinion (they were, of course, also Muslims in the literal sense).

The position of market head was not a standard municipal office such as that of market inspector or head of the night watch, offices that made up the roster of local state appointments and tax-farms. It instead appears to be a creation of the local community, with its holder, nicknamed Uzun ("Long) Ahmed," popularly nominated. The market headship was not unique to Aintab. In his studies of urban administration, Özer Ergenç illustrates the process of popular nomination for this position with examples drawn from the Bursa court records: in 1598, for example, an unsatisfactory market chief was replaced by one Uğurlu b. Haci Abdullah, his appointment contingent on approval of "the people"—meaning all those manufacturing and selling goods in the market.[60] No market chief appears in the Aintab records before Long Ahmed's appointment, although the city may have had market chiefs in the past. What his popular nomination suggests is that people regarded present circumstances as meriting the activation of this optional office.

Following his appointment, Long Ahmed appeared frequently in court as communal witness in a variety of cases, ranging from such major public scandals as a murder and a woman teacher's banishment from the city, to commercial transactions involving prominent tax-farmers, to more ordinary property sale and debt transactions. In a word, he seems to have functioned as a kind of community ombudsman. I am inclined to see this office as a deliberate counterweight to the range of political offices populated by the Aintab elite, or, more specifically, as a counterweight to the politicization of what were regarded as local offices. It is difficult not to read these cases in which a generalized voice articulates popular sentiment as assertions of local legitimacy—as claims to the right of the community to regulate its affairs, or at least to monitor the processes of regulation. Both the timing of these cases and the highly unusual representation of a communal voice draw attention to them.

It may not be coincidental that one week after the appointment of the market head, the Armenians of Aintab adopted a similar kind of communal strategy. Six men came to court to form a mutual guarantorship—*kefalet,* in legal language—for the whole Armenian population of the city. They stated before the court:

> If any harm or damage is done by any Armenian from our district, we collectively assume responsibility for it. And we assume responsibility for those [Armenians] who come among us, those from outside. Henceforth if anything contrary is done by any of our community, hold [the six of] us accountable.[61]

The specific impetus for this move may have been an investigation one week earlier by the provincial governor's subaşı into a crime that had allegedly occurred within the Armenian community five years previously. Somehow the police had come by the allegation that an Armenian who had converted to Islam had been murdered by his former co-religionists.[62] This intrusion of the provincial governor's office into what was probably perceived as finished business within the dhimmi community seems to have precipitated the formation of the mutual guarantorship.

Other troubles may also have been brewing among the Armenian community—for example, the question of the local tavern, run by and for the local dhimmis. Two weeks after the mutual guarantorship was established, on January 15, another Armenian, Yahya b. Hızır, appeared in court to record payment for the tavern tax-farm. The yearly fee, 40,000 akçes, was a very large sum, far exceeding what the cadastral surveys listed as the authorized tax (16,000 akçes in the 1536 survey; 32,000 in the 1543 survey).[63] In short, there were in 1540 enough issues *within* the Armenian community to generate concern about their situation and to focus attention on communal strategies, such as the formation of a legally constituted representative body. However much their public lives might have meshed with those of the Muslims of Aintab, as a minority community of less than 400 in a total provincial population of some 36,000, the Armenians no doubt felt the pressures of uncertainty more acutely than did the province's Muslims. However, Armenians were not alone in fronting a community-generated mediating authority. The logic of such a self-protective move was no doubt reinforced by the general atmosphere within the city.

Let us close this section by considering the practice of *kefalet*—appointing or acting as guarantor or surety for another's whereabouts or debts—and its critical role in the process of bargaining for legitimacy through the law. This legal concept generated a central strategy in the formation of communal linkages in Aintab. In the court records, the most common form of kefalet was the appointment of a fiscal guarantor or bail agent *(kefil bi'l-mal)*. Some Aintab merchants, for example, never concluded a sale without requesting a guarantor for the purchaser's debt, and sellers of expensive houses often required such a guarantor (in this case, as a kind of mortgage surety). Another form of kefalet was the appointment of a guarantor for a person's whereabouts *(kefil bi'l-nefs)*, defined in the court record as someone "delegated to guarantee the presence of the individual whenever it might be requested." The Aintab judge appointed such a guarantor for the Kurdish man released from prison, and in earlier chapters we have seen other uses of this procedure. Additionally, kefalet emerges as a flexible and widely used practice that could also be invoked by groups who wished to assert a collective legal identity, as did the Armenian community of Aintab in the example above. This form of kefalet I have termed "mutual guarantorship."

The practice of mutual guarantorship appears to have undergirded the structure of guilds in Aintab. While no term for guild as such appears in the records, we do find terms for heads of professional collectives, such as the "sheikh" of the merchants or the bakers, or the "steward" *(kethüda)* of the butchers. It was the ritual of mutual guarantorship—a solemn swearing of an oath to uphold standards of the profession and to guarantee each other's financial health—that appears to have given legal or constitutional sanction to professional collectives in Aintab. A group of fifteen butchers, for example, renewed their oath when disciplined at court in June 1541 by their steward and the sarraf Matuk, who figured in this case in his capacity as farmer of the tax on butchers. It seemed that some butchers had been disregarding market practices by going directly to drovers to purchase stock, thus evading the tax that would be levied at the slaughterhouse and causing a shortage of stock for other butchers. Rather than impose a punishment on the guilty butchers, Matuk and the steward demanded that they take a self-disciplining oath not to behave in such a manner and to ensure a steady supply of meat in the city's butcher shops. The oath was entered by the court scribe into the register: "If henceforth we purchase stock directly from the drover and evade the tax, let each one of us be fined a thousand akçes."[64]

The case of the butchers, unlike the collective-forming act of the Armenians, appears to be an instance of repair and reinforcement of an existing mutual guarantorship after a breach of professional standards. Both cases, however, demonstrate the self-regulating and self-protecting elements of the mutual guarantorship, and its assumption that the mutual pact would be treated as a publicly recognized and legally valid entity. What I am emphasizing here is the role of the mutual guarantorship as an assertion of legitimacy—as a legally, economically, and morally constituted site of authority and administrative autonomy. In the context of the cases discussed above, the mutual guarantorship appears as a valuable communal resource in challenging the inroads of the imperializing power.

Taken together, all these events suggest that the Aintab community was gearing up in anticipation of further tension over claims to legitimate control of local resources and local society. At the end of May, city and province experienced a sharp intervention of state authority.

THE EVENTS OF JUNE 1541: DISCIPLINING SUBJECTS

On May 25, Aintab received the news that a new judge, Hüsameddin Efendi, had been appointed to the province's court. Although the judge did not actually arrive until June 23, the inscription of his appointment into the court record was marked by an unusual formality.[65] For one thing, it precipitated the opening of a new court register.[66] Most strikingly, it emphasized the presence of imperial power as the frame for the court's activities.

Notice of the appointment was inscribed at the head of the register's first page and signed by five witnesses (see figure 5). Of the five, three were the leading officials of the garrison stationed in the Aintab citadel: the warden of the citadel, the company commander, and the steward of the citadel. Another witness was the chief of police, who was the principal agent of the provincial governor of Aintab, the latter also a military appointee of the sultan. Only one signatory—the steward of the city—was a local "civilian" figure of authority.[67] This manner of hailing the new appointment served to remind all concerned that the court was a legitimate domain of state action.

The dedicatory page also provides a discursive echo of the investiture ceremonial, described by Jon Mandaville for late-Mamluk Damascus, in which a new judge was welcomed by the governor and his officials, who sometimes rode out to greet the judge as he approached the city.[68] Here, it is Ottoman military and administrative officials in Aintab, like the Mamluk governor the delegates of sultanic authority, who hail the appointment of the new judge.

But why not wait until the judge's actual arrival to inaugurate a new register? The news of the appointment actually heralded more than a new judge, for what took place between the announcement of the appointment and the judge's arrival a month later was a direct intervention of state authority in the person of a special agent assigned to discipline local tax-farming notables who were in debt to the state. The agent's identity and his mission were repeatedly inscribed in the register, in both Turkish and Arabic: "the imperial slave Ahmed Beg, appointed by royal memorandum for the purpose of collecting the arrears of the revenue-collectors named Mehmed b. Tapıncık and Ali b. Sikkak . . . "[69] Ahmed Beg took up office two days after the announcement of Hüsameddin Efendi's appointment and ended his work two days after the new judge's arrival. It is difficult not to regard the two appointments as linked.

This conjunction of events appears to signify an important stage in the incorporation of the Aintab court into the empire-wide network of provincial courts. Earlier chapters have noted the changes that occurred under these two individuals: namely, the expanded scope of the court's domain, the increasing volume of its business, its firmer defense of the integrity of property, and its increased scrutiny of contact between the sexes; the following chapter examines the court's growing control over violent crime. Without knowledge of the identity of judges preceding Hüsameddin Efendi—whether they were local mollas or outside appointments—it is difficult to know how significant the events of June 1541 were for the legal life of Aintab. But if developments in late-Mamluk Damascus, where judgeships became the province of a closed corporation of local families, are indicative of a general phenomenon in the northern Mamluk domains, the Aintab judgeship may well have been a local office, and Hüsameddin Efendi the first, or one of the first, to be appointed to the province through the central administration of the Ottomans.[70] Moreover, given the coincidence of dates and the shifts observable in the climate of the court, it is hard to resist speculating that Hüsameddin Efendi introduced Süleyman's newly issued law book to the court of Aintab.

The two principal targets of the special agent's mission—Mehmed b. Tapıncık and Ali b. Sikkak—had served from 1537 to 1539 as trustee and secretary of crown lands, respectively. (The secretary, Ali Çelebi, we have already met as the current head of the distinguished Sikkak family.) These offices were not referred to as tax-farms, most likely since they were granted directly from the state (as opposed to farmed out by the provincial governor, from his own stipendiary grant from the state). Yet because the individuals who held them were local and because local notables obviously competed for them, they can be considered a kind of "super tax-farm" for the purpose of this study.[71] The two former agents were, it seems, delinquent in paying up tax revenues due from their three-year tenure.[72] An imperial order directed that their "property and possessions" *(emlak ve esbab)* be sold to cover that portion of the imperial revenues *(mal-ı sultanî)* that they had withheld.[73] It was this process of divestment that the special agent was appointed to oversee.

In various transactions recorded at court, the two men sold off a variety of items: Mehmed b. Tapıncık sold nine shops in the Merchants' Bazaar for 27 gold florins, two horses for 20 florins, and to his daughter a house whose price was not recorded. Ali Çelebi sold two female slaves for 50 florins, two horses for 13 florins, and to his brother a quarter share of a house for 3 florins. Additionally he called in a 10-florin loan as well as payment for 15 florins worth of nutgalls (used in leather tanning—the purchaser of the nutgalls sold off 120 pieces of fine leather to cover his debt).[74] The total amount recovered through court-managed sales and debt-recovery came to 138 florins plus the price of the house purchased by Mehmed b. Tapıncık's daughter. Shortly before his departure, the special agent appears to have turned these moneys over to the Maraş fortress toward the quarterly salary payment for its garrison.[75] This latter transaction was typical of the local circulation of state funds, collected and disbursed within the bounds of a single regional governorate-general.

Special agent Ahmed Beg appeared quite anxious to see the two agents' debt fully covered. He himself purchased one of Mehmed b. Tapıncık's horses, for 5 florins. And he called in a tax-farm debt owed to Tapıncık by five men, including Hamza b. Sikkak, Ali Çelebi's brother.[76] On two occasions, he was stymied in his efforts to implement the sultan's firman. He tried to repossess a house that was allegedly the property of the former trustee, but it was proved in court to be a family waqf. And his attempt to force the sale of the former secretary's shares in an oil press and a horse was foiled when it was proven that the alleged partner was in fact the sole owner.[77] The court's role in this whole affair was, it appears, to ensure the legality of the implementation of the sultan's order. Mehmed b. Tapıncık and Ali Çelebi were not members of the ruling class, viewed in theory as slaves of the sovereign, over whose property and possessions the sovereign retained the right of seizure. They were ordinary, if locally influential, subjects with legal rights guaranteed by Islamic law. Hence the process of liquidating the two agents' property needed to be carried out under the auspices of the local court, which ensured that the sultan's disciplining of his subjects accorded with the dictates of a higher law. This attention to the niceties of legal procedure was particularly important in the years around 1540–1541, when the Ottoman sultanate was beginning to stake its claims to legitimacy as much on public elaboration of a rule of law as on conquest and force.

From another perspective, however, this use of the court to discipline errant agents can be seen as a critical element in the conspicuously public process of firming up the state's fiscal and political control. The sum of money raised from selling off horses, houses, slaves, and so forth was not particularly large (by way of comparison, in October 1540 the court imposed the sum of 575 florins as blood money on a villager who had committed murder).[78] Nor is it clear what portion of the two men's debt was actually covered by the liquidation of their property. Rather, the most significant aspect of the punishment may not have been the recovery of the debt itself but the conspicuous nature of the guilty parties' arraignment in the provincial court, which dragged on for several weeks, day after day. Moreover, numerous residents of Aintab and its villages were touched by the June events: those who purchased the items sold, some apparently at more than their market value (one of the slaves was shortly resold for a lesser sum);[79] those who scrambled to pay back debts to Ali Çelebi (the leather manufacturer had to sell the 120 pieces of leather at auction); and those whose affairs the liquidation procedure indirectly threatened (the alleged oil-press partner and the co-owners of family residences). We might think of the process by which Ali b. Sikkak and Mehmed b. Tapıncık were called to account as a kind of fiscal *siyaset*—the exemplary punishment of deficient servants of the crown. But in this case, the punished were not disobedient pashas or failed generals; instead, they were less-than-scrupulous tax-farmers.

The activities of the specially appointed prosecutor no doubt generated a good deal of speculative conversation in the city. Indeed, in the late spring of 1541, there was perhaps even more concern about the balance of power between Aintab and its sovereign than had been generated by the events of the previous fall. During the special agent's tenure, a number of developments occurred that cannot simply be accounted for as random events. Their general thrust was twofold: to ensure greater control of local revenues claimed by the state and to enlarge the domain of legal action to which the state or its representatives had access.

One means of accomplishing both ends, as we have seen, was the disciplining of delinquent fiscal agents. Mehmed b. Tapıncık and Ali Çelebi were not the only local notables whose debts to the crown were prosecuted in June. On the same day that the special agent first appeared in court to carry out his mandate, the sheikh of the Haci Baba dervish complex, Seyyid İsmail, was called into court to begin the process of paying back his own debt to the state: Seyyid İsmail owed 48 florins for the tax-farm to the revenues of Mervana, a village in the crown domain.[80] Like Ali Çelebi of the Sikkak family, Seyyid İsmail was senior member of a locally prominent lineage. His family's ancestral identity lay in the domain of religion—specifically, in the spiritual management of local dervish institutions (zaviye). The Haci Baba zaviye was the third-wealthiest dervish institution in the city and its environs, while the sheikh of the second wealthiest, the Dülük Baba zaviye, was Seyyid İsmail's son, Seyyid Şemseddin. Both zaviyes offered food and shelter to the indigent and were thus public service institutions as well as pilgrimage sites.[81] Engaging in the service of God and the poor among his children, it seems, was a barrier neither to serving Caesar nor to being reprimanded for failing to do so punctiliously.

Less sharply prosecutorial but almost as obvious and as consistently focused in the court records was the effort during the special agent's tenure to tighten up administrative procedures with respect to the Aintab market. The very first case to be recorded in the new register opened on May 25 involved the setting of a standard price by the market inspector, Şarabdar Abdurrahman. The inspector almost never appeared in the court records during the preceding eight months covered by the registers available for this study; indeed, the only time he came to court was the case of the press owners who refused to pay higher taxes the previous October. Henceforth, however, the disciplinary duties of the market inspector were to be carried out in court. Four days later, on the day following Seyyid İsmail's and Ali Çelebi's first appearances in court, Şarabdar was himself summoned on account of his 162-florin debt to the provincial governor for the market inspectorship tax-farm. The dual pressure on this particular tax-farm—forcing payment of its arrears and drawing its activities into the domain of the court—goes to the twofold thrust of the June court posited above. The market inspectorship, an office elaborated under Islamic law and historically a prominent element in urban culture, was a critical office in Aintab as well. It was the largest of all tax-farms, purchased for an annual sum of 115,000 akçes. In Aintab, the revenues of the market inspectorship included the traditional taxes on the scales and stamps used by shop owners as well as fines on substandard products; additionally, it included levies on merchandise coming into Aintab's markets to be sold and purchased goods going out (at the rate of 2 akçes per camel load, 1.5 per donkey or ox load, and 1 per horse or mule load).[82]

The rationale for exerting greater supervision over the office of the market inspector in 1541 was obvious: the revenues it controlled were rapidly increasing. This increase was testimony to the economic expansion of the province, a phenomenon that the central government failed neither to notice nor to exploit. The potential annual revenues of the market inspectorship had clearly been underestimated at 40,000 akçes, or 500 gold florins, in the 1536 cadastral survey of the province (as already noted, the tax-farm was actually going for nearly three times that amount in 1541). This error was rectified in the cadastral survey in 1543, where the market inspectorship was listed as generating 136,000 akçes annually.[83] Moreover, in 1543, revenues from the market inspectorship were no longer listed as part of the provincial governor's income, but instead had been transferred to the crown, where presumably they could be more directly and effectively supervised.

Aintab was a city with a tradition of legal sophistication, as its epithet of "little Bukhara" suggests. But its court was now also one node in an empire-wide legal system, a circumstance that required adjusting the local legal culture to new constellations of power and new issues. The assignment of the state prosecutor and a powerful judge to the Aintab court in the spring of 1541 was a more or less forced aspect of Aintab's legal acculturation into the Ottoman system. Yet the dynasty took pains to operate—or to *appear* to operate—within a discourse of higher legal authority. One of the points that the historian Neşri wished to make in his account of Osman Gazi's resistance to the notion of taxation was that the Ottoman sultanate had always been mindful of the need to reconcile its policies with God's law. Neşri's anecdote was a prescient prefiguring of Süleyman's project of promoting legalism and respect for law as key to the dynasty's ongoing campaign for legitimacy, a project that was gearing up in the late 1530s and early 1540s.

But in a provincial venue, legalism could also be a tool for articulating a *local* rhetoric of legitimacy. Tax-farms and other state-generated offices were ambiguously located. They occupied the sizable middle ground where the interests of the local elite, or at least those with access to such offices, overlapped with the interests of the state. When the latter tightened up fiscal and legal administration, revenues were likely to go up, enriching the coffers of local tax-farmers as well as of the state. On the other hand, when the state disciplined the errant among its local agents, revenues were likely to be transferred, as we have seen, from private pockets to local defense, or from private vineyards to public institutions such as the Mihaliye college. Like the trickle-down channels of tax-farming, local defense created jobs for middle-level members of local society, as did local educational and religious institutions. One of the most important results of the intervention of the state was thus the redistribution of resources, a process that might benefit the middle levels of the community as well as the elite and the state itself.

Obviously, there was bound to be tension as the central government made choices among the local candidates to fill the roster of state-generated offices. The public disciplining of the Sikkak family's most prominent member may have been linked to the government's attempt to smooth the entry of Matuk, the fiscal agent from Aleppo, into the management of Aintab's affairs. Did the actions of the state permanently affect balances of power in Aintab by altering membership in the influential elite that enjoyed control over local society and local resources? If we trace the fortunes of these individuals following the departure of the special agent, we find that most of those adversely affected by the year's events were soon back in the swing of things.

Take, for example, Ali Çelebi b. Sikkak. He and his brothers Hamza Çelebi and Kara Beg (a tax-farmer himself) disappeared from the court records for about three months after Ali's days at court, suggesting that they were waiting out a period of public humiliation or keeping a low profile so as to avoid the law, or perhaps both. But on September 16, 1541, Ali Çelebi made his first of several appearances as communal witness in court, a function that suggests his public rehabilitation (the other two witnesses of the case were Ahmed Ağa b. Demirci, a scion of one of the other two ayan lineages of Aintab, and the steward of the Maraş garrison—both locally influential individuals).[84] Three days later, we find Ali Çelebi in court to record a loan of 3,000 akçes to Seydi Ahmed b. Boyacı, scion of the third ayan family.[85] In other words, Ali Çelebi was once again a visible and active member of Aintab's elite. However, we do not again meet Ali Çelebi's erstwhile partner, Mehmed b. Tapıncık, the former trustee of crown lands. Perhaps he enjoyed neither the family name nor the family resources that enabled Ali Çelebi to resume his local position and accumulate enough money within three months of the divestment procedures to make a sizable loan. Clearly it was the most amply endowed of local citizens who succeeded at high levels of the tax-farming business.

And what of Matuk, the newly appointed provincial treasurer? By the summer of 1541, some nine months after the resistance he initially encountered, Matuk appears to have integrated (or reintegrated) himself into the local business and financial community. We find him dealing with local merchants in cloth and in the expensive commodity of blue dye. For a purchase of 108 florins' worth of the latter, he put up as collateral houses in Aleppo and in the Kadi district of Aintab (the house he owned in Aintab appears to have been a historic dwelling—it was known as "the Haci Enbiya house"). It would seem that Matuk overextended his resources, for almost immediately he appeared in court to deal with arrears in payment for his sarraf tax-farm and for his two municipal tax-farms (the weighing scales and slaughterhouse revenues). His debts did not prevent him from backing local individuals bidding for small tax-farms, however. And toward the end of August 1541, Matuk joined forces with the market inspector, Şarabdar Abdurrahman, and his partner[86] to consolidate the three largest municipal tax-farms (the market inspectorship and his own two tax-farms), a move that may have helped Matuk cope with his tax-farm debts.[87] In other words, Matuk reemerged as an influential local player around the time that Ali Çelebi b. Sikkak also reappeared in the court records.

The fortunes of these individuals elicit two observations. First, while the state disciplined, it was not overly punitive, in Aintab at least. The case of Ali Çelebi suggests that individual notables were not permanently disabled, even though they might be made the object of the state's lessons. Indeed, the central government had an interest in maintaining a local pool of potential tax-farmers, and was unlikely to entirely alienate a resource as valuable as the Sikkak family. And second, the local community had the capacity to "naturalize" outsiders into its networks and rules of conduct. Resisted as official sarraf by the city's authorities, Matuk was not resisted by the village headmen and textile manufacturers who took advantage of his role as banker and his commercial connections with Aleppo. Moreover, in debt to the state like so many other Aintab tax-farmers, Matuk was eventually called to account by the same legal machinery that put him in office in the first place. Indeed, his alliance with the market inspectors was cast in the court record as a mutual guarantorship, suggesting that this protective legal mechanism, typically employed by the less powerful, was appreciated by high-level entrepreneurs as well.[88]

These two observations lead to a third: for a historically borderland locality like Aintab, adjusting to the reign of a new overlord and accommodating to consequent reconfigurations at the local level was nothing new. The Ottoman regime in 1540–1541 may have been more effective than recent regimes in efforts at local control, but the community also had its own internal mechanisms of response that provided a certain flexibility in dealing with shifting circumstances. Accommodating to the Ottoman state's claims of legitimacy may not have been so difficult for those who could count on a share of its bounty.

But what of all those residents of Aintab province who did not occupy the middle ground of interests shared between state and local society? What of those who did not belong to the *eşraf ve ayan*, the urban elite whose stature derived either from their religious pedigree, training, and office or from their membership in recognized entrepreneurial lineages? As we saw in the matter of protecting property in chapter 6, ordinary individuals had to maneuver within narrower parameters. By way of epilogue, let us examine one more cluster of cases whose similarities and timing demand our attention. These cases involve the mutual guarantorship, whose self-regulating and self-protective aspects have been discussed above.

Within one week of the special agent's departure and the new judge's assumption of office, three groups—the bakers of the city, the butchers, and a group of eight military pensioners—appeared in court to register mutual guarantorships.[89] (The new judge took up office on June 23, and the guarantorships were registered on the 25th, 27th, and 29th.) Each record in the court register consisted of a list of the group's members and the statement that they had become "guarantors and responsible parties for one another" (*birbirlerine mütezaminin ve mütekafilin*). The records for the bakers and butchers were a bit more elaborate than that of the pensioners: their lists (containing fifteen and sixteen individuals, respectively) were headed by the sheikh or steward of their guild, and their oath of mutual guarantorship included a statement of the professional standard they pledged to abide by. For example, the bakers' statement read: "The aforementioned individuals have mutually guaranteed and accepted mutual responsibility for the uninterrupted production of bread, such that their bread will be without defect and bread will always be available in their shops . . . "; the butchers also pledged a steady supply of meat in their shops, and added the poetic note that they would be mutual guarantors "in good times and bad."

Why the apparent rush by these three groups to the new judge's court? The most plausible answer is that they hoped to assert, or reassert, a claim to legitimate self-representation and self-regulation, thereby preparing themselves for the kind of intense scrutiny of market practices that had been taking place during the tenure of the special agent. Given that both bakers and butchers had been disciplined at court during the previous month, their collectives were perhaps serving notice to the new judge of their awareness of the shifting environment of the court. Lacking the stature of such longtime tax-farmers as Ali Çelebi and the market inspector Şarabdar, who had the individual resources to bounce back from disciplinary action, butchers, bakers, and pensioners sought relief from their greater vulnerability in joint action.

Perhaps these groups were influenced by the Armenian community of Aintab. Once again, it is the matter of coincidental timing that alerts us to what may be shared legal strategies. On June 12, two weeks before the three pledgings of mutual guarantorship, the local Armenian community appeared in court to renegotiate the tavern tax-farm. Instead of the single tax-farmer, Yahya b. Hızır, who had renewed his lease in early January, now twenty-nine Armenians (quite possibly the entire population of household heads in the city) [90] appeared in court to form a mutual guarantorship for the tavern tax-farm. This move to consortium management was the only change in the tax-farm contract, as the yearly fee remained the same.[91] Given the context of the special agent's efforts to tighten up the regulation of tax-farms, the Armenians appear to have once again employed the principle of legal solidarity, in this case protecting the integrity of the tavern and the community's control of it. Perhaps they also wished to forestall the possibility of a bidding war among themselves over the tavern tax-farm, which might have undermined communal solidarity from another direction.

What stands out about these cases involving mutual guarantorship is that the guarantors were all persons on the margins of Aintab society. That marginality was not economic, since the butchers and bakers were shop owners and the Armenians were apparently all willing to assume a significant financial responsibility. Rather, it was a question of religious, ethnic, or tribal identity (the latter two overlapped). The minority status and small numbers of the Armenians in a city of some 1,850 households is obvious. As for the butchers and bakers, their names suggest that a number of them were of Turkmen background—that is, persons with tribal loyalties and perhaps a religious identity tinged with shi'i elements.[92] The butchers especially might be expected to have ties with nomadic groups who purveyed animal stock; indeed, it was contacts of this nature that apparently encouraged their tax evasion. As we will see in relation to the murder cases discussed in the next chapter, government authorities were uneasy about the potential of tribal groups to spawn regional conflict, hence the effort during the June court to bring tribal dissension into the purview of the court. Possible, or even imagined, cultural connections that provoked the association of nomadic tensions with the butchers and bakers may have added to their marginality. The apparently unjustified imprisonment of the Kurd who was released as a result of community protest suggests popular suspicion of the state's criminalizing bias against another ethno-tribal population.

Religious and ethnic difference placed these groups outside the circle of the urban elite. Unlike another outsider, the Jewish sarraf Matuk, they enjoyed neither the financial leverage nor the state backing that allowed Matuk to move within elite circles, even if he could not claim insider status. The frequent formation of legal solidarities among non-elite circles suggests that those lacking high urban status experienced a greater threat from incorporation into an expanding empire. Especially threatening may have been the administrative and legal consolidation that was taking place in these years, particularly the integration of local courts into the political hierarchy of the empire and the enhanced capacity of the court to scrutinize local affairs. For groups in the population located outside the circle of bounty that linked local elites to the state and protected them from permanent damage at the hands of the law, collective action was the most effective way to claim a legitimate public voice. The mutual guarantorship permitted marginal groups to announce their existence, to validate the defense of their interests under the law, and thus to enter public debate. It compensated somewhat for the absence of class solidarities that enabled entrepreneurial and religious elites to enter into productive alliances with the state. The frequent deployment of this legal mechanism suggests that these groups were not powerless: they readily made proactive use of the venue of the court. At the same time, however, the widespread reliance on legal solidarities among the non-elite demonstrates the uneven impact of imperialization at the provincial level.

8

Punishment, Violence, and the Court

Physical violence was a common affair in Aintab province, at least among men. The court records inform us that men hit each other, pulled beards and yanked collars, beat each other with a variety of objects, drew knives on each other, and killed each other with arrows, shovels, and other instruments. Yet the court record for 1540–1541 lacks any note of any violence visited on the bodies of Aintabans during the punishment of the guilty. While it mentions the criminal penalties of jailing, payment of blood money, banishment, and public humiliation it alludes only indirectly to the floggings routinely prescribed in Ottoman penal law and never to more dire bodily punishments or to execution. All of the latter were prescribed by sharia as well as kanun.

What we see at work here is a division between trial and punishment, between judge and police—*kadı* and *ehl-i örf*—and, more broadly, between the religio-legal and imperial sources of authority in the empire. One of the thrusts of Süleyman's legal reforms was to promote the expanding system of local courts as the principal venue of legal administration and in fact of all public business. According to the division of labor promoted by the regime, the court established the innocence or guilt of a suspect, while the executive authorities sentenced and punished the guilty in accordance with Ottoman kanun. This effort to separate judgment from punishment may seem routine and natural at first glance, but two habits needed to be broken before the system envisioned by Süleyman and his legal advisors could be fully realized (if indeed it ever was). One was the popular habit of looking to governors and local political leaders for the resolution of disputes, and the other was abusive meddling by the ehl-i örf in aspects of local judicial administration outside its jurisdiction. A habit that the regime wished to cultivate, on the other hand, was getting people to look instead to the court for the management of crime and its aftermath.

The absence of records of punishments to parallel the abundant records of court hearings is one reason why the question of punishment is rarely raised in studies of court records.[1] Nevertheless, it is a question that is nearly impossible to avoid for the mid–sixteenth century, a time when the consolidation of judicial administration was such a salient preoccupation of the Ottoman regime. So was the formulation of sultanic kanun, which not only laid out criminal penalties but also worked to clarify the relationship between judge and police. To ignore punishment in a study of court culture is in effect to leave out half the story. We have already seen how criminal codes formed a textual field for displaying notions of social hierarchy. Ottoman criminal regulations can also be read as a map that locates punishment in the architecture of imperial justice and that highlights a central feature in the constitution of sultanic sovereignty—the regime's control over its subjects. Such questions inevitably recall Michel Foucault's study of punishment and its exploration of the ways in which the disciplining of individuals in their bodies is implicated in larger issues of power and modes of control.[2] Moreover, if we are concerned with users of the court and their strategies, the question of punishment cannot be neglected. It was the invisible frame for many cases at the Aintab court, since awareness of what awaited the guilty affected how people conducted themselves at court.

The matter of punishment intimately connected the Ottoman regime with local society. While promoting the rule of law was a goal of Süleyman's reign, the reverse side of the coin was controlling local violence, whether it arose from the legitimate exercise of police authority or from the armed resistance of the disaffected. There was a noticeable shift in emphasis from the reign of Selim I, conqueror and avenger of violence with violence, to that of Süleyman, who was able, over the course of his long reign, to substitute legal controls for brute force. Nevertheless, the Ottoman dynasty jealously guarded its license to *siyaset,* the exercise of summary punishment in the name of law and order. The chapter opens by considering the question of siyaset.

The sultan could not be everywhere at once, however, and so the problem of delegating executive authority over a vastly expanded empire was critical. Much of the chapter is devoted to issues that were raised by law enforcement at the grassroots level. The prosecution of crime and the imposition of criminal penalties at the provincial level were largely the work of local people, with the important exceptions of the provincial governor and the governor-general. In the years covered by this study, local authorities might abuse their mandate in various ways, extorting excessive fines from the guilty, framing the innocent as guilty, applying judicial torture in an unauthorized manner, and imposing fines where they had no right to do so.

The Ottoman regime apparently hoped to meet the challenge of regulating provincial law enforcement, in part at least, by promoting use of the courts as a venue for adjudicating crime.

The chapter ends by looking at the treatment of murder at the court of Aintab. Murder cases are a laboratory for exploring a number of themes of the chapter as well as of the book: the links between court and police, the local culture of violent crime, and the existence of a sophisticated repertoire of dispute-resolution techniques in Aintab. The analysis of five murder cases and two instances of suspicion of murder suggests that this was a community that had more or less successfully worked out—or was in the process of working out—a modus vivendi among legal resources at hand.

SIYASET, OR THE RIGHT TO PUNISH

By the Ottoman sixteenth century, the right and duty of sultans to keep order by punishing crime and civil disorder was well elaborated in theory and practice. The imperial prerogative of siyaset (*siyâsa,* in Arabic) as it was practiced by the Ottomans can be defined as the right to inflict severe corporal or capital punishment—almost always violence to the body, sometimes execution—if the public interest or the integrity of the state or its religion demanded it. The concept of siyaset had a long history in Islamic states, and this Ottoman usage represented only one of its range of meanings and applications.[3] In the premodern Ottoman context, the term is sometimes translated as "administrative punishment" because of its noncanonical nature: in other words, it was not a prerogative originating in sharia. Siyaset gave the ruler the authority to execute rebels, enemies, apostates and schismatics, and others who, though they might merit a lesser punishment under sharia, were construed as threatening the commonweal. For example, habitual thieves were liable to execution under siyaset but not under sharia.

Neither the concept nor the practice of siyaset was an Ottoman innovation. Rather, siyaset was a sovereign prerogative long recognized by Muslim thinkers as necessary to public order. The justification of siyaset was based on the acknowledgment that Islamic law would be ineffective without the executive arm of the state. Siyaset was also conceded to be necessary because sharia was far from comprehensive in terms of penal law. This sovereign function had been given authoritative rationale under the Mamluks. The influential Hanbali scholar Ibn Taymiyya (d. 1328) called for *siyasa shariyya*— "sharia-sanctioned siyaset"—that is, the reconciliation of the authorities' inevitable pursuit of law and order with the principles of sharia. While stressing the superiority of sharia, Ibn Taymiyya's work had the effect of sanctioning the reality of political power. Yet not all Muslim religious authorities conceded the legitimacy of siyasa. Ibn Taymiyya himself, a Damascene, pointed to regional differences in its scope, noting the contrast between "the custom prevailing in these lands of Syria and Egypt" and "other countries, like the Maghreb, [where] the military authority has no jurisdiction whatever, its function being merely to execute decrees of the judiciary."[4] Moreover, there were always opponents among the religious classes of the Mamluks and the Ottomans who were fearful of the potential excesses of siyaset, and who saw reasoning such as that of Ibn Taymiyya as a debasing of sharia. In the Ottoman sixteenth century, the arguments of Ibn Taymiyya and his disciple Ibn Qayyim Al-Jawziyya were repeated by a religious scholar named Dede Efendi and resisted by another, Kınalızade Ali Efendi.[5]

What was the jurisdiction of Ottoman "military authority" in relation to the judiciary, to use Ibn Taymiyya's formulation? Perhaps the best way to characterize Ottoman legal administration is as a system of two justices, one for members of the ruling class (the *askerî*, or "military authority") and one for ordinary citizens of the empire. The former were directly subject to the sultan's judgment, the latter to judgment by the judge and his court. In other words, the sultan exercised the right of summary punishment—of execution without trial by a judge—over high-ranking state officials and military commanders who helped him govern, a right that he did not enjoy over the mass of his subjects.[6] Ordinary citizens were also subject to punishment under the authority of the sultan and his agents, but only *after* a trial in court. Siyaset as capital or severe corporal punishment could be inflicted on subjects after trial in cases of dire or habitual offense. With respect to the law, then, there were two Ottoman populations governed by two separate constitutions. The sultan's right of siyaset in the one was absolute; in the other, circumscribed.

This practice of separate justices—ruling-class justice and subject justice—is related to the political heritage of earlier Middle Eastern regimes. The existence of a separate legal regime for the ruling class is related to a theory of state inherited by the Ottomans in which ruling dynasties were considered to exist as a political layer independent of and suspended above the various groups that made up society.[7] In the Ottoman view, sovereignty inhered in the dynastic family as a whole—*Al-i Osman,* the "House" of the eponymous founder of the dynastic state, Osman. The dynasty was practically conceived as a vast household and privileged members of the ruling elite as part of this household—indeed, as its slaves. Scholars still debate whether the Ottoman practice of ruling-elite or "military" slavery, a seasoned Islamic political tradition, observed the niceties of Islamic jurisprudence regarding slavery; whatever the technical illegalities, however, military commanders and pashas who served the sultan as ministers of council and governors-general, as well as the women of the imperial harem, were considered slaves of the royal household. Slaves were acquired as war booty, as gifts, through purchase from slave dealers, and through the legally dubious levy of children imposed on the subject Christian population of the em-

pire. These captives, none of Muslim origin, were converted to Islam, re-
named, and trained to serve the dynasty. The most promising among them
were educated within the royal palace complex in the mores of Islam and of
elite culture, and, if male, in martial skills; if female, in domestic skills.

The privileges of elite slavery were temporary. Slaves were denied many
of the rights of ordinary subjects—for example, the right to pass their estates on to their heirs. Those who rose through the elaborate system of education and training to hold the highest offices of government might be
enormously wealthy during their lifetimes, but their estates reverted back
to the imperial treasury upon their death; their wealth, in other words, was
largesse temporarily granted as befitting the servant of a great household.
Just as he controlled his slave servants' religious and cultural identity and
their material environment, the sultan controlled their right to life, taking
it if they were judged to have violated their bond of servitude. This was
a paradox at the heart of the Ottoman system—that ordinary subjects enjoyed rights denied to those by whom they were governed. One of their
rights was immunity from the sultan's direct power of life and death.

As sultan, Süleyman showed no reluctance over the course of his forty-
six-year reign in exercising siyaset. Conspicuous objects of his imperial discipline included defeated rulers, rebel pashas, religious deviants, and even
two of his own sons. To avert a threat to the integrity of his rule, Süleyman
executed his famous grand vezir and intimate companion, İbrahim Pasha,
accusing him of designs on the sultanate. For betraying the interests of
empire, he executed two other grand vezirs, like İbrahim his brothers- or
sons-in-law. For threatening the sunni religious foundations of the empire,
the sultan executed a number of schismatics. And he had an enormously
popular prince, Mustafa, killed in 1553 because he represented a political
threat to his father, and the rebel prince Beyazit executed in 1561. In his
exercise of summary punishment, Süleyman was not so different from his
fellow monarchs of the sixteenth century, with the possible exception of the
execution of his sons. By Ottoman standards as well, the latter was an extraordinary and much lamented measure.

While many of Süleyman's acts of siyaset occurred later in his reign,
Aintabans in 1540 would have been aware of a number of earlier instances
of punitive authority. Among the pashas executed at Süleyman's orders before 1540 were Janberdi Ghazali, the rebel governor of Syria who doubted
Süleyman's capabilities when he first came to the throne; Hain ("Traitor")
Ahmed Pasha, the rebel governor of Egypt who was angry at not being promoted to grand vezir, executed in 1524; and the grand vezir İbrahim Pasha,
executed in 1536 shortly after his brilliant conduct of the two-year military
campaign against Iran (during which he had wintered at Aleppo). A number of the rebel "heretics" who lost their lives led armed uprisings that had
originated in central Anatolia, where their followers included large num-

bers of Turkmen tribesmen; they may even have numbered followers in the Aintab region. The most widespread uprising was that of Shah Kalender in 1525; in the struggle against him, several governors-general and provincial governors lost their lives, including the governor of Bire, Aintab's neighbor to the east.[8]

Foucault has identified the grisly public spectacle of physical torture and eventual death through mutilation of the body as the hallmark of premodern punishment. The spectacle of death by public defilement and dismemberment certainly existed among the Ottomans, where it was enacted in inverse proportion to the status of the criminal. For those of greatest status—members of the royal household, including the highest-ranking pashas—execution was a muted event, carried out in private. The mode of death was strangling by bowstring, an act that visited a minimum of violence on the body without bloodshed and used as its instrument an honored weapon in Ottoman chivalric culture. This ritual act belonged to the semiotics of imperial household honor. Part of the code of conduct among the slave elite was to accept death with dignity; in turn, a dignified death was provided. In this way, the moral and cultural unity of the imperial household was preserved, for public disfigurement in death of the august among the sultan's servants would have been an unseemly betrayal of the private rituals of sovereignty. Their fall from grace was marked in other ways, most conspicuously by the denial of public honor in burial: the executed were generally interred in an isolated location and without the dignity of a tomb.[9]

Grisly death was the mark of lesser beings. It was the bodies of those who openly rebelled against the public interest that were visibly and publicly mutilated in death. When Selim I executed the Dulkadir ruler Alaeddevle for betraying the Ottoman cause, he sent the prince's head together with the heads of his son and his vezir as victory trophies to the Mamluk sultan Al-Ghawri (an incident described more fully in chapter 1). The heads of political rebels were typically mounted on pikes at the outer gates of the imperial residence, the Topkapı gate in Istanbul, the Bab Zuwayla in Cairo. When Janbirdi Ghazali, the rebel governor of Damascus, was executed, his head was dispatched to Istanbul, along with 1,000 ears cut from his supporters.[10] A public execution that aroused a great deal of public antipathy was that of Sheikh İsmail Mashuki, who had acquired a large and devoted following, particularly among soldiers, through his preaching at major mosques in Istanbul. When he and twelve of his disciples were beheaded for heresy in the Istanbul Hippodrome in 1529, popular opinion over his guilt was split, with one faction holding him to be a martyred saint.[11]

In one sense, the sultanic prerogative of siyaset was absolute, for siyaset was justified as a power necessarily unique to the sovereign. Yet in another sense it was limited, for chronic abuse of this power could bring a sultan down. While he possessed the terrible weapon of summary execution, the sultan was at the same time expected to display the virtues of forbearance, generosity, and mercy.[12] Execution was only the last resort: heretics were to be given the opportunity to recant, and members of the ruling elite were first disciplined through measures such as reprimand, demotion, and temporary banishment. Moreover, the sultan was expected to seek the counsel of his advisers in so grave a matter as execution: schismatics, for example, were not punished until actual heresy had been established by the top-ranking religious officials of the empire. Ethical writings stressed the importance of combining force and forbearance, and a lack of balance between them was considered a flaw in the exercise of sovereignty.

But what of actual controls on the sovereign's exercise of siyaset? Among the Ottomans, disciplining the sultan was largely a matter of moral suasion, at least through the sixteenth century. Tempering the sultan's use of his awesome powers was the role of his closest advisers—his grand vezir, his mother, and especially his religious counselors. The nature of moral controls over the sultan are well illustrated in a story told about Selim I and his chief mufti, Ali Cemali (who between 1503 and 1525 served three sultans in that capacity). Because of the story's relevance to a number of the issues considered in this section, I quote Richard Repp's account of the incident in full:

> [The story] involves an order by Selim for the execution of 150 treasury officials whose offense, however, is not made clear. Ali Cemali heard of this and went to the divan [imperial council] where he was greeted with some surprise as it was not customary for the Müfti to appear in the divan except for an affair of some moment. He was given the chief seat, and word was sent to the sultan of his desire to speak with him. He was permitted by the sultan to enter alone, and when he had greeted him and sat down, he said: "The duty of the Müftis is to watch over the after-life of the sultan. I have heard that you have ordered the executing of 150 men, the execution of whom is not lawful under the sharia. You must pardon them." Selim was angered and replied: "You are interfering in the affairs of state *(amr-i saltanat)*. This is not part of your duty." Ali Cemali then answered: "Nay rather I interfere in the matter of your after-life; that is part of my duty. If you pardon them, you will have salvation; if not, you will suffer a great punishment." At this Selim's anger passed and he pardoned all of them. Ali Cemali conversed with him for an hour, and then, when he rose to go, said: "I have spoken about the matter of your after-life; it remains for me to speak about generosity of spirit *(al-murû'a)*." When Selim asked what he would say, Ali Cemali replied: "These men are the slaves of the sultan. Does it befit the integrity ('*irḍ* [also, 'honor']) of the sultanate that they should beg from the people?" When Selim replied that it did not, Ali Cemali said: "Then set them again in their offices." The sultan agreed to this but said that he would punish them for their dereliction in their duty. Ali Cemali agreed that this was lawful since such punishment *(al-ta'zîr)* was entrusted to the judgment of the sultan; and so saying, he departed.[13]

Ali Cemali could not subject the sultan as ruler to a higher order of siyaset. (Contrast this with the story related in chapter 5 of Molla Feneri, the chief religious authority under Bayezid I, who could reject the sultan as witness in a court case—a civil as opposed to sovereign function.) Rather, Ali Cemali's success in persuading the sultan to a position that was legally and politically tenable lay in appealing to his spiritual welfare as well as to the honor of the dynasty.

Real controls—that is, institutionalized mechanisms for limiting sultanic authority—came only later, in the seventeenth century, when the Ottoman state was governed less by the fluid structures supporting the charismatic leadership of a ruler who was principally a conqueror than by the more bureaucratic structures and procedures of a state geared toward the stable administration of far-flung territories. From the beginning of the seventeenth century onward, the overthrow of an abusive or incompetent sultan became a central feature of an unwritten Ottoman constitution: more than half the sultans who came to the throne during the last three centuries of Ottoman rule were deposed. But during the long period when the empire was expanding through conquest, the sultans were more or less absolute. The public was nevertheless quite ready to make distinctions among them. Popular opinion faulted Süleyman's great-grandfather Mehmed the Conqueror (d. 1482) and his father "Yavuz" ("the Stern") Selim (d. 1520) because they abused the rights of some of their subjects. Their siyaset, in other words, was not tempered by sharia. On the other hand, Süleyman's grandfather Bayezid II (d. 1512) was known as "Veli" ("the Saint"), while Süleyman himself was "Kanunî" ("the Legislator," "the Legally Minded"). It worth noting that Bayezid II and Süleyman, remembered for their piety and justice, were perhaps the most active sultans in compiling kanun, or law that had as one of its purposes the elaboration and codification of siyaset. Even Süleyman's record of executions did not diminish his reputation for justice. Four years before the sultan's death in 1566, the Venetian ambassador to Istanbul commented that he was "held by all to be very wise and very just but extraordinarily cruel toward those who attempt, or in his judgment might attempt, anything against either his sovereignty or his person."[14] That the sultan could be simultaneously very cruel and very just was a function of the separate systems of Ottoman justice.

SIYASET AND SEX

Süleyman was rightly jealous of the prerogative of siyaset, for it was a key symbol of sovereignty. Especially during the pacification of newly conquered territories, it was essential, from the regime's point of view, to establish a monopoly on the means of violence. Both the instruments of and the justification for violence needed to be conspicuously removed from the hands of local lords and others dislodged from power by the Ottoman conquest. This process had only recently been accomplished by 1540, if indeed it was ever accomplished in full. Among the most intractable areas were those dominated by Turkmen tribal groups that had been part of the Dulkadir domain of which Aintab had formed a southern boundary. A document dating from sometime between 1529 and 1536—a call for help addressed to the sultan and grand vezir from one Musa Beg, governor of the central Anatolian province of Bozok—demonstrates the difficulties encountered by the regime in imposing its authority on these populations.[15] In Bozok, the local tribal chiefs *(boy begleri)* were seizing criminal fines now due to the Ottoman governor and, furthermore, abusing the local population in order to extract excessive and unwarranted taxes and criminal penalties. Musa Beg listed ten such areas of abuse and then closed his petition by stating that this sort of disorder had never occurred when the Dulkadir lords had ruled over the region. In other words, he was complaining about the lack of Ottoman support in backing up his assignment in the area.

Musa's list repays our close attention, since his allegations reveal much about the local culture of crime and punishment, particularly its involvement with sexual conduct and moral reputation. They also cast indirect light on the relationship between judicial and punitive processes. Abuses committed by the tribal chiefs included the following: They forced girls to marry whichever local male offered the highest dower, thus jacking up the marriage tax and violating the wishes of the girl, her family, and the fiancé they might already have chosen. Alternatively, the chiefs extracted bribes from fathers in exchange for letting them arrange their daughters' marriages without interference. They seized fines from unmarried women suspected of sexual misconduct before guilt was established, and they illegally took fines from married adulterers, thus preventing the provincial governor from enacting the siyaset penalty that was his duty and his due. If a thief was caught in someone's house, they claimed he'd gone there for sex, thus turning the crime into one whose fines were due to them; by so doing, they stood in the way of the prosecution of theft and once again prevented the governor from executing his duty. They even incited young unmarried men to sexually assault women of social standing or their daughters so as to render the latter vulnerable to high fines for illicit sex; with the same goal they incited women to involve themselves with the (unmarried) sons of prominent families. Finally, they claimed that they themselves were exempt from punishment (siyaset) should they commit rape or murder, because they were figures of authority.

We might ask why the tribal chiefs had any hand at all in local judicial administration. The answer can be discerned with the help of the Dulkadir law book. Known as the *kanunname* of Alaeddevle, this law book was confirmed by the Ottomans as operative for the Dulkadir region after the death of the last Dulkadir ruler in 1522. The tribal chiefs could claim to be figures of authority (and therefore, so they asserted, exempt from prosecution) because the Ottomans had confirmed their rights to collect taxes and punitive fines. Moreover, the Ottomans had made some of them timariot soldiers (Musa Beg referred to the troublemakers as *boy begi, sipahi,* and *sipahizade*). The law book can also explain why the chiefs were preying on specific groups, since it clarifies whose crimes they could profit from: among the fines that Dulkadir practice had awarded to the ruler (now assigned to the Ottoman provincial governor) were those for theft, homicide, and sexual offenses by married men; fines going to chiefs of the different tribes (confirmed by the Ottomans for the chiefs) included those levied for sexual offenses by unmarried men and women.[16] Hence the chiefs' efforts to construe theft as sexual misconduct and to stir up sexual trouble involving unmarried males.

The illegal and socially destabilizing conduct of the tribal chiefs had several repercussions for judicial procedure. The chiefs violated legal practice by harassing the local population and by subverting the governor's authority. They also prevented the work of whatever authority—judge, governor, or local elder—was charged with deciding the innocence or guilt of potential offenders. No wonder that the Ottoman regime eventually abolished the Dulkadir code, substituting the *Kanun-ı Osmani,* the imperial Ottoman law book, in its second "reform" wave of issuing local law books.[17]

A striking aspect of Musa Beg's petition to the sultan is the degree to which crime and punishment in Bozok had to do with sexual relations and honor. Women and men were vulnerable even when they attempted to legitimate their intimate lives in marriage. Those lives were not so intimate, it turns out. The level of control endorsed by Musa's letter—it argued only that control had been distorted into oppression—had as its corollary the unceasing scrutiny of social relations through the twin processes of taxing marriage and punishing indiscretion.[18] Lawlessness in these processes posed a direct and dangerous threat to individuals and families.

Were the problems in Bozok, a region that perennially challenged central authority, paralleled in Aintab? The next section will explore this question through the court records, although they are not ideal for that purpose since abuses in legal enforcement were probably most often handled within the hierarchy of executive, not judicial, authority, as Musa's letter shows. However, we do have an important clue in the law book issued for Aintab in 1536, in the following clause: "Money should not be taken as siyaset-substitute from those who have incurred siyaset; when people commit a crime, let them punish [them] according to what they deserve. For every finable crime which occurs, great or small, the Ottoman Kanun shall be consulted and [the fine] exacted; force shall not be used to exact anything more than that."[19] Such an order could well have been issued against the Bozok tribal chiefs, who stood in the way of legitimate punishment by

siyaset and who also exacted illegally high penalties from the local population. The clause thus suggests that similar abuses were being perpetrated in
Aintab province. Perhaps they were widespread in the whole region.

Why was the problem of controlling insubordinate ehl-i örf officially addressed in Aintab earlier than in other parts of the former Dulkadir domain? We may learn something from comparing the dates when different
provinces were assimilated to standardized legal administration—that is,
when the Kanun-ı Osmanî, the periodically updated imperial law book, began to be applied locally for criminal justice, thereby displacing former
codes. The law book for Bozok, a version of the law book of the Dulkadir
ruler Alaeddevle, was apparently not revoked until 1558 or 1559.[20] As for
Maraş, capital of the Dulkadir principality in its later years and capital of the
Ottoman governorate-general of the same name (to which Aintab was
administratively subordinated during the 1530s), it may have been as late as
1563 that Alaeddevle's law book was displaced.[21] Uprooting Dulkadir practice was perhaps particularly difficult in Maraş, which was apparently the
prime referent for Alaeddevle's law book: the latter's catalogue of fines was
headed "in the district of Maraş [the regulations] concerning fines [have]
since ancient times [been as follows]."[22] But the law book for Aintab was issued in 1536, and, as noted above, it specifically instructed local officials
to refer to the Kanun-ı Osmanî in awarding criminal fines. Was Aintab
brought under Ottoman law relatively early because it was more easily paci-
fied? or because it was more amenable to cultivation as a regional legal
center?

In connection with the question of whether Aintab experienced the
kinds of problems plaguing the people of Bozok, it is useful to remember
that Aintab city, an old and relatively sophisticated urban settlement, lay
at the southern reaches of Dulkadir control and was thus not as influenced
by the cultural regime of the largely tribal principality as was Maraş. At
the same time, Aintab province contained a significant population of both
nomadic and settled Turkmen. It also appears to have had its own group
of tribal chiefs-turned-timariot. We have to wonder what it meant for
Aintab to be removed from the governorate-general of Aleppo to that of
Dulkadir, as it was sometime in the 1530s. Was the transfer made because
of Aintab city's ability to instruct Maraş in civilized urban behavior (its
acquisition of the Kanun-ı Osmanî as its penal standard was early), or because Aintab's tribal population was best overseen by a pasha who carried
the Dulkadir title? The tribulations suffered by Aintab in later centuries at
the hands of predatory local lords suggest that old habits were not easily
eradicated.[23]

In the light of Musa Beg's petition and the questions it raises, the regime's efforts under Süleyman to strengthen local courts was a critical move
in promoting different habits of dispute resolution and law enforcement.

One goal was to get deliberations about innocence and guilt into the court and out of the hands of the executive authorities. Promoting justice by judges was no doubt in part a sincere effort to support the Islamic moorings of legal administration, but it was also a strategy for breaking the power of local lords. Moreover, it helped control, through a system of checks and balances, the authority that the regime had bestowed willy-nilly on its own pashas and begs. For some subjects of the sultan, taking one's problems to the judge was a new habit, particularly in the matter of sexual offenses. Old habits are revealed in the Aintab court in the statement made by one Fatma bt. Cuma in August 1541 when she withdrew an accusation of rape she had made earlier: "If I ever complain again to the governor *(beg)* or to any of the authorities *(ehl-i örf)* or to anyone else," she said, "I'll pay penance of 1,000 akçes . . . and you can also publicly shame me by blackening my face."[24] Not surprisingly, the penalty of face-blacking, absent in the Kanun-ı Osmanî, was a feature of the Dulkadir law book ("if a person's false witness against another . . . becomes evident, his or her face should be blackened and a fine of 5 gold pieces imposed").[25]

Musa Beg's petition also casts light on some of the issues raised earlier by İne's story. The kinds of abuse of marriage arrangements revealed in Bo-zok—interfering with a family's ability to arrange alliances for its children, manipulating engagements so as to extort a higher marriage tax—make the attention paid by Süleyman and Ebu Suud to the matter of arranging marriage understandable. Their insistence on the need for marriages to be sanctioned by the local judge, particularly when a person other than a girl's father or grandfather gave her in marriage, goes directly to the issue of family control and indirectly to the issue of proper implementation of the marriage tax. What the elders of Cağdığın perhaps saw as just another form of Ottoman interference in local lives could, from the regime's point of view, be construed as protective both of families and of administrative integrity.

QUIS CUSTODIET CUSTODES; OR, HOW TO KEEP LOCAL POLICE IN LINE

The sultanic prerogative of siyaset was necessarily delegable. In the provinces, the sovereign's power was represented by the pashas and begs who executed siyaset where prescribed. But because pashas governed vast areas and begs were often away at war, they too delegated their power downward and outward. Like the army of tax-farmers described in chapter 7, the hierarchy of executive officials in Aintab, the *ehl-i örf,* was made up mostly of local individuals. But how judiciously did these representatives of the sultan's power enforce the law? Bozok was a largely rural and tribal area, but even cities in these years were not spared harassment by the sultan's own men. The depredations of soldiers stationed in Aleppo were so disturbing that inhabitants of the city threatened flight, or so they wrote the grand vezir sometime in 1533 or 1534.[26] Petitions such as Musa Beg's and that of the people of Aleppo raise the question of how widespread lawlessness was among local authorities in the years after Selim I's conquests. The flight of people from the city of Erzurum, for example, may have been as much the result of abuses by local officials as of the vagaries of life on an embattled frontier (on Erzurum, see the opening of chapter 7). Containing the authority of law enforcement officials was a palpable concern of Süleyman's law book, as we will see. A number of new statues inscribed in his law book aimed at working out relations on the ground between judges and local executive officials.

Just who were the executive officials in Aintab? A clause in Süleyman's law book that forbade the collection of fines by "executive officials" before a judge's hearing gives us a sense of the range of local officeholders who could be included under that label. In variant manuscripts of the law book, the text ranged from the generic "ehl-i örf" to the more specific "tax-collectors" and "tax-collectors and timariot fief-holders" to one manuscript's apparently exhaustive list—"the provincial governor's man, the police chief, rural police, fief-holders, tax-collectors, and others."[27] In Aintab, the provincial governor was an outsider, and so perhaps was his police chief, but the lesser agents of authority were from the city and province's villages. There was, therefore, a large class of individuals endowed with some level of executive authority at the provincial level, whether delegated directly by the sultan or indirectly by his delegates. In other words, executive authority, albeit in a watered-down form, was as close as one's city neighbor or fellow villager who had the money and connections to acquire the position of agent to an agent.

There were at least three lines of executive authority operating in the province of Aintab. The first encompassed the city, where authority lay with the provincial governor and his police chief, or "city subaşı," a powerful individual. The latter had his own "men" and, more important, controlled the office of head night watchman (asesbaşı) and his staff. The latter's job encompassed more than the security of the city's streets at night, for the asesbaşı was a frequent figure at court, often appearing in connection with illegal drinking, cursing, and brawling. In 1540–1541, there was considerable turnover in the city's law enforcement agencies, in large part because there were three provincial governors during the course of the year, and each filled the police offices attached to his governorship with new staff. Local offices, such as that of night watch, were offered as tax-farms, and therefore were open to periodic bidding from members of the community.

Rural executive administration was more complex, since villages had a variety of administrative identities, depending on the status of their land— crown domain, military fief, freehold property, waqf foundation, or some combination of these. The links between the empire's fiscal and judicial systems are quite visible at the level of the village. What we might call the village's responsible authority was charged both with the collection of its tax revenues and with law enforcement. Indeed, these responsibilities were inseparable because of the Ottoman policy of promoting fines as criminal punishment: fines formed part of the revenue generated by the village and as such were listed as an item in the cadastral surveys' estimates of each village's total output. In the Ottoman formulation, "criminal penalties belong to the land" *(cürm ü cinayet toprağa tabidir)*, that is, the land on which the offense was committed.[28] In the case of crown, freehold, or waqf villages, criminal fines went to the crown, to be paid out to local fortress garrisons (at least in mid-sixteenth-century Aintab). In the case of military fiefs belonging to timariots, fines were split between the timariot and the provincial governor; if the fief were a larger one, belonging directly to the provincial governor, governor-general, or other high-ranking official, the fines belonged entirely to him. However, neither the collection of fines nor the settlement of disputes was necessarily carried out by these individuals themselves. Indeed, as persons of local authority and stature, they were inclined to delegate routine duties to members of their retinue, taking personal charge only of the weightier aspects of their jobs. All this had the consequence that villagers were linked to a wide range of executive officials in their encounters with the law.[29]

The official responsible for villages belonging to the crown domain was Mustafa Çelebi, trustee of crown lands *(hassemini)* and one of the most influential individuals in the province. He was an Aintaban who had held this office for several years running. The trusteeship was something of a family enterprise, since Mustafa's son Hamza Bali Çelebi was his right-hand man, and the sizable fortune of his wife Aynişah helped keep him in office. The trustee's staff was large, including his own men and police officials (the terms *adem* and *subaşı* may have been used interchangeably when applied to the trustee's staff). In addition, the court records suggest that the province's larger villages (almost all of which belonged to the crown domain) had headmen *(kethüda)* who were linked to the trustee; whether they were appointed by him or locally chosen is not clear.

Many Aintab villages belonged to timariots, members of the Ottoman provincial cavalry; eighty-six were listed in the 1543 cadastral survey as assigned to Aintab. Even within this class of "responsible authorities," there was a good deal of variation. Some villages were shared by up to four or five timariots—for example, the village of Göllüce was held by Halil, Hüseyin, Mahmud, another Mahmud, and Murad, all members of the garrison stationed in the Aintab fortress.[30] Other villages were the fiefs of wealthy timariot members of the sultan's slave elite, including Ferhad Çavuş and Kasım Beg. Scions of minor Aintab lineages—the sons of Gazi Beg, Tarhan Beg, and Üveys Beg, for example—also held rural fiefs as timariots, their rural domain sometimes encompassing as many as six villages. The villages and mezraas held by Piri Beg and Mansur Beg, sons of Tarhan, spread across two of the province's subdistricts, while the holdings of Üveys Beg's sons encompassed all three.[31] These men were most likely the sons of former tribal chiefs who had been rewarded by the Ottoman government with timar grants.

The Aintab records tell us less about law enforcement among nomadic tribal groups in the region and its connection to revenue in criminal fines than about city or rural administration. In general, the administration of tribes, both Turkmen and Kurdish, appears to have been handled at the level of the governorate-general, by the pasha's head police official and by various agents (also subaşıs) directly assigned to tribal administrative duties.[32] In criminal matters, these agents sometimes used the local courts of the province.

The attempt to set the judge's court alongside these lines of authority mandated to enforce law and order led inevitably to friction between them. This is evident from Süleyman's law book, which laid out rules for the necessarily cooperative relationship between judges and executive officials but warned each not to interfere in the jurisdiction of the other. The general thrust of these rules was that, on the one hand, judges were not to interfere with the imposition of severe punishment by executive officials, and, on the other hand, executive officials were not to exceed the bounds of their authority in exacting unjustified or excessive criminal fines. No single section of the law book deals explicitly and sequentially with the relationship between judge and ehl-i örf, though some of the law book's clauses dealing with the mechanics of legal administration were grouped together. As we saw in chapter 3, the imperial law books were collections of statutes, sometimes redundant and even sometimes contradictory, and not intended to be comprehensive legal expositions. (For the convenience of readers who may wish to consult Uriel Heyd's edition and translation of the penal section of Süleyman's law book, in what follows I have included the numbers introduced by Heyd as he separated the continuous text into discrete clauses or statutes. I have most often used Heyd's English translation, though sometimes I have made slight alterations or fully retranslated the Turkish text.)

The authority of the judge vis-à-vis the ehl-i örf was spelled out in two clauses in particular. They were aimed at protecting individuals from punishment without a hearing by the judge and from being forced to pay unjustified or excessive fines. According to the first,

> Officials may not interfere with a person or impose a fine with nothing being proved in accordance with the sharia and merely on suspicion of misconduct. If they do exact [a fine], the judge shall give an order and recover it [115].[33]

The second clause warns against excessive fines:

Officials shall impose a fine according to the offense a person has committed and take nothing more. If they do impose [too great a fine], the judge shall give an order regarding the excess and recover it [116].[34]

This second clause assumes that a judge was able to keep track of those whom his court had found guilty and ensure that the penalties imposed were appropriate.

The problem with the ehl-i örf is obvious. It is spelled out here in Süleyman's law book, implied in the Aintab law book, and graphically illustrated in Bozok. The problem with judges is less obvious because less often documented. The law book informs us of interference by judges in the punishment of theft, which was a crime of particular concern to the state:

If theft is proved by means of customary practice, he who serves as judge shall give a certificate [to that effect] to the executive officials, in accordance with which the executive officials shall hang the person who incurs hanging and shall cut off a limb of the person who incurs the cutting off of a limb. The judge shall not interfere in this matter and shall not cause the punishment [siyaset] to be postponed. Let them carry out the punishment in the place where the crime occurred [88].[35]

It seems, then, that local enforcers—the tribal chiefs and timariots who tried to prevent siyaset in order to put fines in their own pockets—were not the only ones who stood in the way of siyaset. Judges too resisted. In so doing, perhaps they were relying on the sharia tradition that urged that dire physical punishment be avoided (see below).

A matter that caused particular friction between judge and police was the practice of judicial torture—that is, torturing suspects in order to extract information or a confession. Within limits, torture was legal according to the law book, especially when theft was suspected: "If a thief confesses under torture and if there are signs pointing to [his guilt], his confession shall be considered valid, and capital or severe corporal punishment [siyaset] shall be inflicted on him in accordance with [the seriousness of] his crime [89]."[36] Suspicion of theft, in other words, made torture a legitimate judicial instrument within limits. As it did for adultery, sharia required eyewitness evidence (in this case, of theft); and thus, like adultery, theft was hard to prosecute. As Qur'anic crimes, the prosecution of both rested in the hands of the state and had long been subject to extra-canonical practices.

Other clauses in the law book spelled out in greater detail the circumstances under which torture in cases of theft was appropriate. For example:

If a stolen item is found in the hand of a thief or in his house, if [he says that] he bought it, they shall find the person who sold it. If he cannot be found and [the other] is suspected, let them torture him, unless they find [the seller] and bring him and turn him over to the judge or unless [the suspect] can prove he found [the item] in a desolate area [82].

The text of the law book then goes on to qualify the application of torture, warning against severe torture that risked the death of the suspect. Should death occur, however, the suspect's relatives could not claim the right of retaliation or compensation.[37] Another clause regulated the torturing of accomplices in the crime of theft: a person named by the prime suspect could also be tortured, but only if he was a person of bad reputation [90].[38]

The judge was not to stand outside the administration of torture. One in the cluster of clauses setting out the judge's checks on the ehl-i örf declares that "Without the cognizance of the judge, the ehl-i örf may imprison and injure no person [116]."[39] ("Injure" here most likely means to torture.) This role of the judge was no doubt connected to his traditional duty to monitor prisons and ensure that prisoners were being held with valid reason. Once a confession was legally extracted, the judge was to issue a certificate to that effect before punishment was carried out (see clause no. 88 above). In other words, there needed to be a written record of "the cognizance" of the judge.

To sum up, the law book of Süleyman employed the division of jurisdiction between court and ehl-i örf to promote a system of checks and balances wherein the authority of each was used to control the excesses of the other. Judges gave the green light to acts of the executive authority. As the arbiters of innocence and guilt, they were required to validate confessions exacted under torture. Thus no act of siyaset could be performed locally without authorization by the judge. The ehl-i örf were responsible for applying penalties, including capital punishment. They had the authority to torture certain suspects, primarily thieves, although they could not proceed to punishment without the judge's green light. Once the appropriate penalty was legitimately determined, however, judges were not to interfere, whatever objections they might have to physical maiming or capital punishment.

Some offenses were so great as to supersede the authority of both judges and local executive officials. A final clause in the law book laying out the domain of siyaset addresses notorious criminals who threatened the commonweal and so were directly subject to state justice, bypassing the judge's hearing:

> If a person is a threat to social order [ehl-i fesad] and is constantly discovered in illegal acts, and if upright people say to his face that they do not find him a law-abiding individual, the judge and the police chief shall withdraw [from the proceedings against him]. The person in whose hands has been placed the authority to inflict capital or severe corporal punishment [siyaset ve yasak] shall punish him [125].[40]

The seriousness of such a breach of public order is indicated by the stipulation that punishment be handled above the level of local executive officials, presumably by the provincial governor or perhaps by the governor-general. In the case of a habitual criminal, it would seem, a court trial was not necessary. The court's function in ascertaining guilt was assumed by "Muslims," members of the community recognized for their trustworthiness and integrity. But they had to accuse the guilty directly, for their probity was bound up in their speech, as chapter 5 has demonstrated. This ruling is a reminder of the near-reverence of Islamic legal tradition for the testimony of honest witnesses, in the eyes of Muslim jurisprudents the bedrock upon which the judgment of the judges was founded.

To what extent and how were Aintabans in 1540–1541 the victims of harassment by the ehl-i örf? Had the abuses in the administration of criminal justice implied in the Aintab law book of 1536 been rectified? Of course, the very power of executive officials may have intimidated victims who would otherwise have come to court to complain, leaving them either to keep silence or to appeal for help from other authorities—and thereby yielding us no historical trace of their effort. Keeping this caveat in mind, one would have to say that there were not a great many complaints lodged at court during the year 1540–1541. (The legal import of the term "complaint," şekva, was a request for an investigation.)

A number of suits were lodged during the year against injustice at the hands of timariots, but these did not involve judicial misadministration or harassment. For example, timariots were summoned to court for hitting a peasant, beating up a man who came to cut grapes in his vineyard, seizing a mezraa illegally, and participating in a gang rape (although the two accused timariots claimed they had tried to stop the rape).[41] The "man" of an Aleppan timariot (no doubt his armed retainer, or cebeci) was arrested for running drunk through the streets of the city waving his sword, whereupon the timariot punched the head night watchman, who had made the arrest.[42] But it is important to note that the timariots of Aintab were no more salient as figures of urban or rural disorder than were the "civilians" of the province (with the exception that civilians did not have swords). Indeed, timariots coped with plenty of disorder in their own lives—namely, border disputes, unruly peasants, and rival timariots. Rivalry occurred in part because of a sociomilitary hierarchy among timariots, who included wealthy slaves of the imperial household, local "beg" timariots, untitled and thus undistinguished individuals, and the fifty-some less prominent "men" of the citadel garrison. An example of rivalry between "slave" and "beg" timariots was a land dispute between Hasan Ağa b. Abdullah and Piri Beg b. Tarhan Beg, won by the former when he obtained a ruling from the sultan as to the validity of his timar claim.[43] Timariots also encountered quotidian sorts of problems, since they were not simply "military" figures but were also involved in business and city real estate deals.

If we turn to the mismanagement of punitive justice, we find two complaints officially lodged at court during the year, both investigated by the judge. The first suit was brought in December 1540 by a Turkmen tribesman wintering in the village of Orul, who alleged that one of the agents of Mustafa Çelebi, the trustee of crown lands in Aintab, had entered his home and assaulted his wife with the intention of raping her. A deputy judge *(naib)* was appointed to carry out an investigation in the village. He found that "nothing was required either by sharia or by kanun," whereupon the complainant dropped his case.[44] We have already taken note of the second case, a complaint about the unwarranted imprisonment by the governor-general's subaşı of a Kurdish man on suspicion of theft. In chapter 7, this case was analyzed for what it suggests about the community's collective resistance to the interference of Maraş in Aintab's affairs. Here the case is relevant as a probable instance of resistance to torture. The record of this incident, which occurred in September 1540, is repeated for the convenience of the reader:

> When they complained that the subaşı Davud, one of the Pasha's subaşıs, had seized and imprisoned Seyfeddin b. Musa, the Kurd, and was committing unlawful aggression *(teaddi eder)* against him on the grounds that he was a thief, the aforementioned subaşı was summoned to the court. After repeated questioning of him and the aforementioned Seyfeddin, nothing could be discovered that could be held [against Seyfeddin] and he was released. Mehmed b. Mustafa, a trustworthy person, was appointed guarantor for him.[45]

Was this case an example of the judge's interference in the ehl-i örf's efforts to deal with a thief, just the kind of obstacle to ensuring public order that Süleyman's law book warned against? Or was it an instance of rightful curbing of police excess, of the judge performing just the kind of check on police work that the law book prescribed? The court's awareness that it was accountable to both sharia and kanun, expressed in the record of the first case, suggests that the critical point on which our attempt to classify the court's action should turn is the law book's qualification about the torture of thieves, namely, that it was lawful only if there was suggestive evidence. The judge's inquiry turned up no such evidence, a fact of which the people who lodged the complaint were apparently aware. Of course, this is measuring Aintab practice by the law book. It may well have been the other way around—that the law book reflected the limits of public tolerance of the use of torture. In any event, the "unlawful aggression" was tolerated neither by the "they" who lodged the complaint nor by the judge.

On the whole, then, the court records present a picture of the ehl-i örf under control in 1540–1541. People complained, measures were taken— in other words, the system envisioned by the sultan's legal team seemed to be working. But the idealized blueprint for justice laid out in the normative world of the imperial law book was only part of the story. If the system was working, its success was due in considerable part to complexities on the ground. The ehl-i örf were not simply ehl-i örf, as we have seen. They were for the most part ordinary individuals enmeshed in the overlapping networks of economy, society, and family, and this embeddedness diluted any monolithic hold they may have had as a body of police on the life of the province. Moreover, police rarely operated in a vacuum. The existence in and around Aintab of a variety of local and regional legal authorities and venues meant that the prosecution of criminal justice was an organic and complex process. The murder cases analyzed below should make this clear.

Another limitation on ehl-i örf autonomy came from their very heterogeneity. The multiplicity of lines of authority—to the provincial governor, to the governor-general, to the trustee of crown lands—within the overall provincial administration of the twinned processes of justice and taxation created distinct jurisdictions and thus an internal system of checks and balances. The protectiveness with which individual members of the ehl-i örf guarded their rights is revealed in a case recorded at court in late July 1541. The city police chief (i.e., the provincial governor's subaşı) had apparently crossed jurisdictional boundaries by arresting a villager living in a crown village on a charge of adultery and taking him and his female partner to court for trial (where they confessed their guilt). About ten days after the adultery trial, the villager again came to court at the behest of the police chief, this time to state that the police chief had taken from him "neither a single akçe nor a single grain" (local vernacular for absolutely nothing in the way of cash or kind). The villager was then turned over to the trustee for crown lands, the "responsible authority" for his village, to whom the fine was due.[46]

This instance of jurisdictional vigilance among executive officials points to the court's role in the system of checks and balances among lines of authority. The judge was a nexus among these lines as well as an authority placed above them, with the power to adjudicate the intersections of their separate domains. That he also had the authority to monitor their individual behavior is evident in the two complaint cases discussed above, in which he dismissed the charges of intended rape but vindicated the charge of illegal imprisonment by the pasha's police. The court was thus critical in the regime's efforts to keep its men in line and to socialize them into an imperially sponsored culture of justice.

HOW WERE AINTABANS ACTUALLY PUNISHED?

The question of what penalties were actually imposed when Aintabans committed crimes is very difficult to answer. The most obvious obstacle is the lack of records: the judge only rarely imposed a punishment that he wrote into the court register, and we have no written record of the great majority of penalties that were imposed by executive officials. Indeed, it is possible that no such records were even kept.

In addition, normative prescriptions themselves were far from straightforward in the mid–sixteenth century. At first glance, prescriptive penal law of the time appears to be full of contradictions, inconsistencies, and ambiguities. Islamic jurisprudence envisioned severe corporal punishment or execution for some of the "fixed" crimes (those explicitly penalized in the Qur'an): death by stoning for Muslim adulterers, amputation of limbs for certain forms of theft and highway robbery, and execution for homicide committed during highway robbery.[47] Yet at the same time, the texts of jurisprudence urged judges and witnesses to find ways to avoid the more violent of these punishments.[48] In other words, violent bodily punishments were both prescribed and treated as unworkable.[49]

Kanun too, in the form of the imperial law book, was replete with ambiguity. Consider the section on sexual offenses, where Süleyman's law book featured two clauses regarding the female adulterer: the first prescribed that she herself pay the fine, the second that her husband be fined for her offense. A larger area of ambiguity in the law book lies in its clear preference for monetary fines, which were indeed assumed to be the basic operating procedure. Yet at the same time the law book sometimes deferred to penalties prescribed by sharia, which might involve extreme violence to the body or even death. For example, the first item in Süleyman's redaction of the law book prescribed in detail a sliding scale of fines for adultery, but qualified the penalty with the brief statement, "provided the sharia punishment is not applied."[50] Similarly, with regard to homicide, the law book prescribed fines but first stated the sharia-authorized principle of retaliation *(kisas)*, which left the decision whether or not to go after the killer in the hands of the aggrieved party: "If a person kills a human being, retaliation shall be carried out [and] no fine shall be collected. If retaliation is not carried out or the killing is not such as to require retaliation—if the killer is rich, . . . a fine of 400 akçes shall be collected, and if he is in average circumstances . . . [41]."[51] Yet the Ottoman regime's policies were aimed at halting the practice of retaliatory feuding,[52] as we will see in the next section.

Another form of ambiguity in normative penal law was the gap between what the sultan was saying in kanun and what Islamic jurisprudence was saying in the person of Ebu Suud, Süleyman's close adviser and chief mufti from 1545 on. For example, while the regime was promoting the fining of adultery, Ebu Suud reiterated the sharia punishment of stoning to death for married Muslim adulterers.[53] He also opposed kanun on the matter of torture, which the law book insisted should be employed within humane limits. The mufti stood strictly for sharia procedure in the matter of evidence and confession. In his opinion, confession exacted under torture was not valid. Moreover, contrary to the law book, the mufti held executive officials responsible for the payment of blood money should a suspect die under torture.[54]

On the other hand, chief muftis of the mid–sixteenth century took a more liberal position on fines, of which only a minority of Hanafi jurists had approved. Both Ebu Suud and Çivizade, chief muftis during the period of this study, acknowledged the legitimacy of fines, provided they were in the public interest or approved by the judge. According to Ebu Suud, "the fine is the customary (örf) penalty for an offence proved before the sharia judge."[55] The muftis' approval was useful, for the state's efforts to "fiscalize" punishment by imposing fines in place of corporal punishment was critical to preserving the option of violent punishment as its own instrument. Violence was to be identified with siyaset, those corporal and capital punishments that the sultan retained in his personal disciplinary arsenal.

Why was there such variation in the area of punishment? And why was a jurist like Ebu Suud, who owed his position to the sultan's patronage, seemingly at cross-purposes with his patron on some matters but not on others? A possible explanation for the apparent inconsistencies within penal law is that the Ottoman regime was still striving toward administrative homogeneity in the mid–sixteenth century. The sheer volume of legal writing under Süleyman and the effort to be comprehensive meant that inconsistent opinions were being ranged side by side. But we are talking here about a state famous for its organizational genius, a period characterized by a regulatory thrust, and a program putatively aimed at the reconciliation of kanun and sharia.[56] We must therefore wonder if the variability in penal law was not to some degree tacitly tolerated or even positively desired. In his studies of law as a cultural and rhetorical system, James Boyd White notes that criminal law is always "in some fundamental way incoherent" because its alleged purposes—deterrence, retribution, incapacitation, and rehabilitation—are not compatible with one another. This incompatibility arises, he argues, because of their "different conceptions of character and relation"— in other words, the nature of the individual and his or her relation to the punishing authority is viewed differently depending on the rationale for punishment.[57] The Ottoman regime, jurists, and ordinary individuals—all perhaps had an interest in maintaining a range of punitive options and in stating them with a degree of ambiguity.

White's characterization of criminal law may be useful in helping us understand some of the "ambiguities" just outlined. Take the dire punishments prescribed in sharia—mutilation of the body, stoning to death, execution. As with biblical injunctions that prescribed similar penalties—stoning for adultery, for example, or the "eye for an eye" principle of retaliation—the violent punishments of sharia served mainly as a warning about the dastardly nature of the crimes for which they were prescribed. The penalty was in effect an inverted assertion of the moral imperative at issue (e.g., "Thou shalt not commit adultery"). As mentioned above, judges were exhorted to avoid imposing such penalties, and witnesses were excused for concealing evidence regarding such crimes. The popular Hanafi jurist Al-Marghinani cited a saying of the Prophet Muhammad—"Seek a pretext to prevent [corporal] punishment according to your ability"—as support for his argument that judges must undertake stringent examination of witnesses in the matter of adultery; the purpose of this special effort was "that (possibly) some circumstance may appear sufficient to prevent the punishment."[58] The threat of drastic punishment was thus intended more as preventative than as penalty—as deterrence, in White's scheme. In this light, the sharia tradition urging avoidance of the fixed penalties is not the outright contradiction it might at first seem. Rather, we could say that it opened the door to rehabilitation.

This argument helps explain a divergence in Süleyman's law book from that of his father, Selim I. Selim's law book did not supplement its statement of fines on adultery with the proviso "provided the sharia punishment is not applied." One naturally wonders why Süleyman added this phrase, which is featured in his law book's very first clause. The answer—that the sultan and his legal team *intended* to introduce different penal standards—also helps explain why Ebu Suud's pronouncements could contradict the imperial law book. Süleyman can be said to have surpassed his ancestors in the practice of "siyasa shariyya" as expounded by the intellectual heirs of Ibn Taymiyya. This orientation fitted the larger goals of Süleyman's reforms in provincial legal administration: expanding the court system, raising the authority of the judge, balancing the powers of local police. It may have been useful to maintain different theoretical justifications, namely, sharia as well as kanun, since each set a limit to the other. Kanun reminded judges of the need for the state's executive arm, the "siyasa" part of the formula. Sharia reminded the ehl-i örf that this was, after all, a religiously grounded legal system, with moral imperatives that transcended the mundane details of jails and fines.

We close this section by reviewing the meager evidence of punishment in the Aintab court records for 1540–1541. Only one criminal fine imposed by the state is directly mentioned—a penalty of 10 gold pieces imposed on a murderer.[59] The jurisdictional altercation described above, in which the peasant testified that the city subaşı took neither money nor grain from him, provides indirect evidence of the imposition of fines for adultery (the hearing to establish the adulterers' guilt was duly recorded in the court register; the fine taking was not). And a case cited in chapter 3, in which the nomad Ahmed pledged to find a guilty relative and bring him before the judge, suggests that people expected to pay fines: "if I don't [find him]," said Ahmed, "I'll pay the penalty that kanun prescribes."[60]

An amusing case that was recorded in June 1541 suggests that people were clever at evading fines when arrested for finable offenses. Two women who knocked each other's teeth out in a brawl gave an account of their fight that enabled them to escape the penalty imposed by sultanic statute. Here is the record of the incident, which was brought to court by the office of the police chief:

> Kavurd, deputy of the police chief Ali, came to court and summoned the women Emine bt. Mahmud and Fatma bt. Mehmed, both of the city of Aintab. Producing two adult teeth, he said, "These women knocked each other's teeth out during a brawl." When the aforementioned Emine and Fatma were questioned, they stated the following of their own free will: "We *did* fight with each other. But both our teeth were diseased and rotten, and they fell out while we were fighting and defending ourselves against one another." The foregoing was recorded at the request of Kavurd.[61]

Brawling was an offense frequently prosecuted in the Aintab court, although almost always the accused were male. Both the law book of Süleyman and that attributed to his father imposed a relatively severe penalty for knocking out teeth: "When a person intentionally knocks out [another] person's eye or tooth: if retaliation (*kisas*) is carried out, no fine shall be collected; if retaliation is not carried out or is not necessary, 200 akçes shall be collected as fine; if [the attacker] is in average circumstances, 100 akçes; and if he of she is poor, 50 or 40 akçes."[62] The punishment is severe not only in equating the loss of a tooth with the loss of an eye but also in imposing a substantial financial burden. To gain a sense of its magnitude, compare the amount of support typically awarded to a divorced woman or orphaned child (1 or 2 akçes daily), or the fine for adultery (300 akçes for a rich person).

In this case, however, the women appeared to talk themselves out of the fine. While the police chief's deputy alleged that they *knocked out* each other's teeth, Fatma and Emine asserted that the teeth simply *fell out* because they were decayed. The women's version of the event, though admitting the fact of brawling, removed the element of intentional harm. It is also possible that their story, by stressing the mutual and equivalent injury, allowed the case to be judged as one in which retaliation had already taken place (literally enacting the punishment of "a tooth for a tooth"). Whether it was an honest account of their pugilistic encounter or not, the women's statement suggests an awareness of legal rules sophisticated enough that they could offer the court an exonerating narrative of the event. Admittedly, it is not certain that Fatma and Emine escaped punishment, but the predominance of the women's narrative in the summary, unchallenged by additional testimony, suggests that they were excused from any criminal fines.

Turning to other forms of punishment, we find no evidence in the records of corporal punishment imposed by the ehl-i örf. However, we cannot therefore conclude that it was never applied (it may have been in some of the murder cases discussed below). Moreover, it was most likely the ehl-i örf who administered the floggings that were routinely prescribed in the imperial law book (see figure 9). There *is* a hint in the records of older forms of punishment—namely, humiliation and paying penance *(nezir):* a hamam owner, guilty of diverting water from the Alaeddevle mosque, vowed to pay penance of 1,000 akçes were he to repeat his offense; like Fatma who promised not to bother the authorities any more, the hamam owner pledged the money to Seyyid İsmail.[63] The pledged moneys were probably intended for the charitable food services of the Haci Baba zaviye, whose sheikh Seyyid İsmail was: feeding the poor was a traditional way of atoning for a broken vow, an act that had Qur'anic sanction (Surah 5, verse 89). As for private settlements that were authorized by the court, the outstanding example is an award of a very large sum— 46,000 akçes—in compensation for murder. Other lesser examples of compensation in cash and kind are stated or implied; for example, a mother received a fig orchard and a house in compensation for her son's death in a blood feud.[64]

Also mentioned are some punishments authorized by the judge. The records indicate that he routinely imprisoned debtors. And during the year, three individuals were banished from their neighborhoods, one for allegedly lying in court and two for sexual offenses. We also find that the judge prescribed ta'zir a handful of times, all in connection with the Qur'anic crimes of sexual license and drinking. The term ta'zir meant "discretionary punishment," typically at the hands of the judge and typically a number of lashes to be set by the judge. Cases in which the court entered a judgment of ta'zir included a man who called a woman a whore, a man who sneaked into a woman's house and bed at night, a man found on the roof of a house at night (suspicion of intended rape was at issue here), three men caught drinking, and the case of Haciye Sabah.[65] It is admittedly a puzzle, at least to me, how exactly ta'zir functions in these records: why, in other words, criminal acts similar to those just listed did not occasion ta'zir; whether the court record was simply did not note all judgments of ta'zir; and whether there was a rationale behind the apparent inconsistency in the existing record.

What version of whose law book was operating in Aintab in 1540–1541? As we have seen, the provincial law book issued specifically for Aintab in 1536, which mainly detailed its taxes, also established the Kanun-ı Osmanî—

the imperial law book—as the authority for criminal penalties. The Dulkadir code, presumably operative in the pre-conquest period, would thereby
seem to have been abolished. But which imperial law book was in force?
A late version of Selim I's law book appeared in 1520, the year he died,[66]
while Süleyman's redaction, as noted earlier, was introduced around 1540.
I have speculated that the judge Hüsameddin Efendi may have brought
Süleyman's text to Aintab in the summer of 1541. However, the mention of
face-blacking and penance in the records for 1540–1541 suggests that
older penal practices persisted and that Aintab's penal culture was probably
a blend of the Dulkadir and the Ottoman. This does not mean that punishment in Aintab was a mishmash or that the province's legal administration
was lax. In earlier chapters we have noted the importance that both sharia
and kanun attached to hewing to basic principles while allowing interpretive flexibility at the local level. Where tolerable, old habits were allowed to
blend into the new; or, to put it another way, modernized criminal law did
not fully displace traditional practices.

MURDER AT THE COURT OF AINTAB

During the course of the year 1540–1541, five cases of murder were registered in the Aintab court records, and two investigations of death by drowning were undertaken to rule out any suspicion of foul play. These adjudica-
tions of murder are among the most complex cases recorded during the
year and perhaps the record's most vivid demonstration that the study of
legal culture needs to be grounded in the dialectic between action and
prescription. The cases also advance one of the main arguments of this
book, that the court was only one site of dispute resolution, albeit the critical venue that gave legitimacy to the legal system as a whole. The prosecution and adjudication of murder at the Aintab court in 1540–1541 provide
an interesting test of how well the legal system envisioned by the imperial
law book was working. Insofar as it is visible to us, the handling of murder
suggests that the Ottoman system of legal administration in fact exhibited a
fairly close fit between blueprint and realization in this place and time.

Much can be said about these cases, but first let us walk through the
salient facts of each. Each murder except the last was the subject of several
entries in the court record, sometimes stretching over weeks, sometimes
months. (I have numbered the cases for ease of reference.)

In an incident occurring in the village of Gücüge (1), a man was attacked
while asleep on his roof; when he pursued his attackers, he was shot dead
with an arrow. His heirs were awarded compensation of 46,000 akçes, the
amount having been determined through the process of arbitration. The
murderer received authorization to defer payment of 19,000 akçes of this
very large sum.[67] This case was brought to court by order of the governor-

general in Maraş, who sent a high-ranking agent, one Haydar Çavuş, to handle it.

The second case (2) was a complex blood feud in the village of Orul. The feuding factions, each responsible for one murder, agreed after back-and-forth negotiations to give up their claims on one another. Or rather, the siblings of each victim agreed to forgo any further violence. The mother of the first victim received compensation *(diyet)* from Dede b. Hasan, the perpetrator of the first murder, who also had to pay a "blood fine" *(kan cerimesi)* to the village's responsible authority. Orul being a village belong to the domain of the crown, the fine of 10 gold pieces went to the trustee of crown lands.[68] In the final sicill concerning this case, the brother of the first victim requested that Dede be placed under bond, and a guarantor *(kefil)* was appointed. The only stage of this multiple-sicill case at which a state prosecutorial agent was present was the registration of the blood fine. All other adjudication took place among the parties, with the judge ruling at the conclusion that no further dispute existed among them.

Another case (3) involved a murder that occurred when a fight broke out between young men from two large Turkmen tribal federations, the Begdili and the Dulkadir. The victim, Hüseyin b. Aba Ali, from the Dulkadir side, was shot by two men from the Begdili side (one gave the command and one shot the arrow). The victim's father, Aba Ali, tried several times to bring a case against the two assailants but was unable to prove their guilt (they claimed to have shot in self-defense). The case was perforce dropped, although the accused were not given the option of taking the oath of innocence. The whole affair was overseen by the governor-general, Ali Pasha, who generally monitored tribal conflicts because of their potential to flare up into large-scale warfare. He appointed a prominent timariot, Şuca Çavuş, to handle the case for him. The case concluded with the two accused men being placed under bond, albeit with a letter from Ali Pasha warning that officials were strictly forbidden to interfere with or harass them.[69]

Each of these cases is remarkable in demonstrating a complex mobilization of legal resources that is not entirely predictable from the prescriptive legal texts described earlier in this chapter. Taken together, they reveal a nexus of legal venues: the court of the Aintab judge, local arbitration, the tribal council, and the office of the regional governor-general in Maraş. A number of legal principles and practices were also at work: retaliation *(kisas)*, compensation *(diyet)*, bond *(kefalet)*, and dismissal through legal process. And a considerable range of legal personnel and persons acquiring legally determined roles through the course of events were involved: not only the obvious (judge, governor-general, provincial governor, police officers) but also the less obvious (the citizen arbiters, bond agents, and behind-the-scene counselors), all of whom were necessary to achieving the intricate arrangements that settled the disputes.

The fourth case, the least straightforward of all, would seem to be an instance of highway robbery (4). This crime *(kat-ı tarik)* was one of the few criminal acts for which the Qur'an fixed a penalty, which ranged from cutting off the right hand and the left foot to crucifixion, depending on whether murder, plunder, or both took place.[70] The Dulkadir law code, which dealt with highway robbery in its very first clause, prescribed hanging accompanied by severe torture.[71] But the law book of Süleyman did not treat the crime of highway robbery as a discrete offense, perhaps intending that it be dealt with as either murder or theft. At any rate, the reaction in Aintab to news of the crime suggests that people regarded it as a dire offense.

The incident in question (4) involved the murder of two Christian textile merchants from Erzincan who had hired a group of men (one of them from Aintab) to escort them to Diyarbakır. They were apparently murdered by their escorts and their goods divided up among the escort party. In the confused aftermath, when word of the Aintaban's role made its way to individuals in the city, two Aintabans effected a kind of citizens' arrest by forcing the brother of the accused to pledge bond for him—that is, to accept responsibility for finding and producing him. The rationale for their action was that the provincial governorship, which was the appropriate authority in the case, was undergoing a change of personnel and the newly appointed governor had not yet arrived in Aintab. Eventually the accused appeared before the governor's subaşı and confessed to both murder and plunder. Or so the governor's office alleged. When the subaşı came to court—apparently to register the confession (here following procedure suggested in the imperial law book)—the accused denied the subaşı's statement, despite the appearance of four witnesses in court to support the subaşı. On the day following the subaşı's appearance in court, the accused made two statements *(ikrar)* at court that were recorded by the judge at the request of another subaşı, presumably also from the provincial governor's office. The accused stated first that he had been off grazing animals when the murder occurred, and then that he had taken and sold some of the merchants' goods.[72] After recording these statements, the court appears to have taken no further action in the affair. Perhaps the two statements constituted a basis for siyaset punishment by the provincial governor's office, but we cannot speak of a court trial in the usual sense. We might also wonder if the alleged confession to both murder and theft reported by the provincial governor's subaşı was obtained by torture and therefore rejected by the judge, to be followed up by compromise confession.

In the final murder case (5), the black slave of a village magnate testified that he had murdered a man from another village at the order of his master's brother. The brother had dispatched the slave along with a black slave of his own to "go find the man and hit him hard." Should the victim die as a result, the master's brother said that he would be answerable for the consequences.[73] Unlike the other four instances of murder, this case is represented by a single entry in the register; it consists solely of the slave's statement, recorded at the request of the provincial governor's agent and the mother and brother of the slain man. Sorting out the penalty, it seems, rested in the hands of the provincial governor. That the master's brother was not summoned to court suggests that the judge's only task was to identify the actual murderer, although the extenuating circumstances may well have been taken into account in determining who was to pay compensation or be held vulnerable to retaliation. (A fatwa of Ebu Suud suggests that sharia would sentence the master to a long imprisonment and the slave to paying compensation.) [74]

The role of the court in these cases varied. Its principal function was to establish guilt or innocence, as it did for the black slave (5), the murderer on the roof (1), and the two Begdili men who murdered the Dulkadir man (3). Another service it offered was to track the work of the larger community in settling murders: it authorized a mediated compensation and set terms for payment (1), it sanctioned and recorded the outcome of each stage of negotiations toward the settlement of the blood feud (2), and it worked with the pasha in Maraş in handling the tribal murder (3). The case of the highway robbery (4) is less clear, but the court appears to have given some rational order to the confused events and rumors that made up this unusual case.

The tribal murder (3) is particularly interesting for the salience of documents that characterized the case. The record demonstrates a kind of documentary pas de deux between the judge and the governor-general. The case opened with the victim's father appealing to the pasha, who issued a ruling *(hükm)* referring the case to the Aintab judge. The next stage was completed with the judge's letter to the governor stating that the father was unable to meet sharia requirements of proof of his accusation. This was followed by another ruling from the governor, ordering the judge to issue a legal document *(hüccet)* to the accused certifying their innocence and warning officials not to harass them or in any way interfere with them. This case thus draws our attention to another service provided by the court: the complete paper trial it could provide to all concerned, including the innocent, the guilty, receivers of compensation, and investigating officials.

Turning to the two investigations of death by drowning, we find that they reveal a similar confluence of legal venues and authorities. Since it was fairly evident from the outset that each incident was an accident befalling an infirm elderly man, the concern of the authorities was to remove suspicion from members of the communities where the deaths occurred. The legal principle involved was the requirement that the community either find the murderer of a victim discovered within its boundaries or pay the compensation due the victim's heirs. The first case concerned an elderly man who fell into the moat surrounding the Aintab fortress. Since this was the jurisdiction of the fortress warden, he and the city police chief supervised the investigation, in which the man's sister as well as representatives from the man's neighborhood testified that he was senile, that he had no enemies, and that he regularly collapsed while walking about. The seriousness of the event was signaled by the fact that there were eleven case-witness signatories.[75]

Like the first, the second drowning case, also involving an elderly man, seems to have been a pro forma inquiry to clear the community of any suspicion of involvement in the death. The two sons of the dead man first requested an investigation of their father's death, then appeared in court to register the fact that they would make no claim for compensation since the death was now determined to have been an accident.[76] Because this case illustrates so clearly the sharing of responsibility between sharia and kanun authorities and because it is a unique record in that the judge seems to speak personally, I give it in full:

> Ali and Eyvala, from the village of Cided, came to the court and said: "When we went with our father to cut grapes in our village because of the rain, our father disappeared. We found him three days later; he had drowned." [Previously,] when they had come to lodge a complaint with Lutfi Beg, provincial governor of the province of Aintab (may his exaltation be lasting) and with this humble one [i.e., the judge], Hüsrev b. Abdullah was appointed by his honor Lutfi Beg and Mevlana Haci İbrahim Fakih was made deputy with a letter of appointment from this humble one to investigate the matter at hand. When they arrived at the village of Cided, others also arrived to determine whether compensation was due for the deceased: Ali Fakih from the village of Kefer Cebel, the headman Cuma b. Ahmed from the village of Meziri in the province of Bire, Hasan b. Hoca and Sundek Fakih from the village of Battal Oluk. They testified that there were no wounds [on the corpse]. When the aforementioned deceased man's sons Eyvala and Ali were questioned, they said, "Our father was a senile . . . person, he drowned [on his own]; we have no suspicion of anyone." Their statement and the testimony of the aforementioned witnesses [being deemed valid], they were recorded upon request.[77]

The check-and-balance aspect of dual legal authority is evident throughout the case: the sons register their request for an investigation with the judge as well as the provincial governor, both authorities assign a delegate to the in situ inspection, and the villages potentially implicated in suspicion of foul play send experts in sharia (the two *fakihs*—the title indicates a person trained in jurisprudence) as well as a representative of the executive line (the headman).

There are a number of aspects of these seven cases taken as a whole that deserve comment. For one thing, ordinary people appear to have been conscious of the dual nature of the legal system and to have recognized that murder (or potential murder) required the activation of both judicial and executive authorities. This awareness was represented almost ritually in words spoken by two individuals involved in the settlements. In the incident involving the Begdili-Dulkadir murder (3), the tribal elder who pledged bond for the two young men cleared of suspicion solemnified his responsibility by stating, "If their presence is demanded in Aintab, I will have them appear, and if I fail to do so, whatever is to be done to them according to sharia and kanun shall be done to me."[78] In the highway robbery incident (4), when the two men who first learned of the Aintaban's involvement went to one Kara Emirza for advice, the latter counseled them not to act precipitously: "Be patient until His Honor the Governor comes; when he has arrived in full state, we'll have [the informant] taken to him and establish what happened; that way the matter will be handled in accordance with sharia and kanun."[79] Of course, we can never know if the two men actually spoke the precise words appearing in the written record. But it is significant that those words were placed in the mouths of two legally circumspect and prominent members of their respective communities (Kara Emirza would shortly become chief of the night watch).[80]

Such legal awareness may have been a product of the times. Earlier chapters have suggested how the process of imperialization—the accelerated integration of Aintab into the judicial, fiscal, and military systems of empire—required adaptation to new circumstances and new practices. The savvy use of documents relating to property ownership described in chapter 6 and the creation of group solidarities—the *kefalet* bonds described in chapter 7—are examples of such adaptation. In this regard, it is important to note that the more complex of the murder cases—the blood feud, the tribal murder, and the highway robbery—were all pending cases that appear to have been held for the arrival of authoritative figures: the special prosecutor appointed at the end of May 1541; the new judge Hüsameddin Efendi, who took up office on June 23; and the new provincial governor, Hüseyin Beg, who assumed his duties five or six days later. It is probably not coincidental that the first hearing of the Orul blood feud occurred on the first day of the special prosecutor's tenure, while the tribal murder followed three weeks later; the court first heard testimony concerning the highway robbery four days after the new governor assumed his duties. The challenges of defending oneself before these figures undoubtedly called forth all the legal awareness that the individuals involved were able to muster.

These cases also remind us vividly of the degree to which the realization of the law was dependent on its consumers and their strategies. Even the accidents of their fear and confusion contributed to the shape of outcomes. In the tribal killing, the flight of the young men who shot the victim in alleged self-defense to another clan whose protection they sought may have been a factor deterring the victim's father from taking up arms in revenge, for now two Begdili clans would be ranged against him. The agitation of individuals caught up in anticipation of the highway robber's fate is palpable in the record—the urgency of the informant, the hesitation of the men informed of the Aintaban's guilt, the distraction of the accused's brother that turned into frustration and anger. This collective agitation enabled the cool-headed Kara Emirza to step into the breach and manage the course of events as he saw fit. His move to postpone exposing the case until the new governor arrived may have contained an element of opportunism, as shortly thereafter he acquired an office that was part of the provincial governor's patronage. The point here is that normative texts and official venues— sharia rulings, law book statutes, the courts of judges, and the audiences of governors—offered guidelines for framing the meaning of tangled disputes in ways that made them amenable to adjudication. But the normative texts and official venues were not fully predictive of actions and strategies on the ground—of why, for example, the siblings of a murdered man gave up compensation but a mother did not, or whether a slave could resist his master's command to commit a crime.

The final observation prompted by these cases has to do with the role of the Aintab court. The fight between the Turkmen tribesmen occurred in the neighboring province of Bire, which had its own judge and was furthermore administratively attached to Ruha; similarly, the city of Maraş, seat of the Dulkadir pasha, also had its own judge. Yet the case was assigned to the judge of Aintab. I suggested in chapter 3 that the Aintab court may have played a regional role extending beyond its strictly jurisdictional boundaries. The fact that this case, a pending case, was first heard at the Aintab court three weeks after the arrival of the special prosecutor and one week before the arrival of Hüsameddin Efendi lends support to that contention. Since one of the biggest challenges in the Ottoman regime's effort to build a judicial system based on a network of courts was persuading people to put their trust in court-sponsored settlements, it is possible that Aintab was deliberately targeted to be the seat of a strong court. The presence of authoritative figures in the Aintab court was certainly a plus in the delicate negotiations surrounding the three complex murder cases that appear to have awaited the court's new appointees.

It is of course true that we know only of those murder cases that came within the compass of the court. Sharia placed homicide in the domain of private law, which left the choice of retaliation or compensation up to the parties involved. And murder committed during highway robbery was the only homicide that the state, as the prosecutor of Qur'anic crimes, was bound to avenge. So it is possible, in theory at least, that other murders occurred that never entered the court. However, there is reason to think that the numbers of such murders were small—that people either were not permitted to handle murder on their own or chose not to. The most obvious factor in drawing murder into public scrutiny was the state's interest in preserving order.

The regime's concern for social order brings us to a critical feature of Ottoman administration: the linking of taxation and criminal justice. It can be said that the Ottoman regime taxed crime. This was so because the fines imposed on a variety of crimes, including the "blood tax" on murder, formed part of the income of the ehl-i örf—of timariots, provincial governors, and pashas. In chapter 6, we saw how the *malikâne-divanî* system—a system of taxation under which the regime was entitled to a share of the taxes from villages that did not belong to the crown—provided the regime with a pretext for inserting its agents into privately owned rural settlements.[81] Penal fines were a part of the state's share in the revenues of such villages. The right to collect the "blood fine" on murder gave executive officials the necessary pretext to investigate murders that, under sharia, did not require the state's intervention. All the murder cases in Aintab, we should note, took place in non-urban areas.

It may not be coincidental that the malikâne-divanî administrative policy is likely to have originated with the twelfth- and thirteenth-century regime of the Rum Seljuks, the first Anatolian Muslim power to confront the challenge of integrating nomadic tribal groups into a state system.[82] Because of the tenacious cultural attachment of tribal societies to administrative autonomy, it was difficult to persuade them to pay the state's taxes and to submit to its system of justice. Furthermore, the heterodox (from the perspective of urban culture) strains of Islamic religiosity prevalent among tribal groups led them to support charismatic figures who often challenged the legitimacy of governing regimes. In addition, the use of violence figured more prominently among tribal cultures than among urban populations, making raiding, abduction, and blood feuds chronic headaches for state regimes, since these actions could escalate into intra- or intertribal warfare. Even when sedentarized or semi-sedentarized, individuals of tribal heritage or affiliation might remain loyal to such cultural practices because they were deeply imbued with notions of honor and moral autonomy. While urban civilization saw tribal society as uncivilized, there was a reverse prejudice: tribal groups regarded urban society as morally impoverished. It is hardly possible to overemphasize the tenacity of such cultural practices in the Aintab region. The reign of Süleyman may have organized social and legal controls efficiently, but it did not eliminate the feuding practices described above. Late-twentieth-century evidence from Gaziantep demonstrates their vitality, even though for all practical purposes tribal identity had by then disappeared.[83]

The governorate-general of Dulkadir, to which Aintab province belonged, was one of the most heavily tribal of the Ottoman empire. The province of Aintab had its settled and settling Turkmen and Kurds, as well as nomadic and semi-nomadic groups that either passed through the province during their migrations or wintered there. Of the five murder cases, only the incident in which the slave was dispatched to do the deed (5) does not appear in any overt way to have involved populations with potential tribal identities. In the first case, the murderer described his two accomplices as Kurds (it is not clear if he also was Kurdish). The names of those involved in the Orul blood feud (2) suggest they were of Turkmen origin, and we know from the case of the Turkmen tribesman who complained that his wife was attacked by a local official that some tribes wintered in Orul. The tribal murder case (3) was the most obvious example, involving as it did two large Turkmen tribal federations. And in the highway robbery case (4), the escort party that murdered the traveling merchants appears from a number of textual clues to have been Turkmen (escorts would logically have been drawn from tribal groups, who knew the physical terrain and were best equipped to provide protection, although this case makes clear the occupational hazards of such hiring practices). The extreme care with which the judge and the provincial governor investigated the drowning death of the man from Cided may have had something to do with the fact that the villages involved were located in the subdistrict of Nehrülcevaz and not far from Orul, an area that seems to have had a sizable Turkmen population.[84] This small sample of murder cases suggests that the challenge to the Ottoman regime's desire to subvert violence as a popular tool of dispute resolution lay in rural areas and particularly among populations characterized by tribal cultural norms.

There is, finally, a larger historical reason why murder cases in Aintab were more or less routinely brought to public settlement: the region's legal culture, which we might go so far as to call venerable. What I am suggesting is that the process of negotiating the settlement of disputes across a complex of legal options was nothing new in Aintab. Chapter 3 presented the Ottoman project of consolidating courts into an empire-wide judicial system as a work in progress at the mid–sixteenth century. But Aintab itself was located in a region that had deep acquaintance with the cultures of both sharia and kanun and, inevitably, with their interaction. Moreover, the demographic chemistry of a relatively sophisticated city set in the middle of rural and tribal populations was neither new nor unique to Aintab (the metropolis of Aleppo was an example of this phenomenon writ large).[85]

That Aintab was rich in what we might call the cultural accoutrements of sharia—the endowed colleges, the many mosques, the molla population, the label of "little Bukhara," and a court that presumably long predated the arrival of the Ottomans—is a point that has already been made a number of times. Let us turn now to the cultural legacy of kanun to which city and province were also heir. Both the Mamluk and Dulkadir regimes had prescribed legal codes for the region, and their legacy was recognized by the

Ottoman administration. Mention has been made in earlier chapters of the prestige of rulers such as the Mamluk Qaytbay, the Akkoyunlu Uzun Hasan, and even the Dulkadir Alaeddevle as models of both military and legal leadership. Traces of the regulations known among the Ottomans as the law book of the Mamluk sultan Qaytbay can be found in early Ottoman provincial law codes in the provision of fines for gashing head wounds and nonmortal knife wounds. These two fines and a Dulkadir fine on severe bruising were the only penalties specifically written into the 1536 law code for Aintab (which otherwise followed Ottoman kanun).[86]

More important and immediately relevant than the Mamluk legacy is that of the Dulkadir regime. Their legal code—"the law book of Alaeddevle"—survived more or less intact under the Ottomans over a wide stretch of territory for several decades. Thanks to the scholarship of Uriel Heyd, the criminal clauses in this code have been transcribed and analyzed in comparison to the relevant sections in the law book of Süleyman.[87] Heyd points out that the Dulkadir code was more rurally oriented than that of Süleyman: lacking in the Dulkadir code, for example, is any mention of slaves or non-Muslims (whom Heyd appears to take as emblematic of cities). Indeed, the presence of a judge is nowhere mentioned, although the code does make some reference to sharia penalties. Heyd also finds Dulkadir criminal law to be more "highly developed" than Ottoman criminal law of the period because of its strong preference for fines over bodily punishments and its inclusion of such legal questions as self-defense against assailants, unintentional offenses, and theft by more than one person.

It is no contradiction that both Heyd's observations—the rural orientation and the "greater development" of Dulkadir law—are plausible. It is not surprising that a legal code tailored to a largely tribal audience was well-developed in certain aspects, and also that it was reluctant to make concessions to a legal tradition as all-encompassing as sharia. After all, a critical aspect of kanun—promulgating legal codes in the name of the ruler as a marker of sovereign legitimacy—is generally attributed to Inner Asian traditions of tribal political formation, where the emergence of a stable polity depended on the subordination of member tribes to the paramount clan. The classic example is the Mongol polity (the first act of Genghis Khan after acquiring leadership of the Mongol tribes was to promulgate a series of laws), but the Akkoyunlu, the Dulkadir, the early Ottomans, and to an extent the Mamluks also exemplify this tradition, and are closer in time and space to the concerns of this book. The problem of controlling the means of violence was a central one for all these polities. To think through this question, we begin with a more purely tribal polity—the Dulkadir—and then proceed to the Mamluks and the Ottomans, whose regimes were based not on a pastoral but rather on a mixed agrarian-commercial economy and the cultural values associated with it.

Since tribal polities did not disarm their member tribes, the means of violence remained in many hands. Controlling the uses of violence was a primary concern for the rulers of such polities—for the paramount clan, so to speak. It is no wonder that tribal polities stayed at war a good deal of the time, directing violence outward in the form of conquest or allowing it to spend itself inwardly in the form of intra-clan rivalry. The importance of controlling the negative uses of violence can be observed in the Dulkadir code: its first clause prescribed death by hanging for highway robbery (adultery, a social crime, came first in the Ottoman codes). Other cultural traits of tribal societies can account for the legal features that Heyd finds "advanced." The attention paid in the Dulkadir code to unintentional injury and to thefts by more than one person reflect the legal needs of a culture more prone to raiding and fighting than the settled world of sharia (and of most of Ottoman society). Moreover, the Dulkadir emphasis on fines may have something to do with their compatibility with tribal cultures, whose heightened sensitivity to the relationship between honor and punishment was perhaps offended by the Ottoman preference for combining fines and flogging (the latter hardly an honorable punishment). That the Dulkadir code bears less resemblance to the law book of Süleyman than to those associated with Mehmed the Conqueror and the earlier years of his son and successor Bayezid II is not surprising, given that Ottoman kanun originated in a period more heavily influenced by the cultural needs and norms of the Ottomans' own tribal origins and early milieu.

By the sixteenth century, the Ottoman regime bore few traces of its origins, but the organization of the ruling class did echo some of the features of tribal political practices. The ruling elite was not disarmed—indeed, it was by definition military, *askerî*. Its potential to do direct harm to the "paramount clan"—the Ottoman dynastic household—was paralleled by a separate system of justice that authorized a direct response to that threat, placing the power of siyaset in the sultan's hands. Like the Dulkadir law code, siyaset within the Ottoman ruling class made few concessions to sharia. The impatient response of Selim that the execution of 150 scribes was no concern of the chief mufti demonstrates how far this severe sultan believed the domain of siyaset should extend. The enshrinement of violence within a ruling "tribal" elite was even more marked in the Mamluk regime, which elevated no "clan" as paramount sovereign but rather retained armed competition among rival households as the core feature of its political constitution.

Yet as rulers of empires situated in highly cosmopolitan areas and encompassing culturally and religiously heterogeneous subject populations to most of whom the social organization of Inner Asian traditions was alien, the Mamluks and Ottomans perforce acted as patrons not only of a ruling-class justice but also of a more complex subject justice based on sharia.

Sharia—or perhaps one should say siyasa shariyya—had the virtue of long experience in regulating complex populations, including non-Muslims, and in accommodating the executive practices of governments to both the theoretical and practical aspects of Islamic legal traditions. Strong executive power was perhaps the key characteristic of both the Mamluk and the Ottoman regimes, arguably the first stable states of the Islamic world to survive the typical 100-year active life span of ruling dynasties. The Mamluk and Ottoman approaches to subject justice were noteworthy for a substantial and well-articulated component of siyaset and a dual system of legal administration.

There was, however, a significant difference in their legal administrations, in that the Ottoman regime built up a network of "sharia" courts and promoted them as the linchpin of the legal system as a whole. In her study of Ottoman judicial administration in sixteenth-century Cairo, Nelly Hanna points out that a major goal of the Ottoman regime was to systematize and standardize the judiciary throughout the empire, so that the work of one court could be transferred to another; this was accomplished in Cairo, Hanna notes, without diminishing the courts' latitude to draw on local customary practice.[88] Heyd has observed that the Ottomans made a serious attempt to suppress the separate stream of secular courts—the *mazalim* courts, or courts of complaint—presided over in the Mamluk regime by rulers and governors. These courts heard appeals against the miscarriage of justice by state officials, and they also tried criminal cases. In his study of late Mamluk judicial administration in Damascus, Jon Mandaville notes that the governor's court (the *mazalim* court, or *dar al-'adl*) was, in the formal hierarchy of judicial organization, the highest court of the province.[89] What the Ottoman regime aimed at diminishing, or at least checking, was the judicial authority of governors. In so doing, it was reversing (or at least suspending) a long-established practice, one that was elaborated as early as the writings of the eleventh-century jurist Al-Mawardi.[90] The 1524 Ottoman law book for Egypt, conquered from the Mamluks less than ten years earlier, instructed people to use the judge's court rather than the governor's court for settling disputes.[91] This law book was the first important work of kanun issued under Süleyman, and it heralded a key feature of his reforms in provincial legal administration. As for Aintab, it is clear that the governor-general in Maraş and the provincial governor were critical figures who still had the authority to act independently of the judge in some areas. But what is most noteworthy about the murder cases reviewed above is the interplay between what appear to be separate judicial authorities.

If raising the authority of the local court was an achievement of the Ottoman regime, a critical element in its success was the unprecedented comprehensiveness in matters of criminal law displayed in Süleyman's law book, which, as we have seen, attempted both to distinguish between and to combine the roles of sharia and kanun.[92] Without the evidence of Mamluk court records, it is impossible to know if this was an uniquely Ottoman approach to judicial administration, or if the Mamluk "courts of complaint" actually cooperated similarly with judges' courts.[93] The bottom line, however, is that Ottoman policy in the sixteenth century aimed to invigorate the system of courts, a goal that is evident in other apparent innovations of Ottoman judicial administration—the stipulation that the court sit in a fixed location,[94] the keeping of the court's minutes as a public record carefully preserved, and the expanded range of issues that were brought into the court's compass. The Ottoman emphasis on the suspect's right to a hearing by a judge in a court with a fixed location is critical to a central argument throughout this study, namely, that one of the court's most vital roles was as a registry for local voices. It was this Ottoman practice that made writing this book possible.

What the Ottoman regime encountered in Aintab was a relatively sophisticated legal environment. Aintab's heritage included both the culture of sharia and familiarity with politically determined modes of law enforcement. It also had centuries of practical experience in dealing with a complex social demography that ranged from notable merchants and mollas to tribal nomads, and the economic ties that linked one to the other. The apparent self-sufficiency of the city and its hinterland had much to do with this *longue durée* experience. If it is true that the Ottoman regime focused on Aintab as a potentially valuable administrative node in the marchland between southeastern Anatolia and northern Syria, it was the city's viable legal culture—its ability to mesh the legal traditions of sharia and kanun—as much as its economically strategic location that attracted that focus. What was new for Aintab was integration into a legal system more carefully articulated and administered than in the pre-Ottoman past.

PART FOUR

Making Justice
at the Court of Aintab

Fatma's Story
The Dilemma of a Pregnant Peasant Girl

In late September 1541, a young peasant girl named Fatma was brought to the court of Aintab because she was pregnant. She was also unmarried, and so it was obvious that she was implicated in some manner in the crime of illicit sex, or *zina*.

But who was the father? As the case unraveled, it turned out that Fatma had named two individuals, and moreover accused one of them of raping her. At no point in the proceedings does it appear that Fatma was suspected of sexual relations with more than one person. At issue then was an instance of false accusation of zina, also a crime in the eyes of both local practice and the formal legal codes articulated by religious and state authorities. At stake was the honor of at least three individuals, and a village scandal possibly in the making.

Fatma's case was brought to court by a high-ranking local official, the trustee of crown lands, whose job it was to supervise that portion of the provincial tax base which paid directly into the imperial treasury. The Aintab trustee, Mustafa Çelebi, was one of several delegates of the sultan's authority who figured in the complex hierarchy of provincial administration, both fiscal and legal. That he would be involved in Fatma's case was not unusual: a share of the revenues from her village, Hiyam, belonged to the royal domain, and Mustafa Çelebi's job included securing not only these taxes but the requisite social order as well. What *was* unusual in this case was that the trustee, one of the most important officials of the province, handled it himself rather than deputizing one of his agents, his normal procedure. And so the dilemma of an unmarried peasant girl's pregnancy became the concern of more than her local community—it was a matter of concern to the state as well.

Despite these various interests, Fatma was the protagonist in the legal drama of her pregnancy, or so it appears in the court record of the case.[1] Hers is virtually the only voice that we hear directly in the written record. In the first of three formal entries that make up the record of this case, Fatma named the father of the child: "I am pregnant, and I am pregnant by this Ahmed." In this same entry, Ahmed denied responsibility for the pregnancy, but his voice did not carry the status of Fatma's. Instead it was recorded in a cursory and indirect manner: "after Ahmed responded by denying [the allegation], the statement of the aforementioned [Fatma] was recorded at the request of the trustee of crown lands, Mustafa Çelebi."

The second entry consists of Fatma's formal confession to the crime of zina some days later: "During the day, at noontime, I committed zina with Ahmed. . . . "[2] The language of the record—literally, "I did zina" (zina itdüm)—establishes Fatma as an active and intentional perpetrator of the crime. This is noteworthy because it contrasts with the passive role generally attributed to women in most normative legal treatments of consensual illicit sex ("he did zina to me").[3]

In the third and final entry, the village imam, spiritual leader and counselor to his peasant flock, came to court to tell a different story of Fatma's situation. In the imam's account, it was not Ahmed who was responsible for Fatma's pregnancy but another villager, named Korkud. Moreover, in the imam's account, Fatma was not a willing partner in the forbidden act, but rather the victim of rape. Recounting what Fatma had told him earlier, back in the village, the imam repeated the girl's words: "When the mother of Korkud was giving birth, I went there to carry water. Korkud shut the courtyard door and took me inside, this Korkud raped me [lit., 'did zina to me by force']. I am pregnant by Korkud."

The judge now had to untangle these two accusations. When he questioned Fatma about the imam's account, she replied with a statement that is remarkable in these records for its length, its moral tenor, and its apparent idiomatic authenticity: "It's not that I didn't make such a statement, I did, but Zeliha, Ahmed's mother, instructed me to say that. That's why I made that statement. The truth of the matter is that I am pregnant by Ahmed. I cannot slander another, it's this world today, tomorrow the hereafter. It is Ahmed who had illicit relations with me."

HONOR, GENDER, AND SOCIAL CLASS

The three entries that constitute the record of Fatma's dilemma are a striking example of the judge's latitude to amplify some voices and mute others as he composes the summary record of a case. If in this particular case the judge of Aintab focused on Fatma's voice, it is presumably because he considered it legally significant. The very structure of the record, with its insistence on inscribing the young girl's words rather than explicitly addressing the issue of male complicity or solving the social problem of the illegitimate pregnancy, suggests that the crime of slander—of false accusation of zina—received as much attention as the crime of illicit sex.

But in the moral and legal thought-world of this society, the two were hard to separate. Thinking about sexual misconduct was embedded in an understanding of the integrity of the individual in which the violation of individual honor was as serious as the violation of the body. Certainly a violation of one's body might constitute a violation of one's honor, but honor inhered as well in words and reputation. Talk about illicit sex might be as socially destabilizing as its perpetration, and slander therefore was punished as severely as physical assault. Hence the judge's investigation of this affair was aimed at exonerating the wrongly accused as much as it was aimed at identifying the guilty.

Fatma's talk, both inside and outside the court, implicated her fellow villagers. It did so by creating two problems that demanded the attention of the court: the illegitimate sex that resulted in pregnancy, and the conflicting allegations of paternity. Let us begin with the question of Fatma's original accusation that Korkud raped her. Why did she tell the story she later claimed was fabricated and foisted on her by Zeliha, the mother of the young man Ahmed with whom she confessed to fornication? A plausible answer is that by pinning the pregnancy on the alleged act of rape by Korkud, Fatma established herself as victim: she avoided the punishment for fornication, and the responsibility for her dishonor was assigned to another. Zeliha's reasons for deflecting blame from her son are perhaps obvious: to exempt him from punishment and also from possible pressure to marry the pregnant girl.

But there is one problem in this hypothesis. That is the fact that the law reflected society's extreme concern with protecting the reputation of the individual against potentially slanderous talk (in our case, the reputation of Korkud). The rules of Islamic jurisprudence on bringing accusation of zina were so strict that some scholars of these texts have assumed that the court would never see instances of adultery, fornication, or rape. According to the standard manuals of the law, for a case of zina to be prosecuted, either the guilty had to confess in four separate sittings of the court or four witnesses of the actual act of penetration had to provide testimony; if the testimony of any one of these witnesses was flawed, all were punished for the crime of false accusation of zina (eighty lashes).

It is therefore a paradox of Islamic jurisprudence that it set up obstacles to the enforcement of the sexual probity it mandated. The thrust of zina jurisprudence was to safeguard the reputation of the individual and to expose those who brought accusation of zina to the risk of being cast as "slanderers." The stringent requirements for proving zina had powerful historical

origins, which may have contributed to their tenacious hold in jurisprudence: they are contained in Qur'anic verses revealed after an attack on the
Prophet Muhammad through the slander of his young wife 'A'isha (Surah
24, verses 11–20). The law of the jurists did not seriously envision active
prosecution of illicit sex; rather, it was concerned with maintaining social
harmony in the face of what was tacitly acknowledged as the inevitability
of zina.

The resultant bias in favor of protecting reputation at the expense of
those victimized by sexual assault accorded with the life experience of the
jurists. In articulating legal protections, jurisprudence assumed the practice
of gender segregation and the seclusion of women. In reality, however, seclusion was a luxury, a standard marker of the elite in Mediterranean and
Middle Eastern societies and an integral feature of a lifestyle presumably
within the reach of prominent jurists. This assumption by formal law is explicit in our period in the treatment of rape at the hands of the chief mufti
Ebu Suud. In fatwas issued by Ebu Suud, rape was envisioned as occurring
together with breaking into a home, not as an assault in a public or semi-
public place: for example, "If Zeyd enters Hind's house, wanting to rape her
. . . ," or "If two men testify that they saw Zeyd in such-and-such a woman's
house, are the judicial authorities empowered to interfere with Zeyd?"[4] The
same scenario was envisioned in Süleyman's law book, where numerous
clauses begin in similar fashion: "If a person enters someone's house with
intent to commit zina . . . ," "A person who abducts a girl or boy or enters
someone's house with malicious intent . . . ," "If a person finds a stranger in
his house . . . "[5] The Aintab court records suggest, however, that as many
rapes occurred outside homes as inside them.

Such a presumption of women's seclusion as normative social practice resulted in a hierarchy of legal protection that less effectively served people
of more modest life circumstances, whose daily routines involved more trafficking in the streets and public spaces of their villages or city neighborhoods. Especially vulnerable were women of these classes, who were more
exposed to unwanted sexual advances because of their greater public presence. It is this obvious vulnerability that Zeliha exploited in constructing the
rape scenario: Fatma allegedly became Korkud's victim while doing work essential to the female cultural economy of the village—attending birth and
carrying water.

Vulnerable not only to sexual assault, women whose labor was public
were less able than wealthier women to guard their reputation and honor.
More visible, they were easier targets of social suspicion and censure, guilty
or not. Accordingly, they were denied the honor that automatically accrued
to women of greater wealth and status merely by virtue of their seclusion,
which was in turn predicated on the ability to retain slaves and servants
to do their public business. As we saw in chapter 4, such women were known

as *muhaddere,* a term that linked honor to elevated social status by simultaneously denoting "chaste" and "veiled/secluded." In the several fatwas Ebu
Suud issued in order to clarify who qualified for muhaddere status (discussed in more detail in chapter 4), one ruling was that women who fetch
water at springs cannot be considered muhaddere.

To return to our case, how could Fatma elicit the help of the court in
finding legal redress for her pregnancy? How could she bring an accusation
against either Korkud or Ahmed, unless she was able to produce four witnesses? In fact, Fatma was far from alone in these records in making such
a claim despite a lack of witnesses—a move on her part that suggests an
awareness that such allegations were not made in vain. Deliberation about
zina in court was possible because in practice judges were able to relax the
stringent rules of witness set out in juridical treatises and manuals, admitting circumstantial and hearsay evidence. In the case at hand, for example,
the imam's account appears to have been admitted on the basis of two
witnesses of Fatma's allegation of rape (the imam himself and one Hasan),
not four witnesses of the act. Yet, while the law in practice may have made it
easier to bring public accusation of sexual misconduct, particularly for victims of rape, it was still difficult to make such an accusation stick because
of the legal principle that the accused were safe unless they had a *töhmet*—
a previous instance of publicly articulated suspicion of, or conviction of,
wrongdoing.

Consider the status of Korkud and Ahmed, the men Fatma accused. Fatma's retraction before the judge of her accusation of rape against Korkud
presumably cleared him of suspicion. (Indeed, this appears to be the principal goal of the court action as reflected in its record.). But an interesting
question arises here concerning the trumped-up story Fatma claimed was
foisted on her by Ahmed's mother: how did the two women expect to make
the accusation of rape stick? Zeliha may have chosen her target well: all she
had to do was find an individual with a reputation damaged by either known
or suspected wrongdoing. As for Ahmed, the exposure of his mother's failed
attempt to exonerate him appears to have weakened his claim of innocence.
Strictly speaking, his denial of zina ought to have been sufficient to clear
him, assuming that he had a clean reputation. But that fact that he was not
offered the possibility of taking an oath of innocence is suggestive (the imperial law book sanctioned the administration of an oath of innocence to
a person who denied having committed zina with his or her accuser).[6] In
this case, unlike similar zina cases in these records, the judge appears to
deny Ahmed the opportunity to dissociate himself from the affair. While
the court record does not explicitly state the outcome, it implies that Ahmed is considered guilty of zina and must acknowledge responsibility for
the pregnancy.

I want to return to the question of why this case is recorded as Fatma's story. If we can answer this question, we will understand what is most at stake in the case, or, more precisely, what is most at stake in its legal articulation. I have been arguing that sorting out and identifying the slander is as important as dealing with the social crisis of the illegitimate pregnancy. It is not only the focus on Fatma's words in the case record that alerts us to the centrality of her act of slander. There is also the nagging question of why Fatma appears to stand alone with her problem. It is virtually impossible in the world of these records to imagine a young girl devoid of a kinship structure that would yield a guardian to intervene on her behalf. Ahmed, for example, has his mother working on his (and no doubt her own) behalf, but where are Fatma's parents or guardians? The natural presumption that Fatma is *not* socially isolated supports the argument that it is not her pregnancy per se that is the central issue but rather her account of it, which only she can sort out for the court. (Perhaps the man Hasan, who was present when Fatma related the rape version of her pregnancy to the imam, was her father, since her patronymic was "daughter of Hasan.")

Finally, the tenor of Fatma's final words—"I cannot slander another, it's this world today, tomorrow the hereafter"—must be considered. The tone of moral urgency imparted by her words, unusual in the court record, most probably stems from the necessity that she retract her false accusation against Korkud. The premise underlying the legal process was that individuals would speak the truth in giving testimony. It was in verbal acts more than in social comportment that personal integrity, conscience, and fear of God played a crucial role. False witness was therefore a greater sin than false appearance, and repentance—*tövbe*—typically took the form of a communally public declaration, a vow never to repeat a sinful act.[7]

THE STATE AND ZINA

I would now like to situate Fatma's dilemma in a larger frame and to see what conclusions we might draw if we ask how it fits into the Ottoman legal system as a whole and how it relates to other instances of sexual crime in the Aintab records.

A central issue is the trustee's personal involvement in the case, as this appears from the record to be a principal element in its structuring. The court record hints that Fatma's dilemma might have been handled at the local village level had Mustafa Çelebi not intervened in bringing the case before the Aintab judge: the girl, it appears, originally took her problem to the village imam with the trumped-up story of rape. It is not clear how Mustafa Çelebi became involved in the case. Perhaps Korkud appealed to him for help in getting his name cleared (this makes sense in terms of the structure of the case), or perhaps the imam alerted the trustee to the situation when it turned out to be beyond his ability to handle.

The intervention of the trustee would have been understood as justified on two grounds. First, as a legal offense, Fatma's dilemma came within his jurisdiction. Her village, Hiyam, the largest in the province, paid a portion of its taxes to the state domain *(hass)*.[8] Mustafa Çelebi, as trustee of the state's domain in Aintab, was the responsible authority for the village. The second justification for the trustee's intervention stems from the status of the crime of zina with respect to the state—or, in the language of the legal texts, to the sovereign. Zina was one of the five crimes for which penalties were laid out in the Qur'an (another was slander, or false accusation of zina). Because these crimes were conceived of as offenses against God and religion, their prosecution—a right or claim of God *(hakk Allah)*—became the duty of the sovereign, who acted on behalf of God.[9] This prosecutorial role of the state—the sovereign and the delegates of his authority—was the principal reason for the appearance of sexual crime in the courts despite the strict witness laws of Islamic jurisprudence. For the Ottomans, legislation by the sultans, disseminated in the imperial law books, amplified or superseded the rules of the juridical literature that authorized the hearing of such cases.

While the relationship between jurists and the sovereign falls outside the scope of this book, we should note that although it was jurists who articulated this role of the sovereign, their relation to the state was often characterized by contestation and struggle for control of the definitions of acceptable and criminal behavior. Zina was a sensitive area of the law from this perspective. While penal law was not at the heart of the jurists' domain, family law was. The construction of zina in jurisprudence, with its implicit notions of the integrity and honor of the family and its explicit call for control of social relations, straddled family and penal law. Zina was therefore a terrain of debate over the moral regulation of the family and of the social order as a whole.

The state's role in the prosecution of zina was theoretically ambiguous. On the one hand, the sovereign and his delegates could interpret their mandate to punish zina offenses as being in the interest of society, allowing individuals themselves to take the initiative to prosecute zina and thereby to define its scope as a sociolegal problem. This was practically possible because, as Fatma's case suggests, individuals might appeal to the authorities for help in untangling their social predicaments. Moreover, the rules for false accusation of zina required that the victim initiate prosecution, thus giving this fixed-penalty offense the aspect of a private claim. On the other hand, the state might exploit its mandate to prosecute zina in order to engage in aggressive social engineering or to impose surveillance on targeted sectors of society. In the light of this second possibility, the jurists' insistence on the impossible rules of witness may have operated as a safeguard, protecting society against government authority. Finally, the state might act as a brake on zealots intent on a narrow, punitive interpretation of the law.[10]

In the realm of zina jurisprudence, for example, a potential for conflicting interpretations lay in the gap between the harsh punishment for adulterers (death by stoning, for most married Muslims) and a tradition that urged judges to avoid those penalties that inflicted dire bodily injury or death. The contest between jurists and the state over the regulation of sexual behavior might therefore generate a productive tension that helped protect society; conversely, a convergence of interests between jurists and the state might result in the imposition on society of strict interpretations of the law.

What was the position of the Ottoman regime toward zina in our period? The law codes issued by the sultans of the late fifteenth and sixteenth centuries increasingly expanded the range of offenses that could be publicly prosecuted in the name of zina.[11] Under the rubric "Zina and Related Matters," Süleyman's law book incorporated the basic definition of zina developed by jurisprudence: by the sixteenth century, zina as a legal category had expanded from its original definition as illicit sex that was both heterosexual and consensual to encompass homoerotic sex and rape. Sixteenth-century Ottoman legal discourse defined rape as forcing a female or male to submit to illicit sex, or, in Ebu Suud's formulation, "using [a person] by force" *(cebr ile tasarruf etmek)*.[12] The law book also included a number of other offenses in the category "zina and related matters" such as abduction, entry of a domicile with intent to commit zina, sexual harassment (unwanted verbal and physical aggression), and false accusation of zina. It is important to note that this broad notion of zina made it easier not only for authorities to prosecute offenses but also for individuals to appeal to the court for its intervention. In other words, the expanded definition of zina sanctioned the treatment in court of issues previously excluded from its compass.

It is this broad definition of sexual crime that is intended by the term *zina* in reference to the Aintab court in the remainder of this chapter. In the court records of the year 1540–1541, approximately forty cases were recorded that can be classified under the broad rubric "zina and related matters." In addition, there were a dozen or so cases of swearing involving sexual slurs (calling someone or someone's relative a whore, pimp, or catamite), some of which were tried as the crime of false accusation of zina. These cases came to court in one of two ways: roughly one-third were brought by private individuals and two-thirds by agents of sultanic authority. The latter included the provincial governor of Aintab, the trustee of crown lands, and their various deputies; the bulk of these cases were brought by agents of the provincial governor, a natural outcome of the fact that his jurisdiction included the entire city of Aintab as well as a share of the province's villages.

These various kinds of cases falling under the rubric "zina and related matters" tended to cluster as more characteristic of either urban or rural society. Cases of sexual slander and violation of rules regulating male-female contact were almost exclusively confined to the city of Aintab. While a gang rape and a prostitution operation were uncovered in the city, nothing similar emerged at court from the rural hinterland. Abduction and fornication (sex between unmarried women and men) were the forms of sexual crime that distinguished rural areas, and were virtually absent in the city. Other types of sexual crime—accusations of rape or of illegal entry into a home, adultery, divorce of a wife convicted or accused of adultery—came to court from both city and rural areas.

Do these categories of urban and rural crime suggest anything more than different social habits? In chapter 8, I argued that criminal justice could not be understood without reference to Ottoman taxation policies, since criminal fines were construed as taxes, providing revenue that went into the pockets of the *ehl-i örf,* that heterogeneous group of executive officials serving the state. Chapter 8 examined the petition of Musa Beg, governor of Bozok province, who complained to the sultan that he could not prevent abuse of unmarried women and men by recalcitrant ehl-i örf; the latter refused to give up the pre-Ottoman arrangement by which criminal fines on the unmarried went to lesser officials (as opposed to fines on the married, which went to the governor). Ottoman taxation of crime erased this division between sexual offences committed by the married and the unmarried; however, it continued to give local ehl-i örf a considerable share of rural criminal fines, while urban fines all went to the provincial governor.[13] The logical implication of Ottoman policy was that insofar as abuses of zina legislation actually occurred in Aintab in 1540–1541, the married and the unmarried were both vulnerable. Yet the rural unmarried continued to show up in court disproportionately. The clusters of urban and rural crime displayed by the court records suggest that old prosecutorial habits in rural areas may have been slow to disappear, in Aintab as well as in Bozok. The possibility that criminal administration might end up in the hands of very local individuals is demonstrated by the tax-farm subcontracted to the two brothers from the Kazak tribe, mentioned in chapter 7, which gave them the right to collect taxes on crime and the marriage tax, as well as the head tax on bachelors and landless married men.[14] The vulnerability of the unmarried to particular scrutiny by officials and the apprehension that vulnerability might arouse could well be a factor in Fatma's case.

In earlier chapters, we saw that the arrival of the judge Hüsameddin Efendi in late June 1541, following the month-long presence of a special prosecutor, coincided with a shift in the kinds of cases coming to court. In the area of sexual crime, too, shifts are evident. The "urban" crimes of sexual slander, improper male-female contact, and homosexual rape (two instances) appeared in court after Hüsameddin Efendi's arrival, mostly likely because of increased surveillance and enforcement. "Hard-core" sexual crimes—actual instances of illicit sex and accusations of rape or illegal entry—occurred throughout the year. In other words, it did not take the expanded authority of the court visible in the records from June 1541 onward for the traditional definition of sexual crime to be prosecuted. What was new was stepped-up regulation of male-female contact, the assimilation of sexual slurs to the crime of false accusation of zina, and the prosecution of homosexual rape and slander. The law books of Süleyman's ancestors did not regulate male-female contact or include homosexual contact under the rubric of zina; hence these matters represented practices newly criminalized in kanun (see figure 10).

This rather dramatic shift in the adjudication of sexual offenses in the Aintab court is an important piece of evidence supporting my speculation in earlier chapters that the new judge brought the new law book with him. Süleyman's law book, which is thought to have been issued sometime around the year 1540, contained both new matter and more detailed treatment of old matters previously included in sultanic kanun. The disciplining of local officials that occurred during the special prosecutor's tenure, the dramatic increase in the numbers of cases handled by the court from June 1541 onward, and especially the appearance of new kinds of cases that reflect new emphases in kanun are all grounds for hypothesizing that the sultan's new law book was introduced to the provincial courts by new judges with strengthened mandates. Or so it would seem in Aintab, although it is important to note that newly criminalized sexual practices were less prosecuted in rural areas.

While the theoretical justification for Mustafa Çelebi's intervention in Fatma's affair should now be clear, we still have not addressed the question that opened this section of the chapter: why the trustee *personally* brought Fatma's case to court. If we examine Mustafa Çelebi's participation in court proceedings in the months prior to Fatma's testimony to see what patterns might emerge, we find that he typically and not infrequently came to court in his capacity as fiscal administrator for the royal domain—to deal, for example, with tax collection problems or to turn local tax revenues over to the commanders of various regional fortresses as salary for their regiments.[15] In the months prior to Fatma's appearance before the judge, the only other nonfiscal matter that involved Mustafa Çelebi personally was another instance of slander—of false accusation of zina—also arising in Fatma's village of Hiyam.[16] According to the brief record of this case, the woman Zeyneb stated in court that she had slandered two village men by saying "you did zina to me" *(bana zina itdün)*. Mustafa Çelebi appeared in this case in two connections, both to appoint a village official as bondsman for the two men (to ensure that they not flee the village or their encounter with the court) and to request the court's hearing of the matter. The exact nature of the problem was less explicit than in Fatma's case: while Zeyneb admitted to falsely accusing the two men of having sex with her, it is not clear if she had accused them of rape or of engaging in consensual sex with her.[17] Moreover, the trustee's request for a guarantor for the two men, recorded in the court record twice (both before and after the villagers' testimony), suggests some concern about their possible guilt. For our purposes, the significance of this ambiguous affair, coming to court exactly one month before Fatma's appearance and from the same village, lies in its suggestion that sexual slander was perceived as particularly warranting Mustafa Çelebi's personal involvement. As a key figure in channeling legal norms into the villages under his control, perhaps the trustee was feeling the pressure of the court's greater attention to sexual propriety.

A PEASANT GIRL'S AGENCY

Let us return to Fatma's plight to see what, if anything, this peasant girl might be gaining from her court experience. Ostensibly, the record portrays her as a guilty party—doubly guilty, of zina and of false accusation of zina. But are there perhaps other outcomes of this case that are not inscribed in the record? Let us speculate on this question by looking to the court record itself for clues.

A remarkable feature of our records is that there was so much talk in the Aintab court about zina. Fatma was only one of many who either confessed to acts of illicit intercourse, accused others of sexual assault, asserted that they were victims of sexual slander, or, less frequently, retracted accusations of sexual misconduct. We need to ask questions about this frequency of zina cases and what it reveals about the use being made of the local court by its constituents. Why, for example, did individuals in Aintab, most of them women, bring accusations of sexual harassment or rape when they were clearly going to fail in their suit through lack of supporting testimony, and moreover pay a fine for slander? More unexpected, why were there so many confessions to illicit intercourse? There are roughly a dozen zina cases in the court record in which the confession of one or both parties to fornication or adultery is acknowledged by the court. That members of this community were acting in court in ways unforeseen by normative law suggests that they were deriving some benefit from doing so. We must remember that for many people, appearing in court was a daunting experience, even if they stood to gain by doing so. The advantages of petitioning the court then must have outweighed the obstacles, at least for those who came voluntarily.

Did Fatma wish for her dilemma to be exposed at court? The structure of the record suggests that she did not directly instigate the trustee's intervention. He was most likely alerted to the case by Korkud or a member of his family, the imam, or perhaps a village informant. But Fatma's exposure at court may have helped provide a practical solution to the illegitimate pregnancy. Codes of honor, widespread in the Middle East and Mediterranean region, made it difficult for a female whose sexual honor was compromised to marry and thereby gain an adult social identity.[18] Fatma needed to find a husband to rescue both her own and her child's honor. Her double accusation may have been her way of drawing attention to her plight— to the pregnancy as well as to the apparent attempt by Zeliha to prevent her son's association with the girl. That wrongful accusation demanded redress was an inescapable legal reality that a peasant girl such as Fatma would have recognized.

In his study of sexual crime in Renaissance Venice, Guido Ruggiero makes the point that premarital sex, while plainly against the law, should not necessarily be seen as deviant or criminal, since it may actually support the institution of marriage. It may be the most effective way for a young couple to precipitate a hoped-for marriage if they are faced with obstacles such as parental objection or lack of sufficient funds to form a dower.[19] Premarital sex may in fact be a move by the couple to achieve a social position of greater status rather than risk a criminalized status. In colonial and early republican New England, not only was premarital pregnancy common but some women were able to manipulate the courts to exact support from the father, and in some places it was fully expected that the couple would marry.[20] In a study of tribal groups in the Aintab area in the 1970s, the anthropologist Daniel Bates suggests that abduction can play the role described by Ruggiero, particularly when the parties are frustrated in their desire to marry—for example, by having to wait for elder brothers or sisters to be married.[21] While the twentieth century is not the sixteenth, it is clear from Süleyman's law book that abduction and other forms of pre- and extramarital sex in the early modern period might similarly operate to precipitate marriage in the face of obstacles. Evidence of this can be seen in the law book's penalizing of officials who marry women to their abductors.[22]

The public exposure of premarital sex or other sexual misconduct no doubt created problems for those involved: at the very least, they now had a *töhmet*—their reputation for sexual propriety, a valuable social and legal asset, had been jeopardized. However, exposure might sometimes work to the benefit of an individual who was socially compromised by an act of zina. In other words, the court could in some instances simultaneously serve as an arena for prosecuting illicit sex and point the way toward rectifying its undesired outcomes (at least in instances of fornication if not of adultery). This dual role is demonstrated by a case that the trustee's deputy brought to court from the village of Telbaş (local vernacular for Telbaşer, the seat of one of Aintab's subdistricts), in which a confession of zina appears to have led to marriage. Two weeks after Ali confessed in court to fornication with the girl Emine, her father appeared in court to register his consent to their marriage: "Previously suspicion of sexual misconduct *(töhmet)* has been imputed to Ali and my daughter Emine. I have now given my daughter to Ali to be his wife. I have no complaint and no suit against Ali for what happened previously. I renounce all claim against Ali."[23] As so often in these cases, the question of agency and intention is opaque: Were Ali and Emine chagrined at the exposure of their alleged affair? Emine's silence in the record implies that she did not deny the truth of Ali's confession. Was Emine's father actively resisting the trustee's interference in exposing the sexual infraction, or was he forced to consent to the marriage in order to avoid further compromising of his daughter's honor? The two possibilities, of course, are not mutually exclusive. What the record *does* imply is that the father would have been considered justified in bringing a suit against Ali but he chose not to. Furthermore, he enacted a solution in the same public forum that exposed the problem.

While we cannot know if Fatma and Ahmed, or Ali and Emine, were deliberately engaging in premarital sex as a ploy toward marriage (or even hoped to be married), such agency on the part of a would-be couple in mid-sixteenth-century Aintab, or even on the part of an individual young woman or man desiring marriage, was certainly plausible. Particularly in a society in which parents exercised considerable control over the choice of marriage partner for their sons and daughters as well as over the timing of marriage, it was to be expected that the younger generation would develop stratagems of resistance to this parental prerogative. Generational tensions over tolerance of premarital sex are suggested in a complaint lodged at the Aintab court by Tanrıvirdi, a villager from Han-ı Kirman, against his fiancée's father: "I [am] engaged to the girl named Meryem, daughter of this Sultan Ahmed. One night I went [to their place], and while I was lying with the girl in the said Sultan Ahmed's shed, the said Sultan Ahmed caught me with the girl as he came home from the mill. He took my cloak and my shirt."[24] What is striking here is the young man's apparent assumption that the father's confiscation of his clothing was an unjustified act.

We may in fact be observing a generational tension over marriage choices in Fatma's case. One of the aims of Zeliha's plot is to head off the possibility of marriage between her son and the girl he has impregnated. A marriage partner was chosen primarily to maximize a family's social and economic benefit, and it may be that Ahmed's parents objected to Fatma as a less-than-optimal match. Mothers had a particular stake in the choice of their sons' brides, since the practice of patrilocality meant that mother and daughter-in-law would be living in close quarters. Moreover, the responsibility for the domestic training of the new bride rested with her mother-in-law, who would in turn be largely dependent on the good will of her son's wife in old age. As to Fatma's intention when she entered into her apparently voluntary sexual liaison with Ahmed, we cannot know if she did so with the hope of marrying him; hence we cannot be sure how she reacted to the scheme to blame Korkud. But Fatma may not have regretted the exposure of Zeliha's plot, for her own sake as well as Korkud's. Indeed, as I have suggested, she may have been responsible for the exposure. In this light, the trustee's intervention in an affair such as Fatma's could be both punitive and conducive to a favorable settlement.

BARGAINING WITH THE STATE

The surprising incidence of confession to zina in the Aintab court records can perhaps provide other clues to the culture of the court that may shed light on Fatma's case. These confessions need to be accounted for, as they contrast so starkly with the expectations of jurisprudence. Indeed, legal manuals insist that the judge do all in his power to discourage confession to zina: according to the legal handbook of Al-Marghinani, it is laudable on the part of the judge to instruct the confessor to deny or retract what he or she has said[25] (this is possible because Hanafi law requires four separate instances of confession). Perhaps in the Aintab records for 1540–1541, we are observing an aggressive effort to punish zina, and the confessions are therefore forced or induced. Our records suggest that such coercion sometimes occurred. The problem of abusive police, discussed in chapter 8, enhances this possibility. But forced admission of guilt was not the whole reason for the striking incidence of confession. A central feature of the law gave the accused a powerful means of resisting prosecution: the alleged fornicator's denial was sufficient to invalidate any allegation of complicity in zina (assuming that she or he had an unblemished reputation). The court records contain an example of just such a denial, suggesting that this legal principle, articulated in Süleyman's code, was also understood and exploited by the local populace. In a case from the village of Mazmahor (also in the trustee's jurisdiction), the trustee's deputy alleged in court that one Hamza and his fiancée Hüsni had committed zina before marriage. But while Hamza confessed to zina, Hüsni denied that they had sex, whereupon Hamza retracted his claim (he had made only one of the four requisite statements of confession).[26] Even if the deputy was attempting to forcibly prosecute this case, the young woman's denial was enough to frustrate his effort. This case underlines the legal reality that it was often easier to publicly accuse individuals of sexual misconduct than to prove and prosecute the alleged crime.

Confession to zina could thus be voluntary. What benefit then might those confessing have derived from public exposure? They are not unlike the individuals discussed in chapter 5 who sought a degree of social absolution from the community by acknowledging their mistakes or their moral lapses in the public arena of the court. To be sure, public confession was not the same thing as sincere repentance, given that it was often forced otherwise induced. Yet expressions of remorse like that voiced in the record for Fatma may well have been more common in court than the formulaic nature of most confessions suggest, with judge and scribe simply omitting statements that were deemed not legally relevant. Confession to zina, furthermore, was most often made by both members of an errant couple, emphasizing the social nature of fornication and adultery. Joint acknowledgment of guilt did not erase personal moral responsibility, but it provided a partner in sin.

Some individuals who confessed before the judge may have deliberately sought the aid and protection of the court. By allying themselves to its legal structure and culture, they might hope to escape a harsher local legal culture. The most dire form local practice might take in the matter of zina was the custom of honor killing: that is, the right of an individual to kill a female member of the family and her lover if they were caught in the act. So intractable was this ancient tradition that it was absorbed into Islamic jurisprudence of the late medieval period.[27] In the period we are examining, a chilling fatwa from Ebu Suud upheld the practice: given the query "If one night Amr and Zeyd's sister Hind commit [zina] on Zeyd's property, and Zeyd kills Amr, and Zeyd's mother kills Hind, can the legal authorities intervene?" Ebu Suud replies, "Absolutely not."[28] Other rulings of the chief mufti supported the legitimacy of honor killing by making it clear that the heirs of the executed lovers cannot exact the retaliation or blood money permissible in cases of murder. Honor killing was justifiable execution, not murder.[29] The law code of Süleyman also upheld the legitimacy of honor killing, although limiting it, as did most jurists, to the execution of wives and daughters (not sisters), and requiring that witnesses immediately be summoned, presumably to confirm the flagrant nature of the transgression.[30]

Was this dire form of private justice practiced in Aintab? The court record contains at least two cases in which husbands were legally justified in availing themselves of this option but did not. Cuckold divorce provided a nonviolent alternative for a man to restore his honor, and its frequency in Aintab—five instances over the course of the year—suggests it may indeed have been a popularly embraced alternative. This is not to say, however, that honor killing did not occur outside the compass of the court. Certainly the reiteration of the legitimacy of honor killing in the mufti's rulings and the sultan's law implies that it was an ongoing practice, at least in some parts of the empire, and also that it was being resisted in some quarters. While Aintab was an ancient urban center with well-developed urban institutions in the sixteenth century, it lay in a region with a large Turkmen tribal population, both nomadic and sedentarized, whose customary law gave greater place to a code of honor. It is noteworthy that in our records the confessions to zina come for the most part not from the city but from the villages and tribal groups in the province.

Confessing before the judge was attractive because the court offered a milder alternative to private justice. Both religious and sultanic law gave the court a number of options in punishing illicit sex. While Süleyman's law book did not entirely dissociate itself from violent solutions (it sanctioned honor killing and never explicitly suspended the punishment of death by stoning prescribed by religious law for Muslim adulterers), the punishment it most explicitly and fully articulated was the imposition of a monetary fine. Fines were calculated according to the civil and socioeconomic status of the offender: adultery was penalized more heavily than fornication, free persons more heavily than slaves, Muslims more heavily than non-Muslims, and wealthy persons more heavily than persons of middling or little wealth.[31] In addition to de-emphasizing violence, the state's justice was relatively cheap. The Ottoman regime exacted far less in zina fines than did the Turkmen principality of Dulkadir, which had governed the area until the Ottoman conquest in 1516. For example, the married Muslim's fine under the Ottomans ranged from 40 to 300 akçes, depending on the individual's socioeconomic status, while the Dulkadir fine for married persons regardless of their wealth was 15 gold pieces, or four times the maximum Ottoman fine.[32]

Reducing taxes and fines and thereby weakening former loyalties was a classic feature of Ottoman conquest, and Süleyman's government appears to have applied the policy in the newly conquered Aintab region (at least in the matter of zina).[33] By providing an alternative more merciful than honor killing and cheaper than that of the regime it displaced, the court could attract people into the political and social orbit of the Ottoman regime. In the pre-conquest regime, fines had been assigned to tribal leaders; under the Ottomans, fines formed part of the income of local administrative representatives of the state: the provincial governor, the trustee of crown lands, the military personnel stationed in the province. By arrogating prosecution to its own authorities, the Ottoman regime was able to undermine local ties to tribal and village potentates. Not only did it thereby gain an additional source of local revenue but it also reduced the possibility that a local dispute might flare up into a larger disturbance (indeed, disputes that went beyond the jurisdiction of the Aintab judge to the regional governor-general tended to be chronic rural or tribal conflicts). Perhaps most important, by attracting the local population to the state's system of justice, the sultan's provincial representatives gained the opportunity to instruct subjects in the civic habits of reliance on the regime's agents and the social habits of a more sedentary, urban way of life.

Could individuals who sought the shelter of the court really count on its protection? or might they still be vulnerable to local or private justice? The very frequency of confession to zina within the space of a single year suggests that recourse to the court, or cooperation with it, was relatively common. A certain amount of protection was no doubt afforded simply by the fact of appearing in the city before the judge, with the public exposure it entailed. Take Fatma's case as an example of how the court experience might result in a useful notoriety. Our protagonists were, as a result of the affair, now known to important officials of the province: its judge, the trustee of crown lands, and his deputy. The affair was no doubt on the tongues of others who had business in the court on the days of the case's formal airing. It would also be remembered by the prominent citizens of Aintab who acted as case witnesses, including the deputy judge, Molla Veled, and a commander of the garrison troops. Moreover, the court drew local attention to the affair by exposing Zeliha's slanderous scheme and publicly involving the village imam. And the village headman, who reported to Mustafa Çelebi, would no doubt keep an eye out for irregularities. It would probably be some time before our protagonists could return to the anonymity of their former lives.

Because it is difficult to discuss questions of agency and motivation in cases such as Fatma's, we cannot be certain that she acted with deliberate intent to collaborate with the authorities and the court in order to gain some advantage in coping with her dilemma. What I am arguing here is the *plausibility* of such intent because of the kind of local knowledge of the law and its possible relevance to one's circumstances that a peasant girl such as Fatma was likely to have. In turn, Fatma's own story would no doubt serve to instruct others in Hiyam, already the most populous of the province's villages and one that would experience considerable growth over her lifetime.

THE LOCAL SETTING

According to a cadastral survey conducted in 1543, two years after Fatma's encounter with the court, the village of Hiyam was one of the two largest in the province of Aintab (measured by the number of taxed male heads of household recorded in the survey).[34] Moreover, Hiyam was located on a tributary of the Euphrates River, a short distance downstream from the neighboring village of Keret, the province's second largest village (in 1543, there were 190 households in Hiyam and 185 in Keret).[35] Both belonged to the waqf of the Ibn Keshani family, notables of Aleppo. With the combined household population of Hiyam and Keret approaching one-fifth that of the city of Aintab (1,896 households),[36] the two villages together constituted the equivalent of a town. By the year 1574, when the next cadastral survey was conducted, Hiyam, one of the fastest-growing villages in the province, had expanded by nearly half. It is not too much to say that Hiyam in 1541 was, or was in the process of becoming, the center of a local population boom.

The serendipitous survival of court records so close in time to such surveys enables us to reconstruct a social context for the events recorded by the Aintab judge. Even within a single province, villages were bound to differ from one another. Their character varied not only according to their location and attendant economic and demographic base but also according to the administrative structure imposed on them—that is, whether their tax revenues went to a local notable, the province's governor, a provincial cavalryman, the sultan's domain, or a waqf.[37] One might speak then of the political economy of an individual village. I am suggesting here that the political economy of Hiyam engendered a set of social dynamics that framed Fatma's dilemma.

What accounted for the size of Hiyam and Keret? Certainly their location on a close tributary to the Euphrates was crucial. Of the three subdistricts that made up Aintab province, Nehrülcevaz—the district encompassing Hiyam and Keret, which was closest to the Euphrates—would grow in population between the survey years of 1543 and 1574 at a much faster rate than the other two (48 percent, compared to 15 percent and 9 percent).[38] In addition to its proximity to the Euphrates, Hiyam benefited (as did the province as a whole) from the fact that Aintab was located some 90 miles from Aleppo and well situated to take advantage of the expansion of trade that the metropolis brought to its hinterland.

As a local boomtown, Hiyam also likely attracted the considerable nomadic and semi-nomadic Turkmen population of the region. The general rise in population of the greater Mediterranean region during this era led to the proliferation of local periodic markets in the Middle East, and the town of Nizip, just south of Hiyam's district and provincial border, was the site of such a market.[39] It is not unreasonable to think that Hiyam also acted as an emporium where Turkmen from the area could sell or trade wool, hides, and meat. (Some traffic in the latter had moved further west to the large village of Orul, which had both a slaughterhouse and a tannery in 1543, while Hiyam's slaughterhouse was going out of use.)[40] The village's location on a waterway provided an opportunity for Turkmen to wash wool, finish carpets, and water their animals.[41] A portion of the population growth in Hiyam and Keret was no doubt the result of the sedentarization of some Turkmen, although it is impossible to determine from the cadastral surveys just how extensive this was. In December 1999, when I made a visit to Hiyam, local residents related their village's long-ago history as a transition from pastoralism (when their ancestors lived up in the mountains and hides served as money) to sedentary agriculture.

All these factors ensured that Hiyam would experience a good deal of economic, demographic, and social flux. New households were being established, creating pressure for land that might lead to conflict with established farmers. In 1543, in addition to containing several families engaged in both farming and nonfarming activities, Hiyam and Keret (like other large villages) had a higher proportion of nonfarm households than most villages in the province.[42] Such nonfarming households, ranging across the economic scale, could be employed in activities such as agricultural day labor, food processing, artisanal production, blacksmithing, or portage and transport. Halil İnalcık makes the important point that the combined labor capacity of the marital couple was for the Ottoman government the defining element in the nonfarm rural household's tax potential.[43] In short, the rising proportion of nonfarm households and the existence of diversified households suggest that gender roles and social norms based on the organization of the family farm, long presumed to be the fundamental institution of rural society and administration in this period, were changing.

One marked aspect of family structure in Hiyam and Keret, as in the other more populous villages, was the large number of bachelors living with parents or elder brothers. In coming decades, the proportion of bachelors to married men would rise dramatically in Hiyam and Keret. Because marriage was essential to achieving adult social identity, these bachelors most likely remained unwed not out of choice but rather because they encountered economic or social obstacles to forming their own households. Young men may have found it difficult to accrue the resources necessary for establishing a marital household, particularly if the growth of population outstripped the capacity of the village to provide full employment. An influx of younger men into the village may also have created a gender imbalance that would make it difficult for a young man, particularly a newcomer to the local society, to find a bride locally.

Males were not alone in facing challenges to their strategies for marrying and establishing households. The model of marriage whereby parents arranged the betrothal of their children—a model reinforced by sultanic legislation in 1544 that required the judge's permission for a female to marry in the absence of her father or grandfather—was no doubt more dominant in cities than in the countryside. Or so it would seem from the Aintab court records, where rural women often played an active, sometimes controlling, role in their nuptial destiny.[44] Things did not always go as planned, however. In the following case from the village of Keret, recorded on September 17, 1541, the woman Kemya had apparently spoken for herself in arranging her marriage, and now sued her erstwhile fiancé for abandoning what she had regarded as a firm agreement:

> Kemya bt. Mehmed and İsmail b. Hasan, from the village of Keret, came to court. Kemya brought the following suit: "Previously this İsmail sent word saying 'I'll marry you [lit., "I'll take you"],' and I said, 'I'll marry you [lit., "I'll come to you"].'" "İsmail said, "Previously I had had an agreement with the girl; I was going to take her and she was going to come to me." Their statements were recorded upon request.[45]

Whether marriage negotiations that were not handled directly by fathers or other elders typically ran greater risk and more often led to legal disputes is hard to say, but enough cases came to the Aintab judge in 1540–1541 to demonstrate that marriage negotiations in general were vulnerable to breaking down in verbal and sometimes physical confrontation.

A significant aspect of the Aintab authorities' involvement in premarital sex—that is, in cases of fornication—is that all these cases involved villagers or nomads. A number of interrelated factors may be reflected here, such as a difference in mores between city and countryside, or a lesser opportunity in the city for consensual sex. The Ottoman regime was not the first to take an interest in regulating premarital sex. The Dulkadir regime, which significantly influenced legal and criminal culture in the Aintab region, separated penalties imposed on adultery from those imposed for fornication: fines paid by married persons guilty of illicit sex went to the Dulkadir ruler, while fines imposed on the unmarried went to local tribal chiefs (boy begleri). As we saw in chapter 8, the Ottoman practice of allowing tribal chiefs to retain their role as local enforcers of the law led to serious abuses of unmarried women and men and their families in the central Anatolian province of Bozok. Among other irregularities, the tribal chiefs exacted fines for fornication where no crime was proved, and even incited young men to involve themselves with women so as to generate finable offenses.[46]

Whether similar abuses by tribal chiefs or other local civilian figures of authority were occurring in the rural areas of Aintab province is hard to say. Nor is it clear whether local police, the delegates of Ottoman officialdom, harassed unmarried individuals with the same goal of lining their pockets that motivated the tribal chiefs in Bozok. The warning in the Aintab law code of 1536, repeated in Süleyman's law book, that executive officials must not collect fines larger than those officially prescribed implies awareness of this temptation. Moreover, the sultan's law empowered the judge to take corrective action, requiring restitution of any excessive fines. In other words, the Ottoman administration, while attempting on paper to reform abusive practices, was not necessarily free of its own version of harassment. The cadastral survey for 1543 suggests that Hiyam and Keret may have been paying substantial penal fines. Penal fines were included in the general category of "windfall taxes" (bad-i hava), as was the tax levied on marriages. It is therefore impossible to gauge how extensive crime was in Hiyam in comparison to other villages, but its windfall taxes were clearly high. The average household share of the windfall taxes levied on Hiyam and Keret in the 1543 survey was 9.5 and 10.8 akçes, respectively, while the mean for the eight largest villages in the province (including Hiyam and Keret) was 7.1 akçes.[47] In the factors affecting the social climate of large villages— rapid growth at midcentury, number of nonfarming households, number of bachelors—Hiyam and Keret were not exceptional. In accounting for their

higher windfall taxes—a matter where the two villages *were* exceptional—
nothing in particular points to a larger number of marriages, although this
possibility cannot be ruled out.

But it is not difficult to imagine the proliferation of brawling and sexual
transgression, forms of law-breaking appearing frequently at court, in a scenario such as that sketched above: friction between the nomadic tribal
pastoralists and sedentary village agriculturalists, with their different social
habits; the presence of large numbers of relatively unsocialized young men;
traffic in the village's public spaces generated by an expanding economy.
Each of these factors intensified the vulnerability of women, particularly if
there were not enough of them. Women must have felt increasing pressure
to protect their honor, especially those who by reason of their social status
were more exposed. One way to do this, as I have suggested above, was to
cast blame and responsibility for compromising situations elsewhere, not
only to escape suspicion of misconduct but also to engage the community
in the solution of a social dilemma. As a consequence, some young men
might also be vulnerable because of their lack of grounding in a stable and
familiar social matrix. The fact that Hiyam was subjected twice within a matter of weeks to the scrutiny of leading provincial authorities in the matter of
sexual slander by women is surely linked to the shifting social dynamics of
the village in the early 1540s.

.   .   .

Fatma's encounter with the court of Aintab was a small moment in the complex legal dynamics of the empire of which she was a subject. But because
the provincial court was an institution simultaneously of the state and of the
community, such a single encounter can open a window for us onto the ways
in which the interests of the governing regime and local society interacted.
Three aspects of this interaction are worth discussing in conclusion: the
structural variability of local justice, popular understanding of the law, and,
finally, the provincial court as mediator of the law.

It is in the records of local courts that we can best observe the intertwin-
ing of the law not only with the social and moral concerns of the community but with its economic and administrative life as well. Yet a single judge's
district might be populated by a number of communities with differing
characteristics. Since sultanic regulations mandated that the judge not go
out looking for cases to try but rather adjudicate only what came to him,
much depended on the links a particular community had with the court. In
the matter of zina, in which representatives of the state could act in a prosecutorial capacity, the particular delegate of the sultan's authority to whom
one paid one's taxes mattered greatly. How was Fatma's case influenced
by her village's being both the largest in the province and overseen by the
trustee of crown lands? Most court interventions into matters of illicit sex

occurred in larger villages, whose revenues belonged in whole or part to the imperial domain and hence were under the authority of the trustee.

What about sexual crime in villages not overseen by the trustee? Did such crime escape prosecution? or were its perpetrators more subject to customary law? Did peasants living in smaller or non-royal domain villages therefore enjoy less opportunity to take advantage of the court and of channels to it? Possibly so. Tanrıvirdi, who in suing his prospective father-in-law for his confiscated clothes appears to have had no qualms about his nighttime rendezvous with his fiancée, lived in a small village. Perhaps the authorities there simply did not scrutinize the lives of their peasants as carefully as did executive officials more closely linked to the state. The Aintab court records demonstrate clearly that the enforcement of the law was not uniform across the provincial jurisdiction, and that the administrative organization of a community affected the nature of justice available to it. It may be no coincidence that many of Aintab's larger villages belonged to the royal domain. While there are a number of possible reasons for such an administrative structure, one might be that the state was keeping a more direct eye on larger concentrations of population, particularly in a recently incorporated area such as Aintab.

Let us turn now to the question of popular knowledge of the law. It was clearly not precise. The parameters of the crime of zina, for example, appear to have been frequently misunderstood: manuals of jurisprudence instruct the judge to be sure that litigants at court understand which acts constitute zina and which do not, since some people think that simply *looking* at a member of the opposite sex in an undesirable way is zina.[48] Perhaps such a misconstrual of the term was operating in the case of Zeyneb from Hiyam, who withdrew her accusation of zina against two fellow villagers. But imprecise understanding of the law was not simply the result of popular ignorance, since legal rules might vary over time and space. In the matter of zina, confusion was probably inevitable given the historical tendency to expand its scope, a tendency observable in the law books issued by Süleyman, his father, and his grandfather. Much of the judge's effort in court was devoted to sorting out different views of what was legal and what was not. In the case of Ayşe and her neighbor Sadeddin (see chapter 4), he appears to have agreed with the defendants that their early-morning meeting was socially appropriate, while in the case of Haciye Sabah he was confronted with a more serious community dispute over rules of sexual propriety.

Yet the major principles of normative law appeared to be commonly understood, even if the language of the local community did not tally precisely with that of jurisprudence. For example, the word *kazf*, the technical term for a false accusation of zina, was used in the Aintab court for nonsexual slander as well. Conversely, the legal notion that previous suspicion of sexual misconduct deprives a person of the presumption of innocence is given a terminological specificity in the vernacular of the court *(töhmet)* absent in the discourses of formal law. As noted above, an appreciation of the practical consequences of töhmet is evident in the strategies of both Fatma and Zeliha. Perhaps they did not need the example of their co-villager Zeyneb to teach them this, but each encounter of a fellow peasant with the court no doubt enriched the village's perceptions of Aintab's legal culture and how it might be manipulated.

In the Aintab records of 1540–1541, the court appears as an arena of mediation. It mediates local disputes and dilemmas, such as Fatma's attempt to deal with her illegitimate pregnancy and İne's problematic relationship with her father-in-law. In the affair of Haciye Sabah, the judge Hüsameddin Efendi arguably acts as mediator among competing cultures in the community and even between the community and the state. But the court also negotiates among the legal traditions and norms that enter its domain: the major works of Hanafi jurisprudence, contemporary fatwas, the sultan's law, and local customary law (itself neither uniform nor static). The judge himself is absent from the written record of the Aintab court; indeed, the records suggest that his role is to secure the medium for negotiation, ensuring that the solution lies within the parameters set by the normative codes he is responsible for. In that way, both the process and the solution are Islamically and administratively acceptable.

One of the court's primary functions is to act as a forum for voices from the community. It gives public status to voices that might not otherwise get a hearing. Even when the court punishes, its recording of the wrongdoer's voice may not be an entirely bad thing. The court record inscribes the guilty party's version of the story permanently in the community's historical memory. Especially in the area of sexual crime, where the attempt to bring an accusation against another can so easily turn into wrongdoing by the accuser, speaking publicly in court may be the only way of defending one's honor, as we saw in chapter 5. Evidence from contemporary anthropological study may again be suggestive: June Starr, who studied dispute settlement in rural Turkey, notes that a woman sometimes uses the court to make an accusation of sexual harassment even when she will gain nothing legally.[49] Such a motivation may be operating in the Aintab cases in which accusations of sexual aggression appear bound to fail.

In creating a forum for the voices of the seemingly powerless, the provincial court is able to mediate the gender and class biases of formal law. As noted above, the language of normative codes typically represents women as passive objects of sex, even of consensual sex. The court, however, furnishes a context in which women can speak as perpetrators. It is this perpetrator status that provides Fatma and her provincial compatriots (female and male) the leverage to induce the court to address their problems. In a surprising reversal of the expectations of formal law, public admission of zina in our records is neither infrequent nor essentially confessional. Rather, it can be an act of agency that establishes a dialogue with the community through the auspices of the court.

The court compensates for the class bias of formal law by protecting the social well-being of women who are disqualified from the shielding function of high social status implicit in that law. As we have seen, this bias was endorsed by the chief mufti Ebu Suud in his fatwas on the status of the muhaddere woman and his limited view of rape as a violation of domestic rather than *female* honor and space. It was the expectation that a village girl raped while fetching water would receive, if not justice, then at least the attention of the court that enabled Zeliha to assume the plausibility of her fabricated story. In other words, the court appears to seriously consider the life circumstances and constraints of those unable to achieve the social ideals of formal law, which were predicated on an urban, upper-class lifestyle. The court also acts as a moral leveler, most often tolerating the range of social and cultural values articulated by the variety of microcultures within the province. By giving public status to voices that might not otherwise get a hearing, the court serves as a forum where the individual can salvage some moral integrity even when punished or dishonored.

These multiple functions of the court may help us understand how normative law may acquire multiple, even conflicting, meanings in application. First, take the rules of witness for zina. On the one hand, jurists' protection of these stringent rules may hurt urban lower classes and the rural population, especially women, by making sexual aggression difficult to prosecute. This hypothesis is confirmed in the Aintab court record. On the other hand, the stringent rules of witness may function as a means to resist potential abuse by the state. We have seen an example of a peasant couple (Hüsni and Hamza) able to use these rules to resist the trustee's attempt to punish them for sexual relations during their engagement.

Second, the governing regime may be imposing a particular social vision for its own ends and specifically targeting some populations for the purposes of political control and fiscal gain. But its intent does not necessarily translate into oppression: for some local subjects at least, its policies offer choices. The fact that the state's policies are filtered through the local court provides an opportunity for individuals in the community to insert themselves into the processes of interpretation and enforcement. Specifically, as I have argued with regard to Fatma's dilemma, the regime's presence in the court may offer local citizens an alternative to customary legal practices, an alternative that may have been particularly beneficial to women. The role of the provincial court, at least in Aintab in the mid–sixteenth century, was thus a complex one, for while it functioned as an instrument for the enforcement of normative law, it acted at the same time as an arena for negotiating the very law it was mandated to enforce.

Conclusion

Fatma's story frames the conclusion to *Morality Tales* because it brings together many of these themes of the book and, more important, because it looks at legal culture in sixteenth-century Aintab from the perspective of an individual unremarkable in the provincial landscape. This pregnant village girl, in trouble for naming two men as the unborn child's father, gains significance for us as a consumer of the law—that is, as an individual engaged with the court in the process of interpreting legal rules. So this conclusion begins locally, echoing the book's close focus on an individual community and its court. To be sure, no single case in the Aintab court records provides a clear window onto this provincial society, its quotidian concerns, and its legal culture. But Fatma's case, appearing among the last three days' entries for the year studied here, is in one sense the culmination of the work of the court as it is represented by the two well-kept registers dating from September 1540 through early October 1541. Considered in the context of the many court cases this book has examined and the portrait of the province generated by cadastral surveys, Fatma's situation helps us look back and see what we have learned about Aintab, its court, and its recently acquired role in the vast Ottoman empire of the mid–sixteenth century.

The mood of the times was the product of a number of tensions: prosperity that came at a cost, the physical security but also the ideological controversies that the "pax Ottomanica" brought to Aintab, and a stronger court that enabled some to finally solve chronic problems but threatened others with surveillance. It is in this atmosphere of opportunity, uncertainty, and anxiety that both Fatma's dilemma and our study as a whole are situated. In Hiyam, the large village where Fatma lived, we can observe the vagaries of recovery from the disruptions of the Ottoman conquest twenty-four years earlier. Like other villages and city quarters, Hiyam experienced the economic and social shifts that accompanied post-conquest mobility, for people were clearly moving around within the province, as cadastral surveys demonstrate. The slow growth at midcentury of Aintab city as well as of the major Syrian cities of Aleppo and Damascus—unusual because of the rapid growth that characterized the times—suggests that the disruptions of the conquest years hit greater Syria particularly hard. Now people who had taken refuge in urban centers could return to rural communities, while urban residents were spreading out into less densely populated city quarters. Some things had changed in the interim, however. Hiyam, for example, was no longer a meat-processing center, having lost that role to the large village of Orul. And some people came back to their villages only to find that they had unwittingly forfeited property left behind in the custody of others.

Other aspects of life in Aintab province were changing. A salient feature of Hiyam's social complexion—its growing population of bachelors—is relevant to the problematic relationship of public authorities to the seemingly private matter of getting married, an issue that is raised by a number of disputes in the court records. The rising proportion of bachelors in the adult male population was a demographic development pronounced in Aintab's larger villages and in the city; it would become a more generalized phenomenon in coming decades.[1] This excess of bachelors and the population flux in general inevitably aggravated the delicate negotiations that making marriages seemed to entail in Aintab. The court record is peppered with cases of problematic engagements and quarrels resulting from failed alliances.

Such cases, and the problems stemming from less customary marriages like that of the child bride İne, no doubt underlay the ruling by Sultan Süleyman in 1544 that marriage be contracted in the presence of a judge if the bride were to be given away by someone other than her father or grandfather. The regime's aim in this legislation was law and order—that is, the prevention of local disputes that could flare up around disputed engagements or marriages. This potential danger is illustrated by a case from the village of Arablar, ultimately settled at court in December 1540. Three fatherless siblings, engaged in an intractable quarrel over marriage negotiations with two uncles and their children, had apparently resisted the "many times orders and agents came from His Honor the Pasha [of Maraş]"; "finally after a great while" they were persuaded to a court-supervised settlement whose eleven case witnesses (including the province's governor) signaled the gravity of the extended family's antagonism.[2] Fatma's story, like those of İne and others, fits into this sociolegal scenario whereby private arrangements could seriously threaten the peace and thus become an object of concern to local government.

In another particular, Hiyam illustrates an important theme of *Morality Tales:* the striking variation in the texture of justice across a single provincial unit. Where people lived had a large impact on the ways in which they interacted with legal authorities. This was so because villages differed in the manner in which they were linked to provincial, and thereby to imperial, administration. To recapitulate this complex matter: contrary to standard representations of sixteenth-century rural administration as resting in the hands of timariot soldiers (those members of the provincial cavalry who were stationed in local villages), Aintab reveals a variety of rural administrative links. Villages could indeed be assigned to timariots, but also—and more likely—to the crown, to the provincial governor, to high-level officials serving the governor-general in Maraş, or to local Turkmen tribal chiefs. Other villages were owned by urban magnates from Aintab or Aleppo, either as private property or family waqf. Villages thus varied in what I have termed their "responsible authority"—the official with the double charge of collecting taxes and maintaining law and order.

Fitting into the category of family waqf (of an Aleppan notable), Hiyam also exemplifies the *malikane-divanî* system—that arrangement whereby even those villages owned by urban magnates were subject to the regulatory presence of the Ottoman regime through its claim on a specific set of revenues (including criminal fines and the tax on marriages). This claim insinuated a "responsible authority" into privately owned villages in Aintab; since malikane-divanî revenues belonged to the crown, this individual was Mustafa Çelebi, the trustee of crown lands in the province. The revenues he collected from Hiyam and other privately owned villages supplemented the substantial revenues from villages belonging directly to the crown domain, including many of Aintab's largest and wealthiest. All this helped make Mustafa Çelebi the most powerful player in the provincial administrative hierarchy. It was Mustafa Çelebi who brought Fatma's case to the court of Aintab.

The implications for the distribution of justice are obvious. Would Fatma's case have received the same treatment if she had lived in the smaller village of Akcakent, downstream from Hiyam, whose revenues were shared by eleven soldiers stationed in the Aintab citadel?[3] Would their low status among the ehl-i örf and their joint authority over Akcakent have dealt her a different legal fate? And might Fatma have employed a different strategy in handling her dilemma?

.   .   .

Let us turn to a last characteristic of Hiyam, one that at first glance might seem a mere curiosity: the eagerness of people to cultivate vineyards, vegetable gardens, and orchards. As we have seen, it was not just in Hiyam that these agricultural enterprises played a central role in people's strategies to maximize their share of Aintab's economic expansion. City residents too prized vineyards and vegetable gardens, which they cultivated mainly along a branch of the Sacur River that curved around Aintab's northern perimeter. As the court records amply demonstrate, women were especially eager to acquire vineyards. Unlike men, however, they often sold the vines in order to amass savings or to purchase the jewelry and domestic items so central to the autonomous world of women's material resources described in chapter 6. We know about women's interest in vineyards in part because they brought suits against male relatives who expropriated this common item in inherited estates.

Women's recourse to the court in the management of their property was not a habit peculiar to Aintab, as many studies of Ottoman-period legal records have shown. But neither was such recourse a routine matter in Aintab, as the arrival of a new judge partway through the year made clear: for the first nine months covered by this study, women brought no property suits against male relatives, beginning to do so only when Hüsameddin Efendi took up office in late June 1541. A major theme of this book has been the change that Aintab's legal life experienced under the new judge—not only in the disposition of property but also, notably, in the regulation of social contact between the sexes, the supervision of market transactions, and the adjudication of murder. The shifts in local legal culture that Hüsameddin's assumption of office touched off support the important point that courts and their records cannot be studied as an isolated phenomenon; rather, because legal institutions and legal practice were affected by changing currents in political, social, and religious life, they need to be studied as one of several overlapping domains.

Specifically, the arrival of Hüsameddin Efendi in Aintab was a significant moment in the province's incorporation into the Ottoman empire's networks of administration. In contrast to major cities like neighboring Aleppo, which underwent this process of imperialization immediately upon the Ottoman conquest, Aintab waited some twenty years until the ruling regime turned its attention to absorbing and developing smaller centers in the region. The year 1536, when Aintab received its own law book (*kanunname*), which mainly codified the local tax regime, was a critical turning point in its absorption into the empire. The events in this small province mirrored what was taking place on a much larger stage. The years around 1540 were a time when Süleyman and the legal team he assembled seriously turned attention to consolidation of the empire's judicial system, one element in which was the linking of local courts into an empire-wide network. In addition, Süleyman's updated and expanded version of the imperial law book (*Kanun-ı Osmanî*) is thought to have been issued around 1540. If my speculation that Hüsameddin Efendi was charged with introducing this revised law book to

Aintab is correct, then his appointment was another critical stage in the imperialization of Aintab.

The invigoration of local courts and the dissemination of a new law book had to do with more than legal life, however. In Aintab, the court was the arena where all lines of authority emanating from the sultan—the military, the fiscal, the judicial—converged and moreover were supervised by the judge. An example of the regulatory oversight performed by the court was the recording of the transfer of local tax revenues to fortresses in the region as payment for the garrison troops stationed in them. While primarily a judicial functionary, the judge of Aintab was one of the parties responsible for revenue raising, and Hüsameddin Efendi was clearly charged with expanding the court's supervision of taxation. As several chapters have noted, the new judge was preceded in this mission of enlarging the court's powers by a special agent appointed from Istanbul, whose principal assignment was to discipline major tax-farmers whose payments to the state had fallen into arrears. During his month-long assignment, from the end of May until Hüsameddin's arrival, the agent, one Ahmed Beg, initiated the work of expanding the court's supervisory role. An immediate and consequential innovation in court procedure was incorporating the work of the market inspectorship *(ihtisap)* into the purview of the court.

This intricate interweaving of administrative lines was a core feature of the Ottoman approach to government that makes studying the legal system in isolation a dubious project. In fact, from the perspective of the ruling regime at least, it is questionable whether the administration of law can be isolated from other elements in the totality of running an empire.[4] The overlap between fiscal and judicial aspects of imperial administration is particularly relevant to this study: the fact that rural administrators collected criminal fines and marriage taxes in addition to taxes on agriculture and nomadic pastoralism blurs the line not only between social and economic life on the ground but also between the state's programs in the domains of law and revenue raising. In Aintab city, where criminal fines formed part of the provincial governor's stipend (as did the marriage tax and fines imposed by the market inspector), these revenues went to support an essentially military appointment.

Seemingly to temper this deliberate overlap, Süleyman's law book carefully delineated the separate, if symbiotic, domains of hearing by the judge and enforcement by policing authorities. In other words, a system of checks and balances was by design a central element in a style of governance that stressed connection: trial and punishment were administratively separate but functionally linked. Because in theory all authority stemmed from the sovereign, it was his job to articulate the manner in which his powers might be judiciously exercised by his local delegates. Hence Süleyman's insistence on the right of the ordinary subject to a court hearing in the judge's presence before punishment was imposed by the ehl-i örf, and its corollary that the judge must not interfere in the imposition of lawful punishment. In Aintab, this blueprint appears to have been more or less working in the year studied in this book. Here, however, a serious caution should be sounded: this was a moment in the Ottoman empire's long life when the ruling regime's ability to influence life in the provinces was considerable; it was not always so.

. . .

The last few paragraphs have emphasized the structures of royal authority in a local province. Law here has been primarily kanun—the essentially administrative law of the sovereign power. It was the regulatory thrust of kanun that provided the Aintab court with greater heft in the summer of 1541. But we must always remember that subjects and rulers alike acknowledged the higher authority of sharia, the body of specifically Islamic legal traditions to which the empire professed allegiance. Süleyman's insistence on the right to trial certainly had much to do with the regime's ongoing preoccupation with circumscribing the powers that it necessarily delegated to provincial governors and the police forces commanded by them, but it had equally if not more to do with the elaborate procedural elements prescribed by sharia, particularly the important roles that the latter acknowledged for individual testimony and community mediation. Consequently, the Aintab court, clearly a venue over which the regime asserted a considerable degree of control, was even more a court that belonged to its community—by virtue, in large part, of the procedural rules of sharia.

A number of arguments have been advanced throughout the book as to why the Aintab court was a community court. Here I summarize some of them, proceeding from the abstract to the concrete. First, because sultanic kanun could never displace the authority of sharia, the court of a judge, who was trained in the Islamic legal sciences, enjoyed a certain ideological immunity. Süleyman's law book paid greater respect to sharia than did those of his ancestors, suggesting that the immunity of judges and courts was growing stronger over the course of his reign. Second, as bodies of normative law, both sharia and kanun assumed a large role for local input into the interpretation of rules. Third, the work of the court, while dependent upon the presence of the judge, could not have been accomplished without the testimony of local people, which sharia regarded as the core input into a judge's rulings. The testimony of individuals, in other words, can be said to be the flesh on the skeletal structure of procedural rules. Fourth, the benefit gained by local individuals who used the court to promote their own interests was as great, if not greater than, the profit to the regime from its attention to systematizing provincial courts. The many private transactions that Aintabans had the judge record—those bits and pieces of information that they wanted permanently registered—are a prime example of such use. Finally, a point about prosecution and enforcement of the law: while governors were centrally appointed, their authority was largely realized by a policing force that was locally recruited.

While the court had a dual identity that could lead to tensions between the local community and the regime, it was at the same time the principal venue for dialogue between the two. As a legal arena, the court naturalized this dialogue by enabling each side to invoke legitimate mechanisms in articulating its own position. The very existence of dialogue was a reflection of the symbiotic relationship between province and sovereign regime. Local places such as Aintab collectively constituted the vast bulk of the empire, a reality that was recognized in the sultanate's name for its realm—"the well-protected domains." The provinces, in other words, were hardly "provincial," for they were where the imperial project was realized. Because the pax Ottomanica promoted a certain convergence of interests between empire and province, the province served its self-interest in serving the needs of empire. For its part, the Ottoman regime might be said to have courted the people of Aintab, for its legal system could be strong only if communities patronized their local court. The regime's goals of social order were now, under Süleyman, to be promoted more by means of law and less through the instruments of force deemed necessary in the years immediately following the Ottoman conquest. This shift entailed building a citizenry willing to work with the organs of the state and also a civic consensus on a shared rule of law. It also entailed discrediting or co-opting other local legal regimes, such as tribal law or the urban codes enacted by earlier rulers over the region. Ultimately, building an Ottoman consensus on the uses of the law depended on attracting people to local courts.

This last point touches on another theme of the book: the existence of a multiplicity of venues for dispute resolution. The court was far from the only resource to which people might apply for the adjudication of their problems: the court records themselves reveal individuals appealing to governors, timariot soldiers, tribal leaders, neighborhood imams, and muftis. The role of such authorities was probably greater in rural communities than in the city, where the court was more familiar and more convenient, and many cases that ended up in court had their start with one of these figures (Fatma's case, for example, and perhaps that of İne). The murder cases discussed in chapter 8, the most vivid illustration of interaction among these legal resources, make clear that while the court was the central legal institution in the province, its ability to do its work was predicated on maintaining connections to other legal venues in the community. These murder cases display a complex mobilization of a range of legal resources in addressing potentially volatile disturbances.

It is important to note that while the Ottoman regime helped its judges make these connections, in part by endowing the court with greater authority and firmer police backup, cooperative networks of communication, policing, and enforcement predated the conquest. Aintab was an old city located in a region that was interconnected as early as the second millennium B.C.E. The elaborate mechanisms for locating and recovering stolen or stray horses, donkeys, and mules described in chapter 2 reveal a regional approach to problem solving that the Ottomans simply reinforced and exploited. What was new for Aintab, which already had the habit of regional cooperation, was location in the middle rather than on the edge of an empire. I have speculated that Aintab was targeted to host a court more influential than the dimensions of this relatively small province might warrant. If so, its ability to handle cases that originated beyond its borders was a significant factor in its selection.

.   .   .

If an important goal of the Ottoman regime was to attract clients into its court system, it needed to provide incentives to render the courts user-friendly. Aintab's was a litigious society, and people were aware of the pitfalls and advantages of the various options for dispute resolution. People did not go voluntarily to the court without some prior calculation. As I have argued throughout the book, one of the court's advantages was that its procedures gave a voice to its clients in the interpretation of rules. This does not mean that it was lenient in enforcing the law: many people were judged guilty no matter what extenuating circumstances they might offer, and were duly punished. But as we have seen, even in such cases, the court might allow the guilty to salvage some bit of moral honor in the face of conviction.

To succeed in their clientele-building efforts, courts needed to attract that half of the population that was female. But as the introduction noted, the law was not a level playing field, and gender was a major one of its dissymmetries. As we saw in chapter 5, women were decidedly disadvantaged by the structure of the court and some of its rules of procedure: in Aintab at least, women never served as case witnesses, they almost never gave the testimony that sharia regarded as the bedrock of the court's work, and they almost never enjoyed the option of taking an oath of innocence. Yet the court appointed them as guardians of orphans and recognized them as financial guarantors of major urban tax-farms, both highly regarded community roles. This paradox in women's status reveals the important point that law as process was considerably less sharply gendered than normative law. A judge could not alter the structural exclusion of women (or of non-Muslims), but he could facilitate their proactive use of the court and give ample hearing to their defense when they were involuntarily summoned before him. Still, the discrepancies in the treatment of women and men in normative law had considerable effect on how legal events played out on the ground, as we have seen in the chapters in part 2. We have also seen that as a consequence, women frequently adopted different strategies in court than men did in order to meet the challenge of their disadvantages.

A good deal of attention has been given in several chapters to looking at the ways in which females and males spoke at court—or rather, at how the court record represented their testimony. An examination of the variations in idiom, rhetorical tone, and content of male and female testimony has revealed that voices at court varied with the nature of the legal problem. Where the matter at issue was relatively routine—for example, property or divorce—male and female voices were recorded similarly. These were "scripted" matters, where legal rules were familiar. It is not that women and men were equal in the realities of property or divorce (women brought suits because men usurped their property or refused to pay the dower due at divorce), but rather that the course of litigation was predictable because rights were clearly spelled out in normative law—or because normative law reflected common practices. If, in the litigation of such matters, tempers ran high and harsh words were exchanged, the record does not let on.

In contrast, male and female voices differed considerably in areas that were less firmly scripted in normative law or more fraught with questions of honor. Gendered voices appear most clearly in cases having to do with problematic relations between the sexes, where women and men typically adopted different strategies before the judge in defending or attempting to exonerate themselves. The boundaries of permissible contact between men and women, and also between adult males and boys, were not precise; as we have seen, Aintabans differed in their opinion of what was moral conduct and what was not. Because of the ambiguities involved, the court tended to decide each case on its own merits. Hence, there was room for creativity in the crafting of testimony. Especially because such cases directly affected moral reputation and honor, a certain degree of persuasive rhetoric was called for. However, as we have seen, the gendering of voices was not wholly about the sex of the speaker, for on occasion men might adopt a "female" tone, women a "male" tone. Voice was also about one's social, moral, and even psychological location in the problem at hand.

The frequency in the court records of sexual crime and also of disputes over contact between the sexes is worth dwelling on, since such cases have played a salient role in this book. The stories of İne, Haciye Sabah, and Fatma all revolve to one degree or another around the legal problem of illicit sex. These cases have been featured in part because they display "raised voices," giving us a fuller sense of the actors, the events at issue, and the broader social context than other types of court business do. But we should not take the presence of such cases for granted; indeed, they are a surprise in view of the fact that sharia makes the prosecution of adultery and fornication *(zina)* virtually impossible by requiring four witnesses of the actual illicit act. But kanun, less scholastic and more pragmatic, rendered sexual crime prosecutable by sanctioning less stringent forms of proof. Closer to the messy reality of human nature, kanun recognized that adultery, fornication, and rape were real problems that might threaten the social order of the community, and that therefore required regulation. Here, there is no surprise, given that rulers were charged with the prosecution of crimes named in the Qur'an, which included adultery, fornication, and sexual slander. The public rather than the strictly theological nature of sexual crime was emphasized in the law books' imposition of its rules on non-Muslim as well as Muslim subjects.

There were other motives for the Ottoman regime's focus on sexual offenses, and therefore other reasons for highlighting these cases. By bringing their prosecution under the purview of the state-regulated court, the regime could hope to limit the vigilante justice that was an intrinsic element in local customary practice, whose most violent expression, arguably, was honor killing. The absorption of sexual crime into the court's jurisdiction probably helped women more than it hurt them, since as the principal locus of family honor they were disproportionately punished by customary practices. A further reason for the Ottoman government's focus on sexual behavior was that it taxed many forms of crime, including sexual offenses, and therefore had to spell out what acts were criminal. Included in the law books under the rubric "Zina and Related Matters" were sociosexual offenses such as improper association, sexual cursing, and sexual harassment. Over the course of some sixty years, from the law book attributed to Mehmed the Conqueror to Süleyman's own version, the list of prosecutable acts grew longer. The regime, in other words, intervened increasingly to regulate the sociosexual behavior of its subjects. No longer were incidents such as that of a unmarried couple seen talking in a remote spot left to local modes of social regulation. The proliferation of such cases in Hüsameddin Efendi's court—and the annoyance and anxiety they aroused among some Aintabans—are a principal factor in my speculation that Hüsameddin Efendi was charged with applying the sultan's comprehensive new law book.

There was yet another reason for the regime's scrutiny of social conduct: it was in part a response to the geopolitics of the times and their ideological consequences. The bold claims of the Safavid regime in Iran to moral, religious, and political superiority inevitably provoked an Ottoman response, which was to accuse the Safavids of practicing heresy that was shot through with sexual license. By controlling its own subjects' conduct—at least rhetorically—the Ottoman regime could pose as the guardian of rightly ordered morality. The affair of Haciye Sabah was a scandal because it directly linked sex, religious identity, and political loyalty.

Culturally speaking, the thrust of this politicization of sexual behavior was to reduce the whole empire to a single moral code. Merged on paper into a homogenous social entity were province and capital, countryside and city, tribe and sedentary, female and male, commoner and elite, Christian, Jew, and Muslim. But the regime's vision of an ordered society did not necessarily translate into rigid control over the bodies and the actions of ordinary people. In Aintab at least, grassroots legal administration allowed individuals to "interpret" their conduct to the judge, and thus to engage with him in the translation of imperial statutes to local social values. In the case of Ayşe and Sadeddin, discussed in chapter 4, the dialogue at court among the judge, the night watchman, the three neighbors, and their two accusers was in effect a negotiation over the applicability of a legal rule, namely, the forbidding of free association between a man and a woman who were not married. It was the sum of thousands of such instances of negotiation that gave the imperialization of law a local face.[5] This "localization" of royal pronouncements was no doubt the intent of the Ottoman regime, and we do it injustice not to recognize this fact.

The frequency of sexual crime and sexual slander, and the preoccupation of both with honor, probably had a great deal to do with relations among the microcultures visible in Aintab. In addition to the social characteristics mentioned above, there is another that threaded through much of Aintab society and through the pages of this book: the cultural and religious orientations of Turkmen. Originally tribal pastoralists, Turkmen had been settling in the region for centuries and adopting the habits of local urban and village life. In other words, they had to varying degrees lost their tribal identities and practices. However, in the Aintab area there were still numerous nomadic and semi-nomadic tribes, whose mobility and reluctance to abide by administrative and legal structures the regime was trying to contain. As we have seen, newly settling Turkmen were linked in the minds of some Aintabans with poverty and also with unorthodox religious proclivities. Cultural clashes, particularly between Turkmen and the religious elite of Aintab, often took the form of slanderous cursing. Tribal women typically show little deference to urban norms of modest conduct, and it may be that the Turkmen cultural element in Aintab accounts in part at least for the raised voices of women and the occasional dramatic use they made of the court venue. The point here is that the salience of sexually framed tensions in the court records is in part a product of the demographic mix in mid-sixteenth-century Aintab. Only further studies of local cultures can tell how widespread these features were.

Examining sexual crime has another advantage: it enables us to see that the judge did not simply proclaim winners and losers, the innocent versus the guilty. Rather, complex cases received a more nuanced treatment in which each protagonist's actions were evaluated separately. İne's story is an example of what I have called this principle of separate justices, with İne ultimately rescued from her problematic marriage while her father-in-law was cleared of her charge of rape. The drama of Ali and Ayşe from Bire, recounted in chapter 3, is another example, with Ayşe divorced by Ali on the grounds of sexual impropriety but apparently exonerated when she claimed she was assaulted. Moreover, we have seen losers win: for instance, the women in chapter 5 who made accusations despite the obvious fact that they could not substantiate their claims and might even pay a fine for slander. Such individuals used the court as a public stage to seek the community's sympathy and perhaps its absolution by asserting the morality of their own intentions and the immorality of their antagonists. Their hope was to gain honor, rather than a favorable judgement, and to lay a foundation for suspicious conduct *(töhmet)* that might haunt their antagonists in the future.

As the court records of Aintab suggest, people exploited the fact that slander—defined in sharia as false (or unsubstantiated) accusation of illicit sex—was a crime the authorities prosecuted with alacrity. We might speak of a "creative abuse" of slander because it was a surefire way of getting one's problems aired at court. İne may well have been raped, but Fatma was not, nor perhaps were some others who brought rape accusations. Such creative abuse was not a strategy only of women, as examples in chapter 5 have shown. It is possible that Haciye Sabah's male neighbors fabricated their allegation of sexual license in her instructional circles; their double accusation of heresy and illicit sex was aimed at getting rid of this popular teacher one way or another. Abusing the terrible power of slander—for slanderers were pariahs, as the ban on their testimony at court demonstrates—may have been an age-old practice, as the Qur'anic sanction against sexual slander suggests. If a dark side of the complex contest for honor was the use of public venues, when available, to fabricate wrongdoing, then the bolstering of the Aintab court under the Ottomans increased its value as a forum for manipulating morality.

·   ·   ·

The title of this final section of the book, "Making Justice at the Court of Aintab," is intended to suggest the cooperative endeavor of the judge, members of the court, and its clients in fashioning settlements that satisfied the law as well as the needs of the community. But what was the nature of justice at the Aintab court in 1540–1541? An important argument throughout has been that justice varied according to a person's location in the social landscape—by gender, by class, by place of residence, by religious orientation. Was justice therefore unevenly available at court?

The justice fashioned at that Aintab court was just that—the work of the court. We cannot know about individuals who did not come to court— whether they were prevented from coming, or chose not to come (thereby presumably gaining some advantage), or were simply unaware of what the court might do for them. With its other sources of legal information and its other venues for dispute resolution, Aintab was not dependent on its court, although in the years of this study it was becoming the province's central legal arena. Justice outside the court was not necessarily of a lesser quality. This book has noted some of the advantages of the court for women and some of the drawbacks of customary law, but it is difficult to speak conclusively about the whole of women's legal lives—or of those of the elite of Aintab, who tended to avoid the court, or of any other subgroup in the population such as the small Armenian community. The autonomous world of property that women constructed raises questions about their choices in other aspects of their lives. When recourse to a legal authority was voluntary, they may, for example, have preferred the more private option of seeking the opinion of a mufti or of their local imam.

Most of the business of the court was straightforward—the recording of routine transactions or the settlement of disputes that had clear winners and losers. But when it was not, the court aimed at the goal of social equity rather than winner-takes-all solutions. The many cases that were settled by mediation brought "peace" to disputants because each received partial, if not total, satisfaction. The principle of separate justices, by virtue of which judges ignored what appear to be logical inconsistencies in the denouement of conflicts, enabled them both to punish and to allow the wrongdoer to recoup some semblance of moral honor. In their hearings, judges sought to preserve the personhood of litigants if only by allowing the guilty to give some account of the constraints operating on them. The sharia exhortation to judges to find some pretext to avoid the severe physical punishments that it in fact prescribed is another manifestation of the profound impulse to salvage the guilty from social marginalization.

Aintab's was a hierarchical society, a class-conscious community with a complex set of markers for the privileged including religion, occupation, lineage, and place of residence. Tensions among classes played themselves out in brawling, cursing, slander, cheating, and religious antagonism (far more among Muslims than between Muslim and Christian). But this acute awareness of social rank was offset by the culturally tenacious assumption that everyone was entitled to assert personal honor no matter what their location in the social hierarchy. People of lesser social status were thus able to defend their legal and personal integrity, although they might have to work harder to assert it than did members of the privileged classes. We might speak of a notion of citizenry that depended not on property or gender or literacy, but on acceptance of the (potential) moral worth of all and of each person's right to be recognized as honorable. Hence the alacrity with which ordinary Aintabans defended their reputation, and, conversely, the powerful temptation (to which they frequently yielded) to slur the reputations of others.

While the court replicated the structures of class by identifying individuals in its records according to their social status, it was democratic in its recording of voices. Once one had made it past any obstacles and finally arrived in the judge's presence, one could count on a fair hearing, it seemed. (As for the imposition of penalties on the guilty, the absence of records makes it impossible to know if considerations of class were reintroduced, given that kanun frequently weighted punishment according to wealth and social status.) The court also helped level the playing field in Aintab by offering protective legal mechanisms to individuals who stood outside the circle of bounty in which the profits of economic expansion were shared by the Ottoman regime with Aintab's elite. The legal solidarities *(kefalet)* invoked by groups of lesser status—butchers, bakers, pensioners, Armenians—enabled them to engage in self-defense and to gain a voice in the communal arena of the court. Gaining voice was important since it was a crucial move toward asserting moral and legal legitimacy. The court can thus be said to have redistributed power and status through the legal tools it offered.

Left out of the formal structures of the legal process, women were unable to formulate a group voice. The one community of women visible in the court records—the teaching circle of Haciye Sabah—was disbanded. However, there were a number of ways in which women compensated for the lack of a group voice. For one, they had a large collective resource in the family. The large number of cases in which females acted together with a parent, siblings, children, or a combination of family members demonstrates the public importance of families, whose collective voice did not require naturalizing through any legal mechanism. Even the fragility of engagement and marriage was an advantage of sorts for females, since the quarrels engendered by failed negotiations drew the attention of the authorities. In addition, the material world of jewelry, caftans, quilts, kettles, and cash that gave women some financial autonomy could be said to be a kind of group enterprise; women made selective use of the court to build it, and in turn it gave them leverage to undertake other transactions or litigation in court. And finally, women were no doubt aided in acquiring a legal voice by the Ottoman emphasis on establishing stationary courthouses. In Aintab, the "safe space" of the judge's residence-cum-courthouse was enhanced by its enlargement upon the arrival of Hüsameddin Efendi. The frequent appearance of women like Esma, who made her way to the court over a piece of property five times in a matter of weeks, suggests that legal action, like making the pilgrimage to Mecca, was a form of public activity positively sanctioned for women.

Although women for the most part dealt straightforwardly at court, they used their legal wiles more often than men did. Indeed, the formal structures of normative law and of the court necessitated that they do so. Normative law tended to represent women as passive, sharia more so than kanun. Manipulating money and property, initiating legal suits, and even committing crime gave them active agency. As we have seen, accusing or confessing in court established a dialogue with the judge and sometimes with one's fellow Aintabans. It is important to remember that law was popular knowledge as much as it was the concern of learned jurisprudents, and gossip about the strategies people adopted in cases like those featured in this book probably entertained and instructed much as today's TV courtroom and police dramas do. For Aintabans, knowing something about the law was especially important in 1540 and 1541 because processes of imperialization were altering its structures. Structures of morality were also shifting, as expressions of anxiety and anger over the uncertain boundaries of class and conduct suggest. Cases where voices were raised reveal tension over who might act as the moral arbiters of local society. Talking out and talking back—at home, in the neighborhood, at court—ensured that one got one's own opinion expressed. Even when the judge imposed the severely dishonoring punishments of public humiliation and banishment on Haciye Sabah, he gave her the last word in the public record, allowing her to say that the acts for which she was punished had been morally acceptable in the past.

Judges had flexibility in situating normative rules among the complexities of local life. As we have seen again and again, customary practice and community input were vital in the process of adapting universal rules to local needs and practices. It is important to emphasize that the relationship between grassroots habits and the normative law of sharia and kanun was less a conflict than a dialectic in which each drew from the other. Some rules may have harmed groups in the population, but they were to an extent balanced by the moral environment of mutual obligations and reciprocities underwritten by sharia. The approach to justice that characterized the work of the Aintab court kept these larger assumptions about social well-being firmly in sight.

But the moral environment might shift, and so it appears to have done as the Ottoman regime and its subjects alike adjusted to the new political and ideological constellations that followed the ruptures of the early sixteenth century. The case of Haciye Sabah reminds us that when moral visions clash, those of the marginal rarely prevail. The new hegemony of the Ottoman sultanate as the standard-bearer for sunni Islam meant a replacement of the colorful cultural palette of the empire's youth by a more sober social orthodoxy.

NOTES

INTRODUCTION

1. The question of what is actually meant by "the court"—who constituted its personnel, where it met, the rhythms of its daily activities—is taken up in detail in chapter 3.

2. In citations from the court records, the abbreviation AS stands for Aintab (Gaziantep) Sicili, or Aintab court register. AS 161 dates from September 1540 to May 1541, and AS 2 from May 1541 to October 1541. For a catalogue of the Aintab court records, see Ahmet Akgündüz, *Şer'iye Sicilleri: Mahiyeti, Toplu Kataloğu, ve Seçme Hükümler* (Istanbul: Türk Dünyası Araştırmaları Vakfı, 1998), 1:190–91.

3. Lawrence Rosen, *The Anthropology of Justice: Law as Culture in Islamic Society* (Cambridge: Cambridge University Press, 1989), 17 and passim.

4. See chapter 3, note 3, for recent critical assessments of using court records.

5. David Sabean, *Power in the Blood: Popular Culture and Village Discourse in Early Modern Germany* (Cambridge: Cambridge University Press, 1984), 2–3.

6. Judith E. Tucker, "Taming the West: Trends in the Writing of Modern Arab Social History in Anglophone Academia," in *Theory, Politics, and the Arab World: Critical Responses,* ed. Hisham Sharabi (New York: Routledge, 1990), 198 (emphasis mine); Tucker is quoting Charles Tilly, "Retrieving European Lives," in *Reliving the Past: The Worlds of Social History,* ed. Olivier Zunz (Chapel Hill: University of North Carolina Press, 1985), 15.

7. For a study of peasant accommodation and resistance to Ottoman administration in the same period, see Amy Singer, *Palestinian Peasants and Ottoman Officials: Rural Administration around Sixteenth-Century Jerusalem* (Cambridge: Cambridge University Press, 1994), esp. chap. 5.

8. See Ronald Jennings, "Kadi, Court, and Legal Procedure in Seventeenth Century Ottoman Kayseri," *Studia Islamica* 48 (1978): 133–72; "Limitations of the Judicial Powers of the Kadi in Seventeenth Century Ottoman Kayseri," *Studia Islamica* 50 (1979): 151–84.

9. Ahmet Yaşar Ocak, "Idéologie officielle et réaction populaire: un aperçu général sur les mouvements et les courants socio-religieux à l'époque de Soliman le Magnifique," in *Soliman le Magnifique et son temps,* ed. Gilles Veinstein (Paris: La Documentation Française, 1992), 185–92.

10. Carlo Ginzburg, *The Cheese and the Worms: The Cosmos of a Sixteenth-Century Miller,* trans. John and Anne Tedeschi (Baltimore: Johns Hopkins University Press, 1980); Natalie Zemon Davis, *The Return of Martin Guerre* (Cambridge, Mass.: Harvard University Press, 1983); Giovanni Levi, *Inheriting Power: The Story of an Exorcist,* trans. Lydia C. Cochrane (Chicago: University of Chicago Press, 1988).

1. LOCATING AINTAB IN SPACE AND TIME

1. On Selim's route of passage and his activities, see Feridun Beg, *Mecmua-ı Münşeat üs-Selatin* (Istanbul, 1264–1265/1848–1849), 1:399. For an account of the battle of Marj Dabik, see Carl Petry, *Twilight of Majesty: The Reigns of the Mamluk Sultans al-Ashraf Qaytbay and Qansuh al-Ghawri in Egypt* (Seattle: University of Washington Press, 1993), 224–27.

2. More precisely, the records span 938 to 1327 (1531 to 1909). This means not that there are records for every year, but rather that there are no gaps of more than a decade over the entire period. For an inventory of Ottoman court records in collections in the Republic of Turkey, see Ahmet Akgündüz, *Şeri'ye Sicilleri: Mahiyeti, Toplu Kataloğu, ve Seçme Hükümler* (Istanbul: Türk Dünyası Araştırmaları Vakfı, 1998), Vol. 1.

3. In yet other places, the records of court proceedings may have remained in the personal possession of the judge or other members of the court, especially where these offices were the monopoly of local notable families. See chapter 3 for a discussion of the preservation of court records.

4. On the registers produced by these surveys *(tapu tahrir defterleri)* as a historical source, see Heath W. Lowry, "The Ottoman *Tahrir Defterleri* as a Source for Social and Economic History: Pitfalls and Limitations," in *Studies in Defterology: Ottoman Society in the Fifteenth and Sixteenth Centuries* (Istanbul: Isis Press, 1992), 3–18. For detailed studies based on sixteenth-century cadastral surveys of greater Syria, see Amnon Cohen and Bernard Lewis, *Population and Revenue in the Towns of Palestine in the Sixteenth Century* (Princeton: Princeton University Press, 1978), 3–18; Muhammad Adnan Bakhit, "The Christian Population of the Province of Damascus in the Sixteenth Century," in *Christians and Jews in the Ottoman Empire: The Functioning of a Plural Society,* ed. Benjamin Braude and Bernard Lewis (New York: Holmes and Meier, 1982), 1:19–66; and Bakhit, *The Ottoman Province of Damascus in the Sixteenth Century* (Beirut: Librarie du Liban, 1982).

5. The 1520 survey is contained in the register catalogued in the Ottoman Prime Ministry Archives as Maliyeden Müdevver 75. Unfortunately, much of the Aintab portion of this survey, including the inventory of the city itself, has been lost from the register.

6. The 1526 survey is included in the Ottoman Prime Ministry Archives in Tapu Tahrir Defteri 998, the 1536 survey in Tapu Tahrir Defteri 186, the 1543 survey in Tapu Tahrir Defteri 231 and 373, and the 1574 survey in Tapu Tahrir

Defteri 161. Cadastral registers 186, 373, and 161 have been analyzed and large portions transcribed in Hüseyin Özdeğer, *Onaltıncı Asırda Ayıntâb Livâsı* (Istanbul: Bayrak Matbaacılık, 1988).

7. Amy Singer, "*Tapu Tahrir Defterleri* and *Kadı Sicilleri:* A Happy Marriage of Sources," *Tarih* 1 (1990): 95–125.

8. These remembered histories appear principally in the journals *Başpınar* and *Gaziantep Kültürü* and in numerous short volumes on various aspects of local history and culture published locally, many of them originally under the auspices of the Gaziantep Halk Evi. I thank Fatma Bulgan, the acting director of the Gaziantep Museum, and Ayşe Nur Arun, the president of Arsan Turizm, for making the latter available to me. I am grateful to Hülya Canbakal for sharing her copy of Cemil Cahit Güzelbey's *Gaziantep Evliyaları* with me, and to Ayşe Nur Arun for providing me with a copy of Güzelbey's *Gaziantep Camileri Tarihi.*

9. Zeugma has been much in the news in recent years because of the construction of the Birecik Dam and the consequent flooding of much of the ancient site. The name of the modern village located at Zeugma is Belkis.

10. Dülük was the ancient Doliche or Dolichenus. According to the 1543 cadastral survey, Dülük was a relatively prosperous village of ninety-nine households (Özdeğer, *Ayıntâb Livâsı,* 293–94).

11. George Ostrogorsky, *History of the Byzantine State* (New Brunswick, N.J.: Rutgers University Press, 1969), 96–98, 314.

12. Besim Darkot and Hikmet Turhan Dağlıoğlu, "Ayıntab," in *İslam Ansiklopedisi,* 2:66.

13. A classic work on Turkmen in Anatolia is Faruk Sümer, *Oğuzlar (Türkmenler): Tarihleri, Boy Teşkilâtı, Destanları* (Istanbul: Ana Yayınları, 1980). See also Tüfan Gündüz, *Anadolu'da Türkmen Aşiretleri: "Bozulus Türkmenleri 1540–1640"* (Ankara: Bilge Yayınları, 1997), and Ömer Özbaş, *Gaziantep Dolaylarında Türkmenler ve Baraklar* (Gaziantep: Cihan Matbaası, 1958).

14. For an excellent short account of the Dulkadir geopolitical situation, see Barbara Kellner-Heinkele, "The Turkomans and *Bilâd aş-Şam* in the Mamluk Period," in *Land Tenure and Social Transformation in the Middle East,* ed. Tarif Khalidi (Beirut: American University of Beirut, 1984), 169–80.

15. On the Dulkadir principality, see Refet Yinanç, *Dulkadir Beyliği* (Ankara: Türk Tarih Kurumu, 1989), and Hamza Gündoğdu, *Dulkadırlı Beyliği Mimarisi* (Ankara: Kültür ve Turizm Bakanlığı Yayınları, 1996).

16. The Dulkadir princess Ayşe is often mistakenly identified as the mother of Selim I. The marriage took place around 1467, when Bayezid was still a prince; thus it was a political alliance between the Dulkadir and Bayezid's father, Mehmed the Conqueror, most likely intended to secure the neutrality of the Dulkadir principality in anticipation of Mehmed's campaign against the Akkoyunlu in 1468.

17. Gündoğdu, *Dulkadırlı Beyliği Mimarisi,* 37. The inscription went on to name Alaeddevle as the patron and to dedicate the heavenly reward for this good deed to his father.

18. Petry, *Twilight of Majesty,* 211. Petry gives a lively account of the Mamluk side of these affairs.

19. İsmail Hakkı Uzunçarşılı, *Osmanlı Tarihi* (Ankara: Türk Tarih Kurumu, 1983), 2:273 n. 2, quoting the Mamluk historian Ibn Iyas.

20. For an excellent series of maps detailing Ottoman expansion, see Donald Edgar Pitcher, *An Historical Geography of the Ottoman Empire* (Leiden: Brill, 1972).

21. Yinanç, *Dulkadir Beyliği*, 102-5. Ali Beg was invited to a banquet in the city of Tokat by the Ottoman commander Ferhat Paşa; he arrived accompanied by his four sons, only to be murdered during the meal.

22. Petry, *Twilight of Majesty*, 57-72. See also Yinanç, *Dulkadir Beyliği*, 63-79. Some idea of the devastation Aintab may have undergone in this prolonged confrontation is provided in a letter written by a Mamluk general sent against Şehsuvar in 1469, describing their encounter in nearby Maraş: "We followed his tracks, razed his fortress, burned his villages, chopped down trees, and plundered his stores we found in underground granaries" (Petry, *Twilight of Majesty*, 109 n. 2).

23. Özdeğer, *Ayıntâb Livâsı*, 10.

24. On Rumkale, see Ernst Honigmann and Besim Darkot, "Rumkale," in *İslam Ansiklopedisi*, 9:777-81.

25. Clifford Geertz, "Centers, Kings, and Charisma: Reflections on the Symbolics of Power," in *Local Knowledge: Further Essays in Interpretive Anthropology* (New York: Basic Books, 1983), 125.

26. For these events, see Feridun Beg, *Mecmua-ı Münşeat üs-Selatin*, 427; the information on Yunus Beg's intelligence services comes primarily from Mehmed Hemdemi Solakzade, *Solakzade Tarihi* (Istanbul: Mahmut Beg Matbaası, 1298/ 1880-1881), 386. The sultan and his army halted at three different sites in Aintab province: the village of Bedirkent (August 20), the city (August 21–22), and the village of Sazgun (August 23) (Feridun Beg, *Mecmua-ı Münşeat üs-Selatin*, 399).

27. According to the expansive cadastral survey of 1526, an early catalogue of the northern layer of Selim I's conquests, the governorate-general of Aleppo consisted of provinces stretching from Aintab and Birecik in the north to Homs in the south, and included the Mediterranean coast from Iskenderun to Trablus (Tapu Tahrir Defteri 998, fols. 293-300).

28. On the possible date of 1531 for Aintab's incorporation in the Dulkadir governorate-general, see İsmail Altınöz, "Dulkadır Eyaletinin Kuruluşunda Antep Şehri," in *Cumhuriyet'in 75. Yılına Armağan: Gaziantep*, ed. Yusuf Küçükdağ (Gaziantep: Gaziantep Üniversitesi Vakfı Kültür Yayınları No. 6, 1999), 111-18, esp. 116.

29. The conflict over the northern Syrian Mediterranean coastal region, part of which was eventually ceded to Turkey, is well known. For Mosul, see Sarah D. Shields, *Mosul Before Iraq: Like Bees Making Five-Sided Cells* (Albany: State University of New York Press, 2000), 189-91.

30. The average household revenue was 213 akçes in 1536 and 288 akçes in 1543 (Tapu Tahrir Defteri 186, fol. 373).

31. For an elaboration of the argument against viewing premodern times as static, see Leila Erder, "The Measurement of Preindustrial Population Changes: The Ottoman Empire from the Fifteenth to the Seventeenth Century," *Middle Eastern Studies* 11 (1975): 284-301.

32. Tapu Tahrir Defteri 988, fols. 279, 292, 293-300, 408-9. In each case, the rev-

enue figure is the total tax income for the governorate-general, while the number of households *(hane-i 'avariz)* excludes households that were exempt from taxes and unmarried adult sons *(mücerred)*, presumed to be living at home, who were taxed at a lesser rate.

33. There is reason to approach these figures—arrived at by dividing total revenue from urban and rural taxes by the number of taxpaying households—with a dose of skepticism: uniform guidelines were not applied by the officials dispatched to the various regions surveyed; moreover, it appears that some areas (Aintab among them) were counted with less scrutiny than others. Nevertheless, the disparities among the governorates-general are striking.

34. Tapu Tahrir Defteri 998, fol. 298. Aintab was one of the less thoroughly surveyed provinces in this register, and so this figure should be used with even greater caution than other statistics stated above.

35. AS 161:160b. For the format of case record citations, see introduction, note 2.

36. AS 2:161a, 182a.

37. Suraiya Faroqhi, "The Venetian Presence in the Ottoman Empire, 1600–1630," in *The Ottoman Empire and The World-Economy*, ed. Huri İslamoğlu-İnan (Cambridge: Cambridge University Press, 1987), 326.

38. AS 2:54a, 52c.

39. For Ottoman confirmation, see Suraiya Faroqhi, *Towns and Townsmen of Ottoman Anatolia: Trade, Crafts, and Food Production in an Urban Setting, 1520–1650* (Cambridge: Cambridge University Press, 1984), introduction; also "Crisis and Change, 1590–1699," in *An Economic and Social History of the Ottoman Empire, 1300–1914*, ed. Halil İnalcık and Donald Quataert (Cambridge: Cambridge University Press, 1994), 440.

40. Özdeğer, *Ayıntâb Livâsı*, 133.

41. Özdeğer, *Ayıntâb Livâsı*, 128. Merchandise was taxed at the rate of 2 akçes per camel load, 1.5 per donkey or ox load, and 1 akçe per horse or mule load.

42. Özdeğer, *Ayıntâb Livâsı*, 128.

43. For the rates in 1520, see Maliyeden Müdevver 75, passim; for the rates in 1536, see Özdeğer, *Ayıntâb Livâsı*, passim.

44. Halil İnalcık, "Ottoman Methods of Conquest," *Studia Islamica* 2 (1954): 103–29.

45. Özdeğer, *Ayıntâb Livâsı*, chap. 3 ("Taxes Assessed on Crops").

46. I am very grateful to Lisa Schwartz for her expertise in helping to analyze the data listed for each village in the Aintab cadastral surveys. Much of this discussion is drawn from our "*Bennaks* and Bachelors: Employment and Household Structure in a Sixteenth-Century Anatolian Village," in *Halil İnalcık Festschrift*, ed. N. Göyünç, J. Bacqué-Grammont, and Ö. Ergenç (Istanbul: Eren Yayıncılık, in press).

47. Margaret L. Venzke, "The Question of Declining Cereals' Production in the Sixteenth Century," *Journal of Turkish Studies* 8 (1984): 262ff. For further discussion of mezraas, see chapter 6.

48. On the policy of sedentarization, see Rudi Paul Lindner, *Nomads and Ottomans in Medieval Anatolia* (Bloomington: Indiana University Press, 1983).

49. The question of bachelors has been treated extensively by Michael Cook in *Population Pressure in Rural Anatolia, 1450–1600* (London: Oxford University Press,

1972). See also Huri İslamoğlu-İnan, *State and Peasant in the Ottoman Empire: Agrarian Power Relations and Regional Economic Development in Ottoman Anatolia during the Sixteenth Century* (Leiden: Brill: 1994), 143-44, 179.

50. This rise in the number of bachelors is clearly discernible in the 1536 and 1543 cadastral registers, and even more marked in the 1574 survey.

51. On the subject of this prosecution, see Colin Imber, "The Persecution of the Ottoman Shiʿites according to the *Mühimme Defterleri,* 1565-1585," *Der Islam* 56 (1979): 245-73.

52. This similarity between accusations in Anatolia and Europe has been suggested by Fariba Zarinebaf-Shahr in "'Heresy' and Rebellion in Ottoman Anatolia during the Sixteenth Century," *Anatolia Moderna* 7 (1997): 1-16.

53. AS 161:54a *(feth katından berü gelüb bu diyarda sakin olub at ilminden haberdar kimesne olub . . .).*

54. AS 2:136b *(merhum Mihaloğlu Aintab beg olduğu zamandan berü).*

55. The income of the Mihaliye institution was 25,074 akçes in 1557 (Tapu Tahrir Defteri 301, fol. 15; Özdeğer, *Ayıntâb Livâsı,* 181). The Mihaloğlu family may have been from the large village of Sam: Yahşi Beg also endowed a Friday mosque *(cami)* in the village (fol. 1).

56. AS 161:68a *(zikrolan mezraa feth-i hakanîden Ali Beg devrine gelince timar tasarruf olunur).*

57. Özdeğer, *Ayıntâb Livâsı,* 440.

58. On this phenomenon—namely, the process by which descendants of a successful entrepreneur adopt his name—see Beshara Doumani, *Rediscovering Palestine: Merchants and Peasants in Jabal Nablus, 1700-1900* (Berkeley: University of California Press, 1995), 63-65.

59. AS 2:223b, 319a.

60. For the mosque of Khushqadam, see Özdeğer, *Ayıntâb Livâsı,* 164; for the mosque and fountain of Al-Ghawri, see Mustafa Güzelhan, "Uzun Çarşı ve Civarı," *Gaziantep Kültürü* 8 (1965): 102. The mosques are both described as *mescid* rather than *cami,* suggesting they were relatively small; both were located in the market area, as was the fountain.

61. Hikmet Turhan Dağlıoğlu, *Miladi XVI.cı Hicri X.cu Asırda Antep* (Gaziantep: C. H. Partisi Basımevi, 1936), 1:4-5.

62. Özdeğer, *Ayıntâb Livâsı,* 303 n. 1.

63. Esin Atil, ed., *Süleymanname: The Illustrated History of Süleyman the Magnificent* (New York: H. N. Abrams, 1986), 16-17.

64. Other cities appearing in the Aintab court records with the appellation *mahruse* were Sivas, Malatya, Maraş, Amid (Diyarbakır), Aleppo, Damascus, Baghdad, and, best-defended of all, Istanbul (or "Kostantiniye," as the Ottomans continued to refer to it in formal documents).

65. For general treatments of Aintab, see Darkot and Dağlıoğlu, "Ayıntab"; Hüseyin Özdeğer, "Gaziantep," in *Türkiye Diyanet Vakfı İslam Ansiklopedisi,* 18:466-69; Nusret Çam, "Gaziantep, Mimarî," in *Türkiye Diyanet Vakfı İslam Ansiklopedisi,* 18: 469-74; Özdeğer, *Ayıntâb Livâsı,* 1-11.

66. On the citadel, see Rıfat Ergeç, "Gaziantep Kalesi," in Küçükdağ, ed., *Cumhuriyet'in 75. Yılına Armağan: Gaziantep,* 295-310; Ergeç includes a list of comments by various travelers and historians about the citadel.

67. The Alleben is today a mere trickle (it was a healthy stream as late as the 1960s); it may soon recover some of its former volume when construction of a reservoir to feed it is completed.

68. Cemil Cahit Güzelbey, "Gaziantep Adları ve Manaları," *Gaziantep Kültürü* 9 (1966): 9–10; *'ain* means "spring" in Arabic, and *tab* means "sparkling" in Persian.

69. Henry Maundrell, chaplain to the British trading colony in Aleppo in the late seventeenth century, noted especially "a fine Stone very much resembling Porphyry; being of a red ground, with yellow specks and veins, very glossy. It is dug just by Antab"; see "An Account of the Author's Journey from Aleppo to the River Euphrates, the City Beer, and to Mesopotamia," 7, appended to the third edition of his *A Journey from Aleppo to Jerusalem at Easter, A.D. 1697* (Oxford: Printed at the Theater, 1714). This stone began to be used in the middle decades of the sixteenth century in the decoration of newly constructed mosques, notably the Şeyh Fetullah mosque.

70. Özdeğer, *Ayıntâb Livâsı*, 125.

71. Evliya Çelebi, *Evliya Çelebi Seyahatnamesi* (Istanbul: Devlet Matbaası, 1935), 9:335.

72. See AS 2:123c for the coppersmiths' market *(demirci bazarı)*, AS 161:58a for the jewelers' market *(kuyumcu bazarı)*, and AS 2:15a for the shoemakers' market *(paşmakçılar suku)*.

73. See AS 2:132a for the broadcloth store, and AS 2:215a for the market in Ali Neccar.

74. See Güzelhan, "Uzun Çarşı ve Civarı," 102ff., for a brief history of the Long Market.

75. I am grateful to Akten Köylüoğlu for acquainting me with the neighborhoods at the heart of old Aintab.

76. That Aintab was not a prince's city has been noted by Nusret Çam, "Gaziantep'te Türk Mimarisi," in *Osmanlı Döneminde Gaziantep Sempozyumu,* ed. Yusuf Küçükdağ (Gaziantep: Gaziantep Valiliği İl Özel İdare Müdürlüğü, 2000), 8.

77. On Al-Malik Al-Salih Ahmad and Aintab under the Ayyubids, see R. Stephen Humphreys, *From Saladin to the Mongols: The Ayyubids of Damascus, 1193–1260* (Albany: State University of New York Press, 1977). I thank Yasser Tabbaa for helping me locate this prince within his branch of the Ayyubid dynastic family.

78. Hulusi Yetkin, "Gazientep Şehrin Eskiden Ne İsimlerle Anılırdı?" *Gaziantep Kültürü* 9 (1966): 57.

79. On Melik Salih's work, see Çam, "Gaziantep, Mimarî," 470. On the archaeological restoration project for the bath, see Rıfat Ergeç, "Gaziantep Kalesi ve Hamamı," in Küçükdağ, ed., *Osmanlı Döneminde Gaziantep Sempozyumu,* 269–93. Ergeç dates the bath to the thirteenth century, most probably before 1270 (280); it could then have been the work of Al-Malik Al-Salih Ahmad or his nephew and ruler of an expanded Ayyubid patrimony, Al-Malik Al-Nasir (r. 1237–1260), who was allegedly responsible for a bridge across the Alleben leading to the neighborhood of the tannery *(Debbağhane köprüsü).*

80. See Yasser Tabbaa, *Constructions of Power and Piety in Medieval Aleppo* (University Park: Pennsylvania State University Press, 1997), on the Aleppo citadel.

81. On Aintab's reliance on local initiatives, see Çam, "Gaziantep'te Türk Mimarisi," 8.
82. See Tapu Tahrir Defter 301, a register of the foundations (*waqf* institutions) in Aintab, compiled in 956 H./1557 C.E.
83. Tapu Tahrir Defteri 301, fol. 16.
84. See especially Cemil Cahit Güzelbey's *Gaziantep Evliyaları* (Gaziantep: İslamî Hizmetler Vakfı, 1990), and also his numerous articles in the journal *Gaziantep Kültürü*.
85. Cemil Cahit Güzelbey, *Gaziantep Camileri Tarihi* (Gaziantep, 1984; reprint, Gaziantep: Türk-İslam Eğitim, Kültür ve Yardımlaşma Vakfı, 1992), 37–38.
86. I have arbitrarily combined two versions of the story of the Boyacı mosque, one related to me by Ahmet Söylemez, its present imam, and the other recounted by Cemil Cahit Güzelbey (*Gaziantep Camileri Tarihi*, 65–67); neither fully establishes the relationship between Kadı Kemaleddin and Boyacı Yusuf. In Söylemez's version, it is the abducted girl who cuts down the bandit; moreover, it is not the bandit himself who abducts her, but rather his accomplices. In Güzelbey's version, the reformed bandit, who is not named, becomes a valiant soldier (but not a judge) and amasses riches.
87. On the Demircioğlu family and their alleged dervish lineage, see Cemil Cahit Güzelbey, *Cenaniler* (Istanbul: Ufuk Matbaası, 1984); I thank Ali Cenani for making a copy of this work available to me. On the status and income of these two zaviyes, see Tapu Tahrir Defteri 301, fols. 19, 22; this register is a survey of pious foundations (*evkaf*) and private property (*emlak*) ordered by the sultan Süleyman in 1557.
88. Tabbaa, *Constructions of Power and Piety in Medieval Aleppo*, 24–25.
89. Güzelbey, *Gaziantep Evliyaları*, 20–23.
90. Güzelbey, *Gaziantep Evliyaları*, 16–20.
91. Evliya Çelebi, *Seyahatname*, 9:359; in Evliya's version, Dülük Baba is still alive when the sultan returns.
92. Güzelbey, *Gaziantep Evliyaları*, 41–45. An exceptionally large portion of Sam's revenues was derived from grape cultivation, giving the role of grapes and vines in the stories about the sheikh a foundation in reality (Özdeğer, *Ayıntâb Livâsı*, 377).
93. There is a growing literature on veneration of the pious and on the importance of tombs; see, e.g., Shaun Marmon, *Eunuchs and Sacred Boundaries in Islamic Society* (New York: Oxford University Press, 1995), and Christopher Taylor, *In the Vicinity of the Righteous: Ziyara and the Veneration of Saints in Late Medieval Cairo* (London: Brill, 1998).
94. Indeed, a story of the sheikh curing the sultan's constipation—by means of prayer, not grapes—suggests that they may have met more than once during Selim's three-day halt in Aintab (Güzelbey, *Gaziantep Evliyaları*, 44).
95. Özdeğer, *Ayıntâb Livâsı*, 377–78. See Güzelbey, *Gaziantep Evliyaları*, 43–44, on two documents in the hands of the present descendants of the sheikh corroborating these events; according to the documents, the Sam family petitioned Selim to confirm their existing revenue rights, which the sultan did in a firman dated December 1516; their rights were reaffirmed by Süleyman in a firman

NOTES TO PAGES 48–51   399

dated December 1520, an intervention that was necessitated by the family's inability to enforce its claim.

96. See Tapu Tahrir Defteri 301, fols. 18–19, for a list of the villages and mezraas whose revenue supported the Dülük Baba zaviye; see Özdeğer, *Ayıntâb Livâsı,* passim, for their status as waqfs endowed by Süleyman. That Selim and his son chose the zaviye of Dülük Baba and the sheikh of Sam for conspicuous honors may explain how the story of a possible real-life encounter with Sheikh Muhiddin of Sam got transferred to the figure of Dülük Baba.

97. For Ayşe, see AS 2:209b, and for Köse Bayram, AS 2:120c, d. The house donated by Köse Bayram was currently occupied by the imam of the mosque, who had paid his rent to Köse Bayram in olive oil; presumably he continued to live in it, either rent-free or else by paying his rent to the mosque itself.

98. Güzelbey, *Gaziantep Camileri Tarihi,* 63, 65. The Mısırzade family would adopt the last name "Kutlar" under the Turkish Republic; a later scion of the family, Hamdi Kutlar, would give his name to a part of the old Long Market thoroughfare, now a main artery (Hamdi Kutlar Caddesi) on which the Boyacı mosque is located.

2. THE PEOPLE OF AINTAB AND THEIR WORLD

1. According to the 1543 cadastral survey, the numbers of villages were 105 in Aintab subdistrict, 99 in Telbaşer, and 21 in Nehrülcevaz (Hüseyin Özdeğer, *Onaltıncı Asırda Ayıntâb Livâsı* [Istanbul: Bayrak Matbaacılık, 1988], 213–19).

2. In 1543, the largest villages of Aintab province were (in descending order, based on the number of taxed households): Keret (188 *hane,* or taxed households), Hiyam (186), Orul (156), Kızılhisar-ı Tahtani (149), Burc-ı Resas (128), Hacer (123), Seylan (114), Sazgun (114), Kızılhisar-ı Fevkani (108), Gücüge (105), Arıl (99), Dülük (97), and Sam (94) (Özdeğer, *Ayıntâb Livâsı,* passim).

3. Özdeğer, *Ayıntâb Livâsı,* 116.

4. This figure is obtained by using 5 as multiplier of the number of taxpaying households (1,836 in 1536, and 1,896 in 1543); see notes 9 and 13 on this method of calculation. When households exempt from paying taxes are included in the calculation (yielding a total of 1,969 households in 1543), we reach the upper limit of estimated population. Household numbers are drawn from Tapu Tahrir Defteri 186 (1536) and Tapu Tahrir Defter 373 (1543), as well as Özdeğer, *Ayıntâb Livâsı,* 115–16.

5. Suraiya Faroqhi, *Towns and Townsmen of Ottoman Anatolia: Trade, Crafts, and Food Production in an Urban Setting, 1520–1650* (Cambridge: Cambridge University Press, 1984), 11, 13. Faroqhi (13) shows Aintab as one of nine Anatolian cities in the second half of the sixteenth century with a taxpaying population of 3,000 or more (the other cities are Bursa, Konya, Ankara, Kastamonu, Tokat, Kayseri, Sivas, and Urfa). Using data supplied by Ronald Jennings ("Urban Population in Anatolia in the Sixteenth Century: A Study of Kayseri, Karaman, Amasya, Trabzon, and Erzurum," *International Journal of Middle East Studies* 7 [1976]: 21–57) and again using 5 as multiplier of the number of taxpaying households, we can

calculate that Kayseri in 1523 had a population of roughly 9,000 and in 1550 14,350. Jennings's figures suggest that Amasya should be added to Faroqhi's list of Anatolian cities with a taxpayer population of 3,000 or more in the second half of the sixteenth century; looking at the rate of growth through the 1570s, I estimate that Amasya was closely comparable to Aintab in population.

6. The only figure I was able to obtain for Ruha is from Tapu Tahrir Defteri 998 (fol. 199), which indicates that the city's population was roughly 6,600 in 1526 (calculated as indicated in previous notes). In 1540, Aintab and Ruha may have been of roughly equal size, if we assume that Ruha grew at the same rate as other cities. Cities further to the east, such as Mardin and Mosul, were larger than either Aintab or Ruha and more or less in the same range as Kayseri, Ankara, and Bursa: according to Tapu Tahrir Defteri 998, in 1526 Mardin had a population of roughly 10,000 (fol. 7), Mosul 8,500 (7), and Hisnkeyf 6,500 (250); in 1540, when Aintab's population was somewhere around 9,300, that of Mardin was roughly 12,400 (Nejat Göyünç, *XVI. Yüzyılda Mardin Sancağı* [Ankara: Türk Tarih Kurumu, 1991], 85). The population of Diyarbakır (Amid) is not given in this register.

7. In 1526, the population of Bire was around 3,330 (Maliyeden Müdevver Defteri 75, fols. 16–22), and in 1536 around 2,700 (Tapu Tahrir Defteri 184, fols. 7–12). The apparent loss of population may be an artifact of the varying accuracy of the two surveys, although it may also be real. The wharf taxes *(mahsulât-ı iskele)* in 1536 were estimated at 180,000 akçes (Tapu Tahrir Defteri 184, fol. 12). For an amusing account of the difficulties of fording the river at Bire, see Henry Maundrell, "An Account of the Author's Journey," 3–5, appended to *A Journey from Aleppo to Jerusalem at Easter, A.D. 1697,* 3rd ed. (Oxford: Printed at the Theater, 1714).

8. The population of Maraş in 1526 was, very roughly, 5,000 (Tapu Tahrir Defter 998, fol. 418, which gives only the number of taxpaying males, making no distinction between head of household and bachelor); in 1563, the population was probably somewhere between 13,000 and 14,000 (Refet Yinanç and Mesut Elibüyük, *Maraş Tahrir Defteri (1563)* [Ankara: Türk Tarih Kurumu, 1988], 1:11–35).

9. Population estimates for Aleppo differ. André Raymond estimates Aleppo's population in 1537 as 80,000 ("The Population of Aleppo in the Sixteenth and Seventeenth Centuries according to Ottoman Census Documents," *International Journal of Middle East Studies* 16 [1984]: 452–53); he makes the case that the commonly used multiplier of 5 is too small for cities, with their uncounted population of slaves, servants, etc., and therefore he uses a multiplier of 8. See also Ira Lapidus (*Muslim Cities in the Later Middle Ages* [Cambridge, Mass.: Harvard University Press, 1967], 79), who puts the population of Aleppo at about 67,000 in 1520 and 57,000 a decade later. Ömer Lütfi Barkan gives a population of 56,881 for 1520–1530, and 45,331 for 1571–1580 ("Essai sur les données statistiques des registres de recensement dans l'empire Ottoman aux XVe et XVIe siècles," *Journal of the Economic and Social History of the Orient* 1 [1957]: 27); like Raymond, Barkan recognizes that the determination of multiplier is a rather arbitrary matter (18), although he continues to use 5 as a factor. Persuaded by Raymond's argument, I have settled on the very rough figure of 60,000.

10. On Damascus, see Muhammad Adnan Bakhit, "The Christian Population of the Province of Damascus in the Sixteenth Century," in *Christians and Jews in the Ottoman Empire: The Functioning of a Plural Society,* ed. Benjamin Braude and Bernard Lewis (New York: Holmes and Meier, 1982),1:25: a cadastral survey of 950/1543 listed 8,271 households and 401 bachelors, which would suggest a population in the low 40,000s. In my rough figure, I have again been influenced by André Raymond's argument (see the previous note). Tapu Tahrir Defteri 998 (fol. 286) indicates that the population of Damascus was around 52,000 in 1526; this figure should be used for comparisons with caution, as it does not include taxpaying bachelors, who were regularly counted in Anatolian surveys. Lapidus (*Muslim Cities,* 79) reports the population of Damascus between 1520 and 1530 to be about 57,000, and also (see previous note) observes a similar decline in population. Barkan notes that Aleppo and Damascus were exceptions among Ottoman cities in the sixteenth century in that by midcentury they were losing, not gaining, population ("Essai sur les données statistiques des registres de recensement," 28).

11. In 1533, Jerusalem's population was roughly 6,600 and in 1562, roughly 11,400 (for numbers of taxpaying households, see Bakhit, "The Christian Population of the Province of Damascus in the Sixteenth Century," 47). Rough population estimates for cities not mentioned above but included in the various surveys and articles cited are Adana (1,900 in 1526), Karaman (2,500 in 1523), Trabzon (6,300 in 1523), Nablus (4,000 in 1548), and Malatya (9,700 in 1560).

12. In the 1574 survey, the number of households was 2,936 (Özdeğer, *Ayıntâb Livâsı,* 124).

13. I wish here to add a comment or two on the vexed subject of transforming data on numbers of taxed households into population estimates, although this question is hardly central to my study. The use of a single multiplier over space and/or time is a dubious method that takes into account neither geographic nor historical contingency. Raymond's point about the demographic makeup of large cities (vs. that of small villages, at the opposite end of the range) argues against a single multiplier over space, and the rising numbers of bachelors (and hence changing patterns of marriage and household composition) noted for Aintab is an example of a development that argues against a multiplier held constant over time. Another historical variable that may underlie the story told in the cadastral surveys cited above is security in rural areas—i.e., the flight of peasants to the city in bad times, and their return to their villages in better times.

14. The cadastral register of 1520 (Maliyeden Müdevver 75) contained these three subdistricts; the survey of 1536 (Tapu Tahrir 186) consisted only of the subdistrict of Aintab, whereas the survey of 1543 (Tapu Tahrir 373) encompassed the complete, three-subdistrict province.

15. Mehmet Yılmaz, *Nizip Tarihi* (Gaziantep: Mazlum Kitapevi, n.d.), 13. This work is a local history of Nizip, now a subdistrict *(nahiye)* in the province of Gaziantep, in 1540 a subdistrict of the province of Bire. I thank Samuel Kaplan for bringing this small work to my attention and for providing me with a copy of it.

16. On the modern political economy of nomads in this region, see Daniel Bates, *Nomads and Farmers: A Study of the Yörük of Southeastern Turkey* (Ann Arbor: University of Michigan Press, 1971).

17. See Özdeğer, *Ayıntâb Livâsı*, passim.
18. The 1520 cadastral survey described Marj Dabik as being divided between *timar* (land in fief to a cavalry solider, in this case one Ahmed Artuk) and *mülk* (the private property of one Zeyni b. Mehmed); its annual revenue was estimated at 300 akçes (Maliyeden Müdevver 75, fol. 13b).
19. Özdeğer, *Ayıntâb Livâsı*, 216.
20. Margaret L. Venzke, "The Question of Declining Cereals' Production in the Sixteenth Century," *Journal of Turkish Studies* 8 (1984): 251–64.
21. AS 161:111b *(ki varub mezraa imaret idüb zirâat ideler).*
22. AS 161:157b; AS 2:188a, 230a.
23. Specifically, in the three subdistricts of Aintab province, Telbaşer had 89 mezraas, giving an approximate ratio (village to mezraa) of 1:.9; Aintab had 124 mezraas, with an approximate ratio of 1:1.2; and Nehrülcevaz had 30 mezraas, with an approximate ratio of 1:1.4.
24. Yılmaz, *Nizip Tarihi*, 14.
25. AS 2:167a. Similarly today, the natural spring known as Akpınar, located just outside the village of Çaybaşı (formerly Cağdığn), is advertised locally as an "excursion spot" *(mesire yeri).* I thank Hüseyin Kanbıçak and his family for showing me around the area, and also for demonstrating the stages by which grapes are turned into pekmez and other products.
26. Cemil Cahit Güzelbey, the foremost local historian of Aintab, describes dreaming about Ali at night after listening to stories of his pious heroism as "bedtime stories" (*Gaziantep Evliyaları* [Gaziantep: İslamî Hizmetler Vakfı, 1990], 17).
27. Cemil Cahit Güzelbey, "Araban Tarih ve Foklorundan bir Demet," *Gaziantep Kültürü* 11 (1960): 20ff.
28. Local folk wisdom in Aintab asserted that bachelors wishing to marry might seek intercession at the mosque of Ali Neccar, while the Ömeriye mosque not far from it was thought to help females in the same quest.
29. The survey of 1543 counted 60 more taxpaying households (1,896) than did the survey of 1536 (1,836), an increase of only 3 percent. If exempt households are included (giving a total of 1,856 for 1536 and 1,969 for 1543), the rate of growth doubles.
30. See chapter 1, "The Price of Stability," for population fluctuations between 1536 and 1543.
31. See Özdeğer, *Ayıntâb Livâsı*, part III.
32. See the comment of Barkan in note 10, above. In a similar manner, recent conflict in southeastern Turkey has swelled the population of the region's cities, most notably Diyarbakır.
33. Aintab's largest neighborhoods in 1543 were İbn Sekkak, Şehreküstü, Ali Neccar, İbn Ammi, Şekeroğlu, Eyyüboğlu, Akyol, and Töbe.
34. For the efforts of the residents of this district (or of the personnel managing the mosque) to build up the *waqf* of their mosque, see AS 2:203aff.
35. For more on the Sikkak, the Boyacı, and the Demirci and their status, see chapter 7.
36. Cemil Cahit Güzelbey, *Cenaniler* (Istanbul: Ufuk Matbaası, 1984). I am grateful to Ali Cenani for making this book available to me.

37. Cemil Cahit Güzelbey notes that the İbn Sekkak neighborhood had disappeared by the end of the seventeenth century ("Gaziantep Şer'i Mahkeme Sicillerinden Örnekler," *Gaziantep Kültürü* 10 [1967]: 276).

38. AS 2:25b.

39. Tapu Tahrir Defteri 301; see also Özdeğer, *Ayıntâb Livâsı,* 139–96 (Özdeğer occasionally omits an entry in the survey).

40. Lapidus, *Muslim Cities,* 37–38.

41. This demographic analysis of religion is based on Tapu Tahrir Defterleri 186, 373, and 231 for Aintab. For the surrounding areas, I consulted Tapu Tahrir Defter 184 (Birecik), 402 (Dulkadriye), and 998 (covering what is today central and southeastern Anatolia, Cilicia, northern Syria, and northern Iraq). Where identified, Christians enumerated in these cadastral surveys for southeastern Anatolia were almost exclusively Armenian.

42. Tapu Tahrir Defteri 998, fol. 279 (Diyarbakır), fols. 408–9 (Dulkadir).

43. The summary statistics for the governorate-general of Diyarbakır indicate 66,732 Muslim households, 11,772 Armenian households, and 207 Jewish households (Tapu Tahrir Defteri, folio 279). One has to wonder if all Christian sects in the region surveyed were categorized as "Armenian."

44. Tapu Tahrir Defteri 998, fol. 199 (Ruha city).

45. Tapu Tahrir Defteri 998: fol. 7 (Mardin); fol. 7 (Mosul); fol. 199 (Arabgir); fol. 250 (Ruha); fol. 250 (Hisnkeyf).

46. In this register, only the section covering the governorate-general of Diyarbakır gives the breakdown of Muslims and non-Muslims (in contrast to the sections on Aleppo, Dulkadir, and Damascus); given that Ottoman surveyors, at least in their first pass through a region, tended to rely upon earlier practices, it is possible that the late Akkoyunlu administration (which included the area encompassed by the Ottoman governorate-general of Diyarbakır) documented its subject population by religion, whereas the late Mamluk administration, at least in greater Syria, did not.

47. Bakhit, "The Christian Population of the Province of Damascus in the Sixteenth Century," 25.

48. According to a list of neighborhoods appearing in the court records during the month of Muharrem 1108 (August 1696), this neighborhood had at some point split into two—"Armenian Heyik" and "Muslim Heyik" (Cemil Cahit Güzelbey, "Gaziantep Şer'i Mahkeme Sicillerinden Örnekler," 276).

49. Tapu Tahrir Defteri 186 (1536), fols. 26–27; 373 (1543), fols. 45–46. Hüseyin Özdeğer, in *Ayıntâb Livâsı,* simply omits any reference to this Armenian population of Aintab from his published version of these registers.

50. Avedis K. Sanjian, in *The Armenian Communities in Syria under Ottoman Domination* (Cambridge, Mass.: Harvard University Press, 1965), notes that throughout the Ottoman period, Armenians in northwestern Syria were mainly peasants; this may have been true of residents of Aintab province as well, who shared many social and cultural traits with Syrian Armenians.

51. Tapu Tahrir Defteri 373, fols. 289–90.

52. Unfortunately, the 1536 cadaster is limited to Aintab subdistrict, so we have only the 1543 statistic for Orul's population.

53. When the Armenian population of Aintab became significant is a question that is beyond the scope of this book. Kevork A. Sarafian suggests that it was at the end of the sixteenth century that the city's Armenian population grew, owing in part to an influx from eastern Anatolian cities and from Iran; see his *Patmutiun Antepi Hayots* (Armenian history of Aintep) (Los Angeles: Central Typesetting, 1953), 1:200. I am grateful to Natalie Balikjian for drawing this work to my attention, and to Stephan Astourian for translating parts of it for me. The traveler Evliya Çelebi remarks of his visit in 1671 that there were no Christians in Aintab city *(keferesi yokdur);* see Evliya Çelebi, *Seyahatname* (Istanbul: Devlet Matbaası, 1935), 9:358. On the one hand, Evliya's comment might suggest variously that the population was still relatively small, that Armenians were socially and linguistically assimilated, or that they were living predominantly in rural settlements; on the other hand, it might reflect Evliya's notorious tendency to exaggerate.

54. AS 2:226a (the poll tax was called *rüsum-i gebran;* the numbers of taxed Christians is not specified).

55. Sanjian, *The Armenian Communities in Syria under Ottoman Domination,* 14ff., 29; Ernst Honigmann and Belim Darkot, "Rumkale," in *İslam Ansiklopedisi,* 9:777–81. Sanjian points out that Armenian associations with the Crusaders as well as their support of the Mongols against the Mamluks were factors in arousing Mamluk antipathy toward them. He also notes that attrition among Armenians, as among other populations, was caused in part by the disasters of drought, famine, pestilence, and earthquakes common in the Mamluk period.

56. Some of the earliest court studies in English focusing on or incorporating non-Muslims are those of Amnon Cohen and Ronald Jennings; see in particular Cohen, *Jewish Life under Islam: Jerusalem in the Sixteenth Century* (Cambridge, Mass.: Harvard University Press, 1984); Jennings, "Zimmis (Non-Muslims) in Early Seventeenth Century Ottoman Judicial Records: The Sharia Court of Anatolian Kayseri," *Journal of the Economic and Social History of the Orient* 21 (1978): 225–91.

57. Najwa Al-Qattan, "*Dhimmî*s in the Muslim Court: Legal Autonomy and Religious Discrimination," *International Journal of Middle East Studies* 31 (1999): 433.

58. Suraiya Faroqhi suggests that a disadvantage suffered by non-Muslims—they could not legally testify against Muslims—led to their using the court in another way: "proof provided by entry into the register," by which she apparently means the use of voluntary statements, or *ikrar*s ("Sidjill, In Ottoman administrative usage," *Encyclopedia of Islam,* 2nd ed., 9:539–45). An example of this is the "voluntary statement" made by a Muslim who had hit a Christian as they traveled together; the statement was made at the Christian's request (AS 2:24b).

59. Cemil Cahit Güzelbey, "Ainî," *Gaziantep Kültürü* 9 (1966): 99.

60. Since the title *seyyid* was often shortened to *seydi,* while Seydi was at the same time a given name, it is often difficult to know if a name such as "Seydi Ahmed" indicates a claim to descent from the Prophet Muhammad—hence the difficulty in estimating the size of the seyyid population. The seyyid population of Aintab would increase enormously by the end of seventeenth century (see Hülya Canbakal, "XVII. Yüzyılda Teseyyüd ve ʿAyntab Sadatı," in *Osmanlı Döne-*

minde Gaziantep Sempozyumu, ed. Yüsüf Küçükdağ [Gaziantep: Gaziantep Valiliği İl Özel İdare Müdürlüğü, 2000], 77–81).

61. There is a voluminous literature on "dervish Islam," notably the work of Mehmet Fuat Köprülü, Irène Mélikoff, and Ahmet Yaşar Ocak. See also the forthcoming book by Ethel Sara Wolper, *Cities and Saints: Sufism and the Transformation of Urban Space in Pre-Ottoman Anatolia.*

62. The importance of noting the hierarchy of religious personnel and the tensions between its upper and lower ranks is stressed by Madeline C. Zilfi, *The Politics of Piety: The Ottoman Ulema in the Postclassical Age (1600–1800)* (Minneapolis: Bibliotheca Islamica, 1988).

63. AS 2:47b.

64. Seyyid İsmail performed as one of the communal witnesses *(şahid ul-hal)* for the case resolving the dispute over candle lighting at Kurban Baba's grave.

65. The classic study of Islamization and Turkification is Speros Vryonis, *The Decline of Medieval Hellenism in Asia Minor and the Process of Islamization from the Eleventh through the Fifteenth Century* (Berkeley: University of California Press, 1971). Also important is Faruk Sümer, *Oğuzlar (Türkmenler): Tarihleri, Boy Teşkilatı, Destanları* (Istanbul: Ana Yayınları, 1980).

66. Tapu Tahrir Defteri 998: fol. 279 (Diyarbakır), fol. 294 (Aleppo), fol. 299 (Bire), fols. 408–9 (Dulkadir). According to this register, the joint province of Hams-Hama, south of Aleppo, contained twenty-seven tribes (fol. 296). These numbers should not be regarded as exact, but rather as roughly comparative: the cadastral survey from which they come is contained in a massive register encompassing central and southeastern Anatolia, Cilicia, greater Syria, and northern Iraq, which appears to have been assembled in 1526; however, the various regions included in the register may have actually been surveyed in different years.

67. Tapu Tahrir Defteri 231, fol. 69; this register is a "summary register" *(icmal)* compiled in the same year as the "detailed" *(mufassal)* register numbered 373.

68. Özdeğer, *Ayıntâb Livâsı,* 131.

69. Halil İnalcık, "The Ottoman State: Economy and Society, 1300–1600," in *An Economic and Social History of the Ottoman Empire, 1300–1914,* ed. Halil İnalcık and Donald Quataert (Cambridge: Cambridge University Press, 1994), 11–409.

70. Özdeğer, *Ayıntâb Livâsı,* 247, 251, 252.

71. For Suruç, see the 1520 cadastral survey of Bire and Aintab provinces (Maliyeden Müdevver 75, fols. 49bff.). Examples of tribal chieftains controlling large numbers of villages or mezraas included the Kurdish Şevket Beg and the Bedouin Sheikh Mendi (?) of the Beni Misr. A note concerning the mezraas under der Şevket Beg is probably meant to justify the atypical practice of imposing individual taxes on Kurdish tribes: "The Kurdish tribes who follow Şevket Beg . . . are engaged in farming and pay the *öşr* [a standard agricultural tax] on the crops that they harvest."

72. Hulusi Yetkin, a prominent local historian, apparently touched off a controversy when, in a public lecture, he cited historic conflict among Turkmen, Kurdish, and Arab tribes as a reason for Gaziantep's lack of development. In "Gaziantep Bölgesinde Yaşayan Türkmenler, Türkçe Konuşan Diğer Türklerden Ayrı Bir

Soya mi Mensupturlar?," an article in the journal *Gaziantep Kültürü* (11 [1968]: 50, 71), he responds to numerous protests by local Turkmen against what they took to be Turkmen-bashing. Yetkin answered by arguing that almost all local Turks were of Turkmen origin: "Gaziantep bölgesinde Türkçe konuşan ailelerin hemen hepsinin soyunun Türkmen olduğu, Oğuz ilinden geldiklerine dair binlerce tarihi belge vardir. Türkmen demek Türk demektir[.]" While his claim that "thousands of documents" prove this point is a rhetorical exaggeration, and while the perspective he represented here was no doubt influenced by the emphasis placed by nationalist ideology on the Central Asian origins of the Turks of Turkey, it is nevertheless significant that Turkmen identity has so recently remained a salient feature.

73. AS2:151b *(İbn Türkmancık)*.

74. The full text of the clause in the administrative regulations *(kanunname)* for Aintab issued in 1574, on the occasion of a new cadastral survey, is as follows: "[As for] the smoke tax on winter residents: in the old register [the cadastral survey of 1536] it was recorded that 12 akçes should be collected [as] the tax on winter residents from every household excepting the resident taxpayers *[reaya];* that is, [it should be collected only] from the Turkmen groups who do not farm but come for winter pasture. However, it appears that they have also been collecting this tax from poor laborers *['ummal taifesi]* who live in the cit[ies] and do not own their own homes. Because this is an unwarranted and oppressive practice it has been forbidden. Hereafter, in accordance with former law, [the tax] should be collected from the Turkmen groups and other groups who come from outside and spend the winter in the villages and mezraas of the said province; it should *not* be demanded of the poor who live in the cit[ies]. Those who are in positions of authority must prevent this from happening" (the original Turkish is cited in Özdeğer, *Ayıntâb Livâsı,* 206).

75. AS 2:280a.

76. AS 161:202d *(hususan küfüv değildir, mezbur Kerd asılıdır ve kız karındaşum ehl-i ilm kızıdır)*.

77. On the general subject of the persistence of tribal identity in family lineages, see Abdulkadir İnan, "Gaziantep İlinde Türkmenler," *Gaziantep Kültürü* 9 (1966): 137ff.

78. On feuding in the rural areas of Gaziantep, see the several articles lamenting the tenaciousness of this practice that were published in the late 1950s and 1960s in the local journal *Gaziantep Kültürü;* see also Ömer Özbaş, *Gaziantep Dolaylarıda Türkmenler ve Baraklar* (Gaziantep: Cihan Matbaası, 1958), 43–44.

79. In October 1999, a reconciliation was brought about between two families in the village of Kazıklı, described as belonging to two tribes *(aşiret)* who had been engaged in a blood feud allegedly going back some seventy-five years, during which tens of individuals had been killed. This "peace" was sealed in an elaborate feast that was featured on local television as well as in the nationally circulating newspaper *Hürriyet.* I am grateful to Ömer Karaman, the Şahinbey *kaymakam* and one of the engineers of the reconciliation, for taking the time to explain the circumstances of this blood feud to me. By an extraordinary stroke of luck, I happened to be in the *kaymakam*'s office when the parties to this blood

feud appeared to air another matter—a dispute over water access—that threatened to disrupt their newly won peace; I was consequently able to witness mediation at work.

80. Or at least there was constant traffic between larger villages and the city; smaller villages and hamlets perhaps had more dealings with neighboring villages than with the city.

81. A map of the city dating from the early twentieth century suggests that vegetable gardens *(bostan)* ringed the northern and eastern borders of the city, following the course of the Sacur, while orchards and vineyards were more concentrated to the northwest of the city. Smaller concentrations of vegetable gardens dotted the inhabited city (Sarafian, *Patmutiun Antepi Hayots,* vol. 1, fold-out map).

82. Kâtip Çelebi, *Kitâb-ı Cihannümâ* (Istanbul: Dar al-Tabaa al-Amire, 1145/1732), 566; Evliya Çelebi, *Seyahatname,* 9:359.

83. Tapu Tahrir Defteri 343, fol. 47; Özdeğer, *Ayıntâb Livâsı,* 132. Huri İslamoğlu-İnan notes the importance of urban agricultural sectors in premodern Ottoman cities and elsewhere (*State and Peasant in the Ottoman Empire: Agrarian Power Relations and Regional Economic Development in Ottoman Anatolia during the Sixteenth Century* [Leiden: Brill: 1994], 47).

84. AS 161:11c.

85. AS 161:26c.

86. For a study of the economic and cultural links between city and rural hinterland in the Nablus region of Palestine, see Beshara Doumani, *Rediscovering Palestine: Merchants and Peasants in Jabal Nablus, 1700–1900* (Berkeley: University of California Press, 1995).

87. AS 161:21c, 56a, 103c, 156b; AS 2:11b, 100d, 167b.

88. AS 2:3b.

89. AS 2:31a.

90. AS 2:46a, 52c.

91. AS 2:131b, 133a.

92. See Cemil Güçyetmez, "Çıkrıkcılık," *Gaziantep Kültürü* 3 (1959): 167ff., on women's spinning wool into thread or yarn, a task that, as this article notes, is often performed by poor families.

93. AS 2:304a.

94. AS 2:307a.

95. AS 161:96a.

96. AS 161:92c.

97. Arıl's population in 1543 was roughly 500; the taxed male population was composed of 37 farmers *(çiftçi),* 62 nonfarmers or day laborers *(bennak),* and 26 bachelors *(mücerred)* (Özdeğer, *Ayıntâb Livâsı,* 440).

98. See, e.g., AS 161:351a. In this case, a villager from Hacer, in Telbaşer subdistrict, had two water jugs stolen from his house while he was at the Nizip bazaar.

99. This region, in effect, encompassed the northern stretches of the old Mamluk province of Aleppo; Barbara Kellner-Heinkele, in "The Turkomans and *Bilâd aş-Şam* in the Mamluk Period" (in *Land Tenure and Social Transformation in the Middle East,* ed. Tarif Khalidi [Beirut: American University of Beirut, 1984], 169), describes the "precarious Northern borders" of the Mamluk province of

Aleppo as a "never well-defined and constantly disputed borderline compris-[ing] the fortress cities of, among others, Tarsus, Adana, Sis, Maraş, Elbistan, Darende, Malatya, Kharput, and Urfa [Ruha]."

100. Claims for missing animals were voiced in the following cases, among others: AS 161:40b (Rumkale), 89c (Elbistan), 97e (town of Harran in Ruha province), 162d (Sis), 177a (Kos), 181e (Karaman); AS 2:227a (Dayr).

101. Traditionally, runaway slaves and stray animals were both the province of an official called the *yavacı.* Neither the cadastral surveys nor the court records indicate that a specific office of *yavacı* existed in Aintab.

102. In the 1536 survey, the estimated annual revenue from the sale of beasts of burden of 5,000 akçes was assigned to the provincial governor *(sancakbegi),* whereas by 1543 the revenue, now estimated at 6,000 akçes, was assigned to the imperial treasury *(hass-ı şahî;* Özdeğer, *Ayıntâb Livâsı,* 123). On animal markets, see also Amnon Cohen and Bernard Lewis, *Population and Revenue in the Towns of Palestine in the Sixteenth Century* (Princeton: Princeton University Press, 1978), 53-54.

103. AS 2:75a.

104. Uriel Heyd, *Studies in Old Ottoman Criminal Law,* ed. V. L. Menage (Oxford: Clarendon Press, 1973), 82, 120 *(ma'rifet-i kadı ile çağırtmasa . . .).* The law book of Süleyman imposed a fine of 40 akçes on a rich person who failed to turn over a stray animal and have the find broadcast, 20 on a person of middling wealth, and 10 on a poor person. According to Özdeğer *(Ayıntâb Livâsı,* 91), the practice was to sell unclaimed animals and turn the proceeds over to the judge or to the local timariot cavalryman; the finder was rewarded and the animal's owner fined.

105. Sarafian, *Patmutiun Antepi Hayots,* 1:70; Sarafian walked this route personally in 1907.

106. Kızılhisar, the fourth-largest village in Aintab province, seems to have been a center of horse dealing; see for example the drawn-out argument over a horse sale between two locals (AS 2:66c; 72b, c, d; 73a, c; 78b; 80c), and the recovery from the headman of Kızılhisar of a horse gone missing from distant Harran (AS 161:97e).

107. Heyd, *Old Ottoman Criminal Law,* 73, 112.

108. Refet Yinanç, *Dulkadir Beyliği* (Ankara: Türk Tarih Kurumu, 1989), 108-9; Ömer Lütfi Barkan, *XV ve XVIıncı asırlarda Osmanlı İmparatorluğunda Ziraî Ekonominin Hukukî ve Malî Esasları, I: Kanunlar* (Istanbul: Bürhaneddin Erenler Matbaası, 1943), 120-24.

109. Heyd, *Old Ottoman Criminal Law,* 85, 107.

110. AS 2:264a.

111. AS 2:307b, 312c.

112. Yinanç, *Dulkadir Beyliği,* 105.

113. See Heyd, *Old Ottoman Criminal Law,* 51-53, on the difficulties experienced by a governor of Bozok province; the document on which Heyd bases this discussion (presently catalogued in the Prime Ministry Archives in Istanbul as Bab-ı defter Baş Muhasebe Kalemi, Dosya 1/30) is further discussed in chapter 8.

114. Muhammad Adnan Bakhit, "Aleppo and the Ottoman Military in the Sixteenth Century (Two Case Studies)," *Al-Abhath* 27 (1978-1979): 27-30.

115. AS 2:230b.
116. AS 161:167b *(ben bir ticarete gider kimesneyim, bir gün evde ve bir gün yaban-da . . .)*.
117. AS 161:35b.
118. AS 161:162a.
119. AS 2:84d.
120. AS 2:274d, 308a.
121. AS 161:37e, 38a.
122. AS 161:56c,d.
123. AS 161:103b.
124. AS 2:152a, c.
125. Selami Pulaha and Yaşar Yücel, "I. Selim Kanunnamesi (1512−1520) ve XVI. Yüzyılın İkinci Yarısının Kimi Kanunları," *Belgeler* 12, no. 16 (1987): 31.
126. Nelly Hanna, "The Administration of Courts in Ottoman Cairo," in *The State and Its Servants: Administration in Egypt from Ottoman Times to the Present,* ed. Nelly Hanna (Cairo: American University in Cairo Press, 1995), 44−59.
127. For an example of haphazard records, see the court records of Manisa, housed in the National Library in Ankara.
128. Tapu Tahrir Defteri 231, fol. 69; this is a summary *(icmal)* register, whereas Tapu Tahrir Defteri 373, also dated 950/1543, is a detailed *(mufassal)* register.
129. AS 161:357 (the inside back cover of the register records random business of the garrison; there are no dates included in these brief records).
130. AS 161:20d.
131. AS 161:100c.
132. Özdeğer, *Ayıntâb Livâsı,* passim.
133. For the timars of these three sets of brothers, see Özdeğer, *Ayıntâb Livâsı,* passim. Gazi Beg is listed in the cadastral survey of 1536 as himself having a large timar *(zeamet)* (Özdeğer, *Ayıntâb Livâsı,* 368); he also possessed slaves, which we learn from the fact that one of his freedmen (İskender b. Abdullah *min 'uteka-yı Gazi Beg)* knocked out four teeth of a man with whom he got into a fight (AS 161:134b).
134. On the pacification of Dulkadir tribal chiefs with timars, see M. Tayyib Gök-bilgin, "Süleyman I," in *İslam Ansiklopedisi,* 11:109. Huri İslamoğlu-İnan suggests a similar rewarding of former elites in north central Anatolia (*State and Peasant in the Ottoman Empire,* 62−63).
135. The cases of Tatar, Meryem, and Fatma are found in AS 2:86c, 87c; 313a; and 240b. Meryem's husband was named in the record simply as *yolkulu*—"fellow traveler"—a term perhaps synonymous to *yoldaş,* often used among soldiers.
136. AS 2:188c.
137. AS 2:128b.
138. On the celebrations attending the return of pilgrims, see Suraiya Faroqhi, *Pilgrims and Sultans: The Hajj under the Ottomans, 1517−1683* (London: I. B. Tauris, 1994).
139. Evliya Çelebi, *Seyahatname,* 9:333−67.
140. AS 2:150b. At court, İl Hatun swore away her parental rights by asserting that should she seek to recover the child in the future, the judge should refuse to hear her suit.

141. Kevork A. Sarafian, *A Briefer History of Aintab: A Concise History of the Cultural, Religious, Educational, Political, Industrial, and Commercial Life of the Armenians of Aintab* ([Boston?]: Union of the Armenians of Aintab, 1957), 17–18.

142. On women's role in these religious endowments, see my *The Imperial Harem: Women and Sovereignty in the Ottoman Empire* (New York: Oxford University Press, 1993), 203–5.

143. St. H. Stephan, "An Endowment Deed of Khasseki Sultan, Dated the 24th May 1552," *Quarterly of the Department of Antiquities in Palestine* 10 (1944): 170–99; also see my "Gender and Sexual Propriety in Ottoman Royal Women's Patronage," in *Women, Patronage, and Self-Representation in Islamic Societies,* ed. D. Fairchild Ruggles (Albany: State University of New York Press, 2000), 53–68. This institution is the subject of a monograph by Amy Singer, *Constructing Ottoman Beneficence: An Imperial Soup Kitchen in Jerusalem* (Albany: State University of New York Press, 2002).

144. See Faroqhi, *Pilgrims and Sultans,* for an excellent account of these strategic aspects of the pilgrimage.

145. Bakhit, "Aleppo and the Ottoman Military in the Sixteenth Century," 30.

146. If the twentieth-century Aintab custom of decorating the facade of one's house with images of the pilgrimage dates back to the sixteenth century, then the streets of Aintab in the years leading up to 1540 would have displayed a rising religious cosmopolitanism.

147. Uriel Heyd, *Ottoman Documents on Palestine, 1552–1615* (Oxford: Oxford University Press, 1960), 163–84.

148. F. E. Peters, *Jerusalem: The Holy City in the Eyes of Choniclers, Visitors, and Prophets from the Days of Abraham to the Beginnings of Modern Times* (Princeton: Princeton University Press, 1985), 484–87.

149. Joseph ha-Kohen is translated in J. W. Hirshberg, W. P. Pick, and J. Kaniel, "Jerusalem under Ottoman Rule (1517–1917)," in *Encyclopedia Judaica;* quoted in Peters, *Jerusalem,* 480.

150. Peters, *Jerusalem,* 479–92. Peters calls early Ottoman overlordship "a new beginning for Jerusalem" (489), although one that would set off new developments within and between religious communities.

151. The toll tax in Nablus generated 20,000 akçes in the survey year of 945/1538–1539, and 22,000 akçes in the survey year of 955/1548–1549 (Cohen and Lewis, *Population and Revenue in the Towns of Palestine,* 150–51). See also Bakhit, "The Christian Population of the Province of Damascus in the Sixteenth Century," 47.

3. INTRODUCING THE COURT OF AINTAB

1. See AS 2:86c, 87c (Tatar); 89c (Minnet); 91a (Kuddam); 88c (Fatma); 90a (Haciye Zeliha); 91b (Harim).

2. See AS 2:90c, 87a, 92b (the horse and donkey sales); 92a (the loan); 87b (the sale of house and stable); 91c (the brothers' dispute); 88b (the water rights); 88a (the butcher).

3. Critiques of the undiscriminating use of court records include Najwa al-Qattan, "Textual Differentiation in the Damascus *Sijill:* Religious Discrimination or Pol-

itics of Gender?" in *Women, the Family, and Divorce Laws in Islamic History,* ed. Amira El Azhary Sonbol (Syracuse: Syracuse University Press, 1996), 191–202, and Dror Zeevi, "The Use of Shariʿa Court Records as a Source for Middle Eastern Social History: A Reappraisal," *Islamic Law and Society* 5 (1998): 35–36; see also my "'She is trouble . . . and I will divorce her': Orality, Honor, and Representation in the Ottoman Court of Aintab," in *Women in the Medieval Islamic World: Power, Patronage, Piety,* ed. Gavin R. G. Hambly (New York: St. Martin's Press, 1998), 267–300.

4. Cemil Cahit Güzelbey, who made an extensive study of the court records of Aintab, claims that the first records date from 935/1528–1529, but he does not say how continuously the records were kept in these years ("Gaziantep'te Folklor Araştırmaları ve Kaynakları," *Gaziantep Kültürü* 7 [1964]: 113.)

5. For example, near-contemporaneous records from Üsküdar, a large district in Istanbul, contain estate inventories; see Yvonne Seng's articles on this subject, including "Fugitives and Factotums: Slaves in Early Sixteenth-Century Istanbul," *Journal of the Economic and Social History of the Orient* 39 (1996): 136–69, and "Standing at the Gates of Justice: Women in the Law Courts of Early Sixteenth-Century Üsküdar, Istanbul," in *Contested States: Law, Hegemony and Resistance,* ed. Mindie Lazarus-Black and Susan F. Hirsch (New York: Routledge, 1994), 184–206.

6. AS 161:50b.

7. See Wael Hallaq, "The *qadi*'s *diwan (sijill)* before the Ottomans," *Bulletin of the School of Oriental and African Studies* 61 (1998): 424–25, on the importance of "anticipation of consequences" as a raison d'être for keeping judicial records. This point has also been noted by Judith Tucker, *In the House of the Law: Gender and Islamic Law in Ottoman Syria and Palestine* (Berkeley: University of California Press, 1998), 18, and by Suraiya Faroqhi, "Sidjill, In Ottoman administrative usage," *Encyclopedia of Islam,* 2nd ed., 9:539–45.

8. AS 2:134a *(kadı-yı sabık zamanında sicilin dahi itdirdüm).*

9. On the question of the "claims of God" vs. the "claims of the individual," see Joseph Schacht, *An Introduction to Islamic Law* (Oxford: Oxford University Press, 1954), 175ff.

10. Schacht, *An Introduction to Islamic Law,* 176.

11. Ibrahim Al-Halabi, *Multaka al-Abhur* (Istanbul: Dar ul-Tibaat ul-Amire, 1873), 366–67.

12. Uriel Heyd, *Studies in Old Ottoman Criminal Law,* ed. V. L. Menage (Oxford: Clarendon Press, 1973), clauses 44, 76–79, 80, 83, 84, and 117 (pp. 106ff.); watchmen and guards were also liable for the value of goods stolen or damaged on premises under their supervision.

13. Heyd, *Old Ottoman Criminal Law,* 92.

14. AS 161:35a.

15. See AS 161:48b, 51d, 340a; AS 2:48cff., 178b, 198b, 199a, 238b, 249a, b, c, 294a, 306b.

16. Ronald Jennings, "Limitations of the Judicial Powers of the Kadi in Seventeenth Century Ottoman Kayseri," *Studia Islamica* 50 (1979): 170.

17. See two instances of divorce in AS 161:188a, 191c.

18. AS 2:93a.

19. Selami Pulaha and Yaşar Yücel, *I. Selim Kanunnameleri (1512–1520)* (Ankara: Türk Tarih Kurumu, 1995), 77.

20. Selami Pulaha and Yaşar Yücel, "I. Selim Kanunnamesi (1512–1520) ve XVI. Yüzyılın İkinci Yarısının Kimi Kanunları," *Belgeler* 12, no. 16 (1987): 31. See chapter 7 for speculation that fees may have been reduced or eliminated under Süleyman.

21. AS 2:25b, 76b, 206b, 302b.

22. For example, in Jerusalem court records dating from the 1550s on, the judge was named in the first line of each entry; see Amnon Cohen and Elisheva Simon-Piqali, eds., *Jews in the Moslem Court: Society, Economy and Communal Organization in Sixteenth Century Jerusalem* (Jerusalem: Yad Izhak Ben-Zvi, 1993), nos. 325, 353; reprinted in Ruth Roded, ed., *Women in Islam and the Middle East: A Reader* (London: I. B. Taurus, 1999), 136–37.

23. AS 2:1a.

24. The major Ottoman biographical compendia for the sixteenth century are Ahmed Taşköprüzade's *Al-Shaqâ'iq Al-Nu'mânîya;* its expanded Turkish translation by Mehemmed Mecdi, *Hada'ik ül-Şaka'ik,* includes biographies of religious figures through the middle of Süleyman's reign; picking up where these works leave off is Nev'izade 'Ata'i's *Hada'ik ül-Haka'ik fi Tekmilet üş-Şaka'ik.* On these works, see Richard Repp, *The Müfti of Istanbul: A Study in the Development of the Ottoman Learned Hierarchy* (London: Ithaca Press, 1986), 3–7.

25. Repp, *The Müfti of Istanbul,* 55–56.

26. Nev'izade 'Ata'i, *Hada'ik ül-Haka'ik fi Tekmilet üş-Şaka'ik* (Istanbul, 1268/1851–1852), 11–12.

27. Arguing to some extent against this identification, the known points of the career of the Hüsameddin of 'Ata'i's biography were in the European part of the empire: his post as teacher was in the Macedonian city of Siroz, and he died in Istanbul. These facts are still compatible with an Anatolian career, however, since the teaching appointment to Siroz was probably an act of patronage by Hüsameddin's mentor in nearby Edirne; that judges were required to return to Istanbul for a spell between appointments might account for his death in the capital.

28. Nev'izade 'Ata'i, *Hada'ik ül-Haka'ik,* 12. The term "300-akçe judge" should not be understood as indicating an actual income received by judges. On the meaning of the ranking of judgeships as "500-akçe," "300-akçe," etc., see İ. H. Uzunçarşılı, *Osmanlı Devletinde İlmiye Teşkilatı* (Ankara: Türk Tarih Kurumu, 1988), 87ff; Repp, *The Müfti of Istanbul,* 33ff.

29. Evliya Çelebi, *Seyahatname* (Istanbul: Devlet Matbaası, 1935), 9:353.

30. Records constituting the first eight months of this study are contained in AS 161, where a week's work took up an average of 10.3 folios. The remaining four months, contained in AS 2, averaged 20.1 folios per week.

31. Feridun Beg, *Mecmua-ı Münşeat üs-Selatin* (Istanbul, 1264–1265/1848–1849), 1:399; the governor was Karaca Paşa, the judge Çömlekçizade Kemal Çelebi, and the treasurer the former *timarlar defterdarı* of Rumeli, Abdülkerim Beg.

32. One of many examples of anticipating consequences is a case in which a certain Hasan sued a certain İsmail to recover three years' worth of child support that İsmail had contracted to pay for his small daughter, engaged to Hasan's son and

living in Hasan's home (AS 2:185b). Hasan won because "he produced a copy of the decree of the former judge, which had been written in the month of Şa'ban in the year 944 [January 1538]; it was found that the sum of 1.5 akçes per day had been decided upon."

33. Jon Mandaville, "The Muslim Judiciary of Damascus in the Late Mamluk Period" (Ph.D. diss., Princeton University, 1969), 20−23.

34. AS 2:50d. See chapter 4 for further discussion of the judge's residence.

35. AS 2:273c.

36. Pulaha and Yücel, "I. Selim Kanunnamesi," 31. The law book of Selim I (d. 1520) prescribed 8 akçes for recording a case in the court register (with the distribution among judge, deputy, and scribe of 5-2-1), 14 for a copy of the proceedings (10-3-1), 25 for the transfer of a case record from one jurisdiction to another (distribution unspecified), 26 for an official decree by the judge (20-4-2), 8 for a letter of appointment by the judge (5-2-1), and between 15 and 50 akçes for marriage and manumission certificates.

37. For speculation that fees were lowered or abandoned during the reign of Süleyman, see chapter 7.

38. See the cases in AS 161, commencing around p. 176. This scribe also used a slightly different opening formula—*sebeb-i tahrir-i huruf budur ki*—instead of the typical *sebeb-i tahrir-i sicil budur ki.*

39. This scribe appears in AS 2, around p. 190; he used the term *icare* rather than the typical *mukataa,* and was partial to the phrase *ihya ve imaret ide* when recording land grants.

40. AS 2:50d.

41. On the education and culture of scribes, see the remarks of Hallaq, "The *qadi's diwan (sijill)* before the Ottomans," 422−24.

42. Cemil Cahit Güzelbey, *Cenanîler* (Istanbul: Ufuk Matbaası, 1984), 26−34.

43. Ronald Jennings, "Kadi, Court, and Legal Procedure in Seventeenth Century Ottoman Kayseri," *Studia Islamica* 48 (1978): 133−72; see also his "Limitations of the Judicial Powers of the Kadi in Seventeenth Century Ottoman Kayseri," 161−63.

44. On pre-Ottoman practices regarding the physical location of judges, see Hallaq, "The *qadi's diwan (sijill)* before the Ottomans," 418.

45. Nelly Hanna, "The Administration of Courts in Ottoman Cairo," in *The State and Its Servants: Administration in Egypt from Ottoman Times to the Present,* ed. Nelly Hanna (Cairo: American University in Cairo Press, 1995), 46.

46. Hallaq, "The *qadi's diwan (sijill)* before the Ottomans." See also Jon Mandaville, "The Ottoman Court Records of Syria and Jordan," *Journal of the American Oriental Society* 86 (1966): 311.

47. D. P. Little, "Sidjill, In Mamluk Usage," in *Encyclopedia of Islam,* 2nd ed., 9:539. The Jerusalem judge's decrees survive in the collection of the Haram-i Sharif; these documents have been studied by Little and Huda Lutfi.

48. Hallaq, "The *qadi's diwan (sijill)* before the Ottomans," 434. The question of binding is perhaps critical. Mandaville suggests that the Damascus records were not bound; the nature of the Aleppo records suggests that bundles of records were bound later ("The Ottoman Court Records of Syria and Jordan"). My own observation of the first Manisa register (ca. 958/1551) suggests that it was a

bunch of separate leaves later bound together (sometimes out of chronological order). The same is true of the earlier register studied in this book (AS 161), which includes several pages of records from 945 and 946, before the register assumes its steady, near-daily nature.

49. Seven registers from the Maraş court exist, beginning in 1292, and for Urfa some twenty-five registers cover the period from 1261 on. Both sets of registers suggest that at some point they were assembled from loose leaves or fascicles, since a given year or group of years is often represented in more than one register. For an inventory of the Maraş and Urfa collections, see Ahmet Akgündüz, *Şer'iye Sicilleri: Mahiyeti, Toplu Kataloğu, ve Seçme Hükümler* (Istanbul: Türk Dünyasî Araştırmaları Vakfı, 1998), 1:203, 214.

50. Akgündüz, *Şer'iye Sicilleri*, 1:190–91.

51. Beshara Doumani, "Palestinian Islamic Court Records: A Source for Socioeconomic History," *MESA Bulletin* 19, no. 2 (1985): 161.

52. Faroqhi has interesting remarks on the problem of the disappearance of records ("Sidjill, In Ottoman administrative usage," 540).

53. Judges sometimes failed even to turn records over to their successors upon leaving office: in his law book Bayezid II complained of the judges of Karaman that "when they are dismissed from office, they don't turn the court records over to the next judge but rather make off with them. [New judges] should press insistently for [the records] to be turned over, lest the affairs of Muslims be harmed" (Ahmet Akgündüz, *Osmanlı Kanunnâmeleri ve Hukukî Tahlilleri* [Istanbul: Fey Vakfı Yayınları, 1990–96], 2:61).

54. Hanna, "The Administration of Courts in Ottoman Cairo," 49.

55. Uzunçarşılı, *İlmiye Teşkilatı*, 94 n. 2.

56. In this regard, it is instructive to read Jon Mandaville's study of late-Mamluk judicial administration of Damascus ("The Muslim Judiciary of Damascus"), when the Shafi'i school of Islamic law was dominant, together with Muhammad Adnan Bakhit's study of the transformations in judicial administration occurring under Ottoman domination, *The Ottoman Province of Damascus in the Sixteenth Century* (Beirut: Librarie du Liban, 1982).

57. Wael Hallaq asserts, drawing on the remarks of sixteenth- and nineteenth-century Hanafi jurists, that present-day Ottomanists are incorrect to use the term *sijill* to refer to court records ("The *qadi's diwan (sijill)* before the Ottomans," 419–21). Yet it is the term that both the scribes of the court and the people of Aintab used to refer to the court register and the records kept in it: the new register that was begun upon news of the appointment of Hüsameddin Efendi bears the inscription "the inception of the *sijill* of the court of Aintab" *(asdâ'-i sijill-i mahkeme-i Aintab)*. It is also the term that Ottoman rulers used to refer to court records, as when they ordered judges to copy imperial orders into the records (Akgündüz, *Osmanlı Kanunnameleri*, 2:141, 233, 236, 253). Whether jurists would find this usage defective or not, the term *sijill* has an historical reality for the Ottoman empire in 1540.

58. I am indebted to Elizabeth Zachariadou for drawing this issue to my attention at an early stage of my research.

59. On the role of written instruments in Islamic law, see Jeanette Wakin, *The Func-*

tion of Documents in Islamic Law (Albany: State University of New York Press, 1972).

60. I thank Najwa Al-Qattan for this observation.

61. On court procedure, see Schacht, *An Introduction to Islamic Law,* chap. 25.

62. On the *ikrar,* see Y. Linant de Bellefonds, "Iḳrār," in *Encyclopedia of Islam,* 2nd ed., 3:1078–81.

63. AS 2:237c.

64. These statements are found in AS 161:43b, 125b, and 2:155a.

65. AS 2:154c, 155a.

66. The rules of jurisprudence require four (male) witnesses of the sexual act itself, thus making the crime of illicit sex unprosecutable. Ottoman kanun allowed circumstantial evidence; here the immediate witnessing of the distressed (and perhaps disheveled?) girl functions as confirmation of the rape. In this case, the testimony of the two women is the equivalent of that of one male. For more discussion of this question, see Fatma's story.

67. For further discussion of the manner of recording verbal testimony, in the context of divorce cases at the Aintab court, see my "'She is trouble . . . and I will divorce her.'"

68. On thresholds and the question of what constituted theft *(sarika),* see Schacht, *Introduction to Islamic Law,* 179–80; Baber Johansen, "La mise en scène du vol par les juristes musulmanes," in *Vols et sanctions en Méditerranée,* ed. Maria Pia di Bella (Amsterdam: Éditions des archives contemporaines, 1998), 41–74; Colin Imber, *Ebu's-Su'ud: The Islamic Legal Tradition* (Stanford: Stanford University Press, 1997), 213ff. Imber clarifies the distinction between theft and "usurpation" *(ghasb).*

69. For similar uses of cursing in nineteenth-century Britain, see Anna Clark, *The Struggle for the Breeches: Gender and the Making of the British Working Class* (Berkeley: University of California Press, 1995).

70. Hüseyin Özdeğer, *Onaltıncı Asırda Ayıntâb Livâsı* (Istanbul: Bayrak Matbaacılık, 1988), 525, 542.

71. On the usefulness of looking at court records and cadastral surveys together, see Amy Singer, "*Tapu Tahrir Defterleri* and *Kadı Sicilleri:* A Happy Marriage of Sources," *Tarih* 1 (1990): 95–125.

72. For further discussion of the shift from conquest to consolidation, see my *The Imperial Harem: Women and Sovereignty in the Ottoman Empire* (New York: Oxford University Press, 1993), esp. chap. 1.

73. On the dating of Süleyman's law book, see Heyd, *Old Ottoman Criminal Law,* 25–27; Imber, *Ebu's-Su'ud,* 48–49. I use the term "law book" here as a literal but, I hope, accurate translation of *kanunname;* the Ottoman term might also be rendered as "statute book" since the "books" originated as collections of statutes, though by Süleyman's reign the imperial law book had expanded to the point that it was a fairly exhaustive law "code."

74. M. Tayyib Gökbilgin, "Celalzade, Mustafa Çelebi," in *İslam Ansiklopedisi* 3:61–63; Heyd, *Old Ottoman Criminal Law,* 23–26.

75. Imber, *Ebu's-Su'ud,* 122.

76. On the relationship of law and land management, see Baber Johansen, "Legal

Literature and the Problem of Change: The Case of the Land Rent," in *Islam and Public Law: Classical and Contemporary Studies,* ed. Chibli Mallat (London: Graham and Trotman, 1993), 29–47, and his longer treatment of this subject, *The Islamic Law of Tax and Rent* (London: Croom Helm, 1988); see also Imber, *Ebu's-Su'ud,* chap. 5.

77. The classic collection of provincial kanunnames is Ömer Lütfi Barkan, *XV ve XVInci asırlarda Osmanlı İmparatorluğunda Ziraî Ekonominin Hukukî ve Malî Esasları, I: Kanunlar* (Istanbul: Bürhaneddin Erenler Matbaası, 1943). On the cadastral surveys, see Heath W. Lowry, "The Ottoman *Tahrir Defterleri* as a Source for Social and Economic History: Pitfalls and Limitations," in *Studies in Defterology: Ottoman Society in the Fifteenth and Sixteenth Centuries* (Istanbul: Isis Press, 1992), 3–18, and Halil İnalcık, "The Ottoman State: Economy and Society, 1300–1600," in *An Economic and Social History of the Ottoman Empire, 1300–1914,* ed. Halil İnalcık and Donald Quataert (Cambridge: Cambridge University Press, 1994),132ff.

78. Repp, *The Müfti of Istanbul,* 192–96, 215ff., 283–84, 300–304.

79. Uriel Heyd, "Some Aspects of the Ottoman Fetva," *Bulletin of the School of Oriental and African Studies* 32 (1969): 46–47.

80. AS 2:32c, 181a.

81. Heyd, *Old Ottoman Criminal Law,* 57–58, 95–96.

82. The divorces are recorded in AS 161:2c, 186a, 335c; AS 2:2a, 155b.

83. Heyd, *Old Ottoman Criminal Law,* 60, 99 (I have slightly altered Heyd's translation of this statute).

84. İbn Kemal (Şemseddin Ahmed Kemalpaşazade), *Fetava* (MS Dar ul-Mesnevi 118, Süleymaniye Library, Istanbul), 16a, 42b.

85. On illicit sex in Islamic jurisprudence, see Colin Imber, "*Zina* in Ottoman Law," in *Contributions à l'histoire économique et sociale de l'Empire ottoman,* ed. Jean-Louis Bacqué-Gramont and Paul Dumont (Leuven, Belgium: Peeters, 1983), 59–92.

86. The manner in which the court received and recorded other women's allegations of rape suggests that by acknowledging the testimony of Ayşe's five witnesses, it accepted her claim that she had been raped.

87. See, for example, the case of the youth who clears his reputation of the accusation that he had a sexual encounter with a man (chapter 5) and the case of Haciye Sabah.

88. Cornelia Hughes Dayton, *Women before the Bar: Gender, Law, and Society in Connecticut, 1639–1789* (Chapel Hill: University of North Carolina Press, 1995), 4.

89. The work of Ronald Jennings and Haim Gerber has been very valuable in casting light on the interaction of legal discourse and law in practice.

90. Various articles in the journal *Gaziantep Kültürü* suggest that there was a resident community of Shafi'i legal experts from the fourteenth century, if not before, through the nineteenth century. For a case handled by a Shafi'i deputy judge, see AS 2:86c, 87c.

91. Uzunçarşılı, *İlmiye Teşkilatı,* 29.

92. On Al-Halabi and the history of his work, see Şükrü Selim Has, "The Use of *Multaqa'l-Abhur* in the Ottoman Madrasas and in Legal Scholarship," *Osmanlı Araştırmaları* 7–8 (1988): 393–418.

93. See Has, "The Use of *Multaqa'l-Abhur,*" on the slowness of the work's dissemi-

nation. The "systematic section" (part 2) of Joseph Schacht's *Introduction to Islamic Law* is based on the *Multaka al-Abhur,* which Schact calls "one of the latest and most highly esteemed statements of the doctrine of the [Hanafi] school, which presents Islamic law in its final, fully developed form without being in any way a code" (112).

94. Uzunçarşılı, *İlmiye Teşkilatı,* 29; according to Uzunçarşılı, Hanafi jurisprudence was the most important subject taught in Ottoman medreses, in particular the work of the twelfth-century jurist Al-Marghinani, *Hedaya.*

95. A 1557 survey of pious endowments counted eleven congregational mosques, fifty-nine small neighborhood mosques, two religious colleges *(medrese),* four other educational institutions *(buk‛a),* and eight dervish convents *(zaviye)* (Özdeğer, *Ayıntâb Livâsı,* 180–85). In the court records, one "buk‛a" is referred to as a medrese (AS 161:106b).

96. Besim Darkot and Hikmat Turhan Dağlıoğlu, "Ayıntab," in *İslam Ansiklopedisi,* 2:66.

97. For a broad definition of sharia and an attempt to convey the levels of its meaning, see Frederick Mathewson Denny, *An Introduction to Islam,* 2nd ed. (New York: Macmillan, 1994), 195–96.

98. Muhammad Khalid Masud, Brinkley Messick, and David S. Powers, introduction to *Islamic Legal Tradition: Muftis and Their Fatwas,* ed. Muhammad Khalid Masud, Brinkley Messick, and David S. Powers (Cambridge, Mass.: Harvard University Press, 1996), 3. This collection of articles on fatwas is an excellent introduction to the subject.

99. On the Ottoman muftis, see Repp, *The Müfti of Istanbul,* and Haim Gerber, *State, Society, and Law in Islam: Ottoman Law in Comparative Perspective* (Albany: State University of New York Press, 1994), esp. chap. 3.

100. AS 161:350b.

101. İbn Kemal, *Fetava,* 42b (Query: If Zeyd divorces his wife when he is ill and delirious, is the divorce valid according to the law? Response: Yes).

102. AS 161:165a, c.

103. In early-seventeenth-century Kayseri, as in mid-sixteenth-century Aintab, few fatwas were entered into the court records (Jennings, "Kadi, Court, and Legal Procedure in Seventeenth Century Ottoman Kayseri," 134). In studying seventeenth-century Bursa, Haim Gerber found that while fatwas from the chief mufti were entered into the court records, there appears to have been no local mufti working at court (which Gerber attributes to the proximity of Bursa to the imperial capital); even the number of chief-mufti fatwas was not large (*Economy and Society in an Ottoman City: Bursa, 1600–1700* [Jerusalem: Institute of Asian and African Studies, the Hebrew University of Jerusalem, 1988], 189–90).

104. AS 2:78a.

105. This duplicative practice is clearly illustrated in the collection of imperial orders to the governors and kadis of sixteenth-century Palestine published by Uriel Heyd, *Ottoman Documents on Palestine, 1552–1615* (London: Oxford University Press, 1960).

106. Tapu Tahrir Defter 231, fol. 69. The provincial cavalry consisted of two *za‛im*s, 86 *sipahi*s, and a total of 159 armed retainers *(cebelü).*

107. See Mary Boyce, *Letter of Tansar* (Rome: Istituto Italiano per il Medio ed Estremo Oriente, 1968).

108. For the great number and variety of law books issued by these sultans, see Akgündüz, *Osmanlı Kanunnâmeleri*, vols. 1-7. On lawmaking and sovereignty, see Halil İnalcık, "Suleiman the Lawgiver and Ottoman Law," *Archivum Ottomanicum* 1 (1969): 105-38, and Cornell Fleischer, *Bureaucrat and Intellectual in the Ottoman Empire: The Historian Mustafa Âli* (Princeton: Princeton University Press, 1986), chap. 6.

109. Tapu Tahrir Defter 186, fols. 3-5; Özdeğer, *Ayıntâb Livâsı*, 201-3.

110. On Qaytbay and Uzun Hasan, see chapter 7, note 31.

111. See, for example, AS 161:13c.

112. Tapu Tahrir Defteri 186, fols. 4-5.

113. AS 2:278c *(kanun üzere cerimesi virayım)*.

114. *Örf*, often translated as "customary law," here refers to the customary assumption that it takes sovereign authority to actually enforce sharia. On Ottoman usage of this term, see Halil İnalcık, "Örf," in *İslam Ansiklopedisi*, 9:480.

115. Heyd, *Old Ottoman Criminal Law*, 88, 127.

116. AS 2:116b.

117. A. Udovitch, "Islamic Law and the Social Context of Exchange in the Medieval Middle East," *History and Anthropology* 1 (1985): 445. This article is an eloquent statement of the importance of local custom in the thinking of Hanafi jurisprudents.

118. AS 2:19a, 20b; a *batman* was approximately 20 kilograms. For the process whereby tax rates were officially established in consultation with the local population, see the governer-general's order of 1535 fixing the tax rate for beehives; this order was copied into the Aintab register of 1541 in conjunction with a dispute over the beehive tax (AS 2:208a).

119. AS 161:344a.

120. Al-Marghinani, *The Hedaya, or Guide*, trans. Charles Hamilton (London: T. Bensley, 1791; reprint, Karachi: Darul Ishaat Urdu Bazar), 2:638-40.

121. I thank Najwa Al-Qattan for this observation.

122. For İbn Kemal's life and work, see Repp, *The Müfti of Istanbul*, 224-39.

123. İbn Kemal, *Fetava*, 31b *(ta'zir-i balig nedir? Her kişinin haline münasip ta'zir-i balig vardır. Ol hususta ra'y kadınındır)*. The italics in the text are mine.

124. On this point, I would like to acknowledge the valuable lectures of Professor Frank Vogel at Harvard Law School.

125. Johansen, "Legal Literature and the Problem of Change," 30-36.

126. Fleischer, *Bureaucrat and Intellectual*, 198; Johansen, "Legal Literature and the Problem of Change," 31.

127. Schacht, *An Introduction to Islamic Law*, 89. Wael Hallaq challenges this assertion of Schacht's ("The *qadi's diwan [sijill]* before the Ottomans," 417).

128. AS 161:114a.

İNE'S STORY: A CHILD MARRIAGE IN TROUBLE

1. AS 161:136c. I thank Professor Şinasi Tekin of Harvard University for his help in understanding the final statement of the witnesses in this case.

2. On child marriage, see İlber Ortaylı, "Anadolu'da XVI. Yüzyılda Evlilik İlişkileri Üzerine Bazı Gözlemler," *Osmanlı Araştırmaları* 1 (1980): 38.

3. AS 161:26a, 27b; AS 2:185b. See also Halit Ongan, *Ankara'nın 1 Numaralı Şer'iye Sicili* (Ankara: Türk Tarih Kurumu, 1958), 334.

4. AS 161:50b. Under Islamic law, females who were legally adult (defined as physically mature enough to enter marriage) had the right to refuse a marriage alliance arranged for them.

5. AS 2:185b. The typical amount of support or maintenance *(nafaka)* was 2 akçes a day.

6. See Ibrahim Al-Halabi, *Multaka al-Abhur* (Istanbul: Dar ul-Tibaat ul-Amire, 1873), 366–67, for the legal situating of rape (which is referred to as forced sex outside the relationship of marriage or concubinage).

7. Uriel Heyd, *Studies in Old Ottoman Criminal Law,* ed. V. L. Menage (Oxford: Clarendon Press, 1973), 62, 101.

8. Al-Marghinani, *The Hedaya, or Guide,* trans. Charles Hamilton (London: T. Bensley, 1791; reprint, Karachi: Darul Ishaat Urdu Bazar), 2:3.

9. AS 161:28a.

10. AS 161:164a.

11. The term *muhsan* (fem. *muhsana*) actually has two meanings in Islamic law: the first is the definition given here, relating to protection against the crime of false accusation of illicit sex, while the second relates to the punishment for adultery. In the latter instance, the *muhsan/muhsana* is the free person in a valid and sexually consummated marriage, who is subject to the punishment of death by stoning (Schacht, *Introduction to Islamic Law,* 125).

12. Heyd, *Studies in Old Ottoman Criminal Law,* 62, 101.

13. The secretary appeared in the Aintab court in connection with village tax payments and border disputes (AS 161:57a, b, c; 130a, b, c).

14. AS 2:300c.

15. Schacht, *Introduction to Islamic Law,* 165.

16. The language used by Tanrıvirdi—"she has no pleasure in life living together with me"—may be a formulaic expression for the unhappiness of a woman in marriage. The words used in the court record—*hüsn-i zindegânesi yokdur*—were altered by the scribe: above the word *zindegâne* was written *mu'aşereti,* and below the whole phrase was written *benimle.* Both *hüsn-i zindegâne* and *hüsn-i mu'aşereti,* parallel terms, were used in eighteenth-century Istanbul in records of women seeking divorce (Madeline C. Zilfi, "'We don't get along': Women and *Hul* Divorce in the Eighteenth Century," in *Women in the Ottoman Empire: Middle Eastern Women in the Early Modern Era,* ed. Madeline C. Zilfi [Leiden: Brill, 1997], 276, 279). In sixteenth-century Aintab, such language is limited to young girls in marriage: in another case, a mother sued for the release of her daughter from a loveless marriage, pleading that "she has no pleasure in life and is utterly helpless" (*hüsn-i zindegânesi yok ve kız kendüden acizedir;* AS 2:6b).

17. The spelling of the name of this village varies considerably in the record, suggesting that the scribes had a difficult time approximating its pronunciation. I have adopted the spelling used by Hüseyin Özdeğer in *Onaltıncı Asırda Ayıntâb Livâsı* (Istanbul: Bayrak Matbaacılık, 1988).

18. Özdeğer, *Ayıntâb Livâsı*, endmap. The current names of these two villages are Acar (Hacer) and Çaybaşı (Cağdığın); they belong to the subdistrict of Oğuzeli, whose *kaza* seat is the former Kızılhisar.

19. AS 2:206b.

20. AS 2:206c, 207c, 208c. The total value of the goods given by Ali to Sultan was 892 akçes, a rural dower typical of these records.

21. Sunullah Efendi, *Fetava-ı Sunullah Efendi* (MSS Hasan Hüsnü Pasha 502, Süleymaniye Library, Istanbul), 7b.

22. Özdeğer, *Ayıntâb Livâsı*, 343–44, 449.

23. If the girls' fathers were *not* deceased, then what was perhaps being guarded against was improper exploitation of the mother's custody, since according to legal norms, girls stayed with their mother until they were deemed marriageable (defined by physical readiness), whereupon they passed into their father's custody.

24. M. E. Düzdağ, *Şeyhülislam Ebussuûd Efendi Fetvaları Işığında 16. Asır Türk Hayatı* (Istanbul: Enderun Kitabevi, 1983), 37–38.

25. Düzdağ, *Ebussuûd Efendi Fetvaları*, 36, 37–38 *(hakim maʿrifetsiz nikâh sahih . . . olmaz)*. On the contracting of marriage, see Colin Imber, *Ebu's-Suʿud: The Islamic Legal Tradition* (Stanford: Stanford University Press, 1997),167ff.

26. The regulations concerning guardianship in the making of marriages restricted the latitude that people enjoyed in this serious business. For example, they prevented mothers from contracting marriages for their children (see the fatwa of Ebu Suud refusing the validity of a marriage contracted by a mother on behalf of her daughter; Düzdağ, *Ebussuûd Efendi Fetvaları*, 38), and they denied the right, acknowledged by some Hanafi jurists, of an adult woman to give herself in marriage. Not only did the rules on guardianship restrict the traditional flexibility in contracting marriage sanctioned by the variations tolerated in juristic opinion, but they also went against practice in Aintab, where marriages were rarely registered in the court record. See Imber, *Ebu's-Suʿud*, 167–71, on the resistance to Süleyman's legislation on guardianship.

27. Özdeğer, *Ayıntâb Livâsı*, 393 n. 1.

28. Other villages owned by Al-Ghawri's heirs were Tüzel and Ahmanus. On the difficulties experienced by Al-Ghawri's son in claiming Ahmanus in the aftermath of the Ottoman conquest, see Tapu Tahrir 301, fols. 30–31.

29. AS 161:69a.

30. Halil İnalcık, "The Ottoman State: Economy and Society, 1300–1600," in *An Economic and Social History of the Ottoman Empire, 1300–1914,* ed. Halil İnalcık and Donald Quataert (Cambridge: Cambridge University Press, 1994), 122–26.

31. Özdeğer, *Ayıntâb Livâsı*, passim.

32. Leslie Peirce, *The Imperial Harem: Women and Sovereignty in the Ottoman Empire* (New York: Oxford University Press, 1993), 201–2.

33. Machiel Kiel, *Art and Society of Bulgaria in the Turkish Period* (Assen: Van Gorcum, 1985), 109–10.

34. Carl Petry, "Class Solidarity versus Gender Gain: Women as Custodians of Property in Later Medieval Egypt," in *Women in Middle Eastern History: Shifting Bound-*

aries in Sex and Gender, ed. Nikki R. Keddie and Beth Baron (New Haven: Yale University Press, 1991), 122–42; quotation, 125.

4. GENDER, CLASS, AND SOCIAL HIERARCHY

1. AS 2:290b.
2. These individuals figure, respectively, in AS 2:7c, 127a, and AS 161:46e.
3. Hemdi, or Hamed as the record sometimes spells her name, was in the business of selling *şira,* a kind of fermented grape juice; her loan from Haci Ali was probably intended to cover production expenses following the grape harvest) (AS 2:288a, 313c, 314c).
4. AS 161:27a. However, the only Jew who figured at court—as the city's official banker, appointed from Aleppo and probably resident there—was routinely labeled with his religion: "Matuk b. Sadullah the Jew." This practice of referring to Christians as *dhimmi* and Jews as Jews was not peculiar to Aintab.
5. AS 161:173a.
6. Tapu Tahrir Defteri 373, fols. 46–47.
7. On ethnicity in the context of eighteenth-century Aleppo, see Abraham Marcus, *The Middle East on the Eve of Modernity: Aleppo in the Eighteenth Century* (New York: Columbia University Press, 1989), 19–21.
8. For an interpretation of Hanafi views on legal maturity and legal competency, see Baber Johansen, "Sacred and Religious Element[s] in Hanafite Law: Function and Limits of the Absolute Character of Government Authority," in *Islam et Politique au Maghreb,* ed. Ernest G. Gellner et al. (Paris: Éditions du Centre national de la recherche scientifique, 1981), 281–303.
9. Joseph Schacht, *Introduction to Islamic Law* (Oxford: Oxford University Press, 1954), 124–25, 185.
10. Colin Imber, *Ebu's-Su'ud: The Islamic Legal Tradition* (Stanford: Stanford University Press, 1997), 239.
11. Schacht, *Introduction to Islamic Law,* 132.
12. Uriel Heyd, *Studies in Old Ottoman Criminal Law,* ed. V. L. Menage (Oxford: Clarendon Press, 1973), 97, 102, 108.
13. Colin Imber notes, however, that strictly speaking there was no basis in jurisprudence for kanun's assigning an inferior status to non-Muslims in these matters or to slaves in the matter of bodily injury; rather, the distinction reflected jurists' generally negative attitudes toward these groups, as well as "a popular rather than a learned understanding of the Holy Law" (Imber, *Ebu's-Su'udd,* 245).
14. Al-Marghinani, *The Hedaya, or Guide,* trans. Charles Hamilton (London: T. Bensley, 1791; reprint, Karachi: Darul Ishaat Urdu Bazar), 2:12.
15. The obvious reference here is to Joan Scott's well-known essay, "Gender: A Useful Category of Historical Analysis," in *Gender and the Politics of History* (New York: Columbia University Press, 1988), 28–50.
16. I thank Suraiya Faroqhi for drawing the category of senile male to my attention.
17. For an extended discussion of the transformation of gender identity, see my "Seniority, Sexuality, and Social Order: The Vocabulary of Gender in Early Mod-

ern Ottoman Anatolia," in *Women in the Ottoman Empire: Middle Eastern Women in the Early Modern Era,* ed. Madeline C. Zilfi (Leiden: Brill, 1997), 169–96.

18. On the relative unimportance of the event of marriage in the formation of households, in comparison to European practice, see Alan Duben, "Turkish Families and Households in Historical Perspective," *Journal of Family History* 10 (1995): 81–82.

19. Heyd, *Old Ottoman Criminal Law,* 56.

20. Kınalızade Ali Efendi, *Ahlak-ı Ala'î* (Cairo: Bulak, 1248/1833), book 2, 20.

21. In his study of seventeenth-century Bursa, Haim Gerber notes that families were not large; he calculates the average number of children at 2.2 ("Social and Economic Position of Women in an Ottoman City, Bursa, 1600–1700," *International Journal of Middle East Studies* 12 [1980]: 244). According to Duben ("Turkish Families and Households in Historical Perspective," 92–93), infant and child mortality may have resulted in only half of all children born reaching the age of twenty.

22. AS 161:26c, 72a.

23. Denise Spellberg, *Politics, Gender, and the Islamic Past: The Legacy of Aisha bint Abi Bakr* (New York: Columbia University Press, 1994), 40–41.

24. AS 2:248a.

25. AS 2:444a. The term *besleme* is thus defined in modern dictionaries as well as in Francisci Meninski, *Thesaurus linguarum orientalium turcicae, arabicae, persicae . . .* (Vienna, 1680), 1:822.

26. For the classical Hanafi view of majority, see Schacht, *An Introduction to Islamic Law,* 124; N. J. Coulson, *Succession in the Muslim Family* (Cambridge: Cambridge University Press, 1971), 11. For Ebu Suud's view, see M. E. Düzdağ, *Şeyhülislam Ebussuûd Efendi Fetvaları Işığında* 16. *Asır Türk Hayatı* (Istanbul: Enderun Kitabevi, 1983), 33. One had to be at least twelve years old to qualify for legal majority, even if physical maturation had taken place.

27. Schacht, *Introduction to Islamic Law,* 124.

28. Cited in Ronald Jennings, "Women in Early Seventeenth Century Ottoman Judicial Records—The Sharia Court of Anatolian Kayseri," *Journal of the Economic and Social History of the Orient* 18 (1975): 77. For another use of this phrase, see a case from the 1590 Ankara court record cited in Halit Ongan, *Ankara'nın İki Numaralı Şer'iye Sicili* (Ankara: Türk Tarih Kurumu Basımevi, 1974), 85, 144.

29. For a general overview of married women and the law in Europe, see Merry E. Wiesner, *Women and Gender in Early Modern Europe* (Cambridge: Cambridge University Press, 1993), 30–34.

30. On coverture, see Cornelia Hughes Dayton, *Women before the Bar: Gender, Law, and Society in Connecticut, 1639–1789* (Chapel Hill: University of North Carolina Press, 1995), esp. 19ff.; Timothy Stretton, *Women Waging Law in Elizabethan England* (Cambridge: Cambridge University Press, 1998), chaps. 2, 4. I am grateful to Barbara Harris for drawing Stretton's book to my attention.

31. Blackstone's *Commentaries on the Laws of England,* quoted in Dayton, *Women before the Bar,* 19–20.

32. Wiesner, *Women and Gender in Early Modern Europe,* 31–32.

33. Stretton, *Women Waging Law in Elizabethan England,* 7–9, 143–50.

34. Separate courts that specialized in inheritance did exist in some periods and places.

35. Judith Tucker, *In the House of the Law: Gender and Islamic Law in Ottoman Syria and Palestine* (Berkeley: University of California Press, 1998), 58–67.

36. For these fatwas issued by Ebu Suud, see Düzdağ, *Ebussuûd Efendi Fetvaları*, 53–54.

37. Düzdağ, *Ebussuûd Efendi Fetvaları*, 56.

38. Louise Marlow, *Hierarchy and Egalitarianism in Islamic Thought* (Cambridge: Cambridge University Press, 1997), esp. 93, 134–39. See also my *The Imperial Harem: Women and Sovereignty in the Ottoman Empire* (New York: Oxford University Press, 1993), 8–9, for the use of the terms *hass* and *amm* among the Ottomans.

39. As Marlow comments, "They [i.e., religious scholars] interpreted the Qur'anic equation of nobility and piety to their own advantage, and the appearance, in a watered-down form, of materials in which the significance of nobility and lineage are denied attests to their success" (*Hierarchy and Egalitarianism in Islamic Thought,* 139).

40. Hülya Canbakal has documented the striking increase in numbers of seyyids in late-seventeenth-century Aintab ("XVII. Yüzyılda Teseyyüd ve ʿAyntab Sadatı," in *Osmanlı Döneminde Gaziantep Sempozyumu,* ed. Yüsüf Küçükdağ [Gaziantep: Gaziantep Valiliği İl Özel İdare Müdürlüğü, 2000], 77–81), while Marcus (*Aleppo in the Eighteenth Century,* 61) notes that the sizable ranks of the *ashraf* in eighteenth-century Aleppo included some who had achieved their status by means of fraudulent genealogies.

41. Johansen, "Sacred and Religious Element[s] in Hanafite Law," 283.

42. The title *zuema* was used for police chiefs (*subaşıs*), *muharririn* for the secretaries of the provincial governor and the trustee of crown lands, and *müteberririn* for administrative officials of important waqf institutions. Typically, religious notables were collectively known as the *eshraf,* but that term was not used in the Aintab records.

43. This distinction has been suggested by Cemil Cahit Güzelbey to have originated with the conquest (*Gaziantep Şerʿi Mahkeme Sicillerinden Örnekler (Cilt 144–152) (Miladi 1841–1886)* [Gaziantep: Yeni Matbaa, 1966], 234).

44. Neşrî, *Kitâb-ı Cihan-Nümâ: Neşrî Tarihi,* ed. Faik Reşit Ünat and Mehmed A. Köymen (Ankara: Türk Tarihi Kurumu, 1987), 2:710–11.

45. AS 2:50d.

46. For a study that situates Ebu Suud in both a legal and historical context, see Colin Imber, *Ebu's-Suʿud.* See also Jon E. Mandaville, "Usurious Piety: The Cash Waqf Controversy in the Ottoman Empire," *International Journal of Middle Eastern Studies* 10 (1979): 289–308.

47. Francisci Meninski, *Lexicon Arabico-Persico-Turcicum* (Vienna, 1780–1802), 4:428.

48. Much of this section is drawn from my "'The Law Shall Not Languish': Social Class and Public Conduct in Sixteenth-Century Ottoman Legal Discourse," in *Hermeneutics and Honor: Negotiating Female "Public" Space in Islamicate Societies,* ed. Asma Afsaruddin (Cambridge, Mass.: Harvard University Press, 1999), 140–58.

For treatment of the subject in the context of Ebu Suud's work in general, see Imber, *Ebu's-Su'ud*, 244–45.

49. Düzdağ, *Ebussuûd Efendi Fetvaları*, 56.

50. Düzdağ, *Ebussuûd Efendi Fetvaları*, 56.

51. These rules on male-female contact are contained in Surah 4, *Al-Nisâ'*, verses 23–24, of the Qur'an.

52. Public Record Office, London: S.P. 102/61/237 (letter of the grand vezir Siya-vuş Paşa dated Ramazan 1000 [1592]; S.P. 102/61/81 (victory letter dated Rebi'ül-Ahır 1009 [1600], at the conclusion of the Kanisza campaign). I am grateful to Bernard Lewis for these references.

53. Imber has likened this attitude toward female seclusion to the penalties discriminating against non-Muslims and slaves, remarking that both represent "what Muslims at large probably believed Hanafi law to be" (*Ebu's-Su'ud*, 245).

54. Heyd, *Old Ottoman Criminal Law*, 70, 109.

55. İbn Kemal (Şemseddin Ahmed Kemalpaşazade), *Fetava* (MS Dar ul-Mesnevi 118, Süleymaniye Library, Istanbul), 78b–79a.

56. Ebu Suud, *Ba'z ul-Fetava* (MS Yeni Cami 685/3, Süleymaniye Library, Istanbul), 170b.

57. Ebu Suud, *Ba'z ul-Fetava*, 167b.

58. AS 2:93b. For more on this subject, see chapter 6.

59. AS 2:48c.

60. Heyd, *Old Ottoman Criminal Law*, 95–97, 102–3. Such variation is possible because punishment for adultery and fornication is determined for each of the guilty parties by his or her civil status rather than by the particular circumstances of the transgression: a male slave and a freeborn Muslim female will receive quite different punishments for engaging in a mutual act of adultery (according to Süleyman's law book, the slave receives one-quarter the punishment of the woman, and perhaps even less if she is quite wealthy).

61. Heyd, *Old Ottoman Criminal Law*, 64–65, 104.

62. There may have been more concrete reasons for the differentiation as well: greater fines on the rich perhaps indicated the regime's intent not to let them off the punitive hook.

63. İbn Kemal, *Fetava*, 33a.

64. İbn Kemal, *Fetava*, 74a *(Tecdîd-i imân lâzım olur, avâmmdan ise).*

65. For a discussion of the conditional vow, see my "'She is trouble . . . and I will divorce her': Orality, Honor, and Representation in the Sixteenth-Century Ottoman Court of Aintab," in *Women in the Medieval Islamic World: Power, Patronage, Piety,* ed. Gavin R. G. Hambly (New York: St. Martin's Press, 1998), 267–300.

66. Marlow, *Hierarchy and Egalitarianism in Islamic Thought*, 39–40.

67. Heyd, *Old Ottoman Criminal Law*, 91, 129 (I have slightly modified Heyd's translation). The statute goes on to state: "and if they deserve to be imprisoned, they shall, if someone stands surety for their person, not be imprisoned and the matter shall be submitted and officially notified by the judge to My Sublime Court. If, however, their offense is a grievous outrage and there is a likelihood of their resorting to flight and, furthermore, there is nobody standing surety for them, they shall be imprisoned."

68. Al-Marghinani, *The Hedaya*, 2:76. For similar views held by the Hanafi jurists Al-

Kasani (d. 1191) and Ibn Humam (d. 1457), see, respectively, Irene Schneider, "Imprisonment in Pre-Classical and Classical Islamic Law," *Islamic Law and Society* 2 (1995): 157–73, and Imber, *Ebu's-su'ud*, 211–12. I thank David S. Powers for the reference to Schneider's citation of Al-Kasani.

69. Marcus, *Aleppo in the Eighteenth Century*, 48–49, 66–67.
70. AS 2:138b, 145b.
71. AS 161:157c, 186a.
72. The meaning of the phrase *sandal taşı* is unclear, although the context suggests it has something to do with curing the little boy. One meaning of *sandal* is white sandalwood (bot., *Santalum album*), whose oil is used for medicinal purposes. I am grateful to Dr. Xingning Zhao of Ithaca, N.Y., for informing me that white sandalwood is used in traditional Asian medicine to treat a variety of illnesses; it is administered primarily in the form of an infusion.
73. This additional note is difficult to sort out, as it is entered in the record rather messily.
74. AS 2:114a, b.
75. During my twenty-one-month stay in Gaziantep in the mid-1960s, neighborhoods were still patrolled at night.
76. AS 2:137a, 205b, 279a, 307c, 323b.
77. AS 2:205b.
78. AS 2:279a. This case was a rare instance of direct sentencing by the judge, rather than by the administrative authorities of Aintab.
79. AS 2:137a.
80. Heyd, *Old Ottoman Criminal Law*, 102.

5. MORALITY AND SELF-REPRESENTATION AT COURT

1. On the practice of recounting the lives of prophets and saints, see Jonathan Berkey, *Popular Preaching and Religious Authority in the Medieval Islamic Near East* (Seattle: University of Washington Press, 2001). See Haciye Sabah's story for a storyteller *(meddah)* who got in trouble.
2. Frederick Mathewson Denny, *An Introduction to Islam*, 2nd ed. (New York: Macmillan, 1994), 159.
3. On Birgivi Mehmed, see Madeline C. Zilfi, *The Politics of Piety: The Ottoman Ulema in the Postclassical Age (1600–1800)* (Minneapolis: Bibliotheca Islamica, 1988); on Kınalızade Ali, see Adnan Adıvar, "Kınalı-zâde," in *İslam Ansiklopedisi*, 6: 709–11.
4. Birgivi Mehmed, *Tarikat-i Muhammediyye Tercümesi*, trans. C. Yıldırım (Istanbul: Demir Kitabevi, 1981), 293ff.
5. Kınalızade Ali, *Ahlak-ı Ala'i* (Istanbul: Kervan Kitapçılık, n.d.), 138.
6. This point has been noted by Barbara Metcalf in her introduction to her edited collection *Moral Conduct and Authority: The Place of Adab in South Asian Islam* (Berkeley: University of California Press, 1984): in defining the term *adab*—the concept of moral discrimination and behavior, she comments that it "not only required the internalization of norms from all spheres of human activities but involved the inner and spiritual life in its fulfillment" (5). Metcalf attributes this observation to Peter Brown, one of the collection's authors.

7. AS 161:28a.

8. AS 161:170a.

9. On the right of neighborhoods to evict undesirable residents, see the law books of Selim I and Süleyman (Selami Pulaha and Yaşar Yücel, "I. Selim Kanunnamesi (1512–1520) ve XVI. Yüzyılın İkinci Yarısının Kimi Kanunları," *Belgeler* 12, no. 16 [1987]: 31, 71; Uriel Heyd, *Studies in Old Ottoman Criminal Law,* ed. V. L. Menage [Oxford: Clarendon Press, 1973], 93, 130).

10. AS 161:35a; AS 2:75c, 76a, b, 78c. The case of the chronic liar is discussed later in this chapter and that of the female teacher in Haciye Sabah's story.

11. Al-Marghinani, *The Hedaya, or Guide,* trans. Charles Hamilton (London: T. Bensley, 1791; reprint, Karachi: Darul Ishaat Urdu Bazar), 2:672.

12. Al-Marghinani, *The Hedaya,* 2:671–73.

13. AS 161:35a.

14. See note 9 above.

15. Muhammed El-Edirnevi Mecdi, *Hada'ik ül-Shaka'ik* (Istanbul: Tabhane-i Amire, 1269/1852), 50. It was said that because of disagreements between them, Molla Fenari subsequently left the service of Bayezid for that of the rulers of the central-Anatolian principality of Karaman.

16. Al-Marghinani, *The Hedaya,* 2:682ff.

17. Al-Marghinani, *The Hedaya,* 2:612.

18. Al-Marghinani, *The Hedaya,* 2:615–16.

19. Birgivi Mehmed, *Tarikat-i Muhammediyye Tercümesi,* 383–87. Birgivi Mehmed notes that filling the office of judge, like that of sovereign and governor, is incumbent not on the individual but rather on the community (*farz-ı kifaye*).

20. M. E. Düzdağ, *Şeyhülislam Ebussuûd Efendi Fetvaları Işığında 16. Asır Türk Hayatı* (Istanbul: Enderun Kitabevi, 1983), 134–35.

21. Nev'izade 'Ata'i, *Hada'ik ül-Haka'ik fi Tekmilet üş-Şaka'ik* (Istanbul, 1268/1851–1852), 11–12.

22. Judith Tucker, *In the House of the Law: Gender and Islamic Law in Ottoman Syria and Palestine* (Berkeley: University of California Press, 1998), 32.

23. On the importance of living as well as knowing the teachings of Islam, see Metcalf, introduction to *Moral Conduct and Authority,* 7; more generally, see the essays collected in the volume.

24. Derviş Ahmed Asıkpaşazade, *Tevarih-i Al-i Osman,* ed. N. Atsız (Istanbul: Türkiye Yayınevi, 1947), chap. 14, p. 103.

25. Walter Andrews, "The Sexual Intertext of Ottoman Literature: The Story of Me'âlî, the Magistrate of Mihalich," *Edebiyat,* n.s., 3 (1989): 31–56.

26. See chapter 6 on mothers as guardians.

27. AS 2:316a.

28. AS 2:26b.

29. Examples of typical phrasing are "mabeynlerinde munaza'a-i kesire vaki' olundukdansonra, musalihun min el-müslimin araya girüb" (AS 2:24c), "ba'd al-munaza'a ve'l-muhasama musalihun mutavassıt olub" (AS 2:134b), and "mabeynlerinde munaza'a-i kesire vaki' olub ba'd el-munaza'a ve'l-muhasama musalihun araya girüb" (AS 2:200b).

30. See, for example, AS 161:134b, 137a, 344a; AS 2:212b, 311c: *el-sulh hayır hadisi ile 'amel idüb/olunub . . .*

31. AS 1:134b.

32. Al-Marghinani, *The Hedaya,* 2:671.

33. On the role of the oath in cementing social and political loyalties, see Roy P. Mottahedeh, *Loyalty and Leadership in an Early Islamic Society* (Princeton: Princeton University Press, 1980), chap. 2.

34. Of some thirty cases of such oath taking at the Aintab court, twenty-five resulted from the plaintiff's request that the defendant take the oath, and five from the defendant's request that the plaintiff do so.

35. In several cases defendants refused to take the oath, or plaintiffs turned down the option of having the defendant take an oath, thereby surrendering their claim.

36. See AS 2:79b, where the Armenian Bahşi, a plaintiff unable to provide proof of his accusation that the defendant Karagöz cursed him, requests that Karagöz take an oath on the Bible *(İncil üzerine vaz'-ı yed idub)*.

37. AS 161:2a.

38. Lawrence Rosen, *The Anthropology of Justice: Law as Culture in Islamic Society* (Cambridge: Cambridge University Press, 1989), 25.

39. AS 2:161a–e, 164a.

40. On bread and its tendency to function as a subject of moral debate, see the classic article by E. P. Thompson, "The Moral Economy of the English Crowd in the Eighteenth Century," *Past and Present,* no. 50 (February 1971): 78–98.

41. AS 161:54b. For an account of this case, see chapter 7, "The Events of June 1541: Disciplining Subjects."

42. AS 2:5a–b.

43. On the misogynist elements in premodern Muslim writing, see Leila Ahmed, *Women and Gender in Islam: The Historical Roots of a Modern Debate* (New Haven: Yale University Press, 1993); Fatima Mernissi, *The Veil and the Male Elite: A Feminist Interpretation of Women's Rights in Islam* (Reading, Mass.: Addison-Wesley, 1991); Denise Spellberg, "Nizâm Al-Mulk's Manipulation of Tradition: 'A'isha and the Role of Women in Islamic Government," *Muslim World* 78, no. 2 (1988): 111–17.

44. Al-Marghinani, *The Hedaya,* 2:667–68.

45. Two women and three men testified with regard to Ayşe's alleged rape (see chapter 3); three women testified that they had witnessed the appointment of a fourth as proxy in the matter of her daughter's divorce (AS 161:37c); a woman testified that she was a witness of her brother's sale of an expensive house, with the man's son as the other witness (AS 2:3a); and two women and a man testified that a house whose ownership was disputed belonged to one of the litigating parties (AS 2:204a).

46. Joseph Schacht, *An Introduction to Islamic Law* (Oxford: Oxford University Press, 1954), 194.

47. AS 2:305a. The quarrel appears to have either stemmed from or resulted in Tac Ahmed's suit to claim custody of his younger (half) sister, which was the next case recorded in the court register.

48. AS 2:74b.

49. AS 2:84a (the mother of an orphan swears that her ex-husband did not pay her the 3 gold pieces he owed her); AS 2:148a (three sisters swear that their uncle

sold their property illegally and that, having reached majority, they do not approve of the sale).

50. İbn Kemal (Şemseddin Ahmed Kemalpaşazade), *Fetava* (MS Dar ul-Mesnevi 118, Süleymaniye Library, Istanbul), fol. 12a: *Hatunlar cemaat olub ref'-i savtla zikretmek şer'an mubah mıdır? Haramdır avazlarını erkeklere işitdürmek.*

51. AS 161:2a.

52. AS 2:1b, c.

53. AS 161:335b.

54. A further reason for the flat tone in adultery confessions is that the law required the confession to be repeated four times, leading inevitably to a summary representation of what was said.

55. AS 2:132b, c.

56. AS 161:186a (İskender); AS 161:335b, c (Şenok); AS 2:1b, 2a (Mehmed); AS 2:155a, b (Ali).

57. For further discussion of boys as the object of male desire in sixteenth-century literature and law, see Andrews, "The Sexual Intertext of Ottoman Literature"; Everett Rowson, "The Categorization of Gender and Sexual Irregularity in Medieval Arabic Vice Lists," in *Body Guards: The Cultural Politics of Gender Ambiguity,* ed. Julia Epstein and Kristina Straub (New York: Routledge, 1991), 50–79; and my "Seniority, Sexuality, and Social Order: The Vocabulary of Gender in Early Modern Ottoman Anatolia," in *Women in the Ottoman Empire: Middle Eastern Women in the Early Modern Era,* ed. Madeline C. Zilfi (Leiden: Brill, 1997), 177–81.

58. AS 2:7c (*Ali takrir-i meram kılub dediki: işbu Davud ben kendü evime gider iken "ruhum, canım" diyü bana bazı kelimat idüb "seni severim" dedikde, ben dahi "nâ ma'kul söyleme! var benden feragat et!" dedüğüm içün . . .).*

59. AS 2:140a, c.

60. AS 2:69b, 70c.

61. If punished according to sharia rules, a slanderer suffered eighty lashes. Ottoman kanun left it up to the authorities to decide the precise level of punishment, but did prescribe a combination of flogging and fine, 1 akçe for each lash (Heyd, *Old Ottoman Criminal Law,* 110).

62. Heyd, *Old Ottoman Criminal Law,* 88, 126. The term that I have translated here as "disruptive young men" is *levend;* for a discussion of the range of meaning attached to this term, see my "Seniority, Sexuality, and Social Order," 179–81.

63. AS 2:45b, c.

64. Is it coincidental that the attacker was named Ali b. Mehmed? While this combination of names was not uncommon, the attacker may be the same Ali who brought the rape accusation a week later. Was his failed suit related to the attack on the students? If so, the judge may have treated him with a certain skepticism in the second case. More important, if this was the same Ali, it raises the question of the character of the chief of the night watch, Arab b. Haci Halife, whose office was one of the principal mechanisms for monitoring men "out of place" in the city streets. If this speculation is accurate, it is hardly surprising that the group of companions accompanying Ali testified to no more than their presence by the waterside.

65. Natalie Zemon Davis, *Fiction in the Archives: Pardon Tales and Their Tellers in Sixteenth-Century France* (Stanford: Stanford University Press, 1987), 84.

66. AS 2:328a.

67. AS 2:245a.

68. AS 161:159d, 160a, 160c, 161a.

69. AS 2:289b (*bu Arab bir helalzade Arabdır, şimdiyedeğin asla nâ ma'kul fa'alın görmedük, bir doğru oğlandır*). It has been suggested that the phrase I have translated "slit my throat" (*boğazum ide*) may have an obscene connotation.

70. AS 2:289b.

71. AS 161:350b.

72. AS 2:231b.

73. AS 2:74b.

74. AS 2:138b.

75. Heyd, *Old Ottoman Criminal Law*, 63, 102.

76. AS 2:117a. This murder is taken up in chapter 8.

77. Heyd, *Old Ottoman Criminal Law*, 136: "If a person practices procuring as his permanent profession, his face shall be blackened and he shall be exposed to public ignominy."

78. AS 161:5c.

79. AS 2:47a.

80. AS 2:157a.

81. The problem of rape is taken up in more detail in Fatma's story.

6. WOMEN, PROPERTY, AND THE COURT

1. English language studies of women based on Ottoman-period court records are legion. The earliest work was that of Ronald Jennings (in the 1970s), followed by that of Haim Gerber, Abraham Marcus, and Judith Tucker in the early 1980s. Current work is represented by many of the authors in two recent collections: Amira El Azhary Sonbol, ed., *Women, the Family, and Divorce Laws in Islamic History* (Syracuse: Syracuse University Press, 1996), and Madeline C. Zilfi, ed., *Women in the Ottoman Empire: Middle Eastern Women in the Early Modern Era* (Leiden: Brill, 1997). Most studies of women and court records focus on women, property, and the cultural meanings of their relation to it. Additionally, most studies focus on the eighteenth and nineteenth centuries, in part because a greater number of records survive from this period. There has been very little work on the sixteenth century, with the notable exception of Yvonne Seng's studies of Üsküdar.

2. On women and borrowing and lending in sixteenth-century Istanbul, see Yvonne Seng, "Standing at the Gates of Justice: Women in the Law Courts of Early Sixteenth-Century Üsküdar, Istanbul," in *Contested States: Law, Hegemony and Resistance*, ed. Mindie Lazarus-Black and Susan F. Hirsch (New York: Routledge, 1994), 184–206; see also Fariba Zarinebaf-Shahr, "Women, Law, and Imperial Justice in Ottoman Istanbul in the Late Seventeenth Century," in Sonbol, ed., *Women, the Family, and Divorce Laws in Islamic History*, 91.

3. AS 2:83d.

4. AS 2:91a.
5. AS 2:148a.
6. AS 2:211c; 212 a, b.
7. AS 2:263b, 278b.
8. AS 2:283b.
9. AS 2:325c.
10. Selami Pulaha and Yaşar Yücel, "I. Selim Kanunnamesi Yüzyılın İkinci Yarısının Kimi Kanunları," *Belgeler* 12, no. 16 (1987): 45.
11. AS 2:283a.
12. AS 161:42c.
13. AS 2:54c, 58c.
14. AS 2:91c.
15. AS 2:192a.
16. AS 2:275d.
17. AS 2:314a.
18. AS 2:213d.
19. AS 2:318b.
20. N. J. Coulson, *Succession in the Muslim Family* (Cambridge: Cambridge University Press, 1971), 195ff.
21. One piece of evidence suggests that Hamza's claim was never validated: in the cadastral survey of 1543, the village of Arıl was listed as the property of Seydi Ahmed, and in the survey of 1574, of his direct descendants (Hüseyin Özdeğer, *Onaltıncı Asırda Ayıntâb Livâsı* [Istanbul: Bayrak Matbaacılık, 1988], 440). By 1574, the village had been turned into waqf *(vakf-ı evlad-ı Seydi Ahmed b. Boyacızade).*
22. AS 161:39c, 41a.
23. AS 161:336c.
24. AS 161:351c.
25. AS 2:24a.
26. AS 2:25c, 26a.
27. AS 2:266c, 269c. In a case recorded earlier the same day, Zeliha proves that a vineyard in her possession was given to her by her former husband when he was still alive.
28. AS 2:316a.
29. AS 2:323c.
30. On women as guardians of orphans, see Judith Tucker, *In the House of the Law: Gender and Islamic Law in Ottoman Syria and Palestine* (Berkeley: University of California Press, 1998), 142ff.; Margaret Meriwether, "The Rights of Children and the Responsibilities of Women: Women as Wasis in Ottoman Aleppo, 1770– 1840," in Sonbol, ed., *Women, the Family, and Divorce Laws in Islamic History,* 219–35.
31. AS 2:6b; AS 161:37e.
32. See my *The Imperial Harem: Women and Sovereignty in the Ottoman Empire* (New York: Oxford University Press, 1993), 201–2.
33. The chief mufti Ebu Suud gave the practice legal status in a fatwa forbidding the items that a now-deceased father had accumulated for his daughter's trousseau from being claimed by his heirs as part of his estate (and thus elig-

ible for division among them); see M. E. Düzdağ, *Şeyhülislam Ebussuûd Efendi Fetvaları Işığında 16. Asır Türk Hayatı* [Istanbul: Enderun Kitabevi, 1983], 35. Eighteenth-century Syrian jurists also debated and regulated the practice (Tucker, *In the House of the Law*, 55–57).

34. AS 161:145a, b.

35. For Hurrem Sultan's material role in Ottoman diplomacy and the training of palace women in arts of the needle, see my *Imperial Harem*, 141, 220–21.

36. AS 2:182b, c.

37. For the Aintab jewelers' bazaar *(kuyumcu pazarı)*, see AS 161:58a. Women typically acted as peddlers of goods to the women of upper-class households. For the Mamluk period, see Ahmad 'Abd ar-Raziq, *La Femme au temps des mamlouks en Égypte* (Cairo: Institut français d'archeologie orientale du Caire, 1973), 42.

38. AS 161:3b.

39. AS 2:219c.

40. AS 2:154a.

41. AS 2:184a, b.

42. Baber Johansen, "La mise en scène du vol par les juristes musulmanes," in *Vols et sanctions en Méditerranée*, ed. Maria Pia di Bella (Amsterdam: Éditions des archives contemporaines, 1998), 55–65.

43. AS 2:150c. This exchange was specifically cast as a trade *('avz)*.

44. Such high interest rates existed even though Süleyman's law book prohibited rates exceeding 10 percent (Uriel Heyd, *Studies in Old Ottoman Criminal Law*, ed. V. L. Menage [Oxford: Clarendon Press, 1973], 122). In sixteenth-century Istanbul, women used various methods to get around religious restrictions on interest-taking (Seng, "Standing at the Gates of Justice," 201, 205 n. 2); in eighteenth-century Istanbul, women charged rates of interest ranging from 10 to 20 percent (Zarinebaf-Shahr, "Women, Law, and Imperial Justice," 91).

45. AS 2:251d, 298b.

46. In the 1557 register listing waqf-supported institutions in Aintab, the mosque's annual income of 584 akçes came from its endowment of five stores, two houses, and two pieces of land (but not the vineyard on one and the houses on the other) (Özdeğer, *Ayıntâb Livâsı*, 157).

47. AS 2:209b, 220b.

48. These strategies are reminiscent of women's savings collectives today that I have observed in Istanbul and Ankara, and that have been documented for Egypt in Nayra Atiya, *Khul Khaal: Five Egyptian Women Tell Their Stories* (Syracuse: Syracuse University Press, 1982), 22–26, and Diane Singerman, *Avenues of Participation: Family, Politics, and Networks in Urban Quarters of Cairo* (Princeton: Princeton University Press, 1995), 124–31, 154–56.

49. Pierre Bourdieu, *Language and Symbolic Power*, ed. John B. Thompson, trans. Gino Raymong and Matthew Adamson (Cambridge, Mass.: Harvard University Press, 1991), and "Les Trois Etats du capital culturel," *Actes de la recherche en sciences sociales*, no. 30 (November 1979): 3–6.

50. For an excellent study of twentieth-century Palestinian women's variable access to property and the uses they make of it, see Annelies Moors, *Women, Property, and Islam: Palestinian Experiences, 1920–1990* (Cambridge: Cambridge Uni-

versity Press, 1995). A number of practices and cultural attitudes discussed by Moors are reminiscent of sixteenth-century Aintab.

51. AS 161:42a.

52. AS 2:191b.

53. AS 161:177c.

54. AS 2:86b.

55. Coulson, *Succession in the Muslim Family,* 214–15.

56. It may be that Hüsni, who protested, did not have her eye primarily on the family dwelling: her father also gave his son two urban garden plots and a share in a shop.

57. Moors, *Women, Property, and Islam,* 53–57.

58. AS 161:102a, b, c, d.

59. AS 2:165a.

60. AS 2:98c.

61. See AS 161:77b, 94, 105a, 161c; AS 2:136b.

62. AS 2:124c, 274b. The vineyard was bounded on the south and west by "the judge's vineyard."

63. AS 2:60b.

64. Most scholars of premodern Anatolia have followed Ömer Lütfi Barkan's estimate of five as the average number of persons per household *(hane)*, although some have argued for a larger figure (see chapter 2, notes 9 and 13). Ronald Jennings has suggested substituting the number of taxpaying males *(nefer)* rather than the number of household heads as the base figure to be multiplied, and using a multiplier of 3 to 3.5 ("Urban Population in Anatolia in the Sixteenth Century: A Study of Kayseri, Karaman, Amasya, Trabzon, and Erzurum," *International Journal of Middle East Studies* 7 [1976]: 52–54). For purposes of comparison, Jennings's suggestion has the drawback that not all cadastral surveys include taxpayers who were not household heads (that is, they give *hane* but not *nefer* totals).

65. Alan Duben, "Turkish Families and Households in Historical Perspective," *Journal of Family History* 10 (1995): 84–86.

66. AS 161:190b.

67. AS 2:247c.

68. For husbands' gifts of vineyards to their wives, see AS 2:125b, 266c.

69. See Tucker, *In the House of the Law,* chap. 3, for an excellent essay on divorce in seventeenth-and eighteenth-century Palestine. On the ease of male-initiated divorce (both sharia-regulated and customary practices), see my "'She is trouble . . . and I will divorce her': Orality, Honor, and Representation in the Ottoman Court of Aintab," in *Women in the Medieval Islamic World: Power, Patronage, Piety,* ed. Gavin R. G. Hambly (New York: St. Martin's Press, 1998), 267–300.

70. I am grateful to Akten Köylüoğlu for this information.

71. AS 161:51a.

72. AS 161:12d, 13a.

73. While *hul* in classical jurisprudence did not necessarily prescribe the surrender of the female's material rights in the marriage, Ibrahim al-Halabi, whose compendium of Hanafi law composed in the early sixteenth century became the most widely used legal reference in the Ottoman empire, insisted on the prin-

ciple of divorce in return for material consideration in his explication of *hul;* see Ibrahim al-Halabi, *Multaka al-Abhur [Multaka Tercümesi Mevkufatî]* (Istanbul: Dar uttibaatil'-amire, 1290/1873), 1:303. On the popularity of al-Halabi's legal treatise, *Multaka al-Abhur,* see Şükrü Selim Has, "The Use of *Multaqa'l-Abhur* in the Ottoman Madrasas and in Legal Scholarship," *Osmanlı Araştırmaları* 7–8 (1988): 393–418.

74. See, for example, Svetlana Ivanova, "The Divorce between Zubaida Hatun and Esseid Osman Ağa: Women in the Eighteenth-Century Shari'a Court of Rumelia," in Sonbol, ed., *Women, the Family, and Divorce Laws in Islamic History,* 118; Madeline Zilfi, "'We don't get along': Women and *Hul* Divorce in the Eighteenth Century," in Zilfi, ed., *Women in the Ottoman Empire,* 271; Judith Tucker, "Ties That Bound: Women and Family in Eighteenth- and Nineteenth-Century Nablus," in *Women in Middle Eastern History: Shifting Boundaries in Sex and Gender,* ed. Nikki R. Keddie and Beth Baron (New Haven: Yale University Press, 1991), 241.

75. AS 161:81d.

76. AS 161:191c.

77. AS 161:346a.

78. AS 2:1b, c; 2a.

79. Düzdağ, *Ebussuud Efendi Fetvaları,* 33.

80. The risks of neglect of small children in the paternal household were made patent in another of Ebu Suud's fatwas (the names are formulaic and standard to the vocabulary of the fatwa genre):

> Query: If one-year-old Amr and three-year-old Bekr, the sons of the deceased Zeyd by his wife Hind, are forcibly taken from Hind and Hind's mother Hadice by Zeyd's father and brothers and removed to the latter's home, and Bekr falls into the fire and dies from burns and Amr dies from being fed cow milk [rather than being suckled], what must be done according to the law to Zeyd's father and brothers?
>
> Response: They must be severely punished by the judge. (Düzdağ, *Ebussuud Efendi Fetvaları,* 34)

81. Two of the cases used the word *sağirce/sağirece,* the same terminology employed by Ebu Suud to establish the mother's legal right to custody.

82. It is remotely possible that the children in these cases were of an age to pass into their fathers' custody; if so, the thrust of the cases is to suggest that customary practice in Aintab gave mothers greater custody rights than did the letter of the law.

83. AS 2:25b *(tahun-ı mezburın suyunda bizum bostanlarumuzun hak-ı şer'i yokdur, bizum bostanlarumuz hadis bostanlardır, değirmen kadimdir, su değirmenindir).*

84. AS 2:32b.

85. See Colin Imber, "The Status of Orchards and Fruit Trees in Ottoman Law," in *Studies in Ottoman History and Law* (Istanbul: Isis Press, 1996), 207–16 (reprinted from *Tarih Enstitüsü Dergisi* 12 [1982]: 763–74).

86. See Colin Imber, *Ebu's-Su'ud: The Islamic Legal Tradition* (Stanford: Stanford University Press, 1997), 139–41, for an explanation of these two types of waqf and their relationship in theory.

87. The survey of waqfs is contained in Tapu Tahrir 301. Much of it is transcribed

(with occasional errors) in Özdeğer, *Ayıntâb Livâsı,* 141–93. In 1557, there were eleven large congregational mosques *(cami),* sixty small neighborhood mosques *(mescid),* seven educational institutions *(medrese, buka),* and eight dervish institutions *(zaviye).*

88. Tapu Tahrir 301, fols. 20–29 (folios 20–23 are bound out of order). The oldest family waqf still in existence at the time of this 1557 survey had been established in 819 H./1416 C.E. (fol. 21).

89. Özdeğer, *Ayıntâb Livâsı,* 440.

90. Claude Cahen, *Pre-Ottoman Turkey: A General Survey of the Material and Spiritual Culture and History, c. 1071–1330* (London: Sidgwick and Jackson, 1968), 182–83; Halil İnalcık, "The Ottoman State: Economy and Society, 1300–1600," in *An Economic and Social History of the Ottoman Empire, 1300–1914,* ed. Halil İnalcık and Donald Quataert (Cambridge: Cambridge University Press, 1994), 117, 167.

91. On this process of reinterpreting land law, see Baber Johansen, "Legal Literature and the Problem of Change: The Case of the Land Rent," in *Islam and Public Law: Classical and Contemporary Studies,* ed. Chibli Mallat (London: Graham and Trotman, 1993), 29–47; Imber, *Ebu's-Su'ud,* chap. 5.

92. Johansen, "Legal Literature and the Problem of Change," 42.

93. Imber, *Ebu's-Su'ud,* 122–25.

94. The subject of royal women's patronage of architecturally distinguished waqf endowments has been well studied in recent years. See Carl Petry, "A Paradox of Patronage during the Later Mamluk Period," *Muslim World* 73, nos. 3–4 (1983): 182–207; Ülkü Bates, "The Architectural Patronage of Ottoman Women," *Asian Art* 6, no. 2 (1993): 50–65. Two new works also deal with this topic: D. Fairchild Ruggles, ed., *Women, Patronage, and Self-Representation in Islamic Societies* (Albany: State University of New York Press, 2000), and Amy Singer, *Constructing Ottoman Beneficence: An Imperial Soup Kitchen in Jerusalem* (Albany: State University of New York Press, 2002).

95. Peirce, *The Imperial Harem,* chap. 7.

96. Gabriel Baer, "Women and Waqf: An Analysis of the Istanbul *Tahrir* of 1546," *Asian and African Studies: Journal of the Israel Orient Society* 17, nos. 1–3 (1983): 10, 26–27.

97. See AS 161:180a, AS 2:209b, AS 2:50d, and AS 2:120c, d, respectively. The house donated by Köse Bayram was currently occupied by the imam, who paid his rent to the mosque in olive oil.

98. Halil İnalcık, "Çiftlik," in *Encyclopedia of Islam,* 2nd ed., 2:32–33.

99. Imber, *Ebu's-Su'ud,* 129.

100. Hedda Reindl-Kiel, "A Woman *Timar* Holder in Ankara Province during the Second Half of the Sixteenth Century," *Journal of the Social and Economic History of the Orient* 40 (1997): 221–26.

101. Reindl-Kiel considers the inverse of this question at the very end of her study of women and rural land title: "If it is true that the administration bowed to this public opinion, a fundamental pillar of Islamic Law was in some degree undermined" ("A Woman *Timar* Holder," 226).

102. For similar effects of dislocation in the Mosul region and consequent uncer-

tainty about rights to rural revenues, see Dina Rizk Khoury, *State and Provincial Society in the Ottoman Empire: Mosul, 1540–1834* (Cambridge: Cambridge University Press, 1997), 82.

103. AS 161:60c. For the cadastral survey, see Özdeğer, *Ayıntâb Livâsı,* 226.

104. AS 161:64d.

105. I am indebted to Amy Singer for first suggesting this question to me.

106. Many records in a 1557 cadastral survey of public waqfs, family waqfs, and private landholdings (Tapu Tahrir 301, *Defter-i evkaf ve emlak-ı livâ-ı Aintab*) mentioned previous inventories of the lands involved.

107. AS 161:67b.

108. AS 161:114a.

109. AS 2:195c, 198a.

110. Irène Beldiceanu-Steinherr, "Fiscalité et formes de possession de la terre arable dans l'Anatolie préottomane," *Journal of the Economic and Social History of the Orient* 19 (1976): 241–48, 300.

111. On the malikâne-divanî system in the sixteenth century, see Margaret Venzke, "Special Use of the Tithe as a Revenue-Raising Measure in the Sixteenth-Century Sanjaq of Aleppo," *Journal of the Economic and Social History of the Orient* 29 (1986): 248ff.; Khoury, *State and Provincial Society in the Ottoman Empire,* 8off.

112. Ömer Lütfi Barkan, "Türk-İslam Toprak Hukuku Tatbikatının Osmanlı İmparatorluğunda Aldığı Sekiller: Malikane-Divani Sistemi," *Türk Hukuk ve İktisat Tarihi Mecmuası* 2 (1932–1939): 144–45; quoted in Venzke, "Special Use of the Tithe," 253.

113. Venzke, "Special Use of the Tithe," 254.

114. Venzke, "Special Use of the Tithe," 317ff.

115. The figures for Arıl, Hiyam, and İkizce are taken from Özdeğer, *Ayıntâb Livâsı,* 440, 523, 227.

116. Venzke, "Special Use of the Tithe," 322.

117. The incomes of these institutions in the 1557 register were as follows: the Demircioğlu zaviye, 14,496 akçes; and the Cedide medrese, 9,960 akçes.

118. Özdeğer, *Ayıntâb Livâsı,* 374, 415.

119. Ömer Lütfi Barkan, *XV ve XVIıncı Asırlarda Osmanlı İmparatorluğunda Ziraî Ekonominin Hukukî ve Malî Esasları, I: Kanunlar* (Istanbul: Bürhaneddin Erenler Matbaası, 1943), 139.

120. Muhammad Adnan Bakhit, *The Ottoman Province of Damascus in the Sixteenth Century* (Beirut: Librarie du Liban, 1982), 5 nn. 21, 22.

121. Özdeğer, *Ayıntâb Livâsı,* passim.

122. Özdeğer, *Ayıntâb Livâsı,* 127–33.

123. Özdeğer, *Ayıntâb Livâsı,* 81. Comparable statistics are not available for the subdistricts of Telbaşer and Nehrülcevaz, since they were not part of Aintab province in 1536.

124. AS 2:93b. In an earlier record, Tatar and Haleb were appointed guarantors for Şarabdar Abdürrahman's share of the debt, along with one Ali b. Demirci (no relation to the notable Demircioğlus), while the guarantors for the second partner were a male and another female, Münevver (AS 2:5a, b).

125. AS 161:67d.

126. For Rahime's claim, see AS 2:48c; for Hoca Yusuf's other debts, see AS 2:30a, 30c, 31a, 43a.

127. For a partnership explicitly labeled *mudaraba,* see AS 2:26d. See İnalcık, "The Ottoman State," 47–48, 209, on the practice of mudaraba in the early modern Ottoman economy.

128. Rifat Ergeç, personal communication with author, October 7, 1999.

129. The official view, stated in the statute book of Selim I (d. 1520), was that dense planting established the status of the land as orchard, not arable land, and thus dictated the kind of taxes the cultivator would pay; it did not turn the land into private property (Pulaha and Yücel, "I. Selim Kanunnamesi [1512–1520]," 25–26).

130. Imber, "The Status of Orchards and Fruit Trees in Ottoman Law," 211, 214.

131. AS 161:333a.

132. AS 2:232c.

133. I am indebted to Lisa Schwartz for much of the interpretation of the cadastral survey data that follows. See Leslie Peirce and Lisa Schwartz, *"Bennaks* and Bachelors: Employment and Household Structure in a Sixteenth-Century Anatolian Village," in *Halil İnalcık Festschrift,* ed. N. Göyünç, J. Bacqué-Grammont, and Ö. Ergenç (Istanbul: Eren Yayıncılık, in press).

134. Margaret L. Venzke, "The Question of Declining Cereals' Production in the Sixteenth Century," *Journal of Turkish Studies* 8 (1984): 255ff.

135. Peirce and Schwartz, *"Bennaks* and Bachelors." In Aleppo, it was mezraa production that filled the gap (Venzke, "The Question of Declining Cereals' Production in the Sixteenth Century," 262ff.). The cadastral surveys for Aintab suggest that there was only a fine line between mezraas and small villages.

136. Fernand Braudel, *The Mediterranean and the Mediterranean World in the Age of Philip II,* trans. Sian Reynolds (London: Collins, 1972–1973), 1:573.

137. Maurice Aymard, *Venise, Raguse, et le commerce du blé pendant la seconde moitié du XVIe siècle* (Paris: S.E.V.P.E.N., 1966), 48.

138. The various steps in making *şıra, pekmez,* and the additional products *bastık* and *sucuk* were explained to me in December 1999 by the family of Hüseyin Kanbıçak, of the village of Çaybaşı (formerly Cağdığın). Many houses in the village are equipped with the rather elaborate equipment required to perform these various stages in grape processing.

139. İbn Kemal (Şemseddin Ahmed Kemalpaşazade), *Fetava* (MS Dar ul-Mesnevi 118, Süleymaniye Library, Istanbul), 23a.

HACIYE SABAH'S STORY: A TEACHER ON TRIAL

1. The case of Haciye Sabah appears in AS 2:75c; 76a, b; 78c.

2. AS 2:60a.

3. Vladimir Minorsky, "The Poetry of Shah Ismail I," *Bulletin of the School of Oriental and African Studies* 10 (1940–1943): 1006a–1053a.

4. Refet Yinanç, *Dulkadir Beyliği* (Ankara: Türk Tarih Kurumu, 1989), 93–94.

5. David Morgan, *Medieval Persia, 1014–1797* (New York: Longman, 1988), 114.

6. On the 1511 uprising, see Çagatay Uluçay, "Yavuz Sultan Selim Nasıl Padişah Oldu?" *Tarih Dergisi* 6, no. 9 (1954): 61–74.

7. Jean-Louis Bacqué-Grammont, "L'apogée de l'Empire Ottoman: les événements (1512–1606)," in *Histoire de l'Empire ottoman,* ed. Robert Mantran (Paris: Fayard, 1989), 144.

8. The apt term "confessional ambiguity" is John Woods's (*The Aqquyunlu: Clan, Confederation, Empire: A Study in Fifteenth/Ninth Century Turko-Iranian Politics* [Minneapolis: Bibliotheca Islamica, 1976], 4).

9. Morgan, *Medieval Persia,* 120–22; H. R. Roemer, "The Safavid Period," in *Cambridge History of Iran,* vol. 6, *The Timurid and Safavid Periods,* ed. Peter Jackson and Laurence Lockhart (Cambridge: Cambridge University Press, 1986), 221–25. The classes of Martin B. Dickson at Princeton University were invaluable as an introduction to the complexities of Safavid origins.

10. Minorsky, "The Poetry of Shah Ismail I."

11. İbrahim Peçevi, *Tarih-i Peçevi* (Istanbul: Matbaa-ı Amire, 1281–1284/1864–1867), 1:120–22.

12. M. Tayyib Gökbilgin, "Süleyman I," in *İslam Ansiklopedisi,* 11:110.

13. Colin Imber, "The Persecution of the Ottoman Shi'ites according to the Mühimme Defterleri, 1565–1585," *Der Islam* 56 (1979): 250, 267. Other places for which investigations are recorded included Ruha (Urfa), Elbistan, Amid (Diyarbakır), and Bozok.

14. The scribe gave variant spelling of İbrahim's patronymic: Nâzîḥ, Nârîḥ, Narûḥ.

15. Huda Lutfi, "Manners and Customs of Fourteenth-Century Cairene Women: Female Anarchy versus Male Shar'i Order in Muslim Prescriptive Treatises," in *Women in Middle Eastern History: Shifting Boundaries in Sex and Gender,* ed. Nikki R. Keddie and Beth Baron (New Haven: Yale University Press, 1991), 115–16; Jonathan Berkey, "Women and Islamic Education in the Mamluk Period," in ibid., 143–57.

16. See the fatwas of İbn Kemal for indictments of sufi practices (*Fetava* [MS Dar ul-Mesnevi 118, Süleymaniye Library, Istanbul], 20b–28a).

17. Imber, "The Persecution of the Ottoman Shi'ites," 248, 255, 261.

18. Uriel Heyd, *Studies in Old Ottoman Criminal Law,* ed. V. L. Menage (Oxford: Clarendon Press, 1973), 92, 130.

19. Tapu Tahrir Defteri 301, fols. 17–23; Hüseyin Özdeğer, *Onaltıncı Asırda Ayıntâb Livâsı* (Istanbul: Bayrak Matbaacılık, 1988), 187–93.

20. AS 2:280a.

21. Jonathan Berkey, *Popular Preaching and Religious Authority in the Medieval Islamic Near East* (Seattle: University of Washington Press, 2001). I am very grateful to Berkey for letting me see this book in manuscript.

22. Ahmet Eflaki, *Menakib ül-Arifin,* trans. Tahsin Yazıcı (Istanbul: Milli Eğitim Basımevi, 1983), 1:531–32.

23. Eflaki, *Menakib ül-Arifin,* 2:326–37.

24. Derviş Ahmet Aşıkpaşazade, "Tevarih-i Al-i Osman," in *Osmanlı Tarihleri,* ed. N. Atsız (Istanbul: Türkiye Yayınevi, 1947), 237–38.

25. The *bacıyan-ı Rum* were one of four groups or networks spanning Anatolia described by Aşıkpaşazade, who is the only source for the existence of the women's group. In his discussion of these groups, Mehmet Fuad Köprülü argues the plausibility of such a women's organization, which was possibly a female sufi order. He also hypothesizes that Aşıkpaşazade had in mind the force of some

30,000 female warriors reported by de la Broquière (*The Origins of the Ottoman Empire*, trans. and ed. Gary Leiser [Albany: State University of New York Press, 1992], 98–99).

26. Ahmet Karamustafa, *God's Unruly Friends: Dervish Groups in the Islamic Later Middle Period, 1200–1550* (Salt Lake City: University of Utah Press, 1994), 83–84.

27. Ahmet Yaşar Ocak, "Idéologie officielle et réaction populaire: un aperçu général sur les mouvements et les courants socio-religieux à l'époque de Soliman le Magnifique," in *Soliman le Magnifique et son temps*, ed. Gilles Veinstein (Paris: La Documentation Française, 1992), 189.

28. Cornell Fleischer, "The Lawgiver as Messiah: The Making of the Imperial Image in the Reign of Süleyman," in Veinstein, *Soliman le magnifique et son temps*, 159–77; see also Fleischer's forthcoming monograph on the subject.

29. Perhaps the market chief, Uzun Ahmed, a kind of community ombudsman and one of the case witnesses, channeled the affair to the court; or perhaps another case witness, Muhsin the steward (*kethüda*, a title employed for neighborhood headmen), was instrumental.

30. AS 2:63b, 69b; 74b.

31. Imber, "The Persecution of the Ottoman Shi'ites," 247, 255, 259.

32. Heyd, *Old Ottoman Criminal Law*, 290–300.

33. AS 2:245a. For more on this case, see chapter 8.

34. Imber, "The Persecution of the Ottoman Shi'ites," 272.

35. Al-Marghinani, *The Hedaya, or Guide*, trans. Charles Hamilton (London: T. Bensley, 1791; reprint, Karachi: Darul Ishaat Urdu Bazar), 2:17.

36. Heyd, *Old Ottoman Criminal Law*, 92, 130.

7. NEGOTIATING LEGITIMACY THROUGH THE LAW

1. On the survey process, see Halil İnalcık, "The Ottoman State: Economy and Society, 1300–1600," in *An Economic and Social History of the Ottoman Empire, 1300–1914*, ed. Halil İnalcık and Donald Quataert (Cambridge: Cambridge University Press, 1994), 132–39. Although claimed by the Safavids upon the Akkoyunlu collapse at the turn of the sixteenth century, Erzurum was shortly afterward taken in conquest by the Ottoman sultan Selim I in 1514.

2. Halil İnalcık, "Ottoman Methods of Conquest," *Studia Islamica* 2 (1954): 103–29.

3. See Ömer Lütfi Barkan, *XV ve XVIıncı Asırlarda Osmanlı İmparatorluğunda Ziraî Ekonominin Hukukî ve Malî Esasları, I: Kanunlar* (Istanbul: Bürhaneddin Erenler Matbaası, 1943), for the confirmation of "Hasan Padishah's kanun" in Erzincan and Kemah in 1516 (181, 184); in Ruha (Urfa) in 1518 (155: *Tafsil-i kanun-name-i livâ-ı Ruha ber muceb-i kanun-ı Hasan Padişah*); and likewise in other provinces that belonged to the Ottoman governorates-general of Erzurum and Diyarbakır.

4. For these early surveys, see Ömer Lütfi Barkan, "Akkoyunlu Hükümdarı Uzun Hasan Beye ait Kanunlar," *Tarih Vesikaları* 1, no. 2 (1941): 91–106; no. 3 (1941): 184–96. On the Akkoyunlu state in general and the career of Uzun Hasan, see

John Woods, *The Aqquyunlu: Clan, Confederation, Empire: A Study in Fifteenth/Ninth Century Turko-Iranian Politics* (Minneapolis: Bibliotheca Islamica, 1976).

5. Tapu Tahrir Defteri 548 (926 H./1520 C.E.), quoted in Barkan, "Akkoyunlu Hükümdarı Uzun Hasan Beye ait Kanunlar," 94. The entire passage reads: "When the new register into which the aforementioned province was inscribed was submitted to the sublime threshold, because the laws that were in force, recorded in the old register and known as the kanun of Hasan Padishah, were unable to be borne by the tribes of taxpayers and the classes of merchants and the peoples of the well-protected domains, and because, under the wing of sovereignty, the protective shadow of justice, the shade of mercy, the peoples of the province and the aforementioned classes [should] enjoy protection and the circumstances of prosperity, which are a necessity for the survival of the regime and the cause of the right order of the realm, some obligations were abolished and some were reduced, in accordance with an imperial order."

6. Barkan, *Kanunlar,* 63.

7. Tapu Tahrir Defteri 700, quoted in Barkan, "Akkoyunlu Hükümdarı Uzun Hasan Beye ait Kanunlar," 95. See the entire kanunname in Barkan, *Kanunlar,* 62–72.

8. M. Tayyib Gökbilgin, "Süleyman I," in *İslam Ansiklopedisi,* 11:109ff.; Ahmet Yaşar Ocak, "Idéologie officielle et réaction populaire: un aperçu général sur les mouvements et les courants socio-religieux à l'époque de Soliman le Magnifique," in *Soliman le Magnifique et son temps,* ed. Gilles Veinstein (Paris: La Documentation Française: Paris, 1992), 185–92.

9. Tapu Tahrir Defteri 186, fols. 3–5; Hüseyin Özdeğer, *Onaltıncı Asırda Ayıntâb Livâsı* (Istanbul: Bayrak Matbaacılık, 1988), 201–3.

10. Tapu Tahrir Defteri 186, fol. 4; Özdeğer, *Ayıntâb Livâsı,* 202 (for Aintab); Barkan, *Kanunlar,* 95 (for Erzurum).

11. See my *The Imperial Harem: Women and Sovereignty in the Ottoman Empire* (New York: Oxford University Press, 1993), chap. 1, for further contextualization of the symbolic reassertion of sovereign control.

12. Clifford Geertz, "Centers, Kings, and Charisma: Reflections on the Symbolics of Power," in *Local Knowledge: Further Essays in Interpretive Anthropology* (New York: Basic Books, 1983), 125.

13. Gökbilgin, "Süleyman I," 118.

14. Mehmet Hemdemi Solakzade, *Solakzade Tarihi* (Istanbul: Mahmut Beg Matbaası, 1298/1880–81), 486–87.

15. AS 2:60b.

16. AS 2:124b, c.

17. AS 2:301b.

18. I am uncertain of the reading of this village's name.

19. AS 161:200a.

20. AS 161:46c.

21. Uriel Heyd, *Studies in Old Ottoman Criminal Law,* ed. V. L. Menage (Oxford: Clarendon Press, 1973), 83, 121.

22. AS 2:242c.

23. AS 161:83a *(İstanbul kadısından hüccet-i şer'iye . . . ve iki adet emr-i hümayûn adaletname . . .).*

24. AS 161:114a.
25. On these fees, see chapter 3.
26. During 1985, I observed an elderly man from Trabzon who had made the journey to the Topkapi Museum Archives, where the court records of Trabzon were then held, to search old registers for documentation of a property claim.
27. See chapter 3, note 73.
28. Celalzade Mustafa, *Tabakat ul-Memalik ve Derecat ul-Mesalik*, ed. Petra Kappert (Wiesbaden: Steiner, 1981), 242a–276a.
29. M. Tayyib Gökbilgin, "Celalzade, Mustafa Çelebi," in *İslam Ansiklopedisi*, 3:61–63; Heyd, *Old Ottoman Criminal Law*, 23–26.
30. See Heyd, *Old Ottoman Criminal Law*, 26–27, for Lutfi Pasha's probable role. One clause in the law book in particular bears the imprint of Lutfi Pasha's efforts: a clause that establishes the branding of a woman's vulva as the punishment if she willingly allowed herself to be abducted (98). Lutfi Pasha was divorced from the sultan's sister Şah Sultan after a heated argument in which she challenged him for punishing a prostitute in this manner; insisting he would continue to inflict this punishment, he then began beating the princess when she lost her temper (Mustafa Âli, *Künh ül-Ahbar*, MS 3406, Nuruosmaniye Library, Istanbul, 123a–b). Süleyman granted his sister's request for divorce and dismissed the grand vezir, thus putting an end to his official career.
31. On the Mamluk Qaytbay, see Carl Petry, *Twilight of Majesty: The Reigns of the Mamluk Sultans al-Ashraf Qaytbay and Qansuh al-Ghawri in Egypt* (Seattle: University of Washington Press, 1993), passim; on Uzun Hasan, see Woods, *The Aqquyunlu*, passim.
32. Tapu Tahrir Defteri 186, fol. 3; Özdeğer, *Ayıntâb Livâsı*, 201.
33. Barkan, *Kanunlar*, 131.
34. Barkan, "Akkoyunlu Hükümdarı Uzun Hasan Beye Ait Kanunlar," 93.
35. AS 161:21b.
36. This point was made by Karl Barbir in 1980 (*Ottoman Rule in Damascus, 1708–1758* [Princeton: Princeton University Press, 1980]); it has subsequently been reiterated in a number of studies, among them the works cited in note 44.
37. On the difference in usage between *iltizam* and *mukata'a*, see Linda Darling, *Revenue-Raising and Legitimacy: Tax Collection and Finance Administration in the Ottoman Empire, 1560–1660* (Leiden: Brill, 1996), 123: *mukata'a* was the source of revenue farmed out, while *iltizam* was the act of farming—collecting the revenues—itself. In the Aintab court registers, the only consistent distinction between the two seems to be that *mukata'a* is employed more often for urban tax-farms (standard farmed sources of revenue). For the term *icare*, see AS 2:178d, 190b, 195a, 197b, 273d; in 263a, the terms *icare* and *iltizam* are used interchangeably (*icare* may reflect the particular usage of an individual scribe).
38. On the proliferation of smaller tax-farms, see Özer Ergenç, "Osmanlı Şehirlerindeki Yönetim Kurumlarının Niteliği Üzerinde Bazı Düşünceler," in *VIII. Türk Tarhi Kongresi Kongreye Sunulan Bildiriler* (Ankara: Türk Tarih Kurumu, 1981), 2:268; Ergenç draws his examples principally from the court records of Bursa and Ankara in the later sixteenth century.
39. AS 2:2–259a. For a complete list of city taxes, see the cadastral surveys: for 1536, Tapu Tahrir Defteri 186, fols. 27–28; for 1543, Tapu Tahrir Defteri 373,

fols. 46–47. These urban revenues are tabulated in Özdeğer, *Ayıntâb Livâsı,* 127–33.

40. AS 2:308c.

41. AS 2:202b.

42. Özdeğer, *Ayıntâb Livâsı,* 446.

43. AS 161:342a.

44. See Halil İnalcık, "Hawâla," in *Encyclopedia of Islam,* 2nd ed., 3:283–85, and "The Ottoman State," 64–66. Tax-farms were often held by prominent citizens typically referred to as "urban notables" *(eşraf ve ayan);* the important role of this group in urban administration and government in the sixteenth century is discussed by Özer Ergenç, "Osmanlı Klasik Dönemindeki 'Eşraf ve Ayan' Üzerine Bazı Bilgiler," *Osmanlı Araştırmaları* 3 (1982): 105–13. See also the useful article by Haim Gerber, which draws on largely on Anatolian court records: "Jewish Tax-Farmers in the Ottoman Empire in the Sixteenth and Seventeenth Centuries," *Journal of Turkish Studies* 10 (1986): 143–54. For a study of tax-farming that draws on central government records, see Darling, *Revenue-Raising and Legitimacy,* chap. 4. For a cogent analysis of developments in tax-farming in a later period, see Ariel Salzman, "An Ancien Régime Revisited: 'Privatization' and Political Economy in the Eighteenth-Century Ottoman Empire," *Politics and Society* 21 (1993): 393–423; for a case study of tax-farming in Mosul, see Dina Rizk Khoury, *State and Provincial Society in the Ottoman Empire: Mosul, 1540–1834* (Cambridge: Cambridge University Press, 1997), esp. chap. 4.

45. Neşrî, *Kitâb-i Cihan-nümâ: Neşrî Tarihi,* ed. Faik Reşit Ünat and Mehmed A. Köymen (Ankara: Türk Tarih Kurumu, 1987), 1:110–11.

46. AS 161:33b.

47. AS 161:4c. On the question of local minters, see Şevket Pamuk, *A Momentary History of the Ottoman Empire* (Cambridge: Cambridge University Press, 2000), 39.

48. See also a 1586 list of tax-farmers in the city of Bursa, in which the four Jewish tax farmers (out of twelve total) were similarly identified (Gerber, "Jewish Tax Farmers in the Ottoman Empire," 148).

49. Gerber, "Jewish Tax-Farmers in the Ottoman Empire," 145–46.

50. AS 161:25b.

51. The 1557 registration of waqf and private property is catalogued in Tapu Tahrir Defteri 301. In various entries in this register certifying ownership, reference is made to previous registrations and surveys under Ottoman administration.

52. AS 161:45a, b; 49c.

53. AS 161:50a.

54. AS 161:54b *(kadimden berü ma'sere iki yüz osmani akçeye virüb geldük, andan gayri bac ve sair ve sair* [sic] *vechle bir akçe ve bir hubbe vireceğimüz yokdır).* The common phrase "an akçe and a grain" alluded to payment in cash and kind.

55. AS 161:67d. In perhaps another case of timing that was no coincidence, Mustafa Çelebi's settling of his debt occurred three weeks after the sarraf Matuk secured his office through the governor-general's intervention. Significantly, one of the sarraf's functions was to transmit revenues from local crown lands to the Aleppo Mint; hence Mustafa Çelebi, as trustee of crown lands in Aintab, may have felt a certain pressure to square his relationship with the state. The exis-

tence of his debt may help explain his own role in the apparent community-wide resistance to Matuk's appointment.

56. AS 161:68a.

57. AS 161:55b. The subaşı was prosecuting Ali both because of his interest in prisoners and also because the village of Dülük belonged to the domain of the governor-general (i.e., its taxes were a part of his grant from the state, and he was responsible for prosecuting crime in the village).

58. AS 161:52c, 76a.

59. AS 161:164b.

60. Ergenç, "Osmanlı Şehirlerindeki Yönetim Kurumlarının Niteliği Üzerinde Bazı Düşünceler," 1273–74.

61. AS 161:173a *(bizim mahallemizden Arameniyâ taifesinden zarar ve ziyan olursa külliyen kefil olduk diyüb ve bizim aramız[a] gelüb hâriçden gelenlere dahi kefil olduk. Ba'd el-yevm aramızdan bir muhalef iş olursa, bizden bilin . . .).*

62. AS 161:173a.

63. AS 161:187d. For the tavern tax in 1536 and 1543, see Özdeğer, *Ayıntâb Livâsı,* 131.

64. AS 2:31b.

65. AS 2:1a. I am grateful to Hamid Algar and Margaret Larkin for helping me with the reading and interpretation of this inscription. Larkin notes that the Arabic of the inscription is rather unsophisticated and in one place grammatically faulty, characteristic of what an individual with non-native fluency might write.

66. The inscription begins: "The news arrived concerning the judgeship of Aintab, granted to Hüsameddin Efendi, may his virtue increase." Following the signatures of witnesses comes another inscription that formally inaugurates the register: "The inception of the record of the court of Aintab the well-protected following the arrival of the letter concerning Hüsameddin Efendi . . ."

67. AS 2:1; the officials were the *kale dizdarı, bölükbaşı, kethüda-ı kale, subaşı,* and *kethüda-ı şehir.*

68. Jon Mandaville, "The Muslim Judiciary of Damascus in the Late Mamluk Period" (Ph.D. diss., Princeton University, 1969), 61–62.

69. AS 2:10c, 13b, 48b, 51d *(Mehmed b. Tapıncık ve Ahmed b. Sıkkak nam amillerüñ bekayaları tahsili içün tezkere-i şerif ile tayin olunan gulamşahi Ahmed Beg . . .).*

70. On the population of late-Mamluk judges in Damascus, see Mandaville, "The Muslim Judiciary of Damascus," 20–23. In Damascus, the Ottoman regime appointed its own judges immediately after the conquest, replacing the quadripartite Mamluk judiciary, with judges from the four sunni schools, with a single Hanafi chief judge (Muhammad Adnan Bakhit, *The Ottoman Province of Damascus in the Sixteenth Century* [Beirut: Librarie du Liban, 1982], 119–20). The government may not have gotten around to systematizing the appointment of judges in provincial areas like Aintab until the "second wave" of administrative reform, which commenced around 1536.

71. Offices held in *emanet* (that is, by an *emin*) differed from tax-farms in that their holders were salaried officials of the government. Darling points out that a single revenue source could shift among the various forms of revenue status *(Revenue-Raising and Legitimacy,* 127–29): later in this chapter, I discuss the shift of the Aintab market revenues *(ihtisap)* from the *timar* of the provincial gover-

nor to the crown domain *(emanet)*. For another example of this fluidity between *iltizam* and *emanet*, see the 1540 administrative code *(kanunname)* for Bozulus, in Barkan, *Kanunlar*, 140.

72. For the length of their tenure, see AS 161:354d (at the beginning of the register), 4c, 170d.

73. AS 2:42a.

74. AS 2:4a; 11b, c; 12a, c; 13b; 15a; 23b; 37a, b; 41b, c; 42a; 48a; 51d.

75. AS 2:48a.

76. AS 2:10c. The amount of the debt was not specified.

77. AS 2:13b, 42a.

78. AS 161:52c, 76a.

79. AS 2:42c.

80. AS 2:3b, 10b. When the debt was finally paid off three months later, it was recorded as 55 florins (AS 2:199a).

81. Tapu Tahrir Defteri 301, fols. 17–18. See also the transcription of parts of this register in Özdeğer, *Ayıntâb Livâsı*, 187–91.

82. Özdeğer, *Ayıntâb Livâsı*, 128. Exempted from this levy were goods taxed at the municipal weighing scales, listed above.

83. Özdeğer, *Ayıntâb Livâsı*, 128.

84. AS 2:228b.

85. AS 2:304b.

86. Şarabdar's partner, one Ali b. Demirci (unrelated to the ayan Demircis), appears to have been a local resident newly breaking into the tax-farming enterprise (AS 2, passim).

87. See AS 2:229a, 264b, for Matuk's alliances with the market inspectors.

88. AS 2:264b.

89. AS 2:50b, 55a, 59c. The group identity of the pensioners—*arpacıyan ve ulufeciyan*—is not clear; it is possible that they were aging members of the former Mamluk elite, or local military personnel retired on Ottoman government pensions.

90. The cadastral survey of 1543 listed thirty-four taxpaying adult males in the Armenian quarter of Heik, of whom twenty-nine were household heads (Tapu Tahrir Defteri 373, fols. 45–46.).

91. AS 2:29a.

92. Aintab was in the broad region whose Turkmen tribes had been deeply affected by the Anatolian propaganda machine of the Safavids, both as a militant sufi order in the late fifteenth century and as a dynastic state in Iran in the sixteenth. The names of many who appear in the Aintab court records suggest adherence (or adherence of the elders who named them) to the religious ideology of the Safavids, if not actual allegiance to their political project.

8. PUNISHMENT, VIOLENCE, AND THE COURT

1. An interesting exception to this general rule is Eyal Ginio's work on seventeenth-century Salonica; see "The Administration of Criminal Justice in Ottoman Selânik (Salonica) during the Eighteenth Century," *Turcica* 31 (1999): 185–209.

2. Michel Foucault, *Discipline and Punish: The Birth of the Prison,* trans. Alan Sheridan, 2nd ed. (New York: Vintage Books, 1995).

3. See C. E. Bosworth, "Siyāsa," in *Encyclopedia of Islam,* 2nd ed., 9:693–94, for a short account of the history of the term; for a longer treatment (from which Bosworth draws), see Bernard Lewis, "Siyāsa," in *In Quest of an Islamic Humanism: Arabic and Islamic Studies in Memory of Mohamed al-Nowaihi,* ed. A. H. Green (Cairo: American University in Cairo Press, 1984), 3–14.

4. Ibn Taymiya, *Public Duties in Islam: The Institution of the Hisba,* trans. Muktar Holland (Leicester: Islamic Foundation, 1982), 25. The passage continues, "This is more in accord with the ancient practice *(sunna)."* For a brief discussion of Ibn Taymiyya's thought, see Marshall G. S. Hodgson, *The Venture of Islam: Conscience and History in a World Civilization* (Chicago: University of Chicago Press, 1974), 2:469–71.

5. On the subject of siyasa shariyya under the Ottomans, see Uriel Heyd, *Studies in Old Ottoman Criminal Law,* ed. V. L. Menage (Oxford: Clarendon Press, 1973), 198–204.

6. Ronald Jennings, "Limitations of the Judicial Powers of the Kadi in Seventeenth Century Ottoman Kayseri," *Studia Islamica* 50 (1979): 151–84.

7. An eloquent statement of this theory of state is given in Roy P. Mottahedeh, *Loyalty and Leadership in an Early Islamic Society* (Princeton: Princeton University Press, 1980), chap. 4 ("Justice, Kingship, and the Shape of Society").

8. İbrahim Peçevi, *Tarih-i Peçevi* (Istanbul: Matbaa-ı Amire, 1281–1284/1864–1867), 1:120–22.

9. İbrahim Pasha's disgrace was symbolized by the fact that his grave was obscurely located and dishonored by the lack of a tomb. According to one tradition, he was buried in a dervish convent located behind the imperial dockyard, his grave marked by a single Judas tree (Mustafa Âli, *Künh ül-Ahbar,* MS 3406, Nuruosmaniye Library, Istanbul, 122b; Hafız Hüseyin Ayvansarayi, *Hadikat ul-Cevami* [Istanbul: Matbaa-ı Amire, 1281/1864–1865], 2:31); according to another tradition, he was buried in Okmeydanı (Mehmed Süreyya, *Sicill-i Osmanî* [Istanbul: Matbaa-ı Amire, 1308–1315/1891–1897], 1:94).

10. Muhammad Adnan Bakhit, *The Ottoman Province of Damascus in the Sixteenth Century* (Beirut: Librarie du Liban, 1982), 33.

11. Richard Repp, *The Müfti of Istanbul: A Study in the Development of the Ottoman Learned Hierarchy* (London: Ithaca Press, 1986), 236–38. It would seem that the lesser the status of the criminal, the greater the role played by numbers in official Ottoman vengeance: when individuals attacked a dwelling in Istanbul one night, killing all its residents and looting the house, some eight hundred vagrants *(levend)* were rounded up in the markets and taverns and publicly executed (Celalzade Mustafa, *Tabakat ul-Memalik ve Derecat ul-Mesalik,* 120a; cited in Heyd, *Old Ottoman Criminal Law,* 194–95).

12. On the qualities of a sultan, see, for example, the prologue to the late-fifteenth-century history of Tursun Beg, *Tarih-i Ebü'l Feth,* available in English as *The History of Mehmed the Conqueror,* ed. and trans. Halil İnalcık and Rhoads Murphey (Minneapolis: Bibliotheca Islamica, 1978).

13. Repp, *The Müfti of Istanbul,* 211.

14. Eugenio Alberi, ed., *Relazioni degli ambasciatori veneti al senato,* ser. 3, *Relazioni degli stati ottomani* (Florence: Tipografia all'insegna Di alio, 1840–1855), 3:164.

15. This document is found in the Ottoman Prime Ministry Archives (Istanbul), 1/30 in the Bab-ı Defter Baş Muhasebe Kalemi classification; it was formerly catalogued in the Fekete collection (89). It is discussed by Heyd, *Old Ottoman Criminal Law,* 51–52; Heyd placed it between the years 1529 and 1536 because of its reference to İbrahim Pasha as *serasker* (loosely, "commander in chief"), a title he held during these years.

16. Heyd, *Old Ottoman Criminal Law,* 52, 144–47.

17. Heyd, *Old Ottoman Criminal Law,* 147. See chapter 7, above, on the second wave of provincial law books.

18. For a study of these two forms of revenue garnered by the state (the marriage tax and criminal fines) in the context of a group of late-sixteenth-century waqf villages in Palestine, see Amy Singer, "Marriages and Misdemeanors: A Record of *resm-i ʿarûs ve bâd-i havâ,*" *Princeton Papers: Interdisciplinary Journal of Middle Eastern Studies* 4 (1996): 113–52.

19. Tapu Tahrir Defteri 186, fols. 3–5; Hüseyin Özdeğer, *Onaltıncı Asırda Ayıntâb Livâsı* (Istanbul: Bayrak Matbaacılık, 1988), 201–3.

20. Heyd, *Old Ottoman Criminal Law,* 50 (n. 5), 147 ("the fines mentioned above have now been abrogated and [fines] have been fixed in accordance with the illustrious firman [i.e., the penal regulations of the imperial law book]").

21. See the kanunname included in the 1563 cadastral survey of Maraş, which states that the "law of Dulkadir" is now replaced by the "law of Rum," presumably the Ottoman law book for the central Anatolian province of Rum (Refet Yınanç and Mesut Elibüyük, *Maraş Tahrir Defteri (1563)* [Ankara: Ankara University Press, 1988], 7). Yınanç and Elibüyük note (xxix) that the first attempt to survey the former Dulkadir domain provoked several uprisings; the first successful survey of Maraş, resulting in a cadastral register dated 938/1532, occurred after the region's pacification by the grand vezir İbrahim Pasha, and presumably restored some landholdings to the unhappy Dulkadir tribal leaders. The authors, who have examined this register and note that it is severely damaged, make no mention of a kanunname. Even if this 1532 register did incorporate a kanunname, it seems unlikely that it would have displaced Dulkadir law, since the grand vezir's policy was in part to soothe the wounded sentiments of the former regime's adherents. According to the authors, the 1563 cadaster, with its accompanying kanunname (the "law of Rum"), was the second and last survey of Maraş.

22. Heyd, *Old Ottoman Criminal Law,* 144.

23. See the various records selected from later Aintab court registers by Cemil Cahit Güzelbey in *Gaziantep Şerʿi Mahkeme Sicillerinden Örnekler (Cilt 144–152) (Miladi 1841–1886)* (Gaziantep: Yeni Matbaa, 1966).

24. AS 2:245a *(eğer bir daha beg yanına ve cemi ehl-i örfün yanına veya [gayri] kimesnelere şikayet idecek olursam, Seyyid İsmaile bin osmani nezir olsun ve hem benüm yüzime kara dertub tecrîs idesiz dedikde . . .)*

25. Ömer Lütfi Barkan, *XV ve XVIıncı asırlarda Osmanlı İmparatorluğunda Ziraî Ekonominin Hukukî ve Malî Esasları, I: Kanunlar* (Istanbul: Bürhaneddin Erenler Matbaası, 1943), 123; Heyd, *Old Ottoman Criminal Law,* 142.

26. Muhammad Adnan Bakhit, "Aleppo and the Ottoman Military in the Sixteenth Century (Two Case Studies)," *Al-Abhath* 27 (1978–1979): 27–30. For more on this incident, see chapter 2.

27. These variations are given in Heyd, *Old Ottoman Criminal Law*, 89, 127: *ummal taifesi; ehl-i örf taifesi; ummal ve subaşı taifesi; sancak begi adamı ve subaşı ve toprak subaşıları ve sipahi ve ummal ve gayri.*

28. Heyd, *Old Ottoman Criminal Law*, 289.

29. For a thoughtful analysis of one subaşı's relationship with the villages he oversaw, see Singer, "Marriages and Misdemeanors."

30. Özdeğer, *Ayıntâb Livâsı*, 365.

31. See chapter 2, note 133.

32. A special agent known *göynük subaşı* handled abduction and other sexual crimes that occurred among tribal groups.

33. Heyd, *Old Ottoman Criminal Law*, 89, 127 (my translation).

34. Heyd, *Old Ottoman Criminal Law*, 89, 127 (my translation).

35. Heyd. *Old Ottoman Criminal Law*, 80, 118 (I have slightly altered Heyd's translation).

36. Heyd, *Old Ottoman Criminal Law*, 80, 118 (I have slightly altered Heyd's translation).

37. Heyd, *Old Ottoman Criminal Law*, 78, 116 *("dam yokdur").*

38. Heyd, *Old Ottoman Criminal Law*, 119.

39. Heyd, *Old Ottoman Criminal Law*, 89, 127 (I have slightly altered Heyd's translation).

40. Heyd, *Old Ottoman Criminal Law*, 92, 130–31 (I have slightly altered Heyd's translation). For Heyd's comments on treatment of the habitual criminal, see 195ff.

41. For these cases, see AS 161:19a; AS2:16b; AS 161:157b; and AS 161:85b, 90b.

42. AS 161:53b.

43. AS 161:113a.

44. AS 161:146c.

45. AS 161:25b.

46. AS 2:141b, 170a.

47. The Qur'anic penalty for adultery is flogging; sharia jurisprudence, however, substituted death by stoning for married Muslim adulterers.

48. Al-Marghinani, *The Hedaya, or Guide,* trans. Charles Hamilton (London: T. Bensley, 1791; reprint, Karachi: Darul Ishaat Urdu Bazar), 2:4, 8 (section on *hudud,* or fixed punishments); 666 (section on witnessing, where it is argued that potential witnesses may legitimately conceal criminal action, excepting theft); 672 (where retaliation is also included as a punishment for which "all possible pretexts of prevention are to be sought").

49. See Joseph Schacht, *An Introduction to Islamic Law* (Oxford: Oxford University Press, 1954), 176–77, for various aspects of penal law that have the effect of restricting the application of such punishments.

50. Heyd, *Old Ottoman Criminal Law*, 56.

51. Heyd, *Old Ottoman Criminal Law*, 105.

52. Heyd, *Old Ottoman Criminal Law*, 105.

53. M. E. Düzdağ, *Şeyhülislam Ebussuûd Efendi Fetvaları Işığında 16. Asır Türk Hayatı*

(Istanbul: Enderun Kitabevi, 1983), 103, 157; Colin Imber, "*Zina* in Ottoman Law," in *Contributions à l'histoire économique et sociale de l'Empire ottoman*, ed. Jean-Louis Bacqué-Gramont and Paul Dumont (Leuven, Belgium: Peeters, 1983), 85.

54. Düzdağ, *Ebussuûd Efendi Fetvaları,* 138–39.

55. Heyd, *Old Ottoman Criminal Law,* 280–81.

56. Colin Imber devotes a whole book, *Ebu's-Su'ud: The Islamic Legal Tradition* (Stanford: Stanford University Press, 1997), to testing the proposition that the famed jurist was attempting to reconcile kanun and sharia.

57. James Boyd White, *Heracles' Bow: Essays on the Rhetoric and Poetics of the Law* (Madison: University of Wisconsin Press, 1985), 192–203.

58. Al-Marghinani, *The Hedaya,* 2:4; see also note 49, above.

59. AS 2:170b. This case is discussed later in this chapter.

60. AS 2:278c *(kanun üzere cerimesi virayım).*

61. AS 2:27a.

62. Heyd, *Old Ottoman Criminal Law,* 69, 108 (my translation); for Selim I's law book, see Selami Pulaha and Yaşar Yücel, "I. Selim Kanunnamesi (1512–1520) ve XVI. Yüzyılın İkinci Yarısının Kimi Kanunları," *Belgeler* 12, no. 16 (1987): 17.

63. AS 2:327a. On the subject of penance for a broken vow, see Imber, *Ebu's-Su'ud,* 35.

64. AS 2:193a.

65. AS 161:28a, 35c; AS 2:76a, 171e, 279a.

66. Selami Yücel and Yaşar Pulaha, *I. Selim Kanunnameleri (1512–1520)* (Ankara: Türk Tarih Kurumu, 1995), 141–46.

67. AS 161:52c, 76a, b; AS 2:294b.

68. AS 2:5c; 6a; 192b, c; 193a, b.

69. AS 2:38c, 39c, 46c, 51c, 89a.

70. Schacht, *Introduction to Islamic Law,* 180–181.

71. In the law book of Alaeddevle, siyaset was prescribed (Heyd, *Old Ottoman Criminal Law,* 132), while in the law book for Bozok, hanging with torture was prescribed (Barkan, *Kanunlar,* 124); both law books described highway robbery as *yol kesüb haramîlik et[mek]* (stopping a person on the road and committing robbery).

72. AS 2:116a, b; 117a, b; 119a; 121a, b.

73. AS 161:95a.

74. Düzdağ, *Ebussuûd Efendi Fetvaları,* 153.

75. AS 2:88c.

76. It is possible that the brothers paid a fee for this investigation: for the fee of 400 akçes assessed for an investigation of drowning in late-sixteenth-century Palestine, see Singer, "Marriages and Misdemeanors," 118.

77. AS 2:260c.

78. AS 2:51c.

79. AS 2:116b.

80. This question leads to another aspect of the representation of speech in the murder cases. While the tenor of testimony delivered in these cases could not be described as highly inflected, murder cases come closer to actual depositions than any other group of cases in the record: with the exception of the slave's case

(5), each consists of several entries, some of which contain what appears to be near-verbatim conversation (especially in the problematic highway robbery incident [4]).

81. See chapter 6, note 111.

82. This origin of the policy is suggested by Irène Beldiceanu-Steinherr, "Fiscalité et formes de possession de la terre arable dans l'Anatolie préottomane,"*Journal of the Economic and Social History of the Orient* 19 (1976): 233–322.

83. See numerous articles in *Gaziantep Kültürü* lamenting these practices of feuding. A seventy-five-year-long blood feud settled only in 1999 is mentioned in chapter 2 (see note 79).

84. My criteria for hypothesizing Turkmen identity are admittedly nondefinitive, although within the context of the records as a whole they cumulatively suggest the general cultural outlines of a Turkmen presence: names associated with Safavid religious proselytizing, dervish baba names, occupations and occupational nicknames (butcher, falconer), and finally, distinctive cultural idioms.

85. Abraham Marcus, *The Middle East on the Eve of Modernity: Aleppo in the Eighteenth Century* (New York: Columbia University Press, 1989), 27–28.

86. Heyd, *Old Ottoman Criminal Law,* 38–40; for the Aintab law code, see Tapu Tahrir Defteri 186, fols. 4–5.

87. Heyd, *Old Ottoman Criminal Law,* 44–53.

88. Nelly Hanna, "The Administration of Courts in Ottoman Cairo," in *The State and Its Servants: Administration in Egypt from Ottoman Times to the Present,* ed. Nelly Hanna (Cairo: American University in Cairo Press, 1995), 44–59.

89. However, it is also relevant to the discussion here that Mandaville questions how regularly the governor's court actually met and points out that the judges of Damascus were members of the court ("The Muslim Judiciary of Damascus in the Late Mamluk Period" [Ph.D. diss., Princeton University, 1969], 66–73).

90. See the elaboration of governors' rights in judging and punishing laid out in a critical work of Al-Mawardi, *The Ordinances of Government,* trans. Wafaa H. Wahba (Reading, U.K.: Garnet, 1996), 238–40.

91. Hanna, "The Administration of Courts in Ottoman Cairo," 50.

92. Heyd, *Old Ottoman Criminal Law,* 3.

93. The lack of any reference to judges in the Dulkadir law code suggests that if judicial administration in Aintab in 1540–1541 did draw on pre-Ottoman practice, it was the Mamluk model that was influential.

94. Hanna notes that having a fixed location for the court was an Ottoman innovation in Cairo ("The Administration of Courts in Ottoman Cairo," 46).

FATMA'S STORY: THE DILEMMA OF A PREGNANT PEASANT GIRL

1. AS 2:320b, 327c, 328a.

2. Written in the ellipsis was the place where the two had sex, illegible in the record.

3. See the interesting discussion of consensual illicit sex in the legal handbook of the twelfth-century Hanafi jurist Al-Marghinani, which was popular among Ottomans of this period (*The Hedaya, or Guide,* trans. Charles Hamilton [London: T. Bensley, 1791; reprint, Karachi: Darul Ishaat Urdu Bazar], 2:32).

4. M. E. Düzdağ, *Şeyhülislam Ebussuûd Efendi Fetvaları Işığında 16. Asır Türk Hayatı* (Istanbul: Enderun Kitabevi, 1983), 158; Ebu Suud's answer to the second fatwa was "They are empowered to impose a severe discretionary punishment [flogging and fine] and to imprison him."

5. Uriel Heyd, *Studies in Old Ottoman Criminal Law*, ed. V. L. Menage (Oxford: Clarendon Press, 1973), 58, 60, 97–98.

6. Heyd, *Old Ottoman Criminal Law*, 62, 101.

7. See Francisci Meninski, *Lexicon Arabico-Persico-Turcicum* (Vienna, 1780–1802), 2:236, for the definition of *tövbe*, a term for repentance or a vow not to repeat an offense.

8. The royal domain's share of Hiyam's taxes was 41 percent in 1543. The tax revenues from Hiyam were divided between the royal domain and two waqfs, that of Alaüddin Ali b. Ahmed b. Şeybani, which controlled half the agricultural taxes, and that of the Ibn Keshani family, which controlled a quarter (Tapu Tahrir Defteri 373, fols. 285–87). The latter family is mentioned in the court register as belonging to the civilian elite *(ayan)* of Aleppo (AS 161:15b); the waqf of the Ibn Keshani family supported a dervish convent (Hüseyin Özdeğer, *Onaltıncı Asırda Ayıntâb Livâsı* (Istanbul: Bayrak Matbaacılık, 1988), 530).

9. In the words of Al-Marghinani, "this right is to be exacted by the prince, as the deputy of the law, or by the judge, as the deputy of the prince" (*The Hedaya*, 2:13–14). For a useful discussion of this subject, see Baber Johansen, "Sacred and Religious Element[s] in Hanafite Law—Functions and Limits of the Absolute Character of Government Authority," in *Islam et Politique au Maghreb*, by Ernest G. Gellner et al. (Paris: Éditions du Centre national de la recherche scientifique, 1981), 281–303.

10. For an interesting case involving harmful misinterpretation of an order regarding the question of female and male contact on Bosphorus ferryboats that was issued by the sultan Murad III, see Ahmet Refik, *Onuncu Asr-ı Hicrîde İstanbul Hayatı* (Istanbul: Enderun Kitabevi, 1988), 41, discussed in my "Seniority, Sexuality, and Social Order," in *Women in the Ottoman Empire: Middle Eastern Women in the Early Modern Era,* ed. Madeline C. Zilfi (Leiden: Brill, 1997), 190–92.

11. On the development of the category *zina* and the relationship between its treatment in jurisprudence and Süleyman's code, see Colin Imber, "*Zina* in Ottoman Law," in *Contributions à l'histoire économique et sociale de l'Empire ottoman*, ed. Jean-Louis Bacqué-Gramont and Paul Dumont (Leuven, Belgium: Peeters, 1983), 59–92.

12. Düzdağ, *Ebussuûd Efendi Fetvaları*, 158. On the problems of defining rape in the premodern period, see Kathryn Gravdal, *Ravishing Maidens: Writing Rape in Medieval French Literature and Law* (Philadelphia: University of Pennsylvania Press, 1991), 1–11.

13. On the apportionment of criminal fines, see the 1536 law code for Aintab (Tapu Tahrir Defteri 186, fols. 3–5).

14. AS 161:342a.

15. AS 2:259a, 294a, 306b. Mustafa Çelebi also served as case witness for various cases at court.

16. AS 2:253e, 254a, 256d.

17. Because women's role even in consensual sex might be represented as passive, Zeyneb's words are ambiguous; usually, however, rape was indicated by the added phrase "by force."

18. On the question of honor in Middle Eastern and Mediterranean societies, see Michael Meeker, "Meaning and Society in the Near East: Examples from the Black Sea Turks and the Levantine Arabs," parts 1 and 2, *International Journal of Middle Eastern Studies* 7 (1976): 243–70, 383–422; June Starr, "The Legal and Social Transformation of Rural Women in Aegean Turkey," in *Women and Property—Women as Property*, ed. Renée Hirschorn (London: Croon Helm, 1983), 92–116; Lila Abu-Lughod, *Veiled Sentiments: Honor and Poetry in a Bedouin Society* (Berkeley: University of California Press, 1986), esp. chaps. 3, 4.

19. Guido Ruggiero, *The Boundaries of Eros: Sex Crime and Sexuality in Renaissance Venice* (New York: Oxford University Press, 1985), 16–44.

20. Cornelia Hughes Dayton, *Women before the Bar: Gender, Law, and Society in Connecticut, 1639–1789* (Chapel Hill: University of North Carolina Press, 1995), 160–61; Laurel Thatcher Ulrich, *A Midwife's Tale: The Life of Martha Ballard, Based on Her Diary, 1785–1812* (New York: Knopf, 1990), 147–61.

21. Daniel Bates, *Nomads and Farmers: A Study of the Yörük of Southeastern Turkey* (Ann Arbor: University of Michigan Press, 1973), 72–79; Bates says that "the immediate causes and contexts of kidnapping are rooted in the rigidity of the normative system of arranged marriages and in the requirements of large cash bride price payments. Elopement gives the girl freedom of choice otherwise denied her in this area, and the boy the ability to bypass the often deliberate and time-consuming plans of his household. An apparent immediate function of the practice is to facilitate the marriage of poorer men faced with raising cash payments in a market economy, thus leveling potential distinctions of wealth" (79).

22. Heyd, *Old Ottoman Criminal Law*, 60, 99.

23. AS 2:105b, 159a.

24. AS 2:153c.

25. Al-Marghinani, *The Hedaya*, 2:6.

26. AS 2:203b.

27. Imber, *"Zina* in Ottoman Law," 64.

28. Düzdağ, *Ebussuûd Efendi Fetvaları*, 158.

29. Düzdağ, *Ebussuûd Efendi Fetvaları*, 158.

30. Heyd, *Old Ottoman Criminal Law*, 59, 98.

31. Heyd, *Old Ottoman Criminal Law*, 56–57, 95–96.

32. Heyd, *Old Ottoman Criminal Law*, 134. The Dulkadir code explicitly penalized rape (the rapist paid double the zina fine), while the Ottoman did not.

33. Ömer Lütfi Barkan discusses specific instances of the reduction or abolition of various taxes and fees following the Ottoman conquest of the Mamluk state (Erzurum in 1520, Diyarbakır in 1540) in "Akkoyunlu Hükümdarı Uzun Hasan Beye ait Kanunlar," *Tarih Vesikaları* 1, no. 2 (1941): 93–95. On this Ottoman policy more generally, see Halil İnalcık, *The Ottoman Empire: The Classical Age*, trans. Normal Itzkowitz and Colin Imber (New York: Praeger, 1973), 12–13, 73–74.

34. The description of Hiyam in this section would not have been possible without the work of Hüseyin Özdeğer on the tax surveys of sixteenth-century Aintab *(Ayıntâb Livâsı)*. I am also deeply indebted to Lisa Schwartz for her expertise in interpreting the data made available in Özdeğer's study; many of ideas expressed in this chapter are the result of our collaboration. For further treatment of this subject, see our *"Bennaks* and Bachelors: Employment and Household Structure in a Sixteenth-Century Anatolian Village," in *Halil İnalcık Festschrift,* ed. N. Göyünç, J. Bacqué-Grammont, and Ö. Ergenç (Istanbul: Eren Yayıncılık, in press).

35. *Tapu Tahrir Defteri* 373, fols. 282–85 (Hiyam), 219–94 (Keret).

36. Özdeğer, *Ayıntâb Livâsı,* 124.

37. For a consideration of local character in the context of a set of villages in the Jerusalem area in the mid–sixteenth century, see Amy Singer, "Marriages and Misdemeanors: A Record of *resm-i ʿarûs ve bâd-ı havâ," Princeton Papers: Interdisciplinary Journal of Middle Eastern Studies* 4 (1996): 113–52, esp. 144–47.

38. Özdeğer, *Ayıntâb Livâsı,* 113.

39. AS 161:351a.

40. Hiyam's slaughterhouse was taxed in 1536 but not in 1543, suggesting its demise in the intervening years. Orul was another fast-growing village in the Nehrülcevaz subdistrict (*Tapu Tahrir Defteri* 373, fol. 291; Özdeğer, *Ayıntâb Livâsı,* 526).

41. I thank Lisa Schwartz for sharing with me the information that in Gaziantep today, special areas outside the city are reserved along the Sacur River (a tributary of the Euphrates) as animal-keeping areas; these were referred to as "goat hotels" by Schwartz's informant.

42. *Tapu Tahrir Defteri* 373, fols. 282–84.

43. Halil İnalcık, "The Ottoman State: Economy and Society, 1300–1600," in *An Economic and Social History of the Ottoman Empire, 1300–1914,* ed. Halil İnalcık and Donald Quataert (Cambridge: Cambridge University Press, 1994), 149–50.

44. For a dramatic instance of a female's ability to hold up the marriage negotiations of two branches of her extended family, see AS 161:153a, b.

45. AS 2:266a.

46. Başbakanlı Osmanlı Arşivi, Ottoman Prime Ministry Archives (Istanbul), 1/30 in the Bab-ı Defter Baş Muhasebe Kalemi classification; formerly catalogued in the Fekete collection (89).

47. Özdeğer, *Ayıntâb Livâsı,* passim.

48. Al-Marghinani, *The Hedaya,* 2:3.

49. Starr, "The Legal and Social Transformation of Rural Women in Aegean Turkey," 109–11.

CONCLUSION

1. In Hiyam in 1543, the male population on whom the poll tax was imposed consisted of 54 bachelors and 185 married men, while in Aintab city, there were 490 bachelors to 1,896 married men (Hüseyin Özdeğer, *Onaltıncı Asırda Ayıntâb Livâsı* [Istanbul: Bayrak Matbaacılık, 1988], 124, 523).

2. AS 161:153a, b.

3. Özdeğer, *Ayıntâb Livâsı*, 549.

4. The significant overlap between fiscal and legal administration is suggested by Colin Imber when he points out that kanun is essentially feudal law in that it regulates the relationship between fief holders and tax-paying subjects (*Ebu's-Su'ud: The Islamic Legal Tradition* [Stanford: Stanford University Press, 1997], 40–41); this overlap is also noted by Linda Darling, *Revenue-Raising and Legitimacy: Tax Collection and Finance Administration in the Ottoman Empire, 1560–1660* (Leiden: Brill, 1996) esp. chaps. 8 and 9.

5. Amy Singer has made a similar point about the nature of peasant resistance to Ottoman authorities—that resistance was the sum of numerous small acts of non-cooperation rather than collective rebellion; she concludes, "Their separate actions added up to shape the empire which seemingly controlled them" (*Palestinian Peasants and Ottoman Officials: Rural Administration around Sixteenth-Century Jerusalem* [Cambridge: Cambridge University Press, 1994], 130–31).

INDEX

Text: 10/12 Baskerville
Display: Baskerville
Compositor: G&S Typesetters, Inc.
Printer: Thomson-Shore, Inc.